Praise for

Queer progress

Queer Progress is a book that will work as a crucial political intervention in the present *and* have lasting value as a vital piece of community history.

— Steven Maynard, Department of History, Queen's University

More than a mere memoir, this work offers an insightful critique of how radical politics can be displaced. This book is essential reading not simply for lesbians and gays who wish to know their histories in Canada. It is mandatory reading for those who seek to learn from activist histories in order to conceive and implement strategies to create a better world.

— Viviane Namaste, Professor, Simone de Beauvoir Institute,
Concordia University

An important, timely, and highly readable book, *Queer Progress* is a thoughtful and passionate memoir by one of Canada's leading LBGTQ and AIDS activists. Importantly, it foregrounds gender, class, and race conflicts and highlights the links between Canadian and international sexual politics. Tim McCaskell has given not only Canadians but the international LGBTQ movement an excellent, fair-minded account of the surprising way in which the efforts of a small band of radicals unwittingly laid the foundations for Pride commercialism and the search for same-sex marriage and respectability.

— Mariana Valverde, Centre of Criminology and Socio-legal Studies,
University of Toronto

Queer Progress is a refreshingly complex, nuanced, and grounded charting of "queerness" that coincides and collides with activist-academic histories of LGBTQ activism in Canada over the past four decades. The book's rich vignettes, meditations, and stories meaningfully probe the horizons of queer liberalism, revealing and questioning the shifting relationship of "queerness" to "the political." It is an invaluable contribution and challenge to the project of queer social justice, pushing its readers to consider the traction and intractability of queer praxis, especially in this deeply pervasive neoliberal moment.

— Amar Wahab, Professor of Gender, Sexuality and Women's Studies,
York University

Queer Progress is a major contribution to queer men's history focusing on Toronto from the 1970s to the present. Melding autobiography and historical documentation with analysis, this is a must-read for those interested in queer struggles, sexual liberation, and social justice.

— Gary Kinsman, activist, author of *The Regulation of Desire*, co-author of
The Canadian War on Queers

I couldn't put *Queer Progress* down once I started. Tim McCaskell's first-hand account of Toronto's major sexuality rights debates and battles is riveting. Moving between the small details of particular events and his broad, convincing analysis of neoliberalism, McCaskell's frank style and wry wit produce a text that is in parts gut-wrenching (the devastation of the AIDS crisis) and charming (his own sexual adventures). *Queer Progress* is necessary reading, especially for folks like me and younger, who arrived late in this story so far: we have, finally, an explanation of how and why things are in the present, and clues about what may lie ahead.

— Andil Gosine, Associate Professor of Sociology, York University

A Canadian political masterpiece. To feel the front line drama that gave birth to and built the Canadian LGBTQ movement, you need to read this insightful book.

— Olivia Chow, Distinguished Visiting Professor, Ryerson University,
Former MP

In his book *Queer Progress*, Tim McCaskell charts the accomplishments, possibilities, and distortions of the "rather queer" progress of LGBT politics in Canada over the past forty years. The book combines personal narrative, grounded in decades of activism, with a lively interpretation of contemporary debates about homonationalism, neoliberalism, and social difference. The result is a thoughtful, engaging, and must-read book for anyone interested in the history of Canadian LGBT politics.

— Eric Mykhalovskiy, Professor of Sociology, York University

queer progress

FROM HOMOPHOBIA TO HOMONATIONALISM

Tim McCaskell

Between the Lines
Toronto

Queer Progress: From Homophobia to Homonationalism

First published in Canada in 2016 by
Between the Lines
401 Richmond St. W., Studio 277
Toronto, Ontario   M5V 3A8
1-800-718-7201
www.btlbooks.com

Library and Archives Canada Cataloguing in Publication

McCaskell, Tim, 1951–, author
    Queer progress : from homophobia to homonationalism / Tim McCaskell.

Includes bibliographical references and index.
Issued in print and electronic formats.
ISBN 978-1-77113-278-7 (paperback); ISBN 978-1-77113-279-4 (epub);
ISBN 978-1-77113-280-0 (pdf).

    1. Gay liberation movement – Ontario – Toronto. 2. Sex – Economic aspects. 3. Sexual minorities – Social conditions. 4. Equality. I. Title.
HQ76.8.C3M323 2016   306.76′609713   C2016-903084-9
                                                         C2016-903085-7

Cover image and cover design by Jennifer Tiberio
Page preparation by Steve Izma
Printed in Canada

Shelfie

An ebook edition is available for $2.99 with the purchase of this print book.

CLEARLY PRINT YOUR NAME ABOVE IN UPPER CASE

Instructions to claim your eBook edition:
1. Download the Shelfie app for Android or iOS
2. Write your name in **UPPER CASE** above
3. Use the Shelfie app to submit a photo
4. Download your eBook to any device

RECYCLED
Paper made from recycled material
FSC® C103567
www.fsc.org
FSC

Between the Lines gratefully acknowledges assistance for its publishing activities from the Canada Council for the Arts, the Ontario Arts Council, the Government of Ontario through the Ontario Book Publishers Tax Credit program and through the Ontario Book Initiative, and the Government of Canada through the Canada Book Fund.

Canada Council   Conseil des Arts
for the Arts   du Canada

Canadä

ONTARIO ARTS COUNCIL
CONSEIL DES ARTS DE L'ONTARIO
an Ontario government agency
un organisme du gouvernement de l'Ontario

For Richard,
my intrepid companion through this journey

Contents

Acknowledgements

There is an extensive group of people without whose assistance this book would have been impossible. First I would like to thank Alan Miller at the Canadian Lesbian and Gay Archives, who facilitated my access to the collection, an indispensable resource for this work. Don McLeod's annotated chronologies clarified the sequence of an often confusing jumble of events. Then there were those who generously agreed to interviews or answered questions lost to the documentary record: Jim Bartley, Andrew Brett, Naomi Brooks, Hilary Cook, Graham Crawford, Debbie Douglas, Jari Dvorak, Maureen Fitzgerald, David Foreman, Bob Gallagher, Susan Gapka, Amy Gottlieb, John Greyson, Jonathan Hadad, Brent Hawkes, Helen Kennedy, Stephen Kerr, Walter Klinger, Akim Adé Larcher, Paul MacPhee, Courtnay McFarlane, Frank McGee, Carl Miller, Jim Monk, Brian Mossop, Ken Popert, Kyle Rae, David Rayside, Mark Smith, Douglas Stewart, Shawn Syms, Mariana Valverde, Rinaldo Walcott, Tom Warner, Lorna Weir, and Art Zoccole.

Others read all or part of various versions of the manuscript and offered comments, corrections, and suggestions: Glen Brown, Ed Jackson, Richard Fung, Gerald Hannon, Jearld Moldenhauer, Gary Kinsman, Natalie Kouri-Towe, Eric Mykhalovskiy, Viviane Namaste, and Gillian Rogerson. David Seitz inspired the title.

Still others assisted me with aspects of the research: Mary Louise Adams, Joan Anderson, Debbie Brock, Patrick Case, Vijaya Chikermane, Elle Flanders, Avvy Go, Prabha Khosla, Alan Li, Gail Posen, Peter Yu, and Peter Zorzi. Tilman Lewis provided meticulous editorial support. Thanks, too, to the team at Between the Lines, who helped see this rambling project through to a finished book.

Introduction

How did we get here from there?

Once again, the Israel lobby was attempting to prevent Queers Against Israeli Apartheid from marching in Toronto's Pride parade. The summer of 2012 was the fourth installment of what seemed to be an annual crisis. QuAIA fought and won on the terrain of freedom of expression. But the process revealed something queer going on.

In the early days of gay liberation, political speech was tolerated, no matter how outrageous. It was always *sex* that got us into trouble, both doing it and talking about it. But in 2012, we were told that Pride was about celebrating sex in all of its outrageous manifestations. It was political speech that was unacceptable.

That is when I was moved to start working on this book.

My involvement with the politics around QuAIA introduced me to the debates about "homonationalism," a concept coined by Jasbir Puar in her book *Terrorist Assemblages*. As a social movement, gay rights had been successful beyond its early strategists' wildest dreams. From a reviled, quasi-criminal class, we were now included in the constellation of minorities valued by Canadian multiculturalism. Our sexual orientation was no longer a barrier to full legal citizenship. We were recognized in a developing international human rights architecture.

But this progress had been rather queer. We had come a long way but hadn't exactly ended up where we expected. First, such progress hadn't affected all of us in the same way. Some parts of our community were just as disenfranchised as ever, while others had become identified with the status quo. As we moved from the peripheries to the mainstream, there was a remarkable transformation in dominant LGBT politics, from one aimed at social transformation to one that celebrated social inclusion. Toronto's Pride parade now featured many of our traditional antagonists: the Conservative party, churches, some of the biggest corporations and banks, the police, and the military.

In terms of the rights struggle, Canada has consistently surpassed the United States in our gains in an imagined liberal and tolerant nation. But in doing so, we have also strengthened that bright image that hides the reality of the lives of Aboriginal, racialized, and marginalized people, regardless of their sexual orientation. Further, we find ourselves implicated in some very unsavoury politics. Our rights are used to portray Alberta oil sands crude as "ethical oil," as compared to that coming from "homophobic" Arab countries. We are caught up in the pinkwashing campaign that justifies Israeli apartheid as liberal and democratic. We are deployed to stoke Islamophobia and racism. Under Stephen Harper's Conservative government, Canada's acceptance of gay Iranian refugees was used as a propaganda weapon to isolate Iran and to extend U.S. strategic interests in the Middle East – interests that are about money and power, not social justice. Inclusion comes with consequences.

That same year I critiqued a manuscript by Andil Gosine that brought a historical and institutional analysis to the question of queer politics in a "post" colonial world.[1] Gosine explored queer organizing in the Caribbean. He praised the Trinidadian group CAISO (Coalition Advocating for Inclusion of Sexual Orientation), which he felt successfully managed to embed queer politics into the "national imaginary" of Trinidad and Tobago. He contrasted it with efforts in Jamaica that had become embroiled in the Stop Murder Music campaign, and ended up being situated as a foreign threat.

But if, as Gosine suggested, the successful strategy for the development of LGBT culture and rights was to integrate into a national imaginary, then wasn't homonationalism the same thing? As described by Puar, homonationalism is the integration of gay rights into the hegemonic values of American imperialism. The relative success of CAISO in Trinidad and Tobago and that of the U.S. gay movement would then both be cut from the same cloth. But integration into the national imaginary in the two countries has very different consequences. Trinidad and Tobago is a small, post-colonial society. Its major cultural export is Carnival. The United States is the world's leading imperial power. Its global cultural reach is as much resented and feared as emulated around the world. To resist the empire has often become to resist its acceptance of homosexuality.

I have been intimately involved in the Canadian and international gay liberation movement since 1974. From 1975 to 1986, I was a member of the collective that ran *The Body Politic* (*TBP*), Canada's iconic gay liberation journal. I chaired the Public Action Committee of the Right to Privacy Committee (RTPC), the group that spearheaded the response to the massive police raids on Toronto gay bathhouses in 1981. In 1985, I was a founding member of the Simon Nkodi Anti-apartheid Committee (SNAAC), doing anti-apartheid solidarity work in the LGB communities. At the end of the decade, I helped start AIDS ACTION NOW! (AAN!), the activist group that put AIDS on the national agenda. In the 1990s, I was involved in the integration of anti-homophobia work in the Toronto Board of Education's anti-racism and anti-sexism efforts, including the establishment of the Triangle

Program, Canada's only free-standing secondary school program serving vulnerable LGBT youth. In 2009, I became a spokesperson for QuAIA, a group that challenges the pinkwashing of the Israeli state. Simultaneously, I was involved in the struggle against HIV criminalization.

When you are plowing forward in such immediate, daily struggles, there is little time to look back at your path or at where it is leading. Now that we are being told that we have "arrived," I felt it was time to do some looking back.

Since I experienced much of this history first-hand, I have structured this book around a personal narrative. This is not to inflate my importance in the process – this movement has had more leading actors than can possibly be named – but to make the account more vivid and accessible. For that reason, much of this book focuses on events in Toronto, while recognizing how those events, while singular, reflected national and global social changes. That approach also entails other limitations. For example, my experience of these changes has been from the standpoint of a cis, white male. I don't have the same first-hand experience as women, trans people, or people of colour. Many stories could be written about the last forty years from many standpoints. This is only one of them. And even within the parameters of my particular embodiment, I have selected events to illustrate a particular trajectory, from a homophobic nation to homonationalism.

A shortcoming of many of our histories has been to paint the gay liberation struggle against a static social canvass. Yet in the forty years this account covers, society – both national and global – has undergone profound transformation. Gay liberation was born into a world of national economies but today finds itself in a globalized market. Most of those national economies were organized around Keynesian or socialist principles that called for wealth redistribution to minimize class disparity. Neo-liberalism has now largely dismantled the welfare state, and class disparities have predictably deepened. Gay liberation emerged at the height of the Cold War and anti-colonial movements. It witnessed the collapse of the Socialist Bloc, the rise of neo-colonialism, the emergence of the United States as the world's superpower, and now serious challenges to the U.S. empire.

From a time when long-distance phone calls were expensive and people sent letters through the mail, we find ourselves in an environment of instantaneous, almost costless global communication. In the 1970s, we still went to libraries to look up facts in encyclopedias. Today, the world is drowning in factoids at the click of a mouse. From a time when any talk about sex was risqué and unseemly, and sexual imagery was routinely the object of legal sanctions, we find ourselves in a society that incessantly talks about sex and where media of all types is saturated in sexual imagery. The rise of homonationalism has been deeply influenced by these forces.

Since I will reference how gay politics has been shaped by such broader social changes, let me introduce some key concepts that underlie my approach.

MATERIALISM

I will begin with the rather common-sense assumption that people's ideas, thoughts, and beliefs are conditioned by their experiences. Our experiences are not of our own choosing; they come from the material world around us. From what we are formally taught and learn, largely as children. From what we have to do to earn a living as adults. From the way other people act and treat us, and the way we are encouraged to act and treat others by the law, media, and culture. Repetition is a form of pedagogy, and day-to-day life repeats its lessons over and over.

This does not mean that changing environments will automatically produce a different consciousness. Materialism has sometimes been understood to mean that everyone's behaviour is governed by sober economic calculation. Our decisions are seldom so rational.

VALUES

Karl Marx wrote that "the tradition of all the dead generations weighs like a nightmare on the brain of the living."[2] Behaviour is often based not on a considered calculation of interests, but on deeply held beliefs and values.

Do we value equality or hierarchy, obedience or freedom, the individual or the collective? Values are basic notions of what is right and wrong, good and bad, what is important and what is not.

Cognitive scientist George Lakoff reduces values to synaptic connections in the brain that are learned, and that are reinforced by social messages and experiences.[3] We can similarly think of values as basic concepts that are linked to positive affective responses. Does the notion of "family" make us feel warm and fuzzy, or queasy? Those responses will affect how we value the family.

Values shape the logic that people bring to decision-making. For those who associate the family with a strong positive affect, family will be important to defend or to be included in. Those, on the other hand, who value the individual will be more likely to focus on personal development and happiness. Their behaviour will be more oriented to individual success and gratification. Family will not have the same resonance, and family relationships that are a barrier to success and gratification will be more easily abandoned.

Common Cause,[4] a 2010 document by a coalition of U.K. environmental groups, draws on social psychology research to propose a model of relations among different types of values. Related values trigger each other, while others are diametrically opposed. *Common Cause* points out that most people have learned a range of conflicting values, and that different values can be triggered by different kinds of messages.

Constellations of values are associated with political philosophies, and people are likely to be attracted to politics congruent with their values. Conversely, the discourses of political philosophies are likely to activate particular values.

LIBERALISM

Traditional or conservative value systems tend to value the group (religious group, family, tribe, nation) over the individual. They tend to value hierarchy over equality. And they tend to value received knowledge from the past. Such values reflect and reinforce traditional social arrangements.

Cultural theorist Raymond Williams reminds us that "liberal" is derived from a Latin word meaning "free man."[5] Liberalism developed in the European Enlightenment in the seventeenth and eighteenth centuries. It evolved as a critique of, and in opposition to, traditional social arrangements and values.

Liberalism saw the free individual rather than the group as its basic unit, and maintained that individuals had the right to "Life, Liberty and the pursuit of Happiness." It opposed hereditary privilege and asserted that "all men are created equal." And it justified this vision with reference to rational or scientific knowledge, rather than received knowledge from the past. In our case, Alfred Kinsey's studies of sexual behaviour trumped the Bible.

CAPITALISM AND LIBERALISM

Liberalism was closely linked to the rise of capitalism, an economic system where property is considered private rather than bound by communal obligations. Feudal lords and peasants, although they were by no means equal, had obligations to each other. The lord could no more sell his land than the peasant could leave it. Under capitalism, on the other hand, everyone is free to sell their labour on the "free" market (or starve). Capitalists are free to employ people or dismiss them, depending on how profitable that may be.

As capitalism emerged, business owners, manufacturers, traders, and entrepreneurs outside of the feudal hierarchy became increasingly dissatisfied with a social order that excluded them from the status and power they felt they deserved. Liberal ideas were therefore attractive. They challenged aristocratic privilege and argued that it wasn't birth but individual success that should determine one's place. Radical liberals challenged the religious dogmas that justified acceptance of one's station. Liberalism was a revolutionary philosophy for which people were willing to fight, die, and kill.

While the feudal world tried to keep trade, religion, and personal life under the thumb of traditional elites, capitalism and its liberal philosophy promoted freedom. Individual freedom, free trade, free markets, and eventually, free elections, freedom of (and even from) religion, freedom of the press – in short, freedom from government interference in the economy and personal life. If everyone was left alone to pursue their own interests, it was argued, the market would sort things out to everyone's mutual advantage.

CONFLICTING AND COEXISTING VALUES

Capitalism grew slowly in a garden of conservative institutions and the values they promoted. As this new social system became established, traditional values that encouraged accepting things as they were became more important to the new capitalist elites. Liberal ideas, when extended to the working class and the poor, could be a problem. What if slaves demanded their liberty? What if workers wanted to elect their bosses? What if women wanted to be paid as much as men?

Traditional institutions like the church helped maintain order in the face of growing dissatisfaction with the new capitalist order. So the new system and its liberal philosophers accommodated themselves to pre-existing institutions and their values in different ways. Slavery was essential to the early capitalist accumulation in the Atlantic Triangle, and liberalism accommodated itself to notions of racial inequality. "Life, Liberty and the pursuit of Happiness" was the prerogative of white males only. American capitalism dispensed with the monarchy for a republic, and established a division between church and state. Capitalism in Britain developed happily alongside a traditional monarchy and an Anglican state church. The French Revolution decriminalized sex between consenting adults, regardless of gender, in the eighteenth century, but Britain and the United States failed to do so until the twentieth.

Despite such accommodations, ideas of individualism, equality, and rational knowledge continued to corrode conservative institutions and philosophies. Slave revolts and the abolition movement finally ended slavery. The right to vote was extended beyond property owners. Workers demanded their right to organize unions. Women's entry into the workforce undermined the patriarchal organization of the family. Urbanization concentrated populations, allowing those disadvantaged by hierarchies of gender or race, or with non-hegemonic sexual desires, to find each other and attain the critical mass to develop identities and demand change.

Western society originally accommodated itself to the regulation of sexual behaviour by family, religion, and the state. Bodies were parts of groups, and sex was a social responsibility. But as the body became more and more conceptualized as private property, and sex as individual expression, a sexual liberation movement could emerge. Developed liberal capitalist countries were therefore more fertile ground for early gay rights efforts in the twentieth century.

SOCIALISM

Between the Russian Revolution in 1917 and the fall of communism at the end of the twentieth century, a large part of the world declared itself socialist. Socialist movements of different stripes were also often important in the capitalist West. The Cold War was ostensibly about which system – socialism or capitalism – would dominate the world.

Socialism challenged capitalism itself. But as an Enlightenment philosophy, it accepted most of the basic liberal values, reconfiguring them in different ways. Socialist societies valued equality between individuals but went beyond formal *legal* equality to work towards *substantive* equality: equal wages, guaranteed employment, universal access to education and health care. Socialism claimed democracy but argued that democracy needed to be extended to the economy. That could only take place when production was under control of the people rather than a small group of capitalists.

The Socialist Bloc also supported anti-colonial movements as a vehicle for social transformation. The capitalist West, which benefited from colonialism, helped sustain the racist colonial system, despite its ostensible support of liberal values of equality.

Whereas most capitalist countries still supported – and in turn were supported by – religious institutions, socialism saw religion as irrational and "the opium of the masses." Socialists expected religion to die out in societies not based on exploitation.

In this context, many early 1970s gay liberationists linked homophobia to capitalism and were influenced by socialist and anti-colonial theories and practice. But although socialism shared some basic values with liberalism, it was not just liberalism in a hurry.

Liberalism valued individual competition; socialism valued solidarity and spoke of "classes" rather than individuals as the main actors in history. Its stance on the individual and the collective was therefore ambiguous. It was often less concerned with individual rights and willing to sacrifice them for the social good. Socialist democracy often displayed little toleration of dissent. Other traditional values crept in. The "great leader" was regularly idolized and entrenched for life. Received knowledge from the writings of Marx, Lenin, or Mao could replace rational social analysis. Such contradictory values within socialism led to contradictory responses to homosexuality. Same-sex sex was decriminalized in 1917 after the Russian Revolution, but recriminalized in the 1930s when more traditional nationalist values came to the fore.

FEMINISM

First-wave feminism, in the early twentieth century, focused on equality – legal personhood, the vote, and so on. By the 1960s a second wave of feminism had emerged. It analyzed patriarchy and sexism in their most intimate manifestations, arguing that "the personal is political." The notion of sexual liberation was tied up with the cutting loose of sex from reproduction, bolstered by women's ability to control their fertility.

There were many currents of feminism – liberal, radical, socialist. Nevertheless, like socialism, feminism generally shared basic Enlightenment values. "The personal is political" focused on the individual but grappled with the individual's immediate social context. Just as socialism proposed solidarity along class lines, feminism proposed solidarity among women as a group. Feminism demanded legal equality between men and women, which sat squarely within liberal parameters. But it also demanded substantive equality, in this case in the most mundane spheres of life – housework, personal and sexual relations. Such politics was an important part of the environment that gave birth to gay liberation and was certainly the core of lesbian political organizing.

KEYNESIANISM

After the disaster of the Great Depression and the Second World War that it spawned, the liberal idea that each individual working to maximize their own gain would produce the maximum common good was revealed as deeply flawed. Wealth disparity, depression, and war were far from being in everyone's best interest.

John Maynard Keynes argued that the boom and bust cycles of capitalism and inequality had to be controlled by state management. Government should spend when the economy was slow, and cut back to cool things down when it was overheated. Banks needed to be regulated to protect investors. Workers' rights needed to be respected. Keynesian economies developed institutions to redistribute wealth and produce a more equal society – social welfare, public pensions, public medical care, public education – and developed progressive taxation systems (where the wealthy paid more) to support those initiatives.

During the Cold War, Keynesianism was seen as undercutting socialist demands. It was therefore accepted by the dominant capitalist elites. Just as capitalism had accommodated itself to traditional institutions such as the church, it now accommodated itself to the socialist challenge. Keynesianism was far from socialism; it was more about saving capitalism from its own excesses. But it reinforced values of social solidarity. Everyone had a debt to society and a responsibility to support the most vulnerable.

After the Second World War, capitalist democracies like Canada largely adopted Keynesian economics and Keynesian-inspired social liberalism. In a society where class disparities decreased, identity politics could emerge. The Keynesian social safety net provided a cushion for early lesbian and gay activists who risked careers and family support by coming out.

SETTING THE STAGE

Although North American women had been drawn into the workforce during the Second World War, when the soldiers came home they were abruptly pushed back out. But the genie was out of the bottle. Women resisted the post-war conservatism. In a buoyant economy they continued to work, and more rejected dependence on men. By the 1960s, birth control meant that women's sexuality was no longer haunted by the spectre of pregnancy. Conservative notions about sexual obligation to the family and reproduction were being undermined by liberal ideas of sex as an individual's rightful pursuit of happiness. By the 1970s, women's liberation was demanding equality in all social spheres. Sexual liberation had begun, and under its logic, the persecution of varieties of sexual attraction was just as unreasonable as persecution of varieties of religion or discrimination on the basis of race.

In the United States, encouraged by Third World struggles against colonialism, the black civil rights movement and Black Power challenged racial hierarchies and demanded equality. Black is Beautiful would be the template for Gay is Good.

Young people challenged the authority of their elders. You couldn't trust anyone over thirty. The 1968 Paris student revolt had paralyzed France. The Vietnam War was in its final brutal stages, and the anti-war movement spread from campuses onto streets around the world. Phil Ochs sang, "It's always the old who lead us to the wars, it's always the young who fall."[6] In China, the Cultural Revolution encouraged a younger generation to question authority and "bombard the headquarters." The counterculture promoted a general rejection of conformist and consumerist values.

The world was in great turmoil, and into this unstable constellation of political forces and conflicting values, gay liberation would be launched.

GAY LIB

In June 1969 the patrons of the Stonewall Inn in New York responded to a police raid with three days of rioting. The gay liberation movement sparked by Stonewall emerged in the 1970s. It was based on the liberal notion that sexuality should be an individual expression rather than a social obligation. But the movement also drew from the social solidarity promoted by socialism, Keynesianism, feminism, the civil rights movement, and anti-colonial struggles to produce the notion of "community." This allowed it to project political power to combat the moralizing discourses of law, religion, and psychiatry.

In the end, we largely wound up challenging conservative institutions and values that had been accommodated within liberal capitalism. In a certain way, our movement became the cutting edge of the ongoing corrosion of the power of traditional, pre-liberal, pre-capitalist institutions and the values they promoted. Our effort was later buoyed by a neo-liberal economy that deployed sex as a marketing tool, and in particular, cultivated a gay market in order to spur lagging consumption, even as the dismantling of the Keynesian welfare state was accompanied by a neo-conservative reaction.

This story begins in 1974 when I came out in a Keynesian world. It finishes in 2014 when Toronto hosted World Pride in a neo-liberal one. It attempts to make sense of the emergence of homonationalism, and how, over a period of forty years, a social movement adapted itself to a radically changing environment. It tries to understand how broader social forces selected particular strategies from the confused primeval muck that was gay liberation and reshaped the character and significance of LGBT communities.

PART I

A New World in Birth

Invisible

JOHN

I have a clear memory of visiting my grandparents. They lived in Orillia, Ontario, a mid-sized town about twenty-five miles from the little village of Beaverton, where I grew up, in cottage country north of Toronto. I must have been four or so. It was spring. For some reason I ran upstairs and darted into my grandfather's bedroom, where I found myself face to face with a young man in my grandfather's bed.

Dappled sunlight was coming in the window through the fresh leaves on the trees. He was sitting up, reading a book, the sheet pulled up to his belly button. He wasn't wearing pajama tops. He had bright eyes, muscles on his arms, and his chest was covered with thick black curly hair. Transfixed by his chest, I wondered what it would be like to climb up on the bed and touch it, to feel the hair between my fingers.

He said, "Hello, Timmy. How are you?"

My mother rushed into the room behind me and took me by the hand. She explained that John was boarding with my grandparents now and that I couldn't just run into people's bedrooms without knocking. She told John she was sorry. By this point, he had pulled the covers up to his neck. He just smiled again and said, "No harm done, Mrs. McCaskell. How are you?"

"Fine, thank you," she replied, and then hustled me back downstairs.

LOUIS

Louis was skinny and pale with wavy blond hair. His voice was high, like a girl's, and he always walked as if he was wearing high-heeled shoes. Everyone said he acted just like a girl. He would have played with the girls, too, except that the schoolyard was divided into boys' and girls' sides, each with a separate entrance and separate playground. The invisible line that divided the two was not to be crossed. At first, when we were both in grade one, Louis would try to sneak over to the girls' side, but the teacher on duty always caught him and sent him back. Then the boys would punish him for crossing the line. A new term entered our vocabulary: "sissy."

There was great speculation about why Louis was a sissy. The rumour was that his parents had really wanted a girl and, when he was young, dressed him like one and let his hair grow. It "turned him that way." Then they sent him away to live with his grandparents, "'cause who'd want to have a kid like that?"

Before class, at recess or after school, the rough boys would sometimes gather around Louis and call him "Louise" and other names. Louis didn't know how to fight. He would get red in the face and pick up little stones to throw at his tormentors, but he threw like a girl and the stones would go up in the air and fall harmlessly on the ground. Then the boys would split their sides laughing and Louis would turn red to the roots of his blond curly hair. He would start to cry and run home with his funny wiggling run.

As he got older, it got worse. Louis's voice got even higher, his walk even wigglier. He didn't play with boys his own age at all, only with the little kids in grade one who didn't know better.

I generally kept as far away from Louis as I could. Sissy was a dangerous word. It could be contagious.

A SHY BOY

I was shy. And I hated hockey. Every winter all the boys in Beaverton Public School were supposed to play hockey in a league at the rink. I devised schemes to get out of it. It didn't take a rocket scientist to realize that a bunch of boys with sticks slashing away at a lump of plastic on a hard, slippery surface would not end well. I'd rather stay home and read a book. I didn't even like watching hockey on TV.

My father was a hockey fan. He was disappointed. I felt guilty.

I also wasn't any good at baseball. Sometimes there would be after-school baseball games. Everyone would have to participate. Captains would pick their teams in class. Once I was the second-last picked. There was just me and Louis left. It was humiliating.

Soccer was okay. It was mostly just running around and tripping people. Since my feet stuck out, I was good at tripping, so people wanted me on their team. I was suspect as a boy, but not hopeless.

SUTCLIFFE

The morning of June 6, 1962, decorated war veteran Major Herbert Sutcliffe went to his Ottawa office. It was to be his last day before moving to Washington, DC, to take up a prestigious posting at the Pentagon. But as he sat down at his desk, he received a call asking him to report immediately to the director of military intelligence.

Sutcliffe walked down the hall to his superior's office. He was told, "You are not going to Washington, there will be no luncheon for you. The RCMP has advised us that you are a homosexual. You'll be out of the military in three days. Return to your apartment and wait for me to contact you."[1]

It was the end of his military career. Sutcliffe considered suicide that after-noon, but finally decided that he wasn't going to let "the bastards" kill him.

That same spring morning I would have been riding my bike to my grade six class at Beaverton Public School, looking forward to summer holidays. I had no idea of a massive national security campaign to purge homosexuals from the army and the civil service. I had no idea what a homosexual was. I was unaware that police and the Royal Canadian Mounted Police were entrapping and black-mailing hundreds of gay men and lesbians and demanding they give up their friends and contacts.

It would be another twenty years before I met Herb Sutcliffe.

SHENANDOAH

One night during my first year in high school, I went to Beaverton's only movie house to see *Shenandoah*, a movie about a large family in a border state during the American Civil War. There were a few slaves, but they were more like family, and the youngest son, a thin blond boy, was best friends with a slave boy about his age.

Although they didn't care about the war, it soon wrecked their lives. The family was split up. Several of the sons ended up fighting or killed. The daugh-ters were raped and murdered. The youngest son somehow ended up in the Confederate army. Near the end it looked like he, too, would be killed in battle.

But in the climactic scene, back on the homestead, as the gruff father was trying to say a thanksgiving prayer with what remained of the family, the door opened. At the threshold stood the young former slave in a Union uni-form. In his arms he carried his wounded young former master/friend. He had saved him.

In the dark of the theatre, I realized I was crying.

I walked back home over the bridge across the river. There was a skiff of snow on the ground. I felt so lonely. I wanted a friendship like that. A friend that I could have adventures with, who would save my life and whose life I could save. A friend I could hold in my arms. A friendship that would with-stand anything, even war.

DIEFENBAKER

John Diefenbaker was the head of the Progressive Conservative party. My father was a Conservative, and our next-door neighbour was a bigwig in the party. So when there was a leadership convention at Toronto's Maple Leaf Gardens in September 1967, he got observer passes for my friend Bob and me. We would take the train to Toronto and stay in the YMCA. It was my first overnight trip on my own.

Bob got good marks in school, like I did. He did better in math and sci-ence, and I was better in English and history. He was quiet like me, and didn't have a girlfriend or play a lot of sports. So we were a good match.

I was packed and ready to go when my mother took me aside. She seemed upset. She said she had been talking to a friend who told her that homosexuals sometimes lurked in the YMCA showers. I was shocked. I had never heard her use the term before. When she said the word, her voice dropped to a whisper and she glanced around as if she was afraid someone might hear her swearing. A friend of dad's had actually been attacked by a homosexual in Toronto. That kind of thing happened down there. He was lucky and had managed to escape. But who could have ever imagined that they might be in a Christian association of all places. She told me to be very careful, and made me promise not to go to the showers, just to wash in the sink in the room.

At night in our little room in the YMCA I lay awake in the dark, wondering about the showers. I got a hard-on. Bob was breathing quietly in his bed beside mine. I wondered if he was awake and if he had a hard-on, too.

TRUDEAU

In 1968 the world was changing. Rebellion was in the air. So was Trudeaumania.

At Brock District High School, except for the diehard Tories, we thought that Pierre Trudeau was cool. He was different from other politicians. He spoke his mind. He made jokes. He travelled the world and had been to Red China. He even wore sandals and turtlenecks.

As minister of justice he introduced a bill to reform the Criminal Code to liberalize laws on divorce and abortion, and to decriminalize homosexuality. He said the state had no place in the bedrooms of the nation. This was all about sex, and as teenagers, we were all interested in sex – especially since it seemed to scare the wits out of our parents.

It was the decriminalization of homosexuality that drew the most heat. Even in high school most of us weren't completely sure what it was. It had to do with sissies, certainly, or as they were now called, queers. Some said it was a sin, and they would all go to hell. Some said it was dangerous for society and children, and they should be put in jail. Others said they were sick and needed treatment. Still others said that they didn't care what they did as long as they kept it to themselves and weren't obvious. That seemed to be the most liberal point of view. The bottom line was that it was really creepy. A couple of times one had actually been interviewed on TV, on the edgy adult news program *This Hour Has Seven Days*. The voices were distorted and they were always backlit so you couldn't see their faces. Certainly "homosexual" was not something anyone in their right mind would want to be.

Normally, I was very engaged in politics and always ready to argue an opinion. But whenever the discussion about homosexuality came up, I got nervous and didn't say much. I wasn't sure why.

STEPHEN

Nineteen sixty-nine was my first year away from home at Carleton University. I was eighteen. I joined the university's Young Socialist Club. We protested the Vietnam War, called for lower tuition, and argued with the Maoists about Stalin. It was great fun. One afternoon I went to help out on a picket line to support the local strike *célèbre*. There was a guy taking pictures for the student paper. He was the most beautiful man I had ever seen in my life.

It turned out we lived in the same residence building. When I rode up the elevator with him afterwards, I felt indescribably happy. We were soon friends. I wanted to spend as much time with him as I could. I thought about him all the time. I wanted him to be that friend that I had always longed for.

When Stephen didn't have his shirt on, his muscles moved like oil under his velvet skin. I found myself imagining what he would look like, naked, in a forest, with dappled sunlight playing on his chest. Then, in a flash, I thought to myself, oh shit! This is what love is supposed to feel like. There was a ball of fear in my stomach. What did this mean? All my life I had worked at not being a sissy. I wasn't one of those faceless homosexuals that couldn't be shown on television. I wasn't one of those mincing, preening, bitter creatures with a cigarette dangling from a limp wrist that I'd seen in the movies. I didn't even smoke. I was normal. But I was in love with a man.

PRIDE

Saturday, August 17, 1974, was a bright sunny afternoon. I was walking towards Allan Gardens, a park in downtown Toronto. My stomach was in a knot. I saw a handful of people on the north side of the park and a pile of placards.

I was just back in Toronto after two years in South America. I had followed Stephen there, like a needy puppy. I even screwed up the courage to tell him I loved him one night. We were both stoned. He said he loved me too and gave me a hug. We were learning Spanish, but in English, we were obviously not speaking the same language. Soon his girlfriend came to join us. I finally left them in Cali, Colombia, where we had been teaching English, and continued south.

After hitchhiking around South America for a year, I had come back to Canada knowing I had two options: deal with this shit, or jump off a bridge.

The Boys in the Band, a 1969 movie about self-hating homosexuals, was playing at a local rep cinema. I sat in the back of the theatre, in the dark, watching the drama unfold. It was not a pretty picture. But as the movie let out, I noticed two young men who had also been in the audience. They were talking happily and for a minute, one took the other's hand. I felt a flood of warmth in my heart. I followed them for several blocks.

I had heard about a newspaper called *The Body Politic*. It was about gay liberation. The word "gay" seemed to be a slightly effeminate term that served to take the edge off "homosexual." But liberation had been my stock-in-trade in the Young Socialists, so I was into that.

I screwed up my courage, went into a store, bought a stack of magazines including a copy of *TBP*, and took them to Riverdale Park. The park spans both sides of the southern end of the Don Valley divided by a highway. The floor of the valley is flat and treeless, with a running track on the east side. I sat in the middle of the track. There, I could see anyone coming within a quarter mile. I figured if someone came too close to where I was sitting, I could stuff the paper in my bag and run away.

The front cover of that issue displayed a line drawing of two young men lounging naked on a carpet, staring into each other's eyes against a romantic background of gladiolas, ferns, and snapdragons. It was beautiful.

I opened the pages tentatively and stepped into an ongoing conversation. Letter writers were upset about articles in previous issues. One attacked a piece that had claimed "personal solutions and alternative lifestyles" had no place in the gay movement. The writer asserted that one of the most crucial messages of the feminist and gay movements had been that the personal is political. Someone from Calgary wrote his thanks for an article about rural gay youth. Another called for gays to abandon the small towns and congregate in large cities where they could constitute majorities and gain economic and political power. It concluded: "Separatism offers us true liberation, while integration with heterosexuals offers only the oppression we have already experienced for 2000 years."[2]

There was a great deal of back and forth about an interview with a doctor called Edgar Friedenberg, whom someone described as "a person elevated by the mechanisms of the ruling class to the position of intellectual authority." That writer was in turn accused of dogmatism and shrill obsessions in his own claims of superiority.

I felt at home. This was just like the left that I knew and loved.

I also learned that the *Toronto Star* was refusing ads from gay organizations (the word "gay" could not appear in a family paper). Support was building for inclusion of sexual orientation in the Ontario Human Rights Code. And a downtown school, Oakwood Collegiate, had prohibited students from inviting a gay speaker to class.

There was a feature article on Roger Casement, an Irish freedom fighter executed by the British in 1916 who, it turned out, was gay. My grandparents were Irish. It had never occurred to me that an Irish revolutionary could be gay. Finally, there was a long interview with Dennis Altman, an Australian who had written a book called *Homosexual: Oppression and Liberation*. Altman talked about "the potentially revolutionary nature of being homosexual," but cautioned that he was no longer sure that it wasn't possible for modern western capitalist societies to assimilate them.

A month later a new issue came out. This time the outside cover made me feel queasy. It wasn't romantic. It was a picture of a paper doll, like the ones little girls played with, but this one was of a man alongside a pin-on leather outfit. I felt the woman at the cash register looking at me. Worse, when I unfolded the paper, the startling full-page inside front cover was a caricature of Prime Minister Pierre Trudeau, leader of the opposition Robert Stanfield, and New Democratic Party (NDP) leader David Lewis, all naked, with large, engorged, and differently shaped penises. I was relieved that I was once again in the centre of the track and no one could see over my shoulder.

Moving quickly to the letters, there were criticisms the paper was too male oriented, dry, and intellectual. In the news, a printer had refused to publish the issue (no wonder, I thought); a new gay church called Metropolitan Community Church (MCC) had been chartered; a lesbian mother was fighting for custody of her kids; and a provincial gay rights coalition was being formed. And *TBP* and the Gay Alliance Toward Equality (GATE) had just opened a storefront office on Carlton Street. That wasn't far from where I was staying. I was thinking about walking past on my way home when I saw, on page seven, an article about Chilean fascists terrorizing gays. I was stunned. Someone in Canada actually knew about what had just happened in Chile.

Chile had been the great beacon of hope for Latin America when the socialist government of Salvador Allende was elected in 1970. I had been in Peru heading south when the coup happened in September 1973. I heard Allende's last broadcast over a crackling radio in a cafe in Cusco. Minutes later he was murdered by Pinochet's soldiers as the air force bombarded the presidential palace. I managed to cross the border into Chile a few months later when things had settled down. I saw the ruins of the palace. There was still a dusk-to-dawn curfew. At night I heard shooting outside my cheap hotel room in Santiago. People I talked to were terrified, if they would talk at all. There were armed soldiers everywhere.

But when I returned to Canada no one seemed to know or care. It was just another coup in some far-off banana republic. *TBP*, however, was covering it. And it was affecting gays. They cared. Then at the bottom of the same page, my eyes fell on an ad for an Ontario Gay Pride March.

Reading the paper had gotten me used to the term "gay." It no longer made my stomach twist like "homosexual." But I didn't actually know any gay people. There were ads for bars and baths in the paper, but the thought of going to a gay bar conjured up terrifying images of drag queens or leather men. I had no idea what a bath was.

But I'd been on my share of marches and demonstrations. I knew what you were supposed to do at that kind of thing.

Still, that hot Saturday afternoon in Allan Gardens, I hung around at a distance for a while before moving closer. None of the folks who were gathering were wearing drag or leather or chains. In fact, most of them seemed relatively normal. I didn't hear any of the sinister music that always came on when a homosexual appeared in the movies. So when they were almost ready to go, I quickly walked over and picked up a sign that said Gay Liberation Now and started marching down the sidewalk thinking, if there's a TV camera I wonder if I can induce a heart attack and die by holding my breath?

But there were no TV cameras. Fifty people walking down the sidewalk with hand-drawn placards was hardly newsworthy, even in 1974. Another advantage of there being only fifty people was that I was recognized as a new face in the crowd. When the march was over, I was snapped up, taken home, had sex with for the first time, given a bunch of gay liberation literature, and told to come back for more when I had finished reading.

I was a quick reader. And was soon back for more. Suddenly it seemed a million pounds that I didn't know I was carrying disappeared. Suddenly I knew that I had always been gay but just hadn't known it. I found out I had been "in the closet." The whole thing was exhilarating. For the first time in my life I had a way to address who I was, emotionally, sexually, politically, as part of a community. For the first time in my life I could be honest. I came out. I was "liberated."

COMMUNITY, A GUIDE

The community that I came out into was still a small space in the summer of 1974. In time for that year's Pride celebrations, the Community Homophile Association of Toronto (CHAT) published *Gay Directions: A Guide to Toronto*. The booklet is a snapshot of gay Toronto four decades ago.

At three and a half years, CHAT was the city's most established gay organization. It maintained a volunteer-run, twenty-four-hour distress and information line "to give comfort to the lonely, referrals to those who need legal or medical assistance, and information about homosexuality to both gays and the general public."[3] It was able to maintain an office, thanks to Local Initiative Project funding aimed at reducing youth unemployment in the recession sparked by the Arab oil embargo. CHAT held weekly meetings on Tuesdays, a drop-in on Wednesdays, women's night on Thursdays, and often dances on weekends.

Eight other groups in Toronto were listed: ANIK (the Inuktitut word for brotherhood), *The Body Politic* Collective, GATE, the Lesbian Collective, MCC, the Unitarian Universalist Gay Caucus, and Homophile Associations at the University of Toronto and York University.

There was a commercial scene largely catering to gay men, most of it straight owned. Eight bars were listed, with the warning that all bars in Toronto were closed on Sundays. The Club Manatee (men only), however, was open for dancing on the weekends, including Sundays, since it had no liquor licence. There were five steam baths, and a sixth, the Barracks, was scheduled to open before Labour Day. *Gay Directions* was financed by ads from a number of these bars and baths.

A page on "Pleasant Places to Stroll" indicated the major gay men's cruising and outdoor sex locales: David Balfour Park in the north, Philosopher's Walk on the University of Toronto campus, Queen's Park behind the provincial legislature, and St. Joseph Street downtown. That section was followed by a "Word to the Wise," reminding readers of legal prohibitions against sex in a public place.

The last eight pages of the thirty-six-page booklet were dedicated to "Answers to some of your questions about homosexuals and homosexuality," followed by an annotated bibliography of some of "the best and most recent" non-fiction on homosexuality and gay liberation.

It might seem odd today that a community guide should give up so much space to a basic Q&A and a booklist. But *Gay Directions* was meant to orient those just entering a new community – a community that was in early formation. This was outreach to people like me, emerging from isolation, struggling with fear and self-loathing, in desperate need of information about who we were supposed to be. The booklet was not just an orientation to a new city; it had a political goal to reassure and to encourage each of us. "Dare to be yourself," advised an André Gide quote that stood alone on the final page.

And daring to be yourself, the quintessential motto of liberal individualism, was part of the 1970s zeitgeist of questioning traditional authority.

THE SOCIOLOGY OF COMMUNITY

Gay Directions, other than alluding to differences between lesbians and gay men, imagined a community that was homogenous. CHAT was predominantly male, white, and English speaking and oblivious to other differences. But in fact, Toronto *was* much more homogenous at the time. According to the 1971 census, almost 96 per cent of the population of greater Toronto was of European ancestry.[4] Canada's whites-only immigration practices had begun to change only in 1967, and Toronto's complexion in the early 1970s reflected that racist history.

Those of us on the left talked about class differences and the need for workers to rise up. But the same census data found 66 per cent of Torontonians living in middle-income neighbourhoods. About 15 per cent were high-income, leaving only 19 per cent in lower than average income areas.[5] Most of the population found itself part of a large middle class, based on the salaries of adequately paid working people. This was an age when even unskilled (albeit male) workers could aspire to save, support a family, and own their own homes on a single wage. Their children could aspire to go to university and to upward mobility. Most were not rich, but neither were they poor. The national imaginary was reflected in the winning slogan of the Trudeau Liberals' 1969 election campaign – The Just Society.

The post-war Keynesian experiment had established a social safety net supported by progressive taxation. Labour legislation such as the Rand

Formula helped facilitate unionization. Post-secondary education was subsidized. Even though my family had entered the middle class, I received a grant to go to university. Despite the 1974 recession, there were still jobs, and most provided a living wage.

This meant that young people were able to strike out and establish independent lives before marriage. And for those of us uninterested in marriage, it was a way of escaping the heterosexual pressures of our small towns and suburbs. My trajectory was not unique. Few of the people I met in my new community were actually "from" Toronto. We had moved to the big city to find ourselves and others like us. Petula Clark's anthem "Downtown" had a special resonance for us.

Toronto's processes of urbanization concentrated us. A building boom of new high-rises in the city centre, sparked by the opening of the subway system in the 1950s, provided affordable single-person apartments in the Church-Wellesley area. I soon learned that the phallic, round high-rise at Alexander and Church streets was referred to as KY Towers, after the popular lubricant. This was the nucleus of what in the 1970s we called the gay ghetto.

Since gay people were drawn proportionally from the rest of the population, more than 80 per cent of us, the men at least, would have enough disposable income to participate in a gay commercial scene. Since anyone who participated was vulnerable to discrimination, there was a tendency to feel that if we were gay, we were all in the same boat.

That is not to say that there were no disparities. Women in the workforce earned approximately 60 per cent of what men earned. Lesbians, independent of men, tended to be poorer. The commercial scene's orientation to men reflected this difference in disposable income. It also reflected the cultural prohibitions against, and actual dangers for, women out on their own after dark.

Toronto was also the country's major immigrant reception area. Immigrants earned about 80 per cent of what Canadian-born workers did. Although most were of European origin and assimilation was realistic, the ghetto could be a very Anglo place. Social divisions and sexual stereotypes proliferated. Aboriginal communities faced much more serious economic and social marginalization, and at the time, tended to be all but invisible in Toronto gay spaces.

Although this Keynesian world was far more egalitarian than what had come before, or would come after, Canada still had its 1 per cent. Wallace Clement profiled this group in *The Canadian Corporate Elite* (1975). Canada's elite had a clear ethnic character at the time. Anglo Canadians predominated (86.2 per cent), 8.4 per cent were French Canadian, and only 5.4 per cent belonged to other ethnic groups. Although one no longer had to be a member of the Orange Lodge to advance in Toronto the Good, the city's elite was still mostly old money and overwhelmingly Protestant. That class of people were unlikely to frequent the often seedy downtown gay establishments.

Toronto was the second-largest city in a white settler state that involved the exploitation of immigrants, discrimination by the Anglo majority, a social hierarchy among Catholics and Protestants and Jews, overarching sexism against women, and ongoing racism against Aboriginal people and non-whites. All of these relationships were reflected in the lesbian and gay community.

ESSENTIAL READING

The man who picked me up at Pride that August afternoon was Jearld Moldenhauer. Still in his twenties, Jearld was already a community elder. He had been a founder of the University of Toronto Homophile Association, the city's first post-Stonewall gay group. He had just completed a cross-Canada speaking tour, helping establish gay liberation groups in cities across the country. He had also been a leading member and writer in *TBP*, although by the summer of 1974 there had just been a serious falling out.

Jearld's passion now was Glad Day Bookshop, which he had founded a couple of years before. Glad Day was a political project. It aimed to make available the suppressed history, culture, imagery, and literature routinely denied to us. Glad Day would feed the hunger for knowledge and nourish the intellectual foundations of our movement for liberation. Jearld took me home to his gay men's communal house at 139 Seaton Street after the Pride march. (Such communes were the way we would all live after the revolution). Glad Day consisted of shelves of books on the wall of the main hallway. It was from those shelves that he helped me select my essential reading.

HOMOSEXUAL BEHAVIOR AMONG MALES

Of the stack of literature that I took away that day after getting and giving my first blowjob, the book that had the deepest immediate effect on me was Wainwright Churchill's *Homosexual Behavior among Males*.[6] It described itself as a "cross-cultural and cross species investigation," although it probably wouldn't pass muster on either of those accounts today. There wasn't much zoology, and the only cultures he looked at were the modern United States, classical Greece, and Rome. Nonetheless, the book clearly and powerfully laid out most of the founding arguments of gay liberation.

Homosexual Behavior maintained that same-sex sexual activity was a common component of mammalian sexuality, and that the motive for all sexual behaviour was an undifferentiated release of sexual tension. Churchill insisted that response to different sexual objects was learned or conditioned behaviour, and that there was no such thing as a "sexual instinct" among humans.

But, he argued, all societies have a "sexual mystique" – the dogmas and taboos that evolve in the interests of a society's aims for sexuality. He divided the world into "sex positive" and "sex negative" societies, and excoriated modern American society as particularly sex negative. Its sexual mystique failed to recognize any function for sex other than procreation. He detailed the deleterious effect this had on young people not ready to procreate, those too old to procreate, women, families, and anyone involved in same-sex sexual activity.

A full chapter was devoted to Kinsey's notion of a sexual continuum. Alfred Kinsey had published two groundbreaking studies, *Sexual Behavior in the Human Male* (1948) and *Sexual Behavior in the Human Female* (1953). Churchill repeatedly referenced the Kinsey findings as evidence of the widespread persistence of same-sex sexual activity, even in the face of a sex-negative mystique. In fact, he argued, sex-negative societies were paradoxically more likely to produce sexual minorities. The suppression of particular sexual responses isolated and therefore reinforced specific sexual behaviours.

For Churchill, a society's sexual mystique was essentially cultural. The acceptance or rejection of homosexual behaviour could not be correlated "with any known circumstance related to geography or the complexity of a given society."[7] He laid the blame for what he called America's "erotophobia" and "homoerotophobia" squarely on its Judeo-Christian tradition. The Hebrews, he argued, developed "one of the most prohibitionistic sex codes ever known in history," and Christian sects such as Calvinism amplified that negativity. Modern psychiatry had given a scientific gloss to such moralistic prejudices. Churchill argued for a liberal approach to sex; each individual had the right to express their sexuality however they might want.

Churchill helped establish what would become two of the major axioms of gay liberation: Heterosexuality was not "natural," just common. And the problem was not homosexuality but homo(eroto)phobia. His focus on conservative institutions – religion, psychiatry, and law – as enforcers pointed to the battlegrounds where the struggle for gay liberation would be fought.

But Churchill's stance challenged one tenet of the gay movement, collective identity. While calling for a cultural shift to a more sex-positive society, he insisted, "in reality there is no such thing as a homosexual."[8] For Churchill, homosexual identity was the unfortunate by-product of oppression. "Especially for those who have an extensive amount of homosexual experience, it is almost impossible within our society not to be pressured in one way or another into a minority status, and within this status, in a great many cases comes the assumption of a 'homosexual way of life.'"[9]

Churchill considered the "homosexual way of life as a definitely inferior emotional adjustment." But, he conceded, "for those who cannot and those who will not abandon their homosexual interests, there must be some recourse to social life with others like themselves, and it is entirely understandable that these people will tend – like all minorities – to create a little world of their own."[10] He went on to dismiss the political expression of that identity, the "so called homophile movement," as "weak, very poorly organized, largely intellectual, very unpopular even among those who might be expected to rally around it, and downright humorous in some of its aspects."[11]

By the time I read Churchill in the summer of 1974, however, gay identity was common sense and was not about to be overturned. The contradiction between the sweeping goal of sexual liberation for all versus the practical liberation of our minority had already been settled. The new movement took Kinsey's continuum and arbitrarily drew a line between homo- and heterosexual at the 10 per cent point, thus producing the minority that Churchill decried. It followed that as a people, we needed a history, tradition, culture, visibility. We needed leadership. We needed allies. The task of gay liberation was to make this minority one that was consciously aware of itself and organized to advocate for itself.

Homosexuality among Males was widely cited. Many of its arguments became the bread and butter of gay liberation discourse. But Churchill's inconvenient passages on identity were ignored or dismissed as self-oppression. After all, we rationalized, the book had been written almost two years before Stonewall. What could you expect? Churchill was our Moses. He led us out of the wilderness, but could not himself enter our Promised Land. Despite his powerful influence, he never personally "came out."

GAY REVOLUTION

If Churchill was a window on some of the foundational ideas of the Stonewall generation, Karla Jay and Allen Young's *Out of the Closets*[12] captured the politics and the mood of the movement immediately after the riots. In her foreword to the anthology, Jay argued that radical lesbians and homosexuals saw their oppression "as a class struggle and our oppressor as white, middle-class, male-dominated heterosexual society, which has relentlessly persecuted and murdered homosexuals and lesbians since the oppressor has had power." She called us "the negation of heterosexuality and of the nuclear family structure."

To build community, we had to deal with our own oppressive behaviour. "Gay men oppress gay women, white gays oppress black gays, and straight-looking gays oppress transvestites.... Some articles manifest our desire to combat our own chauvinism, our own sexism, our own racism, as well as our oppression by straight society."[13]

In his introduction, Young outlined what he saw as some of the core beliefs of gay liberation politics. The struggles against sexism and against war. That the Roman Catholic Church had been a deadly enemy of the homosexual throughout history. And that the traditional left, both old and new, had been as oppressive to homosexuals as had establishment America.

He explained that while (liberal) homophile and civil rights groups worked primarily towards the elimination of laws that prevented gays from "doing our own thing," gay liberation was more far-reaching. Its premise was "consciousness-raising about sexism with the goal for sexual liberation for all." Finally, "gay liberation also has a perspective for revolution based on the unity of all oppressed people – that is, there can be no freedom for gays in a society that enslaves others through male supremacy, racism, and economic exploitation (capitalism)."[14] Gay liberation needed to join the pantheon of often socialist inflected women's, black, and national liberation struggles that were at that point shaking the world. We would not just be a liberal movement. We were partners in a fundamental social transformation.

While most of *Out of the Closets* assumed gay identity as a given, several articles shared something with Churchill's rejection. According to Carl Wittman:

> We continue to call ourselves homosexual, not bisexual, even if we do make it with the opposite sex also, because saying, "Oh, I'm Bi" is a copout.... We'll be gay until everyone has forgotten that's it's an issue. Then we'll begin to be complete.[15]

Wittman also echoed Churchill in his critique of the "gay ghetto."

> We are refugees from Amerika. So we came to the ghetto – and as other ghettos; it has its negative and positive aspects. Refugee camps are better than what preceded them, or people never would have come. But they are still enslaved, if only that we are limited to being ourselves there and only there.
>
> Ghettos breed self-hatred. We stagnate there, accepting the status quo. The status quo is rotten. We are all warped by our oppression, and in the isolation of the ghetto, we blame ourselves rather than our oppressors.[16]

Wittman asserted that gay people are both part of and in alliance with other struggles, foreshadowing notions of "intersectionality" and "assemblage" that would enter the lexicon years later.

> Many of us have mixed identities and have ties with other liberation movements: women, blacks, other minority groups; we may also have taken on an identity which is vital to us: ecology, dope, ideology. And face it, we can't change Amerika alone.[17]

He asked, "Who do we look to for coalition?" While listing the barriers and difficulties, his answer was "Women's liberation," "Black liberation," "Chicanos," "White radicals and ideologues," "Hip and street people," and "Homophile groups."

In "Somewhere in the Right Direction: Testimony of My Experience in a Gay Male Living Collective," John Knoebel talked about the hopes, trials, and tribulations of being part of New York's 95th Street Collective, an experiment in communal living. The collective was non-hierarchical. Members shared chores, and decisions were made by consensus in long house meetings featuring criticism-self-criticism. It did not end well, but that did not dampen Knoebel's optimism. "I do not consider the failure of the collective to work out its internal contradictions an indication that the group process itself is a failure, or that I don't have to struggle anymore to change myself. . . . I learned a great deal from what happened to me and have written this to share the experience."[18]

The book's final chapter, "Manifestos," was a distillation of the revolutionary rhetoric that electrified the early 1970s. In its affirmation that the personal is political, 1970s radical discourse stressed the reciprocal relationship between transformations in personal consciousness and political transformation. In "What We Want, What We Believe," the Third World Gay Revolution Collective from New York asserted:

> Together, not alone, we must explore how we view ourselves and analyze the assumptions behind our self-identity. We can then begin to crack the barriers of our varying illnesses, our passivity, sexual chauvinism – in essence, our inability to unabashedly love each other; to live, fight, and if necessary, die for the people of the earth.[19]

The "Gay Revolutionary Party Manifesto" even saw gay people as *the* revolutionary force.

> In the past we gay people have never been allowed to associate openly with any nation, race, ethnic group, religion or social movement. All have denied our gayness, even while using our abilities. The result of this exclusion has been that we have had no vested interest in dogmatism, sexism, racism and nationalism. . . .
>
> Gay revolution will not lead to freedom of association for gay people in a predominately straight world, nor will it lead to straight-defined homosexuality with marriages and exclusive monogamy. Gay revolution will produce a world in which all social and sensual relationships will be gay, and in which homo and heterosexuality will be incomprehensible terms. . . . At this point increasing numbers of straight men will be forced to make a choice between becoming gay or attacking gay feminists in order to restore the previous imbalance of power. This reaction would then produce a collective insurrection by gay-feminist revolutionaries which would seek to end the power of straight men.[20]

Such revolutionary writings were heady. They asserted our role in a universal process of human liberation to fundamentally change society. But even by 1974 they were beginning to seem utopian and naive. The flurry of Gay Liberation Fronts that emerged after Stonewall had already given way to more practical forms of organizing. The revolutionary phase of gay liberation turned out to be a kind of Higgs boson, created after the initial big bang of Stonewall, essential for what was to come later, but too ephemeral and unstable to last for more than a flash.

At the time, though, such revolutionary rhetoric was not as outlandish as it now might appear. It was not just part of the left that assumed gay liberation was revolutionary. The establishment was just as likely to see homosexuality as a harbinger of the end of its civilization, and as something to be repressed at all costs. Both the left and the right considered the stakes around attitudes towards homosexuality to be pivotal.

OUT

Coming out wasn't supposed to be like joining a club. It was supposed to be an epiphany about who I was and therefore, who I always had been. I was to look back and see my shyness, lack of interest in sports, studiousness, all those inchoate desires, crushes, my feelings for Stephen, as signs that I had been too stupid or too cowardly to recognize. "Gay" was the truth about me finally revealed.

But despite that, it did sort of operate like a club. Gay was a culture, a tribe whose values, customs, and mores I had to acquire. There were new rules and vocabulary. For instance, "straight" for me had meant conformist, short hair, and not smoking dope. The opposite was "freak." But now it meant heterosexual as opposed to gay.

I learned that the Stonewall riots had changed the world. When the queens fought back against the New York City cops in June 1969, they had come out. Since then, "closet" as a noun, or as an adjective – closet case, closet queen – was a derogatory term.

In terms of values, monogamy was bad, promiscuity was good. But then there was the feminist notion of "objectification" – men turning women's bodies into sexual objects for consumption. Should that apply to gay men's promiscuous sexual behaviour with other men, or was it problematic only when men had power over women? Did liberated sex require love or require dispensing with it? Could love itself be promiscuous?

Butch and fem were out, androgynous was in. Relationships should be equal. It was better for people having sex to come together. If you came first this time, your partner should come first next time. No one should be exclusively top or bottom. For a guy to be too masculine, or a woman (you should never say girl, only woman) to be too feminine was suspect, even though they could be really hot. Drag was a relic of an oppressive past, but disliking drag was "internalized oppression."

Before, my sexual feelings could not be talked about. Now, they *had* to be talked about. Being discreet was out. We needed to ram our existence down their throats. According to *TBP*'s Gerald Hannon:

> Throat-ramming . . . must become the social extension of our public struggle for civil rights. . . . It means never hearing a fag joke or seeing a limp wrist parody without protesting the insult. . . . It means bringing it up at work whenever it seems remotely natural to do so. . . . It means *never* appearing in public with another gay person (or persons) unless it will be obvious that you are gay people. The easiest way to do that is to hold hands.

It means never appearing in public *alone* unless it is as obvious as you can make it that you are a gay person."[21]

Before I had felt ashamed and afraid; now, I had to be proud. Before I had been glad that no one could tell. Now anything that contributed to invisibility indicated cowardice.

I got the coming out part. Soon few straight people got away without knowing I was gay. I hung out at Jearld's commune, like an anthropologist, carefully observing the men who came and went. Most of them you couldn't tell, but I watched carefully for signs. "Turn on your gaydar," Jearld said.

I was taken to the Parkside Tavern with its sawdust-covered floor. The men in leather in one corner, the old queens in another, the young druggies in yet another. The white-shirted waiters who brought the beer to the table because you weren't allowed to walk around with a glass. "Keep out of the washroom," I was warned. The cops have a peephole.

The St. Charles was more upscale. I felt slightly intimidated there. One night we went to the Manatee. The entrance was at ground level, but the dance floor was lower. I saw hundreds of sweating men dancing. I didn't know there were so many of us in the world. It was orgasmic. And occasionally the music got slow. Dancing a slow dance with another man felt utterly weird, but at the same time touching, demonstrating my excitement or most tender emotions in public, without fear, was a breathtakingly novel and affirmative experience.

As tightly as I embraced this new identity, I was not always the best of students. It could all be very confusing. I was not properly fashion conscious, camp, nor interested in show tunes, opera, or leather. Truth be told, I found the bar scene and drag shows boring. I was still shy about sexual talk and sometimes scandalized by the banter of my new friends. My gaucheness around how to be gay was sometimes seen by my comrades as quaint or backward, or deplored as "straight identified." But the access to sex, the potential of love, a network of friends and community all anchored me. And while I might be awkward in a bar, gay liberation politics was a cultural space where I fit in.

At the time, no one seemed to recognize any contradiction in an identity that we were supposed to already be, but still had to learn *how* to be. If my new comrades and I recognized that gay had come into existence at a particular time and place, with a particular history and in a particular society, it was because, we felt, society had progressed to a point where what had formerly been hidden was now becoming visible. We were, after all, living in revolutionary times. Everything was changing. For most of us at that point, gay was a universal category, just now being revealed by history. We were drunk on identity, and after what we had been through, it tasted very sweet, indeed.

LIFE LESSON ONE, YONGE STREET

It was early in September and still hot. We were riding our bikes along Welles-ley Street and having an argument. Jearld had said that gay people were oppressed, just like blacks and women. I said it wasn't the same. Black people and women were treated differently from the time they were born. Gay people mostly just slipped under the radar. We might be lonely and isolated, but we weren't really oppressed.

As we crossed Yonge he said, "Okay, stop here. Lock your bike." I was puz-zled but did what I was told.

"Hold my hand," he said. My jaw dropped. "Hold my hand. We're going for a walk."

He took my hand, and on a hot sunny afternoon in the fall of 1974 we walked south down Yonge Street, downtown Toronto's major commercial artery, two young men holding hands.

I had never felt so terrified in my life.

People stopped. They gaped at us. They pointed. They glared. They gig-gled. They shrieked. They screamed "faggots" from the other side of the street.

I could feel the sweat running down my sides.

After two interminable blocks, Jearld turned to me and said, "Had enough?"

"Yes," I whispered. He smiled sweetly. "That's what oppression feels like."

LIFE LESSON TWO, WOMEN

Initially, I was so enthralled to find myself in a world of other gay men that I hardly noticed that there weren't many women around. Jearld's collective house was all men. Certainly you didn't see women in the bars. Most of the Parkside was actually "men only" as a requirement of the liquor licence.

I asked Jearld, and he explained that it was only natural. The basic thing that brought men and women together in the straight world was sex. So when people weren't interested in that, why would they socialize? Gay men tended to hang out with gay men and lesbians with other lesbians.

Those were the days when gay men often socialized in large house parties. Sprinkled in with their ribald talk, I would often hear jokes about the smell of fish and how gross women were. Not among the younger, more political set, mind you, but these parties drew all kinds and ages. I began to realize that some gay men didn't seem to like women much.

There was sexism, Jearld admitted, but it went both ways. A lot of lesbians didn't like men, either, because they had had bad experiences. But politics had to overcome that. Our experiences of being outsiders were key. They meant you could see things about society that people who fit in couldn't. Lesbians and gay men could see things about heterosexuality. Women could see things about sexism. Black people could see things about racism. We all needed to bring those understandings to the revolution if it was going to succeed.

That made sense, but when I went to help out at *The Body Politic*/GATE office, I was surprised there weren't women there, either. The paper said the right things. It had articles about feminist revolution and reviews of lesbian books (although they were often written by men). When I looked through back issues there had been occasional women on the collective, but they never seemed to stay long. There was constant talk about the need to get more women involved, but it just never seemed to happen.

One night Jearld took me to an event at the CHAT centre. There were various amateur performances. One involved a song about fruit where the men pretended to try to swallow whole bananas. Then some lesbians got up and complained that it was sexist. The men couldn't understand why women were so uptight about sex, and things got really heated. It was quite uncomfortable.

I think one of those women was Patricia (Pat) Murphy. Murphy was part of the Brunswick Four. In January, half a year before I came out, she and three friends had sung "I Enjoy Being a Dyke" at the Brunswick Tavern's weekly amateur night. The Brunswick catered to university students and was not a gay bar. The management asked them to leave, and when they refused, they were arrested and roughed up by the police. Acquitted of all but one charge, the women then charged the police with assault. But when the cops involved "couldn't be identified," the furious women called the trial a farce and wouldn't stand when required to do so by the court clerk. Murphy ultimately spent thirty days in jail for contempt. She was a martyr to the movement. No one crossed her.

I slowly began to realize that lesbian politics was coming from a very different place. It was anchored in a broader feminist movement challenging the basic values of male-dominated society. Even our reading lists were different. I didn't really know many lesbians in those days, but whenever I found myself in a lesbian household, I always noticed a copy of *Our Bodies, Ourselves* on the bookshelf. *OBOS* was the ground zero document of an exploding women's health movement that challenged the "expertise" of the male-dominated medical system as central to women's oppression. It sought to educate women about their own bodies based on their own experience. *OBOS*, first produced by a Boston women's collective in 1970, had by mid-decade been commercially published and sold hundreds of thousands of copies. There was nothing comparable for men, certainly no straight men's movement that we wanted to be part of.

While lesbians had always been central to the women's movement, the relationship was not always smooth there, either. After the notion of coming out gathered steam, Betty Friedan, president of the U.S. National Organization of Women, called lesbians a "lavender menace," reinforcing the stereotype that feminists hated men. Her phrase was appropriated by Radicalesbians, who protested the lack of lesbian visibility at NOW's 1970 Second Conference to Unite Women in New York, and distributed the pamphlet *The Woman Identified Woman*. It opened: "What is a lesbian? A lesbian is the rage of all women condensed to the point of explosion."[22] For a young gay man, all that rage could be a little scary.

LIFE LESSON THREE, HALLOWEEN

By Halloween 1974, I was still seeing Jearld off and on. He said we should go over to Yonge Street.

"It's for kids," I replied. "What's it got to do with us?"

"It's the night the drag queens come out. It's the only night of the year you can't be busted for wearing a disguise in public."

I said I wasn't really into drag. It seemed kind of disrespectful to women.

He told me it was something I needed to see.

We walked north on Yonge. There wasn't much traffic. Then I saw something happening in the street up ahead. It looked like a demonstration. When we got closer, I realized that a crowd had gathered in front of the St. Charles Tavern, the city's most famous gay bar. They were angry and loud.

Then, somehow illuminated, maybe by flash bulbs or maybe just by the street light, a drag queen appeared. Sequins, beehive hairdo, makeup for days. Just as she reached the front door, the crowd realized she was there. There was a volley of eggs. Someone tried to grab her. She elbowed him. The crowd went crazy, screaming. But they had missed her, and as she disappeared inside, she stuck her arm back out, giving them the finger. Eggs and a bottle smashed on the door as it closed.

We stood at the back of the mob, invisible. There was no holding hands here. I could taste the hate in the air.

Jearld gave me questioning look. "Why don't they just go in the back door?" I managed to stammer.

"Are you kidding? There aren't any lights in the alley. Anything could happen back there. And why the hell shouldn't they go in the front door?"

There were a couple of cops standing across the street, looking bored. They were just making sure that the street wasn't blocked and cars could get through.

After a half-hour of soaking up the hate, Jearld motioned that we should go. As we walked away, I glanced back over my shoulder at the hotel overlooking the street across from the bar. "Next year we should all chip in and rent a room up there," I said. "And when they gather, we can dump garbage on them. Balloons full of shit and piss."

Jearld smiled. "I like that," he said quietly.

THE POLICE AND THE LAW

We were scarcely five years away from decriminalization, and still considered an outlaw caste, despised and feared. Not to mention vulnerable. For many young, straight men, queerbashing was a community service. If anyone was actually charged, he only had to say "he made a pass at me" to get off. That seldom needed to happen, though. No gay man in his right mind went to the police in such situations. They were not our friends.

One of the first pieces of lore I learned was the Cherry Beach Express. Cherry Beach was an isolated area on the lake, cut off from the rest of the city by industrial and port lands. Anyone who looked too queer whom the police caught out alone late at night risked being taken there, roughed up, and left to make their own way back to the city. There were reports of lesbians being raped.

Jearld reprimanded me sharply when I said something about the 1969 legalization of homosexuality. I was never to forget that decriminalization and legalization were two different things. Not prosecuting "indecent acts" between two people in private if both were over twenty-one did not mean we were legal. If someone saw you, it was no longer private and therefore illegal. If there were more than two people, it was illegal. If someone was under twenty-one, it was illegal. We still faced legally condoned discrimination, police harassment, violence, and socially sanctioned contempt.[23]

Human rights protection was a far-off dream. It was perfectly legal to evict us from our apartments, fire us from our jobs, or refuse us service in a restaurant simply because we were or appeared to be gay. All that the Criminal Code amendments had done was to recognize the obvious. The state could scarcely effectively surveil all the bedrooms of the nation. The law enforced the social contract of the closet. Keep it hidden and we won't come after you.

THE MORAL ECONOMY OF THE CLOSET

If urban concentration and the commercial scene provided places to gather, at least for men, most in this community were still not "out." My new comrades saw coming out as a badge of courage, and deployed the term "closet" with the derision worthy of any moral failure. But for most, coming out still seemed utterly foolhardy. The closet was a survival strategy, a rational adaptation to an oppressive situation. "Daring to be oneself" was a dangerous enterprise.

Sexuality had been largely relegated to the control of conservative institutions dominated by traditional values – the church, the courts, the cops. Although the relationship between lesbian and gay people and the rest of society entailed a dramatically uneven balance of power, the oppression/closet relationship was a functioning system with a social contract. If we conformed to gender norms, if we were discreet, if we kept hidden, then we would not be humiliated, excluded, prosecuted, tortured, or killed.

Within gay society, notions of what was fair, acceptable, valuable – our moral economy – had evolved in that context. Value was placed on being able to pass, on being able to conform to social expectations in general and those regarding gender in particular. The closet valued individual discretion, the double entendre, conforming to hegemonic values, and not rocking the boat.

Success was measured by normative criteria and often displayed by conspicuous consumption.

In a way, this was a liberal response to a repressive situation. Each individual was mainly out to save their own skin. But even closeted gay society had its own forms of solidarity. While bitching and gossiping within the group were commonplace, betrayal of someone's sexuality to the outside world was monstrous. And although "straight acting" was valued, the drag queen or the bull dyke earned a grudging respect relegated to the rebel.

COMMUNITY POLITICS

The Judy Garland "Somewhere over the Rainbow" generation was facing a new Bob Dylan "The Times They Are A-Changin'" cohort. The risks associated with coming out could be high. But for some of us, especially young, single white men with a sense of entitlement, they were becoming more tolerable.

Shifts in values take place unevenly. The community was small, but that didn't mean that everyone was on the same page. The Pride Week Events listing at the end of *Gay Directions* did not include the Saturday afternoon march that occasioned my coming out. The march was not organized by CHAT, but by the new Gay Alliance Toward Equality.

GATE formed in February 1973 to replace Toronto Gay Action, originally an activist caucus within CHAT. But there had been growing tensions between those focusing on social services and those pushing for political reform. The disappearance of TGA and the formation of GATE signalled a divorce that ended that uneasy relationship. GATE considered itself a radical, activist civil rights organization, and its march to the Ontario legislature at Queen's Park that August was to demand the inclusion of sexual orientation in the Ontario Human Rights Code.

While CHAT supported the civil rights strategy, they were far more cautious. Rocking the boat too much might land us all under water. Their main focus was on providing services to promote community growth, help people in distress, and educate the general public. This sometimes worked as a division of labour, but GATE activists were often dismissive of CHAT's less political homophile approach and its ties with ghetto business interests. Those in CHAT tended to see GATE and *TBP* as a bunch of young hotheads whose radical ideas might well make things worse.

CHAT was organized on traditional lines with a board, and George Hislop as director and president. GATE and *TBP* operated more as collectives, although GATE did subsequently develop an executive after squabbling between members of different left parties involved became intolerable. The division was also generational. Hislop was in his forties in 1974. Most of GATE and *TBP* were still in their twenties. Since I, too, was in my twenties, and considered myself a radical, it was easy to choose a side.

Despite its radical claims, gay liberation was grounded in liberal values. The idea of the importance of sexual freedom was certainly liberal. Sexuality was the property of the individual and its goal was to maximize personal happiness.

But gay liberation, based on gay identity, also had a strong sense of community. Only by building and strengthening community could our goals be realized. Those who would not identify as gay were letting the struggle down. We asked people to assume the risk of coming out in order to achieve the greater good for all. This combination of liberal values around an individual's right to express their own sexuality and the collective values required to produce a coherent group to fight for that right was a key tension in the gay liberation project. But that was nothing compared to the tension between gay liberation values and those of the community it aspired to lead.

In place of discretion and passing, gay liberation valued coming out, openness, and throat-ramming. In place of the double entendre, it proposed directness. In place of conspicuous consumption, it proposed self-sacrifice and communal action. Instead of asking for acceptance and fitting in, it rocked the boat and challenged hegemonic values. Gay liberation saw the ghetto as a prison. For those in the closet, it was a refuge.

A letter from Ron Dayman in the spring 1973 issue of *TBP* even expressed outrage at the publication of a map of Toronto gay spots featuring bars and baths. "I think you owe your readers an explanation of your attitude towards these gay ghettos. Surely it is not your role to encourage their existence."[24] The next month, a letter from Arthur Whitaker called out what he felt was the paper's arrogant attitude towards the same ghetto.

> If the Gay Lib revolution is to succeed then it could probably use the help of the 90% of the gay population that so far sees you as a bunch of condescending university kids, who, for the mere fact you can intellectually rationalize being gay, feel superiority to what you refer to as Ghetto, Bar, Bath, Club Queens. Idealistically we shouldn't need the Ghetto, but when you are horny and lonely on Saturday night these places can be awfully tempting. Some of us, in fact a lot of us, don't have the same avoidance as the high principled Jesus Christ Farts of the Movement.[25]

In the first few months after I came out, I had been introduced to the main questions that would challenge the new politics. The nature of identity. Revolutionary change versus liberal reforms. Communal living. Collectives versus hierarchies. The relationship between different kinds of oppression. Where to look for allies. The connection between personal and social transformation, and the difficulty of keeping all these balls in the air at once. The next forty years would be a long process of learning and relearning the answers to such questions.

2

Getting Noticed

THE BODY POLITIC

Things move fast when you are twenty-three and coming out. In the September/October 1974 issue of *The Body Politic* (issue 15), I was already listed as a contributor. The paper seemed the best fit for me. I had helped out at *Guerilla*, the city's counterculture newspaper, before I headed off to South America in 1972, so I knew how community papers worked. And I found the people at *TBP* interesting. They were mostly young men who had come to Toronto to find a community, about my age, bright, and fearless about social change.

Like me, most of them were also the first in their families to go to university, something made possible by the expansion of post-secondary education and healthy student grants. We were a generation that had come of age in a period of rapid social change. We felt entitled to a just world, and we were not going to take no – or even not yet – for an answer. No prejudice or superstition was going to stand in our way.

The first person I met when I nervously presented myself at the Carlton Street office to volunteer was Robert Trow. Trow had grown up in suburban Thornhill, north of Toronto, and had come downtown to study library science at the University of Toronto. He had a long, horsey face and a suggestive impish smile that made me uncomfortable, since I wasn't yet used to being flirted with.

At the time, Trow was lovers with Gerald Hannon. Hannon had grown up in the village of Marathon, Ontario, a small pulp mill town on the north shore of Lake Superior. He had managed to escape with a scholarship to U of T. Hannon had a quiet, gentle laugh, seemed completely guileless, and always called me "Timmy."

Then there was Ed Jackson, who had finished his BA at the University of New Brunswick and managed to get a student loan to do a master's at U of T. That got him to Toronto, but he soon got interested in activism and never finished the MA. Jackson seemed to know all things literary, but he was less of a dreamer than Hannon. He sported an identical moustache with his boyfriend Merv Walker, who was also small in stature, quiet and intense. Walker had grown up on a farm near Kamsack, Saskatchewan, before he was drawn to the lights of the big city. He arrived in Toronto in 1973 with Tom Warner, from Prince Albert. They had met at the gay group at the University of Saskatchewan in Saskatoon. Warner was tall and gawky, and when I arrived, was already spending more of his time in the shared office working on GATE. He, too, came from a working class background and was studying to become an accountant.

Ken Popert was one of the few actually born and raised in Toronto. The first in his family to have more than a high school education, he had joined the counterculture and came out while studying at Cornell in New York State. People made jokes about him dropping acid, but he was no fuzzy dope head. Hannon described him as having the "coolest, most clinical intelligence of anyone on the paper." Popert also did not suffer fools and had a sharp tongue. I found him intimidating. His partner, Brian Mossop, was a shy translator who, like Warner, divided his time between the paper and GATE. Both Popert and Mossop were members of the Communist Party.

Walter Bruno, on the other hand, was a Trotskyist who worked in the post office. He had a mane of tousled black hair, and people joked behind his back that he was trying to pass himself off as a Latin lover because he had changed his name from Blumenthal.

There were two Americans. Herb Spiers, who hailed from Columbus, Ohio, came to Toronto to work on his doctorate. Spiers had drafted the *We Demand* manifesto presented to the federal government at Canada's first public gay demonstration in August 1971. He was high energy, quick-witted, unabashedly sexual. And although Columbus is a relatively small town, he had a big-city American edge to him.

Michael Lynch wasn't actually on the collective, but he was a regular contributor and was often around the office. From North Carolina, he was a prodigy who had arrived in Toronto to teach English at the University of Toronto at twenty-seven, accompanied by his wife, Gail. He and Gail had a two-year-old son. Although Lynch identified as gay, his continuing marriage did raise eyebrows.

Another odd man out was Ian Young. Young, a poet and critic, ran Catalyst Press out of his Scarborough home. Along with Jearld Moldenhauer, he had been a founder the country's first gay group, the University of Toronto Homophile Association, in 1969. He and Moldenhauer detested each other by the time I came on the scene, and Moldenhauer warned me off him when he was giving me a rundown of the characters at the paper. Young was a libertarian and follower of Ayn Rand. He had little patience with the left-wing tilt of most of gay liberation. He was also rumoured to be into sado-masochism (S/M), still anathema to a movement that judged relationships on strict sexual equality. He was privately tolerated as the Curmudgeon of Scarborough, and would soon be penning the paper's longest-running column, Ivory Tunnel, which reviewed gay literature from small presses.

Lots of others came in and out of the little Carlton Street storefront to help out, argue, and cruise. They all seemed smart and funny and sexy – and to know more than I did. Despite the paper's reputation, there had only been one attempt at a collective orgy, well before my time. Moldenhauer had agreed to be the official photographer because such things needed to be documented. But it hadn't turned out well and was never repeated. Ed Jackson and Herb Spiers were the only ones I ended up sleeping with. One-night stands in both cases. I generally tried to avoid sex with people I was politically involved with.

Although I had nothing to do with it, issue 15 was also the first time that that the 1921 quote from German gay rights pioneer Kurt Hiller appeared in the paper. "The liberation of homosexuals can only be the work of homosexuals themselves." It graced the masthead from then on.

This first time, however, it was accompanied by a caveat in case anyone might misunderstand its intent.

> The sentiment expressed . . . might be taken to exclude the possibility of homosexuals allying their struggle with other forces for social progress. It is clear, however, from Hiller's activities as a pacifist and advocate of women's rights that his words were a warning to homosexuals against reliance on "leaders" and liberal "friends" for their rights. He emphasized that autonomous gay organization is a necessary precondition for the achievement of gay liberation.[1]

CIVIL RIGHTS

We might have caught the wave of the revolutionary 1960s, but by the mid-'70s, we were left high and dry on the beach. The revolutionary rhetoric of early gay lib didn't actually give you much to do, except to recite it as a kind of catechism. Nor did it find much purchase among the large part of a community whose values had been formed within the moral economy of the closet.

If the movement was to mobilize people and grow, it needed to articulate more concrete demands. The notion of civil rights seemed much more reasonable. Rather than a universal transformation of society, its more limited goal was minority rights. It therefore mirrored other minority rights struggles and was congruent with liberal values of individual autonomy and equality.

Even as early as the first national gay march on Parliament in August 1971, it was evident that civil rights demands were the movement's default strategy. The historic *We Demand* brief called for the removal of vague terms like "gross indecency" and "indecent act" from the Criminal Code, a uniform age of consent, and amendments to anti-gay provisions in the Immigration and Divorce Acts. It demanded an end to RCMP witchhunts of gay civil servants and asserted that lesbians and gay men should have the right to equal employment in the public service, and to serve in the armed forces. This was a call for equality, not revolution, a demand that liberal rather than conservative principles organize the logic of sexual regulation.

In 1972, *TBP* member Brian Waite argued that the fledgling gay movement needed to get serious and set priorities, and proposed fighting for the inclusion of "sexual orientation" in the Ontario Human Rights Code as the strategy. Waite's focus on the Human Rights Code was inspired by the women's movement's recent success in getting Ontario premier William Davis to promise to include "sex" in the code. Waite's article compared winning human rights protection to the ongoing fight to decriminalize abortion (which was still illegal except under stringent conditions and with widely varying access). It would give people the right to choose to come out without fearing reprisals. Waite was also taking a page from the book of American activists. New York City's Gay Activist Alliance was fighting for municipal legislation to outlaw discrimination. There might be differences in tactics, but not even those with a real commitment to the closet could oppose the notion of rights.

By the mid-1970s, the civil rights strategy had become common sense. But one could catch glimpses of nostalgia for the excitement and stirring rhetoric of the early days.

"Even if I saw it as only a part of gay liberation, I was all in favour of civil rights, and that was GATE's meat and potatoes," recalls one of the early pioneers, Peter Zorzi.

> On the one hand, no-one ever accused the group of being exciting. To my mind if you put the civil service in charge of the gay movement that would be GATE. On the other hand I suppose the way they operated had much to do with the ends they were working towards. They did provide a structure for the push towards rights, and for pushback.[2]

ANXIETIES

Waite was a member of the League for Socialist Action (LSA). Like most of those in the early *TBP* collective, he had been inspired by the revolutionary rhetoric of early gay liberation. The move towards civil rights was therefore not unproblematic. Theoretically, things were supposed to move in the other direction, from reformist to more radical revolutionary strategies. The U.S. civil rights movement had been superseded by the Black Panthers and radical black liberation. The women's movement's fight for the vote was followed by radical feminist critiques of patriarchy. Any movement in the opposite direction could be perceived as backsliding.

So Waite's piece ended with the following coda. Civil rights were not an end in themselves, but only a means to an end.

Winning this demand will give life to the words "gay pride." It will impel and enable thousands more brothers and sisters to join us in future campaigns for full sexual liberation for humankind ... children, adolescents and adults, no matter what their position on the sexual continuum.[3]

Waite's need to justify the shift to civil rights belied a certain anxiety. First, not everyone bought his justifications. In a 1973 *TBP* article on early Canadian feminist Nellie McClung, Bob Wallace wrote:

Like McClung ... the contemporary liberationist attacks the symptoms, not the causes of sexual oppression. To the suffragist, it was the vote which was important: to the contemporary activist, it is job and immigration restrictions.... It is an end to capitalism alone which can effect equality, and not the agitation for and procurement of ritualistic legal rights.[4]

On the other hand, much of the community was content with civil rights as an end in itself. They did not share the idea that homosexuality was fundamentally inimical to existing society. For them, the fight was about overcoming barriers to participation. Those leading MCC or CHAT or running businesses were more likely to think that homosexuals were just misunderstood. Civil rights would put an end to discrimination, eventually more people would come out, and prejudices and stereotypes would begin to melt away. We radicals called them assimilationists, but every time there was a victory, such beliefs were strengthened.

One way that anxious activists could prove they weren't backsliding was to focus on militant tactics rather than lobbying. In the lead-up to the Third National Gay Rights Conference in 1975, Popert argued that only the *public* process of fighting for rights would produce the necessary change in public perceptions of homosexuality.

The history of minority rights reveals that civil rights accomplish little without a corresponding change in public opinion. But the effectiveness of civil rights is much less important than the effectiveness of the public campaign which demands those rights.... By a campaign for civil rights, we can penetrate the media and advance the reeducation of the public on the subject of homosexuality.[5]

Rights demands also encouraged alliances with those in power – known as vertical alliances. (Horizontal alliances would be connections at the same level of the social hierarchy.) Popert, on the other hand, argued for in-your-face tactics to build pressure on those in power. Assimilationists called for caution and conciliation, but our movement would be militant and brash. We were demanding a new moral economy. We were no longer asking to be left alone. We were demanding to be public.

I was still pretty wet under the ears on a grey Sunday morning in November 1974 when I found myself in front of the suburban home of *Toronto Star* publisher Beland Honderich. Looking back at the photo in the November/December issue of *TBP*, a dozen of us are posing in front of the house. Our signs read "Star Sells Hate," 'Star spreads bigotry," "Star anti-gay sexist," and "Beland is a Bigot." We talked to neighbours and left signs on Honderich's front lawn. Other than the Pride march that previous August, it was my first gay demonstration. Although I look composed in the picture, inside I was scared stiff. Picketing someone's home in the suburbs seemed a bit over the top.

The demonstration had been organized by the Committee for Media Fairness to Gays, a coalition that cobbled together *TBP*, GATE, the Young Socialists, the LSA, the Revolutionary Marxist Group, and several unaffiliated individuals. In the picture, Walter Davis of the RMG is standing at my side.

It had all started more than a year before in February 1973 when the *TBP* submitted an ad to the *Toronto Star*'s classifieds: "*The Body Politic*: Gay Liberation Journal. $2.00 for six issues. 4 Kensington Ave., Toronto, Ont. M5T 2J7." At that time, newspaper ads were the standard way of communicating to a broader population. The *Star* refused the ad, claiming that it was against policy "to accept advertising which would identify or tend to identify a person as a homosexual or to carry advertisements relating to homosexual activity."

The collective appealed to the Ontario Press Council, which ruled that the *Star* was indeed guilty of discrimination. That provoked a meeting with the classified ads manager, who reiterated that as a "family newspaper" the *Star* would not carry ads of a "proselytizing nature regarding sex," since they might be inadvertently encountered by children. He did hold out a small olive branch. The policy was being reviewed, although that process that might take as long as five years.

But then the *Star* upped the ante. A few days later, when *TBP* issue 8 was taken to Newsweb, the usual printer, it was rejected on the orders of the *Star*, the printer's 80 per cent owner. Not only was the *Star* refusing the ad, it was now trying to prevent *TBP*'s publication entirely. As the collective scrambled to find another printer, demonstrations were organized at the *Star*'s offices.[6]

With this much fuss, it didn't take five years to review the policy. Five weeks later there was another meeting, this time between Honderich, several *TBP* collective members, and the *TBP* lawyer. It did not go well. Honderich advised the group that the ban would continue indefinitely. The meeting personalized the issue. For *TBP*, Honderich's "bigotry" was the directing mind. For the *Star* to claim to champion values of tolerance and free expression while making decisions based on homophobic bias was hypocrisy.

Honderich's justification for the ban on *TBP* ads was an article published a year before by Gerald Hannon, "Of Men and Little Boys." Hannon argued that children were sexual beings but endured enforced celibacy as property of the nuclear family.

> A child's sexual life turns him *outward* from the family . . . once begun, the child is in the process of leaving home, psychologically at least. The straight world considers us to be dangerous where children are concerned. The irony is that they are *right* – not to the physical well being of their offspring, however, but to the family structure that imprisons them.

He concluded, "Loving a child and expressing it sexually is revolutionary activity. The activists of tomorrow are more than likely in someone's arms today."[7]

As might be expected, the article had produced a reaction. Kenneth Bagnell, a regular *Globe and Mail* columnist, linked *TBP* to CHAT with its federal Local Initiative Project grants for the counselling line, and demanded that funding be cancelled. The *Globe* editorialized that "the homosexual seduction of a child is a loathsome, pernicious thing." The *Star* wondered out loud if the Criminal Code amendments decriminalizing homosexuality should be rescinded. The *Toronto Sun* trumpeted, "I told you so."[8]

CHAT found itself on the hot seat. CHAT president George Hislop released a statement dissociating the group from Hannon's article, stating that CHAT opposed the "jeopardizing of children." It was to no avail. The federal grant was not renewed. CHAT blamed *TBP*. MCC's Rev. Robert Wolfe also distanced his new church from the paper in their newsletter.

But Hannon was not about to back down on an issue he felt was central. In the next issue, he penned "Children and Sex," arguing that the furious reaction from the press was just more evidence that children were perceived as property. Citing Kinsey's findings that 32 per cent of boys reached orgasm between 2 and 12 months, and 80 per cent between 10 and 13 years, he concluded:

> Given all of this – that children are highly sexual beings, that they are deeply attracted to homosexual activity, that they spend some great part of their time among adults who, consciously or not, find them "downright enticing," it is rather a surprise and certainly a tribute to the repressive excellence of our society that more adult/child sex play does not occur.[9]

Hannon's arguments were completely theoretical (he himself had no sexual interest in children) and hyper-liberal. Children were individual rights-bearing subjects, and their rights to sexual expression were being infringed by a repressive patriarchy. This struck an emotional chord among some gay men who remembered the repression of their budding childhood sexual curiosity, incapable of consent.

But his argument always assumed the child was the sexual actor and over-looked the role of adult desire. It neglected the substantive inequality of capacity between adults and children, and how the resulting power relations affected a child's ability to consent. Nor did his approach deal with gender. Many lesbians had a very different take on the issue, grounded in their experience as unwilling objects of male sexual desire, or as mothers caring for vulnerable children. But in a male collective, such voices went unheard, and the demands of solidarity in the face of the attacks, along with the value placed on sounding the most radical, stifled internal debate.

WINDS OF CHANGE

Despite *TBP*'s antagonizing of the establishment, the Gay Alliance Toward Equality kept its focus on the civil rights strategy. GATE had scored a major victory at city hall the year before. In October 1973, Toronto city council responded to GATE's lobbying and amended the city's anti-discrimination policy to include discrimination on the basis of sexual orientation. It marked the first time that any level of government had protected gays as a minority. But the *Star* failed to report the story. For *TBP* this was more evidence of the paper's anti-gay agenda, not to mention proof of the inadequacy of quiet lobbying.

Still, the issue had also led GATE to build concrete alliances for the first time. Ken Popert was among the group assigned to get support from CUPE (Canadian Union of Public Employees), the union that organized city inside workers. Popert admitted initial reluctance because of his "prejudice against working class people." But, he wrote, "when three of us walked into the office of the local's president . . . to my surprise [John] King seemed just as nervous as I was, flustered and unable to decide whether to remain standing or to sit down. . . . After listening to us, he readily agreed that sexual orientation should not be a consideration in City employment."

The GATE deputation was later invited to address the union executive. Popert continued:

> As the meeting proceeded, I noticed that they called each other "sister" and "brother" just as we sometimes do in the gay movement. When our turn came and we presented our case, I glanced around the table from time to time. Attentive faces, some discomfort. No one was reading a newspaper. And no one headed off for the washroom. Some questions following our presentation revealed respect for our struggle, a desire to defend our rights, and an honestly expressed fear of involving the union in the controversial question of gay rights.

He concluded:

Like us, these people knew what it meant to be engaged in a ceaseless struggle against powerful and antagonistic forces. Like gays, they were driven to organize themselves in self-defense. And like gays, they were constantly being shat on by the powers that control the media and most other institutions. In fact, it seemed that they were more like us than the collection of influence-peddlers who fill legislatures and city councils could ever be.[10]

SERENDIPITY

The two issues – council support and the *Star* – unexpectedly came together. In January 1974, MCC's Bob Wolfe got a panicked call from city hall. A young gay man whom Wolfe had been counselling was threatening to jump off the building's east tower. Wolfe managed to talk the youth down and in February he received an award of appreciation from city council. In his address to council he revealed that the *Star* had just turned down an ad from MCC inviting gay Christians to worship with the church. City councillors were stunned, the media picked up the story as a scandal, and a few days later an embarrassed *Star* agreed to accept the MCC ad.

That was the end of the *Star*'s blanket refusal of gay ads. But when *TBP* dutifully resubmitted its ad a few days later, the *Star* first asked for recent copies of the paper for review. After a month, *TBP*'s ad was again rejected on the grounds that the *Star*'s policy on "proselytizing advertising has not changed."[11] By this point the *Star* had accepted ads from GATE, although substituting the word "homosexual" for "gay," but had turned down another ad from Glad Day Bookshop.

AGAIN TO ARMS

That fall, Hannon again took up the issue of pedophilia. He expressed outrage at the life sentence given to John Roestad, who was convicted of having sex with boys between eight and fourteen. Hannon scolded the gay community for being embarrassed by pedophilia and not rising to Roestad's defence. He described Roestad as "imprisoned and tortured because he was gently and not very carefully giving of himself to these boys." Hannon concluded:

> If you accept that sexual relationships are not intrinsically dangerous, then you must accept that John Roestad's sexual preferences are as legitimate and as potentially fulfilling as your own.... There can be only one cry: Free Roestad! There can be only one object: destruction of a system so utterly perverse.[12]

The *Star*, no doubt still smarting from the exposure of its discriminatory policy, saw an opening. An editorial, "Homosexuals: Where the Star Draws the Line," claimed its attitude was "one of tolerance," citing its support of decriminalization in 1969. It asserted it was in favour of "full civil rights for homosexuals in employment, housing and public accommodations, and in free speech, publication and assembly." But it drew the line at "encouraging the spread of homosexuality," "aggressive recruitment propaganda," and legitimizing "homosexual relations between adults and children."[13] Although the *Star* called for readers' comments on the issue, it refused a letter of rebuttal from *TBP*.

TBP responded with a four-page special issue with the headline "The Star Sells Hate," and distributed it to *Star* employees on their lunch break. The issue argued that the *Star* was urging the curtailment of the civil rights of gay people, "justifying this on the basis of the wide-spread misconception that gay people have both the desire and the power to convert others to their own way of life."

It was a battle of competing, anxious liberalisms. *TBP* insisted it was only referring to consensual sex and evaded the question of the unequal capacities of children. The Committee for Media Fairness to Gays retreated into the terrain of freedom of expression to evade the issue of child/adult sex entirely. The *Star* portrayed itself as supporting adult gay rights and focused on children to evade the question of its homophobic ads policy.

Although *TBP* personalized the issue as being about Honderich, the problem of censorship in the press was more general. In October 1974, GATE Vancouver attempted to place a similarly innocuous ad for its newsletter, *Gay Tide,* in the *Vancouver Sun.* They, too, were refused. GATE won a complaint at the newly minted British Columbia Human Rights Commission, but a series of appeals by the *Sun* ended up five years later in the Supreme Court of Canada, which affirmed the *Sun's* right to discriminate.

Despite the standoff, it was remarkable that the small volunteer-run collective had provoked a major conversation with the city's largest newspaper. Although many in the community felt the exchange was far from productive, there was obviously something about being outrageous that worked.

DIVISIONS

The battle also played out in the community. Theoretically, the media fairness basis of unity should have been acceptable to just about everyone. In practice, CHAT, MCC, and key business leaders were by this point alienated by *TBP's* radical postures. Specifically, they felt its stand on child sexuality contributed to stereotypes of gay men as child molesters and undermined work for acceptance. The Committee for Media Fairness to Gays developed a statement condemning the *Star's* policies. *TBP* reported, "endorsements were being sought, but few have so far been forthcoming."[14]

TBP had hardly been conciliatory. Bridges had already been burned a year before when CHAT's social service staff and four board members, including vice-president Pat Murphy, resigned to protest president Hislop's "authoritarian" management style and sexism. *TBP* had editorialized: "CHAT can no longer be called a moderate organization. It is a reactionary organization...

CHAT has solidly aligned itself with business interests and with middle class respectability."[15] Until that point, Hislop had been a regular contributor to the paper.

The escalating rhetoric between the *Star* and *TBP* widened this gulf. In autumn Peter Maloney, manager of the Club Baths and owner of the Barracks, withdrew advertising and refused to allow *TBP* to be sold in his establishments. Other baths followed suit.

This was the same Peter Maloney who, after coming out at a Liberal party policy convention in 1972, had received "political kisses" from regular *TBP* columnist Twilight Rose. Maloney had written the CHAT brief to the Ontario Human Rights Commission (OHRC) and was the first openly gay candidate to run for a seat on the Toronto school board. He was hardly an Uncle Tom, but the contradiction between the radical "liberationists" and liberal "assimilationists" had become a take-no-prisoners battle.

This civil war didn't make anyone's life easier. The most popular bar at the time was the St. Charles, with its iconic clock tower on Yonge Street. Its main entrance was on Yonge, but for those not wanting to risk being seen entering a gay bar, there was also a back door in the alley behind. A group of us were handing out some sort of flyer. We knew the bar would not give us access, so we gathered at the front door and synchronized our watches. Half went around to the back door. Those at the front gave them five minutes before we went in. As expected, all the bouncers had rushed to the back of the bar in order to throw out the intruders, who were now raising a fuss about their right to free speech. We were quickly able to leaflet more than half the patrons before the bouncers realized they had been tricked and threw us out.

Such tactics certainly got the adrenalin flowing. But they did little to improve relations between activists and businesses.

A year later, in September 1975, Maloney and Hislop would launch *Esprit*, a glossy competitor to *TBP*. *Esprit* aimed "to present to the gay community and to the community at large, a positive perspective of people who are going places and are doing things, who are sometimes gay and sometimes not."[16] *Esprit* lasted only three issues, but its launch represented both a political and an existential challenge to *TBP*. It amplified the feeling that the business community and its representatives were the enemy.

For *TBP*, this was a battle for the heart of the movement. The collective saw the worldview of MCC, CHAT, and the business community, valuing acceptance and incremental change, as deeply conservative. For *TBP*, patriarchal authority was fundamentally unjust, and gay liberation needed to challenge and overthrow it, not seek reconciliation. Those who accommodated themselves to such authority did not deserve to lead.

When David Foreman moved to Toronto he soon joined both the University of Toronto Communist Party Club and GATE. He found evening work cleaning rooms at the gay-owned Richmond Street Baths. As Foreman learned the hard way, the limits to community solidarity were not just around intergenerational sex and tactics.

The pay wasn't great, but evening hours suited him and there were occasional sexual perks. As time went on, though, it became evident that management was playing favourites in terms of shifts, pay, and the better jobs. Inspired by party ideals, he decided to organize a union to ensure equal treatment. The Hotel Employees and Restaurant Employees Union knew nothing about the baths but agreed to let him try to sign up members. When management caught on, Foreman was fired.

The union filed an unfair dismissal complaint, but just before the Labour Board hearing, the bath proposed a thousand-dollar settlement. On the advice of union lawyers, Foreman accepted. But he failed to read the fine print. Later, when he was refused entry in another establishment, he realized he had been banned from all the baths in town. It was thirty years before the ban was lifted.[17]

BRINGING IN RELIGION

The November/December 1974 issue of *TBP* did little to bridge the divide. The theme was gays and the church. The cover displayed a cartoon of a prelate seated on a stack of Bibles attended by two acolytes, one kissing his foot, the other peering up his robe. The issue kicked off with an editorial on MCC that pointed out that the church was not a democratic organization and that it carried two contradictory messages, "gay is good" and "the content of Christian belief." After declaring that Christianity was "both antipolitical and antisexual," the editorial concluded:

> MCC stands with one foot in gay liberation and the other in Christian faith. Both MCC as an institution and its members as individuals are conflicted. Forced to a choice, which way will MCC move? Reverend Wolfe, minister of the Toronto congregation, has already given the answer: "We're not so much of a gay church as a Christian church administering to gay needs."

Although the issue included a half-page comment by Rev. Wolfe himself entitled "Liberation Faith," the collective's position was made clear in both the editorial and the selection of articles. In her feature, "The Lesbian and God-the-Father," Sally Gearhart concluded, "As a woman, as a Lesbian, I invite you not to attempt reform of the church. I invite you either to destroy it or to desert it. Personal integrity allows no other alternative."[18] "Kisses Blow-jobs, Sweet Surrenders" recounted the experiences and disillusionment of a gay seminarian. Popert's review of John Lauritsen's *Religious Roots of the Taboo on*

Homosexuality was illustrated by a graphic of a mouth vomiting out a church. And not to be outdone, Hannon's "Was Jesus Christ a Cocksucker?" speculated whether Christianity was an expression of the Freudian death wish or simply an obsessional neurosis arising out of the Oedipus complex.

CGRO

At the formation of the Coalition for Gay Rights in Ontario in Toronto in January 1975, the accent was not on division but unity. Luckily, the issue of age of consent was a federal Criminal Code matter and could therefore be tactfully sidestepped. Sixty delegates from nine groups in five Ontario cities attended. But other differences needed to be bridged. According to *TBP*:

> The newly political groups were anxious that membership in CGRO not be made contingent upon the willingness of an organization to engage in demonstrations and pickets. . . . The activists tried to allay those fears, pointing out that not every group would have to engage in every kind of activity. Nevertheless, the GATE (Toronto) and GO (Gays of Ottawa) delegations argued again and again that public protest is the key to the gay civil rights struggle.[19]

. Popert, in that issue, explained there were actually two gay movements. In Toronto, one fought for "freedom and an open social life for gays, a life of fully human dimensions, grown far beyond the cramped existence permitted in the city's commercial gay ghetto." But in smaller towns one worked "to provide in a cooperative and more humane form that which gay Toronto already took for granted and had even begun to despise: the Ghetto."[20]

TILTING AT SHRINKS

Michael Riordon was another of those who were often in and out of the *TBP* office. A willowy, energetic man with a nervous laugh and perennially tousled hair, Riordan always seemed intensely ethical. The January/February 1975 issue of *TBP* published "Capital Punishment: Notes of a Willing Victim," a fictionalized account of his experience with aversion therapy at the hands of his psychiatrist.

"Dr. Isherwood" is portrayed as a smooth, subtly sinister character trying to help "Martin" cure his homosexuality. The self-hate and self-denial of the tortured Martin was too close to my own experience. It made me shiver. I had never been to a psychiatrist; such things were not part of my small-town Presbyterian upbringing. After I read the piece, I was glad that I hadn't.

After Stonewall, newly formed Gay Liberation Fronts had targeted meetings of the American Psychiatric Association (APA) to protest its position that homosexuality was a mental illness. Issue 1 of *TBP* had listed "the institutions of gay oppression" as "the government, the school boards, the psychiatrists, the landlords and the employers."[21]

So the critique of psychiatry featured prominently in early issues. In a review of *The Radical Therapist* in issue 3, Jearld Moldenhauer exhorted, "It's time we stopped listening to Big Brother and the Experts (shrinks) . . . instead of realizing that an individual's problems often stem from the oppressive nature of society and then working to change those conditions."[22] The only therapy we needed was politics (and sex).

In issue 7 Herb Spiers wrote "Psychiatric Neutrality: An Autopsy." His article called psychiatrists "mind police" and demanded an end to their "preposterous and immoral theories" about homosexuality as sickness. The piece concluded with a quote from pioneer activist Frank Kameny: "Psychiatry is waging a war of extermination against homosexuals. The psychiatric profession is the major enemy of the . . . community."[23]

Then the unexpected happened. In December 1973 the APA removed homosexuality from the list of disorders. Although *TBP* declared it "perhaps the most significant victory for US gay movement to date,"[24] for those who saw gay oppression as a pillar of capitalism and psychiatry as one of its major institutions, it was disconcerting. Capitalism itself seemed quite nonplussed by the change. In fact, although psychiatry traditionally focused on helping people adjust to norms, it was a relatively modern liberal profession with a focus on the individual. Sander Gilman pointed out that one of Freud's (no doubt subconscious) motivations was to displace the common racial and anti-Semitic explanations of mental illness of his day with a theory of human psychological processes that were supposedly universal – common to all groups and cultures. Although in Freud's view, gender was still a determining factor, the notion of the universal psyche was the egalitarian foundation of psychiatry.[25] Psychiatric knowledge was supposed to be scientific and rational. Kinsey's work in the 1940s and research by Evelyn Hooker in the '50s disrupted the notion that homosexuality was connected to mental illness. So it was perhaps not surprising that psychiatry was one of the first pillars to crumble. The change in the APA definition heralded a change in sexual regulation to a more liberal model not yet imagined by most activists.

In that context, Riordon's article was somehow reassuring. It reminded us of psychiatry's continuing brutality. The story had an interesting coda. A year later, Riordan ran into his former psychiatrist at a GATE dance and confronted him. This time the story was not fictionalized.[26] But it was no longer a tale of the brutality of a profession; rather, it was one of betrayal and the weakness of a closeted gay man.

The same issue turned the tables on psychiatry with a reprint of a Gays of Ottawa pamphlet *Understanding Homophobia*. "Homophobia" was a new term, only coined by George Weinberg in his *Society and the Healthy Homosexual* in 1972. From then on, it was the irrational fear of homosexuality that was the pathology.

PUBLIC POLITICS, PUBLIC SEX

With psychiatry vanquished, a new enemy became prominent. The first time the *TBP* offices had been visited by the police came after the 1974 portrayal of the three federal political leaders with large and excited penises. Although the portrait was an adapted Aubrey Beardsley drawing, morality officers who visited the *TBP*/GATE offices were not impressed by high art. They threatened obscenity charges unless the issue was removed from the display window. The collective refused, but covered the offending members with a "censored" banner. Charges were not laid.

The 1975 May/June issue republished a "Harold Hedd" cartoon by well-known counterculture cartoonist Rand Holmes. The full-page cartoon showed two men in bed laughing at anti-gay passages in David Reuben's *Everything You Always Wanted to Know about Sex*. They then proceed to give each other blowjobs over four graphic panels.

The issue was already on the stands when the Morality Squad arrived again, with an ultimatum – remove the issue from all outlets, or the issue would be confiscated and the paper charged. During his visit, Sergeant Brantford explained that fellatio was the problem. "You can't show it, you can't write about it, you can't describe it."

Admitting a "gnawing feeling of cowardice and capitulation" but faced with the threat of a lengthy and costly court case, the collective complied and removed the remaining issues from the stands. When Brantford and two other officers returned to inspect the results two weeks later, they left with a threat. "If you do this thing again, we'll seize it and charge you and close you down." We could talk revolutionary sexual politics all we wanted. But representing sex itself was still beyond the pale.

AGE OF CONSENT

The hill that the fight between radicals and conservatives would take place on was not about throat-ramming or depictions of hard cocks. It was age of consent – whether it should be abolished or made equal for straights and gays.

For the radicals, supporting abolition was of value precisely because it was unwinnable. That demonstrated how family, patriarchy, and capitalism were entwined. Everyone could agree to civil rights. But the abolition issue became the way to determine whether people were hoping to make their own lives immediately better or struggling to change the world for everyone. It hearkened back to the universalist rhetoric of gay liberation.

TBP editorialized:

> At the centre of the Gay Liberation Movement is the whole burning question, which we cannot ignore, of sexual rights for gay youth and youth in general. That simple right – to freely express one's sexual being unfettered by family, church, school, and government – can't be easily granted or achieved in the context of repressive social relations that limit and stunt us

at every point. The realization of the right implies a fundamental change in social attitudes and social interacting.[27]

The Third National Gay Rights Conference in Ottawa in June 1975 was the largest Canadian lesbian and gay gathering to date. Two hundred participants from across the country developed the program for a National Gay Rights Coalition (NGRC).

My memories are of interminable discussions in institutional rooms and bad coffee. I had been out less than a year and barely understood the politics. But Ken Popert prepared a riveting blow-by-blow report of the proceedings for *TBP*, portraying an epic battle between social forces and asserting its profound significance for the future of the movement.

Popert noted five currents in the conference – religious, service-oriented, rights-oriented, anarchist, and leftist. The dominant current was civil rights, led by GATE Vancouver, Winnipeg Gays for Equality, and GATE Toronto. The anarchists soon split off to organize their own workshops and street theatre. The service-oriented groups were bored and called for a follow-up conference on social services. The leftist caucus was unable "to put forward an alternative view of gay liberation." Popert noted with ill-disguised satisfaction that the only resolution to be defeated at the final plenary was one from the religious caucus that "implicitly criticized the gay movement for failing to recognize that gay people are 'spiritual beings.' "[28]

But the real battle lines were drawn around age of consent. MCC Ottawa led those arguing for a uniform age of consent, and GATE Vancouver and Toronto called on the conference to adopt abolition. In the end, the abolitionist side won a two-to-one plenary vote, a victory for militants and a shift from the demands of the 1971 *We Demand* document.

Abolition of age of consent stood out among the other NGRC demands. Most of them were about equality and changes to improve the lives of lesbians and gay men, while having little impact on anyone else. Abolishing age of consent laws would theoretically impact the lives of all children and families in the country, no matter their sexual orientation. It went beyond a liberal appeal to equality.

TBP's subsequent editorial praised the NGRC for adopting abolition, and for its resolution calling for the immediate release of Henry Morgentaler, who had been jailed for establishing free-standing abortion clinics. "Sexual freedom for youth, for women, for gays – these are all part of the same struggle. We can ill afford to ignore their interconnection. The same elements in our society conspire to control us all."[29]

In retrospect, it was unclear why, if equality set the stage for more fundamental sexual liberation struggles in all other areas, calling for a uniform age of consent could not play the same role. The desire to demarcate the new movement from anyone associated with the old homophile guard seemed to take precedence. Popert explained:

The conference also reflected the growing divisions of the gay movement, and indeed advanced them. Despite frequently expressed regrets over the lack of gay unity ... the emergence and collision of discrete currents of thought and action are the inevitable prelude to the development of an effective and coherent programme for gay liberation. To sacrifice this development in a compromise for the sake of illusory unity would be to reduce gay politics to the lowest common denominator. The growth of division must be welcomed as a sign that the gay movement is alive and well.[30]

But if abolition was a useful pretext to demarcate with conservatives, it went nowhere. The NGRC never developed any campaigns to promote it. Civil rights was taking off. Abolition of the age of consent was an outlier to the logic of equality.

JOHN DAMIEN

One of the new stars of the conference was John Damien. In *TBP*'s conference coverage, he is pictured beside Chris Bearchell, co-ordinator of the Committee to Defend John Damien. I remember Damien as a slight, unassuming man. A former jockey, he was in his early forties in early 1975 when he was fired from his job at the Ontario Racing Commission because he was gay. He was offered hush money and a letter of recommendation to go away quietly. But a new sense of entitlement was sweeping the community. Although he had not remotely been an activist, Damien contacted GATE.

For GATE this was the perfect case. Damien had been a competent and admired professional for twenty-five years before he was abruptly let go. This was clearly discrimination on the basis of sexual orientation. Horses, not children, were involved. Damien was sympathetic and willing to speak publicly. It was a case that the whole community could unite around. And it put a human face on the need to include sexual orientation in the Ontario Human Rights Code.

GATE organized the first press conference on the case. Damien immediately garnered national media attention. In March, the Committee to Defend John Damien was set up and Damien announced he was suing the commission for one million dollars.

Damien was not only sympathetic to the general public. His case was an object lesson to anyone who was still abiding by the social contract of the closet. Damien had been discreet and normative and had followed all the rules. "I've never flaunted my gayness. I've never gone around advertising that I was gay. ... I just led my own private life and that was it," he explained.[31] Yet after years of faithful service, the system had reneged on the contract. Now he had to turn to the young activists to fight for justice. The message was clear: the closet and privilege were no protection. Activism was the only way forward.

Still, the logic of the closet did not die easily. Damien remarked:

The organized gay community has gone overboard, really to push my case and defense. But some of my gay friends don't understand . . . why I wanted to fight this thing. They agree I was right in refusing the money and letter of recommendation, but not about going public. My straight friends, though, are giving me a lot of support.[32]

The case would also be an object lesson for the activists. The only logical way to get redress was through the courts. But once entangled in a legal battle, activists were outgunned. Government resources paid the racing commission's bills. The committee needed to spend time and energy on fundraising, and were dependent on a fickle media to keep the case in the public eye. Tom Warner described the trajectory of the case as "one of frustration, legal delays, waning support and personal pain."[33] The new movement had neither the structure nor the resources to advance its aims through the legal system.

DOUG WILSON

A few months later, a second case surfaced. Doug Wilson was a true gay liberation poster boy. His flawless face, long blond hair, and open farm-boy looks graced the front cover of *TBP* issue 21.

Wilson had grown up in rural Saskatchewan. He was a master's student in the University of Saskatchewan's College of Education when, in September 1975, he posted an ad in the student newspaper about forming a campus gay group. When the ad came to the attention of the university administration, he was called into the dean's office and informed that public identification with the gay movement was "damaging to the college" and that he could no longer supervise in-classroom practicums of student teachers.

Wilson went public and immediately received support from the university's student unions. The Committee to Defend Doug Wilson was successful in having the Saskatchewan Human Rights Commission investigate. It was the first time that the provincial commission had agreed to accept a gay rights case.

But the university managed to get an injunction to stop the commission's investigation on the grounds that "sex" did not include "sexual orientation." The university won a battle, but it had already lost the war.

Unlike the Damien committee, which found itself locked into a legal process, the Committee to Defend Doug Wilson wisely did not pursue the legal route to challenge the injunction. It built horizontal alliances, garnering support from labour, women's, and social movement groups. Overnight Wilson became a media celebrity. The growth in the Saskatchewan movement was exponential, and in March 1976 the university was forced to include sexual orientation in its anti-discrimination policy.

The cases were quite different. Damien was middle-aged and had lost his livelihood. Although the case was significant for the community, it was still very much about achieving individual justice. As a young man, Wilson was less concerned about his own career. He dropped out of the master's program and turned his notoriety to the service of grassroots activism. Wilson corresponded with isolated gay people in rural areas, for whom he was the first public gay figure in the province. He joined the board of directors and ultimately became executive director of the Saskatchewan Association on Human Rights, and helped found both the Saskatchewan Gay Coalition with its innovative rural outreach program and the Metamorphosis cultural festival.[34]

GAY MARXIST PERSPECTIVES

I came of age during the student movement, the Cultural Revolution, national liberation struggles, and the anti–Vietnam war movement. Although I learned a lot during my brief apprenticeship with the Young Socialists at Carleton, I had little stomach for sectarian left-wing parties. I found them insular and self-righteous. Each one, I noted, developed its own particular accent and inflection, a sure sign that members spent most of their time talking to each other. And when they weren't talking to themselves, their time seemed dedicated to intergroup denigration.

When I returned to Toronto from South America in the spring of 1974, as well as coming out I discovered the Marxist Institute. This collective offered courses and sponsored lectures and debates. I went to the Introduction to Marxism course to get my feet wet, and then joined a *Capital* study group. I got on with people I met there and soon found myself part of the Marxist Institute collective.

Sometime in the spring of 1975, Walter Davis of the Revolutionary Marxist Group wondered out loud if the institute would run a class on Marxism and gay liberation. It seemed a brilliant idea. The two of us got together with Walter Bruno to figure out what such a course would entail. After worrying to death the problem of how much to go over the central tenets of Marxism and how much to dive into analyzing gay oppression and the movement, we came up with a proposal that I took to the Marxist Institute collective. I remember being nervous when I presented it, not sure exactly what to expect. Although I must have consulted with allies beforehand, I don't remember how "out" I had actually been in the institute to that point. But I got the go-ahead. The institute was gestating a split between the libertarian Marxists and those more oriented to Leninist forms of organization, and both sides wanted my support.

The group that came together for Marxist Perspectives on Gay Liberation was small and known to each other: Ken Popert and his partner, Brian Mossop, both in the Communist Party at the time, Davis and Bruno, me, and a few others.

The first three weeks we concentrated on basic Marxist ideas, including Engels's work on the history of the family. Then we looked at Wilhelm Reich and the Freudian left, Herbert Marcuse, the early German homosexual rights movement, and the Russian Revolution. The final session addressed modern debates. Course evaluations noted a lack of clear direction, difficulties in relating theoretical issues to practice, and the lack of women's participation.

But with one course under our belts, we were ready to take on the world. A second course was organized, this time advertised both through the Marxist Institute networks and *TBP*. The turnout was much better – about a dozen at the first meeting in early October 1976, including people we didn't even know and more women.

As I gave the introduction, I noticed a young Asian man across the room. He introduced himself as Richard Fung. Later I learned that he had actually come with a straight friend to attend the Introduction to Marxism course. The Marxist Institute's little office had two rooms, railroad style, and two courses could run simultaneously. Richard and his friend had both signed up for the introductory course, but at the last minute, as the groups finished mingling in the larger front room, he scratched his name off that list and darted into the back gay room, leaving his befuddled buddy behind. It was his coming out. He later told me that I was dressed so unfashionably that he was sure I was a straight member of the institute who had been assigned to deliver the course. Forty years later Richard and I are still partners.

This time we had scrapped the basic Marxist concepts section. We spent the first meeting on the course outline and the different ways gay men and women experienced sexism. The course dealt with the canonical texts but also analyzed new feminist writing, psychology, and anthropological work on sexual behaviour.

A young Gary Kinsman, scarcely out of high school, gave a presentation on Reich's theories of the family. He explained earnestly that for Reich, the family was the "primary source of sexual repression" and that "compulsory abstinence leads to the creation of a character structure primed to obey authority. The family was the fundamental training ground for capitalist society."[35]

Having established the family as the source of both women's and gay oppression, and as crucial in maintaining the capitalist social order, we discussed the relationship between gay liberation and the women's movement, and at the early gay rights movement in Germany. Our final session looked at *The Political Perspective of the Lavender and Red Union* and Don Milligan's *Politics of Homosexuality*. Both asserted that gender roles, heterosexuality, and the family were indispensable for capitalism and that therefore, homosexual liberation constituted a revolutionary force.

After the course finished, most participants continued meeting as a Gay Marxist Study Group and rallied to support striking University of Toronto library workers during the winter of 1975. One of the issues in the strike was the inclusion of discrimination protection on the basis of sexual orientation. It was unsuccessful. The university offered a raise but adamantly refused to agree to the non-discrimination clause.

As this was going on, I convinced the Marxist Institute to organize a spring

1976 lecture series on Sexism and Capitalism, and have the series co-sponsored by GATE and The Women's Press. The goal was to bring together the left, gay liberation, and the women's movement. Our theory told us these three movements had a common target – capitalism – however fraught our practical relationships might be. The lecture series kicked off with Eli Zaretsky, who was just about to publish *Capitalism, the Family and Personal Life.*

At the final lectures, the new Gay Marxist Study Group distributed the first of a series of position papers that members produced "as a starting point for the discussion of many important questions of left politics and women's and gay liberation."

The paper rehearsed our basic propositions. "Superstructures" such as institutions, ideologies, and moralities rested upon relations of production and served specific class interests. The conditioning of human sexualities was part of that superstructure. And, since the social organization of sexuality in modern capitalist society was the privatized nuclear family, "the oppression of women and the oppression of gays are two aspects of the organization of sexuality to serve the ends of capital in our society."

Sexism was therefore a bourgeois ideology that reproduced unequal relationships. It convinced women they were inferior and labelled gays as unnatural. Sexism divided the working class, and to condone or ignore it was opportunism. The paper finished by quoting Lenin: "Working class consciousness cannot be genuine political consciousness unless the workers are trained to respond to all cases of tyranny, oppression, violence and abuse, no matter what class is affected."[36]

This conclusion was a broadside against the left. Even the nominally supportive Trotskyist organizations were hemorrhaging gay members. A purge was already in the works in the Communist Party that would see both Mossop and Popert expelled because of their gay rights activities. The "Marxist-Leninist" (Maoist) parties were even worse. A friendly comrade from the Workers Communist Party earnestly explained to me that gay sex wasn't natural and was a reaction to exploitation. Gay relationships abandoned the struggle between men and women over sexism, and there were members of the party who had been gay before they joined, but were now happy heterosexuals. The Workers Communist Party's main competitors, In Struggle / En Lutte, maintained a stony silence on such questions so as not to be distracted from class struggle. The Communist Party of Canada (Marxist-Leninist) considered us a product of bourgeois decadence.

Gay Marxists had a hard row to hoe. Although the lectures did produce some interesting debates, an evaluation letter from The Women's Press noted, "The series raised important theoretical questions for us which we would not otherwise have confronted on the relation between these two forms of sexism, but we don't feel that many answers were arrived at."

The study group didn't last long. As long as we were just a study and discussion group, we could agree to disagree while mutually deepening our knowledge. But those affiliated with the RMG felt it was time for action. Their Trotskyist conception of a "transitional program" required them to "radical-ize" popular struggles. Since gayness was inherently anti-capitalist, the civil rights struggle was at best a first baby step. The movement was being held back by timid and reformist leadership. Such leadership constantly had to be challenged, pushed to go farther, or replaced.

The rest of us argued for a clear distinction between struggles for demo-cratic rights, aimed at equality within an existing social framework – like the women's or gay movements – and revolutionary struggles aimed at funda-mentally changing that framework. Both were progressive, but they had dif-ferent aims and involved different kinds of people. Running them together would lead to divisions in democratic struggles or watering down revolution-ary ones.

If the debates in the courses and the study group seemed peripheral to the broader community, they served as a training ground for a number of indi-viduals who would play important roles in queer politics. And at least some-one was watching. An RCMP file later unearthed reported, "It has been learned [*blanked out*] that GATE is one of 7 gay groups in Toronto and one of these is the Gay Marxist Study Group [*blanked out*] which originated from the NMI [New Marxist Institute]."[37]

BASIS OF UNITY

Although the certainty about the family as the material basis for homophobia was soon challenged, the discussions did consolidate some basic concepts that would stand me in good stead. The first was "basis of unity," the set of princi-ples or goals that everyone in an organization needs to agree on in order to move forward. For example, in single-issue groups, members advocate for a shared goal despite differences on many other issues. Other groups require members to agree to a longer list of principles and ideas. Generally speaking, the more items there are in a basis of unity, the harder it is to get people to agree on them all. Or at least, the process of getting everyone on the same page can require interminable discussion – "too many evening meetings," as Oscar Wilde famously quipped about socialism. On the other hand, once that discussion is concluded, it produces a strong group of like-minded people.

Mainstream activists usually tried to develop a basis of unity that brought together the maximum number of people to work on a concrete issue, a nar-row basis of unity. Such concrete goals could be won without fundamental social change. Getting the *Star* to accept a gay ad, for example, wouldn't mean the end of capitalism.

Some groups, like *TBP*, tried to fudge the issue by keeping the basis of unity intentionally vague. "Gay liberation" could mean different things to dif-ferent people. The collective would agree on the gay liberation position in relation to a particular issue on an ad hoc basis. Generally that worked, but when a contentious issue came up, such vagueness meant that people could sometimes find themselves in serious disagreement.

OPPORTUNISM

Related to basis of unity was "opportunism," which Wikipedia defines as "the conscious policy and practice of taking selfish advantage of circumstances – with little regard for principles, or with what the consequences are for others." I began to perceive different kinds of opportunism. Right opportunism was abandoning principles for immediate gain. That generally meant becoming more right wing to be more acceptable to those in power. The NDP was often accused of right opportunism, since it would abandon principles to appeal to conservative voters.

Left opportunism referred to those who would always take the most rigid, hard-line positions full of leftist rhetoric. They weren't sucking up to those in power, but they were so uncompromising that they remained isolated. What did they have to gain from such behaviour? I began to recognize that individuals got a psychological benefit from always being the most politically correct and radical sounding person in the room. And since it kept their groups small, they continued to be the big fish in a small pool.

Both right and left opportunism were rewarded by immediate personal benefits, material or psychological. Neither thought much about the long-term effects on building a movement for social change. And since they were both motivated by individual rewards, there was also an unsettling propensity to flip from one to the other without warning.

The correct line between different kinds of opportunisms, though, was often hard to determine. It depended on long- and short-term goals. If the goals were immediate, it would be more necessary to get the support of the powers that be. The danger was slipping into right opportunism. If the only thing that mattered was the final revolution – rather than working to make life immediately better in a concrete way – you were probably slipping into left opportunism.

A KISS IS JUST A KISS

We soon had a real-life example to deal with. The Alternatives to Alienation collective claimed to be a fusion of Marxism and Fritz Perls's gestalt psychology. It published a bimonthly newspaper, as well as running the Spice of Life Restaurant on Yonge Street. Alternatives was led by a rather anti-charismatic "psychiatrist," Ernie Barr, who constantly spit into a handkerchief when he talked. The young devotees lived together communally. In exchange for their labour in the restaurant, they received free therapy for their many neuroses as identified by Barr.

In February 1976 two male members of the Alternatives collective were arrested and charged with blocking the sidewalk and committing an indecent act for kissing at the intersection of Yonge and Bloor, the heart of the city's high-end shopping district. They had been posing for pictures to illustrate an article on homophobia for the group's newspaper. The sidewalk at that corner is more than twenty feet wide. It was physically impossible for two people to block it, no matter what they were doing.

With the help of *TBP* and GATE, a meeting was called to set up a defence committee. Forty people attended, half from Alternatives and half from the gay community. GATE and *TBP* advised that the two should get a good civil rights lawyer and launch a public campaign to expose the arrests as homophobic harassment. But the Alternatives collective had more grandiose ideas. This had to be a campaign against all moralism and sexual repression in capitalist society. All the lawyers we suggested were rejected, and Alternatives settled on one of their own choice, who advised them that publicity might jeopardize the case. The defence committee dissolved.

When they quietly came to court in July, both men were found guilty and fined fifty dollars each. They announced that they would appeal, but ultimately paid the fine and let the case drop, leaving behind a precedent that two men kissing in public was an indecent act.

Here we had the radical rhetoric of anti-capitalism (left opportunism) covering the right opportunism of not wanting to identify homophobia because, as one Alternatives member explained, "her mother wouldn't understand." Then further right opportunism refusing to develop a public campaign and leaving things up to the lawyer. And finally refusing to appeal, leaving the gay community to face the consequences.

A week later, in an attempt to challenge the precedent, GATE and *TBP* organized a kiss-in on the same street corner. I was among twenty same-sex kissers (none of us from the Alternatives collective) who bemused passersby and drew a half-dozen police officers. But there were no further arrests.

UNION ORGANIZING

The 1975 strike by library workers at the University of Toronto revealed another process that was going on. Lesbians and gay men were coming out at work. Far from the headlines, this was an intimate process that involved individuals talking to their workmates about their lives. The gay rights movement involved a vertical address, an appeal to governments to live up to liberal principles of equality. It drew its power from the publicity generated by demonstrations and briefs. The work in the unions, on the other hand, was more horizontal. It was based on principles of solidarity.

A 1973 *TBP* article by Walter Blumenthal (aka Bruno) about working at the post office had already described this process. For the first year on the job he had largely been "content to take note of the sheer numbers of gay fellow-workers. . . . And there were dozens in the place, playing every role – from the

House Faggot to Solid Citizen and from Stompin' Dyke to Lovely Lady." But after they got to know each other things changed. He was "less and less inclined to remain in the closet." "Sometimes it was a real trip-and-a-half, sitting together 15-to-a-table in the cafeteria, cruising the new employees and screaming up a storm, to the general discomfort of other tables. I suppose that was one small stage on the road to liberation – just being together and 'doing our thing' openly."

At first Blumenthal was ostracized. One co-worker, Jim, called him "queer" and then turned and walked away. But when the local faced a strike and Blumenthal became a union militant, Jim turned around. "Seems he hated the boss as much as he claimed to hate homosexuals."[38] When management began harassing another employee for being too openly gay, the local rallied and put a stop to it.

The first concrete result from this kind of work was at the Metropolitan Toronto Public Library in 1974 when CUPE demanded protection for lesbian and gay workers. Although the union secured endorsements from a number of social service agencies, management refused to budge until it was threatened with public demonstrations by the gay community. They finally agreed to attach a separate letter of intent to the contract.

Like the CUPE 1230 strike at the University of Toronto Library in 1975, a similar fight by the United Auto Workers Local 195 was not immediately successful. After several incidents of violence against lesbian and gay workers, the local's human rights committee recommended that sexual orientation be added as a protected category in the contract. The union supported the demand, but although negotiators held out as long as they could, the employer insisted that the language be dropped. Harold Desmarais, president of Windsor Gay Unity, himself an auto worker, took the long view. It was "quite usual" for a demand to be rejected by management at first, he said, and the issue would be soon on the negotiating table again.

The John Inglis Company had converted from weapons manufacture to washing machines and appliances after the Second World War. That shift coincided with the dismissal of most of the women who had worked there during wartime. But by the 1960s, women were re-entering the labour force, including in male-dominated manufacturing.

Bev Brown joined Inglis in 1976. A feisty dyke, she quickly earned a reputation as a strong voice for women's and workers' rights. Unions are generally more democratic than corporations; leadership comes up through the rank and file. When Brown ran for chief shop steward in 1979, her male opponent began a whisper campaign that she was queer. But the campaign backfired and Brown won. She went on to form the first United Steelworkers women's committee in Canada, and was eventually elected vice-president of the local.[39]

Win or lose, by the mid-1970s, lesbians and gay men were coming out in unionized workplaces and asking for their co-workers' solidarity. The union movement already recognized that divisions along racial lines weakened it, and was instrumental in establishing the first Ontario Human Rights Code in 1962. The same logic was soon being argued by women workers and eventually, by lesbians and gay men. A foundation was being laid that would position unions as a major ally in gay rights struggles.

COMMUNAL LIFE

If the privatized family was our enemy, one solution was to set up alternative ways of living. Some of us from the now defunct Gay Marxist Study Group – jokingly described as the Stalinist faction – felt we had more to learn about a Marxist analysis of homophobia. And one way to accomplish that would be to intensify our relationships and conversations by living together. In May 1976 we founded a commune as the site of our experiment. We rented a house together on Seaton Street in a yet-to-be-gentrified part of Toronto's Cabbagetown neighbourhood.

It wasn't the first time I had lived communally. When I returned from my first trip to India in 1970, I moved into a three-storey house on Palmerston Avenue, with seven adults, two children, some cats, and a regular supply of crashing hitchhikers. But that venture had no political goals. The house at 188½ Seaton Street was part of a process to develop the gay liberation movement within a broader anti-capitalist left.

The cheaply renovated Victorian row house had five bedrooms, one each for me; Richard, who was working on his degree at the Ontario College of Art; John Manweering, a law student, and his dog, Puppy; David Gibson, a designer for the provincial government who helped design *TBP*; and finally my sister, Lisa. Lisa was the odd straight woman out, but for her, it was a temporary housing solution. She and I were scheduled to head to Africa in the fall to experience the newly successful revolution in Mozambique. She had just finished university, and had been active in the Toronto Committee for the Liberation of South African Colonies (TCLSAC).

Meanwhile we had a commune to organize. The first thing was how to share costs. At first blush, the communist answer would be "from each according to their ability." But we didn't live in a state of communism, so that would be utopian. We therefore settled on equality. Rent was divided into two shares, an equal communal share for the common areas of the house, and a private share that differed according to the size of the bedroom. Bedrooms were allocated in a discussion of both need and ability to pay.

We had supper together as much as possible. Cooking, shopping, and house-cleaning responsibilities rotated on a chore wheel. A house meeting, usually over brunch on Sunday mornings, organized the week's cooking schedule, dealt with any issues, and planned joint projects. The downstairs was decorated with revolutionary Cuban posters that Gibson had acquired, and the political conversation was ongoing and stimulating.

On weekends we occasionally took walks together. We often ended up wandering among the stately houses of Rosedale to the north of our neighbourhood, fantasizing about the one we would appropriate "come the revolution," when such mansions would be turned into communal living spaces. We also discussed reconfiguring the high-rise apartment buildings in St. James Town to accommodate communal living and discourage privatized family life. In spring, everything seems possible.

TRANSFORMATIONS

The Body Politic, now completing its fifth year, had come a long way. Issue 1 had been put together in a backyard shed by an ad hoc group, and, according to one of the writers, it was mostly "political harangues." It cost $350 to print, had no ads, and was sold in the streets by collective members for twenty-five cents. Issue 24, June 1976, listed eleven collective members, including myself, twenty contributors, and six news correspondents. It included national and international news coverage, features, cartoons, and a cultural section called Our Image, and it had national and international distribution. There was a full page of classifieds; although display ads were carefully scrutinized for sexism and limited by an agreed-upon copy-to-ad ratio, they now featured mainstream businesses as well as the usual baths, bars, and lesbian and gay periodicals. There was even one paid staff member (actually two, who took turns cycling between being paid and continuing to work while collecting unemployment insurance). The paper had also become a repository for movement material and had spun off the Canadian Gay Archives.

TBP was now a small business. Despite reservations, the need for a legal framework to develop our activities had become pressing. In January 1976 *TBP* announced the incorporation of Pink Triangle Press (PTP) as a non-profit legal entity to include both the paper and the archives. We assured readers that we had no intention of modelling our business practices on those of Canada's press barons. Corporations are legally required to have officers and directors but despite the new structure, both *TBP* and the Canadian Gay Archives would continue to be directed by their own autonomous collectives. The announcement also appealed for funds to allow the paper to publish monthly, and to support the archives and other projects.

Donors to the press were rewarded with an enamel pink triangle pin. This symbol was an attempt to broaden gay history beyond an American narrative that usually began with the 1969 Stonewall rebellion. We had always tried to promote the notion of a pre-Stonewall history. Early issues of *TBP* had included feature articles by Jim Steakley on the gay rights movement in pre-war Germany. Using the pink triangle worn by homosexual prisoners in the Nazi camps gestured towards this history.

As we were moving into our new commune on Seaton Street, the paper also moved from the cramped storefront office on Carlton. The new offices, shared with the archives, were on the top floor of an old warehouse building at 24 Duncan, just south of Queen Street. We were well situated. Queen, which had been depressed for years, was just becoming a new hub for the city's expanding arts scene. The building had a freight elevator for those daunted by the five-storey climb, high-beamed ceilings, and a bank of windows that filled the open-concept room with light. It was quickly appointed with second-hand furniture, layout tables, armchairs, filing cabinets, and volunteers.

It wasn't just *TBP* that was growing. New groups and businesses catering to lesbians and gay men were springing up in the city and across the country. *TBP*'s Community page, listing groups that "primarily direct themselves toward alleviating or struggling against gay oppression," recorded seventy organizations and coalitions from coast to coast. As more people came out, the community was becoming what sociologists call "institutionally complete," with a variety of services and organizations to meet different needs.

REPRESSION

In July 1976, Montreal hosted the summer Olympics. The games were a boondoggle, raking in money for contractors and leaving the city with a billion-dollar debt that would not be paid off for thirty years. As well, African nations boycotted the event to protest the International Olympic Committee's refusal to ban New Zealand, after that country's rugby team violated the growing boycott movement and toured apartheid South Africa.

But for an increasingly visible gay community, the issue was repression. Under the guise of Olympic security, Montreal police launched a crackdown on gay establishments. It began with a raid on Montreal's Aquarius Sauna and the arrest of thirty-five men as "found-ins" in a bawdy house February 1975. In October, six gay bars were raided, including the city's most popular women's bar. Surveillance was stepped up at public washrooms, leading to an unprecedented wave of arrests for sexual activity. In January 1976, it was the turn of the Club Baths, where men were charged and forced to take venereal disease tests. In May, two months before the games opened, eighty-three men were arrested at the Neptune Sauna. In both places there was extensive property damage. That weekend saw five more Montreal clubs raided, and by June all of the city's gay baths were facing charges and closed. The repression extended to Ottawa, where twenty-seven men were arrested at the Club Baths and the membership list was seized.

In May, a local employee of the Olympic organizing committee leaked a directive confirming that "non-conforming elements" were to be "driven underground" in the Quebec City–Toronto corridor for the duration of the games. Guy Toupin, the Montreal police officer co-ordinating Olympic security, claimed that the raids were only "a part of our normal police work." But he went on, "if such action helps us in turning up potential terrorists, so much the better."[40]

The RCMP also got in on the act with a visit to the GATE Toronto offices. Two officers questioned president Tom Warner about what might be planned for the games. And it wasn't just about us. Mounties also showed up at the Centre for Spanish Speaking Peoples, where I worked, to enquire what mischief Latin American immigrants might be planning. Other immigrant service organizations reported similar visits. Homeless people in Montreal and Kingston were picked up and given six-month jail sentences to get them off the streets for the duration of the games. Our new commune began receiving boxes of documents from the largely Quebec-based Marxist-Leninist group In Struggle, which feared a raid on its Montreal offices and was squirrelling its archives to Toronto for safekeeping.

In Montreal, traditional divisions between the anglophone and francophone gay communities were bridged with the formation of the Comité homosexuel anti-répression / Gay Coalition Against Repression (CHAR). The group organized a demonstration that marched passed the premier's office, Olympic headquarters, and city hall. A solidarity demonstration took place in Vancouver. Gays of Ottawa effectively challenged the Ottawa raids in the press. *TBP* remarked, "We may have pulled it off. Gay people drawn to the movement in numbers as never before may have just aborted this country's most organized and vicious attack on gay people."[41]

IN OR OUT

In 1975, David Goodstein had bought the U.S. gay periodical *The Advocate*, at the time the world's most widely distributed gay liberation paper. He rapidly remade it to appeal to a more mainstream readership, cutting back on news coverage and featuring stories on media personalities. Goodstein believed in gay pride, but for him, "the most obvious examples of this new pride are the many new, well-lighted, expensively decorated bars and clubs that are rapidly replacing the dingy toilets of old."

In a January 1976 editorial, Goodstein launched a broadside against gay activists as "unemployable, unkempt and neurotic to the point of megalomania." He claimed that the "silent majority" of gay people were still in the closet, and speaking publicly on their behalf, he opined that they "actively dislike most of the people speaking publicly on their behalf."

He attacked the notion of horizontal alliances with other oppressed groups. "Gay men and women do not believe achievement of gay civil rights has anything to do with fascism, imperialism, socialism or other aspects of Marxist rhetoric. They are enraged by gay contingents in leftist or 'Third World' demonstrations." Ironically, for someone who had just accused other gay leaders of megalomania, he signed off "it's damned lonely on the front lines."

TBP was not the only gay liberation group to pick up Goodstein's challenge. Six of *The Advocate*'s most important writers penned a joint letter calling his depiction "distorted and highly reactionary in tone and intent." New

York's Gay Activist Alliance adopted a statement of censure entitled "In Defense of the Gay Liberation Movement." In Canada, their statement was endorsed by thirteen member organizations of the Coalition for Gay Rights in Ontario, including *TBP*, which printed it in full.[42]

TBP editorialized that Goodstein's attack targeted the "the *public* struggle for gay rights." To his assertion that municipal rights ordinances were being won through quiet lobbying, *TBP* replied, So what if no one knows about them? That point was prescient. When people did find out, such ordinances came under attack by a resurgent homophobic right wing. Many would be rescinded.[43]

Although the editorial didn't refer to it, *TBP* and *The Advocate* also represented very different organizational models. *The Advocate* was privately owned and profit driven. *TBP* had no owner, was collectively controlled by those who worked on it, and was part of a non-profit organization.

If Goodstein's acerbic right opportunist comments provided a clear target, it was more difficult to figure out how to deal with the fact that as acceptance grew, the movement was becoming more mainstream. A story entitled "Damien's Exile" appeared in the February 21, 1976, issue of *Weekend Magazine*, a Saturday supplement carried in twenty-one newspapers read by five million people across Canada. It claimed, "What John Damien represents is not homosexuality but human dignity." In response, the defence fund received letters of support from across the country and almost $1,500 in donations (not small change for 1976), mostly in small amounts and cash.

Yet Gerald Hannon was worried. In a feature entitled "The Marketing of John Damien," he mused:

> I have to keep telling myself how important the support that article has gathered is, and how necessary the money is, before I can stomach what John Hofsess, the author of the article, had to do to make gay, homosexual, cock-sucking John Damien acceptable to *Weekend Magazine* and its 5 million readers coast to coast.

The "trick," Hannon pointed out, was drawing attention away from "the radical specificity of Damien's homosexuality . . . and raising the whole thing to the safe, abstract and metaphysical level of 'human dignity.'" Hannon argued that Damien had been sanitized and called it gay liberation "where homosexuals are unnecessary." When Damien gets his job back, "it will be clear that a momentary and unfortunate breakdown in the smoothly running machinery of the system will have been remedied."[44]

If we needed more evidence that we weren't in Kansas anymore, Ken Waxman's September 1976 cover story, "The Rise of Gay Capitalism," in glossy *Toronto Life* identified "gay purchasing power" as "real power," and described a new class of entrepreneurs that "serviced" the "booming gay market." At the top of Waxman's pyramid of notables hovered "media-oriented" Peter

Maloney, "guru" of Toronto's gay marketplace and potentially "Canada's first acknowledged gay millionaire."

This time Michael Lynch penned the review.

> Alas, I don't recognize *my* gayness in the fact that we "spend more money than straights on grooming, entertainment, clothes, drink and travel." If it's "self-righteous" and "left-wing" to question this characterization of gayness . . . then shucks mom I guess I'm self-righteous and left-wing.

Lynch pointed out the impact of the gay consumer power approach on those who didn't wield such power because they simultaneously face other forms of systemic discrimination.

> And I wish – Is this left-wing? – that Waxman had made a fourth Discovery: women. In this article, as in the "gay marketplace," women only exist as "girls." . . . Telling evidence isn't it, that when gayness is defined as no more than consumerism, it aids and abets the macho exploitation of women.[45]

Lynch identified women, but his point would become increasingly relevant to others within the community who were marginalized because of racism or other forms of discrimination.

THE WOMEN

Lynch's concern about the absence of women in the article was more than just a critique of Waxman's sexism. It also reflected a nagging anxiety about how few lesbians were involved in *TBP*, a hard fact that reflected badly on our supposed anti-sexism.

In a two-page feature, "Nudity and Sexism," Ed Jackson remembered an early *TBP* collective discussion about a nude picture of a young man in issue 2. At the time, one of the two women on the largely male collective had objected that the picture was sexist. The majority, all men, thought it was a sensitive and tender photo. "So we never really understood each other, the photo was printed, the women drifted away. *The Body Politic* became more male-identified by default rather than by intention."[46]

The piece went on to contrast women's and men's relationships with nudity. The nude female body was deployed for the pleasure of men and to sell products, while gay men faced the suppression of sexualized male images. For women, not having to deal with sexualized images might be liberating, while gay men might consider access to comparable images as part of their liberation. As a result, male-dominated gay liberation media often carried sexualized images of men, and women were made to feel out of place.

Sexualized imagery was not the only thing that kept us apart. Our experiences of sexism were really quite different. Lesbians often found themselves out of place in the gay lib movement, not so much because of active sexism or misogyny (although that did exist) but because of the incomprehension of women's issues among the majority of gay men.[47]

When gay men thought about the right to control our own bodies, we thought of our right to have sex. When lesbians thought about their right to control their bodies, they more often thought of abortion and birth control and the right not to be treated as sexual objects. If gay men wanted to dispense with the family, many lesbians worried about custody of their children and cuts to family allowance benefits. When gay men thought about age of consent, they remembered the suppression of early sexual desires. Lesbians were more likely to think about protecting children from male sexual coercion. While coming out was a badge of courage for gay men, the risks to economic stability could be far higher for lesbians, who were therefore more likely to understand staying in the closet as a survival strategy.

As a result, most lesbians had better things to do than spend their time working with gay men. The more political lesbians – the equivalent of the political gay men who found a home in the gay liberation movement – tended to gravitate towards the women's movement.

There were a few, however, like Chris Bearchell, who made bridging the divide a priority. She wrote:

> Gay women represent an organic link between two forces that have a basic interest in the complete re-structuring of our society – women and homosexuals of both sexes. These two groups constitute two very powerful potential mutual allies. The natures of their respective oppressions share many common factors, and the institutions they face in fighting that oppression are often the same: the church, the family, the state, marriage, the media. Lesbians by their very existence are crucial to one day forging this alliance.[48]

LESBIAN AUTONOMY

Radical feminists, who focused on fighting patriarchy, were likely to see men – gay men included – as the problem rather than as potential allies. Socialist feminists, with their anti-capitalist analysis, were more open to working with men. Though lesbian separatism never reached the same critical mass in Canada as it did in the United States at the time, there was growing support for lesbian autonomy, even by those who argued for working with gay men.

Wages Due Lesbians was connected to the Toronto Wages for Housework Committee, a group demanding compensation for women's unpaid labour in the home. They argued that this labour, including sexual services and emotional support, was essential to capitalism. Wages always fluctuated around what was necessary in order to reproduce the labour force: feeding, clothing, educating, sexually reproducing, and so on. The fact that much of this work was done by women for free allowed capital to pay less to male breadwinners.

In the process, this system made women dependent on men and devalued women's labour – the material basis for women's inequality. Out lesbians specifically were poor because they weren't supported by a male wage. Although it was women-focused, Wages Due saw capitalism rather than men as the enemy.

As it evolved, Wages Due concentrated on questions of child custody and the fight for women to live as lesbians and still raise children. This had both economic and legal aspects. Throughout the summer of 1976, Wages Due went door to door with petitions protesting family allowance cuts as part of the government's anti-inflation program. Family allowance was seen as direct compensation to women for their reproductive work. It was especially important for women raising children without a male wage. In 1978, Wages Due established the Lesbian Mothers' Defence Fund, a support system that provided financial help, referrals to sympathetic lawyers, and personal support for those fighting custody battles in courts that still largely saw lesbians as unfit mothers.[49]

In an op-ed piece for the August 1976 *TBP,* Wages Due urged gay men to support lesbian autonomy.

> Although men are also exploited by capitalism, they are the instruments of capital against us. Men will dominate us unless we are strong. They will use us as long as we are weak. We will be weak as long as we are not an autonomous force in both the women's and the gay movements. . . . Unless we lesbian women can build our power we will always risk gay men building their power at our expense.[50]

Marie Robertson of Lesbians of Ottawa Now (LOON) also spoke from an autonomist perspective.

> People don't work unless it affects their lives. There should be a lot of alternatives – people should work where they want to be. Listen, the gay movement should stay where it is in terms of priorities – don't adopt women's issues. Support them – yes. But the gay male movement is not going to get men out if it adopts abortion as a priority. Or even lesbian custody for that matter.[51]

Many gay men couldn't understand why lesbians wanted to organize autonomously, and they considered it divisive. But lesbian autonomy was supported by most of the male leadership of the movement. One could scarcely argue that the gay movement needed to be autonomous while disputing the same arguments for lesbians.

LOOT

By 1976, the critical mass of activist lesbians reached a tipping point. In October, the Lesbian Organization of Toronto (LOOT) was launched after a meeting of fifty or so women at the CHAT offices on Church Street. Despite the fact that women such as Pat Murphy had dramatically left CHAT in 1972, there were still probably more women involved there than in the more radical groups such as GATE and *TBP*. Women such as CHAT board member Tin Lowes were torn between loyalty to their own mixed-gender organization and the enthusiasm of the crowd for building a new lesbian-only group. According to Becki Ross, "She and other CHAT women quietly sat back."[52] Their premonitions were not unfounded. CHAT was already in financial crisis and would fold in less than a year.

A task force was set up to investigate establishing a centre. Six months later a location was found, a rundown Victorian building at 342 Jarvis Street. The LOOT house opened in May 1977, sharing space with *The Other Woman* and the Three of Cups Coffeehouse. Pat Murphy called it a "shabby, dilapidated, but glorious castle."[53]

"The LOOT building was right across from Jarvis Collegiate, my high school," remembers Naomi Brooks.

> I spent a lot of grade thirteen across the street. The first floor had two rooms that opened into each other so you could have bigger meetings. There was a kitchen at the back. On the second floor there were smaller rooms for smaller meetings. On the third floor, there was a two- or three-bedroom apartment. There was usually lots of beer as well. Sometimes we had liquor licences and sometimes we didn't.[54]

The LOOT house quickly became a hive of activity. Superbia Press operated out of the basement, and Mama Quilla II, the precursor to Lorraine Segato's Parachute Club, also rehearsed there. The centre was a meeting place for brunches, dances, a drop-in, and a lesbian phone line.[55] There was peer support counselling and a lending library, and the coffee house offered social space to hang out. LOOT published a newsletter and organized potlucks, brunches, concerts, and performances. "It was a place to find haven in a world that seemed to be very unfriendly and hostile," remembers Amy Gottlieb, another regular. "It was amazing to have a house you could go to rather than a more commercial place where you had a little corner or a bar. It was much more friendly, run by women, run by lesbians, very welcoming and full of political discussion."[56]

"It was a dream, a dream of a lesbian space that was different from the bar scene," Brooks recalls.

> The bar scene was either disco, or '50s/'60s butch fem old school. The more traditional women's bars like the Blue Jay were really hostile to feminism. That's where the working class folks were definitely. The disco clubs were all about making money. I think LOOT succeeded in bringing together the working class dykes and the feminist academics. Not completely, but in a way that hadn't happened before for sure.

As welcoming as it was, the centre also found itself dealing with the changing city demographics. "We didn't even notice we were almost all white," Brooks notes. "There were a few black women. One we called Black Lisa to distinguish her from the other Lisa."

Day-to-day operations were managed by a "fairly amorphous" collective, and there were monthly open meetings run on a consensus model where major decisions were made. Overnight, 342 Jarvis Street became autonomous lesbian central.

AUTONOMY AND YOUTH

Late in 1975, Huntley Youth Services (formerly Big Sisters) organized a discussion group for youth dealing with sexuality issues. Under the guidance of George Hislop from CHAT and a straight female social worker, eight young men, all gay, began attending the regular meetings. Two of the young men (who had to remain anonymous in the *TBP* report because they were both under twenty-one) decided there was a greater need than the small, closed group could provide, and that youth should be meeting the need themselves.

In the summer of 1976, they applied for membership, as Gay Youth Toronto, in the newly opened, city-run neighbourhood centre at 519 Church Street. The application sparked a crisis. Straight people on the board were "appalled by the idea of people as young as fourteen 'deciding' to be gay."[57] They worried about bad press and accusations of contributing to criminal behaviour. Despite endorsement letters from a half-dozen agencies and individuals including Liberal politician Margaret Campbell and two city aldermen, the board was divided.

A bisexual member of the board realized that he would have the deciding vote. Although his wife was also a board member, and he had not come out to her, he did so by voting to accept the group. Gay Youth Toronto became a member of the 519 in a vote of seven to six.

Gerald Hannon reported in *TBP*:

> It was certainly a victory of sorts: gay people winning the right to use community facilities as any other legitimate group could. But there were drawbacks. The Centre insisted that the lower age limit for membership had to be 16. That cuts out a lot of young people. . . . But the group has decided to live with it for the time being. After all, some board members wanted a psychiatrist and a social worker present at all Gay Youth Group meetings.[58]

Gay Youth blazed the way for others at the 519, and the centre would soon become a de facto lesbian and gay community hub, contributing to the shift in community activities from Yonge to Church Street.

Tensions between lesbians and gay men came to a head at the Fourth National Gay Conference over Labour Day weekend in September 1976, inflamed by what I considered left opportunist interventions by the Revolutionary Marxist Group.

The Toronto conference was the largest to date; an estimated four hundred were in attendance. Plenaries were held in the Jarvis Collegiate's cavernous auditorium, with its heroic 1929 murals. Under the images of famous white men erecting crosses and making gallant gestures while Indians sat entranced at their feet, participants – including an increasing number of women – tried to thrash out the way forward for gay liberation.

The growth in women's participation had been strengthened by a major lesbian conference in Kingston the previous May. Things got off to a good start in Toronto with the formation of a Women's Caucus that successfully proposed the conference support a group of women occupying Nellie's women's hostel to protest government funding cuts. A second meeting of the caucus drew more than sixty participants, and more than 150 attended the Sunday panel discussion of women's and gay liberation.

That panel opened with the reading of a provocative statement by the Rights of Lesbians Subcommittee of the British Columbia Federation of Women. The statement suggested that lesbians should put off the struggle over sexual orientation until women's equality had been won. Gillian Chase of *The Other Woman* warned that both the women's movement and the gay movement were in danger of being co-opted by capitalism. "Sexual liberation has become an industry capitalizing on hedonism, straight or kinky."[59] She also criticized the move towards individualizing political campaigns, an allusion to the John Damien case. Terry Faubert of GATE Toronto discussed the economic and social factors that were a barrier to women joining the movement. Finally Marie Robertson argued that lesbians needed to develop their own issues within the movement in the same way that gay men were.

The meeting cemented the consensus about the need for autonomous lesbian organizing. At a follow-up session, "suggestions ranged from starting businesses which would make money for and hire only women, to public actions around lesbian rights, to the formation of an anti-capitalist lesbian movement."[60] Connections were made, and plans put in place to continue discussion at the upcoming National Lesbian Conference in October.

But any atmosphere of productive debate unravelled in the final plenary thanks to the intervention of the RMG. First, RMG member Gary Kinsman introduced a rambling motion accusing the National Gay Rights Coalition of being male oriented and demanding that it endorse a range of lesbian issues, which he went on to enumerate. The motion was defeated. A second motion by Robin Metcalfe of Halifax GATE called on the coalition to consider endorsing the demands that would emerge at the upcoming National Lesbian

Conference. That passed unanimously. But RMG members had already stormed out of the plenary. They soon returned with a group of angry women who had been told the conference had refused to endorse lesbian issues. The plenary quickly "degenerated into disorderly name-calling, much of it among the women."

There was a similar defeat of a last-minute RMG motion to recognize Quebec's right to self-determination. In its place, a resolution was passed confirming that it was up to Quebec gays "to determine the particular form of the gay rights struggle in Quebec."

A follow-up *TBP* editorial began by praising the work of socialists in the gay liberation movement. But it fulminated: "Unhappily one socialist group has abandoned all political principle to engage in divisive tactics against coalition politics. During the Fourth Annual Gay Conference, several gays from the Revolutionary Marxist Group displayed a remarkable talent for disruption."

The fireworks continued in a series of letters over the next issues of the paper. A joint letter from activists in Winnipeg, Toronto, Ottawa, and Montreal was blunt.

> The RMG's tactic is to show up at conferences and attempt to divide us by introducing controversial and emotional resolutions at the end – not as a constructive move, but as a disruptive contribution to our debates. Moreover they attempt to guilt-trip us into supporting their particular political analysis by pretending to represent women, Quebecois, and other groups who do not yet have a representative voice in our movement.[61]

In the December/January issue, *TBP* published excerpts from a fifteen-page letter from former RMG member Walter Davis. He called the paper's account of the conference "sexist slander" and disputed the contention that RMG only showed up at conferences to disrupt. He described RMG as the only political organization in Canada that "openly supports gay liberation in its fullest sense."[62]

For me, the debacle was an object lesson on the fruits of left opportunism. While I agreed with many of their ideas, RMG always managed to present them in a way that guaranteed they would go nowhere. If the group hoped for its interventions to build support for the women's movement or Quebec's right to self-determination, they were sorely misguided. Instead, they had isolated themselves, polarized issues, probably amplified sexism among some male delegates, and deepened mistrust between men and women and Anglo and Québécois activists. The only benefit of their actions was to reinforce their own self-image.

HIATUS

The conference marked the end of the summer. By this time, Richard and I found ourselves in a full-blown relationship. We never made any vows or promises. We just slowly grew together. We didn't advertise it. Monogamy was frowned on at the time.

Nevertheless, we were a couple, so the separation of my open-ended trip to Africa was hard. My sister and I had been planning the trip overland from Europe to southern Africa for a year. But wars and closed borders got in the way and I returned to Europe. Richard and I rendezvoused in Paris the following May. We ended up hitchhiking south and east, finally making our way to India. When we returned to Canada at the end of 1977, the terrain of gay politics had fundamentally shifted.

3

Noticed

BLOWBACK

"Things have been really bad," Ed Jackson explained to me when I reported to *TBP*'s Duncan Street office in December 1977 after almost a year and a half away.

A fourteen-year-old boy had been raped and murdered on Yonge Street. It had started out as some sort of sex scene. Three of those involved were caught trying to get out of town. Another had gone to the CHAT office, and George Hislop had brokered his turning himself in.

The media, especially the *Toronto Sun*, went wild, characterizing the murder as a "homosexual orgy slaying" and linking it to gay activists' demands for inclusion of sexual orientation in the Ontario Human Rights Code. The child, Emanuel Jaques, was a Portuguese immigrant. The Portuguese community held two huge demonstrations. There were demands for the return of the death penalty and the eradication of homosexuals. Hislop received personal death threats, and there were bomb threats to the *TBP* offices, Glad Day, and the CHAT centre.

There had been a community response. *TBP* had pointed out the homophobic press coverage. CGRO held a press conference. But it was like shouting in a hurricane. There was already a campaign to clean up Yonge Street to get rid of the body-rub parlours. This was gasoline on the fire. "You picked a good time to be away," Jackson concluded. And a bad time to come back, I thought grimly.

I skimmed through a year and a half of back issues. Things did look bad. Just after I left, the Catholic Church had launched an anti-porn campaign with the support of Ontario attorney general Roy McMurtry. Canada Customs had started blocking innocuous gay books and magazines at the border. Legal rulings after the Olympic bath raids in Montreal confirmed that baths could be considered "bawdy houses." In October, machine-gun-wielding police had arrested a further 146 men in a raid on another Montreal bar, Truxx. The men were held overnight and forced to undergo venereal disease tests as a condition of release. In Ottawa and Kitchener, the Canadian military had expelled at least nine lesbians from bases over the summer. The federal Liberals defeated an amendment to include sexual orientation in the Canadian Human Rights Act. It was revealed that the RCMP still kept files on gay civil servants.

The movement wasn't doing all that well, either. Two long-standing feminist magazines had folded: Toronto's *The Other Woman*, with its largely lesbian collective, and the Montreal lesbian journal, *Long Time Coming*. The Damien campaign was bogged down in procedural manoeuvres. Damien himself had been reduced to poverty, and his defence committee was unravelling amid fights over how gay the campaign should be.[1]

Nor was the wave of reaction just in Canada. Anita Bryant's Save Our Children campaign had successfully repealed Miami's anti-gay discrimination ordinance. In California, the Briggs Initiative called for the firing of all gay teachers. In the United Kingdom, *Gay News*, England's major gay paper, had been convicted of "blasphemous libel" for publishing a homoerotic poem about Christ. Italian activist Angelo Pezanna had been deported from the USSR for protesting that country's anti-gay laws and the imprisonment of gay film director Sergei Paradjanov. For the first time, the world seemed to be taking us seriously. And it was seriously trying to stamp us out.

In truth, not everything was bad. More than two thousand Montrealers took to the streets to protest the Truxx raid – the largest gay demonstration in Canadian history. In response, the newly elected Parti Québécois government in Quebec hastily added sexual orientation to the provincial Human Rights Code. In its *Life Together* report, the OHRC had called for the inclusion of sexual orientation in Ontario's code, and the Canadian Labour Congress (CLC) expressed its support, although given the hysteria around the Jaques murder, that seemed unlikely now. Two women expelled from the military, Barbara Thornborrow and Gloria Cameron, had come out publicly and were fighting back, and a sizable gay contingent had joined labour protests against Prime Minister Pierre Trudeau's wage control program.

The paper, too, seemed healthy. The office buzzed with activity and subscriptions were up. There were new faces on the collective, among them a very serious ex-Trotskyist law student, Paul Trollope, and Rick Bébout, a gentle, diminutive American draft dodger who had given up his job at a gay-run bakery to work on the paper. Pink Triangle Press had purchased a new typesetting machine and its typesetting service was turning a profit. A mail order book service was distributing important gay literature, and the press had just republished a Canadian edition of the iconic British booklet, *With Downcast Gays*. If we were under attack, we were so far holding our own.

MOUSTACHES

I noticed one thing about all the new faces. Everyone seemed to be wearing a moustache. As Rick Bébout noted in his memoirs:

> [The early 1970s] politics of polymorphous perversity, backing up androgynous display, had also faded. Now queens were outnumbered by "clones" – satin traded for denim and leather; bijoux for studded belts and armbands; flowing locks for neat crops; languorous, ethereal bodies for big butch pumped up ones. The gym was a new gay shrine.[2]

There was a debate about this, of course. Was it just a superficial matter of style? Were gay men asserting the masculinity we had always been denied? Or were we becoming more conservative and aping our macho oppressors? Was the Village People's new hit "Macho Man" ironic or not? Political analysis aside, something was changing, and gay men seemed to be voting with their feet – or rather with their upper lips.

RAID

TBP now had significant international distribution, and we were receiving exchange subscriptions from papers around the world. Mostly they came from the United States, but also from the United Kingdom, Europe, Australia, New Zealand, and occasionally Latin America. We had always tried to cover international events. We were everywhere, after all. Gerald Hannon explained that in my absence, the collective had discussed beefing up this coverage, and he proposed that I take on co-ordinating a new international news section.

I was delighted. Reporting on international events in the turbulent world of the late 1970s would allow me to talk about the relationship between our liberation and other struggles. All I had to do was read all the lesbian and gay papers in the world every month and compile a digest of the most interesting stories.

That's what I was doing the evening of December 30. It was the Friday before the New Year's long weekend. Only Jackson, myself, and another volunteer were left in the office. A number of others had gone to catch a ferry to the Toronto Islands to have dinner at Michael Riordon's place with budding gay historian Jonathan Ned Katz. Katz had just published his groundbreaking *Gay American History,* and was starting a relationship with collective member David Gibson.

Richard and I had only been back a few weeks, and both of us were still looking for work. That evening at 6:30, I had an interview at Woodgreen Community Centre for a job managing a homeless drop-in program, but I had decided to stop at the office on my way to start reading the pile of international periodicals. My plan was to leave around six and catch the streetcar to my interview.

With almost everyone gone, the office was uncharacteristically quiet. I was deep into my stack of newspapers towards the back, when someone came in the door beside the elevator. Jackson was working up front, so I didn't pay much attention until I heard a trace of alarm in his voice.

77

Noticed

It was the cops. Five of them. They had a warrant.

Jackson tried negotiating, but to no avail. There was nothing to negotiate. The warrant empowered them to seize any documents pertinent to the "business relations" of Pink Triangle Press. They started methodically going through everything, including the archives, boxing up whatever they thought might be of interest. "Can I make a phone call?" Jackson finally asked. The head cop just shrugged. Jackson called Riordon's place, where the others were just arriving. He told them we were being raided and not to come back until the police had left. At that point we didn't know if we were going to be arrested or not. It seemed wise not to have the whole collective in the same place at the same time. On hearing the news, Katz exclaimed with operatic prescience, "This is gay history."

Jackson also called lawyer Clayton Ruby.

Ruby was on tap because we had been expecting something. The December/January issue had included a new article by Gerald Hannon on intergenerational sex, "Men Loving Boys Loving Men." It was originally conceptualized as a way of confronting the hysteria about children and sex that was being drummed up by Bryant's campaign. Although the piece had been ready in the summer, publication was postponed because of the frenzy surrounding the Jaques murder. Six months later, after the Bryant victory in Florida, the collective had finally decided to run it in the end-of-year double issue, arguing that there would never be a "right time." "In retrospect," Ken Popert later mused, "that didn't mean that every time was right. But it was the grand argument at the time, an argument for bravado."[3]

In "Men Loving Boys Loving Men," Hannon interviewed three men about their relationships with boys as young as twelve, as well as a man, now adult, who'd had an adult lover as a child. The relationships he described were playful, sometimes romantic, often banal, and always consensual. They were portrayed as pedagogical, teaching young men about the joys of their bodies and sex. He probed – but not insistently – the question of power with some of those he talked to. Finally, he compared the men to famous youth worker C.J. Atkinson, whose portrait hung in the downtown YMCA. "He loved boys. He had dreams for them. He made them his life's work. If you are what you do, C.J. Atkinson, benefactor and 'leader in boys work' was very much a pedophile."[4]

At first, the article seemed to go unnoticed. Then, just before Christmas, *Toronto Sun* columnist Claire Hoy let loose with a column headlined "Our Taxes Help Promote Abuse of Children." (*TBP* had received small grants from the Ontario Arts Council to promote arts coverage.) On Christmas day he intoned, "Kids, not rights is their craving." On the twenty-eighth, the *Globe* reported Attorney General McMurtry was "appalled" by the article, which he had not read, and on the thirtieth, the *Sun* said that charges were being considered.

As the search continued, it became clear that this was not going to be over by six o'clock. I phoned the community centre and explained that I was working at a gay paper that was being raided by police and couldn't make the interview. So much for that job prospect.

Ruby talked to the cops over the phone and offered to turn over whatever they wanted if they just told him what they were looking for. He even managed to reach someone in the attorney general's office to make the offer, but was stonewalled. The police were determined to loot the place. They left about 8:30 with twelve shipping boxes of financial and advertising records, corporate files, classified ads, manuscripts for publication, archival material, unopened mail, all the copies of *Loving Man, The Joy of Gay Sex*, and *The Joy of Lesbian Sex* for the mail order service, and worst of all, the subscription lists.[5]

When the dinner party from the island got back, they surveyed the damage. Without subscription lists, financial records, or even the chequebook, it was unclear how we could keep functioning. But Bébout managed to find a box with the original subscription computer cards under the shipping table, and over the next week, while Ruby prepared a challenge to the search warrant to get back at least some of the seized materials, we worked to reconstruct the pieces necessary to keep on publishing.

FREE THE PRESS

The breadth of materials seized by police made it clear that these were not normal criminal charges. Their intent was to cripple and ultimately close down the paper. So now we had two tasks: to keep publishing, and to organize and pay for the legal defence. It was obvious that we needed new energy and a clear division of labour.

On January 3, a press release went out to GATE's media list and our contacts in gay media around the world. It closed with a plea for funds payable to The Body Politic Free the Press Fund.

While the collective went on with publishing the paper, the fund's job was to publicize the case and raise money for legal bills. And while *TBP* might want to continue to address the issue of child-adult sexuality or not, the Free the Press Fund was simply about defending press freedoms against government attacks.

That, too, involved a debate. Were we retreating from the real issue by making the basis of unity about press freedom rather than pedophilia? Even among the collective, opinions on the question of child-adult sex were far from homogeneous. What we could agree on was the importance of discussing the issue. Pedophilia was being used as a pretext for attempting to close us down. To make it the issue was to fall into their trap, let them define the agenda, and leave us isolated. A fight around press freedom broadened our basis of support.

The fund's initial directors were selected by the collective to try to build community unity. Most important was gender balance, with five women and five men.[6] Tim Guest and Naomi Brooks, members of Gay Youth Toronto, represented youth. I was assigned as the collective liaison and "secretary."

Donors needed assurance that their money was going to fight for press freedom. So donations were held in trust by lawyer Lynn King and could only be used to cover legal costs for the case.[7] The fund's decisions could be vetoed by the three defendants, and its operating costs were covered by Pink Triangle Press.

Our first appeal was remarkably successful. The editors of *Books in Canada* and the *Canadian Journal of Communication* and *Content,* and Osgoode Hall Law School professor Fred Zemans signed a joint Statement of Concern. Media personalities June Callwood, Pierre Berton, and Charles Templeton and representatives of the Periodical Writers Association of Canada and the Canadian Periodical Publishers' Association also voiced their support. Eight city councillors called on the attorney general to "direct the police to immediately return all materials taken from *The Body Politic*, not directly needed as evidence."

CHARGES

It took a week for the police to figure out whom to charge. Collectives befuddled them. On January 5, charges were finally laid against the officers of Pink Triangle Press: Ken Popert, Gerald Hannon, and Ed Jackson. Popert got the short end of the stick. He hadn't been on the collective for a while by that point, but his name still remained on the Pink Triangle Press corporate records.

There were two charges. The first was use of the mails to distribute "immoral, indecent, scurrilous or obscene" material. That was for mailing the paper with Hannon's article. The second, possession of obscene material for the purposes of distribution, was for our supply of *Loving Man*, a book already cleared by Canada Customs.

By then we were ready to hold a press conference. Hannon defended his piece. "Pedophilia is a taboo topic, and I suppose that one can be expected to be pilloried for opening discussion. But I insist without reservation on my right to discuss it."[8]

A second letter to subscribers alerted them that their names and addresses had been seized, and assured them that everything legally possible was being done to retrieve them. Money began to pour in from across the country and around the world, mostly small amounts from individuals, often with touching, handwritten letters of support.

One man from rural British Colombia wrote:

> Even though I thought the timing of your article on Men and Boys was inappropriate given the climate of public opinion exploited by the press in Ontario, I was outraged by the subsequent raids and bust perpetrated by the government. The article itself impressed me even though it was clearly a

very one-sided view of the total picture. Nevertheless, it did manage to explode the popular image of predatory men pouncing on boys in dark alleys. For myself, I was not previously favourably disposed toward the subject, but your article has succeeded in forcing me to see it in another light and to reexamine my attitudes. Thank you for breaching the ramparts.

A hotel worker from Denver, Colorado, sent five dollars "in the hopes that we can [keep up] the international struggle against fascism everywhere." A women's collective in Seattle also sent five dollars.

Radical Women knows that Body Politic has always covered a lot of feminist issues and we have always been very involved in the gay movement. We see the movements as being integrally connected and likewise see an attack on one as an attack on all. We also see the need for building alliances and united fronts to fight the right wing now. If we wait it may be too late.

The raid was front-page news in the international gay press, and gay and lesbian organizations across the country raised money. There were pickets at the Canadian consulate in New York and Canada House in London. Newly elected San Francisco city supervisor Harvey Milk suggested a tourist boycott of English Canada, and a major tour company cancelled its Canadian offerings in response.

LOOT AND PEDOPHILIA

While the civil libertarian strategy of the Free the Press Fund was effective at bringing liberals on side, the question of cross-generational sex was profoundly divisive, especially among lesbian feminists. In January, there was a long and heated discussion at the LOOT centre. For most LOOT members, it was not just a matter of the article's "bad timing." There was considerable fury about its romanticization of intergenerational sex. "It was like a tidal wave of denunciation," recalls Amy Gottlieb. "Maybe there was somebody who didn't agree, but they weren't speaking up. When it came to 'Men Loving Boys Loving Men,' despite all our differences, women took a very similar line."[9] Members of the Lesbian Mothers' Defence Fund were especially vocal.[10]

According to Pat Murphy, a key LOOT member, "[Gay men] didn't see the relationship between power and sexuality. . . . They'd have sexual relationships with a young kid that they'd taken to McDonald's for a hamburger and they'd say he's all willing and likes it. . . . It was all romantic sexuality that was to their own advantage."[11] The consensus temporarily overcame what Becki Ross saw as a growing division in LOOT between the socialist and radical feminists, as women drew on their own experiences of "unwanted, forced sexual pain and humiliation at the hands of straight adult men."

If there was unanimity in LOOT about the wrong-headedness of "Men Loving Boys Loving Men," the formation of the Free the Press Fund exposed a division that foreshadowed problems to come. Despite their disagreement with the article, some of the women understood the raid as a homophobic attack on the whole community and were willing to defend the paper against the state. Others, like Darleen Lawson, argued, "*The Body Politic* boys brought the bust on themselves. . . . So if we are going to talk about the rights of lesbians and LOOT, maybe we shouldn't take a position at all on this thing."[12]

Women who joined the Free the Press Fund had a difficult time of it. Brooks recalls:

> They filled two slots with me, young and female. I supported them because they were gay. For me that was the bottom line why they were raided. Even though I really had trouble with the article, it was about freedom of speech and freedom of the press. I remember being really attacked for supporting *TBP* by a lot of lesbians. I tried to argue the bigger issue, that this wasn't just about pedophilia, that was just the excuse for the raid, but that didn't get a lot of traction.[13]

PICKING UP THE PIECES

As might have been expected, the next issue, February 1978, came out several weeks late. It led off with a full-page editorial entitled "Crisis: In the Midst of Danger, a Chance to Unite." The editorial situated the raid within a wave of attacks on the community: gay activists arrested for postering and leafleting, the Bryant campaign, the press coverage of the Jaques murder, all in the light of the upcoming debate on the inclusion of sexual orientation in the Ontario Human Rights Code.

It closed:

> Danger. The forces arrayed against us are gaining strength. They want to turn the clock back, to put gay people back in the closet, women back in their "place" and youth even more firmly under the "protection" of adults. And opportunity. Lesbians and gay men, feminists and the young themselves, united and strong in the face of this threat.[14]

This was not just empty rhetoric. Confirming Mao's axiom that "it is not a bad thing to be attacked by your enemies," despite the divisions around pedophilia, such unity was already being displayed. Anita Bryant was coming to town.

THE BRYANT CRUSADE

The Ad Hoc Coalition to Stop Anita Bryant had formed in June 1977 after the former Miss America and orange juice promoter led a successful campaign to repeal anti-discrimination protection for gay people in Dade County, Florida. Co-ordinated by CGRO, the coalition included GATE, the Committee to Defend John Damien, MCC, and CHAT. Over the summer it organized a march that went in and out of the bars chanting "Out of the bars, into the streets, gay liberation now!" and held a rally of seven hundred at city hall.

Then, late in December, it was announced that Renaissance International had invited Bryant to kick off a cross-Canada Christian Liberation Crusade with a rally at the People's Church in suburban North York. North York mayor Mel Lastman announced plans to award her a medal for "her crusade against homosexual activists."

With only weeks to organize, the coalition decided to hold a rally at the downtown St. Lawrence Market Hall on January 14 and a protest at the People's Church the following evening. The press conference announcing the events included Pat Murphy and Linda Jain from Women Against Violence Against Women (WAVAW), Ed Jackson from *TBP*, Chris Bearchell representing LOOT, CHAT's George Hislop, Brent Hawkes, the new minister at MCC, and Francie Wyland from Wages Due Lesbians. Considering all the bad blood that had been spilled among this cast of characters, the fact that they sat side by side on the same panel was nothing short of remarkable.

More than a thousand people attended the Saturday night St. Lawrence Hall event. LOOT's Natalie LaRoche addressed the crowd: "It's an historic night. Look around you – never before in Toronto have we seen so many lesbians and feminists come together with gay men to confront our common enemy."

Male dominance wasn't an issue. Three banners framed the stage: Lesbian Rights, Women Against Violence Against Women, and Lesbians for Wages for Women's Work. The evening was hosted by Pat Murphy of WAVAW, and a majority of speakers were women who stressed the anti-feminist character of Bryant's campaign. The vigorous women's participation was at least partially intended to head off what Murphy and other LOOT and WAVAW members characterized as "misogynist" attacks on Bryant by gay men.

The march up Yonge Street in snowy, minus-ten-degree weather alternated chants to "Defend *The Body Politic*," boos as the crowd passed the strip's body-rub and porn outlets, and "Women and Gays and Children Unite: Same Struggle, Same Fight." It was the horizontal alliance of oppressed groups that the movement had always dreamed of.

It was also a learning experience. Many of the lesbian feminists had not worked with men for years. For many gay participants, this was their first event with such a strongly feminist orientation. In her analysis, LOOT's Pat Leslie challenged gay men to come out to the upcoming International Women's Day to "visibly express that they really do understand the connections between the two movements."[15]

The following evening – despite the parallel ecumenical Celebration of the Joy of Liberation organized by MCC's Brent Hawkes that drew MCC members and others from gay Jewish, Anglican, and Catholic groups – more than five hundred people braved the freezing weather and the long transit ride to the suburbs to take the protest to the People's Church. The church's pastor was even successfully pied by a demonstrator.

Bryant's campaign also had unexpected consequences. Tom Warner noted:

> As threatening to gays and lesbians as the Bryant crusade was, it also provided unprecedented opportunity . . . the media, which up to this time had largely ignored or trivialized gay and lesbian liberation, needed another point of view to balance their coverage. That meant seeking out lesbian and gay activists for their views, thus affording them the media exposure that had until then been elusive.[16]

A NEW PASTOR IN TOWN

The role of MCC Toronto in the Bryant protests demonstrated a shift in the organization and new leadership. Brent Hawkes grew up in the tiny village of Bath, New Brunswick, in the 1950s and '60s, with the local Baptist Church as his second family. In his teens, he felt a call to the ministry. But as he became aware that he was gay, he realized that being a Baptist minister was not an option. He became a high school teacher instead. Then, through one of those little ads that groups placed in newspapers at the time, he discovered a gay community centre in Halifax. He cut out the ad, memorized the phone number, destroyed it, and, in case a long-distance call could be traced, drove to Halifax to call.

The friendly woman who answered told him where the bars were. There he met a university friend who showed him gay literature hidden in the back room of the "adult" bookstore. In a copy of *The Advocate* he found an ad for MCC, a gay-friendly church founded in 1968 that was spreading across North America. "As soon as I saw that ad," he recalls, "I knew that was where I belonged."[17]

In 1976, Hawkes moved to Toronto to find his community and to study for ordination. The Toronto church had grown from three people in 1973, when the first minister, Bob Wolfe, arrived, to a congregation of about eighty, but all was not well. Wolfe's successor had been a bad fit. The congregation split and a narrow majority demanded his resignation after only three months. Hawkes agreed to fill in as interim pastor until a permanent replacement was found, but ended up being asked to stay.

Involvement in the anti-Bryant protests demonstrated that Hawkes intended to take the church in a more activist direction. While some of us grumbled that the ecumenical service drew people away from the People's Church protest, for MCC, it was a resounding success. The service included the first woman ordained as an Anglican priest in Canada, and the moderator of the United Church. There was lots of press. New people were attracted and the congregation began to grow again. Political involvement paid off.

JAQUES AND THE CODE

The elation of the Bryant protest soon gave way to a new round of media hysteria as the Jaques trial began on February 8. It was mercifully quick. On March 12, the verdicts came down. While one of the accused was acquitted, two were found guilty of first-degree murder and one of second-degree murder. All three received life imprisonment.

But in his sentencing statement, Justice Maloney linked the case to the debate about the Human Rights Code.

> There is one feature in your case that disturbs me more than a little. It is your acknowledged tendency to seek out ever-younger homosexual partners. I wonder how common that is among homosexuals. There are those who would seek legal protection for homosexuals in the Human Rights Code. You make me wonder if they are not misguided.[18]

There seemed less and less hope for the amendment. Early in the year, Dorothea Crittenden, a career civil servant with no human rights background, took over as the new chair of the OHRC. Her appointment by Tory premier Bill Davis was widely criticized as political ploy to scuttle the recommendation of the *Life Together* report for inclusion of sexual orientation. This was not just a perception among lesbians and gay men. Four of the eight sitting commissioners resigned in protest.

Crittenden did not disappoint her patron. She soon told the *Toronto Star* that because of the Jaques murder, it was not the time to deal with the sexual orientation issue. In a March interview with *TBP*, she stated that sexual orientation was a non-issue, since gay people were not complaining to the commission. She seemed oblivious to the fact that the commission had rejected the complaint from John Damien on the grounds that sexual orientation was not covered by the code.[19]

INTERNATIONAL WOMEN'S DAY

International Women's Day had first been proposed at the 1910 Conference of Socialist Women in Copenhagen and was honoured in the Socialist Bloc. There had been small-scale celebrations in Toronto in the past, but in the fall of 1977, the Trotskyist Revolutionary Workers League brought together a range of feminists to discuss reviving the day in the city. Lesbian participation, largely through LOOT and WAVAW, exposed serious differences within LOOT.

The question of male participation in the march was a fault line. Radical feminists who dominated LOOT and WAVAW argued that women shouldn't have to march with their oppressors. Socialist feminists, who saw capitalism as implicated in women's oppression, wanted supportive men to turn out as allies. The discussion was heated. When they lost the vote, most of the LOOT and WAVAW women walked out. Pat Murphy accused the International Women's Day Committee of homophobia. "We can't even get together to have one big day all our own without causing freak out . . . without women turning on us and calling us . . . 'man hating dyke separatists.' " WAVAW co-founder Eve Zaremba, an activist, bookstore owner, and author of lesbian feminist detective novels, later wrote about the " 'contaminating presence' of the left, and the 'sidelining' of 'pure' feminist concerns at IWD."[20]

Socialist feminists in LOOT such as Natalie LaRoche found themselves caught in the middle. "IWD had always been a worker's holiday to celebrate women workers. And as socialists and lesbians we wanted to keep it that way. But that didn't mean that we weren't torn and unhappy about the walk out of our lesbian sisters."[21]

LOOT and WAVAW organized their own women-only celebration at the 519 Church Street Community Centre and marched to a women's concert at the University of Toronto. Neither participated in the main March 8, 1978, demonstration. The event demanded women's control of their own bodies, quality child care, and an end to cutbacks in social services, violence against women, and the deportation of Jamaican domestic workers. It also called for undefined "lesbian rights."

THE PORN WARS BEGIN

TBP attempted to build on the notion of a feminist-gay alliance. The April 1978 issue ran a full-page article with photos of International Women's Day. But despite a desire for unity, two tectonic plates were about to collide. As *TBP* was calling for unity on the basis of freedom of the press, much of the feminist movement was taking on a campaign to strengthen obscenity legislation as part of the fight against pornography.

Women Against Violence Against Women was founded by LOOT members Pat Murphy and Eve Zaremba in November 1977 after a Toronto screening of *Snuff*, a splatter film marketed as depicting the actual murder of a woman. Many WAVAW members worked in rape-crisis centres and emergency hostels for battered women, and the group identified pornography as a major incitement to male violence. It was a short step to demanding government intervention.

March 22, 1978, the federal Parliamentary Standing Committee on Justice and Legal Affairs tabled its report on pornography in the House of Commons, recommending a significant tightening of anti-porn laws. The committee had heard more than twenty-five witnesses, including church groups, police, publishers, and representatives from the National Action Committee on the Status of Women.

In *TBP*, Gerald Hannon did not dispute that much pornography was sexist. But he called the deputations from the women's groups "thoughtful, intelligent, articulate, impassioned – and wrong." Wrong, he explained, not in terms of what they said, but because in appearing before the committee, they gave feminist cover to anti-sexual recommendations.

The women had in fact argued that sexual explicitness itself should not be considered obscene or pornographic, only material involving "the use or threat of violence as a means of achieving sexual gratification, or an inappropriate object of sexual gratification." Nevertheless, the committee recommended extending the definition of pornography to include "undue exploitation of crime, horror, cruelty, violence or the undue degradation of the human person as well as sex," or "any depiction of real or simulated masturbation, sexual intercourse, gross indecency, buggery or bestiality if the individual is under 18."

Hannon noted that in committee discussions, "degradation" seemed to include almost anything other than missionary position, and that fellatio was frequently mentioned as a repulsive act. He argued that obscenity laws were always used "to harass and stifle" erotica that is experimental or serves minority tastes. A sidebar to the *TBP* article quoted a series of particularly homophobic statements by witnesses at the hearings that went unchallenged. He concluded that the only reason to appear before the committee should be to call for the abolition of all obscenity legislation.[22]

The debate contributed to the unravelling of the short-lived lesbian and gay unity. Within less than a year, for example, the Free the Press Fund was completely male. Naomi Brooks remembers her experience there as frustrating. "After a while I felt I was there not even as a token. I really had no voice. I'd suggest things and there was no room for discussion or opinion. I was just a name on a piece of paper."[23] Nevertheless, by March 1978, the Free the Press Fund had raised over $21,000, more than two-thirds of the $30,000 first estimated as necessary for the legal defence.

IT'S THE ECONOMY, STUPID

The *TBP* collective was developing an analysis that connected these events. An April 1978 editorial noted that for the first time in history, more than one million people in Canada were unemployed. "Unemployment makes governments shake. It exposes the basic flaws in the economic structure and underscores the split between rich and poor, between those who make decisions and those who don't, between the powerful and the rest of us."[24] The editorial argued that talk of "moral decay or pornographic filth flooding the land" was a distraction arranged by the powerful to divert attention from the real issues. Gay people were especially vulnerable at these moments. We could be scapegoated as symbols of moral decline, and economic uncertainty made it more difficult to come out.

The economy certainly wasn't doing well. We didn't know it at the time, but the Keynesian era of high employment, economic expansion, and wealth redistribution was coming to a close. "Stagflation" – high inflation plus high unemployment – was the word of the day. According to Keynesian economics, those two things weren't supposed to happen at the same time. Inflation meant the economy was overheating and needed to be cooled down, usually by increasing interest rates. High unemployment meant the economy needed to be stimulated with lower interest rates and higher government spending. But now, cooling the economy would increase unemployment, and heating it up would swell inflation. The economic consensus that had held sway since the end of the Second World War was paralyzed.

Although we had no idea of the sea change we were experiencing, the social crisis was palpable. And in that context, *TBP* argued, both minority communities and civil liberties themselves were vulnerable. News from abroad reinforced that perception. In April, a four-year-old gay rights ordinance was repealed in Saint Paul, Minnesota. In May, similar ordinances were struck down in Wichita, Kansas, and Eugene, Oregon. Oklahoma passed a bill allowing school boards to fire anyone "advocating, soliciting, imposing, encouraging, or promoting public or private homosexual activities in a manner that creates a substantial risk that such conduct will come to the attention of school children or school employees."[25] In Britain, the far-right National Front called for homosexuals to be exterminated in gas chambers, and neo-Nazi thugs began attacking gay bars. A private member's bill to decriminalize homosexual activity in Scotland was defeated in the House of Commons.

The May 1978 editorial built on this theme, reminding readers of the revelations from the MacDonald Commission, established in 1977 to investigate RCMP law-breaking. The commission had found evidence of "warrantless break-ins . . . illegal mail opening, illegal police access to confidential medical files, illegal secret agreements with Revenue Canada, theft, arson, and the obstruction of justice through the destruction of evidence."[26] The police could not be trusted.

Meanwhile, our first line of defence, attempts to quash the search warrant, was rejected. Yet each loss helped strengthen the argument that the state and the police were out to get us, and that this was part of a larger erosion of civil liberties.

DIFFERENT PATHS

American events amplified strategic differences. In an "earnest" editorial in *The Advocate* in March 1978, David Goodstein expressed fears that 1978 would be Year of the Backlash and exhorted readers to get behind a Republican candidate in Illinois who was supportive of gay rights. "If you live nearby, put on your three-piece (if you are a man) or a dress (if you're a woman) and volunteer at his headquarters."[27]

On the other hand, the same *TBP* editorial that linked the backlash to the economy was entitled "A Time for Indecency." It concluded: "To go back into the closet now, not to come out, or even to be out and not involved, is to court a disaster unparalleled since being out meant wearing a pink triangle on the right cuff and the left shoulder."[28]

The paper also lionized the more militant cultural response to the backlash. The Tom Robinson Band played Toronto's El Mocambo in June 1978. Robinson was openly gay and part of Britain's Rock Against Racism movement. At his concert he dedicated a song to *TBP*. According to reviewer Tim Guest, Robinson sang about "gay liberation, the Stonewall riot, . . . Britain's neo-Nazi National Front, racism, fascism, police harassment and most of all, about a world where right-wing forces like Anita Bryant are becoming so strong that we have to question our own survival." Guest described Robinson's work as an antidote to "the tyranny of disco, which is the curse of the gay community."[29] Battle lines were drawn in the face of crisis – the new militancy versus the new closetry, rock 'n' roll versus disco.

THE FEMINIST RIPOSTE

If, for *TBP*, the war on porn was a sign of a resurgent right-wing conservatism, for many feminists, pornography was a real issue, not a distraction. In a letter to the paper, Mariana Valverde took on Hannon's arguments:

> Sometimes such legislation is used for the suppression of *bona fide* erotica; but the excessive zeal of certain authorities should not blind us to the fact that sometimes legal controls may be necessary.
>
> Today, *TBP* has of course good reasons for loudly defending civil liberties, freedom of the press and so on; but it should not debase the gay rights movement by implying that it is on the same level as the "struggle" of certain capitalists to sell more varieties of sex to more people. By upholding the "right" of the porno industry to cater to "minority tastes" *TBP* is implicitly supporting the view so dear to the hearts of capitalists everywhere – that sexuality is a commodity, to be freely bought and sold on the open market. If we leave sexuality in the hands of free enterprise, the sex industry may well do to sex what the food industry has done to food: give us chemical substitutes instead of the real thing.[30]

TBP's August 1978 issue continued the debate with the headline "Pornography: Erotic Liberation or Sexual Terror?" Featured was an article by Andrea Dworkin, a polarizing figure if ever there was one. Dworkin likened pornography to fascist and racist propaganda.

> This propaganda does not only sanction violence against the designated group; it incites it. This propaganda does not only threaten assault; it promises it. . . . A woman, nearly naked, in a cell, chained, flesh ripped up from the whip, breasts mutilated by a knife: she is entertainment, the boy-next-door's favourite fantasy, every man's precious right, every woman's potential fate. The woman tortured is sexual entertainment.[31]

Dworkin went on to assert:

Fascist propaganda celebrating sexual violence against women is sweeping this land. Fascist propaganda celebrating the sexual degradation of women is inundating cities, college campuses, small towns. . . . Images of women bound, bruised, and maimed . . . are death threats to a female population in rebellion. . . . Feminists refuse to cower in the face of this new campaign of annihilation. . . . What does it mean that yet again – and after years of feminist analysis and activism – the men (gay, leftist, whatever) who proclaim a commitment to social justice are resolute in their refusal to face up to the meaning and significance of their enthusiastic advocacy of yet another women-hating plague?[32]

Susan Cole and Eve Zaremba argued that it was time to "end the charade" and face up to the basic political conflict between gay men and feminists.

Feminists and gay liberationists do have much in common, can and should work together as allies on many issues. However the basic self-interest of women as expressed through feminism and the self-interest of gay men do not always coincide. . . . Hannon insists that if our society adopted a *laissez-faire* stance on pornography and a simple no-censorship line, we can expect to live happily ever after. We have found that this is not so. In fact, as women, we expect that the abolition of censorship laws would give us few advantages and a lot more of *Snuff*.[33]

Hannon responded, "*TBP*'s case is a clear example of the way obscenity laws will be used. They will do nothing to attack the roots of the oppression of women."[34] As if to bolster his arguments, Canada Customs stopped the importation of *Christopher Street,* an innocuous New York gay cultural journal. *Word Is Out*, a groundbreaking documentary without a hint of nudity or sex, was given a Restricted classification by the Ontario Censor Board, simply because lesbians and gay men were being interviewed.

COULD IT HAVE BEEN OTHERWISE?

Could the growing contradiction have been resolved less antagonistically? On the one hand, both the gay and feminist movements had begun to recognize that there would be no immediate fundamental reorganization of society. They therefore opted for vertical alliances with the state to ask for protection. Women, for protection against pornography. The gay rights movement, for protection against discrimination.

But the gay movement also had a recent history of fighting against discriminatory laws. We were, at this point, only a decade away from decriminalization. Most gay men had a visceral appreciation that the police, the courts, and the state were not our friends. Hence, there was resonance to Hannon's accusation that parts of the women's movement were making common cause with the state without regard to the impact on sexual minorities. But from the point of view of the women's movement, gay men were trying to protect their sexual interests without regard to the impact on the sexually more vulnerable.

In retrospect, the debate was less about pornography than about whether the state or the market should regulate erotic material. Hannon saw the justice system as a conservative institution that wished to control sexual expression and that would use any power given it to suppress sexual minorities. He opted for the liberal free market and political discussion to shape consumption patterns. Valverde pointed out the dangers of an unregulated market to those most vulnerable to sexual exploitation, and saw at least some state regulation as justified to protect the common good.

It was also a debate about the character of the state. Was the state a neutral body that could be used to curb dangerous impulses of the socially more powerful, or a reactionary body whose growing power needed to be curbed? Others had been debating that question for years. It wasn't much wonder that gay men and lesbians couldn't come to agreement. But the alliances involved in both positions were entangling. Gay men's alliance with those suspicious of the state pulled us in more liberal and libertarian directions. Anti-porn feminism's alliance with the state pulled it in a more traditional direction where women needed protection of the "strict father."

GROWTH AND CHANGE

The question of pornography also surfaced at the sixth annual conference of the now renamed Canadian Lesbian and Gay Rights Coalition (CLGRC, formerly NGRC) in Halifax that summer. The position common among gay men predominated. The conference passed a resolution opposing any form of obscenity legislation, prefaced with the statement "Whereas the suppression of erotic material does nothing to attack the roots of the oppression of women." It came in the context of yet another battle around lesbian participation, when a motion calling for a prorating of lesbian votes to 50 per cent was defeated. No consensus was possible on how to balance the unequal numbers and interests of lesbians and gay men.

Other issues were also surfacing. One delegate said, "We have created a machine for the passing of resolutions. Two years from now you won't be able to tell us from the NDP." According to David Garmaise of Gays of Ottawa, "The conference quickly became a procedural and organizational nightmare – people kept losing track of the central issues they came to discuss."[35]

One problem was size – over two hundred delegates from forty organizations from coast to coast – and the expectation they would agree on a series of motions proposed by attending groups and individuals. Another was trying to squeeze cultural, recreational, political, and business activities into one long weekend. A third was confusion about which issues were local and which needed national attention. Underlying it all was the growing complexity of an expanding community.

Growth was also becoming an issue in Toronto. In the April *TBP*, Ken Pop-ert decried the organizational explosion of specialized lesbian and gay "grou-plets." "It is an ominous fact that general purpose organizations are being starved of members as the grouplets spring up." He asked who would do the "leafleting, postering, telephoning, meeting writing and mailing – the staples of political organization?" He suggested that this was a retreat from politics in the face of right-wing attack.[36]

Popert's article did not go unchallenged. John Argue replied, "I believe firmly that the more sophisticated our collective life becomes, the more effective will be our response to our powerful enemies."[37] Others, like Hugh English, Gary Kinsman, and Paul Trollope, chimed in from the left. They acknowledged a "kernel of truth" in Popert's argument, but proposed that the problem was not so much the new organizations, but rather the inadequacies of the old ones. Specifically, the inability of GATE "to meet the needs of radicalizing gays and to develop a militant perspective on how to combat the attacks upon us."[38]

Tom Warner discerned a generation gap:

> Almost all the people putting forward the concept of crisis are the people who have been most active in the movement for a long time. This leads me to wonder whether the fear of a "crisis" is not merely the fear of change – change in the structures and strategies that we have held near and dear for so long.[39]

This growth was not just about new groups. The gay ghetto that early activists had viewed with suspicion continued to expand. A class of gay entrepreneurs was emerging to service a growing market. In May 1978, George Hislop opened a new gay bar, Buddy's, at Church and Gerrard. Buddy's joined The Barn, a leather and denim bar that another gay entrepre-neur, Janko Naglic, had opened just up the street the year before.

Church Street's cheaper rents were attractive to such small gay businesses. With the 519 community centre north of Wellesley and two new bars to the south, Church was replacing Yonge as the centre of gay life. Gay entrepreneur-ship was no longer restricted to bars and baths. *TBP* ads reflected an ever-wider range of services and businesses catering to the gay market. In 1978 the Toronto Lambda Business Council was formed, giving voice to this new stra-tum of small business people – or in Marxist lingo, gay petite bourgeoisie.

BROADSIDE

Another new voice that spring was *Broadside: A Feminist Review*. The Interna-tional Women's Day Committee was dominated by socialist feminists, but the *Broadside* collective was largely drawn from radical feminist circles. Although made up mostly of dykes (the paper later coyly noted "In fact, there never was a time when the Broadside collective didn't include heterosexual women"[40]), the basis of unity was feminism, not sexual orientation.

With half the population as its potential audience, *Broadside* embraced a wider range of issues than *TBP*. The introductory issue, May 1979, included articles on nuclear power, the Iranian revolution, sexist popular culture, the federal elections, unemployment, and women in theatre, film, and literature. It featured congratulatory ads from a wide range of women's and lesbian and gay organizations, including *TBP*.

The idea for a feminist paper was hatched at Eve Zaremba's home by members of WAVAW and LOOT. But although it was conceived as a community project, collectively organized and volunteer-driven, *Broadside* emerged in a different world from the one that gave birth to *TBP* almost a decade before. It did not start as a rant sheet in someone's back shed. Before it published, *Broadside* incorporated as a for-profit business, raised capital, sold subscriptions, and rented an office. Its collective members were all legally directors of the corporation. The masthead listed Philinda Masters as the paper's editor.

Broadside saw its role as activist journalism on behalf of women, and although it featured radical feminist positions, its pages would be open to the lively and sometimes acrimonious debate characteristic of the women's movement of the time.

REJOINING THE DEBATE

After my botched interview the night of the *TBP* raid, I ended up getting a job as executive director and only employee of the Riverdale Intercultural Council. RICC had been set up by the Ministry of Culture and Recreation to combat anti–South Asian racism in the working class east-end neighbourhood. That I had travelled in India apparently qualified me for the job. Although the ministry preferred multicultural festivals as an antidote to "Paki bashing," the job at RICC allowed me to work with people to combat racism and relate it to other forms of discrimination.

In the meantime, Richard had found a job working with neighbourhood groups to make programming for the Rogers Cable community access channel. This was the beginning of his trajectory into documentary and experimental video. We had been renting the top floor of a house on Simpson Avenue, in Riverdale, down the street from the communal house where many of the core *TBP* collective lived. But that spring, there was an opening at the commune at 188½ Seaton Street and we moved back in.

The Seaton Street commune retained its character as a centre for eclectic left-wing gay activism. David Gibson, from the original Gay Marxist Study Group and now leading the design team of *TBP*, was still there. David Mole, a British student completing his doctorate in economics at the University of Toronto, had also joined the house. He was close to the Marxist-Leninist group In Struggle, although the group's ambiguous silence on issues of gay liberation helped keep him on the periphery. His ex-wife, however, was a member in good standing. A third David, David Roche, lived across the hall from David Mole. David R. was a gender-bending performance artist and professional house cleaner, or "maid," as he put it. His unrequited love for David M. was later immortalized in Jeremy Podeswa's award-winning short film *David Roche Talks to You about Love* (1983).

Finally, there was George Smith, a brilliant if unconventional Marxist sociologist working on his doctorate at the Ontario Institute for Studies in Education. The oldest of us at forty-three, he had grown up in a poor, anglophone Montreal neighbourhood. Like most of the *TBP* cohort, he had managed to break into post-secondary education. But his academic career had been thrown into a tailspin when, while working on his doctorate on a scholarship in the United States, he was entrapped by American police and deported.

If debate is a form of mental exercise, 188½ Seaton Street was a gymnasium. At breakfast, Smith, who was usually first to get to the daily newspaper, was ready to challenge anyone on any topic, no matter how trivial. Our communal dinner conversations ranged across history, sociology, current events, party building, politics, philosophy, culture, and economics. And of course, sex. Nothing was above or below critique, including the strengths and shortcomings of *TBP*. It was comradely criticism, however. David Gibson and I were the only two actually on the collective, but everyone else regularly helped out in one way or another.

MARXISM AND GAY LIBERATION REDUX

It seemed ungenerous to restrict such conversations to our home, so we arranged to do another Marxism and Gay Liberation course at the Marxist Institute in the spring of 1978. The course again attracted pillars of the movement like Popert, Mossop, Kinsman, and Bearchell, and women newer to the scene, including Mariana Valverde and Lorna Weir. George Smith brought his analysis based on the method of sociologist Dorothy Smith (no relation), and David Mole his sophisticated grasp of classical Marxist economics.

This time we could assume that everyone had both a basis in Marxist theory and a practice in movement politics. We began by producing and sharing short statements on what we thought were the crucial questions.

It was Brian Mossop's statement that in hindsight was most prescient. He suggested that the fights around "rights" had actually been a surrogate for the acceptance of homosexuality. Few people who hated us thought we deserved rights. Few who supported gay rights hated us.

It was a startlingly simple but acute observation. It led him to propose that we needed to go beyond rights to directly confront people's fears about homosexuality – our capacity to raise and teach children, for example. He also pointed out that while the struggle for rights had widespread support in the community, it had not mobilized large numbers and had been incidental to community growth. That growth had been around non-political social groups – sports teams, commercial services, and so on. Yet it was growth that provided us with visibility and social weight. Activists needed to encourage this social growth rather than dismiss it.

Finally, Mossop noted we were no longer confronting "the dead weight of tradition, but actual organized attacks by the state." People were more willing to fight to stop having something taken away than they were to spend time getting some words in a Human Rights Code. We needed to put our energies into mobilizing resistance to repression.[41]

There was also a serious re-evaluation of the role of the family. George Smith argued that the idea that the family was the source of gay oppression was "mostly wrong." Talking about "the nuclear family" turned it into a thing (reified it) and attributed to it the power to cause other things. It didn't account for gay oppression under other kinship systems. Nor did it involve an analysis of changing family forms or dynamics under capitalism. Finally, it alienated working class people who often found in their families a refuge from work and the capitalist marketplace.

We read Stuart Ewen's *Captains of Consciousness,* which analyzed transformations in American family organization in response to monopoly capitalism, consumer culture, and the advertising industry. In the original course we had debated crude causalities from economic base to culture and superstructure. This time, there was a more sophisticated examination of how family structures and their roles were transformed.

George Smith also insisted on a new way of using the term "ideology," not just as a set of ideas, but as a particular (unscientific) method of interpreting the world. Ideologies were narratives and discourses that were built on other narratives or discourses. When Marxists justified their pronouncements by quoting something that Lenin or Marx had said, they were being ideological. To be truly Marxist, one had to refer to the actual social relations one was analyzing. That took fieldwork and investigation, not quotations from authorities – "the concrete analysis of concrete conditions."

A final point was the need to clearly distinguish between oppression/discrimination and exploitation. Discrimination was treating certain identifiable groups unfairly. Exploitation was the process of appropriating wealth from the labour of others. Even well-paid workers were exploited, since their labour made money for their employers. Discrimination certainly made it easier to exploit people, and it increased the rate of exploitation, since it meant lower wages for an oppressed group. But it was not indispensable to capitalism. Demands to end discrimination therefore fit within the parameters of liberal politics. For capital, only the process of exploitation itself was non-negotiable.

GAY DAYS

We had all been anxious about the upcoming *TBP* trial, but soon got news that there would be a reprieve. The trial, which was to take place at the end of June, was postponed until January 1979. Without a trace of irony, Crown attorney Jerome Wiley announced that he would not be available to proceed. He was getting married during the summer and would be leaving on his honeymoon shortly afterwards.

So, rather than a court case, the highlight of the summer was a huge community party – Gay Days – held on the last weekend in August. The event was envisioned by Gordon Montador of Glad Day Bookshop, Harvey Hamburg of the Toronto Area Gays phone counselling line 923-GAYS, and Val Edwards of LOOT. Together they assembled a group of more than fifty men and women, many of whom had not been involved in community organizing before. Gay Days kicked off with a women's music concert on Friday night. On Saturday, a day-long fair attracting thousands filled Queen's Park with balloons and banners on a sunny summer's afternoon. Thirty-five Toronto organizations were represented under the trees. Richard designed the *TBP* booth, and everyone chipped in to build it in our living room at 188½. All the community displays were similarly DIY. That evening boasted the biggest gay dance in the city's history, with 1,400 people cramming the St. Lawrence Market Hall, bouncing to the new hit of the season, the Village People's "YMCA." (My mother had been on to something.) Sunday's picnic on Hanlan's Point, the sheltered beach on the west coast of the Toronto Islands, traditionally a summer gay cruising spot, attracted more than five hundred.

Gay Days was an antidote to a difficult winter. Its existence in the centre of the city was a political statement that did not pass unnoticed. *Toronto Sun* columnist Claire Hoy called on citizens to protest the use of such public facilities by homosexuals.[42]

At the end of the community fair, a hundred or so of us gathered for an official picture around Queen's Park's sombre equestrian statue of Edward VII, festooned with balloons and a giant pink triangle reading "Out of the Closets" hanging around the horse's neck. This was the core of the city's growing gay movement. It now far eclipsed the handful of activists I had met coming out only four summers before.

Montador concluded that Gay Days helped "encourage the exploration of gay culture on a positive basis" and "could change the direction of the movement . . . because more people can be attracted by cultural involvement than by straightforward political causes."[43] It was an oblique challenge to Popert's worries about the loss of political focus, and an affirmation of the position that Mossop had argued in the Marxist study group. As time went on, people were talking less about "movement" and more about "community." The existence and visibility of community was itself coming to be seen as a political act.

That produced another round of discussion back at Seaton Street. What was this "community"? Did gay people have something substantial in common, a sensibility, for instance? Did community really exist, or was it just an illusion we used for political purposes, a temporary class alliance in order to deal with our oppression? Whose interests did this concept serve?

That autumn, *TBP* published a three-part series by John D'Emilio on the history of the Mattachine Society. In its search for history, *TBP* had lionized Magnus Hirschfeld's Scientific Humanitarian Committee in turn-of-the-century Germany. Hirschfeld's group began the campaign for repeal of paragraph 175 of the German penal code outlawing homosexual sex in 1897, and established the groundbreaking Institute for Sexual Research in 1919. But the closety Mattachine Society of the 1950s had always played the role of foil to real gay liberation, launched by the Stonewall riots in 1969.

D'Emilio argued that Mattachine was much more than that. Founded by Harry Hay and other gay American Communist Party members and sympathizers in 1950, it was the first group to conceptualize gay people as an oppressed minority and to demand social change. Members had opted for a secretive, cell-based organization, not because they were cowardly closet cases, but as a rational security measure in the face of police repression against lesbians, gay men, and leftists in McCarthyist America. It was humbling to recognize that our generation hadn't actually invented gay lib.

In the same issue, Lorna Weir wrote a full-page report on a new book, *The History of Sexuality* by someone called Michel Foucault. Gay liberation had always thought of itself as struggling against a sexually repressive society, but Foucault disputed this "repressive hypothesis." He pointed out that "what is peculiar to modern societies . . . is not that they consigned sex to a shadowed existence, but that they dedicated themselves to speaking of it *ad infinitum*, while exploiting it as *the* secret."

Foucault saw power as not necessarily repressive but as a technology for producing "useful" individuals. Rather than repressing homosexuality, he claimed, modern society actually produced us as a species. Drawing from Foucault, Weir concluded: "I am suggesting also that a celebration of gay and lesbian sex, while it may eventually lead to our acceptance as a 'minority group,' will ultimately serve the expansionary needs of a cramped bourgeoisie."[44]

This was heretical, or unthinkable, for those of us immersed in the struggle for gay liberation. Our understanding of the world and our place in it was organized by the practicalities of fighting what felt very much like repression. That understanding was only to be reinforced in the following months.

A COLD FALL

Despite police promises to control the homophobic crowds on Yonge Street, Halloween 1978 was the usual hate fest. A screaming mob lined both sides of the street near the St. Charles. The front door of the bar was smashed in, and by the end of the evening the building's facade and the sidewalk were slick with broken eggs. The only difference was that an ad hoc group of gay activists patrolled the alley to protect drag queens trying to enter by the back door.

A month later, November 27, San Francisco's first openly gay city supervisor, Harvey Milk, was assassinated along with Mayor George Moscone. Milk had defied the odds, welding together a coalition of lesbians and gay men from the Castro district, labour unions, and black and Latino voters to win a seat and shake up San Francisco city hall. In office, he had won the city's first anti-discrimination ordinance. He was instrumental in the defeat of the Briggs Initiative, the statewide referendum calling for the firing of gay and pro-gay teachers in California. Now he was dead, murdered by an openly homophobic ex-cop and former city supervisor, Dan White. Milk's death seemed to confirm the deep homophobia of the political system.

A little over a week later, Toronto police raided the Barracks.

THE BARRACKS

I was not at that time a bath boy. Richard and I had never promised fidelity, and while both of us occasionally played with others, we were in practice monogamous. I was vague on the city's bathhouse scene.

The Barracks was one of the smaller of Toronto's half-dozen gay saunas. It specialized in S/M, leather, and bondage play. The police stormed in at 1:30 early Saturday morning, December 9. Twenty-six men were arrested; several were roughed up. Police kicked in doors, ripped ashtrays from the walls, and punched holes in the drywall. They also made off with an undisclosed number of sex toys and the bath's eight-hundred-name membership list. The following morning, George Hislop, who was a 10 per cent shareholder, was also arrested. Toronto baths had operated for decades without problems. This was a new development.

That afternoon, GATE and *TBP* organized a meeting at the paper's offices including activists, bath owners, and the Lambda Business Council. *TBP* reported:

> The combination of gay businessmen and gay activists represented an uneasy alliance, and a few bath owners quarreled at first with the proposal that the case be given a high profile as an attack on the gay community. However that tactic was finally accepted by all those present.[45]

There was, in fact, a political realignment taking place. On its own, the government's reluctance to amend the Ontario Human Rights Code could be seen as Tory intransigence. For many, the raid on *TBP* was the result of the paper's own irresponsibility. Claire Hoy's anti-gay rants in the *Sun* were just a way to sell papers. Anita Bryant's visit just a media ploy by a few Christian fundamentalists. The Halloween near riot was a tradition of suburban rowdies blowing off steam. The Barracks raid was a reaction to a particularly unsavoury sex venue.

Considered cumulatively, however, it really did seem that we were under attack. And with Hislop's arrest, "legitimate" businesses began to feel that they, too, could be targeted. The traditional gulf between activists and the commercial ghetto was narrowing.

On December 11, hundreds gathered at the 519 Church Street Community Centre to discuss the raid. The meeting voted to hold a press conference the next day and a march and rally the following Saturday. Although the *Toronto Sun* predictably made much of "the paraphernalia of perversion" and the "whips, chains and leather" seized by police, *The Globe and Mail* actually called the bawdy house laws "Victorian and out of date."[46] Much of the media also seemed ready to buy the assertion made at the press conference by new *TBP* member Mariana Valverde that "an attack on any gay establishment is an attack on the whole gay community, and that includes lesbians."

The support changed the equation. The police had expected most of those charged to plead guilty in order to avoid the publicity of a trial. But when the men appeared in court December 12, none did.

At the rally the following Saturday, Michael Lynch ridiculed the *Sun*'s fascination with sex toys by exposing a bag of innocuous household utensils that he described as "whips, chains and paraphernalia." Despite my bath inexperience, I was tapped to speak at the conclusion of the rally at city hall. I told the crowd that in raiding the Barracks the police hoped to divide the "dirty" from the "decent" homosexuals. I reiterated Valverde's message that the community had to stand together.

The police were obviously annoyed by the unexpected blowback. On December 18, Staff Sergeant Gary Donovan started calling Toronto school boards with the names of six teachers who had been swept up in the raid, hoping to get them fired. Donovan said he found the idea of homosexual teachers "disturbing." But one of the teachers, Don Franco, refused to be cowed. He went to talk to MCC minister Brent Hawkes. Hawkes went public, demanding Donovan be disciplined. Activists demanded the sergeant's outright dismissal. Toronto Board of Education chair Fiona Nelson issued a statement saying that "a teacher's sexual orientation and personal life are none of the school board's business unless they interfere with that person's job."[47] Donovan received a slap on the wrist, but the police were clearly on the back foot.

BAWDY HOUSES

Few of us knew much about the bawdy house laws at that point. We were aware that the archaic-sounding legislation had been used in the 1977 Truxx raid in Montreal, but this was the first time it had been used against gay men in Toronto. Barracks patrons were charged as "found-ins" in a common bawdy house, and the owners and staff were charged as "keepers." Found-ins could get six months in jail. The keeper charges could result in two years of imprisonment.

According to the Criminal Code, a "common bawdy house" was any place resorted to "for the purposes of prostitution or the practice of acts of indecency." Acts of indecency, however, were not defined. Trudeau had decriminalized "gross indecency" in 1969, as long as it took place between two consenting adults in private. But theoretically, according the bawdy house laws, although such acts themselves might no longer be criminal, they were still indecent. So anywhere they took place could be considered a criminal establishment, and anyone found there could be arrested. It felt like we were falling down the rabbit hole. Jearld Moldenhauer's earlier insistence that decriminalization did not mean that gay sex had become legal began to make more and more sense.

A few weeks later, January 2, 1979, the *TBP* trial would begin. Given the climate, we steeled ourselves for the worst.

RALLYING THE TROOPS

The collective understood that the court case would hinge not so much on questions of law as on public opinion. We needed to build broad community support. The Free the Press Fund organized a rally. A number of local artists agreed to perform, but we still needed an emcee. I was surprised when someone suggested George Hislop. Ever since I had come out, Hislop had been associated with the conservative homophile approach. The paper had denounced him as a reactionary. Though I was mouthing the rhetoric, I was slow to understand the new imperative for community unity.

We would also need a keynote speaker, someone who would demonstrate mainstream support. Now in the swing of things, I suggested, "What about the mayor?"

John Sewell had taken office only weeks before. He had a reputation as a gadfly, and as a reformist alderman had helped poor neighbourhoods fight predatory developers. He narrowly won the mayoralty race when two conservatives split the right-wing vote. Although everyone we knew voted for him, gay issues had not figured in the campaign. Personally, I hadn't expected that his election would make much of a difference.

"Do you think he'd actually do it?" someone asked.

"Who knows? He sold himself as a progressive. It's a test to see where he stands. It can't hurt to ask. The worst he can do is say no."

I was charged with writing a letter, and to everyone's astonishment, a week later the mayor replied that he would be happy to speak.

The trial began January 2, and the rally was the next evening, January 3, my twenty-eighth birthday. The auditorium at the University of Toronto Faculty of Education building on Bloor Street was packed. Hislop emceed in inimitable style, relaxed, chatty, flirting, with slightly bawdy humour. I was still a bit of a prude and remember being shocked when he referred to "so many men, so little time." The crowd lapped it up.

But it was, according to the *TBP* report, "when lanky Toronto Mayor John Sewell sprang onto the stage [that] everybody knew it was An Event."

Sewell spoke, framed by a giant logo of the paper in handcuffs, brilliant under the lights of a half-dozen TV cameras. In five minutes he turned the world upside down. As a long-time defender of Toronto communities, Sewell declared that the gay community was one among many that "contribute significantly to the vitality and versatility of the city." He also addressed the issue of the alternative press:

> As you all know, *The Body Politic* plays a very useful role in helping to clarify issues for members of the gay community – in helping to discuss controversial matters within that community. As in the case with other members of the alternative press, people who are not interested in these issues do not have to read these papers. . . . The trial now going on in regard to *The Body Politic* is seen by many as an attack on the freedom of the press. . . . I hope that my attendance here tonight can help ensure that an attack on the alternative press in Toronto must not be countenanced, and that we all must act strongly when any kind of attack is suggested.

His closing remark brought the crowd to its feet. "We know it's not illegal to be gay," he said. "We should take the next step and make it clearly legitimate to be gay."[48] No politician had ever said such things before.

Sewell left the hall with the press and the cameras tumbling behind him. Without the TV lights, for a moment, the stage seemed absolutely dingy. It took a bit before our eyes adjusted and what had happened began to sink in.

Hislop gamely retook the stage. Feminist journalist Joanne Kates denounced the nuclear family as "a training ground for loyal workers and dutiful consumers." The three defendants were introduced and Hannon told the crowd, "Though the arm of authority has very often reached out to stifle the voice of dissent – and has often shamefully succeeded – it has never stopped its heart."

Lorraine Segato started the entertainment. Felix Partz and AA Bronson of General Idea, an up-and-coming artists' collective, gave a running commentary on slides isolating different body-parts and their relationship to censorship. Multimedia artists Randy and Berneche saluted yellow journalism. Musician Clive Robertson rhythmically chanted *TBP* clippings as poetry, and performance artists Lisa Steel and Marion Lewis delivered eerie monologues. But it was The Clichettes who brought the house down. A group of women impersonating female impersonators in 1960s drag, they forged a battle cry out of Leslie Gore's "You Don't Own Me!" making it the anthem of the rally.

The event closed with David McClean speaking about the problems facing gay youth and Chris Bearchell analyzing the political backlash the movement faced across the country. Richard captured the whole event on camera and edited it into a one-hour program, *The Body Politic on Trial,* which screened in thousands of homes on Rogers Cable community access channel.

Somehow we had combined support from the city's most important mainstream politician, the cutting edge of the Queen Street arts scene, mixed in gay liberation politics, and managed to communicate our message through a major public broadcaster. It was a resounding victory.

For us, Sewell's support was an important alliance. For him it was a nightmare. He became a lightning rod for homophobes. Right-wing reverend Ken Campbell broke down in tears on the Bible-thumping *100 Huntley Street* TV broadcast, and the mayor's phone number was repeatedly flashed across the screen. City hall switchboards lit up with venomous calls. "I never knew there was so much hate in Toronto," Sewell was reported as responding. (Welcome to our lives, Mayor Sewell.)

Campbell went on to lead a rally at city hall linking the mayor to the Jaques murder. The *Sun* accused Sewell of giving authority to the radical homosexual movement. The *Star* and the *Globe* grudgingly applauded his courage, but criticized his "bad timing."

DISORDER IN THE COURT

The rest of the trial was an anti-climax. Every morning of the six days of hearings, men and women wearing pink triangles jostled for courtroom space with born-again Christians praying for their souls. Ruby argued that the real issue was freedom of the press. Crown prosecutor Wiley suggested that "Men Loving Boys Loving Men" counselled people to commit criminal offences. Wiley's witnesses included both Ken Campbell and the *Sun*'s Claire Hoy, who described their disgust for homosexuality. (The Crown had attempted to recruit new MCC pastor Brent Hawkes as a witness against the paper, but he turned them down flat.) Ruby made mincemeat of such obviously biased witnesses. The Crown also called several homophobic physicians. Their sometimes lurid testimony was interrupted by Judge Sydney Harris questioning its relevance to a charge of "using the mails."

On our side, sex researcher Dr. John Money praised the article as informative and non-judgmental. Four progressive theologians countered the religious fundamentalist arguments. Sociologist Thelma McCormack suggested that the article should be read at all home and school meetings, and journalist June Callwood, who was vice-president of the Canadian Civil Liberties Association, testified to the paper's journalistic integrity.

A month later, February 14, Judge Harris came down with his verdict. Harris had his own sense of theatre, deliberately reading his forty-five-page judgment for an hour and a half as tension built in the packed courtroom. When he finished with the words "not guilty," we were stunned. The courtroom broke into whoops of applause, and supporters swept the three defendants outside for a statement.

"It's been clear from the beginning that the charges were an attack on the whole gay community," Ed Jackson explained, "and it's the whole gay community that won here today."[49]

The celebrations went on at Hislop's bar, Buddy's, late into the night. Everyone was deliriously happy and enormously relieved. But acquittal didn't fit with our narrative of the homophobic, authoritarian state. Hannon stressed that the win was by no means a tribute to the Canadian judicial system, more a matter of luck and public support. He reminded us that the continued existence of obscenity legislation remained a concern. Jackson pointed out that "the liberation of gay people will never be a matter decided in the courts."[50] The next *TBP* celebrated the victory by republishing "Men Loving Boys Loving Men" along with a new article, "Another Look," that took into account feminist concerns with the power imbalances in adult-child relations.

Three weeks after the verdict, Attorney General McMurtry announced that the acquittal would be appealed.

IWD II

Organizing for the city's second International Women's Day was just as difficult as the year before. At a February 1979 committee meeting, a motion was introduced to remove lesbian rights and abortion from the list of demands in order to make the day more "respectable." It was defeated, but the gaggle of lesbians who had stuck with the coalition ended up feeling even more isolated. The radical feminists again boycotted the coalition and held their own women-only march on the Thursday before the official event. There, despite the fact that most of the participants were lesbian, lesbian presence was almost invisible. Worse, the following Saturday, at the official rally of more than three thousand people, lesbian rights were introduced as a "touchy issue" and the dyke who spoke about her fight to retain custody of her children wore a hood to disguise her identity. Chris Bearchell wrote in *TBP*, "Lesbians in that auditorium were confronted with an image of themselves as pathetic and invisible."[51] Lesbians had been erased in both marches. The relationship between the two camps was worse than ever.

In an effort to repair the damage, a small committee drawn from LOOT, WAVAW, and the International Women's Day Committee organized a community forum. A hundred and twenty women attended the meeting, dubbed The Hetero-Mackerel Meets the Lavender Herring: A Fine Kettle of Fish. The day got off to a good start with a skit satirizing stereotypes of the different factions, and a commitment to dialogue, working together, and addressing the issue of female sexuality. But when the discussion began, it quickly broke down into a shouting match: radical lesbian feminists versus straight socialist feminists, with the lesbian socialist feminists caught in the middle. Valverde called it "the most appalling event I'd been to in my entire life."[52]

In a subsequent *TBP* opinion piece, Bearchell, herself squarely associated with the lesbian socialist feminists, put most of the blame on the radical dykes. She drew links between "lesbian chauvinism" and closetry. *TBP* was now seen as taking sides, not that we had much credibility with the radicals anyway. Worse, the split in the LOOT leadership, and the growing alienation of those who saw LOOT as a social and cultural space, began to corrode the spirit of the organization itself.

THE BINATIONAL LESBIAN CONFERENCE AND THE END OF LOOT

LOOT had a major project in the works, a Binational Lesbian Conference. Much of the radical feminist energy was being drawn off by WAVAW and the new magazine, *Broadside*. With more conservative and socially oriented members not particularly interested, the conference organizing committee was dominated by LOOT's socialist feminist faction.

There was no government funding. The finance committee raised money through benefits, dances, donations, and registration fees. Another sub-committee polled women across the country to ask what they needed. Simultaneous translation was arranged, and the conference program was in English and French. Billeting, transportation, food, and workshop committees were set up.

More than four hundred women attended. Day one focused on community, including coming out, minorities, lesbians in prison, and addiction issues. Day two discussed the movement and its factions and divisions, and day three, directions for future organizing. There were skills-building workshops on everything from bicycle repair to basic sound and lighting, and cultural workshops on poetry, film-making, body awareness, and theatre. There was controversy, such as when Lilith Finkler, still a teenager, introduced a motion calling for the abolition of age of consent. That didn't get far. Later a squad of uniformed cops marched into the final banquet to investigate possible liquor law violations. But in the end, attendees were ecstatic, and there was an agreement to establish a new national magazine, *Lesbian/Lesbienne*, and to develop a lesbian bill of rights.

"Everyone was so high on this amazing energy and even women who would never have been caught dead at political events were hanging around the conference," recalled Naomi Brooks. "We felt we had built a national lesbian movement. This was it, it was happening."[53]

But when the dust settled and delegates returned home, it was evident that LOOT was in trouble. No one was coming to the house any more. The project was exhausted. The bitter political split had destroyed trust at a leadership level. Many of the radical feminists were now involved in *Broadside* or the new Feminist Party of Canada. Pat Murphy and others had set up a new women's bar, the Fly by Night, which attracted women primarily interested in socializing. Desperate appeals through the newsletter for women to step forward and save the centre went unheeded. LOOT would close its doors less than a year later on May 1, 1980.

Reactions to LOOT's passing recorded in *Broadside* went from sadness and a sense of loss to disillusionment: "Have we anything to say to the world as lesbians qua lesbians, rather than as gay liberationists and feminists? Or are we simply a maze of intersecting social circles, void of any real political or cultural content?"[54] More optimistically: "I have come to accept the lesbian community as the many headed hydra sprouting new life every time an old limb withers. . . . We are spinning webs, not building pyramids."[55]

Lesbian politics seemed to be in serious disarray and, despite Foucault's new theories, gay men were experiencing serious state repression. To be fair, Foucault never argued that there was no repression, only that in its attempt to repress, the state had to define and therefore talk about homosexuality, thus invoking it as an identity. For *TBP*, however, it was hard to see any long-term bright side to another round of legal battles. Nevertheless, the acquittal had buoyed everyone's spirits, and McMurtry's appeal reinforced our narrative that the attack on the paper was an attack on the community.

The impression of a community under attack was given further credence that spring by a wave of porn busts across the country. The RCMP raided the homes of gay men in Montreal, Timmins, Oshawa, Toronto, Mississauga, Winnipeg, and Saskatoon, seizing personal porn collections. Metro police also used a *TBP* ad to target the home of a straight Ajax man who was trying to sell a porn collection he had inherited. Toronto washroom entrapments were also on the upswing. *TBP* published a short advice column to help people challenge a search warrant if the cops came to the door.

And for anyone who still thought the police could be our friends, the March 1979 issue of the Metro police association newsletter, *News and Views,* set the record straight. In an article entitled "The Homosexual Fad," Staff Sergeant Tom Moclair called homosexuality a "sickness or aberration" that "should never become a right." He accused the mayor of sanctioning "acts of perversion which symptomize the decadence of our society in his liberal and flippant show of appreciation to a few hundred homosexuals who helped him get elected." Moclair continued: "Just listen to them talk (if you can stomach them), and they sure like to talk, because talk is a penchant of homosexuality especially in the physically deprived and cowardly male." He concluded: "Selling their condition as if it were virtue; acting it out; prancing and wiggling, and sometimes dressing in effeminate garb; smelling like polecats; these are not involuntary acts. These are sick, volitional despicable actions."[56] A companion article took swipes at blacks and Jews.

RTPC VS. THE POLICE

A new group in town, the Right to Privacy Committee, stepped in to mount a response. The RTPC was the final name of the committee that had formed immediately after the December 9 Barracks raid in 1978. Peter Maloney and Brent Hawkes were involved, along with veteran activists Tom Warner, Brian Mossop, George Smith, and Michael Lynch. That mix hadn't stopped Ken Popert from describing the organization as a vehicle for gay business interests, a characterization hotly disputed by others.

Gary Kinsman grumbled about the name. Privacy was too close to closetry for him. He wanted something more militant sounding. But it was congruent with the values of many bath patrons, for whom baths were a safe place, and for whom the Barracks raid was an outrageous violation of the social contract of the closet. It also gestured to the legal question of whether the baths were public or private places. If they were private, then what happened there should be exempt from interference under the 1969 decriminalization of private homosexual activity. Finally, privacy resonated with the fundamental liberal value that each individual's personal life should be free of group (state) interference, and shifted the frame of the raid from the apprehension of criminals to the violation of the intimate rights of citizens.

Somehow George Smith corralled me into chairing the March 20 public meeting at the 519 to determine a response to the Moclair article. A couple of hundred angry people crammed into the main auditorium. I had spoken to crowds before, but I had never tried to facilitate a discussion in one. Somehow, with a mix of being a traffic cop and an orchestra conductor, I managed to pull it off. My only misstep was when I recognized a blond man at the back, and "he" turned out to be a young dyke.

By the time the RTPC packed the Police Commission meeting on April 25, both the police chief and the head of the police association had been forced to issue statements distancing themselves from the article. Peter Maloney again demanded the dismissal of the cop who had called school boards after the Barracks raid, and called for a permanent gay liaison committee. The commission sullenly heard the submissions, but refused to make any commitments.

It was becoming clear that this was not a matter of the homophobia of individual police officers. The force was simply not accountable to civilian oversight. It was, in fact, a right-wing political force in its own right. In Ottawa, the Canadian Police Association was lobbying for a return to capital punishment and the lash. Project "P," which conducted the raid on *TBP*, also had a lobbying arm pushing for stronger obscenity legislation. The police had become adept at using the media to justify their actions and orchestrate public opinion. They were fundamentally opposed to the process of gay liberation.

SAN FRANCISCO'S NIGHT OF RAGE

Our new appreciation of police power was thrown into relief by events in San Francisco. On May 21, 1979, the Dan White verdict came down. Although White had come to city hall with a loaded gun and murdered the mayor and gay city supervisor Harvey Milk, he was acquitted of murder and found guilty only of the lightest possible charge, manslaughter. He could be out of jail in less than three years. White was an ex-cop.

Within hours, a crowd of five thousand converged on San Francisco city hall chanting, "He got away with murder." After hours of rioting, doors and windows were left shattered and the shells of thirteen police cars were smouldering in the streets.

The police retaliated. By 1:00 a.m. police cars began moving into the Castro, far from the melee at city hall. Screaming homophobic insults and "Sieg

Heil," cops in full riot gear began attacking people indiscriminately. They smashed the glass doors of Elephant Walk and trashed the popular gay bar. When the deputy chief tried to physically restrain some of his men and organize a withdrawal, they called him coward and refused to obey orders. The assault went on for more than an hour. It was war.

The next escalation in Toronto came June 6.

NOW OUR HOMES

Don Franco, the teacher arrested at the Barracks who went public after police contacted the board of education to try to get him fired, was an active member of the RTPC.

He was also into S/M. He had a makeshift dungeon off the bedroom in his suburban bungalow and regularly advertised for partners in *TBP*. On June 6 he got a call in response to his ad. "Wally" came over later that evening, but after a short conversation, pulled out a badge and told Franco he was under arrest for keeping a common bawdy house. Six more plainclothes cops burst in and ransacked the house, making off with a dozen garbage bags of his possessions, including Christmas card lists and membership lists for both the RTPC and the local NDP gay caucus.

TBP reported, "That the police might one day charge our private homes as 'bawdy houses' has always been one of our most paranoid fantasies. It's happened."[57]

THE END OF HUMAN RIGHTS?

If Toronto and San Francisco were any indication, the gay movement was now in hand-to-hand combat with the repressive forces of the state. Despite CGRO's best efforts, there seemed to be little hope of getting sexual orientation included in the Ontario Human Rights Code in the foreseeable future. The Damien case was, depending on your perspective, either dead or dying. In Ontario, the only legislative victory had been back in 1973 when the city included sexual orientation in its anti-discrimination policy. In this context Michael Lynch penned "The End of the 'Human Rights' Decade" in *TBP*'s July 1979 issue.

Despite beginning with the Stonewall riots in 1969 and ending with the San Francisco riots of 1979, Lynch characterized the time in between as a decade of moderation aimed at lobbying "for two words in a human rights code of severely limited applicability." Yet, after a decade of work, of the eleven human rights acts in Canada, we had been successful only in Quebec.

Lynch reminded readers to distinguish between human rights as a goal and as a strategy. We may not have achieved the goal, he argued, but as a strategy, the fight for human rights had three achievements. It helped produce a gay community that "sees itself and is seen by others as a political 'minority' "; gay life had been "brought to public consciousness"; and "the facts of oppression, real and undeniable have been made known."

Lynch traced the history of the gay human rights strategy in Canada from the 1971 *We Demand* demonstration in Ottawa, through Brian Waite's seminal article in *TBP* in 1972, to the founding of the National Gay Rights Coalition in 1975. The fact that human rights had "mainline political respectability" had allowed even more conservative gay groups to embrace it.

But now, he argued, the strategy was "linked to defeat" and only served to demoralize. It had become the new "homophilism" that sought assimilation. "The isolation of this one issue from all the rest that concern us" should no longer be a priority. Lynch suggested that if any strategy could unite the cluster of groups and organizations that had emerged over the last decade, it might be the "containment of totalitarian power, particularly that of the police." That would mean seeing "police power as the strongest arm of racism and patriarchy. That study may lead us to strategic coalitions against those institutions and values, not just tinkering with the police bureaucracy."[58]

Not everyone bought the argument. Jim Monk from Windsor Gay Unity suggested that Lynch "confused our own exhaustion with our estimate of the remaining utility of the human rights strategy." Abandoning human rights now, he said, would be a sign of vulnerability that would encourage the homophobes. It would also undermine the movement's leadership in the eyes of previously uninvolved sectors of the community who were rallying to the strategy in the wake of Anita Bryant and the raids on *TBP* and the Barracks.

No one raised the underlying class dynamic. Police violence is always disproportionately directed against the poor and marginalized, or at least those whom the police assume to be so because of their race, location, or dress. A focus on police would produce different alliances than a civil rights strategy, which would protect more conservative and middle-class sectors of the community from discrimination.

But despite the debate, in the face of the lack of concrete progress, something was clearly unravelling. Although the National Gay Rights Coalition had changed its name to the Canadian Lesbian and Gay Rights Coalition in 1978, a number of prairie groups had already resigned in the face of the coalition's continuing paralysis on the question of lesbian participation. The 1979 annual conference in Ottawa was described as lacklustre. Few women attended, and delegates passed yet another resolution for an "active campaign" to involve women. A growing disillusionment with efforts around human rights codes was evident. The final resolution that would have made the inclusion of sexual orientation the priority was changed to make it *a* priority. There seemed to be much more interest on local issues, and a commission was set up to collect information on grassroots organizing.

NEW ALLIANCES

When a group of prominent Toronto gay activists occupied McMurtry's offices on King Street on August 20, the agenda was police issues, not the government's refusal to include sexual orientation in the code. And with the August 26 police murder of an unarmed black man, Albert Johnson, in his own home a week later, the focus sharpened on an out-of-control police force. An October 1979 *TBP* editorial, "Black Power, Pink Triangles," called the Johnson killing the "latest in a series of incidents involving racism and homophobia" and urged readers to support an October 14 city-wide demonstration against police racism and violence. The RTPC joined with anti-racism groups to form the Working Group on Police Minority Relations, which called for the laying of criminal charges in the Johnson case, and demanded a civilian review board to investigate police shootings.

The need for such alliances was reconfirmed October 11, when police raided another bath, the Hot Tub Club. This time the RTPC was holding a meeting only two blocks away. When a breathless man arrived to report the raid, Peter Maloney, who was chairing, closed the meeting and led the charge to the bath. Other runners headed to the nearby bars. Soon, more than a hundred people gathered, including city aldermen Dan Heap and Allan Sparrow. Maloney led the crowd in blocking the paddy wagon trying to carry away the arrested men, and after some pushing and shoving, the outnumbered police released those arrested on their own recognizance. That night, four private homes were also raided, and more than forty bawdy house charges laid against twenty-six men.

Tom Warner of CGRO linked the raids to the impending reform of the code, as "an obvious attempt to discredit gay community demands that sexual orientation be added."[59] But for more and more of us, the police themselves were becoming the major issue. As Mossop had pointed out, we had moved from a period of confronting the dead weight of tradition to one where we were facing organized attacks by the state.

Three days later, gay community members joined thousands of others to protest police racism at city hall. Despite opposition from the Canadian Party of Labour, a small Maoist group active in anti-racist work, and the hesitations of some Sikh organizers, with strong black community support, Brent Hawkes spoke about police attacks on the gay community on behalf of the new working group. Police violence was providing a platform for horizontal alliances between gay groups and other minorities.

It was an alliance that the police and their supporters would do everything to undermine. The following week, Catholic Archbishop Cardinal Carter submitted a report commissioned by the Police Commission about how to improve community-police relations. Although he reluctantly met with gay community reps in preparing it, Carter specifically stated in his report that lesbians and gay men did not constitute a community that may legitimately demand special consideration, and limited his recommendations to improving race relations.[60]

4

Shifting Sands

WASHINGTON

In October 1979, Richard and I and our friend Tony Souza drove to Washington for the first National March on Washington for Lesbian and Gay Rights. It was the tenth anniversary of Stonewall. The march also coincided with the first National Third World Lesbian and Gay Conference.

We managed to get across the border (always a worry for three gay men in those days), and after a long drive, arrived at our seedy downtown hotel in the U.S. capital. The next day we walked over to the site of the Third World conference at Howard University. As we approached the entrance, a young man ran up to Richard and said, "The Asian caucus is meeting on the second floor." Richard was taken aback. Growing up in the Caribbean, he had always thought of himself as Trinidadian. In Canada people expected him to be Chinese, at least until he opened his mouth. Now he was rushed off to the Asian caucus.

The conference was convened by the National Coalition of Black Lesbians and Gays. There was significance in the choice of the conference name. In Canada, the phrase used for people of non-European background was generally "visible minority." The term "Third World" signalled that the marginalization people were facing was due neither to their numbers nor to how they looked. "Third World" tied racism to the effects of hundreds of years of European colonialism, and linked people to the anti-colonial struggles against it.

Audre Lorde gave the keynote to five hundred delegates.

> In the affirmation of our coming together and the potential power of our numbers, remember also how much work there is still to be done in our communities. In the present, vision must point the way toward action upon every level of our varied existences: the way we vote, the way we eat, the way we relate to each other, the way we raise our children, the way we work for change. This weekend we are here not only to share experience and connection, not only to discuss the many aspects of freedom for all homosexual peoples. We are also here to examine our roles as powerful forces within

109

our communities. For not one of us will be free until we are all free, and until all members of our communities are free. So we are here to help shape a world where all people can flourish, beyond sexism, beyond racism, beyond ageism, beyond classism, and beyond homophobia.[1]

The next day was clear and cold. The huge protest, estimated by organizers to be a quarter million, was led by a group of Third World lesbians, the Salsa Soul Sisters, followed by a contingent from the Third World conference that had already marched through Chinatown and black neighbourhoods. Richard and his new comrades from the Asian caucus carried a banner reading "We're Asians Gay and Proud." *TBP* reported that the presence of so many Third World lesbians and gay men "laid to rest any remaining stereotype of the movement as an essentially white, male, middle-class phenomenon."[2]

It took three hours before the back of the march reached the shadow of the obelisk. The five-hour rally was broadcast coast to coast on National Public Radio, closing with Tom Robinson leading the crowd in a rousing chorus of "Glad to Be Gay." The following day, hundreds of participants from every U.S. state met with congressional representatives to lobby for an end to discrimination.

The remarkable event had only been conceived the previous November. The result of grassroots organizing across the country, it almost didn't happen after the main national organizations – the National Gay Task Force, Gay Rights National Lobby, Dignity, and MCC in the United States – refused to endorse the idea, fearing a backlash. But after the Milk assassination, the organizing had gained momentum. The mainstream groups reversed their decision just over two months before the event.

Inspired by the Third World conference, when we returned, Richard put a personal ad in *TBP* seeking Asian lesbians and gay men to form a group. Several months later Richard, Tony Souza, Nitto Marquez, and Gerald Chan (who had come out in a landmark article in the pan-Asian magazine, *Asianadian*) founded Toronto's first ethno-racial gay group, Gay Asians Toronto. Souza was originally from India, Marquez from the Philippines, and Chan from Hong Kong. The new group was overwhelmingly male. One of the earliest members was Tony Cheung, a working class youth who had grown up in Chinatown. When GAT boldly postered Chinatown seeking new members, Cheung ensured they steered clear of Triad-owned businesses and restaurants.

Although originally envisaged as pan-Asian, GAT soon evolved into an East Asian group. As Asian communities in Toronto rapidly expanded, it would be an incubator for community organizing for almost twenty years.

GAT opened up a discussion of racial hierarchies of desire within the community for the first time. Richard wrote in *TBP*:

> I feel like a fortune cookie in a tray of cheese Danishes. . . . I can't grow a
> moustache, I don't make a convincing cowboy. I'm stuck with the costume

I was born with. It's a costume because I have been to Asia only on holidays and I don't speak any Asian language. Yet someone can tell me seriously that he "really gets off on Orientals."[3]

Racial stereotyping in the gay male sexual marketplace – both rejection for not embodying white models of masculinity, and rice queen fetishization – would be an enduring preoccupation of gay Asian organizing over the next decades.

THE VOLCKER SHOCK

Jimmy Carter was in the White House as we marched past that afternoon, but he didn't come out to wave. It was a Sunday, and after church the president was busy having lunch with the first lady. Although he must have known we were passing, Carter probably had more pressing things on his mind. For several years now the economy had been in a mess.

Carter had appointed Paul Volcker to head the Federal Reserve Bank a few months before. Volcker had decided that inflation was the main problem and dramatically raised interest rates to cool down the economy. That was music to the ears of the rich, because inflation ate into their savings. But as Keynesian economics predicted, the "Volcker shock" sparked a recession. Small and medium businesses could no longer afford to borrow money. People lost their jobs. Many could not afford to pay their mortgages. Carter knew that the voters were likely going to take it out on him. The election was just a year away. Since Carter was a Democrat and a liberal, the country's economic problems and Volcker's solution to them were putting the wind behind the sails of his Republican opponents.

Months later, in her analysis of the new decade in *Broadside*, Myrna Kostash noted:

> I am also coming to believe that we will be in the streets not so much for the joy of it this time, but in desperation, dread and wrath. We will be there because we have no choice ... in the urgency of the economic crises the demands of the women's movement will be dismissed as a "luxury," as anti-social even: how dare we demand higher wages, daycare centres, women's studies courses and access to abortion when all about us is inflation, bankruptcy, closure and disintegration?[4]

But as we marched in front of the White House, we didn't realize that we were at the beginning of a sea change. The Keynesian era that I had grown up with, which valued economic balance and equitable distribution of social resources, had ended. This was the beginning of neo-liberalism – a world where the rich would get fabulously richer, corporate power would be unrestrained, and the rest of us would be left to our own devices. This shift would have profound effects on the trajectory of the gay movement.

Carter quietly did another thing earlier that year. He signed a directive for covert aid to traditionalist rebels opposing the Soviet-backed government in Afghanistan. The left-wing Afghani government had angered large landowners and Muslim clerics with its aggressive land reforms and secular policies to improve the lives of women. Aligned with the Americans were the Saudis, promoting their version of conservative Wahabi Islam in a jihad against atheistic communism. In October, the USSR invaded Afghanistan to support its beleaguered allies. The resulting civil war between traditional Islam and Soviet imperialism would have profound effects on world politics.

IRAN – A NEW KIND OF REVOLUTION

Next door in Iran, another example of conservative anti-imperialism was playing out. In January 1979, Shah Mohammad Reza Pahlavi ignominiously fled Iran after a popular rebellion against his twenty-five-year autocratic monarchy. The Shah had been put in power by the Americans and the British in a CIA-managed coup against the democratically elected government of Mohammad Mossadegh in 1953. Mossadegh had tried to nationalize British and American oil companies exploiting Iranian oil fields, but the Shah reestablished the oil giants' access to Iranian oil and embarked on his White Revolution, a brutal process of "modernization" that displaced thousands of peasants, swelled Tehran's slums, and undermined the traditional bazaar economy. His rule became more extravagant, corrupt, and authoritarian as time went on, and his secret police filled the jails with the political opposition.

In our commune on Seaton Street, we cheered the fall of another U.S.-sponsored dictatorship. Until that point, all the revolutions we had known, despite their regular failings in terms of gay rights, were led by socialists and nationalists who espoused enlightenment values such as secularism, equality, women's liberation, and modernization to overcome underdevelopment. Few of us had any knowledge of another long-standing current of anti-imperialist thought that reached back to Al Afghani in the nineteenth century.

This current contrasted the secular, individualistic West with the spiritual, communal East, and saw the West's colonial machinations as a threat to traditional social values. It was largely a reaction to the hypocrisy of a West that talked about freedom and democracy, but inevitably imposed compliant dictators or used military might to enable its economic exploitation of weaker countries. Rather than basing resistance on Enlightenment-influenced ideas such as socialism, this current saw the traditional religious values of the common people as an antidote to the corrupting influences of the West. Western imperialism had thoroughly discredited western liberalism for much of the world's population.

The Iranian revolution also involved liberal, socialist, and secular forces, but it was the new leader, the Ayatollah Khomeini, who spoke the language of the rural and new urban poor. After the Shah was gone, the country overwhelmingly approved the establishment of an Islamic Republic in April 1979, and the new regime soon began to tighten the screws on the secular opposition. That May, *TBP* reported an International Women's Day demonstration in Tehran opposing Khomeini's orders that women wear the traditional chador in public. The story also ominously noted reports of the execution of men who were variously reported to be gay, child rapists, or organizers of a child prostitution ring.

Although the Iranian revolution was grounded in Shia Islam, its example also encouraged religiously based anti-imperialist organizing in the majority Sunni Arab world. For these movements, secularism and sexual licentiousness went hand in hand with colonialism. Ironically, as the lesbian and gay movement felt itself under attack in the West, we were becoming a symbol of the dangers of western society in the Middle East. Although Iran seemed a singularity in 1979, it represented the beginning of another sea change that would have profound effects on international sexual politics.

In November, U.S.-Iranian relations worsened. Islamic students seized the U.S. embassy in Tehran, releasing documents detailing American support of the Shah. The United States retaliated by giving Saddam Hussein, the secular dictator of neighbouring Iraq, a green light to invade Iran. A chain of events that would exacerbate the conflict between the secular West and traditionalist Islam had been initiated.

THE DAILY GRIND

Back at home, *TBP* had established regular routines to keep on top of production. The collective met every Monday night from eight to ten or eleven. We planned the upcoming issue, crafted editorials, troubleshot, and occasionally vetted display advertising. We still aimed at consensus, occasionally bringing an issue to a vote when that wasn't possible.

Advertising was no one's favourite discussion. We desperately needed it and equally resented depending on it. We occasionally had to turn ads down just because we had too many. The ratio of copy to advertising could not be crossed. Periodically there were fraught discussions about what that ratio should be.

Then there was politically problematic advertising. When body-rub and porn entrepreneur Honest Joe Martin asked to run a full-page ad outlining his mayoralty platform in the upcoming election, the collective turned him down because of his "libertarian" politics. One of Martin's policy planks was an end to government interference in the sale of porn. The collective argued that it did not accept advertising that exploits women.

> "Freedom for everybody," in Honest Joe's books, sounds a lot like the freedom the powerful need to increase the power they've already got. . . . We don't think those are ideas worth promoting – even if someone wants to buy the space to do it. Maybe that's the difference between libertarian and liberation politics.[5]

We began a series of subscription ads featuring well-known personalities recommending *TBP*. But we stopped after running two – with historian Martin Duberman and with fiction writer Jane Rule – deciding that such ads contributed to the "star system." There was a move, on our lawyer's advice, to censor classified ads. After the Don Franco case, we knew the police were using them to arrest people. Then there were a lot of second thoughts.

Often these discussions were detailed in an introductory This Issue section. Our goal was always to be as transparent as possible about our process. Issue 49 explained, "Though we don't wish to foster capitalism, we do operate within a capitalist system in a number of ways, one of which is having to sell our paper to subscribers (and advertisers) to keep it going, even as we try to reveal how this works."[6]

Collective members took charge of specific parts of the paper. In issue 55, Gerald Hannon and Bill Lewis co-ordinated local and national news, I did international, Alex Wilson was in charge of Our Image, the cultural section, and Ed Jackson and Paul Trollope ran letters and the community page. Rick Bébout co-ordinated layout and production, and he, Robin Hardy, and Ross Irwin were in charge of advertising and promotion. Bébout and Hannon also managed the office.

I often felt guilty because everyone else seemed to do so much more. All I did, beyond the collective meetings and the shared drudgery of opening and sorting mail, was spend several nights a month reading dozens of lesbian and gay papers from around the world. I spent at least one full weekend, buzzing on yerba maté, compiling my pages of international news shorts. And then the tedious task of coming up with headlines of a length that would fit a column. At production time, always a rush, we all pitched in to lay out the waxed strips of copy on the flats for printing.

After each issue, everyone who had contributed, collective members or not, got together for a potluck. Fortified with food and drink, the issue and the process of producing it was dissected, critiqued, and theorized, and lessons drawn for the next one. Such meetings could be intense. But people were clever, funny, and passionate, and the conversations were almost always remarkably without rancour.

Reflecting on this period, Bébout drew on Lewis Hyde's *The Gift: Imagination and the Erotic Life of Property* to describe *TBP* as an example of "gift culture." Other than whoever was putting in twelve-hour days to staff the office for minimum wage, all this time, all this work, and all this writing was done for free – gifts to the community and to the movement. Such was the new way of organizing that *TBP* sought to embody – collective, democratic, transparent, participatory, non-hierarchical, generous, and yet able to get things done. We still thought of it as a model of the future. Unfortunately, the model was more and more out of sync with the world that was taking shape around us.

The real fly in the ointment, though, was that the collective continued to be overwhelmingly male. In January 1979 two women joined the collective, Chris Bearchell and Mariana Valverde.

Bearchell had contributed to the paper for years. A committed feminist and socialist, a vocal opponent of lesbian separatism, and a powerful debater and orator, she was involved in dozens of struggles in various movements before she finally took the plunge.

Valverde came from a left-wing Spanish family and was working on her doctorate at York. Sharply analytic of the social context shaping the feminist and gay liberation movements, her sophisticated arguments seldom toed any party line. But in an indication that the gap between feminist and gay men's understandings of the world was far from bridged, Valverde left the collective after only six issues.

"My leaving was not a reaction to any one event or issue," she explains.

> My main problem was that I felt I was being asked to re-explain feminism 101 over and over again. . . . I felt that it was not right for a "gay liberation" magazine to treat feminism as a totally external movement/intellectual current that could be occasionally included in a particular event, or could be represented in a particular article, but that was not a component of gay liberation itself. I did not feel hostility toward feminism as much as a sense of great tiredness and disappointment. Having to constantly argue for a feminist perspective from scratch, as if the guys had never heard the arguments before, was just too frustrating.[7]

The Binational Lesbian Conference in 1979 called for *TBP* to dedicate more space to women's views on intergenerational relationships. In response, *TBP* reps announced plans for a special feminist issue. It was timed in October to celebrate the fiftieth anniversary of the legal decision that made women "persons" under Canadian law. Editorial control of the features section was turned over to an autonomous group of women.

It would have been utopian to expect such a process to be smooth, given what was happening at LOOT at the time. Differences among the women's committee precluded even a common evaluation of the process. Although a number of those involved thanked the *TBP* and welcomed "this chance to make ourselves known to you," the names of other women who had worked on the issue were conspicuous by their absence. The experience was never repeated.

There seemed to be growing recognition that gay men and lesbians represented "two distinct cultures," and there were as many divisions among lesbians as there were among gay men. But while that might have explained the difficulties in co-operating, it could also be used to justify male sexism and indifference to working together.

One person who could cut through the period's politically correct pretense like a hot knife through butter was Jane Rule. Rule, living with her long-time partner on rural Galiano Island in British Columbia, was Canada's best-known lesbian author. By the time she started writing her regular So's Your Grandmother column for *TBP*, she had published six successful novels, including her 1964 *Desert of the Heart* and the 1975 *The Young in One Another's Arms*. Rule was both iconic and iconoclastic. In her first *TBP* column she focused on being an out lesbian surrounded by the small-town life of Galiano. Rule declared, "If I ever did find myself in an artists' colony or lesbian community, I'd move."[8]

RURAL OUTREACH

Divisions between men and women weren't the only issue. Toronto, with its commercial ghetto and an expanding range of organizations, had been the birthplace of our political unrest. But as a provincial coalition, CGRO needed to knit together organizations in smaller centres without a commercial scene. Melding the isolating and often hostile realities of small-town life with the brash politics of Toronto was no mean task, but CGRO decided it needed to deal with the issue.

In early 1980, it applied for a small grant from the inter-church coalition, PLURA (an acronym of its Presbyterian, Lutheran, United Church, Roman Catholic, and Anglican sponsors), to do organizing in small towns and rural areas of the province. Although PLURA traditionally supported progressive grassroots activism, a grant to a gay organization was a bit of a breakthrough. But Jim Monk, chair of CGRO at the time, was also part of the PLURA board, representing the Windsor Coalition for Development as community non-church rep. Monk was surprised how easily the application passed, with only token reservations from one of the Catholic representatives.

As a result, CGRO was able to hire Robin Hardy, a twenty-eight-year-old gay man who had grown up in Winnipeg and Ottawa. Hardy, sometimes accompanied by Bearchell, criss-crossed the province in a rattletrap Honda holding meetings, encouraging people to develop networks, and visiting individuals in their homes. Sometimes gatherings were advertised in local media.

Hardy was clear that he was not there "from big gay Toronto" to tell everyone what to do. He encouraged people to identify local needs and figure out how to address them. He found that setting up a phone line was usually a priority. "People contact you, you begin to get a membership list and you are on your way to building the base for a club."[9] But he did not buy the stereotype that only city people could be political, reporting that "the militancy of gay women and men in small town Ontario is enough to put a lot of big-city gay people to shame."[10]

Over the summer of 1980, Hardy contacted more than five hundred lesbians and gay men in the north. New organizations were set up in Thunder

Bay and Sudbury. Gay men and lesbians in farms and villages were put in touch with local organizations. Hundreds were added to the CGRO mailing lists. Market forces might have been responsible for bringing gay people together in the first place, but now the movement was reaching out to areas that the market had little motivation to penetrate.

THE APPEAL

As 1980 and the appeal of the *TBP* verdict loomed, the Free the Press Fund was thinking about next steps. Overcoming community divisions on questions of child/adult sex had preoccupied the first phase of the fight; the solution had been to focus on freedom of the press. Almost two years later, the fund was confronted with different problems. How to remind a forgetful public that the case was ongoing. How to put together a coalition that would be significant, not so much to the community but to the attorney general. It was an almost imperceptible shift from a strategy of horizontal alliances to more vertical ones, imposed by the realities of having to deal with the courts.

It meant we needed to be high-profile and demonstrate more mainstream support. A plan was hatched for a full-page ad in *The Globe and Mail*, Canada's national journal of record. It would cost in the neighbourhood of $9,000 (approximately $25,000 today), a hefty sum given the fund's major responsibility of raising money for the costly legal defence.

We decided to develop a simple statement for people and organizations to endorse. It would be the centrepiece of the ad. Endorsers would donate a small amount to cover the cost, and their name would be publicly displayed. Since the target group was largely straight people, the money should not interfere with ongoing fundraising for legal defence. It was a kind of crude pre-Internet crowdfunding effort.

After much back and forth we devised a statement that began with a simple message: "We urge the Attorney-General of Ontario to drop the appeal against *The Body Politic*." It went on to briskly describe the facts of the case, and quoted Judge Sydney Harris's ruling that *TBP* was a "serious journal of news and opinion." It closed by characterizing McMurtry's decision to appeal the verdict as an attack on minority expression and further punishment against a non-profit group already found not guilty in the courts.[11]

Key people were asked to sign on first – iconic liberal journalists and commentators June Callwood and Pierre Berton, political theorist C.B. Macpherson, radical Catholic theologian Gregory Baum. (Berton, a major Canadian radio and TV icon, initially quibbled not about the spirit of the ad but about the word "gay," the proper meaning of which he felt was being corrupted. But after I sent him an etymology tracing its use to describe sexual behaviour to the fourteenth century, he relented.)

On the strength of such support, the Canadian Civil Liberties Association, the Periodical Writers Association of Canada, the International Women's Day

Committee, the Law Union of Ontario, and Art Metropole allowed the fund to contact their substantial mailing lists. Gay and lesbian groups across the country were also asked to solicit names from their regions.

The ad appeared February 6, despite a brief last-minute panic when, as the *Globe* was going to press, we received a phone call from the advertising department demanding a notarized document certifying that all the names on the ad were legitimate. I raced over to the *Globe* offices on my bicycle with a hastily drawn up document just in time.

Most signers donated between ten and twenty dollars; a few, more than a hundred. More than eight hundred individuals and organizations signed on, an estimated two-thirds straight identified. Of the five thousand or so people we mailed to, we got a very respectable 10 per cent return rate, and the knowledge that thousands of others were reading our material for the first time.

It was remarkable to rally such wide support within a couple of months. It also had a special significance to those who remembered the battles to get dailies to accept even a classified ad less than a decade before.

The goal of the ad was to broaden our support and raise the profile of the case. No one expected the attorney general to withdraw the appeal. But although we had won a political battle, the legal one did not go so well. On February 29, 1980, the appeal judge overturned the acquittal and ordered a new trial. After a community meeting the following week, there was consensus that we had no choice but to appeal the appeal verdict. The work of the Free the Press Fund was far from over.

HUMAN RIGHTS

Meanwhile, slogging at its endless battle to get sexual orientation into the Ontario Human Rights Code, CGRO made a breakthrough. The 1977 *Life Together* report had recommended the inclusion of both "handicap" and "sexual orientation" as prohibited grounds for discrimination. Both disabilities communities and the gay community had mobilized in support of their own issues. But CGRO took the initiative to make cold calls to the Coalition for Usable Transportation (CUT) and the Blind Organization of Ontario with Self-Help Tactics (BOOST), the two most vocal disability rights organizations. After a series of meetings, there was mutual agreement to support the inclusion of both issues as a package.

Such unity was not necessarily a given. When CUT and BOOST met with Liberal opposition leader Stuart Smith in the summer of 1978, he suggested it would be "politically wiser" for them to push only for the addition of handicap at the time. Both CUT and BOOST publicly rejected the advice.[12]

In November 1979, Labour Minister Robert Elgie tried to dodge the whole Human Rights Code issue by introducing special legislation to protect the disabled. With both Liberal and NDP support, it was expected to pass easily. But disability groups quickly opposed the approach, calling it "segregationist and discriminatory." CGRO joined the campaign, insisting that human rights protection for the disabled belonged in the code. The alliance was formalized with the creation of the Coalition for Life Together.

The media ridiculed the government for its ham-fisted attempt to avoid the issue. The Liberals and NDP did an about-face and refused to support the bill. Faced with certain defeat, Elgie withdrew it and the coalition stepped up lobbying for the full implementation of *Life Together*.

Although the unity between the gay and disability movements had been a conscious decision, *TBP* also pointed out the bridging influence of gay people with disabilities, who were part of both communities. Gerald Hannon published "No Sorrow, No Pity" in February 1980. *TBP*'s first major feature on gay people living with disabilities, it looked at the stereotype that people with disabilities couldn't be sexual. The article examined the experience of growing up gay in institutions, the difficulty of coming out if you are dependent on others, and prejudice against people with disabilities in the gay community. It included an accessibility survey of Toronto gay bars.

The alliance between the two movements was a textbook case of the richness of a horizontal approach. It challenged both homophobia among the disabled and caregiving groups, and ableism among gay men and lesbians.

CRUISING

In February 1980, William Friedkin's new movie *Cruising* opened in Toronto. One wag said that Friedkin, who had also made *Boys in the Band*, had moved on to gay corpses. *Village Voice* columnist Arthur Bell, who was leaked a copy of the script, called it "the most oppressive, ugly, bigoted look at homosexuality ever presented on the screen."[13] Near riots had been generated in New York's Greenwich Village the previous summer when gay demonstrators ran onto the movie set, blowing whistles and pulling plugs. Local gay bars had denied Friedkin permission to shoot on their premises, and twenty gay extras quit the film.

But attempts to close down *Cruising* were problematic for a movement fighting for freedom of expression. Scott Tucker, who had participated in the protests, wrote a feature in the November issue of *TBP*, rhetorically asking if it was censorship when a marginalized group challenged the production of hate propaganda. He noted that free speech was often used to protect the power of free enterprise to denigrate the powerless. He wondered about a media system that had suppressed our images and now portrayed us as psychopaths and murderers. In a later article, Vito Russo raised other issues.

> When Billy Friedkin decided to film what Hollywood has always decided to film – the visible gay ghetto – they [respectable middle-class gays] freaked out. We don't want *those* people representing us on the screen while we're trying to tell the world that we're just as All-American as everyone else.[14]

Cruising wasn't the only controversy. Earlier that month, women from the Toronto Rape Crisis Centre and WAVAW protested the opening of *Windows*. The film's storyline featured a lesbian who hires a man to rape a woman she is in love with, in order to convince her not to sleep with men. In an article about both movies, Susan Cole wrote in *Broadside* that "*Cruising* has no business on the screen." As for *Windows*, "women don't rape. Men do. But *Windows* tells us that lesbians, not men and male institutions, threaten the security of women."[15]

American gay glossies *After Dark, Blueboy,* and *Mandate,* on the other hand, came out in favour of the film, and *Mandate*'s feature "The Men of Cruising" claimed that the film challenged the traditional "limp-wristed" stereotypes and promoted a positive, masculine image of gay men. The article proposed that gay liberation had nothing to do with questioning or challenging gender roles. "The whole gay movement is about freedom of expression," argued editor-in-chief John Revere.

Ken Popert alerted *TBP* readers to the censors "among us and within us," and talked about the ambiguity of any movie. Since there was no hope of actually closing down the film, gay men should see it and work for others to see it "through our eyes."[16]

When *Cruising* opened in Toronto, February 15, mainstream media were abuzz about the possibility of violent protest. That night, however, a dozen gay men distributed a pamphlet in the lineup calling the film "a gross distortion and misrepresentation of our lives and loves" and charging that it "can only serve to perpetuate prejudice and encourage this climate of hatred against us."[17] After a week of leafleting, a demonstration on February 29 drew forty gay men and lesbians calling for a boycott.

As a coda, Gary Kinsman and Leo Casey wrote an opinion piece in *TBP* opposing a "free market" notion of freedom of expression and distinguishing censorship by governments from boycotts by community groups. They argued that the underlying issue was the "question of the media's relationship to the community they serve" and called for "the widest possible community input and control."[18]

The traditional media stereotype was that gay men were weak and passive, certainly not a physical threat, except perhaps to even weaker children. But the image of the super macho, possibly violent gay man promoted in *Cruising* heralded a new narrative: the gay man as dangerous. The next media onslaught would portray us as not just a physical, but a political, danger.

GAY POWER GAY POLITICS

On April 26, 1980, CBS Reports aired a new documentary, *Gay Power Gay Politics*. Ostensibly an investigation into the emerging gay voting bloc in San Francisco, the program portrayed gay leather men taking over children's playgrounds for sex, murdering each other in S/M encounters, and intimidating municipal politicians. Reporter George Crile began his interview with San

Francisco mayor Dianne Feinstein by asking, "How does it feel to be the mayor of Sodom and Gomorrah?" Activist Cleve Jones was asked, "Isn't it a sign of decadence when you have so many gays emerging, breaking apart all the values of a society?" The program closed with footage from the March on Washington, as narrator Harry Reasoner intoned:

> Gay political organizations are acting all across the country. The right of homosexuals to organize like any other minority seeking to further its own interests is no longer in question. The question is, what will those interests be? Will they include a demand for absolute sexual freedom, as they did in San Francisco? ... It is no longer a matter of whether homosexuals will achieve political power, but what they will attempt to do with it.[19]

Gay Power Gay Politics portrayed the community as a single-minded, homogenous bloc. It ignored lesbians, never mind that San Francisco had only managed to elect one openly gay politician, who was murdered eleven months later. But it was effective. There was an immediate jump in bashings in San Francisco after *Gay Power* was aired. Bootlegged copies were widely circulated by right-wing groups like televangelist Jerry Falwell's Moral Majority and were instrumental in defeating gay rights initiatives in a number of California cities.

The fallout was by no means restricted to the United States. Stephen Lewis, human rights advocate and former head of the Ontario NDP – the only party to endorse even a limited version of gay rights – was among those to react. On his radio program he described his "sense of revulsion" and warned listeners about the "horribly menacing" gay lobby. In a *TBP* commentary, Michael Lynch called the program a "well crafted sermon with one lesson: wake up America, or gay voters will terrorize your city too."[20] If Lewis could be taken in by the program, Lynch suggested, we were in real trouble.

In response to complaints, the U.S. National News Council ruled that *Gay Power Gay Politics* "tended to reinforce stereotypes ... exaggerated political concessions to gays, and made them appear as threats to public morals and decency." But despite a CBS apology, the horse was out of the barn. The frame was set for a new wave of anti-gay politics. The motto was no longer "Save our children." It was "Don't let *it* spread."

THE NEW RIGHT

Gay Power Gay Politics was music to the ears of a powerful new political force emerging in the United States and spilling into Canada. The "new right" focused on social rather than economic issues. It was often organized through evangelical churches and their media empires, and trumpeted "traditional family values." In response to a cosmopolitan, urban, liberal elite, and its individualist and egalitarian values, the new right reactivated traditional conservative values of family and nation under the authority of God and patriarch.

It had immediate resonance with those the economic crisis was most hurting: the middle class whose fortunes were declining, non-unionized working people, small businesses, and the rural poor.

So the family became an ideological battleground. The right supported a traditional version, while the gay left attacked it as the root of homophobia. The success of Bryant's Save Our Children campaign in Florida demonstrated to new right tacticians how homophobia was important high ground to be exploited.

Others on the progressive end of the spectrum tried to reappropriate the term. Bumper stickers and buttons proclaimed "Hate is Not a Family Value," and we danced defiantly to Sister Sledge's "We Are Family," with the accent on the "we." But family values soon took on a clear social meaning, and it was not gay friendly.

The new right was far from spontaneous. It was the result of years of work and strategizing by right-wing think tanks such as the American Enterprise Institute and the Heritage Foundation. Privately funded organizations had always sought to advise government and political parties on policy, usually with advice that reflected the interests of their funders. Think tanks began to proliferate in the 1970s, after the anti–Vietnam war movement, Black Power, and the women's movement began to take on anti-capitalist rhetoric. In 1970, in a memo to the U.S. National Chamber of Commerce, Supreme Court Justice Lewis Powell called on business leaders and conservatives to fund institutes that would stem the tide and promote a more conservative business perspective. In response, the Heritage Foundation was set up in 1973 by beer magnate Joseph Coors. Its mission was to "formulate and promote conservative public policies based on the principles of free enterprise, limited government, individual freedom, traditional American values, and a strong national defense."[21] Dozens of similar think tanks soon followed.

Although its ostensible focus was culture, the new right dovetailed perfectly with the small government, free enterprise, anti-union message central to the neo-liberal economic turn. Although neo-liberal policies would undermine traditional family life and corrode national economies in the name of globalization, ideologues deployed "family values" and nationalism to help outmanoeuvre their rivals in the Washington establishment. This was a fight between elites over the future direction of capitalism.

So even as it presented a down-home grassroots persona, the new right was based on significant moneyed and conservative elite support. With such funding, it employed cutting-edge marketing strategies. It soon recognized that rather than doing any sober analysis of their material interests, people were more likely to vote for parties they felt reflected their values. Those promoting business interests began to speak the language of social conservatism and to seek support in developing networks of religious conservatives.

One of the leading new right groups was the Moral Majority. Founded in

June 1979, its aim was to overcome the division between church and state. Falwell's *Old Time Gospel Hour* gave the Moral Majority immediate outreach and fundraising capacities. It soon boasted four million members and two million funders. It was always strongest in the South, but it established Christian Political Action Committees in twenty states using direct-mail campaigns, telephone hotlines, rallies, and Falwell's religious television broadcasts to extend its influence.

The new right had its eyes set on the White House, and Republican presidential candidate Ronald Reagan spoke its language. The Moral Majority endorsed Reagan and spent more than ten million dollars to portray Reagan's opponent, Jimmy Carter, as un-Christian and a traitor to the South.

Such political aspirations were further bolstered by a shift to the right in the other Anglo democracies. Margaret Thatcher's Tories won the British elections in May 1979, and Joe Clark defeated Trudeau's Liberals in Canada the same month. We were seeing a sea change in both economics and politics.

WHO ARE "WE," ANYWAY?

The new right saw gays and lesbians as a dangerous minority. We saw ourselves as an oppressed minority. Other than the adjectives, we were very much on the same conceptual page.

In the spring of 1980, *TBP* scraped together enough money to fly me to Barcelona to represent the newspaper at the Second Annual Conference of the International Gay Association. The IGA had formed two years before in Coventry, England. The 1980 conference was organized by the Front d'Alliberament Gai de Catalunya (Catalan Gay Liberation Front, FAGC) and the Grup de Lluita per l'Alliberament de la Lesbiana (Group in Struggle for Lesbian Liberation, GLAL).

Barcelona was tremendously exciting and exhausting. In some ways it was very familiar. There was an inconclusive debate on age of consent, and another around the role of lesbians and whether the term "gay" already included lesbians or "lesbian" should be added to the group's name. What was different, however, was the Spanish movement's understanding of what gay liberation was all about.

Spain was just emerging from the Franco dictatorship and the underground lesbian and gay movement was closely entwined with, and spoke in the accents of, the underground left-wing movement, whether communist, Trotskyist, or anarchist. That took me back to the small group of activists that I had become part of after coming out in 1974. In addition, both FAGC and the main group in the Basque country, Euskal Herriko Gay Askapen Mugimendua (Basque Gay Liberation Movement, EHGAM), understood the role of the gay movement as part of a larger struggle for social change to liberate everyone's same-sex desire. That was in real contrast with the ethnic minority concept that was hegemonic back in Canada, the United States, and northern

Europe. We took for granted that gay people were a distinct minority. They took for granted that everyone had the capacity for gay relationships.

It was a moment that made me question my own cultural assumptions and aware of how much had changed since I read the early gay liberation materials of the 1970s.

Mariana Valverde had pointed out the same thing in an earlier report after a visit to Spain. "The FAGC argues ... that 'liberation does not consist of being tolerated' and that a true revolution will spell the end of the very distinction between homo and heterosexuality. . . . All people have the potential for a pluri-sexual orientation."[22]

Ken Popert wasn't at the conference, but at about the same time he wrote an article in *TBP* about the dangers of the minority "game." He pointed out that gay people had used different concepts to make sense of homosexuality – "[Hirschfeld's] Third Sex (analogy with women), the Minority Community (analogy with racial and ethnic groups) and the Lifestyle (an analogy with patterns of commodity consumption)."[23] He argued that the Minority Community concept was plausible, fit with multiculturalism, and was palatable to liberal rights discourse. But it was a game, nonetheless.

Fewer and fewer of us, however, were capable of thinking about it in that way. The fact that we were a minority community was just common sense.

ESSENTIALISM

A review of a new book, John Boswell's *Christianity and Social Tolerance*, opened up a related front. Boswell's book was an early example of a new wave of gay scholarship emerging from the universities. In the early 1970s, activists like Dennis Altman were the movement's theoreticians. But Gay Academic Unions had fought to legitimize lesbian and gay themes in various academic disciplines. That was now bearing fruit, even as it shifted the locus of power from the streets to the ivory tower, from activists to professors.

Boswell's book claimed to find surprising tolerance for, even celebration of, same-sex relationships in medieval Christianity. That was a challenge to theories that claimed religion as the fount of sex negativity and homophobia. The book was favourably reviewed in *TBP*, but there was a significant criticism:

> Boswell constantly assumes that human sexuality is, at root, essentially fixed and that the modern tendency to divide humanity into homosexuals and heterosexuals is valid for earlier periods as well. This leads him to believe that historical variation is a matter of ideology alone – that is *attitudes* towards homosexuals – rather than the very nature of sexuality and its organization. Thus for him, homosexual acts are performed by "gay people" and one can legitimately speak of "gay subcultures" differing from our own only in detail.[24]

Here we had an opening salvo in the ongoing debate. Essentialists felt sexual orientation was a constant through time and space; social constructionists felt sexuality itself is socially and culturally organized and fundamentally different across time and space. Boswell was being accused of essentialism. This was a variation on a yet older debate about whether nature or culture was primarily responsible for human behaviour.

The battle even surfaced on the dance floor. While Diana Ross took the essentialist position with "I'm Coming Out," Sylvester gestured towards social construction, in "You Make Me Feel, Mighty Real."

The essentialist position easily slipped into sociobiology to trumpet the existence of a gay gene. In practice, essentialist positions, including the search for the gay gene, were attractive to those who sought assimilation. They coincided nicely with the notion of a fixed gay minority and served as an antidote to homophobic positions that saw same-sex sex as bad behaviour that could be corrected. If there was a gay gene, we were "natural" and should be accepted in the same way that other minorities were accepted.

Left activists were more likely to promote the social constructionist position. There was a long history of those in power positing biological difference to justify their privilege – men were biologically dominant, women subservient, whites biologically superior, non-whites inferior. Popert warned, "Sociobiology is the ideological consort of the Right. It suggests that the social order is biological, natural, immutable. Movements for social change, which assume that the social order is artificial and alterable, labour in vain."[25]

While social constructionist ideas quickly dominated in the academy, essentialist ideas were more likely to find resonance on the ground. The notion of gay people as a stable minority had become widely accepted. Although in 1980 the debate still seemed academic, it would prove to have more direct political consequences in the future.

THE END OF AN ERA

As if to signal a changing world, several venerable organizations disappeared. GATE Toronto passed with hardly a whimper. It last appeared in the *TBP* community page in July 1979 with a post box but no phone number. GATE Vancouver formally dissolved, citing financial pressures and an overtaxed membership. A final statement criticized the shift towards social services and lobbying and reiterated that real freedom was not possible "without a complete restructuring of society's institutions."[26]

A few months later, over the July 1 weekend, 1980, the national coalition that both GATE Vancouver and Toronto had been instrumental in creating also disappeared. The Canadian Lesbian and Gay Rights Coalition dissolved at its eighth annual conference in Calgary. Fewer than half of the organization's member groups even bothered to attend.

The CLGRC's dissolution came just a year after Michael Lynch had presciently announced the end of the human rights decade. In the end, the

CLGRC could not resolve either its internal contradictions or adapt to a changing external environment.

Internally, the CLGRC supported both equality and democracy. When it came to gender, the two could not be squared. Equality between lesbians and gay men foundered on the fact that lesbians were always significantly in the minority. Giving women equal weight in the organization ran up against the democratic principle of one organization, one vote. But a coalition dominated by men could never adequately represent lesbians.

From the beginning, there had been tension between service and recreational organizations and the political groups that first convened the coalition and initially set its national agenda. But as service and recreational organizations catering to immediate local needs continued to grow, and the political agenda stalled, the coalition – with its incessant debates about strategy, tactics, and gender balance – seemed less and less relevant.

There was brave talk of two new groups. One would continue to organize yearly national conferences. Another, the Canadian Association of Lesbians and Gay Men (CALGM), would continue to lobby the federal government, but without unpalatable demands for abolition of age of consent and pornography legislation. Both groups felt more like something everyone was pretending to believe in, in order to make the whole thing seem less depressing.

The idea of a mass movement of lesbian and gay groups from every part of the country uniting for a common program of legislative change was effectively dead. For the foreseeable future, issues and efforts would be local or provincial. The old activist core that had dominated the CLGRC could no longer shape the movement, if indeed it could be said that a movement continued to exist at all.

RE-EVALUATIONS

Brian Mossop was one of the old guard, but he did not mourn the death of the CLGRC. He might have also been picking up on the development of the emerging "liberated territory" along Church Street. His comments in *TBP* signalled a shift in fundamental strategy. The long discussions of lesbian participation had gone nowhere, he argued. They had been based on the assumption that feminism and gay liberation flowed from the same source.

> Instead there should be a discussion of how gay men are going to organize other gay men. Can it be done by associating ourselves with the women's movement, or do we have to look at places we haven't looked at seriously before – like the ghetto? We've got to stop rejecting the [Church Street] ghetto as being contrary to some golden-age view of what gay lib was like before the commercial scene became a force.[27]

It was a position that he put forward more thoroughly later in an article, "Gay Men's Feminist Mistake." Feminism, he argued, was drawn from the experience of women in a sexist society. Gay men's experiences were different, and they required a different theory that spoke directly to that reality. For example, rather than condemning the "moustache-and-check-shirt look" as sexist, gay men needed to recognize its ambiguity. "It's hard to imagine a movement of gay men getting anywhere without the fundamental bond of 'men loving men' *just as they are,* with all the contradictions of people raised in a sexist society. To hate ourselves as men is as harmful as to feel guilty about being gay."[28]

There were two entwined issues here. The first was that gay men had to unapologetically organize around the issues that were directly important to gay men. The second, that we should no longer see the business sector as the enemy. The original movement had reviled gay business and the commercial scene and ideologically embraced feminism. It hadn't worked. While we could unite with feminists on certain issues, we fundamentally needed to embrace the issues of men involved in the ghetto. While many feminists would decry S/M as a manifestation of male violence, for example, gay men needed to fight to keep places like the Barracks open.

Mossop received a lot of blowback in the letters pages, but his points echoed one that many lesbians had made. Gay men and lesbians were different and had different interests. Meanwhile, the new alliances with gay businesses were reshaping gay politics.

COMING OUT

For activists, coming out had been the litmus test for commitment to the movement. In another heretical move, Jane Rule gored even that sacred cow, pointing out that the risks involved were very different for different people. While being gay and proud had made "an enormous difference to a generation of urban gay people," for others, "self acceptance can't come from the gay community alone but must include the understanding of parents, husbands, wives, children, co-workers." She warned against using coming out as "moral club to threaten people still in the closet. . . . It is neither true nor kind to suggest that their silence is necessarily part of our oppression."[29]

This time Mossop spoke up for tradition, calling Rule's column "appalling." "Nonsense," he replied, "The best time to come out is *right now*! And we should be encouraging everyone to do so, not telling them they really needn't since we are carrying the torch for them." He asserted that he had never encountered anyone "who *regretted* burning their closet." A few of us coming out would never be enough "to create a climate so changed that there is really no danger even for the most vulnerable."[30]

At the time, the back and forth was assumed to refer to the urban versus rural divide. Rule's position was conditioned by her life on Galiano Island. Mossop's community was the world of downtown Toronto. But the debate foreshadowed conflicts that would become important as society and the community became less homogenous and intersectional notions of social power came into focus. Not everyone ran the same risks in coming out. Risk often correlated with other social locations including race, immigration status, or gender.

CENSORSHIP

In April 1980, Winnipeg police advised two major book retailers, Coles and Classics Bookstores, to take the *Joy of Gay Sex* and the *Joy of Lesbian Sex* off their shelves or face prosecution. In July, Toronto's Glad Day Bookshop was notified by Canada Customs that five titles shipped from the United States had been seized and banned as "immoral or indecent."

We had framed the raid on *TBP* as an erosion of existing civil liberties. But the provincial and federal governments had always felt that restricting what people could say or see or read was in their purview. The Ontario Censor Board was set up in 1911 to preview all films publicly screened in the province. In 1975 its power was extended to the approval of videotapes as well. By the 1980s, the board rated films and videos to restrict viewers by age, could require cuts to scenes deemed objectionable, and could ban films altogether if they failed to comply. To add insult to injury, the board charged distributors to assess their films, making it prohibitively expensive to legally screen small-scale, independent productions. Failure to follow the censor board's strictures could result in the intervention of Project "P."

The censor board's members were appointed by the province, and since the Progressive Conservative party had held power since 1943, the board reflected a traditional notion of morality. In 1978 it banned Louis Malle's award-winning film *Pretty Baby*, and in 1980, the Academy Award–winning *Tin Drum*.

By the 1980s, as the prices of both making videos and purchasing tape decks decreased, videotape became the medium of preference for an emerging arts scene in the city and the major medium for gay porn. The censor board and the police struggled to exert their control under the muscular leadership of chair Mary Brown. Art galleries, artist-run centres, video co-ops, community centres, and alternative cinemas began to be targeted. This put the board in direct conflict with Toronto's burgeoning video arts and film festival scenes.

A new set of alliances arose between the gay movement and the arts community. Video and film artists such as Colin Campbell, John Greyson, Midi Onodera, and Richard Fung helped bridge the gap. *TBP* joined a new Coalition Against Censorship that planned to "illegally" show *The Tin Drum* without the required cuts. Only a last-minute compromise deal between the distributor and the board resulted in the film's release. Questions of censorship and pornography would become increasingly important, even as they helped erode the notion of a fundamental gay/feminist alliance.

Canada's Constitution, The British North America Act, was created in 1867 by the House of Commons in London. It was a relic of a colonial past, and while many had called for its repatriation and a made-in-Canada constitution, it had never happened.

Pierre Trudeau wanted a legacy, and to be the prime minister who brought the Constitution home would certainly fulfill that goal. As well, it was an end run around Quebec nationalists. A made-in-Canada constitution would undermine their argument that the existing act was a British colonial document, and could reaffirm the position of French as a national language. But a new constitution opened up questions of federal/provincial jurisdiction, and by 1980, after four years of fruitless negotiations, Trudeau decided to proceed unilaterally.

If Trudeau considered Quebec nationalism parochial and backward, his new constitution would be the antithesis: modern and reflecting liberal values. A key element would be a charter of rights.

In the fall of 1980, televised all-party committee hearings were held to solicit public input on the proposed charter. Over 267 hours of testimony, the committee heard more than three hundred presentations, largely from organizations representing women, Indigenous communities, people with disabilities, and ethnic and cultural minorities.

Lesbian and gay voices at the hearings were weak. Many women's and minority organizations were well established and received federal funding. They had research and legal budgets to strengthen their submissions. The only national lesbian and gay group, the Canadian Association of Lesbians and Gay Men, had been formed only months before with the demise of the CLGRC, and had no funding.

CALGM addressed the committee on December 11, arguing that the charter should specify sexual orientation as a ground for human rights protection. The position, developed by Vancouver law professor Robert Black, was about equality. Gone were the old CLGRC demands for abolition of the age of consent and pornography legislation. But even if CALGM had not already dropped those hot potatoes, the rights framework of the hearings made such demands largely irrelevant.

It was be CALGM's only major political intervention before fading away. The group was both lacking resources and beset by internal tensions. Chris Bearchell, George Hislop, and Peter Maloney were among those attending the hearings from Toronto. Bearchell was a leading voice for the radicals and socialists at *TBP*, Maloney a fixture of liberal gay small business. The two mixed like oil and water.[31]

The identity politics of the era also contributed to the isolation of lesbian and gay voices. Each group that addressed the committee spoke about the importance of its own inclusion based on a history of discrimination. Women's groups, for example, which could have raised lesbian issues, did not. We were not completely without allies, however. Gordon Fairweather, chair of the Canadian Human Rights Commission, spoke forcefully for inclusion of sexual orientation.[32]

The committee was hearing none of it. Progressive Conservative member of Parliament Jake Epp suggested inclusion would allow the promotion of the gay lifestyle to students. The Liberals, who as a party had previously passed gay rights resolutions, didn't want a can of worms opened in an already difficult process. When NDP member of Parliament Svend Robinson moved to include sexual orientation in the committee's report, the motion was soundly defeated by the other parties. The final text of the charter did not include it.

But the pressure had not been completely in vain. The final text of the Equality Rights section was left open-ended.

> 15. (1) Every individual is equal before and under the law and has the right
> to the equal protection and equal benefit of the law without discrimination
> and, in particular, without discrimination based on race, national or ethnic
> origin, colour, religion, sex, age or mental or physical disability.[33]

The "in particular" wording meant that the list was not exhaustive. Sexual orientation might later be understood as included. The task of prying open that window of opportunity would further transform the LGBT movement.

SHOWDOWN IN SAN FRANCISCO NORTH

Toronto was often described as San Francisco north. Now it looked like we could have our very own version of Harvey Milk, hopefully without an assassination.

There was to be a municipal election in 1980. In February, John Sewell gave *TBP* a feature-length interview in which he talked about his support for different kinds of communities. Sewell had certainly shown he was willing to stick his neck out to defend his principles. Although his understanding of the gay community still left a lot to be desired, the generally sympathetic interview was aimed at consolidating his support among gay voters. A subtext was the idea that the "next step" would be to elect an openly gay alderman to city hall. George Hislop was positioning himself for just such a bid.

Hislop's first move was to get himself elected as a citizen rep to the Toronto City Planning Board, an advisory body elected by city council to make recommendations on development issues. Hislop managed to corral support from both left- and right-wing factions on council to win a first-ballot victory. His election generated a media buzz.

Long-time alderman Allan Sparrow was not running for re-election, and Hislop set his sights on downtown Ward Six, which encompassed most of the gay ghetto. In March, a new group, the Association of Gay Electors, held a nomination meeting and proclaimed Hislop their candidate. *TBP* described the meeting at the 519 Church Street Community Centre as a "noisy, applause filled, emotional event punctuated by thunderous bursts of foot-stomping and cheers," and a "personal triumph for Hislop ... a popular gay activist since 1971."[34] Hislop had come a long way since being denounced as sexist and authoritarian by women at CHAT. "At City Hall we must ensure that women achieve equality," he explained at the beginning of his campaign. "Equal opportunity is not enough. Women start from a disadvantaged position so they must be offered more in order to bridge the gap."[35]

In April, Hislop won a second crucial nomination from the Ward Six Community Organization, defeating political newcomer Jack Layton. Although Hislop's platform reflected a range of downtown issues, his campaign was managed by Peter Maloney, and his support was drawn largely from the gay community. Activist Clarence Barnes called it "a tribal thing." For the city it was a public claim of gay territory. Ominously, however, as the final nomination vote was taking place, CBS was beaming *Gay Power Gay Politics* into thousands of Toronto homes.

Nevertheless, the Hislop campaign picked up steam. In September, at the opening of his campaign office, he was endorsed by Mayor John Sewell. The media described it as a Sewell/Hislop alliance. Despite Hislop's insistence that he was not "the homosexual candidate" but "the candidate who among other things, happens to be gay," media stories were full of references to San Francisco. The spectre of *Gay Power Gay Politics* would haunt the campaign.

That frame was reinforced by Sewell's only significant opponent, Art Eggleton. A lacklustre alderman, whose only council achievement had been passing a stoop-and-scoop bylaw for dog owners in city parks, Eggleton represented developer interests who had agreed this time not to split the vote between two conservative candidates. Eggleton played the gay card. Describing himself as "a tolerant person" but traditional in his values, he declared, "I can't agree with flaunting sexual preference." He accused Sewell and Hislop of "facilitating San Francisco–style politics at a time when parents in this city are concerned with the recent action of the Toronto Board of Education." He declared he didn't want Toronto to become another San Francisco where "the gay community pushed its way into city hall," and warned that if the Sewell/ Hislop campaign won, gays would hold "a mortgage on the mayor's office."[36]

Eggleton's reference to the board of education highlighted trustee elections taking place at the same time, where fears of a San Francisco gay takeover were being fanned as well. The wave of change that had brought Sewell to power in 1978 had also been felt at the Toronto board, and a narrow majority of reformers were in control. Combatting the effects of racism, sexism, and class bias in the education system had become a major focus of their work. Liaison committees between the board and certain ethnic and racial communities had been set up, and in the spring of 1980, a group led by activist John Argue asked for a lesbian and gay liaison committee on the same model.

There had been a great deal of prevarication. Homosexuality and children was a volatile mix, even for progressives. Tony Souza, then the board's new adviser on race relations, took it upon himself to educate the progressive caucus, most of whom had not previously known he was gay. After much back and forth, a majority voted to begin looking into setting up such a committee. Right-wing trustees were horrified. The *Toronto Sun* reacted with fury. It published a centrefold with photos of the trustees who wanted to let homosexuals into the classroom, calling for their defeat. The progressives tried to reframe the issue as one of human rights by including sexual orientation in the board's anti-bias statement. But the right wing then secured enough votes to pass a motion that the board "will not countenance the proselytization of homosexuality," and demanded a legal report on the advisability of including sexual orientation in the anti-bias statement.[37]

The gay issue permeated the election. The liaison issue at the school board, Sewell's support of *TBP*, and Hislop's campaign mutually amplified the hysteria.

The police also got into the act. Sewell had infuriated them by supporting calls from racialized and gay communities for greater accountability and civilian oversight. For the police, Sewell was anti-cop. Police association president Paul Walter sent out a confidential memo to members asking them to volunteer for Hislop's opponent, Gordon Chong. Anti-Sewell material was distributed from several downtown police stations.

A bevy of right-wing groups was activated. Renaissance International published a two-page ad in the *Sun* calling people to vote to preserve Toronto the Good. Metro's Moderate Majority distributed anti-gay fact sheets door to door across the city. Positive Parents held a Decency rally at city hall, and distributed leaflets warning parents, "Your children are the bait in a deadly game of gay power politics." The Family Freedom Foundation collected signatures and handed out anti-gay cards in evangelical churches. Protest candidate Anne McBride, who had worked in the Anita Bryant campaign in Miami, took out newspaper ads warning against "the homosexual takeover of our school board and city council." The headline of a pamphlet distributed by the League Against Homosexuals was "Queers do not produce: they seduce."[38] Many of the "statistics" used in this material were drawn from *Gay Power Gay Politics*.

In September, *TBP* lent me to the Sewell campaign. Sewell's campaign manager was John Piper, an apparatchik whose job was to win the election. My feeling was he wanted Sewell to play things down as much as possible. When I watched the televised debate with Eggleton, the mayor seemed uncharacteristically evasive and unsure of himself when questions about policing and support of communities were raised. Why doesn't he stand up for his principles? I asked myself. That's his strength. I was sure it was Piper's influence.

If *TBP* had wondered how deeply Sewell understood the gay community, I began to wonder how much the campaign understood any communities at all. I was assigned to co-ordinate the Chinese, Filipino, and Latin American wings of the campaign. The Latin American side made some sense. I spoke Spanish and had worked for years at the Centre for Spanish Speaking Peoples, so I had lots of contacts. Still, it wasn't like there weren't very competent progressive Latin Americans around who could do the job. The Chinese effort was led by a seasoned community organizer with deep roots in Chinatown. When I met him, I was sure he wondered why they had sent this white gay boy to keep tabs on him. I certainly did. Filipinos were still a fairly small community, and I knew many of those who had been organizing against the Marcos dictatorship back home. I basically turned things over to them and tried to keep out of the way.

I sensed the Sewell campaign felt that such immigrant groups weren't particularly important or competent, and probably wouldn't or couldn't vote, anyway. Since I was part of another group they didn't quite know what to do with, they put me in charge.

That feeling was reinforced at the first meeting of the Latin American group. In the middle of our meeting, Piper burst in, fresh from the opening of Hislop's campaign office. He was obviously worked up and had come to reassure the Latin Americans that lots of other groups were supporting Sewell besides gays. I felt uncomfortable, but the group was used to large white men who spoke patronizingly in English to them. They listened politely.

The discussion began in earnest in Spanish once Piper left. People did need to figure out how to talk about gay issues in their communities. This wasn't a politics they were used to. Finally, a Salvadorian refugee spoke. He was straightforward. He admitted many people in his community, as in all communities, didn't understand gay issues. But he pointed out that gay people in San Francisco had just raised five thousand dollars for Nicaraguan solidarity. If these people are allying with our struggles, he said, it shouldn't be such a big deal to talk about gay issues in our communities. The rest of the group nodded in agreement and then got on with planning their work.

In October, Val Edwards conducted a feature interview with Hislop for *TBP*, "The Time, the Place, and the Person." Hislop's face graced the front cover and *TBP* endorsed both him and the mayor. The pundits were confident of a Hislop victory. Gone were the days when he had been denounced as a reactionary and allying with liberal politicians an anathema. The prospect of real influence at city hall overcame any compunctions about vertical alliances. The editorial closed with a warning: "So even if Sewell and Hislop win, we cannot sit back and let John and George do it." But it concluded, "During the next few weeks, the gay people of Toronto must either reach for the future or cling to the past. We cannot turn away from the choice."[39]

At the end of October something extraordinary happened, or rather, the usual Halloween homophobic ritual didn't. There were no attacks on the St.

Charles. Not an egg was thrown. Police set up barricades to narrow the sidewalks and kept pedestrians moving. They also patrolled the back alleys. Although they claimed this had nothing to do with the election, after so many years of inaction that seemed hard to believe. The St. Charles was smack in the middle of Ward Six. It looked like gay power was already paying off. We were on the cusp of a political breakthrough, and the hit song in the discos was Kool and the Gang's "Celebration."

Who was paying attention to the fact that a few days later, south of the border, Ronald Reagan, backed by the new right, defeated incumbent Democrat Jimmy Carter?

Hislop was not to be Toronto's Harvey Milk. On election day, November 10, he came in "a credible third" in a race for the two Ward Six council seats. Although Sewell substantially increased his popular vote from 1978, that had been a three-way race. This time he, too, lost, by just under two thousand votes. Several progressive trustee candidates also went down to defeat, shifting the school board dramatically to the right. The gay liaison was dead.

Sewell urged supporters not to give up on the city, defending his stands on "good and valid issues." Hislop told supporters that "the amount of love that has been shown toward me and towards the people who have worked in the campaign and towards our community in Ward Six has vastly outweighed that hate we have seen demonstrated." But the blaming began almost immediately. John Piper was the first to say, "It was a bit too early in the 20th century for *that* issue." Defeated progressive school board candidate Sheila Meagher complained bitterly, "The homosexual thing did it."[40] The right-wing press was jubilant. The barbarians had been driven back from the gates.

Two weeks later, the provincial government introduced sweeping changes to the Ontario Human Rights Code. As expected, sexual orientation was not part of the package. Then, December 11, Michael Cassidy, head of the Ontario NDP, the only party to have called for the inclusion of sexual orientation, announced that it was "not a priority at this time."[41] The NDP would not even propose an amendment.

We had moved from being the irresistible force that threatened city hall to political pariahs. The worst was yet to come.

PART II

The Rise of the Right

5

Onslaught

RAID

I was just drifting off to sleep when a housemate knocked on the bedroom door. Richard was travelling in South America and I had moved into the tiny room at the back to save on rent.

I had spent the night studying for a mid-term the next morning. I was trying to finish off the BA I'd started at Carleton a decade before, and ECO 101 involved graphs that danced around depending on the values of the variables. It was a killer course, with a 60 per cent fail rate. I had turned in early to make sure I got a good night's sleep.

"I'm asleep," I groaned.

"It's Gerald."

"I'll call him back tomorrow."

"He says it's urgent."

Grumbling, I climbed out of bed and went to the phone.

"They're raiding all the baths."

"What?"

"All of them, all at once. Get over to the Club and see what's going on."

The Club Baths Toronto was about a fifteen-minute walk from Seaton Street. My roommate and I cut across Allan Gardens. It was freezing. The bare branches rattled violently in the dark. Rounding the corner to the Club entrance on Mutual Street, we were hit by an icy blast of wind. There was a police wagon and lots of black-coated cops. Like animals who had just finished a successful hunt, they ignored us. They had their prey.

A man walked out. He was short, stocky, in his forties. He seemed disoriented. I asked what was going on.

"They're arresting everybody. I don't know why . . ." He had a Portuguese accent.

"They let you go?"

"Yeah. They gave me this paper. I have to appear in court. I was just sleeping, not doing anything. I was there because it's a cheap place to stay. I always

137

stay there. Why pay fifty bucks in the Holiday Inn when you can get a room for ten? How am I supposed to know the place is illegal? It's been open for years. If people find out I'll lose my job."

"What did they do?"

"Who are you, anyway?"

"I'm from *The Body Politic*. The gay newspaper."

"You're gay?"

"Right."

"They can't do this to us. They got no right. This place has been open for years. It's not hurting anybody. They came in like an army. They called us faggots. What am I going to do? I've never been in trouble in my whole life. What's going to happen? Will they put our names in the newspaper?" He was close to tears.

Others began to trickle out. I tried to get names with varying success. Some were in shock. Others enraged. "Sure, you can have my number. You phone me, you hear. You phone me and tell me what we're going to do to get back at those bastards."

"Come on, man, let's go," his friend said. "Why did you give him your name? We're in enough trouble as it is."

Gerald Hannon arrived in a taxi. He confirmed it was happening everywhere. "There's going to be hundreds arrested." He headed off to the Romans, another bath on Bay Street.

Then they started bringing out others who were not being released. Burly cops loaded them into the paddy wagons. They were all shapes and sizes and ages. Some were handcuffed. My fingers and toes were getting numb from the cold when a young man stepped out the door, wedged between two cops. He paused for a moment as the icy air hit him in the face. He looked pale and exhausted. He was beautiful. They shoved him roughly into the paddy wagon. It triggered something. Suddenly, I no longer felt the cold. I fought back tears. I was enraged.

Needless to say, I didn't sleep much that night.

RAGE

The next morning, February 6, 1981, was grey and drizzly. The wind had died down. I blearily dragged myself through my exam and then raced down to *TBP*. The office was a madhouse, full of people, all the phones ringing at once. The meeting was just preparing to break up. Most of the collective was there, as well as Brent Hawkes, Don Franco, and old-timers like Peter Zorzi.

The discussion was now trailing off into speculations about why this had happened. Chris Bearchell said it was about portraying us as criminals, an excuse to keep us out of the Human Rights Code. Others pointed out that the Tories never had any intention to include us, and with the NDP running for cover, they already had what they wanted. "Hislop is calling it the 'gang of sergeants,'" someone offered. "With him and Sewell out of the way, there's nothing to stop them now." Someone else objected, "This is too big to be decided at that level. There were hundreds of cops. You can't arrest three hundred people unless it comes from the top. It's the election."

The group decided on a demonstration at Yonge and Wellesley, at midnight. Bearchell had insisted. I thought it was crazy. You couldn't organize a demonstration in twelve hours. How were people going to find out about it? And if we weren't a big crowd, Friday midnight on Yonge Street, we were going to get slaughtered.

"Everyone will know about it," Bearchell said. "There's four thousand flyers being printed. We're swamped with volunteers who want to do something. They'll distribute them. The phones haven't stopped ringing. There's a group doing phone trees. The media are all over the story. We've got the co-operation of the businesses. People will show up."

I was still not convinced as I headed to the intersection at about eleven o'clock to meet with the marshalling team. At least it wasn't as cold as the night before. Church Street seemed unusually empty, but flyers for the demonstration littered the sidewalk and covered the telephone poles. A few people were milling around when I arrived. The marshals had decided not to use armbands. It would make us too vulnerable. We all knew each other, anyway.

By 11:45 a couple of hundred people were squeezed onto the sidewalk. That was a respectable crowd. Maybe Bearchell was right. Several uniformed cops stood in the shadows across the street. By this time, every bar, every disco, every possible place that gay people hung out on a Friday night was being leafleted. That night there was no need to synchronize watches. No bouncers ejected anyone.

Once the sound system arrived, a squeal of feedback echoed through the intersection. People responded with a roar. More were arriving. Just as the first speaker started, the sidewalk could no longer contain us. People spilled into the street. One of the marshals rushed up. "We're blocking Yonge Street. We need marshals over there."

Yonge Street was an icon. The only thing that was allowed to close it down was the Santa Claus parade. We had no permit. But there was no place else for people to go. There were thousands of us. Tonight Yonge Street was ours.

Starting with a timid "Gay Rights Now," the spontaneous chants from the crowd got stronger. "Fuck You 52!" – a reference to the Toronto police's 52 Division, the staging point for the raids. Then there were the whistles, thousands of people blowing whistles. It was deafening.

Speaker after speaker harangued the still-growing crowd. Bearchell took the podium. "They think that when they pick on us that they're picking on the weakest. Well, they made a mistake this time! We're going to show them just how strong we are. They can't get away with this shit anymore! No more shit!" The crowd took it up. "No More Shit! Fuck You 52!"

The marshals were trying to figure out what to do. Someone signalled to Bearchell to stretch out her speech. We huddled. The original plan was to go north on Yonge and then over to Jarvis to police headquarters. It would be relatively short and would take people closer to the safety of Church Street. But by this point the crowd had a mind of its own. "Fuck You 52! Fuck You 52!" There was no choice. We were going south to 52 Division. Jim Monk made the announcement. We scrambled to make sure we had marshals at the front, back, and both sides, trying to keep people together. At this time of night, Yonge Street belonged to queerbashers.

It was also usually busy with traffic. But tonight it was an empty canyon, echoing with the sounds of whistles and chants. Tonight it was ours.

One thug along the side did try to throw a punch. He was immediately surrounded. The crowd had murder in their eyes. A cop materialized to try to pull the thug away, then several more. But they were all quickly pinned in a doorway. "Fucking fascist pigs!" Only the intervention of several marshals managed to save their asses. We swept on.

The police set up a line of cars at Yonge and Dundas. The crowd just rolled over them. Someone jumped up on the hood of one and pissed on the windshield as an ashen-faced cop inside stared straight ahead. We turned west when we got to Dundas. An eastbound streetcar felt it had the right of way. It stopped when a demonstrator pounded on the front window and it cracked. We swept on. A line of teenaged thugs formed across University Avenue just before the police station. Some had linked arms. Others took karate stances. The crowd didn't even slow down. The thugs scattered.

The police had formed a cordon around 52 Division, just past University. We came nose to nose with them. Peter Zorzi, who was in the front lines, described the moment:

> We come right up to them. SIEG HEIL! SIEG HEIL! We shout, give them the Nazi salute. FUCK YOU 52! NO MORE SHIT! The chants go on and on. Old memories floating around in my head. Cops pulling me out of gay bars to check my ID, the same ones who've done it time and again before. Snickering over names and messages they find in my wallet. Trying to humiliate me. Cops grabbing me from behind as I walk out of the St Charles, jerking my sleeves up before I even realize what's happening. Looking for needle marks they say. Cops, as I walk the streets in Toronto, calling me faggot, queer, as they walk by, drive by. Cops coming at me with guns pointed as I leave a gay bar in Montreal. Cops dragging people past me, out of the Parkside and Bloor subway washrooms. Cops telling me to move away or they'll arrest me, as I try to sell a gay newspaper to gay people outside a gay bar. . . .
>
> Now for once they have to stand there and take it from us.[1]

But it was a standoff. By this point the marshals had only nominal control.

Someone shouted "Queen's Park." The next thing I knew we were all heading up University towards the legislature buildings. I stayed with a small group of marshals at the back trying to keep people together. We now had a pack of queerbashers following us, waiting for anyone to fall behind. The crowd began to move faster. By the time the park was in sight, we were running. I got to the lawn, the grass crunching under my feet. I could see people hurling themselves against the doors of the legislature, the scene illuminated by the light of a single TV camera. I was sure the door was going to buckle. Then a phalanx of police arrived and drove everyone back down the steps. Once again there was a standoff.

But by this time it was close to three in the morning. The crowd was burning out its fury. We spent the next hour trying to get people to go home, or to head for transit or the relative safety of Church Street, making sure they moved in groups. There were only eleven arrests, most of them later in the morning when police and queerbashers went after stragglers.

We may have missed our Harvey Milk, but we had had our night of rage.

RIGHT TO PRIVACY

George Smith was responsible for turning rage into an effective response. As esoteric as his sociological Marxism might have sounded, he knew how to analyze concrete conditions.

The Barracks was one of George's favourite haunts, and he had been active in the Right to Privacy Committee since the beginning. He took over as chair after the first demonstration and set the agenda for the follow-up meeting held in the auditorium of Jarvis Collegiate, February 10. The anger needed to be channelled into ongoing activities or it would dissipate.

More than a thousand people showed up at the venerable school on the edge of the ghetto. The facts were becoming clear. Operation Soap had resulted in the arrests of 266 men as found-ins and twenty as keepers. It was, at that point, Canada's largest mass arrest since the War Measures Act during the 1970 October Crisis in Quebec. Damage caused by the police was extensive, and the cops' behaviour during the incursions had been viciously homophobic.

Smith began the meeting at Jarvis by opening up the floor to the audience. One by one, men who had been arrested told their stories of abuse at the hands of the cops. Perhaps the most powerful testimony came from John Burt, the son of Holocaust survivors, who explained he had never understood how his parents had gone passively into the Nazi concentration camps until he found himself being herded, naked, into the showers with other terrified men that night. That reinforced a remark made by one of the police at the Barracks: "Too bad these showers aren't hooked up to gas."

These first-hand stories had more impact than anything that was reported in the papers. This was an attempt at making gay sex illegal again through the bawdy house laws. The cops hated us and were trying to destroy us. We had to fight back.

We had organized straight support to demonstrate that we were not alone. Fran Endicott, Toronto's first black school board trustee, took the podium to speak about police violence and harassment of minorities. Menno Vorster, president of the Toronto Teachers' Federation, reminded us that the Toronto board had endorsed sexual orientation protection. A statement of concern signed by twenty-five city aldermen, writers, and civil libertarians closed, "Please be assured that there are many in Toronto, among whom we are but a few, who will stand behind you." Among the signers was Stephen Lewis, who had snapped out of his *Gay Power Gay Politics*–induced stupor.

After a general discussion, the crowd broke off into classrooms to organize aspects of the response – legal co-ordination, court monitoring, fundraising, media work, counselling and support for those arrested, and public action. Each classroom came up with a plan and those involved exchanged contact information. The legal committee would identify lawyers who would pool their expertise to ensure everyone got the best possible defence. The Court Watch program would figure out how to read daily court dockets and identify those who might not have been in touch, encourage them to plead not guilty, and let them know we could provide free legal representation. The fundraising team would raise money for legal bills, and would set up a trust modelled on the *TBP* Free the Press Fund. Counselling and Support made plans to deal with the emotional fallout of the charges. For many men, this was going to be their coming out to friends and family. Each of these committees would send representatives to the RTPC steering committee to co-ordinate the work.

Everyone at the Jarvis meeting was asked to fill out a volunteer sheet with contact information, skills, interests, and availability. The results were coded and computerized by volunteers. Overnight the RTPC became the largest gay organization in the country, with a mailing/volunteer list of 1,200 names.

THE STREETS AGAIN

I ended up chairing the Public Action Committee. We decided to target the Police Commission meeting February 12 and stage a second major demonstration February 20.

Media images of the damage to the baths fanned growing outrage. *The Globe and Mail* called the raids "ugly," describing them as "more like the bully-boy tactics of a Latin American republic . . . than of anything that has a place in Canada." Even Dick Smyth, the usually right-wing news director of popular AM radio station CHUM railed against the "ham-handed brutality and lunk-headed vandalism" of the police, and called them "pigs" on air.[2]

On February 12, while a hundred chanting protesters stared down the mounted police outside, the Police Commission heard demands for a public inquiry. They came from Alan Borovoy of the Canadian Civil Liberties Association, a group representing the majority of city councillors, journalist June Callwood, Jack Layton from the Working Group on Minority-Police Relations, and reps from downtown churches. Five days later, with no inquiry in sight, MCC pastor Brent Hawkes began a hunger strike.

On February 20 we again lucked out on the weather. The evening was mild with a light off-and-on drizzle as we formed up in front of the provincial legislature at 6:30. We soon realized that there were even more people than on the sixth. There had been time to organize. We had a decent sound truck with speakers. Hawkes, now into the fifth day of his hunger strike, reiterated the demand for an inquiry and vowed not to eat until one was called.

Alliances with other communities were a priority. Wally Majesky, president of the Toronto Labour Council, took the mic on behalf of 180,000 union members. A middle-aged Italian housewife, Josephine Godlewski, set the tone. "I'm a housewife and I'm not gay, but the people who were arrested . . . were minding their own business in a place of their own choosing. First it was the Blacks. Now the gay people. Who is the next? Me?"[3]

We linked arms and headed over to Yonge Street. Once again we took the street south to 52 Division. The station was surrounded by cops. David White spoke from the Working Group on Minority-Police Relations. A greeting was read from Allen Ginsberg, who suggested the police should try out the baths themselves. Pat Murphy from WAVAW told the crowd not to fear violence and to be ready to fight back. There was a rousing reception for Lemona Johnson, the widow of Albert Johnson, the black Jamaican immigrant shot and killed by the police in their home in the summer of 1979. It was an impressive display of unity.

We knew that the police were infiltrating the crowd with plainclothes cops. I was marshalling at the back again, so I didn't know that four had slipped in and positioned themselves to hold the main banner at the front. Gary Kinsman, co-ordinating the front line, first thought they were drunks. But when one tried to cut the banner, marshals confronted them and they disappeared. The extent of it wasn't revealed until days later when we looked at the news photos and realized that the same suspicious faces had appeared at the Police Commission. There had been six arrests at the second demonstration, three of them marshals who had tried to intervene in fights that, it turned out, were provoked by the same plainclothes provocateurs. We soon got their names. Chief Jack Ackroyd lamely tried to suggest they were "community liaison officers," but admitted that it was "improper" for them to be carrying signs during demonstrations.

BOARD ROOMS

At the board of education, progressives had lost their narrow majority in the November elections. The right wing was eager to settle scores. Tony Souza, the new adviser on race relations, was in their crosshairs. He had arranged the permit for the RTPC to use Jarvis Collegiate for its post-raid meeting, and had publicly expressed exasperation over police racism and homophobia.

The solicitor's report on the inclusion of sexual orientation in the board's anti-bias policy came to the February 23 board meeting. It argued that since the Ontario Human Rights Code did not include sexual orientation, the board had overstepped its authority in adding the term to the anti-bias statement. After some debate, the board struck sexual orientation from the statement, allowing it to stand only in relation to employment practices (to avoid a battle with the teachers' unions). Still remaining, however, was a policy that prohibited the "proselytization" of homosexuality. That effectively foreclosed any anti-homophobia discussions or gay speakers in Toronto classrooms. Souza, at least, thanks to the intervention of Fran Endicott, was not fired. He got away with a reprimand and instructions to restrict his work to racism.

At city hall, however, pressure continued to mount. On March 12, Mayor Eggleton agreed to set up an inquiry into police–gay community relations. He tapped well-known sociologist Dan Hill for the job. It was not quite the inquiry into the raids that Brent Hawkes had demanded, but it allowed him, after twenty-five days, to end his hunger strike.

OPEN SEASON

On March 31, after two years of legal skirmishes, police got to roll their trolley of boxes of seized sex toys and lubricants into the courtroom. The Barracks trial, from the December 1978 raid, had begun.

Before a verdict was reached, an array of charges arising from the new raids were laid against co-owners George Hislop, Gerry Levy, and Rick Stenhouse, who had also been charged in 1978, and Peter Maloney and two American investors in the Club Bath chain, Jack Campbell and Raymond Diemer. The new charges involved conspiracy to possess the proceeds obtained by crime, to keep a common bawdy house, and to publish, distribute, and sell obscene matter. Under conspiracy laws drafted to capture Mafia activity, each charge could carry a ten-year sentence. At a press conference the following day, April 23, nearly three dozen lesbian and gay organizations called the charges an attempt to silence police critics and to characterize the gay community as criminal.

Police also stepped up harassment of gay bars, charging several with liquor licence violations. And after he complained to police that a pick-up had stolen his wallet, a second man was charged with keeping a common bawdy house in his home.

Just as worrying were increased reports of queerbashings. Young thugs were taking their cue from the cops that it was open season on gays. Gay men's self-defence trainings had been offered since 1979, and graduates came together to organize an RTPC Gay Street Patrol. The patrol sent out squads on weekends to prevent or at least document incidents, since many of those attacked were understandably unwilling to go to the police. Naomi Brooks was a member. "That was a really interesting group," she recalls. "It was very mixed, men and women, a bunch of people who cared about the community and didn't want people getting hurt. We patrolled the gay neighbourhood, mostly the men's areas because places like the Rose [a women's bar] were over on Parliament and out of the way. We wore pink triangles."[4]

The reverberations of the raids touched almost everyone. Gay businesses felt threatened. Ordinary "bar and bath queens" who had never given a second thought to gay politics found themselves on the streets. Anyone reading TBP recognized that their homes and apartments could be declared bawdy houses. Hawkes's involvement brought MCC into the action.

The traditional social contract of the closet was broken as the safe spaces that people had always taken for granted came under attack. Anger and fear pushed the centre of gravity towards activism. The traditional small political core of the community was revitalized with new recruits, and through the RTPC, dozens of previously uninvolved gay men began to apply their skills to political struggle.

Not all of those recruits were inexperienced, however. Bob Gallagher had come to Toronto to do his master's in 1977. Like most of the early TBP crowd, he was from a working class background; his was a large Irish Catholic family. Gallagher had been involved in the anti-war movement in the United States and was an experienced marshal. His skills were invaluable in managing the large and often tense demonstrations that marked the rest of the spring.

The raids also echoed around the world. The TBP raid had brought Toronto to the attention of the International Gay Association. Now, those contacts helped facilitate protests at Canadian embassies in Rome, The Hague, and Stockholm. The Dutch Ministry of Foreign Affairs asked the Canadian embassy for a report on possible human rights violations. Groups in Australia, Austria, Belgium, Denmark, Finland, Germany, Ireland, Israel, and the United States delivered letters of protest to Canadian embassies.

ELECTION

The upcoming provincial election was almost forgotten in the fury of the raids. Hislop announced plans to run as a protest candidate in the downtown riding of St. George, but the mainstream parties were taking no chances. Rev. Bruce McLeod was chosen over gay activist Peter Maloney as the Liberal candidate, and the NDP picked Dan Leckie over gay activist John Argue. All the candidates, including the Progressive Conservatives' Susan Fish, ostensibly supported gay rights, but no party was willing to field a gay candidate.

Betrayed by the NDP, under attack from the Progressive Conservatives, and stonewalled by the Liberals, the CGRO opted to condemn all three parties. It urged lesbians and gay men to withdraw support as volunteers and redirect their party contributions to the coalition itself. In practice, that mostly hurt the NDP.

On March 6, CGRO held a Gay Freedom Rally, filling the St. Lawrence Market hall. Acting director of the Canadian Human Rights Commission Maryka Omatsu compared silence on the addition of sexual orientation to the code to the silence of politicians at the internment of Japanese Canadians during the Second World War. Hislop asked the crowd to "put a faggot in the legislature." Sparks flew when Toronto Labour Council president Wally Majesky obliquely scorned "single-issue candidates" and federal NDP justice critic Svend Robinson urged people to vote for the NDP. Neither of them understood the depth of the anger against the NDP for abandoning sexual orientation in the code and staying silent on the bath raids. Robinson was loudly booed. The hero of the evening was writer Margaret Atwood, who began, "When I heard the police had raided the baths, I asked, 'What do they have against cleanliness, anyway?' "[5]

Two weeks later, March 19, the Tories were re-elected with a majority. While the Liberals held their own, it was the NDP that suffered most, dropping from thirty-three to twenty-one seats. Despite the party's retreat on the issue, radical right-wing groups continued to target NDP candidates with anti-gay hate literature, and gay people refused to donate, vote, or work for the party that had abandoned them. Party leader Michael Cassidy resigned in disgrace. If the Hislop experience showed we were not strong enough to launch a politician's career, Cassidy demonstrated we were strong enough to destroy one.

OUR HOLOCAUST?

When John Burt recalled his parents being shipped to the concentration camps and a police officer at the Barracks referred to showers being hooked up to gas, both cemented a chilling frame around the bath raids that contributed to the mobilization.

The politically involved among us had long been aware of Hitler's persecution of homosexuals; hence the name Pink Triangle Press. The February 1980 issue of *TBP* had advertised the published script of Martin Sherman's new play, *Bent*. The play, about a fictional gay character in the Nazi death camps, was getting rave reviews in its Broadway run staring Richard Gere. That same year saw the publication in English of Heinz Heger's *The Men with the Pink Triangle*, the first non-fiction first-hand account of a gay man's experience in the camps.

In the November 1980 issue of *TBP*, I interviewed Gerd Blomer, a prominent gay activist in Cologne, Germany. Blomer had discovered that police in major German cities were still keeping a "pink list" of suspected homosexuals. Such inventories had been the administrative foundation of the Nazi roundup of gays after 1935. The article opened: "It takes substantial administrative capacity to run an efficient extermination campaign. Certainly terror, betrayals, spies and informers are all important. But the real basis of any good holocaust is something far more simple: a list."[6]

We knew police in Toronto now had in their possession the *TBP* subscribers and classified advertisers lists (seized in 1977), the Barracks membership list (seized in 1978), the Toronto Centre NDP gay caucus list, an early version of the RTPC membership list, and Don Franco's personal address book (all seized in 1979), and a list of all those arrested in the bath raids (1981). Together, those were the names and addresses of several thousand gay men and many lesbians.

A full-page ad for *Bent*'s run in Toronto filled the inside cover of *TBP*'s March 1981 issue, the same issue featuring the bath raids. The play opened March 12, just over a month after the raids. Michael Lynch made the comparison explicit in an April feature titled "Bent under Hitler, Bent under Ackroyd," and there was a follow-up review of the play in the next issue.

So it wasn't surprising that homemade signs replacing the maple leaf in the Canadian flag with a swastika began appearing at RTPC demonstrations. Pastor Martin Niemöller's famous poem beginning "First they came for the Communists, and I didn't speak out because I wasn't a Communist" was modified to mention homosexuals. At a Gay Asians Toronto benefit for the RTPC, Lim Pei Hsien choreographed and performed a dance piece called "Never Again." In the context of a resurgent right wing in both Canada and the United States, comparing the activities of the police in Germany in 1935 and in Toronto in 1981 did not seem far-fetched. This time we were not going down without a fight. The next few months provided plenty of opportunity to demonstrate that resolve.

THE BATHS

Richard was still travelling in South America, so back in Toronto, I found myself on the sexual marketplace. I wasn't interested in dating. That could lead to all sorts of complications, and Richard was planning to come back in the summer. I didn't like alcohol a whole lot, and as George Smith pointed out, bars had a very poor cost-fuck ratio. You could spend all night paying for drinks and then go home with someone who might or might not turn out to be fun. At the baths, however, you didn't have to drink. You paid your entry fee, and then had eight hours and dozens of possibilities of play. After the raids, I was spending a great deal of time working on the RTPC to defend the places. Smith's logic seemed sound, so I thought I would give them a try.

The baths opened up a whole new world. For the first time I felt immersed in this community that I had been doing politics around for the last six years. It wasn't just the variety of sexual options. I also soon learned that once they had come, it was relatively easy to get guys talking about their lives. With my background in sociology, I was like a kid in a candy shop. People had such fascinating stories, such different histories, identities, and views of the world. I found myself interviewing, counselling, hearing confessions, sharing intimate joys and sorrows, and debating with students, manual workers, actors, waiters, doctors, teachers, lawyers, engineers, bureaucrats, married men, single men, out, deeply in the closet, from all corners of the globe and of all political persuasions. I developed camaraderie both with those I slept with and with those I met but never slept with. Despite our differences, we shared a common lust.

At that heady moment, the baths also seemed a world capable of dissolving social difference into a shared gay identity. When we stripped off our clothes and put on a towel, what divided us seemed to fade away. It would take a while before I figured out that this "sexual communism" also had its own economy. Not all signs of social difference could be discarded with one's clothes, and social difference also marked differences in sexual "value."

A HOT SPRING

At 1:35 a.m., Saturday, May 30, 1981, dozens of police raided Edmonton's Pisces Spa, arresting sixty men on bawdy house charges. Edmonton cops had consulted with their Toronto colleagues and learned from their experience. When they kicked in doors and probed the darkrooms, they came armed with lights and video cameras. Men were captured on tape and told to remain where they were, until they were photographed with a paper indicating name, age, and occupation. Most were photographed twice, once naked and once clothed. There would be no difficulties in identification here.

All sixty were transported to a courtroom at 5 a.m. to be questioned under oath in front of a provincial court judge about sexual activity in the bath, without benefit of a lawyer. Although no one's testimony could be used against him personally, everyone's could be used against everyone else. The men were only released around 8:30 that morning.

This time the police actually had a complaint. Fred Griffis, a twenty-four-year-old gay man, said he went to police because places like the Pisces gave gay people a bad name. In a later interview with *TBP*, Griffis explained that he thought group sex was disgusting and that while it was "too bad" men were arrested, they should have foreseen the consequences. When asked if he would do it again he replied, "I guess I would, yeah. It's a matter of being a good citizen. I'm proud of this city."[7]

The Edmonton community was much smaller and more closety than Toronto's. Many men were from nearby small towns. The local MCC minister and GATE called an emergency meeting the next day, but the Pisces owner convinced the gathering against any public reaction. A week later he and another owner pleaded guilty, jeopardizing all the found-in cases.

The news enraged Toronto activists, but our focus was on organizing around the Don Franco home bawdy house trial on June 5. Then, a week later, June 12, the first Barracks trial verdict came down. The judge strangely acquitted owners Hislop, Stenhouse, and Levy, but convicted two employees of keeper charges. That night, thousands again took Yonge Street to voice their displeasure with the verdict and show solidarity with Edmonton. A major riot was narrowly averted by marshals when billy-club-armed police charged the crowd to pursue a man who had knocked off an officer's hat.

A week later, the cops struck again. Two remaining small baths, missed the night of February 5, were raided on Tuesday, June 16. Twenty-one more men were arrested. That Saturday, June 20, the RTPC returned to the streets, but it was getting harder for marshals to channel community frustration. Five months after the original raids, the police were unrepentant. The mayor's promised inquiry into police-community relations was stalled after Dan Hill turned down the job. Nothing had changed. To make matters worse, as the crowd again blocked Yonge and Wellesley, the police issued an ultimatum: clear the streets or they would seize the sound system and disperse the crowd by force. Hawkes, who was on the speaker's platform at the time, informed the crowd and asked what they wanted to do. No one was in the mood for compromise. We held our ground and called the cops' bluff.

When the speeches were done, we moved north on Yonge, heading for police headquarters. The marshals' attention was on an increasingly rowdy group of youths harassing the edges of the crowd, and we were taken unawares by a spontaneous sit-in at the city's main east-west intersection, Yonge and Bloor. When we got things moving again and arrived at police headquarters, a police line finally separated the queerbashers. There were more fiery speeches, and effigies of the police chief and attorney general were burned.

As head marshal, Gallagher had asked police to keep an eye on the toughs as the crowd broke up. But when we reached Church Street, the gang was back, this time armed with pickets torn from a fence. No cops were in sight.

I was one of a handful of marshals who tried to form a line between the crowd and the bashers to keep the demonstrators together. If people started to scatter they would be vulnerable to individual attack. But the crowd was not about to scatter. There was too much anger. We were quickly outflanked as people surged forward screaming "Kill them!" The bravado of the would-be queerbashers suddenly changed to panic. They ran like rabbits back up Church Street, several hundred demonstrators hot on their heels.

North on Church, the police reappeared, establishing a line across the street to protect the thugs from the demonstrators. We threw up a marshalling line to keep our side away from the cops. But things were out of control. When we were attacked, there had been no police. When the queerbashers were in danger, cops miraculously appeared to protect them. The crowd began to chant, "Where were you?" Behind our marshalling line people started rocking a police car abandoned in the street.

I didn't even see the billy club coming. My arms were linked with other marshals on both sides. I heard it rather than felt it. And you actually do see stars. Suddenly I was staggering, blood coursing down my face. The police had broken our line, charged the crowd, and were battering people to the ground. Complete mayhem. A cruiser accelerated into the demonstrators and Ken Popert, also marshalling, was thrown over the hood. People who tried to protect their friends were targets of police clubs.

I missed most of it. I was disoriented and some friends managed to get me to a nearby emergency department where I was stitched up and put on concussion watch. Popert and I compared notes from our respective gurneys. A young woman demonstrator appeared to have a broken leg. The emergency waiting area was full of others with cuts and bruises.

Six demonstrators were charged with assault that night. Despite clear photos of police violence, no officers were disciplined. The police were unable even to determine who had driven the police car that had tried to run people down and hit Popert.

The next RTPC meeting was difficult. It emerged that a number of our marshals had been involved in both the unscheduled sit-in and in trying to overturn the police car behind our lines, which had been the pretext for the police attack. I took for granted that when we called a demonstration, marshals had to do everything in our power to keep people safe. This was not just ethical. Practically, if people felt demonstrations were dangerous, they would not come. Marshals needed to be disciplined and follow the agreed-upon plans. It was unacceptable for them to provoke situations that put others in danger.

A few spoke about the need to express our anger. I replied that they could do it on their own time. Once they put on a marshalling band, their responsibility was not to their own feelings but to others. If civil disobedience was on the agenda, everyone had to agree beforehand. Those involved needed to be properly trained and ready for possible consequences. To do otherwise would be left opportunism of the worst sort and seriously damaging to the movement.

MOVING

Our house at 188½ Seaton Street, where we had lived for five years, was ground zero for RTPC organizing. Without warning our landlord announced that he would not renew our lease. We never knew if the police were behind it or not. Luckily, Jearld Moldenhauer came to the rescue. He still owned the large Victorian house just down the street where he had brought me after the 1974 Pride parade. His attempts at communal living had never quite worked out, and he wanted to move to an apartment. He offered to rent the house to us. Between planning legal strategies and organizing demonstrations, we spent the early summer lugging boxes across Dundas Street to our new digs.

In August, Richard returned from eight months in Latin America. We needed to renegotiate our relationship. My life had changed with the bath raids, and it would be hard to return to the tacit monogamy that characterized our first five years. We worked it out, and by the beginning of August, we were sharing a large front room on the second floor of 139 Seaton. The new

of the RTPC. I connected us to *TBP*; Richard, to Gay Asians Toronto and an
emerging Caribbean lesbian and gay community.

NEW ALLIANCES

The raids did not only transform the internal politics of the community. The
focus on the police as the enemy also generated new alliances. "You are at the
cutting edge of the struggle to get the police under control," opined former
mayor John Sewell. Civilian control and police accountability did not only
concern gay people. Toronto police were also seriously racist. The city's demographics had changed. By the early 1980s, the "visible minority" population
had already increased to more than 12 per cent. Yet the police force was still
lily white. Various formal and informal hiring practices kept it that way.

Most new immigrants lived in poorer inner-city neighbourhoods, areas
always subject to more aggressive policing. The association of poverty with
visible minorities and the vulnerability of such populations gave police a
green light to put prejudice into practice.

Complaints of police abuse were handled by the force's own Complaint
Bureau. Police investigated themselves with predictable results. In 1980 only
3 per cent of complaints were substantiated. Of these, fewer still reached a
court of law. When they did, the city paid police legal costs and convictions
were rare. Few people even bothered to try.

Albert Johnson's death in 1979 had intensified demands for an independent complaints process, but Attorney General McMurtry stonewalled
attempts at reform. In May 1981, the new majority Tory government introduced new complaints legislation. Representatives of forty Toronto minority
organizations including black, South Asian, and gay community groups held a
press conference to deplore the bill's inadequacies. Lawyer Clayton Ruby
quipped, "It should be called the Police Protection Bill."

A little over a month later, that coalition came together with progressive
city councillors and the Law Union of Ontario to announce the Citizen's Independent Review of Police Activities. CIRPA set up a phone line to collect and
publicize stats on police abuse and assisted complainants in pursuing cases. It
educated communities about citizens' rights and lobbied for police reform. It
demanded transparency and accountability in the police budget process.
Police Commission chair Phil Givens bolstered the group's credibility by
accusing it of "espionage and sabotage."

The RTPC's leading role in CIRPA helped legitimize the gay community
within a constellation of multicultural and immigrant groups. But extracting
formal recognition of the gay community from reluctant political structures
would be another matter.

THE RIGHT AND THE KLAN – AN EPIPHANY

I had left the Riverdale Intercultural Council in the summer of 1980 to finish off my BA. But I was soon pulled back in. The Ku Klux Klan, emboldened by the rise of the new right, opened an office in the neighbourhood in the spring of 1981. My successor, Bobby Siu, called me to help organize a community response.

Most Canadians considered the Klan an American phenomenon. They were, however, one of many incarnations of a long-standing far-right tradition in Canada that was racist, sexist, anti-Semitic, and anti-gay. In May 1972, for example, one of the first public gay meetings in the city had been tear-gassed by the Western Guard, an earlier far-right formation.[8]

I hadn't thought a lot about the connections between racism and homophobia. The Klan just seemed an extreme example of a general hostility to minorities. But when I heard them referring to gay people as "race traitors," the penny dropped. The Klan subscribed to a notion of biological racism and imagined itself defender of the "White Race." Race was reproduced biologically – through sex. So white lesbians and gay men, whose sexuality was not focused on reproduction, were betraying the race. In a flash the connection between racism, the sexist notion of women as only useful for child bearing, and the contempt of gay men and lesbians became clear. There was an underlying logic to their madness.

The Riverdale Action Committee Against Racism canvassed door to door with an anti-Klan petition, and in May 1981 held an afternoon protest in Riverdale Park. I was in charge of security. There was a brief moment of panic when a large group of leather-clad bikers appeared on the lip of the park, silhouetted against the afternoon sky. I rushed up to investigate and was relieved to find that the lesbian Amazon Motorcycle Club had arrived to support the demonstration. Later, when we marched past the Klan house, we were greeted by Klan members, some in full regalia, who stood on the porch screaming obscenities. But with our motorcycle escort revving, our side seemed at least as threatening as they were.

Dykes on Bikes, as the Amazon club was known, weren't the only queer presence that day. There was also a significant contingent from a new group, Gays and Lesbians Against the Right Everywhere (GLARE). It had been formed by some socialist-minded former members of GATE during the municipal election. GLARE linked the rigid enforcement of sexual norms, the emergence of religious and neo-fascist right-wing groups, and police harassment. The group warned that "the same forces that attack the gay and lesbian communities pose a threat to everyone who wants a freer, fuller life – especially workers, women, immigrants, blacks, and all who oppose the arms race."[9]

GLARE also helped resuscitate lesbian organizing, still reeling from the collapse of LOOT. Lesbians attending an April GLARE forum entitled Coming Out Is Not Enough organized a women-only follow-up a month later. That afternoon began with a panel of lesbians active in the women's and gay movements, trade unions, and anti-imperialist and anti-nuke groups, followed by workshops. "In the sober political judgement of the participants, the day was an outrageous success," organizer Lorna Weir wrote in *Broadside*. "Women who had not spoken to each other in years because of political disagreements and personal arguments were giving each other bearhugs by the end of the day." The conference eventually resulted in a new formation, Lesbians Against the Right (LAR), which defined itself as a lesbian feminist organization. "Externally, attacks on lesbians from the right, and internally, a process of political maturation, are combining to reconstitute the autonomous lesbian movement in Toronto," Weir concluded.[10]

THE BRUNER REPORT

The escalating hostilities and CIRPA's example of citizens taking things into their own hands increased pressure on city hall. After Hill turned down the offer to report on police–gay community relations, the proposal had fallen into limbo. On July 13, more than six months after the raids and the same day that CIRPA was officially announced, city council approved the appointment of Arnold Bruner for the job.

Bruner, a straight fifty-four-year-old articling law student and former journalist, was utterly naive about gay issues. On his first tour of gay bars, he expressed surprise that there were so many of us and that we looked so normal. But he was willing to produce a report in sixty days with a budget of $22,500, something that Hill felt was unfeasible.

Before he agreed to the task, Bruner asked for and received assurances of co-operation from both police brass and an ad hoc group of "gay leaders." The head of the Police Association, however, neither met with him nor made any such commitment. Many in the community remained deeply sceptical. George Smith pointed out that Bruner was approaching the issue like a journalist rather than someone heading up a public inquiry or a social scientist. "There is no investigation of police culture, but lots of investigation of gay culture," he said.[11]

Two months later, however, *TBP*'s editorial admitted, "Arnold Bruner surprised us." The report, released September 24, placed most of the responsibility for the crisis on the police and politicians. It called on the chief of police to clarify to citizens and the force that gays and lesbians constituted a "legitimate community" that was "entitled to the same rights as other minorities and whose individual members are entitled to the same respect, service and protection as all law-abiding citizens."[12] This call for legitimation would be one of the hardest of the recommendations for the police to accept.

The report also called for a police-gay "dialogue committee," and an end to undercover surveillance of washrooms and parks until the committee found a solution to such "problem areas." Police officers should undergo "awareness training," their general educational levels should be raised, and a program should be established to recruit lesbian and gay officers. City hall should include lesbian and gay reps in the Mayor's Committee on Community and Race Relations, and minority representation on the Police Commission. Finally, Bruner called on the government to include sexual orientation in the Ontario Human Rights Code.

There was widespread distortion of the report in the mainstream press, with talk about "quotas" for gay police and "special treatment." The *Toronto Sun* fumed that the report was "a sop to homosexuals."

One recommendation stuck in the craw of gay and lesbian community reps – that "the leaders of gay community organizations, in a spirit of dialogue, urge on the gay community the value of a moderate stance toward police, law officials and government."[13]

"We've already taken a moderate stance toward the police," retorted Chris Bearchell, speaking for the newly formed Toronto Gay Community Council. "We haven't taken the law into our own hands like some of them have." She also expressed scepticism that the problems between the police and the community could be solved by dialogue. "It's like expecting a rape victim to sit down and have dialogue with a rapist," she said.[14] Brent Hawkes, on the other hand, professed himself "ecstatic" with the report.

Serendipitously, Bruner's report was released the same day as the Don Franco verdict. After two years of court appearances and fears of losing his job and pension, Franco was acquitted of keeping a common bawdy house in his own home.

The following evening the RTPC took over Yonge Street again, this time as a street party with disco music, noisemakers, balloons, and dancing. It was both a celebration and a calculated counterpoint to the June 20 violence. It was the end to a tumultuous summer. The fall would find the fight shifting from the streets to the courts.

COMMUNITY BUILDING

The bath raids united gay businesses, activists, and formerly apolitical gay men in the face of a common enemy. Where *TBP* had once railed against gay capitalists and activists would be turfed out of bars, the RTPC organized discussion groups in the common areas of the baths and bars held fundraising events. And social activities were now seen as complementary to, rather than in competition with, political organizations.

The Toronto Gay Community Council, formed in March 1981, brought together most of the city's lesbian and gay organizations. Its basis of unity was broad – to share information and debate important community issues. The council provided a regular forum of communication between the political activists, social and recreational organizations, and community businesses represented by the Lambda Business Council. By January 1982, the TGCC was increasingly speaking for the community on important public issues such as police relations. Sub-committees focused on social services for youth, fundraising, the feasibility of a lesbian and gay community centre, and planning a national conference for the summer of 1982.

The Gay Community Appeal, on the other hand, had begun in the fall of 1980 as a low-key fundraising effort for the many new small gay organizations. It brought together an experienced crew of men and women. Harvey Hamburg, of the 923-GAYS phone line and Gay Days, became executive director; Dr. Rosemary Barnes, a founding member of LOOT, president; Thomas Beechy, an accounting professor at York, treasurer; and Karen Prins, of the Toronto Women's Bookstore, secretary. The group's slide-tape show was brought into homes on the model of a Tupperware party. After watching the show, guests were asked to make pledges. The appeal accepted applications from community groups and distributed funds once a year.

The first year, $19,000 was raised. The funds were disbursed at a gala at Toronto's faux Gothic castle, Casa Loma, in January 1981, just before the raids. Buoyed by the explosion of activity after February 5, the second year's amount exceeded $35,000.

The huge Gay Days dance in 1978 had demonstrated another possible fundraising model. In late March 1981, six groups pooled resources to host the first Gay Community Dance Committee fundraising event at 519 Church. Turnout was small – only 125 people – but when it was over, there was a small profit to divvy up.

In June 1981 an expanded GCDC took over the cavernous St. Lawrence market for a Pride dance that drew more than a thousand. A year later, the committee had a membership of more than twenty groups and regularly attracted up to two thousand people to two dance floors at the Concert Hall. The large upstairs area surrounded by a balcony played hardcore disco. The smaller downstairs room featured a lesbian deejay catering to more eclectic and mellower tastes.

Each dance involved over two hundred volunteers from member groups and six hundred volunteer hours. Ticket buyers checked off the group they most wanted to support on the back of their tickets. Profits were distributed based on a formula that took into account both volunteer shifts and ticket credits. For many groups, the GCDC was soon a significant source of funds.

A new women's concert production company also burst onto the scene, making Toronto a regular stop on the women's music movement circuit. Womynly Way, the brainchild of Ruth Dworin, brought in acts like the Wallflower Order Dance Collective, Rita MacNeil, Holly Near, and Heather Bishop, cultivating audiences for politically engaged women's music in the city. "Cultural work is one of the least threatening ways to get a message to people," Dworin told *Broadside*.[15]

TBP also turned to a broader community with the launch of the Out in the City section in May 1981, a calendar of events and activities spanning theatre, the arts, meetings, dance, music, and cinema. Important court dates for the bawdy house cases were listed to draw out supporters, as well as major progressive events such as peace rallies and solidarity actions. Another section listed restaurants and cafés, bars, baths, and discos. Businesses belonging to the Lambda Business Council were highlighted. A community section gave contact information for twenty-six social/political action groups, nine health and social services groups, five professional organizations, five religious congregations, four sports leagues, and fourteen women's services in the Toronto area alone. We also began to print more features on non-political activities such as the baseball and bowling leagues, gay choirs, the state of lesbian bars, gay science fiction, and the arts.

PRIDE

The summer of 1981 also saw Toronto's first Pride since 1974, initiated by the renamed Gay Liberation Against the Right Everywhere (GLARE) and the new Lesbians Against the Right. Both groups had formed as a militant response to the new right. But after a spring of confrontational male-dominated nighttime demonstrations against the police, GLARE and LAR conceived Pride as more celebratory, relaxed, and inclusive of women and children. More than a thousand people gathered in downtown Grange Park on the sunny afternoon of June 28 to hear music, speeches, and entertainment, and meander past information tables set up by local organizations. Child care was provided.

GLARE and LAR had to hold a special meeting around the participation of a newly formed "convent" of gay men who dressed as nuns, the Sisters of Perpetual Indulgence. Since many considered drag sexist, the Sisters weren't given stage time, but they worked the crowd in full habit without incident. When the march, led by the Amazon Motorcycle Club, stopped briefly in front of the 52 Division police station, the Sisters performed an impromptu exorcism.

Under the radar was another religious controversy. When Brent Hawkes decided that MCC should participate, part of the congregation resisted because Pride was "too leftist and too radical." But Hawkes was adamant. "If we're not going to be there then we're giving it over to those folks. We've got to be there."[16]

This was the first time Toronto Pride was held on the anniversary of the Stonewall riots, and it joined a growing number of centres celebrating the date across Canada, the United States, and Europe. The event's success encouraged the formation of a permanent Lesbian and Gay Pride Day Committee to prepare the next year's festival, with GLARE member Kyle Rae as a prominent voice.

Despite their role in re-establishing Pride, LAR and GLARE did not have long lifespans. LAR organized a Dykes in the Streets march in October 1981, and participated in the Gay Community Council, CIRPA, Pride, and International Women's Day. But it dissolved early in 1983, unable to develop a clearly defined set of goals or a unifying political strategy.[17] GLARE produced educational materials about right-wing, anti-gay myths and participated in similar coalition work, but with many members drawn to the work of RTPC and Pride, it, too, lost capacity and dissolved.

TO LIAISE OR NOT TO LIAISE

Halloween again. With the already increased number of queerbashings, and the relationship with the police at an all-time low, no one knew what to expect. Nevertheless, the police met with the Toronto Gay Community Council to develop a crowd control plan to keep things moving in front of the St. Charles. The RTPC street patrol was taking no chances. Four squads with walkie-talkies co-ordinated by a base station in a nearby high-rise patrolled the back alleys, kept in touch with each other, monitored police communications, and ensured the cops were aware of any trouble spots. As a result, there were no serious incidents and Yonge Street took on almost a carnival atmosphere. The police grudgingly admitted that our communication system worked better than theirs.

The de facto co-operation with the police provoked differences in strategy within the council. One issue Bruner had put on the table was a community-police liaison committee. The RTPC steering committee was opposed. A liaison suggested the problem was a lack of communication between two parties, rather than a state-funded, quasi-military organization using powers under the Criminal Code to systematically attack us. Laws and police procedures needed changing. That was not going to be achieved over tea and biscuits.

TBP quoted one Vancouver activist on the unspoken ground rules that had developed in that city. "We'll help to make it easier for you to ignore the parks if you don't raid our bars and baths." The article concluded: "The single and dubious accomplishment of the Vancouver Gay-Police Dialogue could simply be the transformation of gay representatives into willing accomplices in the policing and social control of their own community."[18]

But significant community voices were interested in exploring the idea. Hawkes argued for engagement. "If we don't have anything to do with them, nothing is going to change. We need the police at their best, not at their worst."[19] In March 1982, *TBP* editorialized about conditions for moving forward. The gay side needed to represent and be elected by the TGCC, with a regular reporting procedure. Council reps should share in developing meeting agendas. Investigating who orchestrated the bath raids should be one of those agenda items. Police, on their part, had to guarantee continuity and high-level participation. The goal was to influence policy, not attitudes. Meetings should have a neutral and mutually acceptable chair and publicly circulated minutes.

But, the editorial concluded, "the dialogue that will finally make the difference is the dialogue we negotiate with labour, with immigrant groups, with women, with civil libertarians – people, like us, who want democratic community control of the police force in this city."[20]

The TGCC set up a sub-committee to study the feasibility of a regular gay-police liaison. But the only immediate action was a meeting between the community council and the minorities committee of the Police Commission to create another committee to implement Bruner's recommendation of gay awareness programs for police officers.

CLASS AND CONSCIOUSNESS

In the midst of all this excitement, I published features in *TBP* about trips to Colombia and Nicaragua. The articles reveal something of a naive missionary quality. I went looking for "the stirrings of gay consciousness," which I more or less satisfied myself I had found. But the experiences also stirred my own consciousness about the conditions necessary for the development of a gay identity and a gay movement.

The Colombia piece was structured around long conversations I had with two young men, both of whom I met in parks, or rather in the *plazas centrales* of two medium-sized cities. The first man was a middle-class student, isolated and closety, not at all comfortable with his sexuality. Although he had had a few furtive sexual contacts, I was the first person he had ever spoken to who was out. He was very much outside any gay networks there might have been in his world. If his sexuality was discovered, loss of family support would have been devastating, socially and economically.

The second was a hustler, the son of poor peasants. He was at the centre of a nexus of sexual transactions with dozens of regular customers from a wide range of backgrounds. Unprompted, he identified as gay and had a sense of history. "Men have had their time. They've reached the top. Now it's women. Women are becoming liberated. They're starting to come out with books and magazines. But we haven't yet. Maybe it'll be our turn next," he told me.

In Bogotá, a city of about four million at the time, there was a critical mass of middle-class men with sufficient disposable income to support the beginnings of a gay commercial scene and recognized cruising areas. There I found several consciousness-raising groups and a small gay magazine, *Ventana Gay*. Most of the people I met were similar in background to my friends in Toronto. They had some university training and could aspire to a profession. Some of the debates were also familiar. Guillermo explained, "For us, a real problem is the false sense of liberation that the ghetto gives people. People say, 'Liberation? From what? Why?'"

Another young man, Manuel, drew attention directly to the question of class. "It's true a lot of bars have opened in the last five years here in Bogotá. . . . But who can afford to go except those rich enough to afford a prostitute or the prostitutes who are investing in their clients? How can you build solidarity between people divided into two such worlds?"[21]

Manuel was overstating the case. There was enough middle-income concentration in Bogotá to produce a critical mass of people who went to bars to cruise and socialize. The scene was not just divided between sex workers and clients. But he was on to something. The greater the class inequality, the harder it was for the glue of sexual orientation to hold community together. The greater the inequality, the harder to establish the critical mass necessary to produce a movement.

That understanding was reinforced eight months later when Richard and I went to Nicaragua. After a bloody civil war, the Sandinista National Liberation Front brought down the forty-five-year-old Somoza dictatorship in the summer of 1979. When we arrived in December 1980 to explore how the revolution was treating gay people, Nicaragua was still very scarred by war. There was a tiny, wealthy elite, a miniscule middle class, and massive poverty.

On New Year's Eve we attended a party at the home of a well-off businessman. We arrived early. His friends were similar in age and class. They complained a lot about how difficult things had become since the revolution. Some were considering moving to Miami. Managua was "such a dump," and it was so difficult to find a lover "of the same background." One talked to me about the "common people." "You couldn't really develop a relationship with one of them," he said. "I've tried, but the cultural gap is just too large. . . . Many of them ask for money because they are so poor. Of course they enjoy it, but they think of it as something like work."

As the evening progressed, more and more younger men began to arrive. From their accents and dress, it was clear they were drawn from the common people. I talked to one, a carpenter's son, about gay youth organizing in Toronto. He was fascinated, but explained that if anyone found out he was gay, "it would be the end of [him]." He would probably get married and have kids like everyone else, despite his desires. Our conversation was shut down by one of the older men, who loudly interjected, "A little faggot like you? Tell me another one."

A few nights later we went to the cruising area, the plaza in front of the Managua bullring. The area was full of kiosks selling food and beer, mariachi singers plying the crowd, and mostly female sex workers. There were a few tables where the men seemed to be gay. We were accompanied by Lucho, a young man who had worked as a runner for the Sandinistas while still in high school. In the Nicaraguan context, the fact that he was a high school graduate indicated he was middle class. After the revolution, the new government had even sent him to Cuba for a few months to study museum administration. Cuba had been a gay paradise, the first time in his life he had met others who were openly gay. He admitted he didn't feel much more comfortable in the plaza than he had at the New Year's party where we had met. "The rich men are against the revolution and exploit poor boys," he said. But the bullring plaza was peopled by "prostitutes and petty criminals."[22]

Class disparities corroded the possibility of gay solidarity. Without solidarity there could be no movement. For me, that meant that gay people had a direct interest in fighting for a society that minimized class disparities.

THE SEXUAL TURN

Back in Toronto, as I became more acquainted with bath culture, I even penned a "theory" piece about the baths in the July/August 1981 *TBP*: "Untangling Emotions and Eros." At 188½ we had been debating how social forces were reshaping people's sex lives. In the piece, I argued that in traditional, straight-dominated society, emotional and sexual relations had been entangled in an attempt to protect women from the abuses of male power, to facilitate stable child rearing, and to consolidate property. But modern capitalism, with its constant development of human needs, was pulling these two things apart. As society became more equal, recreational sex and emotional attachment were becoming independent, and capital was flowing in to meet and amplify the former.

Because gay men were not divided by gender inequality, our male income privilege put us at the forefront of this development. Straight people were still divided by gender difference, and the continuing vulnerability of women made sites of purely recreational sex a potential danger. Lesbians didn't have that same power imbalance, but were less likely as a group to have the required disposable income for the profitable development of similar institutions as gay men.[23]

The baths were the prime example of such a development. There, for a fee that made their organization profitable, gay men could find other men for sexual play, safely and efficiently, and in ways that either didn't disrupt or could be complementary to more long-term emotional relationships located in other sites and institutions. I even did a public talk on "the baths as the highest stage of sex under capitalism." Most people thought I was being a gay chauvinist and missed the reference to Lenin.

In the same issue, Gerald Hannon wrote "The Heart of The Mineshaft." The Mineshaft, one of New York's most famous fuck bars, was known for fisting and water sports. Hannon talked about the need to develop a new language to express the intimate emotions of such public sex: "I pissed in his face" versus "I tied myself to his body with the hot rope of my own piss." He continued:

> A great deal depends on how you say these things, and we have to learn to say these things together. . . . Our community is still something of a sexual baby that hasn't learned to talk, and one of the places gay men are going to learn to talk is the baths. . . . The baths and bars are the closest things gay men have to community centres. We go there to invent ourselves.[24]

I was trying to do a material analysis of evolving sexual organization; Hannon wanted to develop a new sexual vocabulary. Both pieces highlighted new interest in the importance of the sexual organization of gay life.

Not everyone was pleased. George Smith took umbrage at Hannon's suggestion that instead of privacy we should be talking about sex.

> While Gerald and the *TBP* collective have the luxury of speculating about new modes of saying, "I care. You are beautiful. I want to fuck you," the RTPC is engaged in the practical task of defending those arrested, building alliances to curb police excesses and demanding legal reform. Defense of "the right to privacy" has been shown to be an effective way of doing that. Speculation about fuck bars has not.[25]

Others had different concerns. Jim Bartley accused Hannon of trying to romanticize recreational sex to justify it, and countered, "sex alone is its own justification."[26] David Townsend pointed out that "entanglement of emotion and eros is from another perspective integration, and for some it is a goal, not a manifestation of oppression." He accused me of accusing the non-promiscuous of being "politically incorrect in bed."[27]

Jane Rule took us all on in a Deliberations piece entitled "Sexual Infancy." "Divorcing sex from love has real but temporary virtues. If we had been allowed to explore all those avenues of desire as children, the exercise might not have any attractions for us." She argued that "discovering that sex can become something other than a sport or a dependency is important because we have learned that by means of it we can express tenderness, compassion, joy, wonder and serenity, even though we are therefore more vulnerable to frustration, pain and grief."[28]

A re-evaluation of sex was gathering steam. Ken Popert elaborated the political implications. In "Public Sexuality and Social Space," he argued that promiscuity and institutions encouraging it were the fountainhead of gay male collective consciousness. He reminded readers that "the current, unexhausted wave of gay struggle began more than a decade ago in a bar," a reference to Stonewall. "Bars and baths are to the gay movement what factories are to the labour movement: the context in which masses of people acquire a shared sense of identity and the ability to act together for the common good." For Popert, "promiscuity knit together the social fabric of the gay male community."[29]

This was a significant shift from the assumptions of ten years before. Then, *TBP* had seen the ghetto as a place of alienation, and gay business owners as a self-interested class often holding back the movement.

This shift had political implications. We had originally taken for granted that it was shared oppression that made community. That was the basis for alliances between gay men and women and other marginalized groups. But if community resulted instead from the web of relationships generated by shared desire for each other's bodies, then the dividing line between friend and foe was about whether or not one supported the institutions that made that promiscuity possible. Popert's new thesis included bar and bath owners as central to the community, and promoted alliances with anyone who would oppose state interference into gay men's sexual lives – largely civil libertarians. The women's movement, once seen as a natural ally but whose majority voices called for greater state involvement in the fight against pornography, were part of the problem. The new formulation lent itself to a fading of attention to women's concerns, or for that matter, to the concerns of anyone else not engaged in promiscuous gay male networks.

Such alliances around sex were easier to theorize than to implement, however. In July, Hamilton police raided Ramblewood, a sexual swing club for consenting straight adult couples, in a circus tent outside the city. More than a hundred people were arrested on bawdy house charges. The RTPC was contemplating a campaign for repeal of the bawdy house laws, and the raid seemed an opportunity to ally with a new group. When I called the Ramblewood owner, however, he was at first noncommittal. When I called again he said that his lawyer had advised him not to get mixed up with the gays.

It wasn't just gay men who were reassessing the importance of people's sexual lives. In *TBP*'s issue 76, historian Joan Nestle argued for a re-evaluation of traditional butch-femme lesbian relationships. The dominant position among lesbian feminists was that butch-femme was "backward," a reproduction of heterosexual models that represented the depth of lesbian oppression. Nestle suggested that butch-femme relationships were "complex erotic statements, not phony heterosexual replicas . . . a conspicuous flag of rebellion and an intimate exploration of women's sexuality."[30] She accused mainstream feminists of trivializing the reality of lesbian lives in a bid for middle-class respectability.

The summer also saw publication of the Sex Issue of *Heresies: A Feminist Publication on Art and Politics*. Sue Golding began her *TBP* review with the statement "A long silenced and underground erotic politic among women is finally erupting." She concluded:

> If it can be said that the early feminism of the 60s was born out of a critique of patriarchy through male/female sexual (and heterosexist) relations, it can now be said that the strengthening and expansion of that critique emerges only when we look at the full erotic dimension of sexual relations by and with women. This means a comprehension of power – our power – and it means nothing less than viewing sex as something in and of itself detached from the old romantic trappings of "love." . . . The Heresies collective has correctly shown us that sex is not just an issue, it is becoming *the* issue.[31]

Finally, Gayle Rubin let off a broadside against the mainstream women's movement and lesbian feminists in *Coming to Power*, published by Samois, a lesbian feminist S/M organization. In part of a chapter excerpted in *TBP*, Rubin talked about coming out twice, first as a lesbian and then as someone into S/M, and how she found the second more difficult. The article spoke about attempts to silence and discredit S/M practitioners in the women's movement. She accused that movement of reflecting common anti-sexual attitudes and shifting to the right. "It has generated a lesbian politic that seems ashamed of lesbian desire." She feared that second-wave feminism was repeating the errors of the first, which had become "increasingly conservative and similarly shifted the burden of its argument onto a reconstructed femininity in the form of alleged female moral superiority. Much of the nineteenth-century movement degenerated into a variety of morality crusades with conservative feminists pursuing what they took to be women's agenda in anti-prostitution, anti-masturbation, anti-obscenity and anti-vice campaigns." She concluded, "What is exciting is that sex – not just gender, not just homosexuality – has finally been posed as a political question."[32]

It seemed that just as the certainties of both 1970s gay liberation and '70s feminism were achieving a modicum of legitimacy in society, they were in crisis among lesbians and gay men themselves.

SEX THEORY VS. POLITICAL PRACTICE

The sexual turn was a continent-wide phenomenon within feminism. But in Toronto, it was the experience of the bath raids that moved it to centre stage and provided practical evidence of its potency. Popert's notion of promiscuity knitting the community together grew organically from his observation of the response to the raids.

Although sex radical women like Chris Bearchell were instrumental in the original response, and many other women attended the bath raid demonstrations to express their solidarity, the RTPC was always a male organization. There were never women on the steering committee. The found-ins it advocated for were all gay men. The RTPC was a practical manifestation of the importance of sexual networks in generating community.

George Smith could theorize the pants off anyone. As a sociologist, he recognized the importance of Popert's thesis. The success of the resistance he helped orchestrate through the RTPC was based on the strength of such sexual networks. But as an enthusiastic (if critical) reader of Foucault, he was also interested in the ways state discourses and practices define and shape communities. As chair of RTPC he was primarily concerned with how police, as an organ of the state, defined and attempted to regulate gay men, and how that provided opportunities for alliances with other communities, similarly defined as "outside the law," principally black and marginalized immigrant groups. As a consensus builder, he saw no reason to antagonize the women's movement that also had beefs with a sexist police force, or those who supported the struggle out of civil libertarian concerns. So there was an attitude in the RTPC steering committee that *TBP* was often more enamoured with highfalutin liberation theory than it was with being accountable to the practical needs of community.

Another part of RTPC practice revealed the limitations of sexual networks. At one point, it was proposed that we organize a series of small socials to bring found-ins together. The hope was to establish stronger bonds between them and ultimately to involve more of them in the day-to-day work of the organization.

I went to one of the first of these socials, hosted by two relatively well-off found-ins who lived in a large condo near the Art Gallery of Ontario. The condo could probably be best described as piss-elegant, the men refined. In came several younger found-ins, retail workers. They hadn't thought to bring wine. They didn't understand the food. They didn't know what their hosts were talking about most of the time, any more than their hosts understood them. The dinner conversation devolved into a series of awkward silences, and as soon as the last course was served, everyone rushed off to other appointments, to mutual relief.

Stripping down to a towel might momentarily occlude class, and sexual attraction might transcend age in the baths. But such factors were no less constitutive of the identities of gay men than they were of anyone else's.

IN THE COURTS

That fall the action shifted to the courts. The last of the original Barracks found-ins appeared October 15, 1981. Two pled guilty and received absolute discharges; another was acquitted on a technicality. The guilty pleas were a wake-up call for the RTPC. While we were organizing demonstrations and ensuring the more recent February 1981 found-ins would plead not guilty, the three-year-old cases had slipped under the radar.

Two weeks later, on November 2, the men charged as keepers at the Romans came to trial. One man pled guilty and received an absolute discharge in return for dropping all charges against the other four, including the bath's owner. Since an absolute discharge was legally not a conviction, it was unclear whether the guilty plea had set a precedent that the bath was a bawdy house, or how it might affect the upcoming found-in cases. The plea bargaining had been arranged at the last minute by an old-school lawyer without input from the RTPC, and the organization scrambled to tighten up its legal co-ordination and improve communication with the defendants.

A third kick in the teeth came November 20 when Jack Campbell, president of the Club Bath chain in the United States, flew into town unannounced, pled guilty to conspiracy and bawdy house offences, paid a forty-thousand-dollar fine, and returned to the States the same afternoon. Campbell was active in the U.S. Democratic party's gay caucus and had helped finance the fight against Anita Bryant in Florida. George Hislop, one of Campbell's accused co-conspirators, called it a "complete shock." Peter Maloney, another accused conspirator, said he had been "actively misled regarding Campbell's intentions."

The RTPC steering committee fumed. If anyone had resources to fight such charges, it was Campbell. His excuses only increased our fury. He hadn't known there was a political struggle. He didn't inform his co-defendants because their phones were tapped. A year later, Campbell was appointed to the board of the U.S. National Gay Task Force. *TBP* editorialized that the appointment of "a traitor like Campbell" was "staggeringly bad judgment." The RTPC wrote to complain, and when it received no response it issued a press release to the American gay media calling on Campbell to resign. "Campbell had showed "total disregard to what effect it would have on his customers, business partners, the gay community and our attempts to change the law," said Hislop. "If they retain him in this role we must conclude that Americans don't give a damn about people in other countries."[33] Campbell continued in his post.

THE HUMAN RIGHTS OMISSION

The year closed almost as tumultuously as it had begun. On November 30, 1981, after years of submissions, demonstrations, false starts, back-tracking, betrayals, apologies, and stonewalling, the much-delayed bill to amend the Ontario Human Rights Code finally reached the legislature. With the Progressive Conservatives in control, everyone knew sexual orientation wasn't going to be included. Still, the now chastened NDP agreed to support an amendment, and a Liberal member of the House, Sheila Copps, agreed to move the motion. She was one of only six Liberals who would support an amendment. Even Liberal human rights critic Jim MacGuigan, a former supporter, caught *Gay Power Gay Politics* fever and backed out, muttering about "militant homosexuals in San Francisco."

On December 1, Copps arrived too late to move her amendment so an NDP member ended up doing that as well. But the moment was not about the vote. It was high gay theatre.

As the vote was concluded, sixty-nine to twenty-three against the amendment, activist Del Mansell stood up in the public galleries and shouted to the startled members below, "This is a human rights omission!" He had handcuffed himself to the railing. Mansell then began to read a list of groups who had supported the inclusion of sexual orientation in the code. Such interruptions were not legislative protocol. With the Speaker pounding his gavel for silence, Mansell was pushed back into his seats by guards.

But just as decorum was re-established, another activist, Paul Murphy, leapt up from the other gallery and took up where Mansell had left off. The Speaker lost control in the ensuing uproar and ordered the galleries cleared. Then Brent Hawkes handcuffed himself to the closest railing and joined the protest. No one was interested in going home.

When the bolt cutters had their way with the handcuffs, the manhandling was over, and burly security guards had cleared the gallery, the bruised but defiant demonstrators gathered on the front steps of the legislature under the glare of TV cameras. "The whole thing was worth it, just to see the look of shock and horror on Attorney General Roy McMurtry's face," said one participant.

DEFIANCE

Despite the early setbacks, the RTPC was able to convince the vast majority of found-ins to plead not guilty. RTPC Courtwatch volunteers checked court dockets daily to make sure everyone had support and proper legal advice. By December, the cases were seriously clogging the courts, and judges began to complain. Provincial Court judge C.H. Paris even suggested to the Crown attorney that the found-in cases simply be dropped. The RTPC legal committee kept the lawyers in touch and developed common strategies. The first was to make it difficult for police to identify those charged. If the arresting officer couldn't identify the accused, the case could not proceed.

In one case, a young Asian man was the defendant. The RTPC contacted Gay Asians Toronto, and the courtroom filled with Asian men. When the arresting officer scanned the room from the witness dock, he was unable to pick out the accused. The Crown complained. The defence lawyer asked sweetly whether his honourable colleague meant to suggest that he thought all Asians looked alike. The attorney turned bright red. The judge chuckled. The case was dismissed.

Defence lawyers also argued that the Crown needed to prove the accused had "prior knowledge" they were entering a bawdy house. In other cases they demonstrated that the accused had "lawful excuse" to be there – physiotherapy, overnight accommodation, or in the case of Robert Trow, running the weekly Hassle Free venereal disease testing clinic.

Dennis Findlay, RTPC Legal Defence Committee co-ordinator, handled at least a dozen cases himself when found-ins showed up without lawyers. Although he had no previous legal training, Findlay won acquittals in four cases and had charges withdrawn in another eight. By the spring, we averaged acquittals or charges dismissed in more than 80 per cent of cases.

Throughout this period, RTPC argued for an expansion of the notion of privacy. The Criminal Code suggested that privacy was about the number of people – two. George Smith, on the other hand, talked about how privacy was *constituted*. If those engaged in sex took precautions to not be seen, then they were constituting privacy, even if the sex was taking place in a "public" place such as a park. If they paid admission and went into a private place, like a bathhouse, then their behaviour should be considered private as well. The strategy was not to demand the right for public sex, something hardly acceptable to liberal allies, but to broaden the scope of privacy to force the police out of community spaces. The devil, however, was always in the details.

Many considered the problem one of police homophobia and argued that the cops were misusing the bawdy house laws. For them, Bruner's call for a liaison committee and better training would solve the problem. Smith, on the other hand, insisted that the problem was the law itself. Although the personal attitudes and beliefs of individual officers might affect the tone of their conduct, organizational behaviour was orchestrated by the text of the Criminal Code. It was that text, not attitudes, that needed changing.

There was an opening to do just that. The code was under review in Ottawa. The RTPC decided to intervene in the process. We needed to focus our effort on building support for a change in the bawdy house laws. But what kind of change?

A bawdy house was defined in the code as a place resorted to "for the purpose of prostitution or acts of indecency." There were two options. One was to ask for the removal of "acts of indecency" from the definition. This would effectively remove the baths from the equation. It would be seen as less radical and would probably attract a broader base of support, including many in the mainstream women's movement who considered prostitution violence against women. But the effect would be to distance gay men from sex workers, who would remain open to harassment and bawdy house charges.

The other option would be to call for the repeal of the bawdy house laws, period. That would generate an alliance with sex worker groups, and emerging sex radical sectors of the women's movement. It would be a harder sell to the general public.

Building on the full-page ad in the *Globe* that *TBP* had organized a year and a half before, we decided on a similar strategy. But what wording would we ask people to sign – repeal or reform?

I convinced Smith that we needed an open debate. It would be divisive for the steering committee to choose on its own. At an upcoming public meeting, I agreed to chair that part of the agenda. I outlined both options and opened it to the floor. Theoretically, this was supposed to be a contradiction among the people that should be worked out non-antagonistically through respectful discussion.

That proved hard to accomplish. Those of the more "radical" camp were less than comradely to those who felt we should just go for removal of "acts of indecency." When Kyle Rae, in high-left dudgeon, called those supporting reform "ignorant," I cut him off and called him on his lack of respect. He sat down in confusion. Unfortunately, the incident meant that fewer people then felt safe to speak openly. When we called the question, the group voted for repeal, the more radical option. But I wasn't happy with the process. Neither was Smith, who grumbled about the polarization that came from my "ideological two-line struggle" approach.

The campaign itself was a success, though. Once the statement was developed, we approached public personalities from different fields to ask them to sign. When that group was on board, we developed materials giving background and introducing our high-profile support, and solicited the mailing lists from organizations whose members we hoped would sign on. Thousands of letters were sent out to those lists soliciting signatures and donations to pay for the ad.

Smith and new RTPC chair Graham Crawford presented a brief to the parliamentary committee at the end of April 1982, and the *Globe* ad appeared June 2. Its headline – "The State has no business in the bedrooms of the nation" – was surrounded by the names and affiliations of 1,400 signatories. Its final two paragraphs read:

> This vague and archaic law threatens the right to privacy of all Canadians. It allows police to portray sexual acts in private as indecent and makes every home a potential bawdy house. It has led to open abuse against sexual minorities and criminalizes private sexual activity between consenting adults.
>
> To end the renewed harassment of gay men and lesbians and to reaffirm its intent to protect the right to privacy of all consenting adults, we urge Parliament to repeal the bawdy house provisions as part of its present reform of the Criminal Code.

It was a liberal appeal demanding respect for individual autonomy in the face of state repression. The police were portrayed as a conservative institution undoing the will of a liberal Parliament. But although it was an impressive show of support, the parliamentary reform process dragged on for years. And there was no bawdy house repeal at the end of it.

BERT SUTCLIFFE

The exciting parts of RTPC history are the demonstrations, but an enormous amount of daily administrative work was also necessary. The Courtwatch program, legal co-ordination, fundraising, and media work were all done by volunteers. Not to mention the many mundane tasks that involved hours of tedious, repetitive work.

Sometimes we mobilized RTPC general meetings. We would set up a makeshift assembly line with envelopes, stamps, and labels, and attendees would mechanically prepare mailings while participating in strategic discussions, listening to reports, and voting on policy. It gave everyone present a concrete way to contribute. Others worked from their homes.

It was during the ad campaign that I met Bert Sutcliffe, then a retired teacher in his mid-sixties, living in a downtown apartment with his partner, Ralph. Sutcliffe figured he was too old to participate in the often tense nighttime demonstrations and wasn't up for long meetings, but he was happy to stuff envelopes in his apartment. I regularly brought over the materials and sometimes stayed to work with him. As we folded, stuffed, and labelled, he would regale me with stories of his younger life.

Sutcliffe had joined the Canadian army in his early twenties during the war, and was soon shipped to England. One night, drunk, he ended up in bed with a fellow soldier. It was his first time. His new friend introduced him to London gay life. "The best was the blackouts," he told me with a twinkle in his eye. "You could hear the German bombers above us. Anybody could be killed at any moment. And all these young men would end up in the back alleys. Everybody was horny. It was wonderful."

Decorated for his bravery under fire, at the end of the war Sutcliffe returned to Canada, earning a degree in history from the University of Toronto before re-enlisting and going to Korea. He rose through the ranks, and in 1962 was about to be posted to a plum job in Washington when his world collapsed around him. A former trick had been arrested in the RCMP anti-gay witchhunts and had been intimidated into naming others. On the day of a goodbye luncheon in his honour, Sutcliffe was called in and immediately dismissed from the army. It was the end of the only life he knew.

He went home and put a pistol to his head and then suddenly said to himself, "Fuck them, I'm not going to let those bastards kill me." He ended up a history teacher in a Toronto high school until his retirement in 1979. It was the first time in his life he finally felt free to come out.

Sutcliffe's stories made our own little war seem less stressful, and the intense comradeship of the spontaneous sexual encounters he described emerged as a constant across the generations. I knew then that the cops would never be able to destroy us.

6

Sex and Death

CANCER?

Since we read through all the U.S. gay papers, Leo Casey (who was now helping with the international news) and I may have been among the first in Toronto to hear about the new "gay cancer." Our story, in September 1981, was headlined " 'Gay' Cancer and Burning Flesh: The Media Didn't Investigate." It opened: "Three recent news reports carried by major . . . news media throughout North America have demonstrated a persistent capacity for major distortions in their coverage of gay-related issues."

The first was a wire service story about a massive fire in a San Francisco "homosexual S&M slave quarters," where firemen smelled "burning flesh" and "were concerned that men chained to beds had been 'burnt alive.' " It turned out that the building was an ordinary hotel under renovation that had briefly been a gay bath years before. There were no bodies.

A second story in the San Francisco *Chronicle* revealed that the city coroner had to conduct safety workshops for gay masochists on "how to avoid injury and death from gay S&M sex." That turned out to be a workshop about avoiding street violence.

The third item was a July 3, 1981, issue of *The New York Times* headlined "Rare Cancer Found in 41 Homosexuals." There was an unexpectedly high incidence of Kaposi's sarcoma (KS) among otherwise healthy young gay men. The *Times* article suggested that the cancer was always aggressive and fatal, and was only found among gay men. But KS was found in a number of other populations and was usually slow moving. The story continued, "The most pernicious section of the article, however, is the manner in which it suggests a causal link between the sex lives of gay men and KS." I closed, "Chalk up three more for the world of objective news reporting."[1]

Unlike the burning bath or the safe torture workshop, the last story wasn't about to fade. The following month, Bill Lewis and Dr. Randy Coates penned a full-page Health article entitled "Moral Lessons; Fatal Cancer." Lewis was a professor of microbiology at the University of Toronto, and partner of Michael

Lynch, who was intimately connected with the New York scene and regularly travelled back and forth. Coates was a physician at Toronto's Hassle Free Clinic, the popular downtown sexual health centre. Although their tone was less flippant than our original report, the focus again was on the media. They accused *The New York Times* of trying to draw "moral lessons" in the absence of scientific information: "if gay men insist on having lots of sex with a variety of partners, they will have to suffer the revenge of cancer."[2]

By this point, there was growing consensus that the outbreak of KS and PCP, a kind of pneumonia, among young gay men was linked to some underlying immune disorder. By 1982 this was being called gay related immune deficiency (GRID). Speculation on the cause was rife in the American gay press – multiple sexually transmitted infections, intestinal parasites or the drugs used to treat them, recreational drug use, poppers, too much sperm up our bums, partying all night, environmental pollution, germ warfare, genetics, and so on. Other commentators dispensed with any pretense of scientific speculation and saw divine punishment.

Although those with connections to New York, like Lynch and Lewis, seemed more preoccupied, the general message in Toronto was that this was just more anti-gay hysteria. There was still only one known case of KS in Canada, and U.S. politics seemed more threatening than a gay-targeted epidemic.

REAGANOMICS

When Carter's Volcker Shock pushed interest rates up to unprecedented levels in 1979, as expected, it slammed the United States (and subsequently Canada) into recession. It also lost Carter the next election to Reagan, who had skilfully constructed an alliance between the social conservatives of the new right and a more assertive corporate elite.

Social conservatives traditionally resented the liberal elite that dominated Washington. They found it un-Christian, distressingly in favour of women's rights, homosexuals, and racial minorities, and associated with general big-city decadence. The corporate elite hated taxes that paid for Keynesian wealth redistribution and regulations to protect employees and the environment. Although these two sectors could not have been farther apart socially or economically, they both clapped with enthusiasm when in his inaugural address Reagan announced, "In this present crisis, government is not the solution to our problems; government is the problem."

Reagan gave each what they most wanted.

To the financial elite he gave huge tax cuts. He argued that if rich people had more money, they would invest more and the benefits would "trickle down" to everyone below. He froze the minimum wage, slashed transfers to the states, and cut the budgets for Medicaid, food stamps, and educational programs. Ketchup, famously, was designated a vegetable for school lunch programs. His tax cuts ultimately increased the federal deficit, which served as an excuse for further cuts to programs. These policies, plus growing unemployment, drove down wages. As a result, the share of the gross domestic product that went to labour began to decline, while the share that went to employers went up for the first time since the Second World War. It was the beginning of a massive redistribution of wealth from labour to capital, from the poor to the rich.

As could be expected, the main opposition to Reaganomics came from unions. Reagan soon let them know who was boss. When striking air traffic controllers refused his order to return to work in the summer of 1981, he fired 11,345 of them, using supervisors and the military to handle commercial air traffic until more pliant employees could be found. It was a clear message to the private sector that unions no longer needed to be feared.

The unions responded with a March on Washington in September that drew a half-million people demanding "jobs, justice and equality." An official lesbian and gay contingent marched under the banners of the National Organization of Lesbians and Gays and the National Coalition of Black Gays. Generally, however, gay people were more concerned about the growing power of the religious right in Reagan's coalition than with his economic policies.

Reagan consolidated his alliance with social conservatives early, appointing Rev. Robert Billings, the Moral Majority's first executive director, as a religious adviser to his campaign. Once elected, Reagan delivered to that constituency, escalating the Cold War and dubbing the "atheist" Soviet Union "the evil empire." A War on Drugs with mandatory minimum penalties for drug offences replaced the War on Poverty.

Promoting traditional family values, Reagan withdrew support for the Equal Rights Amendment (ERA) and focused federal sex ed funding on abstinence-only programs. His Adolescent Family Life Act tied support to pregnant and parenting teens to promotion of "chastity" and "self-discipline." In 1983, while a sitting president, he found time to publish *Abortion and the Conscience of the Nation,* calling for recognition of the sanctity of life and citizen awareness of the far-reaching implications of abortion.

One of the first pieces of legislation introduced during his presidency was the Family Protection Act. The bill's co-sponsor was Reagan's campaign manager, Paul Laxalt. Its primary goal was "the restoration of family unity, parental authority and a climate of traditional morality." The bill stipulated that "no federal funds may be made available under any provision of Federal law to any public or private individual, group or other entity for the purpose of advocating, promoting or suggesting homosexuality, male and female, as a life style." Although it was too extreme to ultimately make it through Congress, it was a major concern for the mainstream American gay rights organizations during Reagan's first term.

Reagan was probably not personally homophobic. As governor of California, he had opposed the Briggs amendment, writing "homosexuality is not a contagious disease like the measles." But as an actor, he knew how to give his crowd what it wanted.

WHO'S READING US?

In February 1981 *TBP* did its first major readership survey. Given everything that was happening after the bath raids, it took until the end of the year to analyze and publish the results. There were more than five hundred responses. It was not a random sample, but it did give an overview of the community we were talking to.

Of those who responded, 76 per cent were Canadians (32 per cent from Toronto), 21 per cent were from the United States, and almost 3 per cent from overseas. That mirrored what we knew from our subscription lists. Only 10 per cent of respondents were women. Despite our hand-wringing, women's features, and regular women on the cover, *TBP* was still largely a magazine read by gay men.

Readers were also relatively young. Seventy-nine per cent of men were aged between 19 and 39, as were 89 per cent of women. Our women's readership was slightly younger than our men. They were also well educated: 83 per cent of women and 81 per cent of men had at least some university education, and only 3 per cent had not finished high school. Male readers in Toronto earned almost twice as much as female readers ($21,900 compared to $11,000), but this gender disparity was less pronounced among respondents in other parts of Canada. Toronto also saw more disparity in income, with fewer people earning closer to the average and more much higher or lower.

More than 80 per cent of readers lived in large urban areas. Twenty-five per cent of men lived in shared accommodation with a group, as opposed to 19 per cent of lesbians, who were more likely to live with a lover. Despite *TBP*'s anti-religious stance, 42 per cent of men and 25 per cent of women readers reported affiliation with a "Western religion," but 10 per cent of men and 20 per cent of women spontaneously expressed hostility to the idea of religious affiliation. Most Canadian readers voted for the NDP (45 per cent), which put them to the left of the general population.

Notwithstanding the gender disparity, this was a snapshot of a well-educated and relatively successful group. The survey did not ask about experiences of discrimination or race.

CENSORSHIP CONTINUED

As *TBP* prepared for its retrial, the struggle against censorship strengthened the community of interest between the gay community and the downtown arts scene. In March 1981 the Ontario Censor Board demanded cuts in a new Michael Snow film, which was to premier at a small experimental film theatre, the Funnel. Two days later, a planned *FUSE Magazine* screening of recent video documentaries was also blocked by the censor board. "The Board of Censors is not only interfering with artists' films and artists' videotapes but is now preventing the working women's community from seeing important research on sexism, labour, women's hostels, immigration and family violence," said Lisa Steele, *FUSE* co-editor.[3] *FUSE* tried to take the board to court, but had to drop the case when threatened with a countersuit.

A week later, another Michael Snow screening at the Funnel was blocked, even though the film had already been shown several times, including at the Art Gallery of Ontario. When the Canadian Images Film Festival hosted a think tank on censorship of experimental film in Peterborough, Ontario, police launched an investigation. This was too much even for *The Globe and Mail*, which editorialized, "The appointment of censors to second-guess obscenity laws and the public's morals is bothersome enough. To have them chase the public into limited screenings and private galleries is outrageous."[4] A new group, the Ontario Film and Video Appreciation Society, formed to challenge the board's powers under the recently repatriated Constitution.

But the board was unrelenting, banning *Vie d'Ange*, a Quebec film that was to be shown at a festival at Toronto's Harbourfront Centre in April, and blocking an RTPC benefit screening of artists' videos in May. That month the Film and Video Against Censorship committee was formed. It demanded the board of censors be replaced with a classification board without the power to cut or ban material.

The Progressive Conservative government stood its ground. Gordon Walker, minister of consumer and commercial relations, claimed that when Sweden abolished censorship, there was a 60 per cent increase in rapes. This assertion built on the theme that censorship not only preserved public morals but also protected women from violence.

SEX WARS

Much of the American women's movement, including the National Organization of Women, had spent the 1970s pushing for the Equal Rights Amendment to enshrine women's rights in the U.S. constitution. Although the ERA passed both Congress and the Senate in 1972, and was ratified by thirty-five state legislatures, by the end of the decade it was still three states short of the support necessary to become law. With the shift to social conservatism that culminated in Reagan's 1980 election, it became clear that the ERA was not going to pass. Several states even withdrew ratification before the effort finally died.

With that unifying goal a shambles, the U.S. women's movement began to fracture. Some went with the growing conservative current and focused on protecting women from pornography. There were lots of willing allies among conservative legislators and law enforcement. Others took the opposite tack and explored the assertion of women's power through sex. There was ever less middle ground.

The landmark Barnard Conference on Sexuality: Towards a Politics of Sexuality, held in April 1982, blew the lid off the simmering debate and began what became known as the Feminist Sex Wars. The Barnard Conference intended "to move beyond debates about violence and pornography and to focus on sexuality apart from reproduction." But its premise was immediately challenged by The Coalition for a Feminist Sexuality and Against Sado-masochism, which accused the conference of being part of an "anti-feminist backlash" and lobbied for its cancellation. When that didn't work, they protested. The "pro-sex" women in turn accused the coalition of "authoritarianism" and of repudiating "the spirit of free inquiry and the basic principles of a democratic radical movement."

Conference organizer Carol Vance pointed out that while for men, sex is usually associated with pleasure, for women it is associated with both pleasure and danger. The women's movement was dividing into hostile camps between those who focused on sex as a social danger, and those who focused on it as a site of agency and pleasure.

A similar debate trickled into Toronto. Incensed by the participation of the Sisters of Perpetual Indulgence at Pride in 1982, several women from Lesbians Against the Right wrote to *TBP* and *Broadside* calling the nun drag misogynist and complaining that it distracted from more important issues. In *Broadside* Eve Zaremba scolded both sides, telling the LAR women that "not everything which we as women find objectionable is necessarily misogynist, a term we should handle carefully so as not to downgrade it through overuse," and asking the Sisters to reflect on their motives.

> Why do they go in for this stuff? My suggestion is that the main impetus is that *it is fun.* And since it upsets many straights and less "advanced" gays, it could even be considered politically progressive, even revolutionary.... Very tempting stuff, especially for the mentally lazy and guilt-ridden. It's time we grasped the fact that not everything which shocks the bourgeoisie is necessarily progressive.[5]

Although the same forces were at work, the right-wing shift was less pronounced in Canada than in the United States, and the women's movement less internally polarized. Among mainstream conservatives, there was more consensus about the importance of social programs and the need for separation of church and state. Radical social conservatives, especially of the religious variety, were a small minority. Although economic policy was beginning to follow the U.S. lead, with hand-wringing about deficits and the need to cut back, it would be years before anything like Reaganomics would arrive in Canada.

Finally, the Canadian women's movement still had a unifying issue – establishing free-standing abortion clinics. Despite differences on pornography, prostitution, S/M, and so on, everyone could agree on a woman's right to choose. Across the country, the strategy was to challenge federal anti-abortion laws by establishing standalone, accessible abortion clinics and keep other disagreements in house.

OBSCENITY REDUX

If anyone hoped 1982 might bring some respite from police attacks, they were quickly proven wrong. On April 21, Senior Morality Officer Thomas Stephen and a colleague arrived at Glad Day Bookshop and browsed the magazine rack for a few minutes. They selected two magazines, *The Leathermen* and *Come Watch*, and charged a young employee, Kevin Orr, with "possession of obscene material for the purposes of sale." Three weeks later, the same Officer Stephen and another colleague arrived at *TBP*'s offices with an open-ended search warrant and spent an hour rifling through our files. Pink Triangle Press and all nine *TBP* collective members were charged with "publishing obscene written matter." The article in question was "Lust with a Very Proper Stranger."

The magazines charged at Glad Day were available in forty-nine other downtown and suburban locations, none of which was charged. "Lust" was a mild description of the hygiene of fist-fucking penned by a *TBP* contributor under the pseudonym Angus MacKenzie.

The entire collective had to report for questioning at Morality Headquarters and the next day to the Jarvis Street police station for fingerprinting and mug shots. We held a press conference where our lawyer, Clayton Ruby, and representatives of the Canadian Periodical Publishers Association and the Toronto Gay Community Council spoke on our behalf. Denunciations came in from the Writers Union, the Civil Liberties Association, and others. May 15 saw an angry demonstration seize the intersection at Yonge and Wellesley and march on police headquarters chanting, "We are all Angus MacKenzie." We already had the *TBP* Free the Press Fund, but now Glad Day had to set up a new one. It was all so déjà vu.

An immediate casualty of the charges was the proposed gay-police liaison committee. Toronto Gay Community Council called the charges "yet another example of selective law enforcement designed to discredit and harass our community." Council spokesperson Harvey Hamburg also noted a change in police tactics to "smaller pervasive busts of gay individuals." A wave of overcrowding charges had been laid against gay bars, and washroom and park arrests were on the upswing. Surveillance in The Bay department store and the Islington subway station washrooms alone had netted more than two hundred gross indecency charges that year. Criminal lawyers also reported a surge in arrests of hustlers and transsexual sex workers.[6] The community council responded by suspending any further talks about a liaison committee.

Two weeks after the new charges, *TBP* was back in court for our retrial on the 1977 charges against "Men Loving Boys Loving Men." We joked that it was hard to tell if they were trying to wear us down or just confuse us into submission. We mustered a parade of defence witnesses, broadcasters, academics, journalists, and "avowed homosexuals." In his summary, Clayton Ruby also cited the new constitution's Charter of Rights and Freedoms.

Judge Mercer delivered his verdict on "Men Loving Boys" on June 15. The case was dismissed for the second time. We won again. But this time there was no grand celebration. We were eager to just put it behind us, get back to the office to work on the next issue, and strategize for the "Lust" trial November 1.

Less than a month later, I was in Washington at the International Gay Association conference. The IGA was attempting to establish itself this side of the Atlantic. Ironically, although the conference was held in the country with the largest lesbian and gay movement in the world, overseas delegates still outnumbered Americans. Worse, since U.S. law prohibited the entry of homosexuals, most of us were in the country illegally. I was talking to some French delegates when someone said, "Look, he's still smiling. He doesn't know yet." The news had just arrived. *TBP*'s second acquittal was also being appealed.

The conference organized a demonstration outside the Canadian embassy, with everyone wondering if we would all be deported. In Toronto, the Gay Community Council called the appeal "an astounding abuse of power." The collective debated how to proceed. If the appeal court found us guilty, the maximum fine was five hundred dollars, a fraction of what it would cost to continue fighting. It was tempting to just plead guilty, pay, and move on. Or, if a third trial was ordered, we could refuse to co-operate and stand mute in the courtroom. Ultimately, however, we decided the risk of capitulating was too great. Repeat offenders often faced long jail sentences, and if McMurtry managed to register a conviction of any sort against us, it would only be a matter of time before the next charges were laid, unless we self-censored ourselves into irrelevance. We would fight.

And public opinion was shifting. *The Globe and Mail* asked, "Does the Attorney General's office intend to go on prosecuting until it finds a court that will convict? Does it think that is justice?" Even the *Whig Standard* from Kingston, Ontario, called the appeal "a further example of the government's abuse of the criminal justice system."[7] McMurtry was looking ever more isolated and foolish.

DOING IT

The attacks only seemed to spur community growth. In the summer of 1982, two years after the last national conference had put the Canadian Lesbian and Gay Rights Coalition out of its misery, the Toronto Gay Community Council organized Doing It, a ten-day festival and conference that drew five hundred lesbians and gay men from eight provinces and observers from the United States and seven other countries. There were workshops on organizing techniques, fighting the right, spirituality, Third World issues, street patrols, gay youth, and dozens of other topics.

Twenty presentations and slide shows on lesbian and gay history were presented at Wilde, a parallel conference organized by the Canadian Lesbian and Gay Archives (CLGA) celebrating the hundredth anniversary of Oscar Wilde's 1882 visit to Canada. That conference brought together key historians of the emerging social constructionist school, including Jonathan Ned Katz, Karla Jay, Gayle Rubin, Jim Steakley, George Chauncey, and Allan Bérubé.

A mini-conference on Lesbians and Gay Liberation attracted over a hundred women. Other mini-conferences brought together the gay press, gay fathers, and the North American Man/Boy Love Association (NAMBLA). Four public seminars drew large crowds to tackle the "big four" sex issues – S/M, pornography, pedophilia, and public sex – with remarkably non-rancorous discussions. Other venues hosted performance art, music, experimental video, and cabarets. Three galleries featured the work of lesbian and gay artists, and a special screening series presented twenty-five films. There were three major dances. The second Pride celebration and march drew twice as many people as in 1981. A sold-out crowd at the Bloor Cinema wildly applauded the world premiere of *Track Two*, a feature-length film on community response to the bath raids featuring stirring footage of the massive demonstrations.

"And in the end," *TBP* reported, "everyone simply collapsed on the beach at Hanlan's point. No wonder."[8]

The event was an enormous undertaking that went off without a serious hitch. It illustrated the extent of the energy that had been touched off by the raids, and the growing sophistication and resources of the community that had evolved over the previous decade.

THE SILENCE OF LAMBS

Despite NAMBLA's participation in Gay Days, pedophilia, the issue that had plagued the 1970s, was largely eclipsed in the new politics of trials, freedom of expression, and confrontations with the police. After the first acquittal and republication of "Men Loving Boys Loving Men," and a second piece reprising a more nuanced feminist critique, the response was a resounding silence. Readers no longer seemed much interested in talking about the issue.

In November 1981, long-time activist Jim Monk had tried to reopen the debate with a two-page review of Tom O'Carroll's *Paedophilia: The Radical Case*. O'Carroll wrote the book while awaiting trial for conspiracy to corrupt public morals. His crime had been to chair Britain's Paedophile Information Exchange (PIE) and edit the group's newsletter, *Magpie*. Monk found the arguments in the book "too compelling to ignore."

O'Carroll reprised the early sexual liberation position linking child-adult sex with children's liberation, arguing that "children should have the right to have sex with adults if they so desire." He disputed that consensual sex with adults was psychologically damaging to children, and pointed out that age of consent laws did nothing to prevent real child abuse. To deal with cases of suspected coercion, he proposed civil proceedings to determine consent.

But O'Carroll also anticipated that the notion of pedophiles as a minority was a dead end. He concluded:

> Ultimately, it is no use fighting for paedophile liberation, though this is a stage that has to be worked through. Sexual liberation can only mean something valuable to most people in the context of their own lives, and the lives of their children, not the lives of some minority group with whom they are asked to sympathize.

Nevertheless, asserting that this was a "subject that refuses to go away," Monk cited the growth of NAMBLA and pedophile groups in Europe.

Pedophile organizing was still broadly accepted by much of the gay movement. For instance, in Boston, when two NAMBLA steering committee members were arrested on charges of indecent assault in January 1982, MCC Boston, Lesbian and Gay Media Advocates, Gay Hispanic Men, the Committee Against Racial Violence, the Boston Alliance Against Registration and the Draft, and *Gay Community News* issued a joint letter of protest. The case was dismissed when the sixteen-year-old boy refused to testify. In October 1982, a coalition of feminist groups called on the Gay and Lesbian Centre of Philadelphia to reverse a decision to allow NAMBLA to hold its annual membership conference on the premises, but the centre's board held firm and the conference went on.

In Britain, the Midland Bank demanded PIE close its account because of publicity about the group's activities, and in 1983, police made intimidating visits to several of the organization's executive. Britain's largest gay group, the Campaign for Homosexual Equality, spoke out on PIE's behalf. The IGA also held firm in the face of the Irish Gay Rights Movement's pull-out in protest of the PIE's continued membership in the international body. The IGA had authorized PIE to be its official liaison with other non-member pedophile groups around the world. In Canada, the Coalition for Gay Rights in Ontario welcomed NAMBLA as a member.

But Monk closed his article by abruptly changing focus. Rather than having the gay movement take up the issue of pedophilia, he suggested, "it is up to pedophiles and boy lovers to organize themselves." The gay movement had other responsibilities.

> The responsibility which the gay movement has shirked up to now is the organization of gay youth, the support of gay children growing up in hostile or indifferent heterosexual families. . . . I believe the time has come for us to

engage gay youth and their parents in a dialogue. This book, and the proposals for reform that it contains, should be the first subject for discussion.[9]

It seemed a rather disingenuous attempt to equate pedophilia with youth work. While Monk was right that youth services were in dismal shape, it is doubtful that O'Carroll's book would be of much use in expanding them.

Monk was a supporter of the original demand for abolition of the age of consent, but the article indicated how the discursive ground was shifting. The same processes that took Kinsey's continuum of sexual behaviours and produced a bounded gay sexual minority were beginning to define pedophilia as yet another distinct sexual orientation. If pedophilia was still anathema to most lesbian feminists, it was also less and less an issue for gay men, except perhaps to distinguish ourselves from it.

HEAD GAMES

Gerald Hannon was talking on the phone and I was working at the desk across from him at the *TBP* office. I knew he was talking to one of the cops about the return of materials or some other administrative matter. I wasn't really listening. Then I heard him say "thanks" in an odd way and hang up. When I looked up, he was staring straight ahead, looking a bit pale. I asked him if he was okay.

"The cop said he liked my new glasses."

"Very gay, but so what?"

"I only met him once, more than a year ago. How does he know I just got new glasses?"

It was a message. We were being watched.

We got ours back, though. James Fraser, the driving force behind the Lesbian and Gay Archives, worked at the city archives as his day job. Somehow, he came across a detailed floor plan of 52 Division. The next RTPC demonstration was going down to 52, so we used it as the graphic on our flyer. According to the grapevine, police brass were completely freaked out and considered it a major security breach.

REALITY CHECK

Summer turned to fall, and on November 1, 1982, *TBP* was back in court, this time for the "Lust with a Very Proper Stranger" trial. My clearest memory is of the testimony of sociologist Dorothy Smith, an expert in communications theory from the Ontario Institute for Studies in Education, and mentor, although no relation, to our housemate and RTPC chair, George Smith. Smith was in her sixties, wore her grey hair up in a bun, and peered through granny glasses resting on her sharp nose. She looked for all the world like an English schoolmarm, and had the accent to match. Smith treated the Crown prosecutor as if he were a somewhat slow schoolboy, patiently explaining once again that *TBP*'s reading level, design, and voice signalled it was a serious, intellectual magazine. That was very different from the kind of language level and voice one found in pornography. She lost her patience when the prosecutor said he still didn't understand what she meant by pornographic voice and could he give her an example. Without missing a beat, she looked down her nose at him and said dryly, "He thrust his throbbing dick into my hungry cunt, for example." The Crown prosecutor blanched. The court stenographer froze, and the packed courtroom and the judge did their best to stifle titters.

Judge Mercer dismissed all charges at the end of the first day of what was supposed to be a three-day trial. This time McMurtry did not dare appeal. Now we had only the original court case ahead of us.

APPROACHING STORM

The name of the mysterious syndrome affecting gay men was now AIDS (acquired immune deficiency syndrome), although for most it was still the Gay Plague. In Reagan's cuts to "big government," the Centers for Disease Control lost 30 per cent of its funding, hampering research and surveillance of the growing epidemic. In August 1982, the president vetoed a bill containing a half-million dollars for AIDS research, though that veto was overturned after a two-thirds vote in Congress. In San Francisco, a congressional hearing was held comparing the response to AIDS, an illness that afflicted "the most stigmatized and discriminated against minorities," to legionnaires' disease, which affected elderly veterans.[10] It was clear that the Reagan administration was disproportionately interested in the veterans. Most resounding was the president's silence on the epidemic. He did not publicly utter the word "AIDS" at any point during his entire first term, a silence that encouraged other western leaders to do the same.

By the end of September 1982 there were fourteen cases reported in Canada, two in Toronto. In our November issue, under the headline The Case Against Panic, Bill Lewis wrote "The Real Epidemic: Paranoia," speculating that the mysterious disease was caused by a transmissible agent. He suggested that many might already be immune, and compared the dangers of AIDS to other risks, like hepatitis, getting queerbashed, or even driving a car.

Michael Lynch did an eight-page feature, "Living with Kaposi's," on a thirty-four-year-old New Yorker called Fred and how he and his partner and family were dealing with his diagnosis. Much of the piece still focused on sensational media reporting. Lynch singled out *Newsweek* and *The New York Times* for pathologizing gay men, but also critiqued coverage in *Christopher Street* and *The Advocate*. *The Advocate*'s irrepressible David Goodstein had editorialized, "The fact is that aspects of the urban gay lifestyle created in the last decade are harmful to our health. . . . Our lifestyle has become an elaborate suicide ritual."[11] This was anathema to *TBP*'s newfound conviction that sex was the glue that held the gay community together.

That fall the porn wars reached a boiling point. Red Hot Video, an expanding West Coast pornography franchise with fourteen outlets in British Columbia, was the target of anti-porn women's groups. There was picketing, leafleting, and demonstrations outside key stores. The groups lobbied the provincial government to prosecute the franchise on the grounds that some of its material portrayed violence and non-consensual sex.

On November 23, 1982, less than a month after the *TBP* "Lust" acquittal, a group calling itself the Wimmin's Fire Brigade firebombed three Red Hot stores.

> Red Hot Video sells tapes that show wimmin and children being tortured, raped and humiliated. . . . Although these tapes violate the Criminal Code of Canada and the BC guidelines on pornography, all lawful attempts to shut down Red Hot Video have failed because the justice system was created, and is controlled by rich men to protect their profits and property. As a result, we are left with no visible alternative but to change the situation ourselves through illegal means. This is an act of self-defense against hate propaganda.[12]

One store was destroyed and another badly damaged. Although mainstream women's groups deplored the violence, most expressed understanding for the Brigade's frustration.

TBP took a dramatically different stance. The problem wasn't breaking the law. We restated our support for women's challenge to the abortion law by setting up illegal abortion clinics, for example, but we deplored the firebombing because it allied the women's movement with religious fundamentalists and strengthened the police's hand. But despite a letter accusing the collective of paternalism and sexism, the issue otherwise died down. Two months later, police raided a number of stores and Red Hot was charged.

Then, on March 4, 1983, Glad Day Bookshop's Kevin Orr was found guilty of "possession of obscene material for the purposes of distribution," despite the widespread availability of the two offending magazines. Orr drew a very conservative judge who considered the seized magazines "lewd and disgusting," and suggested that if police weren't charging other stores, they probably should. Although Orr was granted a conditional discharge with two years' probation, Glad Day appealed the case on principle. A month later, the bookstore received notice that a shipment of the magazine *Pan* had been seized by Canada Customs and declared "immoral or indecent." Glad Day had been importing and selling the "serious international non-pornographic magazine about paedophilia" since 1979 without incident. *Pan* typically contained news, film and book reviews, short fiction, and some fully clothed photos of boys.

In April, I waded in with an article that compared how an earlier generation of women activists had thrown themselves into the fight for temperance, or prohibition, arguing that male violence against women was fuelled by drunkenness. It was a similar position to that of women who saw male violence fuelled by porn. Prohibition of alcohol did little to improve the lives of women. The same, I speculated, would be true for the anti-porn movement.[13] But *TBP*'s next move closed down any possibility for further debate.

In June 1983, as the Red Hot trial began in Vancouver and we waited on a date for the second appeal of the "Men Loving Boys" verdict, *TBP* ran an ad for the video chain. The decision had produced heated debate in the collective. In 1979, when we had turned down porn entrepreneur Honest Joe Martin's political ad, we argued that *TBP* did not accept advertising that exploited women and stressed "the difference between libertarian and liberation politics." But something had imperceptibly shifted in the collective's basic values in the intervening four years. Fighting for our right to publish, belonging to a community facing state interference after the bath raids, and the ongoing censorship of gay material at Glad Day had reconfigured our political landscape. It had amplified the long-existing position that anyone who sided with the state to suppress and control sexuality was not our friend. Experience was reshaping our consciousness.

By publishing the ad, we forced a polarization that, as could be expected, was not in our favour. It was especially difficult for many long-time feminist supporters. In the next issues of *TBP* and *Broadside*, a who's who of long-time activists, volunteers, contributors, and an ex-collective member denounced the publication of the ad as "unnecessarily heightening and polarizing a climate of tension between and within our movements." The anger was palpable, and a subsequent editorial response – "Sometimes [solidarity] is messy. Well so be it" – did little to build bridges. For several more issues, letters featured scathing criticisms and cancelled subscriptions.

In Vancouver, the Red Hot trial was quick. Ontario censor Mary Brown flew out to be a witness. The porn shop was convicted of a summary offence and fined a hundred dollars. But at *TBP*, our network of support had been irrevocably damaged.

TRANSITIONING

In the same issue as the Red Hot Video ad, Jim Bartley's "Charting a Course between Male and Female" appeared. This was the first significant *TBP* piece on trans issues. Unlike the ad, "Charting" sparked no comment. Perhaps the other issues drew the fire, or perhaps it was the style of the article itself. It focused on reportage, without theoretical pretensions.

"Charting" consisted of interviews with three trans women: Diane and Paula, two roommates awaiting surgery, and Wanda, who had lived as a woman without surgery for twenty years. The article personalized the women, describing their voices: "husky, edging toward sultry, a few notches closer to femme ... a mellow, throaty caress somewhere in the realm of Tallulah Bankhead. . . . Her laugh fills the room – a rich, bitter-sweet lament for the absurd polarities of 'maleness' and 'femaleness.' " It concluded, "and yet their femaleness is notably un-stereotyped."

The women talked about their early experiences, negotiating the psychiatric system, their generally unhelpful relationship to gay liberation groups, and their choices in life. The article attempted to be affirming.

It had not started out that way. Bartley remembers going to the interviews with the idea "that trans identity was a condition triggered by entrenched and polarized gender roles, and maybe homophobia." That was a typical position at the time.

The relationship between gay people and transsexuals was historically fraught. For most of the straight world, we all belonged to the same general "pervert" category. Gender performance/identity and sexual orientation were indistinguishable. Pre-Stonewall, when the shared goal of most transsexuals and gay men had been to pass, there was at least a tacit understanding of similarities. Trans women also often started out in some relationship with gay drag networks. There was little conception of trans men. That social space was occupied by bull dykes or women who simply lived as men as best they could.

But when gay liberation made coming out its core political right of passage, anyone trying to pass at anything became suspect. The gay clone look of the 1980s further promoted hyper-masculinity and abandoned '70s gender critique. In Spain after the IGA conference in 1980, a friend remarked that a young man we met was planning to transition. I was shocked, and put it down to how backward gay consciousness still was after a quarter-century of Franco's fascism.

There was also a very different relationship to the medical profession. Psychiatry had been designated by the gay liberation movement as a principal agent of homophobia. Yet transsexuals needed the approval of a psychiatric diagnosis before beginning their transition. That, and the fact that many trans people initially identified as gay, seemed like abject surrender to the enemy. In terms of gay liberation's always shaky alliance with feminism, this was potentially dangerous terrain.

When asked about stereotypical behaviour, Wanda laughed about how a trans friend only ordered liqueurs, because "they're what ladies drink." Bartley pointed out, "the fact that the sex changes involved in transsexualism can tend to affirm and perpetuate oppressive sex roles has long been the principal feminist objection to surgical and hormone treatment of TSs [transsexuals]."[14] It was an understatement.

Only five years earlier, LOOT had voted to reject a lesbian trans woman's formal request to join the organization, and declared that it welcomed womynborn-womyn only. Trans women were seen as "inauthentic imposters" and called "sex-change he creatures." Graffiti on the LOOT notice board read, "So what makes a woman – a castrated penis or a life of male oppression?"[15] Feminist theorist Gloria Steinem famously quipped, "If the shoe doesn't fit, must we change the foot?" And in a 1979 book, *The Transsexual Empire: The Making of the She-male,* Janice Raymond was incendiary: "All transsexuals rape women's bodies by reducing the real female form to an artifact, appropriating this body for themselves. . . . Transsexuals merely cut off the most obvious means of invading women, so that they seem non-invasive."[16]

For those who insisted that gender was socially constructed, a culturally learned performance, and therefore something that could be radically transformed, it was an existential challenge when someone declared that they so deeply considered themselves to be of a particular gender that they required surgery to have their body conform. But as Bartley got to know the women, he became convinced that "whatever the source of their dilemma, the only response and 'fix' was to support them and their transitioning." It was a breakthrough.

The fact that such an article could be run in 1983 was another indication of the tectonic shifts going on. Personally, Bartley was won over by the women's presence. He found himself recognizing, in their insistence on being true to themselves, something of his own coming out as a gay man.

But this was facilitated by a more general shift from a gender analysis of social oppression to one that placed individual rights at the centre of analysis. If feminists worried about the social implications of transgender, liberals saw it as simply another expression of individuality. An individual's body was private property to be disposed as they saw fit. In a more liberal world, the gay movement was distancing itself from the iconic positions of the women's movement.

RACISM

The sexual turn elevating the importance of individual desire had a number of impacts. It helped overcome the traditional divisions with gay business. It permitted a more sympathetic exploration of trans issues. It opened us up to address concrete issues important to the lives of ordinary gay men.

On the other hand, it widened the rift between gay men and the majority of lesbians who did not participate in the same sexual subculture. The *TBP* collective became less sensitive to the feelings of women and less careful of our alliances there. Finally, elevating sexual desire to the centre of community formation potentially alienated those who found themselves excluded from those circuits, since it appeared to put sexual desire above criticism.

In the same issue as the Red Hot Video ad and Bartley's piece on transsexuals, Ken Popert's "Race, Moustaches and Sexual Prejudice" brought the issue of race to a head. The article began with the collective's rejection of an ad for a magazine entitled *White Assed Super Pricks (WASP)* with the subtitle "Unethnic and Unorthodox." While not necessarily disagreeing, Popert said he felt that the discussion had been simple-minded. Without the apparently racist, possibly ironic headlines, the actual images were little different from most gay skin mags that we advertised.

He argued that sexual preference and desire were "mysteriously" established early in life and were beyond conscious control. However that happened, different "characteristics which define the edges of social conflict: age, sex, race and class" emerged as important. Therefore, "we can easily see that the society around us must exert a large influence." The results of that influence could be found in personal ads, where desire for particular racial groups was often mentioned. (*TBP* only turned away ads singling out groups for *rejection*.) "These phrases lie at the centre of a web of racially tinged desire whose subtle filaments cling to many of us."

If desire was a passion, something that comes over us, that we suffer, then the individual couldn't be held responsible. "If my sexuality is racially tinged, then it is not because I am racist, but because I have grown up in a society which attaches great importance to race."

Popert didn't approve of such racialized sexuality, and pointed out that it reduced choice "whether we're the excluder or the excluded." He drew an analogy with the limitations of being a top, since it limited the number of men he slept with. But he asked what it would mean to struggle against racism in desire – having "sex with individuals we're not attracted to as a way of breaking down the barriers?" He went on, "and doesn't the notion that we should modify our sexuality according to morality or politics subvert the intent of gay liberation? . . . Gay liberation, before anything else stands for the integrity and inviolability of sexual desire, the right of men and women to choose their sexual partners according to their needs."

Popert concluded:

> We cannot change the negative aspects of our sexuality and no purpose is served by feeling guilty about them. . . . The most constructive target in the fight against racism is not our own desires, but the institutionalization in our own community and the surrounding society of racial inequalities. . . . Racism will go out of our sexuality when racism goes out of society, and not before.[17]

Popert made thoughtful points, but his piece was inflammatory. A feverish identity politics was developing with the rising frustration of people of colour over their continued exclusion, marginalization, and discrimination in an ostensibly multicultural Canada. And it was always risky for a white person to wade into such a debate, especially if they challenged accepted truths. In this case, Popert's whiteness drew attention to the fact that the collective was also all white, as were the vast majority of *TBP* volunteers. This might have been unremarkable in 1970, but by this point, so-called visible minorities were approaching 15 per cent of Toronto's population. For a white man from an all-white collective to lecture others on racism seemed the height of insensitivity, just the kind of thing one would expect when a bunch of white boys spent their time talking to each other in their segregated club.

Second, the article seemed to trivialize the issue. Popert began by declaring himself a "moustachosexual" – someone attracted to moustaches. He asked, since moustaches were not equally distributed among racial groups, if that made him a racist. When he suggested that racialized desire restricted white choices, too, he seemed to equate that with the regular exclusion and rejection experienced by minorities.

In his attempt to focus on the institutional aspects of racism, Popert was in sync with developments in anti-racism at the time. But the experiences of rejection or exoticization, daily occurrences for members of racialized groups, were intensely personal. By his own standards, if sex was the glue that held the community together, such interpersonal racism was profoundly corrosive in a community that was less monochromatic by the day. Finally, by suggesting that nothing needed to be done in the personal sphere, he seemed to dismiss the experiences raised by visible minorities. Their concerns were relegated to secondary status to be dealt with "after the revolution."

The response was overwhelmingly negative. Some, like Richard Fung, were relatively generous.

> I agree with Ken Popert's suggestion that racism cannot be effectively combated at an exclusively personal level and that this is an institution of our society that must be fought in the context of larger social change. However, I don't think that we can therefore say there is nothing we can do or should do in the meantime.

Tony Souza concluded, "Racism is about power. I wish *TBP* would present its readers with a better analysis and understanding of this issue, one which would help us all work together to fight the oppressor common to us all."

Eng K. Ching stated:

> For me, gay liberation does not stop at men loving men or women loving women. It provides me with the condition from which I act towards the end of all other kinds of oppression. . . . By refusing to struggle against the racism in our homosexuality, we let straight society define our sexuality and also block the further advances of gay liberation.

"The disquieting element," wrote John Clifton,

> is Popert's apparent denial of any personal responsibility for the nature of our sexuality. Of course it is true that many environmental forces influence the ultimate shape of our sexual character. Does this, however, mean that we are such altogether passive receptacles as Popert implies?
>
> Popert's implication that anti-racists with racialized sexuality have only two options, either they should give in to racism in sexuality or they should

pinch their noses, swallow their revulsion and dutifully seek sex with the members of whichever race they like the least. This is, I think, a very narrow idea of what consciousness raising about race involves.[18]

A group of twenty-three women demanded a full retraction of the article and apology.

> If we expect heterosexual people to be responsible for their homophobia, if we are not content with them saying "that's the way I was raised, and I am not responsible for that," then how can we justify or ignore our own racism by using the same excuse?[19]

Finally, the board of directors of Gays of Ottawa wrote, bringing together the Red Hot Video ad and Popert's article. GO expressed "its deep concern and fundamental disagreement with *The Body Politic* on two very important issues – racism and misogyny." Its letter said:

> We feel that, in giving the issue of censorship precedence over the broader issues of racism, violence against women and straight male power, *TBP* is losing sight of gay liberation itself. . . . With your apparent positions on racism and straight pornography it is becoming increasingly difficult to maintain this feeling of solidarity as you continue a single-issue preoccupation with censorship and "freedom of the press."[20]

Gays of Ottawa discontinued the sale of *TBP* in its Ottawa community centre.

LOCATION, LOCATION

Because of Richard's deep connections to both the Asian and Caribbean communities, much of our social circle identified as people of colour. I was used to my friends' conversations about experiences of prejudice, marginalization, and discrimination. For most white Canadians, however, it was still possible to live in completely white environments, either unwittingly or by design.

My work also took me outside the circuits in which most people of my background circulated. At the time, I was the legal secretary at the Centre for Spanish Speaking Peoples. We largely dealt with refugee claimants and the difficulties faced by immigrants. Even when they looked as white as I did, most Latin American immigrants faced a range of barriers invisible to the average white Canadian.

Tony Souza had been appointed the Toronto Board of Education's first adviser on race relations, tasked with implementing a range of new policies to challenge pervasive racism in the education system. As part of this work, he had set up a regular "race relations camp" for secondary school students. The retreat was run twice a year at an off-season summer camp called Kandalore in the Haliburton highlands, three hours north of Toronto. I first went as a facilitator in 1981, and by 1983, I was a regular. That September, Souza offered me a part-time contract to do logistics, refine the curriculum, train other facilitators, and follow up with student groups after they returned to school. I left the Spanish centre to reorient myself towards anti-racist education.

Despite the board's injunction that Souza's programs could only deal with race, the process was open-ended. So gender, sexual harassment, homophobia, class, and immigration issues regularly came up. By the summer of 1983 we had been mulling over the similarities, differences, and connections among those issues for several years. So although I still experienced the conditioning that came from moving through the world as a white man, both my personal and professional life helped give me a vocabulary that allowed me to participate in conversations.[21]

The Kandalore process drew on differences to build up a more complicated social picture. No matter how generative, no individual experience could reflect more than a fragment of the whole. Popert had drawn from his own experience, but the collective's largely segregated social world provided little opportunity for cross-reference. His article predictably stumbled across red lines and pushed buttons.

By the time letters on Popert's article started to come in, I was already dealing with a lot of angry friends. It was distressing to realize how little most of my long-time comrades at the paper had thought through these issues. They expressed genuine surprise at the reaction, while I could only be surprised by their surprise.

But I also knew that the formulaic expressions of outrage that characterized early anti-racist work were not very useful in opening up discussions. Telling people what the correct line was and punishing them when they got it wrong was not effective in changing hearts and minds. A public exchange of letters led to entrenchments, and with everyone worked up and defensive, there was little opportunity for even a temporary forum for discussion. I could see no way of establishing a more productive exchange.

The sexual turn that was the basis for Popert's position actually fit well with an approach where the process of knowledge formation began with individual experience. Since sex was often the major thing that gay men had in common, I agreed with Popert that it needed to be investigated, not disciplined. It would ultimately be more fruitful to challenge institutional discrimination in the community. But that didn't mean that we could ignore the impact of racialized sexuality on individuals and on the community we were trying to build.

This discussion was an ill omen for what was to come. A number of white-dominated progressive organizations founded in the 1960s would soon be torn apart by poorly handled debates over race characterized by defensiveness, denial, misunderstanding, and entrenched interests.

On November 21, 1982, Fred, the young man with KS whom Michael Lynch had written about, died. Lynch made the announcement in a second feature in the March 1983 issue. For the first time, he talked about the ritual of mourning.

In February, Positive Parents, a Toronto anti-gay organization (that in retrospect was rather ironically named), demanded the banning of blood donations from homosexuals. Channelling widespread fear and echoing demands of the U.S. religious right, the group also called for testing of restaurant employees, the closure of gay baths, and public warnings of the risk of contamination in gay-frequented premises.

In the March 14 issue of New York's largest gay paper, the *New York Native*, Larry Kramer published his famous article "1,112 and Counting." It opened:

> If this article doesn't scare the shit out of you, we're in real trouble. If this article doesn't rouse you to anger, fury, rage, and action, gay men may have no future on this earth. Our continued existence depends on just how angry you can get. . . . Unless we fight for our lives, we shall die. In all the history of homosexuality we have never before been so close to death and extinction. Many of us are dying or already dead.[22]

Kramer denounced the Centers for Disease Control, the National Institutes of Health, politicians at all levels, and gay men for failing to take the epidemic seriously. But he was already somewhat of a pariah for his 1978 book *Faggots*, in which he had excoriated gay men's promiscuity. Critics charged that the subtext of Kramer's work was always "the wages of gay sin are death." But people were dying, and no one knew why. Hysteria was mounting. In May 1983, five thousand people marched in New York to demand that Reagan allocate more to AIDS research funding.

That same May, two years after the initial Centers for Disease Control report, Health and Welfare Canada set up a fourteen-member Ad Hoc Task Force on AIDS. Alistair Clayton, director of the Laboratory Centre for Disease Control, was appointed chair. The government's lack of urgency was demonstrated when the committee's secretary addressed the issue of applications for research funding. "The usual closing dates are in November or December and grants are awarded six to nine months after submissions have been received." He went on to say, "Economic restraints mean the government will be looking at sharing information and facilities as well as cooperative research."[23]

The committee was made up entirely of doctors and scientists. There were no representatives from any of the "risk groups" that had now been identified – homosexuals, Haitians, or hemophiliacs.

There were, however, representatives from both the Canadian Red Cross blood transfusion service and the Canadian Blood Committee, indicating the government's real concern – that whatever was causing this immune suppression could spread to the general public through the blood supply. In fact, that horse was already out of the barn. Hemophiliacs were falling ill from something in the blood factor they had to take.

The Red Cross was very much in the hot seat. First it announced that volunteer donors thought to be at risk for AIDS would be screened. But when the Haitian community reacted with demonstrations and pickets, the proposal was scrapped. Eager to avoid a similar debacle with the gay community, Red Cross representatives phoned the only gay phone number they had heard about – *TBP*. Ed Jackson picked up the phone and ended up organizing a meeting March 12 that included several *TBP* collective members, reps from Hassle Free Clinic, Michael Lynch and Bill Lewis, leading gay doctors and social workers, and CLGA archivist Alan Miller, who had put together "what was then the world's only bibliography on gay men and AIDS."[24]

COMMUNITY RESPONSE

With a lack of urgency at all levels of government, community members stepped up to the plate. Gays in Health Care called a forum on HIV and hepatitis B at the beginning of April. More than three hundred people came out. Jackson's group proposed the creation of an ongoing AIDS committee, and a follow-up meeting sketched out a blueprint for the AIDS Committee of Toronto.

AIDS was conceptualized as the crisis that followed the bath raids, and ACT first modelled itself after the RTPC. Five working groups were struck: community education, patient support, fundraising, medical liaison, and media and public relations. Participants at the public meeting signed up for ongoing committee work. An executive with representatives from each group would co-ordinate efforts.

Like the RTPC, ACT focused a new wave of energy and a new coalition. Old political hands like Lynch and Jackson now joined with health care professionals, social workers, and young people who had come out since the bath raids. Much of the work was based on a "health from below" model developed by the feminist health movement. Women headed several committees. ACT was volunteer-based, with a skeleton staff to co-ordinate.

TBP concentrated on combatting the kind of hysteria sweeping the United States and treading the line between panic and complacency.

> There are those among us who would deny the political dimension, who say that because people are dying it is irresponsible to raise political questions. But as yet, the medical experts have very little concrete knowledge about AIDS and we have every reason at this stage to be skeptical of definitive pronouncements from that quarter. Especially when they dovetail so readily with a disapproving sexual ethic that has sought to control our lives for other reasons.[25]

By September 1983, half of *TBP*'s world news was dedicated to AIDS.

Virginia Apuzzo, executive director of the U.S. National Gay Task Force, openly condemned the Reagan administration's "policy of gestures." She cited six areas of government failure: failure to expedite research funding, to provide proper funding methods, to stem AIDS hysteria through public education, to address the safety of the blood supply, to include affected groups in decision-making, and to recognize patients' rights of confidentiality and privacy.

While Reagan signed a bill for a public health emergency fund, he expected funds to be transferred out of other programs. He resisted the most hysterical calls from the religious right, but neither did he want tò antagonize them by giving in to gay demands. The safest thing for the president was to do as little as possible. He remained silent.

At the end of the year, *TBP*'s front-page headline read, "Is There Safe Sex?" A month earlier, a team at the Pasteur Institute in Paris had announced the isolation of a new virus that they suspected caused AIDS. But the official answer was still "we don't know." Even the growing consensus about a "single agent" wasn't helpful if it wasn't known for certain how that agent spread.

The best advice seemed to be to follow a hepatitis B model and assume only blood and semen were involved, but no one knew for sure. Sneezing? Sweat? There was a range of advice circulating: limit partners, choose partners carefully, don't exchange fluids, use a condom, don't fuck at all, jack off from a distance. The article advised, "Don't seek advice. *Seek information.*"[26] We were trying to be rational, but the message had a distressing undercurrent of every man for himself. Was this to be survival of the smartest?

AN EPIDEMIC OF DREAD

As a John Greyson safe sex video would later put it, we were in the midst of an ADS epidemic – acquired dread of sex. The ethic of sexual liberation was in retreat. In the July/August 1983 issue, *TBP* did a feature on cruising, riffing on the publication of *Cruise to Win,* an American how-to book about picking up men. The piece consisted of six men describing cruising experiences in big cities, bars, streets, small towns, and tourist traps. Most were in their thirties, one older, one Asian, one Maltese, the rest white. The article was in no way a glorification of cruising scenes. The introduction expressed scepticism about cruising "to win." The men talked about insecurity, their dissatisfaction with various scenes, the racism they encountered – as well as excitement, fun, and camaraderie.

A flurry of letters came in from men expressing their distaste for cruising. The term "sex addiction" entered the debate. One letter cited AIDS and warned about "the consequences of such behaviour." Another cautioned, "Tricking can and will leave one lonely, in doubt of your own value as a person, and possibly cause you to acquire a disease that has no known cure." A letter described the emptiness of the bar scene. *TBP*'s celebration of sexual play and its importance for community seemed to be losing its appeal.

Jim Fouratt, legendary New York nightclub promoter, Stonewall participant, and founder of Wipe Out AIDS, directly challenged the notion that sex
was what held gay communities together.

> Is our identity just sexual? . . . It's not only sex. That's what it was in the
> closet. The illusion has been that what we do in our bedrooms and what we
> do in our private lives is somehow different from the rest of our lives and it's
> not. We bring all of that into our private lives, into our sexual encounters.

Promiscuity is "simply not good enough as a rallying cry for gay liberation." He accused *TBP* of "getting caught on a line built on ten years of gay
liberation, if you can't see reality today and synthesize that, then you get
stuck. . . . Conditions have changed."[27]

Changes in attitude were also reflected in gay men's sex lives. A Colorado
study showed a rapid decline in gonorrhea cases, a good indication that gay
men were having less or at least different kinds of sex. A Wisconsin study on
sexual partners of gay men showed a decline from a mean of 6.8 per month in
1982 to 3.2 in 1983. A questionnaire at Toronto's Hassle Free Clinic found that
fewer clients were going to the baths and more were using condoms. Fifty-
eight per cent said their sex lives had changed because of AIDS.

Meanwhile, everyone was feeling for lymph glands. A year before, most of
us didn't even know we had them. I was sitting at the international desk reading some U.S. paper when I felt the first one in my neck, and experienced a
flash of dread followed by denial. Lots of things could make a lymph gland
swell, apparently. And besides, there was nothing anyone could do about it.

FOR OLD TIMES' SAKE

The police took one last kick at the can with a raid on the Back Door Baths in
April 1983. Perhaps after two years, they were testing our resolve in the face of
the new health crisis. They must have known that they were unlikely to win
any cases. Ironically, the raid took place just before the Toronto Gay Community Council was to debate reopening discussions with the police about a gay-
police liaison.

Instead, the community council and the RTPC reacted with the last of the
huge demonstrations to take Yonge Street. Once again we won the test of
wills. We gathered at Yonge and Wellesley and took the street, but when the
crowd prepared to head north to police headquarters, the cops tried something new. They threw up a line on an angle across Yonge. Unless we actually
broke through their line, we would squeeze ourselves back on the sidewalk as
we proceeded.

There was a brief standoff as the marshalling team huddled. Then the
order was given: simply sit down. *Gandhi* was playing in all the theatres.
Everyone knew the routine. Unless they wanted the street closed all night, to
clear us out, the cops would have to wade in and drag off a thousand sitting

people under the harsh light of the TV cameras. The image wouldn't be an angry mob attacking police lines; it would be police attacking peaceful demonstrators. It was their turn to huddle. They withdrew their line and we proceeded to police headquarters.

This was no longer just an angry crowd. The RTPC had a crack marshalling team with solid communications equipment. We could count on a core group of a thousand disciplined, battle-tested demonstrators. Two years after the original raids, we were a match for any police tactics.

In terms of the proposed liaison, *TBP*'s June 1983 editorial demonstrated how much the lines had hardened.

> Our police problem is not one of mistrust and misunderstanding. Its roots are not a lack of knowledge or sensitivity. They lie in the way the police are organized (so that the brass can say one thing while allowing the force to do another – knowing they can get away with it). And how they are controlled (by the provincial Tories, rather than the specific communities they are supposed to serve and protect). And how they fit into society (as an armed force promoting its own interests, not a neutral administrative agency).
>
> The solutions are political, not educational. They include community control of the police, and defeat of the Tory government which is blocking any kind of structural and organizational change.... Dialogue with our oppressors serves their interests, not ours.[28]

THE MORGENTALER BOMBING

As the gay movement was besieged by AIDS and the cops, the women's movement experienced its first right-wing terrorist attack. Toronto Women's Bookstore, on the first floor of a Victorian building on Harbord Street near the University of Toronto, was a fixture of the Toronto feminist community. In June 1983, Henry Morgentaler opened an abortion clinic on the second floor of the building as part of his ongoing challenge to Canadian abortion laws. Police raided the clinic July 5, seizing records and dragging the doctors off to jail.

The clinic defiantly remained open, but in the early morning of July 29, anti-choice activists broke in the back door and, unable to access the clinic, scrawled some death threats and set the building alight. The clinic itself was relatively undamaged; the Toronto Women's Bookstore was almost completely destroyed. The police were unable to track down the perpetrators. If anyone needed convincing that the right-wing threat to gay and women's liberation was real and serious, the arson put that scepticism to rest.

SPEAKING OF DIALOGUE

Twenty-three-year-old John Greyson was rushing to the bus station to catch the last bus to London, Ontario, to visit his parents on a hot August evening. He had just returned from several months in northern Nicaragua, where he had been filming for a documentary on the Sandinista government's agrarian reform program. His parents had been worried sick. The papers were full of stories of brutal attacks by the U.S.-backed Contra insurgency that was trying to overthrow the left-wing Sandinista government.

Greyson had just crossed Bay Street and was heading south to the bus station when he heard a voice. "Why'd you cross on the red light, faggot?" Two cops stepped out of the shadows. He was bewildered. First, the light had been green. Second, there was nothing about him that would lead anyone to identify him as gay.

The cops asked for identification. Since he'd only arrived from Nicaragua that morning, the only thing he had was his passport. It was a new passport and the Nicaragua entry stamp was the first thing they saw. They started asking him what he'd been doing there and where he was going. He was explaining that he was going to catch a bus when one of the cops knocked the passport out of his grip. When he bent over to pick it up, the other one stepped on his hand. He shouted in pain. They accused him of threatening them.

Nursing his swelling hand, he knew he was in trouble. He said that if they started beating him he was going to scream really loud. They slapped handcuffs on him and threw him into the back seat of a cruiser. It was only as he was being driven to 52 Division that he realized what was going on. The Romans bath was just a couple of blocks north of the bus station. The cops must have assumed that's where he was heading.

He didn't have a number for a lawyer so, although he hardly knew us at the time, he called our commune, RTPC central. I happened to pick up the phone, and was able to rouse Bob Kellerman, one of the lawyers who had been working on the bath raids. Kellerman called the station to negotiate, and after signing a document to promise to appear in court, Greyson was eventually released after three in the morning. He had been charged with disrupting the peace.

When the case came to trial months later, Kellerman had found another gay man who had been beaten by the same two cops under similar circumstances. Their modus operandi was to wait in the shadows and pick off men going into or coming out of the Romans.

When the Crown and the arresting cops saw Kellerman's witness in the courtroom, they immediately huddled, and then asked for some time to speak with the judge. They soon returned with an offer to drop all charges. Greyson wanted a trial to expose what had happened, but Kellerman, probably sagely, advised him to take the offer. There was no trial, no testimony, and no consequences for the cops. Sometimes the system was so rigged it wasn't worth the fight.

In July 1983, the International Gay Association held its fifth conference in Vienna. Gillian Rogerson, now working with me on the international news, attended for *TBP*.

The conference opened with a demonstration demanding that the World Health Organization remove homosexuality from its list of diseases. Austrian law at the time made it illegal to spread information about homosexuality or to organize a gay group, so things were low-key. The demonstration marched quietly to the site of the World Psychiatric Association conference, and since the WHO listed homosexuality as disease number 302.0, they sat down in the street forming that number.

The conference also struggled with the perennial issues of women's participation (12 women delegates, 150 men), how to subsidize travel for those coming from Third World countries, the weakness of North American participation, and pedophilia. But those issues were dwarfed by a new controversy that was a signal of things to come.

The Gay Association of South Africa had applied for IGA membership. GASA was an overwhelmingly white organization that defined itself as "non political, non militant and non sectarian," and would therefore "not concern itself with political issues."[29] The Scottish Homosexual Rights group opposed GASA's membership, arguing that any South African group that claimed to be non-political was supporting the apartheid system by default. By 1983, international campaigns calling for boycott, divestment, and sanctions against South Africa were well established. Nations were cutting off economic, cultural, and athletic relations with the apartheid regime. Unless it could show that it was actively part of the anti-apartheid struggle, the Scots maintained, GASA's membership would violate both the IGA's clearly stated opposition to racism and the international boycott campaign.

Others argued that gay solidarity ought to override national politics, and that GASA could not be held responsible for its government's actions – "The IGA cannot be the police of the governments of the world." The apartheid regime was both racist and homophobic. Gay sex could result in a seven-year prison sentence, but organizing against apartheid was considered treason and could result in the death penalty. GASA was trying to do its best under difficult circumstances and needed to focus.

In the end, GASA's application was deferred until the 1984 conference in Helsinki. In the meantime, the group was asked to document that it was a multiracial organization and did not discriminate against non-white members. That was not good enough for GASA's main supporter, Israel's Society for the Protection of Personal Rights, IGA's only Israeli member group.[30] The Israeli group resigned its IGA membership to protest the deferral. Israel was a major international ally of the apartheid regime, with close military and economic ties.

The international gay movement found itself facing fundamental questions: Did gay solidarity override other struggles for human rights? Should it lend its support to gay people who participated in and benefited from a system that oppressed other groups? How was the IGA to navigate international struggles in a polarized world?

CLOSING ACT

In September 1983, Judge Patricia German upheld the second acquittal on *TBP*'s original "Men Loving Boys" charges. The deadline for a reappeal quietly passed a month later. After three trials, six appeals, two trips to the Supreme Court, and over $100,000 in legal costs, *TBP* was finally out of court for the first time in almost six years.

The paper was already looking to the future. The collective had remained relatively stable for those six years, with eight to ten members. But given the number of volunteers now working on an issue, usually about fifty, rather than being the democratic expression of control by all who laboured to put out the magazine, the collective had evolved into a de facto editorial committee. There was feeling that we had become insular and, at least among some of us, that if there were more voices around the table we might have avoided debacles such as the Red Hot Video furor. So with the September issue, the criteria for membership were relaxed and the collective jumped from eight to twenty-four, twelve new men and four women. It also included its first person of colour, Lloyd Wong.

Thanks to the perseverance of RTPC's legal co-ordination, the last of the original bath raids found-ins had had their day in court, with an 87 per cent victory rate. George Smith had passed on the chair to new blood after almost two years of guiding the organization, and had gone back to working on his long-neglected PhD thesis.

We had won. The police had little to show for their effort. The Richmond Street Baths was the only bathhouse to close. It had been badly damaged, and no bank would provide a sufficient line of credit for repairs. *TBP* continued to publish. Hundreds of people had been pulled out of the closet by the raids, others had been encouraged to come out by the response. Our community networks were immeasurably stronger – the Toronto Gay Community Council, the Gay Community Dance Committee, the street patrol, the Courtwatch program, and Pride were all born in the direct aftermath of the raids. Sports leagues, choirs, social services, and groups aimed at youth to academics to members of various religions or with disabilities continued to proliferate. The historic divisions between activists and gay businesses had largely been overcome. The unofficial anthem of the next few Prides would be Parachute Club's "Rise Up."

TBP had survived the onslaught, but we were now facing a very different world than when the ordeal had begun in 1977. And we ourselves were different. *TBP* and its readership were no longer a group of underemployed twenty-somethings. We were older, more established, and relatively more privileged. Our whiteness, once invisible, was ever more apparent. Every day it was less necessary to be a radical to come out. The community was now dominated by non-political social organizations.

Years of battles against state censorship had shifted movement values to more libertarian positions against state control. That had widened the gulf between gay men and much of the women's movement that called on the state to protect women from pornography.

We had also become a movement that was just as comfortable arguing our case in courtrooms as in the streets, and often more accustomed to cultivating liberal power brokers than working on difficult alliances with other oppressed groups on broader social changes. We were learning to live with immediate, concrete, incremental changes – the next trial, the next court case – rather than dreaming about a fundamental reorganization of society.

There was a shift to more conservative social values in society at large. Reagan's revolution was doing everything it could to promote that, and Canada was far from immune to its influence. So while within the community a minority championed by *TBP* still celebrated uninhibited sexuality, for many gay men, AIDS reinforced the linkage of sex and danger and reactivated a desire for more traditional relationships, putting them in sync with more normative social values.

The response to the bath raids had been a countervailing force. It had brought the non-political community groups together and many people into the streets for the first time. Its focus on the police had generated alliances with other groups subject to arbitrary police power. But as the raids receded into the past and the courts ruled largely in our favour, both community unity around police issues and those alliances began to recede. AIDS would continue to reshape community, identity, and alliances over the next period.

7

Plague and Panic

THE DYING BEGINS

The IGA declared 1984 International Year of Lesbian and Gay Action. Not much happened. A glossy poster was mailed out to member groups. In Europe there were a few actions. The "massive" march on the United Nations headquarters in New York planned for September 30 ended up drawing fewer than two hundred people. AIDS was beginning to overshadow everything.[1]

Deaths were no longer just American statistics. On January 7, 1984, Peter Evans died. Only six months before, he had come out as Canada's first public face of the epidemic. A *TBP* interview dubbed him "Canada's National Person with AIDS." Despite declining health, the soft-spoken young man did a whirlwind of talks and interviews across the country calling for understanding and respect in the face of panic and misinformation.

Evans had been inspired by a reading of the Denver Principles at an AIDS forum in Toronto. The principles, a foundational document for later AIDS activism, were drafted by a group of people with AIDS (PWAs) at the Second National Forum on AIDS in Denver, Colorado, in June 1983. The prologue read: "We condemn attempts to label us as victims, which term implies defeat, and we are only occasionally patients, which term implies passivity, helplessness and dependence upon the care of others. We are people with AIDS." A new identity was in formation.

Evans was the thirty-fifth Canadian to die. He was twenty-eight.

Michel Foucault died in September. Few of us at *TBP* were his close friends, but most of us had met the iconoclastic French philosopher during his 1982 sojourn in the city when he taught a summer course at the University of Toronto. Everyone who aspired to be on top of things had now read his work. He was the leading intellectual of the age. In Toronto, he had preferred The Barn's cowboy and leather ambience to the more preppy bars, and his favourite bath was the Barracks. His obituary said he died of a nervous disorder, but everyone knew it was AIDS.

With every month the blows started landing closer to home. In March

1985, James Fraser was gone. James was the founder and heart and soul of the Canadian Lesbian and Gay Archives. Tall, gawky, garrulous, with a bushy beard and perennially tousled hair, he was a New Brunswicker who could talk anyone's ear off with his rapid-fire East Coast accent, although I always found him a little shy. James had gone to Vancouver in the fall of 1983 to work on a degree in Archival Studies. He died there at thirty-nine.

Don Bell was the roommate of my first boyfriend after Jearld. He was sexy, funny, speedy, and had been the "deejay to the movement," tirelessly lugging his equipment to the early gay dances and other events. He was a regular early contributor to *TBP* and the first to try to computerize our subscription list. He died in May at thirty-four.

ACT

The first years of the AIDS Committee of Toronto were not easy. ACT initially tried to model itself on the RTPC. But the RTPC had conducted a political campaign and, as massive as the task was, it only needed money for a finite number of court cases. ACT, on the other hand, was providing ongoing services with no end in sight. Unlike the RTPC, with volunteers operating out of people's homes, ACT needed staff and an office, and that had to be paid for. Despite misgivings from some of the old political hands, ACT managed to secure a small grant from a joint federal-provincial job creation program.

It also made sense for the group to develop a board of directors, incorporate, and apply for charitable status. Like Pink Triangle Press, ACT found itself needing to conform to the requirements of broader corporate and government structures.

Gary Kinsman, an early ACT employee, helped draft a proposal for "two-level incorporation." There would be a charitable foundation, but ACT itself would not apply for status so that it could engage in political advocacy. The board rejected that proposal. As Kinsman feared, it took only months for board members to cite this charitable status to argue that they could not support a pro-choice action. The organization almost died twice in the first two years. In June 1984 the money ran out after a hoped-for grant was rejected. Only with the help of Susan Fish, the local provincial Progressive Conservative member of the provincial legislature, was enough scraped together to keep the fledgling organization afloat. A year later, another short-term grant from Metro Council (which oversaw Toronto and its surrounding boroughs) pulled ACT back from the brink of closure.

At first, staff largely co-ordinated the work of volunteers. But a need for more consistent standards soon became clear. When a screening and training process for volunteers was set up, however, many volunteers saw it as a loss of control over their organization. The dispute wracked the board.

A third issue was the independence of sub-committees. Like the RTPC, ACT had a number of autonomous committees. The Support Work committee attracted women from rape-crisis and anti-violence work and, often, men with a religious background. Stephen Manning, who later became executive director, was actually a priest during part of his term. The women brought with them years of experience in the women's health movement and an understanding that health was something to be fought for, not the property of experts.

"I think so many women got involved in ACT because a lot of our friends were getting sick and dying," Naomi Brooks remembers.

> It cut to everybody's hearts. Even given all the historical animosity between lesbians and gay men, we all had lots of intense friendships across gender lines that were really important. I can't think of one of the guys that I knew who was sick or died who didn't have a lot of women involved in his care. I think that also goes back to the roles that we take on.[2]

Another group of gay men more connected to ghetto life dominated the Education committee. Fundraising required different specialized skills and connections. The loose structure and demographic differences produced different solitudes, and volunteers often identified more with their working group than with the organization as a whole. Those frictions also expressed themselves at the board level, since the original board included representatives from the various working groups.[3] Manning, dealing with the conflicting factions within ACT, said it was sometimes like "*The Body Politic* meets Rape Crisis Centre."

Early education efforts were aimed at convincing gay men to limit our number of sexual partners to reduce risk. But the April 1984 announcement by the U.S. secretary of health and human services of the discovery of HTLV-III (later known as HIV, or human immunodeficiency virus) as the cause of AIDS, and the growing consensus that the virus was transmitted like other blood-borne infections, required a complete revamping of educational materials to talk about "safer sex" and condom use. At the 1983 Pride, Harvey Hamburg had been called "alarmist" for advocating condoms. By Pride 1984, ACT was handing them out. Such an abrupt change was a challenge. For most gay men, condoms were associated with birth control, and the idea that we might have to use them seemed bizarre.

By the end of 1984, San Francisco baths and sex clubs had been closed, and the city tried to subpoena membership lists to determine the number of "sex monitors" necessary before allowing them to reopen. Similar demands were being heard in New York. As hysteria mounted, it fell to ACT to take a difficult stand. Kevin Orr, now ACT spokesperson, had to explain to a suspicious media that closing baths would be counterproductive. By driving sex underground, it would only make AIDS education more difficult. ACT's position reflected the influence of *TBP* 's sex-positive outlook, the huge effort put into defending the baths after 1981, and the co-operation developed between bath owners and activists. Toronto baths soon became a site for safer sex education, reaching men who had sex with men but who remained outside established gay networks.

RELIGIOUS RE-EVALUATIONS

In March 1982, *TBP* had reviewed *Homosexuality: In Search of a Christian Understanding*, a book published by the United Methodist Church in the United States. It opened with the expected *TBP* line, "Gays who have chosen not to abandon institutional Christianity have also chosen – so what else is new? – to live with a profound contradiction." The reviewer, David Townsend, went on:

> The author's concern to meet gay people "where they're at" boils down to a willingness to leave them where he thinks they are – mired in self-loathing and a desire only to change their orientation, or to make the best of a bad job by living with their handicap. . . . The author's compassion is cheap; his "neutrality" would be comic if it weren't so destructive.

However, Townsend concluded: "Still, I wouldn't dismiss the book; any group discussion of the issue in the institutional church is a step in the right direction."[4]

A year later, Townsend penned a feature called "Staying On" that began, "Through everything there is the perception that to abandon the church would be to lose ourselves." Townsend came out as a Lutheran, "of a reasonably traditional stripe. . . . I put stock in the metaphysical truth of orthodoxy, and am inclined to see the Church, its sacraments and its ritual as essential to my wholeness as a person." He reminded readers of the importance of Christianity's "vision of social responsibility."

His article discussed the "equilibrium" achieved by Paul Murphy, former president of the Toronto chapter of Dignity, the gay Roman Catholic organization, Sue Mabey, an open lesbian struggling to be ordained by the United Church of Canada, and "Bob," a still closeted Lutheran minister in a small city near Toronto. Townsend argued that "rapprochement with the Church is politically expedient." He suggested, "I would rather have Bob counseling a gay seventeen-year-old than leave him to Bob's replacement."[5]

Finally, he framed the church as a site of struggle, citing John Boswell's *Christianity and Social Tolerance* to argue that homophobia is not "inherent" in Christian tradition. Churches were being targeted by the new right, and gay people needed to be on the ground, inside the institution, to make counterarguments and resist.

An interesting play of basic values underlay these arguments. The sexual turn was consolidating a more liberal orientation in the gay movement. This same liberal shift that valued individual decisions, whatever they might be, opened up space in *TBP* to challenge the "self-obsessed and dogmatic" prescriptions of early gay liberation towards religion. At the same time, those

committed to social responsibility found themselves coming to terms with
institutions such as the church, which, despite their practical failures and
homophobia, still emphasized communal values.

Over the next three years, *TBP* would give much more coverage to religious questions. A major issue was a United Church draft statement on homosexuality prepared for its General Council in August 1984. The bone of contention was in the conclusion: "In and of itself, sexual orientation should not be a factor in determining membership in the order of ministry of the United Church of Canada."[6] The report called on the church to "repent" for its persecution of lesbians and gay men in the past, and to work towards the end to discrimination on the basis of sexual orientation.

The core argument was that homosexuality was not sinful since it was not a "choice," but rather something "discovered" by the individual. "Homosexuals are made in the image of God like anyone else." While such a position didn't sit well with notions of the social construction of sexuality, "I was born this way" would increasingly be deployed to justify gay acceptance. Ironically, while racialized minorities had gained acceptance as explanations of difference based on nature and biology gave way to notions of culture and nurture, gay acceptance seemed contingent on the opposite movement, towards biological and natural explanations.

The importance of this argument was underscored by church moderator Clarke MacDonald, who told the General Council that he had spent three hours with a geneticist at the University of Toronto discussing whether being gay was a choice or involuntary. Since the geneticist refused to say categorically that it was involuntary, MacDonald said, "as one who has been the recipient of grace," he objected to the dismissal of the possibility of healing through prayer and the Holy Spirit. The draft statement wasn't adopted, and the council could only agree to commit the church to more study until the next General Council in four years. A motion to recognize the church's gay caucus, Affirm, as a valuable resource in this process was defeated.

A year later, a full-page *TBP* article, "Out from Behind the Veil," reviewed *Lesbian Nuns: Breaking Silence.* While critical of the Catholic Church's anti-sexual positions, the review also noted widespread prejudice against nuns and ex-nuns among many lesbians. "If *Lesbian Nuns* opens up a dialogue within the lesbian community about spiritual practice and prejudice, then the work will have broken another ugly silence . . . the work is a major contribution to the development of women-identified consciousness."[7]

Another article highlighted the growth of Affirmation, the Mormon gay group. "While many gay Mormons have left the Church, not all want to abandon it." Fired from his job at church-affiliated Brigham Young University, "Steve" explained that he still loved the church and accepted most its teachings "except for the gay business." He expressed hope that "maybe through Affirmation and in fifty years when all the 80- and 90-year-old leaders are long gone – we might get a fair hearing. The Church needs to be educated."[8]

The tone of all these articles was to express sympathy rather than disdain for those committed to religious institutions, no matter how homophobic, and to frame their situation as a struggle against oppression from within. This was a long way from the ill-disguised hostility to religion that characterized the paper in the 1970s.

BOYS IN BLUE

On January 28, 1984, *TBP* and the Canadian Lesbian and Gay Archives hosted a goodbye party to our offices at 24 Duncan Street. When we had moved in to the top floor of the old warehouse building seven years before, the Queen Street arts scene a block north was just starting. Now property values were rising and the landlord could make more money selling the building than renting it out to scruffy tenants. The whole arts scene was being forced west as the area became the Entertainment District. (Being at the cutting edge of gentrification is a thankless task.) The party was an effort to raise eight thousand dollars in moving costs to replant us, still on the Queen Street strip, but farther to the west at Bathurst.

Over the course of the evening, more than 350 people scaled the stairs and paid a donation to come to the bring-your-own-bottle party. By 3:00 a.m. only the most intrepid were still on site. At 3:15, two police officers rudely pushed their way into the room and forced the deejay to cut the music. Two obnoxious cops in the *TBP* offices with seventy-five inebriated gay activists was not a good party mix. Faced with a heckling and jeering crowd, they called in reinforcements. That didn't help cool things down. Ed Jackson and Kevin Orr were charged with "unlawfully keeping liquor for sale," and *TBP* volunteer Danny Cockerline, "boasting a striking frock of bold blue," was led away in handcuffs singing "I Love a Man in a Uniform." Down at 52 Division, when ordered to strip, Cockerline accommodated with "a routine the officers won't soon forget."[9]

All charges were eventually dropped. And thankfully, *TBP*'s new digs were just outside the boundary of 52 Division.

We had beaten back the attacks on the baths and *TBP*, but individual washroom busts continued at an all-time high. Despite this, or perhaps because they felt dialogue could produce change, Peter Maloney and Brent Hawkes again proposed the Toronto Gay Community Council consider establishing a gay community–police liaison.

The evidence for the utility of dialogue was not strong. Despite that city's liaison committee, Calgary police set up hidden cameras in April 1984 in the Eaton's department store washrooms and arrested men on charges of gross indecency. They had not raised the issue or explored other options at the committee. A week later, Calgary cops raided Numbers, a store selling cards, sex toys, and magazines, and the only outlet in the city for gay literature. There was also a notable upswing in harassment of sex workers. Many Calgary community members felt that committee meetings were being used by police to gather information rather than to explore new policing strategies.

Maloney's justification was the appointment of a new Toronto police chief. "I think it would be just good politics for us to talk to him," he said, and offered himself up for the job. Glen Wheeler, writing Copwatch for *TBP*, opined, "Perhaps Peter Maloney is right – maybe now is the time for dialogue. No one would be sorry if the hassles and entrapment stopped."[10] CIRPA and RTPC, however, remained opposed. "There is no evidence from past contacts with the police that there is any serious intent to change behaviour or attitudes toward the gay community . . . those who concluded some time ago that the formal liaison must await a change in police behaviour have no reason to change their minds now."[11] The no-dialogue position commanded the majority on the community council, but the never-ending debate was eating away at the organization.

THE WAVE RECEDES

Increasingly, both sides were speaking into a vacuum. The organizations thrown up in the aftermath of the bath raids were melting away. In the summer of 1984 the Gay Street Patrol announced that it was suspending operations because of "declining interest." For three years, the patrol had organized teams to tour the back lanes around Yonge Street, intervening in cases of queerbashing or police harassment. It had marshalled the major demonstrations, run security for the Gay Community Dance Committee, and conducted popular Defensercise classes.

Only five people showed up to an evaluation meeting for the Toronto Gay Community Council in July. An emergency meeting was scheduled for September, but when that meeting failed to draw quorum, it was agreed to suspend operations until April 1985. That left no accountable organization to speak for the community. Ironically, Mayor Art Eggleton had finally asked the TGCC to nominate a representative to his sub-committee on policing. Now there was no one to respond.

Even long-standing organizations were in trouble. CGRO announced it was running an eight-thousand-dollar deficit and laid off its only employee, office manager Christine Donald. Donald's small salary had been covered by grants from the Gay Community Appeal, CGRO's own fundraising efforts, and fees from member groups. Tom Warner explained that many of CGRO's member groups "aren't too secure themselves."

Nor was the Gay Community Appeal in good shape. For the first time since its inception in 1980, the 1984–85 fundraising campaign fell short of its goal.

As the adrenalin from the bath raids and the euphoria of resistance wore off, volunteer-run groups were increasingly under stress. AIDS contributed to the sense of gloom and drew off scarce human and material resources. While CGRO tried to keep things alive with a skeleton of volunteers, the Gay Community Appeal began to experiment with a more professional model. At the end of its unsuccessful 1984–85 fundraising cycle, it hired a part-time executive director.

TBP also felt it. There was rent and a staff of six to pay, even if at moments of financial crisis they still cycled on and off unemployment insurance. But subscriptions were stagnant. We needed to reach out to new audiences. In September 1984, we launched *Xtra*, a twice-a-month, free, four-page "bar rag" that promised "up-to-the-minute reports on upcoming events and local controversies, spotlights on community personalities, sports, gossip, fun photo spreads . . ." While *TBP* had always treated advertising as a necessary evil, *Xtra* made a direct appeal to advertisers and had no compunctions about taking on all comers. "Interested in reaching this city's most active and aware gay men and lesbians – what they call in the ad biz lingo a 'targeted urban market,' *XTRA* readers are Toronto's largest and most sophisticated group of gay people."[12] The model proved astonishingly successful, and was soon keeping *TBP* financially afloat.

RITES

While *TBP* was considering new models, others had already decided we had drifted too far from our original vision. May 1984 saw the launch of *Rites*, pointedly a magazine "for *lesbian* and gay liberation" (my italics). *Rites* gathered those who felt the need for an alternative voice, and tried to be both consciously and assertively feminist and left-wing.

Issue 1 staked its ground.

> Rites stands for: lesbian and gay liberation, feminism and progressive social change. . . . The equal involvement of lesbians and gay men. . . . The expression of the connections between lesbian and gay oppression, the oppression of all women and the experience of other oppressions such as class, race and age.[13]

Rites was organized on a collective model. It included a number of friends including Mary Louise Adams, Gary Kinsman, Heather Ramsay, and Doug Wilson, who had just moved to Toronto from the Prairies. Unlike *TBP*, its collective had an equal balance of women and men. It had more lesbian content, gave more extensive coverage to general feminist and women's issues, and its subscription base, although smaller than *TBP*'s, was also more evenly divided between women and men. *Rites* seemed less compelled to reach out to a non-political audience. Articles were longer, wordier, and more earnest, and its design lacklustre. It avoided messy conflicts around advertising imagery because it hardly had any display ads.

Other than tone, there was remarkably little difference between *Rites* and

TBP on major issues. Both covered the ongoing debates about pornography and both opposed censorship, although *Rites* took care to be less offensive to feminists concerned with sexism and violence in porn. Both covered the battles about ordination in the United Church approvingly, RTPC court and policing issues, the right to serve in the armed forces, and AIDS. Although *Rites* didn't have the networks to generate the same breadth of international coverage as *TBP*, it ran regular news shorts and occasional longer articles.

While *TBP*'s fights with state censorship had cultivated a more libertarian-inflected politics, and it attempted to be intelligible to a broader, less politicized audience, *Rites* reflected a more traditional socialist conception of a community needing to be politicized. *TBP*'s alliances were around the immediate practicalities of fighting censorship or the police; *Rites*' cultivated women and people of colour, groups that supposedly had stakes in fundamental social change.

LESBIAN SEX CONFERENCE

For anyone harbouring a stereotype of dour, political lesbians, the first major lesbian conference to be held in the city in five years was a surprise. The Lesbian Sexuality Conference, held June 8 to 10, 1984, drew three hundred women from across the province and beyond. Mariana Valverde reported for *Broadside* that the conference attracted a whole new crowd. "It had been ages since I had seen a group of lesbians I didn't know, *in the daytime*."

The conference was not without its political edge. Susan Cole opened with a keynote about how lesbian desire was distorted by the reality of life in a sexist society, and warned that "we can be bought off by orgasms." She also reiterated her opposition to S/M, but said she could tolerate it as a private vice similar to her own addiction to major league baseball. She left listeners with a question: "How do we eroticize equality?"

Workshops fell into two categories: sex workshops that included role-plays and skits where women shared stories of their erotic adventures, and mutual support groups designed to address particular needs. Valverde concluded that the conference "put the fun back in sexual politics"[14] but wondered about the significance of talking exclusively about sexual issues in the only lesbian conference held in years.

PRIDE '84: WE JUST WANNA HAVE FUN

In 1984, for the first time, Pride celebrations took place in what was beginning to be referred to as the "gay village." Although there were still more bars and gay-friendly restaurants on Yonge, cruising and hanging out was now firmly entrenched a block east on Church. Just south of Wellesley, a new Second Cup coffee shop's red-tiled steps became a popular spot to sip coffee and socialize on summer afternoons and late into the night. "The Steps" were immortalized in a number of *Kids in the Hall* sketches broadcast nationally on CBC. A block north was the 519 Church Street Community Centre, the de facto lesbian and gay community centre. Cawthra Park, site of the 1984 Pride, surrounded the 519 on three sides. Pride had embraced the ghetto.

TBP's two-page spread on Pride featured an article by Sonja Mills, a young volunteer at the paper. It had been her first Pride. The headline was "Sonja Just Wants to Have Fun!" Mills represented a new generation. She had a "wonderful time" but noted that the event commemorated resistance "to a kind of oppression that seems a little remote to me," describing an "almost painless" coming out "into a relatively secure, established community." She asked, "What does Stonewall mean to you if you were only seven when it happened?" Her generation, like Emma Goldman, wasn't much interested in a revolution they couldn't dance to. It had to be fun.[15]

Mine wasn't the only eyebrow raised among the old guard. Things hadn't started in the 1970s because we wanted to have fun. It was because without a movement, without change, our lives were intolerable. The trials, fighting with the police, long meetings, sleepless nights, working eighteen-hour days to meet deadlines had been exciting, satisfying, ultimately rewarding – but often far from fun. The AIDS crisis certainly wasn't fun. But we held our tongues, not wanting to sound like old fogies or to discourage new blood at the paper.

Something was changing, however. The April issue of *TBP* had announced the formation of the Notso Amazon Softball League. The Notsos would soon become the largest lesbian organization in the city with at least a dozen teams of twenty to twenty-five members plus administrative organizers and umpires. Like the LOOT house on Jarvis Street had, the Notsos functioned as an autonomous lesbian meeting place. "That was where the feminist intellectuals and the working class dykes met," recalls Naomi Brooks, a long-time player. "There were always lots of spectators. Everybody went to the bar together afterwards."[16] LOOT had envisioned lesbian autonomy as a political project. The Notsos implemented it as a recreational one.

Mills's article did nothing to assuage the anxiety that I felt every year as Pride approached. The event had emerged as our major expression of visibility. Yet the often fractious, all-volunteer committee seemed so fragile. In the weeks leading up to Pride, I became obsessed with the forecast. If people were only interested in fun, a cold, rainy weekend might bankrupt the group and the whole effort would fall apart. After my first Pride in 1974, there had not been another for seven years. If Pride disappeared at the same time that so many other venerable organizations were floundering, and AIDS destroyed our sexual networks and drove people back into the closet, I feared losing the ground we had gained over the last decade and a half.

Mills's article was not the only thing to signal a growing generation gap. The 1980s brought changing styles – new wave, punk, new romantic, Boy George look-alikes, gender bending – all quite distinct from the moustached Castro clone look that dominated the '70s generation. The September issue of *TBP* carried a story about "new wavers" picketing two popular downtown gay bars, Cornelius and Chaps, after being turned away by bouncers. The group also booked a table at Pride, got hundreds to sign a petition against bar discrimination, and marched as a contingent in the parade. The manager at Cornelius explained that they were not admitted because their appearance "intimidated" other patrons. Also, new wave people only came to dance and didn't drink enough.[17]

In January 1985, *TBP* writer Danny Cockerline published a feature on his experience in Toronto bars. He asked, "Are the enforcers of gay bar door policies the new queerbashers in our midst?" Cockerline was already in Cornelius one night when the bouncer told him to leave, since "guys aren't supposed to wear make-up. Only girls are." Cockerline was wearing eye makeup, as well as men's overalls, running shoes, and a military haircut. In the piece he noted that Chaps was now regularly excluding new wavers, and Boots had adopted a "men in men's clothing and women in women's clothing" policy. Even a former Mr. Boots had been bounced because he wasn't considered sufficiently manly. The management at Club 101 had begun excluding unaccompanied women. An *Xtra* survey found that drag was no longer welcome in any of the city's bars unless confined to the stage.

Cockerline wrote that beneath the excuses was a desire to sanitize the image of the community. He cited a letter to *TBP* that argued, "We need good leaders to promote a positive image to the straight community. In order to better educate them, they have to feel comfortable with us.... Society has these stereotypes because we refuse to speak out against our own community members." It seemed like the bars at least were getting over their reluctance to do just that.

Cockerline concluded:

> While brooding at Yonge and Wellesley that summer night [after being thrown out of the bar], I thought back to the winter of 1981 when 3,000 people had gathered at that same intersection to protest the arrest of 300 of us in the police raids on our bathhouses. That was my debut as an openly gay person; at the age of 20, marching with all those people I felt powerful and free for the first time in my life.... Sitting there again under very different circumstances in 1984 and feeling anything but free, I wondered what had happened.[18]

There was no real recourse. Bars were free to set dress codes. But two lines in Cockerline's piece that went unexplored revealed far more than a problem of style or generations. "Reports have also been received at *The Body Politic* over the past year of discrimination against people on the basis of sex, skin colour, age and class. Gay Asians Toronto circulated a flyer during the summer informing people of discrimination at Chaps."

Mainstream culture in the 1980s rejected the androgyny of the '70s and reaffirmed strict gender differentiation. Men wore muscles and women wore big hair. The gay mainstream was following suit. We were not that much different from broader society, it turned out, and not just in terms of dress. The fact that *TBP* foregrounded discrimination on the basis of style while race was relegated to an add-on foreshadowed difficulties to come.

DOPE TO COKE

In the 1970s the recreational drug of choice among gay men was marijuana or its more concentrated sister, hash. The high was generally contemplative, dreamy, and mellow. Many combined it with the deep relaxing rush of poppers, either on the dance floor or during sex. But by the mid-1980s, cocaine was emerging as the leading party drug. Coke produced an electric burst of high-octane energy, a feeling of invulnerability and inflated self-confidence.

There was much rumination about whether this shift was linked to AIDS. Who wanted to mellowly contemplate a terrifying epidemic? It was much better to feel confident, invulnerable, and full of life. But such speculation overlooked the material economy of drug use. Once restricted to the relatively wealthy, the price of coke was plummeting. Reagan's Nicaraguan Contras were financing their efforts to overthrow the Sandinistas by channelling vast quantities of cocaine to the North American market. Their CIA handlers looked the other way.

An even cheaper and highly addictive cocaine derivative, crack, was soon part of the mix, flooding America's poor black ghettos. The crack epidemic and Reagan's War on Drugs were a pretext for a massive increase in the incarceration of black men in the United States. Whether this was a strategy aimed at crushing the resistance of black communities or just an inevitable outcome is still debated. The fact that the Contras were involved and the CIA knew about it is now incontrovertible.[19]

As crack use seeped across the border, it also spread among gay men in Toronto. I began to notice more hustling in the baths as the unfamiliar smell of crack replaced that of marijuana, and users turned a trick to pay for their next hit.

LESBIANS AND GAYS SUPPORT THE MINERS

Across the Atlantic another kind of polarization was emerging. Margaret Thatcher came to power in 1979 when her anti-immigrant statements bled off votes from the racist, far-right National Front. Like Reagan, Thatcher was committed to a neo-liberal program of reducing government spending, privatizing state-owned utilities, lowering taxes to business, and cutting deficits. And like Reagan, she was swept to power thanks to an alliance with right-wing social conservatives.

Thatcher's famous quote "There is no such thing as society, there are only individual men and women" reflected the liberal individualist underpinnings of her economic strategy. But the final part of that quote often goes unmentioned: "and there are families." Thatcher didn't just believe in liberal individualism. As a deeply conservative person, she felt loyalty to traditional family relationships. Lesbians and gay men were a threat. Police harassment and queerbashing intensified.

Thatcher's first term seemed destined to be her last, until the Argentinean junta invaded the Falkland Islands in 1982. She sent in the Royal Navy, retook the islands, and rode to a second victory on a wave of patriotism. Then she got down to business. Unions were a major barrier to restructuring, and in her second term she took them on, characterizing unions as "the enemy within."

In March 1984, Thatcher announced the closure of twenty coal mines and a long-term plan to shut down seventy more. The mines, nationalized in 1947, were the economic life-blood of dozens of small communities. The National Union of Miners responded with mass walkouts and strikes. Thatcher tried to crush the union with brutality and arrests, and sequestered union funds to starve out the strikers. In June there was a battle between five thousand miners and five thousand police officers. A few weeks later at London's annual Pride march, a group of lesbians and gay men began collecting funds for the embattled mining communities. They soon became Lesbians and Gays Support the Miners.

In the words of one LGSM member, the group worked to bring "socialism onto the agenda of sexual politics in the London lesbian and gay community . . . [and] sexual politics onto the agenda of trade union politics."[20]

The group's driving force, Mark Ashton, a twenty-three-year-old Irishman, belonged to the Young Communist League. According to Roy James, an LGSM member:

> There was a clear strategy on Mark's part to align himself with the labour movement in order to get gay politics, sexual liberation, HIV and AIDS treatment on to the political agenda. . . . Thatcher and Reagan were seen to be in cahoots. They were resisting any requests or demands that would start research funding. . . . We, as gay people, saw it as a form of genocide.[21]

Most of the group's energies were focused on raising money for the small Welsh mining town of Dulais. Members took collection buckets to gay areas, often finding themselves in a cat-and-mouse game with police who tried to stop the collections.

There were other difficulties, too. Much of the London community had fled the homophobia of their small towns. Why should gay people support the same communities that had made their lives hell, or a labour movement that had never supported gay rights? LGSM responded that lesbians and gay men and the miners were both being abused by the Thatcher government and needed to stick together. It was an appeal to solidarity – a horizontal alliance.

The high point of the campaign was the December 1984 Pits and Perverts concert at the Electric Ballroom in Camden, headlined by Jimmy Somerville and Bronski Beat. Somerville had recently topped the charts with his gay anthem "Smalltown Boy."

Dai Donovan, a union leader from Dulais, spoke to the concert crowd.

> You have worn our badge, Coal Not Dole, and you know what harassment means, as we do. Now we will pin your badge on us, we will support you. It won't change overnight, but now 140,000 miners know that there are other causes and other problems. We know about blacks and gays and nuclear disarmament and we will never be the same.[22]

The concert raised almost six thousand pounds. I gave it the featured picture in the world news in the February 1985 issue of *TBP*, and the International Socialists organized solidarity rallies in Toronto. By the end of 1984 there were at least eleven LGSM groups across the United Kingdom.

But the LGSM wasn't without its internal difficulties. Gay men from various socialist groups soon joined, and meetings often turned into a pissing match to see whose politics could dominate. In November 1984, most of the lesbians broke away, bored of the male-dominated infighting. Lesbians Against Pit Closures wanted to stress the growing independent role of women in the strike.[23]

After a year, in March 1985, the strike was broken, but the impact of the solidarity was long-lasting. At London's 1985 Gay Pride, a large contingent of miners and their families from South Wales led the march (as depicted in the 2014 film *Pride*). The same year, Britain's powerful Trades Union Congress passed a resolution supporting gay rights, and a year later at the Labour party conference, a motion to support equal rights for lesbians and gay men was proposed. Although opposed by the National Executive Committee, it won a vote from the floor with the support of the National Union of Mineworkers. While the solidarity shown to the miners had theoretically been a horizontal alliance, in practice, the British union movement was a major social force. Its reciprocal solidarity was a huge boost to the embattled gay rights movement in desperate times.

Mark Ashton died a year later of AIDS. He was twenty-six.

IMPROPER CONDUCT AND THE BIRTH OF HOMONATIONALISM

Nestor Almendros, the award-winning Spanish filmmaker, moved to Cuba with his family after the revolution, but returned to Europe when two of his early short films were banned by the Cuban government. In 1984 he came to the Toronto International Film Festival (then known as the Festival of

Festivals) with *Improper Conduct*, a documentary he had co-directed with Orlando Jiménez Leal.

Improper Conduct focuses on the Cuban government's deplorable treatment of homosexuals, well known since the early gay liberation writings of the 1970s. The worst example was the period between 1965 and 1967, when gay men and other "undesirables unfit for military service" were sent to re-education camps. That program was shut down after considerable criticism within the country, and homophobia returned to the common or garden variety found in much of Latin America and the Caribbean. But Almendros made state-sponsored homophobia the centrepiece of his attack on the Cuban government. For him, it was emblematic of revolutionary repression, and showed that Cuba was an unredeemably vicious totalitarian state.

Although widely praised by mainstream U.S. media, and winner of the audience award for Best Documentary at the 1984 San Francisco International Lesbian and Gay Film Festival, the film also received criticism. Ruby Rich, director of the film program at the New York State Council of the Arts, said that many of the film's claims "ring true in reverse proportion to the viewer's familiarity with Cuba. I was astonished by one émigré's description of Cuba's rigidly enforced tourist routes, having myself just come back from days wandering Havana unattended."

Richard and I interviewed Almendros for *TBP*. Our review scrupulously made no effort to deny or justify the repression on the island. But we asked pointed questions about Almendros's overall portrayal of the situation. He made much of the 125,000 Cubans, some of whom were gay, who jumped at the chance to leave during the Mariel exodus in 1980 when U.S. immigration was briefly opened. But we asked, "Wouldn't the opportunity to do the same thing produce a comparable immigration from any one of many Caribbean or Latin American countries?" There was no denying homophobia in Cuba, but from all accounts, it didn't seem much different from other countries in the region. The film also failed to consider the huge gains in literacy, health care, housing, and education that the revolution had produced, which benefited all Cubans, gay and straight alike.

Richard Goldstein, writing in New York's *Village Voice*, managed to capture the core of the problem.

> There is another agenda in this film, perhaps more central than its liberationist aims and surely more problematic. That agenda involves the delegitimization of the present Cuban government, a prospect we may well be forced to contemplate if Reagan is re-elected. To progressives in North America who might be expected to oppose any overt or covert assault on the Cuban state, a film like *Improper Conduct* could be a powerful deterrent. It makes personal and "progressive" what right wingers always say about Communist societies.[24]

This was something quite new for the gay liberation project. We were being deployed in a Cold War battle to discredit America's enemies.

In 1984 this was still a hard argument to make. At least half the U.S. states still punished "sodomy" with long prison sentences. Only a handful of cities had human rights protection. Gay foreigners were not legally allowed to enter the United States. Homosexuality was grounds for dishonourable discharge from the army. Some states had laws against teachers saying anything that might be construed as promoting homosexuality. And the anti-gay witch-hunts of the McCarthy era were not far in the past.

But a strange mixture of American patriotism and gayness was definitely in the air. In June 1985, a TWA plane was hijacked by Lebanese militia.[25] More than a hundred passengers, including two gay men, Jack McCarty and Victor Amburgy, were held for seventeen days. McCarty, owner of the popular San Francisco bar Elephant Walk, was also a volunteer at the Shanti Project, a peer counselling centre for PWAs.

Fearing what might happen if their kidnappers found out they were gay, the two posed as brothers. Ironically, their captors apparently expressed admiration for the couple's butch Castro Street clone look of tank-tops and olive fatigue pants.

When the two returned to the United States with the last group of hostages to be released, they stepped off the plane arm in arm to be greeted by President Reagan. Neither man had been previously out to their parents, but they were welcomed as gay heroes. Back in San Francisco, the heroes became a media sensation, receiving an official city reception. The Gay Men's Chorale sang "America the Beautiful" to set a "patriotic tone." Then, according to the *Bay Area Reporter*, Kramer led the crowd in singing "The Star-Spangled Banner." "Eyes grew moist as the national anthem became a statement of renewed patriotism for many, gay and straight." The music was requested by the heroes in order "to keep politics out of the ceremony."

Much of the press used the story as an opportunity to chorus about how homophobic Muslims executed gay people, in contrast to the freedoms of America. Others were more critical of the patriotic bandwagon. Allen White ended his report in the *Reporter* acidly, noting that despite McCarty's association with the Shanti Project, when asked about the U.S. government's record on AIDS funding, he "refused to say anything that would cast a negative view of America."[26]

RESISTING CENSORSHIP

With this promise of scarcely comprehensible new bedfellows upon us, some issues stayed depressingly the same. In February 1984, the Development Education Centre had to appeal the Ontario Censor Board's attempt to classify Lizzie Borden's feminist sci-fi film *Born in Flames* as Restricted, requiring cuts before screening. The film had been scheduled for a week's showing, including benefits for *FUSE* and *Broadside* magazines. On May 31, police seized the projector and copies of a number of tapes shown as part of the British Canadian Video Exchange '84 at A Space gallery. Among them was *Framed Youth*, a tape produced by the London Lesbian and Gay Video Project. Both Richard and I were there when the grim, dark-suited men hauled away the projector and the tapes.

A Space and the Ontario Film and Video Appreciation Society cited the new Constitution in their challenges to the censor board. As a result, the board was recast as the Ontario Film Review Board in December 1984, and its vague guidelines were clarified. Unfortunately, the clarification actually extended its powers. The review board continued to tighten the screws on independent film and video producers.

In response, a province-wide coalition of artists, feminists, and lesbian and gay community groups went on the offensive and organized Six Days of Resistance Against the Censor Board. John Greyson emceed a Toronto event wearing a fetching cocktail dress emblazoned with the slogan "Fuck you Mary Brown." The banned film *Taxi zum Klo* was screened without interruption.[27] Law professor Brenda Cossman referred to Six Days as "the largest group civil disobedience in Ontario history."[28]

We were also fighting on another front. A Progressive Conservative government had won a federal landslide in September 1984. The Trudeau years were over. Canada Customs stepped up its targeting of imported magazines. American magazines that weren't banned completely began appearing with blank pages sprinkled through their Canadian editions. Even the word "glorp" was deemed obscene and whited out in a comic strip picturing a blow job. *The Joy of Gay Sex* was banned, and the mainstream U.S. monthly *The Advocate* was occasionally blocked. Materials sent to Glad Day Bookshop in Toronto and Little Sisters, the Vancouver lesbian and gay bookstore, were singled out for special scrutiny. The Canadian Committee Against Customs Censorship was formed. More demonstrations, more appeals, more court cases.

ZAMI

I thought *TBP* was turning the corner after the heated rhetoric around Ken Popert's article on race in 1983. The community was beginning to reflect Toronto's growing racial diversity. Gay Asians Toronto was now joined by Zami, a group for Black and West Indian lesbians and gay men.

Zami's arrival was covered in *TBP* with an attractive picture of Douglas Stewart, Debbie Douglas, and their partners. Stewart had grown up in an immigrant neighbourhood in the suburbs. Douglas had come out to Richard and me after attending one of the board of education anti-racist camps as a high school student. She was already married with an infant daughter at the time, and when her marriage broke down and she needed a place to live, we put her in contact with Makeda Silvera and her partner, Stephanie Martin.

Silvera and Martin were a lesbian couple from Jamaica who owned a large house on Dewson Street in the west end. They transformed the house into a Caribbean feminist commune. Whenever Richard and I dropped over, there was a pot of food percolating on the kitchen stove, Caribbean music on the record player, an indeterminate number of young men and women, mostly women, hanging out, and intense conversations. The couple also founded Sistervision Press, which would become an important publisher of works by women of colour marginalized by the white Canadian publishing business.

The Dewson Street commune was ground zero for black and Caribbean lesbian and gay organizing in the city. Doug Stewart was the first man to be invited to move in, and for most of the time the only man who officially lived there. He credits the house as the foundation of his political education. "An aspiring middle-class kid," he had met Silvera and other black feminists when volunteering at a Black Youth Hotline run out of the Immigrant Women's Centre on College Street.

> My volunteering was more of a charity model . . . why don't we help the less fortunate in the community . . . but the women at the centre were like, okay, we've got to school this brother. . . . [They] educated me about how lovely it was that I wanted to do all of that, but there's a larger political analysis and context. This is not about charity, it's about solidarity because you are also saving your own ass. They started problematizing that politics.[29]

For Stewart, black feminism filled a political void that allowed him to bring together his gay and black identities.

> In terms of bars, the black gay men I met were not very much interested in being around black people. They felt the black communities were very much a place of discomfort or danger or rejection. So many of them were around white men. . . . And the other brothers that I met at apartment parties were very clear that they didn't want to be out, and had a critique that if you wanted to be out you must think you're a white guy. Only white guys can afford to be out there that way.[30]

The idea for Zami came out of conversations at Dewson Street. Debbie Douglas remembers:

> We had all just met each other and we began thinking of other folks like us who didn't have a space to have this conversation and to get to know each other. . . . We wanted a group who could speak to gay and lesbian issues in the black community and to issues of blackness and racism within the lesbian and gay community.

Zami started meeting at 519 Church, as a support and discussion group for those just coming out or dealing with racism in the white-dominated gay ghetto. "We never knew who was going to come through the door, and all sorts of people came through the door," recalls Courtnay McFarlane, who joined the group while still in high school.[31] Zami always walked the line between personal support and political activism. As "the visible black queer organization in the city," Zami took part in Pride, held social events, spoke out in the Caribbean community, and was the black presence in lesbian and gay community events. "The early movement was led by black lesbian feminists, and they are still crucial today," remarks Rinaldo Walcott, years later.[32]

As time went on, however, Zami became more male dominated. Women still participated, but they were also involved in a range of other organizations such as the International Women's Day Committee or the Black Women's Collective, a black feminist organization made up largely of lesbians. For black gay men, however, other than apartment parties, Zami was one of the few spaces where they didn't have to deal with the racism of white gay spaces. Until the late 1980s, Zami was the training ground for a cohort of activists who would go on to exert a powerful black presence in Toronto's lesbian and gay communities.

GAT

Gay Asians Toronto played a similar role. In 1981, Chopsticks, the group's first major cultural event, was a fundraiser for the RTPC. Alan Li, then a medical student at the University of Toronto, joined that same year and soon became a dynamo in the Toronto community. Li was a keynote speaker at the 1982 Pride, and in 1983 helped organize the first Celebrasian, a cultural night that drew an audience of hundreds. (Li would return to Hong Kong for a period in 1986, and help spark a wave of gay organizing there.) GAT was soon publishing a regular *Celebrasian* newsletter. Lloyd Wong, another key member, was only seventeen when he joined in 1980. He went on to be a member of the *TBP* collective and a writer for *FUSE Magazine*, and was featured in Richard's videos. Although officially a men's group, GAT also maintained close relationships with Asian lesbians such as Mary-Woo Sims, who would go on to play a leading role in LGBT politics and human rights in Canada.

In an attempt to document the moment, in November 1984 Richard premiered his first documentary, *Orientations*. The tape, made with the co-operation of GAT on a $2,500 grant from the Gay Community Appeal, explored the lives of a range of East, South, and Southeast Asian lesbians and gay men in Toronto. Philip Solenki, one of the few of people of colour who wrote for *TBP*, called it "pioneering" in his review. *Orientations* dealt with coming out into a white community, racism, family expectations, and a range of other issues. Interviews featured Alan Li, Prabha Khosla, Mary-Woo Sims, Tony Souza, Nitto Marquez, Lloyd Wong, and others near the beginning of their trajectories as community activists.

Then the shit hit the fan. "BLACK MALE WANTED. HANDSOME, SUC-CESSFUL, GWM would like young, well built BM for houseboy. Ideal for student or young businessman. Some traveling and affection required. Reply with letter, photo, phone to . . ."

It was the text for a classified ad to be placed in the February 1985 issue of *TBP*. The volunteer who opened the envelope flagged it, and Solenki, who also helped out with the classifieds, was the first to object. But since the collective wasn't meeting until after the publication date, and the ad didn't contravene the paper's policy about not *rejecting* people on the basis of race, it ran in the February issue.

Solenki asked that the ad be discussed at the next collective meeting, three days after the February issue hit the streets. He also spoke to friends in Zami about his discomfort. At the meeting, the collective was seriously divided between those of us concerned with racist stereotyping and those more concerned with freedom of expression. We agreed to host another meeting in two weeks with members of Zami, Gay Asians Toronto, and another new group, Lesbians of Colour.

The meeting was a disaster. First, it was poorly attended by collective members. According to Alan Li, representing GAT, "those of us representing non-white minorities felt that the proceedings . . . and the attitudes of certain collective members were far more offensive and dangerous than the ad itself . . . with the collective as the jury and with Zami and Gay Asians Toronto having to convince them of our feelings that the ad was racist." He noted that Popert restated that while he felt "the inviolability of sexual desire" was the ultimate goal of gay liberation, he would agree to pulling the ad so as not to offend potential friends. "Gerald Hannon, on the other hand, was not intellectually convinced . . . and would not change his stand [to print the ad] because of pressure from other people's emotional reactions. . . . We were made to feel that our arguments were non-representative, our objections hysterical and our feelings defensive."[33]

Richard agreed.

> The fact that a racist ad appeared in *TBP* is not the main issue any longer. . . . The concerns raised later by Zami and Gay Asians Toronto met with an incredibly patronizing dismissal. . . . As someone who has witnessed a lot of heavy debates around gay, race and women's issues, I was actually shocked by the level of arrogance and the cliché responses at that meeting.[34]

After the joint Zami/GAT/*TBP* meeting, the issue was raised at a public screening of *Orientations* at 519 Church Street. The overwhelming majority of those in attendance criticized *TBP*. A flurry of memos was exchanged between collective members, and at a tense collective meeting on February 25, a large majority voted not to reprint the ad until a new policy could be developed. A motion to issue an apology, though, was defeated. A five-page feature in the April issue gave a synopsis and included letters and edited versions of some of the internal memos circulated among collective members.

Popert led off, explaining that he had been experimenting with S/M and that the often homophobic scenarios should not be confused with real homophobia.

> I think the study of desire is the most interesting thing that there is; it is not there to be morally evaluated and either glorified or condemned. . . . Desire is inviolable. . . . If black males as house boys are expelled from our pages today, I fear that black males as slaves will be given the boot tomorrow. And the appetite for scissoring people's desires down to the size of pusillanimous political agendas will grow. . . . I wrote of myself that "he once thought his politics should guide his sex life, but has since found out that they both work better if his sex life guides his politics."[35]

In my extract I said:

> Our masthead does not read "a magazine for the inviolability of desire." It says a magazine for gay liberation. . . . The attempt to conflate them seeks to replace the rich and complex politics which our movement and this paper have developed for the last decade and a half with a narrow and short-sited libertarianism. . . . Although we demand the freedom to play with the symbols of social power, our goal is to overcome the abuse of that power in the real world. . . . The ad does not ask someone to *pretend* to be black. Nor is the successful white male fantasizing about his colour. . . . We must . . . see to it that the "desire" of dominant sectors does not run roughshod over the sensitivities of others and contribute to more fragmentation and division.

Richard Summerbell challenged Popert's dichotomy between reality and fantasy. "Is it reasonable to be offended, threatened, frightened or made angry by a depiction of a racist scene, even if this scene were just a sexual fantasy? My contention is that it is reasonable."[36]

Alan O'Connor concluded, "We need a sense of responsibility and care along with fun and enjoyment. The old arguments in terms of the inviolability of desire leave out too much ordinary experience."[37]

Gerald Hannon was firmly in favour of reprinting.

> That meeting with Zami and Gay Asians . . . certainly clarified that the ad did, in fact, offend them very strongly. I am quite sure that if we publish the ad and others like it, they would consider us arrogant and insensitive and refuse to have anything to do with us. But I still feel we must publish the ad. Our responsibility in these cases is to listen to the people who are wounded, explain why we are taking the actions that we are taking (explaining that it

is not a gratuitous insult or a mindless swipe, but that it is a critical part of our politics) and say we hope we can work together, given that we are going to do this for these reasons. And if in fact we can't, that simply tells me our political agendas are not sufficiently similar for us to work together in any productive way right now. . . . But surely the ad represents only a particular form of a very widespread fascination with interracial sex. *I* feel it – I don't want a houseboy, but I think I would like a big black stud to fuck me because I know he's going to be passionate and have a big dick, and that's also a little scary, and I'm also afraid he's going to smell and how am I going to handle *that*, and I don't really want to have sex with most Asians, although a lot of them are cute but they're so damned quiet and exquis- ite. . . . All right – I don't believe these stereotypes, and I think they are harmful. But I recognize that they are *feelings*, which intercede, particularly at sexual moments when feelings are more likely to surge forward than my rational beliefs on the matter. . . . If I didn't know better, I'd feel ashamed of myself. . . . I would like not only to accept this ad as it is, but remove what restrictions we presently put on ads. Accept people saying "no blacks." Accept "no fats or fems." Then find some way, editorially, of making people aware of what they're doing in the ads, particularly if they're doing it mind- lessly.[38]

Chris Bearchell recalled our refusal to run the Honest Joe Martin ad in 1980.

Martin thought our politics were enough like his (favouring an abstract notion of freedom that includes the freedom to discriminate and exploit) that he could expect to be welcomed. . . . Gay liberation is as much about power and freedom as it is about sex, because it is informed by our daily experience of oppression and rebellion. Libertarian theory was, and is, clearly inadequate to gay reality. The libertarian impulse promoting the "inviolability of desire" is a denial of the significance of social power . . . focusing on the unacceptability of racism implies that individuals can and should take responsibility for changing the world.[39]

The next two issues were filled with letters. We were called sanctimonious, excoriated, and congratulated for opening up a much-needed discussion. Doug Stewart noted:

The other thing that bothers me about this whole issue is when people sup- porting the ad use the word "we." Who are "we"? It seems to imply the gay community. At the same time it excludes the people of colour within the same community. . . . I now understand why Black gay activists define themselves first and foremost as Black and as gay second. Because not only does the gay community write around us a lot, but also because there are choices involved in revealing our sexuality, but not when it comes to race.[40]

> Who wants to be patronized and treated as a gadfly minority, a nuisance? Who wants to be automatically confined to the periphery of the newspaper and of the movement, while white men without any sense of how they hold and use power go about their "normal" business? A few people from the hyphenated gay communities might keep talking and writing; their opinions will undoubtedly be relegated to the letters page. But most of them will give up hope, and stop trying to make a difference.... Then the advocates of abstract desire, those who forget that all desires are rooted in certain power structures, will breathe a sigh of relief, having achieved hegemony over the definition of gay liberation.... A few months or years later they'll sincerely ask one another; why can't we get more women to work with us? Why can't we get lesbians of colour and gay Asians and all those people to come to *our* meetings and write for *our* paper?[41]

A month later in the June 1985 issue, *TBP* announced its new ads policy. The houseboy ad would never run again. We would not accept ads "which seem racially abusive or stereotypical (or which are abusive or discriminatory on other grounds), and which appear to be asking for a relationship of *real* subservience. Ads which are clearly directed to fantasy alone would not be turned away."[42] The decision, once again, required a majority vote rather than consensus. The collective remained divided.

For people of colour, the experience fit a familiar scenario. A white boys' club in control of the country's principal gay liberation voice, insensitive, uncomprehending, and dismissive of the concerns of others, holding on to their power. But in the collective what was at stake, as several memos pointed out, was the meaning of gay liberation itself. A fault line had emerged. It was not generational. It was the core of old hands, those of us who had been around since the 1970s, who were at loggerheads.[43]

The increasing assertiveness of people of colour was demonstrated that July when the International Gay Association once more tried to gain a foothold in North America, holding its seventh international conference in Toronto. Members of Zami, GAT, and Lesbians of Colour organized nine conference workshops, and liaised closely with Third World delegates, putting questions of race and racism squarely on the IGA agenda. A concurrent history conference, Sex and the State, organized by the Canadian Lesbian and Gay Archives, made "broadening the scope of lesbian and gay history to encompass and be defined by the experiences of people in the third world and of lesbians and gays of colour"[44] a major objective.

AN OPENING

Although the Tories now controlled the federal government, something remarkable happened at the May 2, 1985, general election in Ontario. After forty-two years in power, the Progressive Conservatives lost an election. Well, they didn't actually lose. They still held most seats in the legislature, but they were a minority in relation to the opposition. David Peterson's Liberals and Bob Rae's NDP struck a deal and defeated the government in June.

Peterson became premier. In exchange, he agreed not to call an election for two years and to pass some NDP-favoured legislation. It was a huge shake-up. For the first time in anyone's memory, we wouldn't be faced with an openly hostile, homophobic government in Queen's Park.

SIMON NKOLI

I was digging through my stack of international newspapers when a small article in *Gay Scotland* caught my eye. It reported that a jailed anti-apartheid activist had come out in prison in South Africa. There were few details, but I was intrigued. A black, gay, South African anti-apartheid activist – given the debate the paper had just been through, that seemed just the kind of story that the community needed to hear about.

Both Richard and my sister were involved in TCLSAC, the main anti-apartheid solidarity group in the city, and I often helped at demonstrations in support of the growing boycott movement. One of our white South African friends had recently returned home to work in the underground. Lisa got me his number in Johannesburg. He sleuthed around and got back to me with a name, Simon Nkoli,[45] and the address of Nkoli's lover.

Nkoli grew up in a poor single-parent family. An anti-apartheid activist since his school days, he was first arrested as a teenager in 1976 after helping organize resistance to mandatory study in Afrikaans. That first time, he was held for 105 days without charge. While at college, he became the first Transvaal regional secretary of the Congress of South African Students (COSAS) and was soon a secret member of the African National Congress (ANC, then illegal) and the United Democratic Front. COSAS became involved in helping organize rent strikes in the black townships. After addressing several meetings and rallies, Nkoli was arrested again. This time he was held for seven months and tortured before being released.

Nkoli had come out to his mother at eighteen, and after unsuccessful attempts to cure him by priests and traditional African doctors, she came to terms with his gayness. He moved in with his first lover, a white bus driver, although in order to live together he had to pose as his lover's domestic servant.

In 1982, Nkoli moved to Johannesburg to work part-time at the South African Institute of Race Relations. There he became involved in a detainees' support committee, providing legal and material assistance to political prisoners. Johannesburg was also the site of South Africa's first public gay organization, the Gay Association of South Africa. Nkoli signed up with the overwhelmingly white organization in 1983, but soon realized that most GASA activities were closed to him and other black gays because they took place in whites-only areas in the evenings. He took the initiative to form the Saturday Group, a GASA-affiliated lesbian and gay support and discussion group in the black township of Soweto. Although the Saturday Group was officially multiracial, in practice because of its location, its membership was overwhelmingly African.

In 1984, Nkoli helped establish the Vaal Civic Association to undertake tenant organizing in the townships. After addressing crowds in the ongoing rallies, he was detained on September 23, 1984. Months later he was charged with treason, murder, and terrorism, along with twenty-one other United Democratic Front activists who became known as the Delmas 22. All of the accused potentially faced the death penalty. The pretext for the murder charges was that several local councillors who were collaborating with the South African government had been killed in rioting following one of the protests.

Though Nkoli had always kept his gay and anti-apartheid activism separate, a heated argument about homosexuality sparked him to come out to his astonished co-accused in prison. He was the first anti-apartheid activist to dare to make an issue of his sexuality. At first, several of his co-defendants feared that his homosexuality would be used to discredit the movement, and wanted him tried separately. Others argued for solidarity.

The headline in my first *TBP* article about the case was misleading: "GASA Head Jailed in Emergency Sweep."[46] Nkoli was not part of the GASA leadership. They were all white. And GASA scrupulously defined itself as non-political. There had been no mention of the case in *Exit*, the affiliated gay South African paper we received at *TBP*. Although Nkoli was a member and had founded GASA's only black discussion group, he was dropped like a hot potato. It took a year before the rest of the world even heard about his arrest. Yet just months before, GASA had finally convinced the IGA that it was opposed to apartheid and had been accepted as a full member.

I managed to get in direct contact with Simon and began sending him copies of the paper and other literature. We made it a major item in *TBP*'s international news, and within months, the story had spread to gay and lesbian media around the world. By that time it was clear that this was more than just a news story. Nkoli had already spent more than a year in prison, much of it in solitary, and was now facing an even longer trial. He needed direct support. That fall a number of us (using an alternate spelling of his name) formed the Simon Nkodi Anti-apartheid Committee: Lesbians and Gays Against Apartheid. Here we had a hero, a gay man struggling against homophobia in the context of a broader struggle for social justice and against racism.

Just as we had a new hero, 1985 also produced a local martyr. Friday evening, June 21, had been one of those warm Toronto evenings that signalled summer was here to stay. Kenneth Zeller, a forty-year-old teacher-librarian at Williamson Road Public School, had been celebrating finishing his master of education degree. On his way home after the party, he dropped into Toronto's High Park, a favourite summer cruising area.

Five young white men from a nearby secondary school, all sixteen or seventeen years old, were in the park that night as well. They, too, were celebrating the end of the school year. After a few beers someone suggested, "Let's beat up a fag."

Zeller came across them on a footpath. One screamed "You fucking faggot!" and knocked him to the ground. Zeller regained his footing and ran back towards his car, the boys in hot pursuit. As he opened his car door, they attacked again. One smashed the front passenger window, another punctured the car's tires. They kicked and beat him in the head and face. When he collapsed unconscious, they fled into the woods. An hour later, Zeller was pronounced dead of severe head injuries.

Homicide detectives arrested the boys six days later, charging them with first-degree murder. By the time of the trial in November, the charges were reduced to second-degree murder. During the short trial, the boys were described as normal kids, courteous, fun-loving, and helpful. A sixteen-year-old best friend testified through tears that there was no attitude of intolerance towards homosexuals among his friends.

Their hockey coach testified that he, too, was unaware of any intolerance towards homosexuals among the boys. He admitted that the term "gay" might occasionally be hurled against an opposing player, but "never was the term spoken with any hostility."

The father of one of the boys blamed it on the beer.

A clinical psychiatrist testified that it was all about peer pressure and insisted "their behaviour was not uncharacteristic. The same action would have been perpetrated by any number of young men under similar conditions." He concluded that the risk they posed to society was "no greater than the average kid." When cross-examined on the use of the phrase "You fucking faggot," he, too, insisted, "Its usage did not indicate a hostility towards homosexuals."

The boys ultimately pled guilty to manslaughter and received nine-year sentences, eligible for day parole after eighteen months.

The defence was successful, but the trial raised serious questions. If these were just normal boys, and their behaviour not uncharacteristic, if school officials could hear "gay" used as an insult and think nothing of it, if the term "fucking faggot" was not seen as indicative of hostility, what kind of environment were these young men growing up in? The questions were playfully rendered in John Greyson's short film *The Making of Monsters* (1991).

TBP asked school board officials for answers. Trustee Alex Chumak, who considered his role in blocking the proposed gay liaison five years before as one of his achievements, replied that it was alcohol, not homophobia, that led to the murder. All the boys attended schools in his ward. Former board chair Fiona Nelson, who had also opposed the liaison, said, "I do not feel the slightest bit of responsibility." She refused to answer questions about the need for anti-homophobia programs.[47]

Trustees preferred to keep their heads in the sand, but daily life was leaving them behind. More youth were coming out within the school system, and the question of homophobia regularly arose spontaneously in our anti-racism camp discussions. In one of the alternative schools, I came across a young man who had just fled from Western Tech, the school that most of Zeller's killers attended. Anthony Mohamed had come out before the murder, but as the boys went to trial, homophobia in the school increased exponentially. He changed schools for his own safety.

Only one trustee, Olivia Chow, was willing to take a stand. Chow conducted her own ad hoc investigation, bolstered by a letter from Ontario Secondary School Teachers' Federation calling on the board to "investigate the possibility of implementing programs that would sensitize students to the basic human rights of homosexuals in our society and counteract the homophobia that is found in their overall social environment."[48] Chow found homophobia rampant and unchallenged. In April 1986, she tabled a series of recommendations to the board, including a counselling service aimed at lesbian and gay youth, teacher training, anti-homophobia curriculum materials, and the inclusion of sexual orientation in the board's anti-discrimination policy. After protracted horse-trading and multiple amendments, all the recommendations were adopted, except for the last. Even the unprovoked murder of a respected staff member could not convince the right-wing-dominated board to take a stand against discrimination.[49]

GAY PLAGUE TO PUBLIC HEALTH MENACE

The mainstream U.S. magazine *Newsweek* put it most succinctly. "Once dismissed as 'the gay plague' the disease has become the number one public health menace." Cover stories in *Newsweek, Time, People*, and Canada's *Maclean's* in August 1985 were all sparked by Rock Hudson's announcement that he had AIDS. While *People* used a pre-illness photo of the screen idol, *Maclean's* and *Newsweek* showed the famous leading man gaunt and hollow-eyed. Then someone realized that on one of his last appearances on the hit TV serial *Dynasty*, Hudson had shared a long and steamy kiss with co-star Linda Evans. Although aware of his diagnosis, he had not informed her or the studio. Ed Asner, president of the Screen Actors Guild, revealed that scripts across Hollywood were being hastily rewritten to eliminate kissing. North of the border, on May 9, 1985, the Red Cross admitted that the Canadian blood supply was contaminated. Two recipients had already died. Hudson rushed off to Paris to try a new treatment, but he was dead in less than two months. *Life* magazine warned, "No one is safe from AIDS." The public attitude shifted from indifference to full-scale panic.

Middle America, long silent on homosexuality, found itself discussing gay life around the dinner table. This was far from the joyful bursting out of the closet that gay liberationists had long awaited. The conversation was coloured with fear and, at best, pity.

In New York, the State Public Health Council overwhelmingly voted to give itself permanent power to close establishments allowing "high risk" sex. The iconic Mineshaft and the New St. Mark's Baths were both shut down. The Anvil closed voluntarily. The New York Coalition for Lesbian and Gay Rights launched a lawsuit against the regulations, but others in the community applauded the move. On the ground, men shifted to jack-off clubs and phone sex.

The Reagan government continued to set the tone. The president's proposed budget for 1987 called for a 22 per cent reduction in funding for AIDS research, treatment programs, and testing. The White House also instructed the Centers for Disease Control to hold back on AIDS education proposals until they were checked by local and state bodies to ensure they were inoffensive. The United States began to use the new AIDS test to screen military personnel and prospective immigrants, and there was ominous talk of insurance companies using it to screen out applicants. Testing for AIDS, they found gay men.

In Toronto, the test provoked another kind of controversy. In December 1985, *TBP* editorialized against testing. ACT was already discouraging people. At the time, it was still believed that only a small percentage of those infected with HIV would get sick. Since finding out that you were positive would produce stress, and stress was harmful to the immune system, testing might increase your chances of becoming ill. More ominously, since HIV was reportable, the name and address of everyone who tested positive ended up on a public health list. With no human rights protection and the *Toronto Sun* already calling for quarantine for anyone testing HIV positive, no one knew what the state might do with such information. Finally, there was no treatment. Knowing you were positive did not provide any practical benefit.

I ended up not having the option. Richard and I had joined a cohort of gay men who enrolled in a University of Toronto epidemiological study in March 1984. Four hundred and twenty of us dutifully reported to Toronto General Hospital once every six months to answer questionnaires about who had stuck what organs into what orifices and how often, while vials of our blood were drawn for comparison, testing, and study.

By that point I had lots of swollen lymph glands, and a year before it had been discovered that my platelet levels were low. This was apparently associated with whatever "it" was. The doctors were worried about spontaneous bleeding, but said there was nothing they could do except give me massive doses of prednisone. That would make me blow up like a balloon. Instead, I started seeing a Traditional Chinese doctor who told me there was a 40 per cent chance he could improve the situation.

They had mostly been interested in Richard, since he was "asymptomatic." The main goal was to figure out how it was transmitted. If he got it, they wanted to know all the details of our sex life that might have led to transmission. We considered being part of the study a public service, but had also been assured that by participating, we would be at the cutting edge of any new therapies. That wasn't the case.

Sometime in 1986 I went in for my regular appointment. By then the new HIV test had come on line. As I was about to leave, I asked the doctor if the study was using the new test. He looked embarrassed and said yes. There was a silence. "So," I asked, "have you tested my blood?" After a pause he said yes again, followed by another embarrassed silence. "So what was the result?" He replied, "Do you really want to know?" "Well," I said, "if you know my status, and the government knows my status, I think that I have the right to know, too." "You've got it," he replied. So much for pre- and post-test counselling.

I didn't yet know how to conceptualize it, but I had just run across the difference between being a patient and a research subject.

MORAL PANICS

In its commitment to exploring sexuality, *TBP* was swimming more and more against the tide. For much of 1984, the Fraser Commission toured the country soliciting input on a new pornography law. Mainstream feminists demanded greater control of material they felt promoted violence against women. Religious groups demanded suppression of representations of sexual activity in general. The commission had been set up by the Liberals, but a Progressive Conservative government headed by Brian Mulroney had won the general election in September 1984 and would decide what to do with it.

Fraser's April 1985 recommendations, characterized as "liberal feminist," supported the repeal of solicitation laws and changes to the bawdy house laws so as to no longer criminalize gay baths. Pornography should be judged in terms of social harm rather than by sexual explicitness.[50]

TBP was especially worried about new pornography legislation. Mulroney himself was a centrist, but he was forced to take his party's western social conservative wing into account. When a bill to revise the Criminal Code was tabled in June 1986, it defined degrading pornography as anything that showed bondage, ejaculation, menstruation, or lactation. *TBP* called it "nutty, absurd – and dangerous." Fortunately, the bill died when the parliamentary session ended on August 28. Women at *TBP* continued to write about, promote, and produce lesbian feminist erotica in the pages of the paper.[51]

SOUTH AFRICA: THE TRIALS BEGIN

The Delmas 22 treason trial began in January 1986, and GASA maintained its silence. As inquiries from the IGA went unanswered, there was talk of expelling the group. In his letters to me, Simon Nkoli expressed anger at the organization's refusal to support him, but didn't want GASA expelled from the international organization on his account.

Nkoli didn't want to be anyone's political ammunition, but from his prison cell he had little control over events. After his arrest, his Saturday Group in Soweto had given way to a new group, the Rand Gay Organization. Unaffiliated with GASA, RGO focused on black lesbian and gay organizing. As RGO jockeyed for legitimacy, and GASA tried to avoid expulsion from the IGA, Nkoli's support became important.

Now the South African gay magazine *Exit* mentioned Nkoli's case for the first time, publishing a letter featuring his opposition to GASA's possible expulsion.

> True, I feel strongly that GASA and its affiliates have not paid enough attention to why they are still massively white despite the composition of the whole community and the gay community in South Africa.... But the place to sort that out is here among ourselves. It is not my desire that this problem should be discussed at an IGA conference.[52]

Nkoli's intervention was crucial in GASA's avoidance of expulsion a few months later.

SNAAC first appeared in public at International Women's Day in March 1986. It was serendipitous that the slogan for IWD that year was "Women Say No to Racism from Toronto to South Africa." That was the result of years of struggle within the IWD Coalition by the Black Women's Collective, many of whom were dykes. It was especially cold that year, so the photos I sent to Nkoli showed us well bundled up. He may have been a hero, but Nkoli was also practical. He wrote to see if we could send him a parka. South African winter was approaching, and it was cold in his unheated cell.

Spring 1986 saw a massive Arts Against Apartheid festival in Toronto, with concerts, art projects, and performances. Bishop Tutu and Harry Belafonte attended. As part of the festival, SNAAC packed the ballroom for an evening of gay performance art at 519 Church. But the anti-apartheid movement in Toronto didn't quite know what to do with us. Although our event was approved, someone forgot to put it in the festival program and it had to be included in a subsequent summary. A few days later, when we arrived at the massive solidarity march, the marshals instructed us to go to the back of the march with the marginal political groups. That was too much. We moved to the front and took our rightful place with the solidarity groups.

At Pride Day, a month later, we felt more welcome. We began to realize that our role was not just expressing our solidarity with Nkoli and engaging in were also doing anti-homophobia work in the anti-apartheid movement.

CHARTER EFFECTS

If the Conservative government seemed true to form on pornography, there was one major problem with any explicitly homophobic legislation – Section 15 of the Charter of Rights and Freedoms had come into effect April 1985. It read, "Every individual is equal before and under the law and has the right to equal protection and equal benefit of the law without discrimination." Legislation could now face a Charter challenge before the Supreme Court. Still, it was a surprise when on March 5, 1986, Justice Minister John Crosbie announced the Government of Canada had committed itself "to take whatever measures are necessary to ensure that sexual orientation is a prohibited ground of discrimination in relation to all areas of federal jurisdiction." Everyone was astounded. This was not the kind of thing Tories were supposed to say. Somehow the rights agenda was becoming uncoupled from sexuality issues such as porn.

That the Charter was taking Canada down a new path in terms of rights was underscored June 30, 1986, when the U.S. Supreme Court ruled that Georgia's anti-sodomy law, on the books since 1816, was constitutional. The Georgia law defined "sodomy" as "any sex act involving the sex organs of one person and the mouth or anus of another." The maximum penalty was twenty years in prison. Supporting the judgment, Chief Justice Warren E. Burger wrote: "To hold that the act of homosexual sodomy is somehow protected as a fundamental right would be to cast aside millennia of moral teaching."[53] The contrast between the U.S. and Canadian positions couldn't have been starker.

EMERGING ALLIES

By the mid-1980s, parts of the Canadian labour movement began to take a more active role in social issues. Lesbian and gay members had been challenging homophobia at a grassroots level in their locals since the mid-1970s. As the struggle for Human Rights Code changes earned a higher profile for lesbians and gay men in, a shift in attitudes began to trickle upwards through the unions. In 1985, the Canadian section of the United Auto Workers split off to form the Canadian Auto Workers (CAW). In its oath of office, the new union included the responsibility to fight discrimination, including discrimination on the basis of sexual orientation. The following year, the Canadian Labour Congress, the coalition of all labour unions in the country, amended its constitution to prohibit discrimination on the basis of sexual orientation as well.[54]

At the same time, the Ontario Public Service Employees Union began raising the issue of employment equity in the province. Up to that point, women were regularly paid less than men for similar jobs and excluded from some types of work altogether. There was similar discrimination against racialized groups and the disabled. When OPSEU set up its Race Relations and Minority Rights Committee in 1986, lesbian and gay workers were recognized as a target group. Although not queer herself, Beverley Johnson, a leading black union activist, was adamant that issues of sexual orientation be at the table. She eventually became chair of the committee.

According to Johnson, the issue of employment equity faced some stiff opposition.

> There was not a lot of support in the labour movement for this work. Some union leaders supported it, but many of the rest reflected the conservatism of Canadian society in terms of equality for racialized or LGBT workers or the rights of workers with disabilities. They were not supportive of employment equity. On the other hand, this work also attracted a lot of workers who had faced discrimination or multiple discriminations and many more of these workers became active in the union.[55]

A right opportunist position might have advised not dealing with lesbian and gay issues in this context. It was already hard enough to get union buy-in around issues facing women and racialized workers, and in the 1980s, homophobia was acceptable in a way that racism or sexism was not. But the union value of solidarity, the fact that women and racialized workers might be simultaneously lesbian or gay, the growing number of lesbian and gay activists in the unions, and the overall shift to "social unionism," especially in the public sector, all helped override such arguments.

PHOBIA

The original advice for lowering AIDS risk was to lower your number of partners. The harsher version was to stop having sex at all. *TBP* railed against panic, but sex radicals were helpless as community mores changed in response to the epidemic. The promiscuity we had once celebrated seemed at best irresponsible. At worst, suicidal. Couples were definitely in. Even the terms were changing, from the sexually focused "lover" to the far more salubrious "partner." Rod Stewart's "Do You Think I'm Sexy" was replaced by the AIDS anthem "That's What Friends Are For." In the landmark 1985 TV movie *An Early Frost*, the protagonist, Michael, is infected by his lover after a single indiscretion. He throws his partner out of the house and returns to his family to die.

For only $19.95, Talisman Design in New York offered *Advocate* readers a handsome, distinctive piece of jewellery in silver or gold finish indicating the wearer had tested HIV negative. And *Jock*, part of the *Torso* gay porn empire, began advertising itself as "an alternative to contact sex . . . discreetly delivered in a plain sealed envelope" and "cheaper than you'll find it in that seamy low-life bookstore. In that armpit part of town. Where just about anything could happen on your way in."[56]

So it seemed that being HIV positive and being gay was not exactly the same thing, at least for those who were negative and didn't live in "that armpit part of town." AIDS phobia swept both straight and gay society. Stan Reed was a doctor at the Hospital for Sick Children who was doing research on HIV in Haiti and Canada. He had access to the latest blood tests, so I started seeing him. Although it was research, he seemed to take an interest in my health.

One morning when I arrived, a young man was already waiting for his appointment. I had not yet mastered the art of cruising in doctors' offices, but I gave him a smile and we embarked on some superficial chat until he was called in. When he left, he said goodbye, and then, in a lowered voice, "It's been nice talking to you. But would you do me a favour? If we ever see each other again, in a bar or someplace, please don't let on you met me here. I don't want my friends to know. I don't want them to think I'm a slut. They're all I've got." Later we would call it HIV stigma.

SAF(ER) SEX AND BEYOND

The event of safer sex was a lifeline to the sex radicals. Rick Bébout's May 1986 *TBP* feature, "The Prophylactic Lover," opened, "Whatever else monogamy may be, it's not a health insurance policy." Only safer sex could make a difference. But the problem was, no one was quite sure what safer sex actually was. The Americans wanted us to use condoms even for oral sex. Canadians tended to classify that as low risk. How low was low risk? Did it make a difference if you swallowed or spit out the cum? Nevertheless, Bébout concluded, "A lover is not a rubber. But a lover – or anybody you care enough to have sex with – is certainly *worth* a rubber."[57]

For the first time, there was also a small glimmer of hope. In the United States, Burroughs Wellcome was testing a new drug, AZT, which seemed to show promise in prolonging life. Members of the Vancouver Persons with AIDS Coalition took to the streets in the spring of 1986 with a petition calling on the federal Health Protection Branch to facilitate access to such experimental drugs. Thousands of ordinary citizens signed. But although the branch promised to release unapproved treatments on compassionate grounds, when doctors applied, they were turned down.

Vancouver PWA's Kevin Brown met with Health Minister Jake Epp to deliver the petition June 27. "We're willing to sign waivers," Brown explained. "We're dealing with a life and death issue here. If we wait for something to be proven, it may be too late. I may not be alive and I want my chance now." Epp promised to "encourage" Burroughs Wellcome to release AZT to Canadian doctors, but was otherwise noncommittal.

Brown left the meeting cynical. "I've heard for nearly a year now why things are not taking place, but my time is running out," he said.[58]

In October 1986, I left the collective after twelve years at *TBP*. I had started work on my master of education degree, and my full-time job at the board was becoming more intense. Both Richard and I had been studying karate since 1981. At first it was an escape. I couldn't go to meetings on nights we had class. But by 1986 I was coming up for my black belt, and that required much more commitment, longer training, plus volunteer teaching. I also was aware that I needed to look after my health. Now living with HIV, I had to admit that I couldn't burn the candle at both ends the way I had in my twenties. And a new volunteer, Charles Phillips, was working with me and seemed more than capable of taking on international news.

There had been another financial crisis over the summer of 1986. Our rickety financial management system just wasn't adequate for the scale of the operation. No one had even seen it coming until the paper was thousands of dollars in debt.

Before, we had always belt-tightened, some staff would go on unemployment insurance, and things would get patched up. But this time, according to Rick Bébout, "the problem was more fundamental." Despite all the attempts to be more popular, less didactic, better designed, and more fun, we simply weren't selling enough copies. Cutting back on staff had also become a problem. While much of the work was done by dozens of volunteers, when push came to shove, it was staff that picked up the slack. As operations expanded and professionalized, staff were already stretched to the limit. We were also producing two papers, *Xtra* twice a month along with the monthly *TBP*.

Over the summer, a series of emergency meetings was called. Several collective members felt we needed to completely rethink what we were doing. Graham Crawford of the RTPC, a management consultant, offered to facilitate the development of a new "mission statement." I found the process tedious and excruciatingly abstract. We spent hours wordsmithing, and I was left wondering if the outcome was worth the trouble. If I hadn't already been thinking about giving my notice, that may have been what pushed me over the edge.

> To engage audiences among lesbians and gay men and those who share their concerns, through a variety of means and media, offering them opportunities to support and participate in the development of ideas and in actions which promote liberating social change, focusing on sexuality in its social, political and cultural contexts.[59]

Despite the new mission statement, I had to admit that the enterprise no longer seemed to have the edge that it did when I came out twelve years earlier. We were more professional looking, but somehow, our content felt less important. The range of issues seemed ever narrower and more predictable – sexuality good, rights good, censorship bad. With everything else going on in my life, I no longer had the energy to contemplate starting from scratch. I felt bad leaving in the middle of a crisis but, on the other hand, I had seen the paper through much worse over the years. We had always muddled through, and I was confident that a younger crew could turn things around.

HUMAN RIGHTS

At the end of January 1986 the Ontario legislature's Standing Committee on the Administration of Justice began discussing Bill 7 – An act to amend certain Ontario statutes to conform to Section 15 of the Canadian Charter of Rights and Freedoms. On the agenda was the Ontario Human Rights Code.

CGRO dusted itself off and stepped up lobbying efforts. The group presented its fourth brief of the decade to call for inclusion of sexual orientation. On May 6, Evelyn Gigantes of the NDP tabled an amendment to Bill 7 to do just that. The amendment passed in committee, with only Progressive Conservative members opposed. The Liberals seemed blindsided by the development. A spokesperson for Attorney General Ian Scott, asked whether Scott would defend the amendment in the legislature, would only say, "No decision has been made on a hypothetical situation."

CGRO's efforts were low-key at first, focusing on representatives considered on the fence. According to Tom Warner, there was a "general feeling that people at Queen's Park would like to do the whole thing quietly."[60] Fat chance of that.

As soon as the committee decision was known, the Ontario Conference of Catholic Bishops, REAL Women of Canada, several evangelical groups, and the National Citizens Coalition came together to form the Coalition for Family Values. Priests started denouncing the bill from their pulpits. Christian television shows encouraged listeners to write and phone the legislature. Key ridings were targeted for mass mailings. In response, CGRO and the RTPC launched a public pro-amendment campaign and solicited the support of labour, women's groups, and civil liberties organizations. On November 20, 1,500 people packed the St. Lawrence Hall to hear NDP leader Bob Rae, city councillor Jack Layton, and author Margaret Atwood speak out in support of change.

After two days of debate, the issue came to a vote December 2, five years after a similar motion was last defeated in 1981. This time the amendment passed 65 to 45. Those in favour included all the NDP members, most Liberals, and even four Progressive Conservatives, including leader Larry Grossman. Almost fifteen years after Brian Waite first argued that the fight to include sexual orientation could mobilize the community around something concrete, it had happened. We had finally won. The question *TBP* asked was, what next?

One outstanding issue was the prohibition of discrimination on the basis of sexual orientation in all areas of federal jurisdiction. A year after Crosbie's promise, nothing practical had been done. In Ottawa, a group of thirty lesbians and gay men who had been involved in letter-writing campaigns to members of Parliament formed a new organization – Equality for Gays and Lesbians Everywhere. EGALE was bilingual, included both women and men, and was unabashedly about lobbying.

The emerging issue was one that the early movement would never have contemplated – spousal benefits. The first to push the issue was Karen Andrews, a Toronto library worker who demanded that her benefits be extended to her lover and their two children. Although the couple had lived together for nine years, jointly owned a home, held joint bank accounts, and named each other as beneficiaries in their wills, the Ontario Health Insurance Plan (OHIP) refused to extend family coverage. Andrews was not alone. After her union negotiated a human rights clause in the collective agreement, a Terrace, B.C., college instructor, Elizabeth Snyder, asked that her partner be covered. In Wolfville, Nova Scotia, two professors launched a grievance against Acadia University demanding spousal medical benefits, and in Vancouver, the school board agreed to benefits after teacher Krin Zook asked for dental coverage for her partner of seven years.[61] In November 1986, a motion to ask the province for permission to extend family benefits to the partners of gay City of Toronto employees lost on a tie vote at city hall. This was clearly the new frontier.

Spousal benefits were especially important to lesbians, who were more likely both to be in relationships that involved children as dependants and to earn lower income than men. When Pride did a survey of participants the following summer, the stark difference between the economic circumstances faced by gay men and lesbians was evident. While 35 per cent of the men surveyed earned more than $30,000, only 17 per cent of women did. Sixty-seven per cent of men earned more than $20,000, compared to 48 per cent of women. Only 7 per cent of men earned less than $10,000, but 23 per cent of women found themselves in that low-wage bracket.[62] The average income for individuals in Canada was just over $24,000 at the time.

As the AIDS crisis deepened, and the 1970s generation began to age, stable partnerships and spousal benefits increased in importance for men as well. Growing material inequality increased pressure for relationship equality.

THE END OF THE ERA

By the end of the summer, the financial situation at *TBP* was considerably worse. Ken Popert had informally been steering the group through the crisis, and it was moved to make him interim publisher. "At the meeting of the expanded collective . . . people were talking about needing someone to make decisions and to be the temporary publisher," he recalls. "When somebody said 'What about you?' I turned around in my seat because I thought they were talking to somebody behind me. I felt put upon because I had never seen myself in such a position. It seemed like an awful lot of responsibility being dumped in my lap. But I went home and talked to Brian about it and I did agree to do it."[63]

For the first time, the collective submitted to hierarchy. The decision had to be ratified, and a general meeting of Pink Triangle Press was called for November 16. Over 180 volunteers, friends, and supporters were invited. Thirty-five showed up. I was one of them. It hardly seemed like a mandate, so yet another committee was set up to look at the structural proposals and a transitional process was outlined.

Everything came to a head at the December 16 collective meeting. Although the cash drain seemed to have been staunched, two of the remaining staff, Gerald Hannon and Andrew Lesk, gave notice. A third staff member announced that she, too, would resign unless her hours could be reduced within a month to something humanly possible. It was the last straw.

The paper was facing collapse. It was suggested that *TBP* be killed to free up energies for *Xtra* and give the collective some breathing space, but Chris Bearchell argued we couldn't do that without community consultation. The final wording was "suspended." *Xtra* would continue to publish.

The decision was not announced, but when a local radio station called up about the upcoming January 1987 fifteenth-anniversary issue, Popert spilled the beans. Within hours the death of *The Body Politic* was all over the media. That's how most of us heard.

After getting over my shock, I was furious. When asked to write a short piece about my "fondest memories" of *TBP* for the last issue, I declined and wrote an angry letter instead. I called the decision "deplorable, irresponsible and improper." *TBP* was not the collective's property. It was held in trust for the community.

> Since when does a slim majority of less than a dozen people, several of whom have already tendered their resignations from staff, presume it has the right to kill something that has been produced and sustained by so many of us for so long, and something which is of undeniable importance to our movement locally, nationally and internationally?[64]

Michael Lynch wrote in the same vein.

> I am particularly bitter at the lack of notice, lack of public discussion, lack of wide community consultation in advance of this decision.... If the Collective had evolved to this point of self-isolation in making such a stupendous political decision, this Collective deserves self-destruction.[65]

Both Lynch and I were now diagnosed with HIV. To have the most respected gay journal in the country, arguably in the world, disappear in the midst of an unimaginable community health crisis was a body blow.

No one on the outside could make sense of it. Some pointed the finger at Popert. With *TBP* and its troublesome collective out of the way, as publisher, he now basically controlled the press. That could make him either a visionary who had amputated a limb to save the patient, or someone intent on a ruthless power grab. Given the state of the press, it seemed more like chaining himself to a sinking ship. Still others saw him as the only one left with the commitment and perseverance to rescue something out of the rubble of *TBP*'s collapse.

Whatever the proximate cause, in his article in the final issue, Rick Bébout laid out the story of long-term decline that at some point or other was bound to reach a breaking point. From 1977 to 1984 no paid staff had ever resigned, but after that year, one by one, long-term committed people started moving on. After we moved to publishing twelve months a year with twenty-three issues of *Xtra*, staff turnover became chronic.

At first, with the revolution around the corner, everyone was willing to spend night after night labouring to make a deadline. The deadlines had been fewer and farther between, and the pace of work more relaxed. By the early 1980s, with the community under attack, people dug in their heels and resisted. They might have to work themselves to death but they would go down fighting. But now, with basic protections and a more tolerant society, the future extended into more of the same. With no sense of epochal change or crisis, why kill yourself working for even a very good paper?

Bébout had to catch himself not to sound like he was complaining about the "younger generation," or the "mammals," as he called them, as opposed to us "dinosaurs." "The truth is they still work hard and still for peanuts. If they won't work hours like Gerald and I did in the late Seventies, well, neither will Gerald nor I anymore." It was, he argued, "a different moment in history."

That was certainly true. The days of Keynesianism were over, and with them easy access to unemployment insurance, secure pensions, or even welfare in a pinch. While in our day, twenty-somethings didn't need to obsess over savings or a career, that was no longer the case. Thatcher had pointed out that the kind of changes she, Reagan, and now Mulroney were implementing were not just aimed at the economy. "Economics are the method; the object is to change the heart and soul."[66] People's values were being transformed.

Popert put it trenchantly. "The productive base of *TBP* had disappeared. It was volunteer labour."[67]

Even without burnout, there was a feeling that *TBP* had lost its way. Bébout continued, "The clear historical moment in which a single magazine could try to be all things to all lesbians and gay men, to touch them with the spirit of something wonderful and new, seemed to have passed. We weren't sure, many of us, what this medium was for any more."[68]

In her final submission, Chris Bearchell wrote of both fond moments and regrets. One regret was "that members of the Collective came to see collectivity – rather than over-expansion, unrealistic spending and increasing bureaucracy – as the root of *TBP*'s problems." As an ex-Trotskyist, Bearchell was bound to mention "bureaucracy." However, that really didn't seem fair. Everyone who worked on *TBP*, volunteers and staff alike, was involved in direct, hands-on work. No one had a plush office or spent their time counting paper clips. But she was on to something about over-expansion, or at least the ability of the collective model to manage such change.

TBP operated within a capitalist economy and, like any small business, it needed to grow to survive. To grow we needed to be relevant and appeal to a wider range of consumers, who would not only buy the paper but would also interest advertisers. Growth wasn't just a decision, it was an economic imperative.

All this affected the content. "In 1979 we published an average of 17.23 pages of features and reviews per issue. By 1984 it was down to 10 and for 1986 – I don't want to look,"[69] Bébout pointed out. Most of this missing content was because of the expansion of display advertising, necessary to keep the paper afloat.

But there was also waning interest. In 1982 we published about seventy letters from our readers. In 1986 there were thirty-eight. Classified ad revenue dropped by more than half between December 1985 and December 1986. Newsstand sales were about 3,000 after the bath raids and plateaued at 2,300 for the next few years, but by 1986 had dropped to fewer than 1,800. Although Canadian circulation was stable, the traditional one-third of *TBP* readers outside the country dropped dramatically in the same period.

The same process affected our politics. In attempting to demonstrate that *Xtra* was "as radical as anything we ever said in *The Body Politic*," Bébout described the messages: "define your life in your own terms; be visible; work (and play) together; trust each other to help make things change – and mistrust authority."[70] While such radical liberal politics had always been part of the message, forgotten was analysis. Power, gender, and race. The role of capitalism. How social structures and sexuality interact to support each other. The gay movement as part of a broader struggle for social justice. Such insights had always been part of the paper's early pages.

TBP lasted much longer than most of the radical gay papers that emerged in the 1970s. Its passing closed the book on a profoundly optimistic moment where everything seemed possible. The new measure of success would not be revolution, but survival.

PART III

Walking with the Devil

8

By Any Means Necessary

ACT UP

One warm afternoon in the fall of 1987 I bumped into Michael Lynch on College Street in front of the board of education. I hadn't seen him since the collapse of *TBP* the previous winter. During the summer, while I had been away, Bill Lewis, Lynch's ex-partner and closest friend, had died. At Bill's funeral, Michael had read a poem by Edna St. Vincent Millay that concludes:

Gently they go, the beautiful, the tender, the kind;
Quietly, they go, the intelligent, the witty, the brave.
I know. But I do not approve. And I am not resigned.[1]

Michael Lynch was far from resigned. He was just back from the October 10, 1987, March on Washington for Lesbian and Gay Rights. Hundreds of thousands had gathered in a show of strength against rising conservatism in the United States. The demonstration was the first public appearance of New York's AIDS Coalition to Unleash Power. ACT UP's contingent wore T-shirts emblazoned "Silence = Death." This was not a group of polite professionals asking governments to consider funding services, please. These were angry gay men and lesbians demanding action on an epidemic that was killing them and their lovers, friends, and fuckbuddies, and devastating their communities.

Lynch asked if I'd heard about ACT UP, or that our old friend, Herb Spiers, was chairing one of the group's committees. I had, but I was largely out of touch with U.S. events since giving up international news at *TBP*. "We need something like that in Toronto," Lynch said. "If I call a meeting, would you be interested?"

Out of respect for him, I agreed. But I wondered how to do politics about a disease. I knew the politics of law change, challenging the police, fighting in the courts, publishing a radical paper. But I hadn't thought of medicine as political. Most of the AIDS work in Toronto was about providing services, palliative care, or education. And since there were lots of service providers, counsellors, nurses, and doctors to volunteer for that kind of thing, I had never felt especially needed.

SAVED BY SHINGLES

And I had my own problems. Around the time that *TBP* was collapsing, my doctor had sent me to a cancer specialist at Toronto General Hospital. She was concerned about my low platelets and the risk of uncontrolled bleeding, urging me to give up karate (one wrong punch could kill me). And she wanted to have my spleen removed.

The spleen is a part of the immune system that acts as a filter, removing diseased platelets, among other things. When you don't have one, platelet levels go up. Chopping off a huge part of whatever immune system I had left seemed counterintuitive, and so far, although I bruised easily, I hadn't had any bleeding problems. But I still hadn't overcome an awe of doctors, and she insisted. Surgery was booked for March break so that I wouldn't have to miss much work.

A couple of weeks before surgery, the skin in my right leg began getting sore – and then excruciating. Soon I had difficulty walking. I was diagnosed with shingles, an inflammation of the nerve fibres caused by a reactivation of the chicken pox virus. My surgery had to be cancelled. Shortly afterwards, studies were published showing that removing the spleen in people with HIV led to faster immune deterioration. Shingles possibly saved my life.

In the meantime, half of my body broke out in angry blisters. It was the most painful thing I had ever experienced. My family doctor said there was nothing to do but wait it out. He recommended painkillers. I went to the Traditional Chinese Medicine doctor who had been trying to treat my low platelets. He said there was little he could do, either. But when I got on the phone with Stan Reed to book a blood test for his research, I mentioned what was going on. He immediately put me on a new drug, acyclovir. The pain began to go away. It was only by chance that I managed to get treatment and avoid possibly permanent nerve damage.

VIRAL POLITICS

I had been away most of the summer of 1987 before my meeting with Lynch. Given my own experience, I should have been more aware of how AIDS was political. Right after Pride Day, Richard and I left for a road trip across the country to visit our old friend, Lim Pei Hsien in Vancouver. Lim had lived with us in the commune on Ontario Street, and we had briefly been fuckbuddies when Richard was away in South America. Lim was a renaissance man: a professional dancer, registered nurse, martial artist, and graphic designer. Extracts from "Never Again," his dance piece that premiered at Celebrasian, were featured in *Track Two* (1982), the documentary about the bath raids, and in *Orientations*, Richard's 1984 video on gay and lesbian Asians. Lim and his partner, Joseph Reid, had moved to Vancouver a few years before, and there, Reid had his first bout of PCP pneumonia. Lim was also positive.

When we got there, Reid had recovered, but was obsessing about rumours that the B.C. government was building concentration camps in the north of the province to intern HIV positive people, the same way they had interned Japanese Canadians during the Second World War. I didn't take it very seriously, but later learned that British Columbia had indeed introduced a bill to give the province power to quarantine us. Elected officials in both British Columbia and Nova Scotia had also discussed turning former island leper colonies into holding areas for HIV positive gay men.[2] Serious discussion of the abrogation of civil rights of HIV positive people at such a high level was certainly a political issue.

Later, in August, my sister and I flew to Finland and travelled by train across the USSR from Leningrad (now Saint Petersburg) to Vladivostok in the Far East, and from there by boat to Japan. The USSR was in the midst of perestroika, Mikhail Gorbachev's attempt to open up and bring change to an increasingly moribund socialism. As in the United States, HIV positive people were barred from entering the country. Because of my low platelet count, I asked my specialist to give me a letter explaining my condition, technically idiopathic (cause undetermined) thrombocytopenia, in case I got into trouble on the trip. Obligingly, and without a clue, she wrote me a letter explaining I had AIDS and might hemorrhage. I threw it away. If the Russians saw it, I would have been immediately deported. Travel with HIV was also a political issue.

There was one piece of good news that summer. Simon Nkoli was released on bail in July after almost four years of imprisonment. The government case against the Delmas defendants was unravelling. SNAAC was delighted, but the situation presented a new problem. Nkoli still had to attend the ongoing trial daily and couldn't work or support himself. He was penniless. SNAAC took on a new task of fundraising. We committed to sending him a hundred dollars per month for the duration of the trial. It wasn't much, but together with the support he received from some European groups, it kept him afloat.

Unbeknownst to any of us, Nkoli had also tested positive. But he had decided that being both gay and an anti-apartheid activist was already a full plate. So he kept his status quiet. That was also a political decision.

AIDS POLITICS

A small group that Lynch convened met a few weeks later to discuss the political issues around medicine. Treatment in hospitals depended on where you ended up. In many places it was deplorable – visitors banned, nurses and orderlies refusing to empty bedpans or serve food, hazard signs on people's doors. Some hospitals would do tests that others wouldn't. There were no standard protocols for treatment. Standards of care and co-ordination were a political problem. I referenced my own good luck at knowing a doctor who happened to know about shingles treatments.

The main killer in those early days was PCP. It could come out of nowhere, and apparently healthy people could be dead within weeks. Pentamidine wiped out the parasite that caused PCP, but in Canada, it was only administered intravenously once people were sick. Pumped directly into the bloodstream, pentamidine was highly toxic. In the United States, however, several small trials had shown that if the drug was mixed with water and turned into mist in a nebulizer, those who breathed it in every week or so before they got sick could avoid coming down with PCP in the first place. Canada had lots of nebulizers and lots of pentamidine, but putting them together had not been approved. It was therefore technically illegal, and hospitals would not administer it. It was not medicine that was the problem; it was red tape. That was political.

Finally, there was access to experimental treatments in general. Nothing was available. There was no government support for research and nothing was happening to speed up access to new drugs. The government was ignoring AIDS. That, too, was political.

Over that fall, an eclectic group came together: old radicals like Lynch, George Smith, Gary Kinsman, and myself; Alan Dewar, a card-carrying Tory and former Oshawa alderman; his younger boyfriend, James McPhee, who worked at Glad Day Bookshop; several gay doctors, Michael Hulton, Dennis Conway, and Wayne Boone; Russell Armstrong, who had been central to the fights against customs censorship at Glad Day; and Chuck Grochmal, who ran the coat check at The Barn, the Church Street leather bar. At least half of us knew we were positive. Dewar had already been hospitalized for PCP twice, and McPhee wasn't well. Grochmal was using bootlegged aerosolized pentamidine to stave off another bout of pneumonia.

We were also all gay men. At that point, AIDS politics and gay politics seemed seamless. We were being left to die because of homophobia. Jake Epp, federal minister of health, who resolutely refused to deal with AIDS, was the same member of Parliament who eight years before baited CALGM with homophobic innuendo when the group had called for the inclusion of sexual orientation in the Charter. Although I raised the issue that Haitians and hemophiliacs were not faring much better, Dewar was especially adamant that whatever we became, we had to be a gay organization. If not, he wasn't interested. I guess he'd lived most of his life in the closet and was determined not to die there.

THE ANC TAKES A STAND

Shortly after Nkoli's release on bail, British gay activist Peter Tatchell put in motion a series of events that would help reshape South African history.

The ANC was a broad tent. It included liberal elements whose belief in individual rights gave some traction to the idea of gay rights, traditional communists who saw homosexuality as "bourgeois decadence," traditional Christians for whom homosexuality was a sin, and elements of traditional African patriarchy that saw homosexual identity as an un-African, western import.

For many of Nkoli's co-accused, the international campaign in the lesbian and gay media was the beginning of their education on the issue. It also turned out to be the beginning of an education for the ANC in general.

As a young man in his native Australia, Tatchell had cut his teeth on the anti-apartheid movement. Over the years he had been disturbed by homophobic currents within the ANC but had always publicly kept his silence. Any criticism might undermine the cause.

But after several unsuccessful attempts at privately raising the issue with the ANC leadership, in August 1987, Tatchell decided to go public. ANC executive member Ruth Mompati was visiting London to promote South Africa Women's Day. She had organized the biggest women's demonstration in South African history, when twenty thousand women marched in 1956 to protest the extension of the pass laws to women. Tatchell arranged to interview her.

After discussing the struggle for women's emancipation, he raised the issue of the human rights of lesbians and their role in the struggle against apartheid. "I hope that in a liberated South Africa people will live a normal life," Mompati replied. "I emphasize the word normal. . . . Tell me, are lesbians and gays normal? No, it is not normal."

She went on, "I cannot even begin to understand why people want lesbian and gay rights. The gays have no problems. They have nice houses and plenty to eat. I don't see them suffering. No one is persecuting them. . . . We haven't heard about this problem in South Africa until recently. It seems to be fashionable in the West." When asked why ANC had no policy on lesbian and gay human rights she replied, "We don't have a policy on flower sellers either." Tatchell followed up by contacting the ANC's chief representative in the United Kingdom, Solly Smith. Smith reiterated, "We cannot be diverted from our struggle by these issues. We believe in the majority being equal. These people are in the minority. The majority must rule."

The interviews were republished in the London gay weekly newspaper, *Capital Gay*, in September 1987, and quickly circulated around the world. The ANC was deluged with letters of condemnation from its liberal allies. The ANC leadership, focused on winning western support for its strategy of boycott, divestment, and sanctions (BDS) to isolate the South African government, was seriously embarrassed.

Tatchell then made a private appeal to Thabo Mbeki, ANC director of information. Mbeki was considered the most liberal-minded of the ANC leaders at the time, and was senior enough to push for a formulation of official policy. Tatchell described his letter as "challenging, but friendly and constructive." He argued that support for lesbian and gay liberation was consistent with the principles of the ANC's Freedom Charter. As well, he cited Nkoli's case, and that of Ivan Toms, a white gay doctor jailed for refusing to serve in the South African army.

Mbeki replied a month later.

> Dear Peter,
>
> . . . The ANC is indeed very firmly committed to removing all forms of discrimination and oppression in a liberated South Africa. You are correct to point this out. That commitment must surely extend to the protection of gay rights. . . . We would like to apologise for any misunderstanding that might have arisen over these issues.
>
> Yours in the common struggle, Thabo Mbeki

For the first time, a major national liberation movement had come out in support of gay rights. At Mbeki's request, Tatchell circulated the letter to gay and anti-apartheid movements around the world. It was a watershed moment.[3]

A NEW CRIMINAL CODE

The Progressive Conservative government of Brian Mulroney didn't have much stomach for reforming sexual offence sections of the Criminal Code. But since traditional legal inequalities could not be squared with the new Charter of Rights, there was little choice. The amendments came into law January 1, 1988.

The term "gross indecency," traditionally used to criminalize gay sex, was removed. The notion of privacy as two persons was relaxed. Orgies were now legal as long as they were not visible to unwitting non-participants. With one exception, the age of consent was equalized to fourteen for gay and straight sex alike. And youths could have sex with each other from the age of twelve, as long as their ages were no more than two years apart.

There were, of course, a few wrinkles. The age of consent for anal intercourse was set at eighteen, a provision that could be expected to disproportionately affect gay men. The bawdy house section of the code was not repealed. It could still be used to criminalize the baths and potentially people's homes. Finally, a new provision made it an offence to "invite, counsel or incite" anyone under fourteen to touch themselves or anyone else. There were fears that doctors, counsellors, or teachers who advised young people about safe sex or masturbation could be prosecuted.[4]

The amendments were the last nail in the coffin of the demand for repeal of age of consent. When consent was set at twenty-one, abolition seemed at least an option. But few people were ready to support sex between adults and children under fourteen. The risks of exploitation were just too great. Further, the argument that age of consent laws criminalized young people experimenting with their peers was addressed by the "laddering" clause that permitted sexual play between children as young as twelve as long as there was no more than two years' age difference.

A new consensus seemed to be emerging. The issue of child-adult sex had always been fraught. But it was as if all the social anxieties that had once been distributed over gay sex in general were concentrated on the pedophile, now imagined as the true monster. That sexual contact between adults and children could ever not be destructive to the child became unspeakable. Even the most innocuous physical contacts between adults and children were increasingly under suspicion.

The change in the law both reflected and reinforced this consensus. Across North America, the boundaries of acceptable sexual activity had widened under the influence of sexual liberation and individual pursuit of happiness. At the same time, the opprobrium directed at those outside the circle of acceptance intensified. This shift laid the groundwork for a series of moral panics across the continent that would disproportionately affect gay men.[5]

AIDS ACTION NOW!

After several months of meetings, our little group of neophyte AIDS activists was prepared to go public, and we needed a name. Some suggested ACT UP Toronto, but not wanting to be seen as mimicking Americans, we decided on AIDS ACTION NOW! It was a name that asked to be shouted, not spoken – a slogan.

In November Lynch published "Silence = Death, US Gays Fighting Homophobic AIDS Policies. What about Us?" in *Xtra*. The article cemented the frame that government homophobia was blocking action on AIDS, a narrative he repeated in a January press conference that announced the formation of AAN! "If this syndrome were affecting 1,500 Canadian Boy Scouts, neither Mr. Epp [the federal health minister] nor Ms Caplan [the provincial health minister] would be reacting with such armchair leisure. They are moving too damn slow. They are letting us die off because we are gay."[6]

The press conference was a careful show of unity. Speakers included Art Wood, chair of ACT; John Hamilton, chair of the newly formed Toronto People with AIDS Foundation; and Dr. Wayne Boone of the HIV Primary Care Physicians Group. In New York, ACT UP and the largest AIDS service organization, Gay Men's Health Crisis, were at each other's throats. The activists were accusing the service organization of complacency and complicity; the service organization was accusing the activists of disruptive extremism. We wanted to avoid such rifts in Toronto.

Two days later, *NOW*, Toronto's free downtown weekly, published a feature titled "Advocacy Action on AIDS." It said, "Like no other patients before them, people with AIDS are organizing against a cumbersome health system to prolong their own lives."[7] By then, the gay village was plastered with a bold image of Thor wielding his hammer. "Too Damn Slow! Our friends are dying as bureaucrats fiddle." The poster advertised AAN!'s first public meeting at Jarvis Collegiate, February 4, 1988.

Four hundred people showed up. George Smith masterminded the agenda. It was modelled on the RTPC mass meeting that had taken place after the bath raids in the same hall, seven years earlier. One after another, people from the audience shared testimonials about hospitals, rejection by doctors, and their frustration at not being able to get concrete information, never mind treatment. A lot of anger was expressed against ACT for its lack of public advocacy. They only want to "hold our hands until we die," one man said.

Smith finished the first part of the meeting explaining what was known about the syndrome, but ended with a call to action against health care cuts threatened by the Mulroney government. "If we are not in there fighting we'll be pushed to the back of the line." He also made sure the audience understood we weren't just fighting for our own lives. "We fight for the IV drug users, for the babies born with AIDS, for the hemophiliacs and for the Third World where HIV infection is rampant."[8]

The crowd then broke into small groups to brainstorm plans for committee work. When everyone came back to the main hall, they endorsed four concrete demands: immediate availability of aerosolized pentamidine to prevent PCP, a consensus conference of medical personnel and PWAs to establish standards and co-ordination of care, government action to make experimental treatments available, and adequate funding to make Canada a leader in AIDS research.[9]

PLACEBO TRIAL

That same week the federal government announced a trial of aerosolized pentamidine. But as details came out, our relief changed to anger. It was to be a double-blind placebo trial. That meant that half the people enrolled would not receive pentamidine, just a mist of bad-tasting water. Neither participants nor doctors would know who was getting the drug and who wasn't. In order to enroll, participants had to have already survived a bout of PCP. Since about half of such people could be expected to come down with a second PCP attack during the trial, comparing the results would show whether or not pentamidine would affect the rate of recurrence.

But the "clinical endpoint" was not just recurrence. Three hundred people were projected to enroll. That meant 150 would wait around for a second bout of PCP, untreated. Given the higher mortality rate for a second bout of PCP, as many as a dozen of us might die in order to demonstrate something we already knew from U.S. trials.

AAN!'s first demonstration took place March 25. Five hundred people left 519 Church Street in a light drizzle. Carrying empty coffins, we marched to Toronto General Hospital, one of the trial sites, for a candlelight vigil. I explained to the media that the purpose was to stop the trial and keep the coffins empty. On the way, we passed the offices of David Crombie, the Progressive Conservative member of Parliament for the riding, where we sealed the doors with red tape and Michael Lynch gave a passionate speech.

But marching on a hospital had been too much for ACT. After a difficult meeting between Lynch and ACT chair Art Wood, ACT refused to endorse the action. Lynch worried that the crowd might express its anger as we passed the ACT offices. But with AAN! determined that there be no open rift between political action and social services, we hustled the crowd past without incident.

A few weeks later, Fisons, the company conducting the trial, announced that a compassionate arm without placebo would be included for those who didn't meet the requisite single previous PCP infection. It was our first, small victory. At least people like Alan Dewar, who already had two bouts of PCP, could now get the drug. But for everyone else, the company held firm on the question of placebos.

RESEARCH ETHICS

Meanwhile, George Smith was immersing himself in the history of science and medicine. He was enormously excited when he explained that after the experimentation on concentration camp inmates in Nazi Germany, the *Nuremberg Code* (1947) developed ten ethical principles for experimentation involving human subjects. Those principles had been affirmed in the *Declaration of Helsinki* (1965).

The first principle read, "The *voluntary* consent of the human subject is absolutely essential." That meant that if there was any coercion or duress involved in recruiting subjects, a trial was unethical. Its results should not be published.

Smith argued that if the only way a dying person could access a possibly life-saving therapy was to enter a trial, they were being coerced. They weren't enrolling voluntarily but because if they didn't, they were condemned to death. If a trial used placebos, to be ethical, there had to be an alternative way to access the therapy for those unwilling to run the risk of getting nothing.

I had first-hand experience in how vulnerable people were coerced. I was visiting my friend Akio in Casey House, the new palliative care hospice for PWAs. His partner introduced me to an Indigenous man there who was recovering from a serious bout of PCP. His doctor had enrolled him in the pentamidine trial. He knew he only had a 50 per cent chance of getting the drug, and admitted he was terrified of coming down with PCP a second time. I told him we could arrange access, but he'd need to leave the trial. He shook his head. What if his doctor got mad? What if they threw him out of Casey House? He'd be homeless, on the street. There he'd soon die anyway. He had no choice but to take his chances and do what his doctor said.

Smith's second ethical argument was more straightforward. Individuals facing life-threatening circumstances should have the right to choose treatments they and their physicians think would be beneficial. The argument that unapproved drugs might not be safe was hardly applicable to those who were doing to die anyway.

Access to pentamidine couldn't be merely a protest issue. We needed an immediate solution. Every one of us who came down with PCP risked death. Every day was a new game of Russian roulette. Only systemic change could get pentamidine to everyone but, in the meantime, we were embedded in a community in Toronto that needed it now.

We found out that one of the doctors who worked with us had a licence to practise in New York and could write prescriptions that were valid there. Pentamidine was not terribly expensive and was available in U.S. pharmacies.

For three hundred dollars, less than the cost of one day in hospital, we developed information packages and set up a phone line to explain how to get a prescription and where to purchase the drug in Buffalo, a two-hour drive from Toronto. In April 1988, we distributed the packages to doctors' offices, AIDS service organizations, and hospitals across the city. We set up a carpool to shuttle people across the border. We liaised with ACT and the PWA Foundation to make sure that there was funding for those who couldn't afford the cost of the drug. Dr. Boone volunteered to supervise. Within a few months, forty people were attending a busy Thursday clinic to inhale the drug.

LIGHTING A FIRE

On May 18 the Canadian AIDS Society opened its national conference in Toronto. CAS was an umbrella group of AIDS service organizations from across the country. AAN! marked the opening with a die-in outside and, when a representative of the federal government addressed the gathering, unveiled a large banner declaring "Epp = Death." The following day we convinced most conference participants to join a march to city hall. The police were angry that we took the street and blocked traffic without warning, and advised me that we would all be arrested if we entered Nathan Phillips Square at city hall without a permit. I rushed back to talk to Councillor Jack Layton, who was marching with us, and he called off the cops. We burned an effigy of Epp in the square; the image of the flaming health minister was carried by media across the country. On May 25, AAN! members travelled to Ottawa and publicly consumed illegal treatments on Parliament Hill, followed by a press conference at the national press gallery.

The end of June 1988 was Pride Day once again. That year I split my time between AAN! and SNAAC. While SNAAC was raising money to support Simon Nkoli, AAN! realized that to give real resonance to the demand for access to experimental and unapproved treatments, we needed to increase demand among potential consumers. We distributed thousands of copies of *Treatment AIDS,* a broadsheet listing potential treatments unavailable in Canada. *Treatment AIDS* would morph into *Treatment Update,* a regular publication summarizing the latest developments in research and treatment compiled by Sean Hosein, an AAN! member and George Smith's partner.

In July, the G7, the leaders of the richest industrial countries, met in Toronto to plot economic strategy. In response, a coalition of unions, students, and anti-war groups organized an alternative Popular Summit to bring demands for social justice. AAN!'s Chuck Grochmal addressed a huge rally at Queen's Park calling for a shift in resources from war and repression to health care.

AKIO

I had met Akio in the baths in 1985. We only had sex once, but became friends. Though he was not out to his family back in Japan, he had led a flourishing gay life in New York before coming to Toronto to live with his partner, Gerry. That summer he found himself with less and less energy. In the fall he was rushed to hospital with pneumonia. It was PCP.

His hospital experience was horrible. He reacted terribly to intravenous pentamidine. Gerry tried to alleviate the side effects with various naturopathic medicines. The doctors didn't approve, and he had to sneak his remedies in. Akio's request for aerosolized pentamidine was refused. The treatment wasn't approved. The doctors were cold and arrogant, the nurses fearful. The hospital had little experience with PCP or AIDS.

Akio recovered and came home, but he was emotionally as well as physically devastated. Since no one in Japan knew he was gay, AIDS threatened to explode the doors of his closet. He was overwhelmed with anxiety and shame, and afraid to tell anyone what was happening. It became a kind of paranoia.

One night I got a phone call from Gerry, a travel agent, who had just come back from Europe. "There's a cure," he explained feverishly. "I've talked to homeopaths in Europe and they can cure it. The drugs they give here are poisons. They just further damage the immune system. They've managed to cure all sorts of people over there."

Akio and Gerry found a highly recommended homeopathic doctor and convinced me to see him as well. Dr. Saine was kind and interested. He spent hours asking questions about my life, the foods I liked, my childhood illnesses, whether I slept with the windows open or closed, and so on, in order to determine my constitution. When I mentioned the fight we were having around pentamidine, he cautioned me against it, declaring it a toxic poison. He'd treated a patient with PCP, he told me. The man came into his office on a stretcher but after a few of Saine's little white pills, he walked out unaided.

Despite Saine's treatment, that spring Akio got worse again. I encouraged him to start aerosolized pentamidine but he was now convinced that allopathic medicines were poison. The toxicity of high-dose AZT had become an urban legend, and its reputation had generalized to all western medicine. An underlying distrust of medical authority – a result of years of medical homophobia – was reactivated.

Saine told him that symptoms were good, part of the body's healing process. They indicated which homeopathic medicines were needed to restore his health. Gerry would phone Saine's office every day to describe the latest symptoms, and Saine would prescribe a new pill. Eventually, Akio's lungs filled up with fluid and he couldn't breathe. Gerry called an ambulance. They managed to stabilize him in hospital, but Akio was a shell of his former self. After a few weeks he was transferred to Casey House. Gerry continued sneaking in the latest alternative medicines, as they were both afraid to ask for permission. The theories became wilder and wilder. At least once a week Gerry would phone me about the latest cure.

I was meeting with two students from a local high school at my home. They were being bullied by their principal for doggedly trying to implement the anti-racism action plan they had developed at our camp, and we were working on a strategy to go forward. Those were the days of tape-recorder answering machines. We always left the sound up so that we could hear incoming messages. Casey House called. Akio had passed, and if I wanted to see the body I needed to come down in the next few hours. The message echoed through the house before I could rush to the phone and turn off the volume. I spent the next half-hour trying to calm down the kids and then rushed over to Casey House to comfort Gerry.

Homeopathy didn't work. But at this point, people were willing to try just about anything. Hosein followed all sorts of unapproved treatments in a regular AIDS Update column in *Rites*, but it was difficult to discern promising treatments from the promises of charlatans.

SHIFTS AND COMPROMISES

Four years after its 1984 meeting that rejected the ordination of lesbian and gay ministers, the United Church of Canada General Council convened in Victoria in August. Once again it was considering a report that recommended the ordination of lesbians and gay men, *Toward a Christian Understanding of Sexual Orientations, Lifestyles and Ministry*. The 1984 meeting had called for more study, and both Affirm, the United Church lesbian and gay group, and the opposition, the Community of Concern and the Renewal Fellowship, had been busy.

A great deal had changed in the intervening years. Liberal values that looked to rationality and science continued to erode traditional approaches valuing revealed scriptural knowledge, even within Canada's largest Protestant denomination. Manitoba, Ontario, and the Yukon had joined Quebec to add sexual orientation to their respective human rights codes. While 1984 was arguably the height of the homophobic panic sparked by the AIDS crisis, by 1988, the same crisis was normalizing talk about lesbians and gay men across society. The notion of the gay community as a beleaguered but legitimate minority was becoming widespread. And while ordaining gays had been scotched by the church's moderator in 1984 on the grounds that sexual orientation was a choice, the idea that being gay was an accident of birth was increasingly hegemonic.

The report was tabled along with a dissenting statement. After a series of boilerplate affirmations about the sanctity of marriage, the report made a clear statement: "We confess before God that as a Christian community we have participated in a history of injustice and persecution against gay and lesbian persons in violation of the Gospel of Jesus Christ."

It also confessed that there was still confusion about "God's intention in relation to human sexuality," and criticized both "an undue emphasis on sexual morality" and "an undue elevation of the sexual aspect of our being ... making this an idol which we worship. ... Neither view is fully consistent with God's intention for us."

But it concluded "that all persons regardless of their sexual orientation, who profess faith in Jesus Christ and obedience to Him, are welcome to be or become full members of The United Church of Canada," and that "all members of the Church are eligible to be considered for Ordered Ministry."[10] All of the recommendations were passed by the General Council.

There were some qualifying statements reminding "that all Christian people are called to a lifestyle which is patterned on obedience to Jesus Christ," which some feared might be interpreted to require gay people to be celibate. But despite such reservations, *Rites* headlined its story "Victory in Victoria." The inheritors of the gay liberation movement that had once railed against both organized religion and the idea of biologically determined sexuality now hailed the deployment of the same arguments about innate sexual orientation to win our acceptance by a progressive church.

EGALE AND A TURN TO THE COURTS

After dissolution of the Canadian Lesbian and Gay Rights Coalition and its short-lived successor, the Canadian Association of Lesbians and Gay Men, there had been no national lesbian and gay organization. EGALE, the Ottawa-based group, had lobbied for the inclusion of sexual orientation in the Canadian Human Rights Act. Since its location gave it easy access to both members of Parliament and national media, its voice became more prominent. In September 1988, EGALE morphed into EGALE Canada. It took on a national mandate to educate the public, conduct research, liaise between media and government, monitor legal actions, and act as a resource for other groups. In practice, its focus would be on legal change. It soon received $25,000 from the federal Court Challenges Program to develop Charter-based legal challenges to the Canadian Human Rights Act, the Canada Health Act, the Immigration Act, and the Criminal Code.[11]

This turn to the courts reflected impatience with the slow rate of political change, and the perception that the Charter opened a window of opportunity. Despite the Progressive Conservative government's 1985 *Equality for All* report, and the government's March 1986 promise to prohibit homophobic discrimination in all areas of federal jurisdiction, nothing had happened. In the face of political intransigence, the courts seemed a possible remedy. That shift was encouraged by the January 1988 Supreme Court decision to strike down Canada's archaic abortion laws. If the politicians wouldn't move, maybe the courts would.

First up was the Karen Andrews case. The Toronto librarian was fighting to have her lover and their children covered by OHIP. When the Liberal health minister refused to act on provincial ombudsman Daniel Hill's finding that denying benefits was "contrary to law and improperly discriminatory," Andrews's union, CUPE, paid to take the case to court. A We Are Family campaign, riffing on the 1979 Sister Sledge song, built community support. The Ontario Supreme Court rejected the plea in spring 1988, ruling that Andrews and her partner were two unrelated individuals and that family coverage was intended for "traditional families." But the issue was now in the public eye. The provincial attorney general, Ian Scott, himself a closeted gay man in a long-term relationship, ordered a review of Ontario laws containing the world "spouse." Still, no legislation was forthcoming.

The two iconic court cases of the 1970s – GATE Vancouver's Supreme Court case against the *Vancouver Sun* and the John Damien case in Toronto – both ended in defeat. However, the early movement had been as interested in getting noticed as in the legal outcome. The Andrews case was about winning. It was a subtle shift that would help reshape the movement.

PREPARING FOR THE LONG HAUL

In the fall of 1988, I took over as AAN!'s chair. Lynch's energy had waned over the summer, and by autumn he was hospitalized with PCP. His immune system was so weak that even the pentamidine couldn't hold it off.

It was a relatively seamless transition. Lynch had spent much of the early summer setting up the new temporary AIDS Memorial, unveiled that Pride Day in Cawthra Park. When he couldn't make meetings, chairing duties had often fallen to me. Twelve years as consensus builder on the *TBP* collective had prepared me for the delicate task of turning anger and frustration into concrete action. I was also lucky that my job at the board of education was flexible enough that I could multitask and slip in a lot of AAN! work. But I had no idea of just how intense it would turn out to be.

At AAN!'s first annual general meeting, October 5, 1988, I was elected chair and a new steering committee was approved. The organization was coming together, but it reflected the demographics of AIDS activism at the time. We were all gay men, except for one woman, Renee du Plessis, and all white except for du Plessis and Sean Hosein. There were two doctors, Michael Hulton and Dennis Conway. Only five of the thirteen steering committee members were positive. A majority were veteran gay activists; the vast majority had a university education.

A new seven-point policy program was approved. The first was catastrophic rights: "access to all drugs and treatments that can be used to treat HIV-positive people . . . free of charge, even when they have not been given government approval for regular distribution."[12] This demand was especially important, since we had learned that there was already a program to clear the use of unapproved drugs in Canada – the Emergency Drug Release Program. But the EDRP bureaucracy routinely refused to accept requests from doctors treating people with AIDS.

The demands also included PWA representation on decision-making bodies and the availability of anonymous testing. We called for an end to placebo-controlled trials. Unlike ACT UP in New York, which saw trials as a way of accessing treatments, AAN! made a clear distinction between treatment and research. Finally, we advocated for a National Treatment Registry, an idea proposed by New York physician Nathanial Pier. Pier argued for a central body to list and evaluate the many treatment ideas being circulated.

The meeting ended on a sombre note when it was announced that Alan Dewar had died the day before. Alan was the first of our founding members to pass away.

LAYING DOWN THE LAW

It didn't take long for AAN!'s first demand to make a splash. In mid-November Chuck Grochmal delivered a message to the first Conference on Clinical Trials for HIV in Canada, held in London, Ontario. Doctors, researchers, drug company representatives, and government officials had come to discuss financing and infrastructure, but Grochmal brought up the issue of placebos and catastrophic rights. As others picketed outside, he warned the gathering, "We can shut down any clinical trial in this country."

In her book *AIDS Activist*, Ann Silversides quotes Dr. Philip Berger, a primary-care doctor who was there: "Grochmal was 'so resolute. . . . He spoke in a calm, deliberate and unambiguous way. The room froze. That was a turning point.'" According to Dr. Michelle Brill-Edwards, the representative of the Federal Bureau of Human Prescription Drugs, both the researchers and the drug companies got the message. Drug trials would become ungovernable if catastrophic rights were not recognized.[13]

TARGETING TORIES

That same fall, a federal election campaign began. AAN! held a rally October 22. This time, it was Prime Minister Mulroney who was burned in effigy. You never get as much media play for a second burning, but we did get national news coverage about the refusal of the EDRP to clear non-approved AIDS drugs. During the campaign, every time Mulroney came to Toronto, we made sure he was greeted by angry AIDS activists. Tory candidates were repeatedly booed in all-candidates meetings when we brought up the government's record on AIDS.

But AIDS was a minor issue in what became known as the free trade election. Mulroney had signed an agreement with the United States that would swamp the Canadian market with cheaper U.S. imports. The Canadian economy would shift back from manufacturing towards resource extraction; this time, our export would be Alberta oil rather than beaver pelts. This would conveniently shift economic power to the Tory heartland in Alberta, away from industrial Ontario. It began a process pushing Canadian politics decisively to the right.

Both the Liberals and the NDP opposed free trade, splitting the majority vote against the measure. The November 1988 federal election narrowly returned the Tories to power.

We had been little more than an irritant, but we had caught the Tories' attention. In January 1989, Perrin Beatty, the new minister of health, announced that the EDRP would be opened to requests for unapproved AIDS treatments. That included aerosolized pentamidine. The pentamidine trial promptly collapsed as its subjects opted out of the placebo roulette and started taking the drug. Six months later, Toronto had a provincially funded aerosolized pentamidine clinic serving hundreds of PWAs. Grochmal's warning had been more than bluster. We had closed down our first unethical trial.

CLOSER TO HOME

Doug Wilson moved from Saskatchewan to Toronto with his partner, Peter McGehee, early in 1983. Although I had hoped he would join the *TBP* collective, his arrival coincided with the Red Hot Video and racism controversies, and he became a founder of *Rites*. But we worked closely after he took on a contract for the board's Equal Opportunity Office. By 1984 he was compiling and publishing *Focus on Equality*, our regular newsletter, and organizing the annual anti-apartheid student conference.

In the same 1988 elections, Wilson ran for the NDP in Toronto's downtown Rosedale riding, which included the gay ghetto. His way had been paved by the coming out in February that year of veteran NDP member of Parliament Svend Robinson. Robinson's gayness had been an open secret on Parliament Hill for years, but his coming out was a tipping point. There was much homophobic reaction. B.C. premier Bill Vander Zalm pointed out that homosexuality was a sin and said, "I don't know whether we should really feel so good about people influencing young girls or young boys in this way." Grant Devine, Progressive Conservative premier of Saskatchewan, said he felt the same compassion for homosexuals that he felt for bank robbers. But most mainstream media framed the coming out as an act of honesty and bravery, and critics found themselves on the defensive. "Robinson's critics are so coarse. Their pathetic little prejudices (and deep fear they reveal) richly deserve to be exposed to public ridicule and contempt," wrote *Ottawa Citizen* journalist Susan Riley.[14]

Without warning, in the middle of the campaign Wilson was hospitalized with PCP. The NDP kept it quiet, and the Tories took the riding in any case.

Wilson's illness was a shock. Although he was positive, his CD4 count (the best measure of the immune system at the time) was still relatively high. He and I began sharing information on complementary therapies, but Wilson was still reluctant to get involved with AIDS politics. It was hard enough being a national gay politician without being the first gay politician with AIDS. He didn't want to be pigeonholed as a one-issue candidate. His commitment to social justice was far more expansive than gay rights or AIDS.

Wilson was just recovering when we heard that Simon Nkoli had been acquitted of all charges on November 18, 1988. An important victory in desperate times, it put a new agenda on SNAAC's plate – organizing a North American tour as soon as Nkoli could get a passport.

Xtra closed 1988 by publishing a special section, Proud Lives, posting pictures of many of those who had died that year. There were thirty listings, many of them friends.

THE MONTREAL CONFERENCE

The spring of 1989 AAN!'s focus was on the upcoming Fifth International AIDS Conference to be held in Montreal. In March, I went on a reconnaissance mission to contact local activists. My timing was bad. Two days before I arrived, Joe Rose, a young gay man living with AIDS, was queerbashed and murdered on the Montreal transit system. Rose's death helped spark the formation of Réaction SIDA, Montreal's first AIDS activist group, a few weeks after I left.

When I visited the main service organization, Comité SIDA Aide Montréal (CSAM) in search of activists, they couldn't help me. They didn't get involved in politics. But they did put me in touch with one young man, Kevin, a former hustler, who had become a patient advocate complaining about shoddy hospital care. He wasn't connected to any organization and had little political analysis, but he had a deep experiential knowledge about local problems for PWAs in the health care system. At one point, he looked straight at me and said something I never forgot. "AIDS is like a lens. When you look through it, you see all the problems of society magnified many times."

I also met Montreal city councillor Raymond Blain, who in 1986 had been the first openly gay candidate to be elected in Canada. After swearing me to secrecy, he managed to get me a floor plan of the convention centre where the conference would be held. That was worth its weight in gold, and we shared it with ACT UP in New York.

We were already corresponding with Herb Spiers at ACT UP. Together we developed *Le Manifeste de Montréal* (the Montreal Manifesto), a declaration of the Universal Rights and Needs of People Living with HIV. A few weeks before the conference, Réaction SIDA found some unused office space to serve as a media centre and organizing hub. ACT UP chartered a bus to bring up New York activists.

Previously, the international AIDS conferences had been about medical research and marketing opportunities for big pharma. People with AIDS, when we appeared at all, were little more than medical exhibits or faceless statistics. AIDS activists were determined that that was going to change.

I took the train to Montreal several days early to represent AAN! at a community conference at McGill University, two days before the main show was to open. The conference was mostly made up of reps from AIDS service organizations and NGOs, but I made some useful international contacts including Alfred Machela, founder of the Rand Gay Organization, then working with Nkoli on the Township AIDS Project in Soweto.

As the ACT UP people arrived from New York, the meetings in the activist centre began to swell and go late into the night. We plotted out a week-long plan. There would be a unified demonstration outside the convention centre as delegates arrived for the opening on Sunday, June 4. Tuesday would focus on the struggle for anonymous testing. Wednesday was about lesbians and sex workers. Thursday would feature a rally with international speakers. Friday would deal with Quebec issues and actions at the closing ceremonies.

The office was filled with people lining up to type and copy press releases and flyers, while others painted banners on the floor. The phones and fax machines were buzzing. Many of us, including me, had not been able to afford the five-hundred-dollar registration fee, but someone had located a colour Xerox and several ACT UP members were busy forging passes.

I was to speak for AAN! at the first rally. As delegates streamed in for the opening ceremonies, activists gathered outside the main entrance. But ACT UP had something more dramatic up its sleeve. As I climbed on the makeshift podium, I realized there was a commotion at the entrance. A flying squad of ACT UP members had just rushed the main doors and pushed past security. The rest of the ACT UP crowd was close behind. AAN! member Glen Brown, head marshal for the rally, was standing beside me. He remembers that he asked me what we should do and I replied, "I guess we should lead them." So we followed with everyone else.

Seconds later, three hundred of us were streaming up the escalators to the main hall. Delegates were settling into their seats to hear opening remarks by Prime Minister Mulroney and Zambian president Kenneth Kaunda. Instead, they witnessed a crowd of activists roll onto the stage carrying banners and signs (many of which had been prepared by John Greyson as props for his video *The World Is Sick (sic)*). Life imitates art.

Once on stage, facing twelve thousand startled delegates, no one knew quite what to do. Since I was chair of the main Canadian organization, someone stuck a mic in front of my face. The address that I had planned for outside hardly seemed appropriate. This was a time for sound bites. So I opened the conference "on behalf of people living with AIDS," and launched into an attack on the hypocrisy of the Mulroney government – my fifteen seconds of international fame.

After a few more speeches, there was confusion about how long we were going to stay. The conference was now well behind schedule. The Canadians left first, an ACT UP spokesperson read the Montreal Manifesto in French and English, and finally, despite protests from security, everyone settled into the empty VIP seats at the front of the hall.

With the activists cleared off, Mulroney came on stage and opened the conference. Hundreds of us in the front rows got up and turned our backs, and a banner reading "Mulroney – You've Left Us to Die / Tu nous as laissées crever" was unfurled. The prime minister's speech was repeatedly interrupted by boos and hisses, especially when he intoned the neo-liberal mantra about limited government resources and the need for private fundraising initiatives. Later I told the media, "We don't believe we should have to hold garage sales to pay for the health care we deserve. The government must fund community based support, education and research initiatives."[15]

The next speaker was President Kaunda, whose son had recently died of AIDS. He received a much warmer reception and a standing ovation when he called on world leaders to divert military spending "to the more worthwhile destruction of AIDS."[16]

The significance of the moment was captured in the ACT UP account of the event.

> I'll never forget the sight of our ragtag group of 300 protesters brushing past the security guards in the lobby of the Palais de Congress [sic], the fleet of Silence = Death posters gliding up the escalator to the opening ceremony or our chants thundering throughout the cavernous hall. There we were, the uninvited guests, taking our rightful place at the heart of the conference. And when PWA Tim McCaskell grabbed the microphone and "officially" opened the conference "on behalf of people with AIDS from Canada and around the world," even the scientists stood and cheered.
>
> But it was only when we refused to leave the auditorium and instead parked ourselves in the VIP section that the crowd realized that our action was more than just a symbolic protest. Despite threats and rumors of a potential "international incident," we remained in our seats, alternately chanting and cheering, and giving notice that PWAs were "inside" the conference to stay. From that point on in the crisis, researchers would have to make extra room at the table for PWAs and their advocates.[17]

It was an exhausting week. The conference started at dawn every morning and the meetings at the activist centre went late into the night. There was some annoyance among the Canadians that ACT UP had neither consulted nor informed us of their plans to take the stage, but that was hard to sustain, given the jubilation over the success of the action. More difficult to manage was planning and prioritizing given the entitlement of the Americans, who seemed to think the whole world revolved around New York. At one point I was accused of homophobia by an ACT UP member after I raised concerns that all the speakers at our international rally were gay or lesbian and did not reflect the demographics of the epidemic. The members of Réaction SIDA, on the other hand, found all the anglophones, Canadian and American alike, overbearing and ethnocentric. Nevertheless, there was enough urgency and generosity to hold us together for the week.

IDENTITY AND THE TYRANNY OF THE UNINFECTED

For me, the Montreal conference also served to awaken an emerging HIV identity. The ACT UP crowd fiercely oscillated between asserting themselves as gay and HIV positive. That was exhilarating. In Canada, few of us had been public about our status. The question came to a head for me when a reporter asked if I had the AIDS virus. I was taken aback. That had never happened before. I stumbled through an answer that my status was a matter between me and my doctor, but afterwards I was far from satisfied with my reply. How could I be out and assertive as a gay man, but in the closet about my HIV status? If I had been willing to take a leadership role and assume the risks of coming out as gay, why was I reluctant to do the same about having HIV? It seemed especially hypocritical since I was chairing the country's major AIDS activist organization.

The need to come out and speak as an HIV positive person was further cemented for me at the community report on the conference that we organized back in Toronto. Still high from Montreal, we spent a lot of time describing the politics, from the takeover of the stage to the daily actions on different issues. Finally, a hand was raised at the back the room and a man tentatively asked, "I'm glad you did all that stuff, but is there news of anything that's going to keep us alive?" We had been so concentrated on looking through the lens of AIDS to expose the underlying social problems – homophobia, racism, the oppression of sex workers, underdevelopment – that we had forgotten about the lens itself and its immediate impact on those infected.

At the same time, George Smith was thinking about identity from a different perspective. He noted that the money government bodies were finally dedicating to AIDS was always within a public health framework. That meant protecting the uninfected (the public) from the infected (us). He called it "the tyranny of the uninfected." The implications were chillingly illustrated in Alistair Clayton's closing speech to the Montreal conference. Clayton was head of the new Federal Centre for AIDS. He outlined his strategy as "isolating the reservoir of infection." Once properly contained, he assured the conference, the epidemic would "burn itself out." For us that meant one thing: we would be quarantined until we died, and then there would be no more AIDS.

Safer sex, AIDS education, and so on, were all important public health issues, but they only included us as a danger. AAN!, Smith asserted, primarily needed to deal with the needs of the infected. No one else was going to do it. Treatment was the common denominator, the basis of unity that could unite all positive people, despite other differences. It was the first sign of a fissure between gay and poz identities.

Three days after our report on the conference, David Marriage, another of our key activists, died. David was an artist and carpenter. He had built the coffins we had carried in our inaugural demonstration. I hadn't really known him prior to AIDS. He was gentle and private and hadn't mixed much with the gay activist crowd. But when AIDS came along, he demonstrated an astounding inner strength. The first time I noticed him must have been in 1986. I was leaving a movie and he was going in. His face was already covered in purple KS lesions, and people were staring at him. I remember feeling a cold rush of fear. Was that going to be me? Yet he walked into that theatre, anticipating the movie with a smile on his face, as if absolutely nothing was wrong.

We needed fucking treatments. Now.

EVA HALPERT

A new treatment, ddI, was announced at the conference. But no one could get it.

Eva Halpert was a tiny Hungarian Jewish woman. Her son Ivan was dying. Ivan had exhausted the usefulness of AZT, and ddI was his only hope. His doctor applied to the EDRP and got permission. But pharma giant Bristol-Myers, who owned the drug, refused to release it until it was approved and ready for marketing. Halpert was incensed. No company was going to deny her son a life-saving drug.

With AAN! support, Halpert, often accompanied by her eighty-year-old father, began picketing the Bristol-Myers office across from city hall. The pair, with their simple messages – Bristol-Meyers, Please don't kill my son/grand-son – were unlikely AIDS activists. The story was soon circulating in national and international media.

It was a hot summer, and we were worried about Halpert's stamina as she spent day after day walking back and forth on the broiling pavement. On July 13 we upped the ante. AAN! held a press conference at city hall demanding the immediate release of ddI, while across the square, as fifty noisy protesters milled in the street below, a crew of activists went to occupy the Bristol-Myers office. Somehow the company had caught wind of the action and the office was locked, so the group occupied the hallway in front of the doors. By the time the police arrived to clear them out, we had led the media across the street to capture everyone being dragged away and charged with trespassing.

We continued to up the pressure, distributing leaflets in the community and providing phone numbers where people could call and fax protests to the company. The leaflets also urged a boycott of a list of Bristol-Meyers's other retail products.

Eva Halpert's picket continued. Finally, on September 28, Bristol-Meyers relented and released ddI to those intolerant to AZT. Ivan got his drug.

We had taken on the government and won the battle to open up the EDRP. Now we had forced the first big company to comply. But as George Smith pointed out in an article in the fall issue of *AIDS ACTION NEWS!*, the struggle for treatment access was far from over.

HIV DENIALISM

An article in *Rites'* conference coverage introduced another element into the debate. Was HIV actually the cause of AIDS? In "Challenging the AIDS Establishment over HIV," Colman Jones extensively quoted Dr. Joseph Sonnabend, a microbiologist and primary-care physician in New York, and his patient, musician Michael Callen. Both decried the conspicuous absence of "alternate hypotheses" to the growing consensus that HIV was the cause of AIDS.

This was not just an academic debate. If HIV did not cause AIDS, then all our work around access to HIV treatment was wrongheaded. Sonnabend was categorical: "The HIV hypothesis has consumed all our resources and yet hasn't saved a single life." Callen was a little more circumspect: "While many who question the HIV hypothesis are clearly misguided and without scientific foundation, there is nonetheless a serious critique of HIV, and there are alternate explanations that are at least as plausible."[18]

Callen may have been referring to Peter Duesberg, a professor of molecular and cell biology at the University of California, Berkeley. Duesberg had gained public notoriety with a March 1987 article in *Cancer Research* proposing that AIDS was caused by long-term consumption of recreational drugs and that HIV was harmless.[19] He had later gone on to suggest that HIV medicines themselves caused AIDS.

At the beginning, AAN! gave some attention to the question, publishing a piece by Jones in *AIDS ACTION NEWS!* and, in October 1990, organizing a screening and panel discussion of Jones's new video *The Cause of AIDS: Fact and Speculation.* Jones presented his work as an investigative documentary, but there was little doubt that his sympathies lay with the denialists. Most of us tried to keep an open mind, but as time went on, the various streams of HIV denialism seemed ever more irrelevant, even potentially dangerous, since they discouraged people from taking medications. Jones continued to be prolific and published in *Rites, Xtra,* and *NOW,* even as the consensus around HIV solidified and anti-HIV drugs showed more promise and fewer side effects.

The attraction of the HIV denialist position seldom seemed to be based on a cool weighing of the evidence. But that evidence was difficult for all but the most adept to evaluate. Rather, denialism resonated with a distrust of anything that was seen as establishment, a suspicion common among gay men after years of establishment homophobia.

COMPLEMENTARY THERAPIES

Because mainstream pharma wasn't able to stop the dying, alternative medicines became popular. Arguments sometimes riffed on apparently anticapitalist positions – the pharmaceutical industry was interested only in profits and preferred to keep selling us drugs rather than finding a cure. George Smith called this classic ideological thinking. It was true that the bottom line for pharma was profits, not people's health, but that did not necessarily invalidate pharma research or mean its products were poisonous.

Such approaches didn't necessarily deny HIV, and they were extensively covered in AAN!'s treatment information efforts. But we did try to change the terminology from "alternative" to "complementary." Personally, while I waited for something better, I tried whatever might help. Although many doctors discouraged their patients from taking substances they didn't understand, mine, Dr. Berger, was more open-minded. He wasn't ready to condemn something because he didn't understand it. I used various kinds of Chinese herbs, n-acetylcysteine, monolaurin, hypericin, kombucha fungus that I grew in the fridge, AL-721, and megadoses of a range of vitamins. What did I have to lose?

We did call for proper testing of such treatments whenever possible. A young Swiss man had done the rounds in Montreal with a "bio-energized saline solution," promising rapid immune restoration. I pulled together a group of friends and we dutifully followed his protocol, using a local chiropractor to oversee results. After three months, everyone's CD4 cells continued to drop. The young man, who was regularly back and forth across the Atlantic, was devastated. We didn't see him again.

Sadly, the distinction between alternative and complementary was lost on many. For several years I was invited to talk at an annual forum on alternative medicine. When I finally asked the audience how many of them were taking antivirals and prophylaxis for opportunistic infections, hardly anyone raised their hand. I gave them a lecture about how none of us was in a position to put our eggs in one basket. We needed to take advantage of advances in mainstream medicine as well. I wasn't invited back.

COLOUR CORRECTIONS

By the end of the 1980s, the visible minority percentage of Toronto's population was approaching 25 per cent. The growth was reflected when Toronto hosted Grassroots '88, the 5th International Lesbian and Gay People of Colour Conference in July 1988.

The conference was a successor of the seminal 1979 Third World Lesbian and Gay Conference that had led to the founding of Gay Asians Toronto. But by 1988, the term "Third World," referencing anti-colonial struggles, had been displaced by "people of colour," conceptualizing its constituency by how people looked and how they fit into a racial hierarchy in the First World. National liberation struggles were fading into history.

The conference helped spark a surge of organizing among racialized lesbians and gay men in the city, much of which focused on AIDS. Toronto's two major AIDS services, ACT and the PWA Foundation, were still largely oriented to white gay men. A combination of racism, cultural incompetence, and language difficulties made them not particularly welcoming for many racialized people and new immigrants.

Zami had generated a Black Gay and Lesbian AIDS Discussion Group, which raised the idea of an AIDS service organization mandated to meet the needs of Toronto black communities. Key to the organizing was Doug Stewart, who became the first executive director of the Black Coalition for AIDS Prevention (Black CAP). Black lesbian feminists once again took a leading role. Initially sponsored by the Harambee Foundation, Black CAP began work in August 1989 and soon secured funding from the municipal, provincial, and federal governments. Like in ACT, a skeleton staff co-ordinated the work of dozens of volunteers.

Black CAP probably contributed to the end of Zami, as many of that group's activists put their energy into the new organization. Zami had also ceased to be the only game in town. There were more black queer spaces as the club scene developed. DJ Black Cat emerged as a major music magnet. A younger generation began organizing events. Zami stopped meeting in 1989.

Khush: South Asian Gay Men of Toronto was founded by young South Asian men in 1987 and burst onto the scene with Salaam Toronto! in 1988. This one-day cultural event at 519 Church was initiated by Ian Iqbal Rashid. Salaam was designed to combat racism in the white gay community and homophobia in the South Asian community. It soon morphed into Desh Pardesh, a cultural event that would become a five-day conference/festival attracting thousands.

Desh was not so much a lesbian and gay cultural event as a South Asian cultural event organized by South Asian lesbians and gay men. While there was lots of lesbian and gay content, Desh dealt with the wide range of issues facing the South Asian diaspora in Canada. In her history of the festival, Sharon Fernandez called it "a festival rooted in the perennial quest of immigrants for inclusion."[20] At Desh, "the complexity of South Asian identity became apparent. It was also a site for White Canadians to be at an event which was sophisticated about arts, racism and politics that set a new standard for how these three spheres could be brought together."[21] Desh was a gift to the whole city from its South Asian lesbian and gay community.

But cultural events were not enough in a growing epidemic. In 1989, after a South Asian couple died unable to access AIDS services in their own language or cultural context, Khush members formed the South Asian AIDS Coalition (later renamed the Alliance for South Asian AIDS Prevention) with support from ACT. Initially run by volunteers working out of a garage, its first co-ordinator was Anthony Mohamed, the young man who had become a gay activist after the murder of Ken Zeller had rocked his high school.

Next to emerge was the Gay Asian AIDS Project (GAAP), an outgrowth of Gay Asians Toronto. It was the brainchild of Dr. Alan Li, who had joined GAT in 1981 while still a medical student. By 1987, Li began working as a doctor at the Regent Park Community Health Centre, serving diverse low-income communities living in Canada's largest public housing complex. He soon realized that other community health centres with the mandate to serve inner-city Chinese communities were unable to deal with the needs of gay Asian men with HIV. He spearheaded an education program to deal with the issue, and in the meantime, GAAP tried to address AIDS education by making material available in a range of languages and offering culturally appropriate support for PWAs from various Asian backgrounds. In 1994 GAAP merged with several other small Asian AIDS groups to form Asian Community AIDS Services (ACAS).

The recognition and profile of such groups also helped inspire other ethno-specific lesbian and gay organizations. By the end of the 1980s, Greek, Italian, Portuguese, Polish, and Latin American groups were springing up.

TWO SPIRITS

Aboriginal lesbians and gay men were also a growing presence in Toronto, as more Aboriginal people began moving to the cities. Art Zoccole came to Toronto in 1979 from Lac des Mille Lacs First Nation near Thunder Bay. He remembers that, at first, Aboriginal gay men "would see each other in a bar but we didn't talk to each other."[22] But by the late 1980s, friendship networks were developing, and "we noticed that people had started getting sick."

Zoccole explains:

> So our humble beginnings were taking care of our friends and going into people's homes as care teams. Then they would pass away and we'd have all kinds of issues. Some communities wouldn't even accept the body back home because of the stigma around AIDS. We realized we needed to do our own ceremonies. We all realized that we came from a place where we had a lot of our culture with us. We started our own celebrations of life, introduced our ceremonies into those, and had them at the Native Canadian Centre.[23]

In 1988, Zoccole and Billy Merasty put up posters in the bars and booked a small room at the 519 Church Street centre for a community meeting. Thirty-five people came. A consensus emerged on the need for an ongoing group.

Since there were participants from several nations, everyone had a different term to refer to people like themselves in their own language. They agreed on an English name, Gays and Lesbians of the First Nations in Toronto.

Zoccole recalls that at the time, when it came to lesbians, he had "no idea." In fact, at the first meeting, he was startled to see Lavern Monette, a lawyer for the Union of Ontario Indians. He thought to himself, "Oh my God, the Union of Ontario Indians has sent their lawyer to see what we're doing." But as the meeting went on, it dawned on him just as suddenly, "Oh my God, she's a lesbian."

Nonetheless, women came to play a strong role in the group. Its first executive director was Susan Beaver. Some funding was secured from the City of Toronto. Then, in 1991, Frank McGee from the newly formed provincial AIDS Bureau offered the group fifty thousand dollars to do AIDS work with the Aboriginal community. That sparked the need for incorporation, eventually under the name Two Spirited People of the First Nations (TSPFN).

It was ironic that it took AIDS to generate a funded, stable, institutional presence for racialized and Indigenous people within Toronto's LGBT communities. It was this engagement with the state that amplified such voices within the community as a whole. But while these groups were often involved in anti-homophobia work in their communities as part of their AIDS education mandate, their work was usually defined as prevention and support. AAN! continued to be the only group with a clear mandate on advocacy and activism around treatment issues.

BROADSIDE CLOSES

A little more than a decade after it burst on the scene, *Broadside* announced it was ceasing publication in August 1989.

From the outside, the magazine seemed healthy. Unlike *TBP* two years before, its subscriptions had remained stable at about three thousand. Its concerns had not narrowed. It still embraced a wide range of issues relevant to women, from violence to free trade. The November 1988 issue struck a hopeful note. While it announced the departure of Philinda Masters, listed as editor of the paper since its inception, as well as two other long-time collective members, it concluded, "Broadside is almost ten years old and what better way to celebrate a full decade of life than with a serious campaign for improvement. We are considering all kinds of dramatic and exciting changes."[24]

In reality, it was becoming harder to pay the bills and to find volunteers. Several other feminist publications had gone under. The women's cultural scene was dwindling. The counterculture was long dead, and the mainstream had shifted back to more traditional notions of femininity signalled by high-heeled shoes and big hair. The Progressive Conservative government was cutting back on funding to women's organizations (although *Broadside* itself had never received significant funding). As the women's movement diversified, the *Broadside* collective had remained white, producing a "lopsided view of things."[25] The number of pages had shrunk from its heyday.

The last issue, August/September 1989, was bittersweet. There were congratulatory ads on the paper's tenth year and letters of dismay from subscribers who had been forewarned of the paper's demise. Eve Zaremba got the last word, proclaiming "the Women's Liberation Movement is here to stay," and warning against negativity as a "cop out for individuals who just want an excuse to quit." She identified the dependence of women's groups on government funding as a major mistake for feminists during the 1980s, a Liberal party tactic aimed at containment, and wondered why anyone would expect such support from the new Progressive Conservative government. She called for a new way of organizing "the many smart women out there in academe, in women's services, in media, in unions, in law, in business."[26]

Her message was a reiteration of the radical feminist call for women's unity beyond class, social location, or race. But under neo-liberalism, more privileged women were breaking through the glass ceilings of sexism and moving on, while many others were being left behind. The demise of *Broadside* was a reflection of the crisis within radical feminism itself.

RELATIONSHIP RECOGNITION

Similar processes were at work in the lesbian and gay movement. The addition of sexual orientation to the Ontario Human Rights Code in 1986 helped protect individuals from discrimination. As the early movement had hoped, that encouraged more people to come out and challenged negative social attitudes incubated by invisibility. But as those who previously had too much to lose now found it less risky to come out, the demographics of who represented the community began to change. The original liberationists had been generally young and in less permanent relationships. Now those with more "normative" lifestyles, both men and women, were at the table. For them, the recognition of stable relationships became a key issue.

Relationship recognition had been important to lesbians raising kids, whose parental rights to non-biological children were not recognized. For gay men, AIDS raised the stakes. As more people got sick, long-time partners were refused visitation rights in hospitals because they were not legally "family." When people died unexpectedly, their partners had no claim to shared assets or pensions. A host of increasingly important economic and social benefits were restricted to heterosexual relationships. A new basis of unity between more normative lesbians and gay men was emerging: the ultimate relationship recognition was marriage. Denmark had just legalized it. Did we want it?

Rites didn't quite know what to make of it. A full-page article by Ingrid MacDonald – "A funny thing happened on the way to the revolution: More lesbians are looking at marriage as an option – Is it for you?" – pointed out that in the 1970s, marriage was targeted as a site of oppression. "Women burned their marriage certificates in demonstrations." But now, she explained, "this is an extremely conservative time. Monogamy and weddings shift our focus away from AIDS." On the other hand, "the renewed interest in marriage might also signal a new courage to demand from the state an equality of access to the benefits and recognition that our straight counterparts receive."[27]

With the attorney general musing about changing the definition of spouse, the cat was out of the bag. One of the last remaining gay liberation groups from the 1970s, the now renamed Coalition for Lesbian and Gay Rights in Ontario (CLGRO, formerly CGRO) took up the issue at a two-day conference, On Our Own Terms, in August 1989.

The opening keynotes were delivered by Karen Andrews and Brian Mossop. Both were part of the organizing committee and had been involved in legal challenges. Andrews had lost her case for family benefits coverage. Mossop worked as a translator for the federal government, and when he was denied bereavement leave to attend his partner's father's funeral, he complained to the Canadian Human Rights Commission. After almost four years, in April 1989, a tribunal ruled he was entitled to compensation, stating "homosexual couples may constitute a family."[28] The ruling was under appeal but it was still considered a major advance.

Mossop and his partner, Ken Popert, publisher of *Xtra*, were early activists. Andrews, on the other hand, was part of the newer generation. While Andrews focused on the issue as one of equity, Mossop reminded the conference that there were "significant differences in how gays and lesbians form relationships compared to heterosexuals," and warned against adopting the heterosexual model. He reiterated that "the actual winning of legal rights was less important than the added legitimacy that this would confer on our sexuality and relationships through public education." Despite their different approaches, both agreed on the importance of equal rights to spousal entitlements.[29]

The debate soon became more heated. Veteran liberationists like Chris Bearchell urged the group to "strive for something more than mere equality." She pointed out that heterosexual relationships were usually based on dependency or "an unrealistic expectation of exclusivity." Lesbians and gays should be free to develop our own forms of relationships, and those not in traditional couples should not be penalized.[30] For others this made little sense. Equality with straights was the only intelligible goal.

In the end, long-time CLGRO organizer Tom Warner reported a "fragile consensus." CLGRO would seek legislative change to allow individuals to designate whomever they wanted as a spouse based on their own values and beliefs. It called for an optional partnership registration system, and the amendment of the legal definition of "spouse" and "marital status" under provincial laws. It was a middle course between those who rejected traditional heterosexual relationship models and opted for alternatives, and those who wanted to be recognized as a legitimate couples equal to their heterosexual peers.

SIMON COMES TO CANADA

I wasn't involved in the relationships debate. With Simon Nkoli out of jail, I was caught up with efforts to prepare his North American tour on behalf of SNAAC. Our budget for the Canadian tour came to just under ten thousand dollars. Between individual donations, local fundraising, and small grants from NGOs, we scraped together the money.

SNAAC established requirements for participating cities. Most importantly, groups needed to host a public meeting co-sponsored by local anti-apartheid and lesbian and gay organizations. The tour aimed to encourage ties between lesbian, gay, and anti-apartheid activists across the continent.

After attending the International Lesbian and Gay Association (ILGA, renamed from IGA) meeting in Vienna and speaking in several European cities, Nkoli flew from London to Toronto on August 8, 1989. After almost five years of correspondence, it was moving to meet him. He was a slight, shy, and fey young man with a ready laugh that concealed an iron determination. We put him up in the latest incarnation of our commune, now moved to Toronto's west end after Jearld Moldenhauer sold the house on Seaton Street where we had lived for a decade.

After a few days, the tour began in earnest. Nkoli flew to Winnipeg, Regina, and Vancouver and then headed down the West Coast to San Francisco and Los Angeles. An old friend, James Credle, took responsibility for the U.S. part of the tour. I had interviewed Credle for a feature in *TBP* about coming out as a young black draftee in Vietnam in the 1960s. Credle had become assistant dean of multicultural student affairs at Rutgers University and was active in Men of All Colors Together, with chapters and contacts across the United States. Over thirty days Nkoli had more than thirty speaking gigs in U.S. cities, ending up in Boston and then back to Toronto via Halifax.

By the time he returned, Nkoli was absolutely exhausted. But there was no respite. The main Toronto event was the evening of September 28 and Councillor Jack Layton had arranged for an official reception at city hall the same afternoon. Both *NOW* and *Xtra* made Nkoli cover boy and published interviews to promote the event. Everyone was so eager to help build local anti-apartheid movements that no one stopped to think what a gruelling ordeal the tour would be. Somehow Nkoli managed to hold up under the strain. I guess four years in prison had made him resilient. But we did reluctantly cancel his last scheduled appearance in Windsor, Ontario, when he said he couldn't possibly continue.

The success of the tour, the packed Toronto event, and front-page coverage in *NOW* brought SNAAC, and with it, the lesbian and gay communities, to the attention of the anti-apartheid movement in Toronto. We were transformed from the marginal group that was forgotten at anti-apartheid events to a major player. Unfortunately, we achieved that at Nkoli's expense.

The tour was both SNAAC's greatest achievement and its swan song. The apartheid regime was crumbling. Nelson Mandela was unconditionally released from prison five months later. After five years of work, SNAAC, along with most of the international anti-apartheid networks, disbanded shortly afterwards.

IDENTITY CRISIS

In early September, the most active members of AAN! went on a two-day retreat at Hart House Farm on the Niagara Escarpment. The weekend produced three important documents: a basis of unity, the organization's mandate, and goals for the next year.

But in his report on the retreat in *AIDS ACTION NEWS!* Bernard Courte noted that a fault line was developing in the organization, posing "the direct needs and interests of people with HIV infection versus . . . more general political issues." He continued:

> Furthermore, a group led by people living with HIV expressed some frustration that the organizational goals being proposed were moving us away from our primary goal, which is to make treatments available to those PLWA/HIVs who want them. If in our struggle for access to treatments or quality health care, social change occurs, we will all be happy. But those of us who are fighting for our lives see *this* – access to treatments – as the primary objective of this organization, its *raison d'être*.[31]

George Smith orchestrated a compromise, and the final version of the basis of unity and mandate seemed to be acceptable to everyone. The basis led off with the empowerment of people living with HIV and the potential for AIDS to be a "chronic manageable illness." But it also recognized "that the politics of AIDS raises profound questions about the way our society is organized" and noted that "it is necessary for us to deal with issues of social inequality around race, sex, class, sexuality, ability etc., both inside and outside our organization." The mandate began with improving the availability of drugs, treatments, and care, but closed with the open-ended "any other activities that AAN! thinks will improve the quality of life for persons living with AIDS or HIV."[32]

A month later at the organization's annual general meeting, everything came to a head. With no warning, some members of the mostly HIV negative group distributed a last-minute sheet of amendments to the AAN! constitution. The original constitution had been drafted to give an elected steering committee decision-making powers, but the amendments allowed only general meetings to make decisions, reducing the steering committee to an implementation body between meetings.

The implications were huge. While the steering committee was now elected with an eye to ensuring the strong presence of people living with AIDS, at general meetings there could be no guarantee that HIV positive people would be in a majority. In such an open forum, whoever talked loudest and longest would dominate. Given the fragile state of health of many of our positive members, long debates at interminable meetings would mean they would likely leave before decisions were made.

Smith felt personally betrayed, since he had worked so hard to build consensus. For me, this was similar to the left opportunist Trotskyist tactics of the early 1980s – caucusing in secret and then springing proposals full of politically correct language on a broader coalition, with little regard to the consequences. At any rate, both of us were furious. It seemed a direct attack on HIV positive people's leadership in AAN!

As chair, I was able to defer the motion until the next general meeting to ensure proper discussion. Over the next two months we made sure that everyone understood the proposal's implications. When the December meeting rolled around, only one of the original backers turned up and the amendments were soundly rejected. Subsequently, we did amend the constitution, but to ensure that HIV positive people constituted a majority of the steering committee.

From that point on, AAN! was an organization run by and for HIV positive people, rather than a vehicle for anyone's version of radical politics. We dealt with relevant social issues, but access to treatments was always the priority. And HIV negative allies were welcome. I was asked to stand for re-election as chair for a second year, but I was worn out. In my experience, the job was too demanding for one person. I agreed to continue on the condition that we establish co-chair positions. Glen Brown, a young HIV negative man of exceptional organizational abilities, would co-chair with me.

THE VEYSEY RULING

Tim Veysey's partner, Les Beu, had been a speaker at the CLGRO On Our Own Terms conference that summer. Veysey, an inmate at Ontario's Warkworth prison, had applied for conjugal visits, but Correctional Services denied the application on the grounds that another man could not be his spouse. Veysey took them to court in 1988, arguing that the decision violated his Charter rights to equal treatment.

A few months after the conference, in November 1989, the Federal Court of Canada ruled in Veysey's favour. Judge J.E. Dube cited provincial human rights legislation and the 1985 *Equality for All* report that recommended sexual orientation be covered by the Canada Human Rights Act. Finally, he noted that while sexual orientation was not specifically mentioned in Section 15 of the Charter, in his view it was an analogous ground.[33]

The recognition that gay people and our relationships were protected by the Charter was a game-changer that would reconfigure the logic of the legal system. The floodgates for redress had been opened, even if politicians were dragging their feet.

Exasperation with politics was reinforced by events at city hall. After much behind-the-scenes effort, city council voted to proclaim June 25 Lesbian and Gay Pride Day. It was a slap in the face for Mayor Art Eggleton. Such proclamations were supposed to be the prerogative of the mayor, but Eggleton had always obstinately refused, perhaps because he still attributed his victory in 1980 to the homophobia stirred up by Sewell's support for the gay community. Now council had done an end run. Then, two weeks later, opponents managed to reopen the question. On a second vote, with different councillors present, the proclamation was rescinded. Sometimes politicians didn't seem to be worth all the trouble.

But if going to the courts seemed the path of least resistance, it also shifted the leadership of the rights movement. There was less need to mobilize people to put pressure on governments. Professionals would do the job in the courts. If the early movement measured success by bodies in the street and media reports, the 1990s would learn to value legal opinions and those who could donate money to pay legal fees.

LOSSES

That fall and winter, AAN! lost more key members. James McPhee, the organization's treasurer, died November 30. I knew James was very ill and had arranged to drop over to his house to see him after work. It was dark when I knocked at the door. A woman answered and said James had died that morning. He was twenty-six.

Tony Vigers had been treasurer of the RTPC after the bath raids, and had taken over James's duties at AAN! when James's health started to fail. After living with KS for four years, Tony died less than a week after James.

Ross Fletcher studied at the Ontario College of Art and was a leading member of the media committee. He died December 12 at age thirty-one.

Then we heard Nathaniel Pier, the New York physician who had introduced the idea of a treatment registry, died December 27. He was a founder for the New York Community Research Initiative that served as a model for a similar effort in Toronto. *Xtra*'s Proud Lives at the end of 1989 listed almost ninety of our friends gone.

January 17, 1990, Gram Campbell died. Gram had designed the Thor poster for our first meeting and did artwork for countless gay and AIDS organizations. He was thirty-one.

Steering committee and founding member Chuck Grochmal was gone February 3. Chuck had been a tireless advocate, did our desktop publishing, and wrote a regular column on AIDS for *Xtra,* as well as holding down his coat check job at The Barn.

At the Montreal conference in June 1989, Health Minister Beatty had promised to put together a National AIDS Strategy within six months. AAN! continued to push for a National Treatment Registry as part of that strategy. But with our friends and loved ones dying all around us, bureaucratic time-lines were far too slow. In January 1990, AAN! launched the Treatment Information Exchange. TIE took over publication of *Treatment Update / Traitement SIDA*, held regular meetings for PWAs to discuss treatment options, encouraged communication among doctors, and began developing a database on cutting-edge treatments, both mainstream and complementary. Eric Mitchell (later Mykhalovskiy), a young graduate student at York University, became TIE's first co-ordinator.

TIE was funded by a grant from the Trillium Foundation, the organization that distributed profits from the Ontario Lotteries Corporation. Trillium was not exactly government, but managing public funding at that scale made many AAN! members nervous. TIE would also provide services, and in the long run, would need other funding sources. Under George Smith's leadership, within a year, TIE became an independent charitable corporation, the Community AIDS Treatment Information Exchange (CATIE).[34]

This distinction between activist work and services, a division of labour first recognized in order to minimize friction between AAN! and AIDS service organizations, became a hallmark of our organizing. The idea for the Community Research Initiative Toronto had been raised at the same early meetings which had founded AAN!, but we decided from the beginning that if CRIT was to have credibility, it needed to be independent. AAN!'s prisons sub-committee also became the Prisoners AIDS Support and Advocacy Network (PASAN) in 1991, when it took up the work of providing support and education to individual prisoners and the prison system as a whole.

ANONYMOUS TESTING

New therapies, at least for opportunistic infections, were beginning to come on line. The cover of the January 1990 issue of *Xtra* advised, "AIDS test now a must."[35] With pentamidine now available, it didn't make sense to find out that you had HIV by waiting to get PCP. But many gay men still feared the consequences of getting their names on a government list.

Those fears were amplified on January 31 when Ontario's chief medical officer of health, Richard Schabas, called on the minister of health to reclassify AIDS as a "virulent" rather than a "communicable" disease. That shift would give public health officials the right to detain anyone they suspected of spreading the virus.

In an interview with the *Toronto Star*, Schabas clarified what he meant by anyone suspected of spreading the virus: "The risk of intercourse with someone who is infected, even when a condom is used, is known to be too high. . . .

My opinion is that the appropriate recommendation or order to someone known to be infected is not to have sexual intercourse."[36] All HIV positive people who had sex, no matter what precautions we took, were to be quarantined. The fears about concentration camps that Joseph Reid had expressed in Vancouver seemed a step closer.

AAN! took the lead to organize a press conference with ACT, Casey House, and the PWA Foundation. We demanded Schabas's immediate resignation. His proposal would threaten the rights and freedoms of all PWAs, and it undermined the public health message encouraging people to use condoms. If the risks were still too high when condoms were used, why bother? Five hundred people marched on the Ministry of Health to demand Schabas be fired. Within weeks, every AIDS service organization in the province had signed on to that demand. In April the AIDS sub-committee of the Toronto Board of Health expressed its opposition to Schabas's proposed reclassification.

Schabas did not resign, nor was he fired. But ironically, his draconian proposal sparked anonymous testing. The City of Toronto had already approved the concept almost a year before. In April, the Ministry of Health bowed to the outcry and approved a trial to establish five anonymous test sites across the province. Hassle Free Clinic, already offering anonymous testing in defiance of the law, was no longer under threat.[37]

WHO OWNS AIDS?

At ACT, executive director Stephen Manning was struggling with what he saw as a drift from grassroots community towards professional control of AIDS service organizations. He raised the issue in a 1990 speech to the Canadian AIDS Society annual meeting. The talk was printed in *Xtra* later that summer as "Owning AIDS."

> Owning an issue means having the moral right to speak about it and to be listened to, to have a say in how an issue is represented and what it really means.... The powerful institutions of government, medicine, pharmaceuticals and social services are becoming more and more involved in the issue of AIDS and HIV infection. Consequently, they are having a greater impact on the lives of men and women living with AIDS ... will our larger helpers become our colonizers? ... AIDS cannot belong to people for whom it is only a professional problem.

Manning argued that the claim to moral leadership is "the proper business of communities; networks of mutual belonging, visible identity and common fate." He proposed three criteria for moral leadership: "communities must be deeply affected by AIDS," they must be "deeply involved in confronting AIDS," and they must have the capacity to sustain an adequate response "in all its complexities." He said, "I believe that the three characteristics I have described best fit the gay communities of Canada."

> Speaking the whole truth about AIDS requires a language for sexual politics. The preference of traditional sectors is to ignore or regulate sex. The volatile mix of gay liberation and lesbian feminism that runs through AIDS movements has provided us with a means to attack the deadly silence and prohibition which government, medicine and social services bring to AIDS responses.

Manning recognized that asserting ownership broke with the impulse to try and distance the gay community from the epidemic. He stated that we were deluding ourselves "if we think that it has escaped the notice of the world that gay men remain the overwhelming majority of PLWAs in this country." He pointed out "the disastrous situation of those who contract HIV by blood transfusion is recognized in cash, the equally real pain of HIV+ gay men and others is apparently not so valuable." In the face of such homophobia, we needed to believe "in our right to exist, to be visible and to be proud."[38]

AIDS seemed like a rather questionable piece of real estate to want to lay claim to. But the new relationship with the state meant it could be leveraged for funds for organizational survival and growth. On one side, Manning's article could be seen as challenging the implicit homophobia that was "de-gaying" AIDS and fighting to ensure that the largest group of infected people received its share of resources. On the other, from the point of view of the growing number of straight PWAs who were largely members of racialized groups, it seemed less than sensitive. Though he did note that gay men needed to remember other affected groups such as "injection drug users, racially different immigrants, women with dependent children, hemophiliacs."

Finally, Manning addressed a "relatively new" diversity. "Some of us are HIV+, some of us are HIV–. . . . The growing self-awareness of, self-definition, and self-assertion of HIV+ people presents a challenge to us all, both as communities and organizations."

AAN! resented our emergence being characterized as a challenge. I worked up a Venn diagram to portray the relationship between HIV and other identities. The central box was HIV+. The major overlapping box was gay men. That overlap constituted about 80 per cent of the poz box, but most of the gay men's box was still outside. The poz box also overlapped to a lesser extent, with boxes for women, hemophiliacs, straight men, and people from "endemic areas," code for racialized immigrants at the time.

A poz identity was emerging as a political project, distinct from gay identity. This fissure had several implications. From the standpoint of public health, it located negative gay men as part of the public, worthy of protection and thus more normative, while poz gay men remained the danger to be surveilled. In terms of organizing, gay men might be the dominant demographic within HIV identity, but that didn't mean gay and HIV positive were the same or that gay men owned AIDS. Lesbians and gay men might be our major allies, but for us, it was poz people who owned AIDS, regardless of orientation. As the dominant group, poz gay men needed to take special care not to marginalize other poz people who were not gay, male, or white. It was encouraging that in the fall of 1990, Darien Taylor, a straight HIV positive woman, was elected co-chair with Glen Brown.

DOCUMENTS AND DEMOS

In April 1990 AAN! scored its next major victory. Federal health minister Perrin Beatty came to Toronto to speak to the Toronto PWA Foundation on the twenty-fourth. We demonstrated outside, pointing out that while nearly a thousand Canadians had died of AIDS since his appointment, there was still no National AIDS Strategy. Under pressure, Beatty made an impromptu promise that funding for a National Treatment Registry would be officially announced as part of the National AIDS Strategy in June. To keep up pressure, George Smith led a group that submitted an organizational chart to show how a registry needed to work. The chart was published in *AIDS ACTION NEWS!* in June.

This was an example of Smith's strategy of "demos and documents." Demonstrations, where people vented their anger against the status quo, were soon forgotten. They often had little effect on clueless and opportunistic policy makers. On the other hand, without pressure, recommendations to politicians regularly gathered dust. But oscillating between the two – clear, well-researched policy options and public action to keep the issue in the media – had at least a chance of producing movement.

IDENTITY AND ITS TRAVAILS

Other than gay men, the other major groups originally infected with HIV in Canada were hemophiliacs and Haitians. Although they were a significant group in Toronto, positive hemophiliacs were never represented in AAN! The majority were straight and didn't form the same close community as gay men. Since they required regular transfusions, most had been infected through the negligence of the Red Cross, which managed the blood supply. The Red Cross and the government were therefore potentially liable. In December 1989, the federal government announced a $150-million package offering a lump sum of $120,000 to 1,250 individuals infected through the blood system on the condition that they waive their rights to sue. Many refused the deal and demanded more.[39]

John Plater, the newly elected president of Hemophilia Ontario, came to an AAN! meeting to feel out our position on the fight for further compensation. He made his pitch but was confronted by a visibly angry Ric Hatt. Hatt, the first straight man to join the AAN! steering committee, was deeply invested in poz identity. The compensation scheme, he argued, divided poz people into two groups. There were the innocent victims infected through blood, and the rest of us, the guilty ones infected through sex or drugs, who didn't deserve anything. He was utterly opposed to any AAN! participation in Hemophilia Ontario's campaign. In fact, he thought we should organize against it. The insistence on poz identity helped provoke an irreconcilable division among HIV positive people.

Although Plater himself was positive, and continued his AIDS work until his death in 2012, he never came back to an AAN! meeting. Cooler heads prevailed in AAN! and we did not publicly oppose the fight for compensation. But we could not reconcile the diverging interests of these two groups of affected people.

On the other hand, most of Canada's Haitian population were relatively new immigrants, French speaking, and living in Quebec. Despite the efforts of our Francophone Team to ensure our materials were available in French, AAN! also never included HIV positive Haitians. Barriers of geography, race, and class further fractured our imagined poz identity.

Although my Venn diagram noted race and gender, like Manning's approach, it failed to take poverty or class into account, as either an identity or a social location. Our focus on treatment, and the short timelines imposed by impending death, required involvement with the pharmaceutical industry, researchers, and the state. In our documents and demos strategy, we valued those who could critique scientific protocols and government policy, prepare policy documents, and speak authoritatively to bureaucrats and reporters. Such skills tended to concentrate among those with professional and management training, who in turn tended to be those with more class privilege. That had racial implications, too. So although AAN! was a volunteer-run organization, we still felt pressure to select a more "professional" leadership.

FLEXING POZ MUSCLE

Despite the difficulties that poz identity generated, it was foundational for our work.

Doug Wilson became seriously involved in AAN! at our retreat in the fall of 1989. The idea of a National Network of People with AIDS had been bouncing around for some time, and Wilson took it on as a major project. AAN! was a local organization. As the debates went on about who owned AIDS, we felt it was necessary to establish a more assertive national presence of PWAs.

The problem was not just identifying competent activists who were well enough to take on an organizing role in different regions. Unlike a local activist group, which could operate on a shoestring, any national group required resources. Bringing people together and even long-distance phone calls were expensive. French/English translation was necessary. Staff would be required.

In consultation with others PWAs across the country, Wilson developed a work plan and a model, but all requests for funding were rejected by the federal government. Ottawa looked to the Canadian AIDS Society as the national voice, and CAS made it clear it was not interested in a parallel and possibly competing group, especially one that might criticize AIDS service organizations. The attempt to produce a national network was a long struggle that ultimately went nowhere. But CAS's obstruction of the project did galvanize a number of PWAs from across the country to intervene.

At the 1990 CAS annual meeting in Winnipeg, a caucus of HIV positive participants succeeded in blocking a proposal from the outgoing CAS board to increase designated seats for PWAs from a tokenistic one to a tokenistic two. Instead, they won a motion that required each of the country's five regions to elect at least one HIV positive person towards its two board seats, bringing the minimum number of PWA members to five of a twelve-person board. It was not an independent national voice for PWAs, but *AIDS ACTION NEWS!* reported, "The new board will put the Society in the lead for commitment to the principle that HIV-positive people must have effective representation not just token representation on all boards and governing bodies."[40]

NATIONAL AIDS STRATEGY

The announcement of the federal National AIDS Strategy on June 28 was a mixed bag. First, it was half a year late. At the June 1989 Montreal conference, Perrin Beatty had promised it would be ready within six months. While the commitments from Beatty's own ministry were not bad, he had been unable to convince his cabinet colleagues to follow through in their respective jurisdictions. The minister of justice was not prepared to support the inclusion of sexual orientation in the federal Human Rights Act. The minister of corrections refused to address the problems of HIV in prisons. The minister of immigration would not address AIDS issues in immigration.

Still, the treatment registry was being developed. That task was assigned to the Physician Behaviour Research Unit at the University of Toronto. Dr. Kathryn Taylor, the unit's director, said the registry would be a "world first" and would integrate "both traditional and alternative therapy." She planned to consult four hundred people about the design through the World Health Organization. If the government acted promptly, she hoped the registry could be functional within nine months.[41]

There was also a commitment to facilitate the participation of PWAs on relevant boards and committees, and a funding package for community-based service organizations. But there was still silence on money for research, and the ethical issues of placebos and ethical research were sidestepped. Finally, the special needs of minorities and marginalized groups in terms of education, prevention, and treatment were not addressed.

In George Smith's analysis, "the national AIDS strategy was designed to solve the political problems [of] the Minister ... rather than the specific problems faced by people with HIV infection. The strategy, in other words, was designed from the standpoint of the federal government." Nonetheless, he noted the role of activism in shaping the strategy.

> One of the political problems the Minister faced was AAN!, especially our demand for better access to treatment. By way of contrast, the needs of groups like the HIV primary care physicians who were not taken to be a political problem for the minister were ignored. . . . It's the squeaky wheel that gets the grease.[42]

A few days later, Eva Halpert's son Ivan died, despite his mother's successful fight to win him ddI.

SOUTH AFRICA AND THE WORLD

Simon Nkoli returned to Toronto during the summer of 1990. He was accompanied by Musa Zazayokewe, a public health nurse from the Johannesburg AIDS Centre. Both of them were studying AIDS education in Toronto.

Nkoli was splitting his time between the Gay and Lesbian Organization of the Witwatersrand (GLOW) and the new Township AIDS Project in Soweto. Mandela had been released in February and South Africa was beginning to dismantle its apartheid system, but the nation was still in deep denial about AIDS. There were at the time only 380 confirmed cases, a number that paled in the face of those suffering from tuberculosis and other life-threatening diseases.

Nkoli presciently warned that the statistics were not capturing the full picture. Health care was so bad among most of the African population that there was massive underreporting. Most went to traditional healers and died of tuberculosis or dysentery before being diagnosed with HIV. AIDS also became a political football when a white government minister accused the ANC of bringing AIDS to the country. Everyone wanted to deny that South Africa was facing an epidemic.

Apartheid also still structured access to treatment. AZT was available for those able to pay – basically whites. For the rest, Zazayokewe explained, "we are trying to look for a holistic method which deals with the mental, emotional and physical aspects to assist in maintaining the immune system until there is a cure. We need to address what to do after infection. We have tended to dwell on prevention and that is not enough."[43]

In fact, South Africa was facing two AIDS epidemics. One, the First World type that largely affected (white) urban gay men; another, the Third World type affecting both men and women living in the deplorable conditions of the Bantustans and townships. Nkoli found himself straddling the two epidemics. He was more integrated into the urban gay scene than most black Africans, but had deep roots in the townships, no-go zones for most whites. He was therefore in a unique position to introduce the experience of AIDS education and activism developed in North American gay communities to a country poised on the brink of both an epidemic and fundamental social change. An indication of that change was South Africa's first Lesbian and Gay Pride march in October 1990. The event received an official message of support from the ANC.

Elsewhere the bipolar world that gay liberation had known since its inception was also coming to an end. The Socialist Bloc was in the midst of its catastrophic collapse, with the Soviet Union the final domino to topple. But ironically, in what should have been its moment of triumph, the now unchallenged neo-liberal world economy collapsed into its first major recession. In Britain, Margaret Thatcher resigned as social disparities generated unmanageable social tensions. In Ontario, a singularity occurred. The NDP, the social democratic and perennial third party, with its traditional support of gay rights, unexpectedly won a majority in the September election.

The NDP victory was little more than an electoral fluke. The party won a majority in the provincial legislature with only 37 per cent of the popular vote, largely because voters had been angry at the Liberals for calling a snap election. Unprepared for power, the NDP found itself in the middle of a recession, in charge of a province already saddled with debt and facing decreasing tax income.

But everyone was intoxicated by hope. For the first time we had elected a government that was supposed to be our friend. Gay liberation, a movement that had always been oppositional to the status quo, was entering uncharted territory.

9

Great Expectations

ONE STEP FORWARD?

The unexpected election of the Ontario NDP was met with astonishment and excitement in the Church Street gay village. We were accustomed to provincial governments that were indifferent to hostile. The Liberal-NDP alliance in 1985 had included sexual orientation in the Human Rights Code, but the following Liberal majority had failed to recognize same-sex relationships.

During its years as the perennial third party, the NDP had developed a reputation as a champion of gay rights, especially in downtown Toronto, where many NDP organizers and foot soldiers were lesbians and gay men. Growing support for LGB issues in the labour movement had also strengthened the resolve of the traditionally labour-aligned party. During the campaign, the NDP had promised both to increase access to new drugs and to develop a provincial AIDS strategy. The party's right opportunist betrayal after the 1981 bath raids was, for most, a distant and receding memory. Overnight, the political route again seemed a worthwhile bet.

AAN! moved quickly. The Provincial Action Committee prepared briefing notes on urgent issues for Evelyn Gigantes, the new minister of health, and requested a meeting. At first there were encouraging results. Within a month of the election, province-wide anonymous HIV testing was approved. Nevertheless, the December 1990 issue of *AIDS ACTION NEWS!* noted that we had still not been able to secure a meeting with the minister, and the government's recent throne speech had made no mention of AIDS.

A KINDER, GENTLER NEO-LIBERALISM

The Pollyanna vision saw the NDP government in Ontario and the disintegration of authoritarian regimes in Eastern Europe as part of a general movement towards a more democratic and progressive future.

But far from ushering in democracy, the collapse of socialism proved an opportunity to impose a catastrophic neo-liberal experiment in Eastern Europe. A new "gangster capitalism" oversaw the privatization of public resources at bargain prices. Former apparatchiks became multi-millionaires overnight. In the former USSR and elsewhere, health care, education, and social services collapsed. Millions lost employment and were thrown into poverty. Life expectancy fell. Under these circumstances, instead of freedom and democracy, authoritarianism quickly returned.

Neo-liberalism was triumphant. With socialism discredited, the pressure for redistribution of wealth in the developed capitalist countries also diminished. The push for cuts to state programs and services, lower corporate taxation, privatization of public property, and deregulation of finance picked up steam. The Keynesian establishment was either co-opted or reduced to a rump. Union resistance was weakened.

In this New World Order, neo-liberalism's alliance with social conservatism was less necessary and at times downright embarrassing. In many cases, social conservative and right-wing positions seemed so extreme and out of touch with consolidating liberal values that they became a liability. Social conservatives were relegated to an opposition role.

In the United Kingdom, Margaret Thatcher was forced from office by a revolt in her own Conservative party in November 1990. Her infamous poll tax had resulted in widespread rioting, while her nationalist opposition to European integration annoyed financial elites. Tony Blair was already waiting in the wings with his New Labour party.

In the United States, Bill Clinton would be elected in late 1992. Clinton had supported the ERA and even occasionally talked about gay rights. His election was seen as a sea change after years of socially conservative Republican administrations.

In Canada the new socially conservative Alberta-based Reform Party split the conservative vote, paving the way for the return of the Liberals under Jean Chrétien.

But everywhere this shift took place within a neo-liberal framework. Under this kinder, gentler neo-liberalism, the inclusion of certain women, lesbians and gay men, and members of racial and ethnic minorities could be contemplated within a consolidating individualist, egalitarian, and rationalist value set. But neo-liberalism had established a new set point for the rate of exploitation that could not be negotiated. Even under these more socially liberal governments, the social safety net and wealth redistribution programs continued to be weakened, corporate taxes reduced, and regulation and oversight of finance and business gutted. In one of her last famous quips, in 2002, Thatcher was asked what her greatest achievement was. She replied, "Tony Blair and New Labour. We forced our opponents to change their minds."

Despite the new NDP government, the neo-liberal experiment of the 1980s had already irrevocably changed Toronto. In 1970, high-income census tracts made up 15 per cent of the city; by 1990 that was 17 per cent. However, middle-income neighbourhoods dropped from 66 per cent to 51 per cent, and low-income areas increased from 19 per cent to 32 per cent.[1] The grow-ing disparity disproportionately affected new immigrants, who were largely racialized people. Since "we were everywhere," lesbian and gay communities would also find ourselves more divided.

PRIDE POLITICS

Pride had continued to grow since its reinvention in 1981. The first official *Pride Guide* in 1982 was a folded 8½-by-11-inch pink sheet listing the pro-gram and the coalition of community groups that made up the committee – Chutzpah (lesbian and gay Jews), CGRO, GAT, GLARE, Gay Equality Missis-sauga, Gay Fathers, LAR, Lesbian and Gay Youth Toronto, MCC, 923-GAYS (phone line), and the Toronto Gay Patrol. In order to help finance its activi-ties, Pride began soliciting ads for the guide in 1984, mostly from community organizations, small business, and professionals oriented to the gay market. The committee continued to be made up of reps from community groups until 1985, when it shifted to a group of interested individuals. The first sig-nificant corporate ads appeared in 1987. Ramses realized that with safe sex, condoms were no longer a heterosexual preserve. Remax noticed that there was a gay real estate market, and Molson Breweries began to appreciate that a lot of lesbian and gay socializing involved beer.

By 1988, a board of directors did the planning, subject to the direction of public committee meetings. But at the end of 1989, with the festival about to enter its second decade, *Rites* reported a "growing schism." At the October 1989 meeting to begin planning for the following year, it was proposed the parade be restricted to "organized floats and marching bands," a change that would exclude many community groups. No consensus was reached.

Also contentious was the slogan for the 1990 festival. There were four sug-gestions: "Into the Gay Nineties," "Counting Ourselves Out" (it was a census year), "Decade of Visibility," and "By Any Means Necessary." After the first two were ruled out, the meeting split. According to *Rites*, "The Party faction did not particularly like 'Decade of Visibility' as they felt that many of their members did not consider themselves visibly gay, but found it better than the other slogan, since 'By Any Means Necessary' might frighten the straights."[2] When the issue was put to a vote, "By Any Means Necessary" won by just one vote. *Rites* did not report whether the two groups, the party faction and the political faction, were identifiable by class, race, gender, or age.

Perhaps the tension had always been there. The 1981 Pride billed itself as a celebratory alternative to the angry RTPC night-time demonstrations follow-ing the bath raids, even as the march stopped to express its anger in front of 52 Division. But in an increasingly disparate society and community, the political consensus of the 1980s was eroding.

While Pride was having trouble coping with growth and change, *Xtra* was adapting quite well. By 1988 it was distributing 17,000 twenty-eight-page copies, had full-time staff, and was in the black. Its 1989 Pride issue had a full-colour cover, ran to forty-eight pages, and had a print run of 18,000.

Although *Xtra* published under the auspices of Pink Triangle Press, the non-profit organization set up in *TBP* days, it functioned under a very different organizational model from the old *TBP* collective. PTP had a board, but when it came to day-to-day operations, *Xtra* and other PTP acquisitions operated like businesses, with Ken Popert as executive director.

Popert, who found himself in charge with "no business background," attributes *Xtra*'s early success to Colin Brownlee.

> He was the real business genius of the reborn organization. My contribution was to recognize his value and work with him. He was the one who infused the organization with that spirit of change and trying things. . . . We managed to produce a critical mass that drew other people to the organization who were smart and knew how to do things. . . . Partly because we were the only game in town, we tended to attract the best of who was available.

Popert refers to PTP's business plan as "a matter of vice paying for virtue." He explains, "We exploit the homosexual impulse and we use the money to do what we perceive to be good things."[3]

PTP began to experiment with other ventures based on that model. In 1990, it opened Cruiseline, a chatline for gay men. In the midst of the AIDS crisis, there was nothing safer than telephone sex, and according to Popert, Cruiseline turned out to be a "Niagara of profits." He says, "It started spewing out hundreds of thousands of dollars, especially at the beginning when there was no competition." Cruiseline not only subsidized *Xtra,* it made possible the development of *Xtra XS,* a regular arts and culture supplement, the *Church Wellesley Review,* a showcase for lesbian and gay writing, and in 1993, *Xtra West* in Vancouver and *Capital Xtra* in Ottawa. For Popert this expansion was a step towards the national constituency that had been lost with the death of *TBP.*

THE IMPORTANCE OF ETHICS

In April 1990, the *New England Journal of Medicine* published the results of ACTG 019, the trial that studied the effect of AZT in more than 1,300 non-symptomatic people with HIV. It was a three-arm, placebo-controlled trial. One group of subjects received 1,500 mg of AZT per day, a second 500, and a third, in the placebo group, received nothing at all.

Thirty-three of the 428 subjects on the placebo went on to develop AIDS, compared to eleven and fourteen in the slightly larger 500 mg and 1,500 mg groups. Both treatment groups suffered bone marrow toxicity, and the higher-dose group experienced more anemia.

But the results, which appeared to show that AZT slowed the progression to AIDS, were undermined when tests revealed that 9 per cent of the placebo group actually had detectable levels of AZT in their blood, even though they were supposed to be receiving nothing. On the other hand, AZT showed up in the blood of only 84 per cent of those on 500 mg and 79 per cent of those who were supposed to be receiving 1,500 mg.[4]

The subjects were actually part of a community of HIV positive men trying to save their lives. Entering the trial was the only way they could access AZT, at that point the only therapy. Not knowing what they were getting, many participants had pooled drugs with friends in the hope of increasing everyone's chances of receiving something. As a result, researchers didn't know who was receiving how much, and the results were thrown into disrepute. Worse, since so many of the high-dose subjects were actually receiving substantially less drug, reducing side effects, the initial approved dose was set too high, leading to serious toxicities.

It wasn't quite what Chuck Grochmal had in mind when he warned researchers that people with AIDS could close down any trial in the country. But it clearly reinforced the message about the problems of placebo-controlled trials forcing us into research as our only hope of avoiding sickness and death.

SPOUSES

With the unexpected election of the NDP and real legislative change a possibility, according to Tom Warner, something that "liberationists of the 1970s would never have foreseen" took place. "CLGRO membership received an influx of lawyers, civil servants, and other professionals who were interested in relationship recognition but not particularly committed to liberation or issues related to sexuality."[5]

Such new members soon dominated the committee preparing CLGRO's *Happy Families* brief. In 1991, alarmed by what they thought was a drift in the working group, Warner and Christine Donald, the long-time CLGRO staff person, produced a new document to salvage the spirit of the original *On Our Own Terms* position. The key statement read:

> CLGRO believes that, whereas our preference would be that benefits be made available on an individual basis (with allowances for the dependence of children, the aged and the disabled), whenever benefits are available to heterosexuals living in couples, these same benefits also must be available to same-sex couples on the same footing.[6]

Although the statement was finally accepted, even such a compromise generated "much heated debate." According to the working group minutes, "There seemed to be several people who were uncomfortable with the issues of dependency and alternative family structures."[7] And the 1992 *Happy*

Families brief, although quoting from *On Our Own Terms*, would ultimately focus only on equality of same-sex and opposite-sex couples.

THE FRATERNITY

A small group of men who were dissatisfied with the "baths, bars and parks" began organizing in 1989. The result was The Fraternity. *Xtra* reported: "Like the gay sports clubs, car clubs and computer clubs springing up these days, The Fraternity brings together a group of gay men with similar interests. Their common interest is not a hobby, however. It is a class." The article went on to describe membership as "an overwhelmingly under-represented group in the gay community: the conservative, professional class homosexual."[8]

Fraternity membership was initially by invitation only. Members were required to pay a membership and initiation fee. But growth was immediate. By 1990, a temporary ceiling of 250 members was imposed. Members were referred to by their first names only to preserve confidentiality. According group president David G., this "was not to make a 'secret society' but to be as 'inclusive as possible.' "[9]

The use of the term "inclusive" was notable. This was not about including historically marginalized groups, and certainly not women. It was an attempt to include men who feared losing traditional privilege by coming out.

While the old bar and bath owners had often tangled with gay militants in the 1970s, gay identity had been their business. The Fraternity was a place for a new, upwardly mobile strata of professional gay men who were materially benefiting from the neo-liberal shift in society. Many were still tentative about coming out. But the group's existence showed the progress that had been made in overcoming homophobic stigma. In 1970 few men of this class background would have dared associate with a gay group of any kind. Their association now, however, did not mean they had adopted the earlier movement's desire for social change.

Although some members were worried about The Fraternity's reputation as elitist and snobbish, at a 1992 discussion others were quite assertive:

> The Fraternity was built on certain standards – now people who can't meet those standards want to drag it down. . . . [We] shouldn't change to satisfy our critics. . . . Opening up the group may change it and make it more like a bar and attract undesirables. . . . How would most members feel, "dress-wise," if a "way-out" person joined. . . . Tired of this issue – sorry that it is a topic.[10]

GAY GAMES III, VANCOUVER 1990

Changing demographics were not only felt in Toronto. In August 1990, Vancouver hosted Celebration '90: Gay Games III, the largest lesbian and gay event ever organized in the country, and the first time the games were held outside the United States. Sporting and cultural events over eight days included 7,300 athletes from 27 countries, 27 different sports, 2,500 volunteers, 1,500 cultural participants, and over 12,000 spectators.

Originally referred to as the Gay Olympics, until the U.S. Olympic Committee sued for copyright infringement, the games had begun in San Francisco in 1982. They were the brainchild of Tom Waddell, a San Francisco doctor and athlete. Despite Waddell's AIDS-related death in July 1987, the games continued to grow and the Federation of Gay Games was established. FGG bylaws stated that its purpose was "to foster and augment the self-respect of gay women and men throughout the world and to engender respect and understanding from the non-gay world through the medium of organized, noncompetitive cultural/artistic and athletics activities."[11]

Sports was seen as a bastion of conservative heterosexist gender roles, and the games were supposed to challenge the stereotype of the effeminate gay man. Less clear was their intended effect on the stereotype of the mannish lesbian or the idea that women's phys. ed. teachers were all dykes.

In Vancouver, the local organizing group was the Metropolitan Vancouver Arts and Athletics Association (MVAAA). Its driving force was Richard Dopson, a school psychologist. So great was the paranoia around AIDS that as soon as the association won the bid in 1986, Dopson contacted the city's chief medical officer of health and convinced him to make a statement reassuring citizens that the games would not pose a health threat. Four years later, as the event approached, the health official reiterated, "The presence of gays in our community poses absolutely no risk to citizens."[12]

Although the threat of AIDS seemed to be allayed, organizing was far from smooth. The MVAAA met with University of British Columbia staff to rent facilities four years in advance, but a few days later, received a two-line letter informing them that university facilities were not available. After eighteen months of requests for an explanation, Svend Robinson, the local member of Parliament, intervened with university president David Strangway. Strangway explained he felt renting the facilities was not in the university's best interest. In a memo that was later leaked, he explained that he "did not want to involve the university in such a social issue."[13]

Robinson and the MVAAA did an end run around the president to the board of governors. The games had set up an "honorary board" of notables who all wrote the UBC board personally. Robinson spoke to Prime Minister John Turner and contacted the UBC Alumni Association. Under a media spotlight, an embarrassed board of governors overturned the president's position.

It was a resounding victory, but the subsequent statement by the MVAAA raised red flags. "Our desire to settle this through negotiations rather than confrontation underscores the fact that we are sports and cultural organization rather than a political activist one."[14] Dopson was also quoted as saying, "We're going to meet people here from all over the world who are very proud to be gay, very proud to be athletes. They are not leather and drag queens but they're athletes."[15]

When an adolescent wrote the games inquiring about participating, the request was rejected on the ground that youth participation was too controversial. "We must avoid accusations that we 'corrupt' or 'recruit' minors for 'deviant and/or sexual purposes.'"[16] The MVAAA's willingness to distance itself from the taint of unconventional sex, politics, or gay youth did not sit well with many of Vancouver's traditional activists.

Unfortunately the stance was not enough to impress funders. Although comparable sports activities regularly received state support, the Fitness and Amateur Sport Directorate, the relevant federal body, refused funding outright. After intense lobbying, the Department of Communications and Culture provided $15,000 of a $130,000 request. The new Mulroney government was in cost-cutting mode.

Three separate grant applications were turned down by the provincial government, still under the leadership of homophobic Social Credit premier Bill Vander Zalm. Only the city of Vancouver came up with substantial cash. Seeking corporate funding was still novel, and few corporations at the time considered the pink market worth investing in.

In the end, traditional homophobia put the games on the map. In November 1989, a coalition of Christian fundamentalists ran a full-page ad in both major Vancouver dailies under the heading "Time Is Running Out." It concluded:

> We therefore with all reverence and serious intention, in Christ's name, make a public statement: That because these Games will bring God's judgment upon us all in this city, we therefore forbid them in the name and authority of Jesus Christ. . . . This is a clear call to spiritual warfare.[17]

The call for warfare backfired. Liberal values of individual rights and rational knowledge were by this time hegemonic, at least in Vancouver's cosmopolitan downtown. Both the United Church of Canada and the B.C. Civil Liberties Association publicly condemned the ad. Even the *Vancouver Sun* – the same paper that had refused GATE ads in the 1970s – apologized, stating "we find its message repugnant." The MVAAA began receiving offers of financial and volunteer support. T-shirts were printed and sold with the ad's hourglass graphic.

The fundamentalists blundered onwards. With the support of U.S. evangelicals they formed Watchmen for the Nation and organized rallies and prayer vigils. On the eve of the games they brought American Christian musclemen to B.C. Place to pump iron, as preachers intoned the message of Jesus. They hoped, they said, to draw "the attention of young people away from the Gay Games." In fact, their efforts did the opposite, constantly keeping the games in the public mind. According to the MVAAA, "Most people were indifferent about the event until the campaign against it. The attacks pushed many people into supporting the Games."[18]

The fundamentalists were even portrayed as un-Canadian in *The Globe and Mail*. "After several stormy debates over morality and human rights, the city of Vancouver is ready to open its arms to thousands of gays and lesbians for the third international Gay Games. . . . Canada is a tolerant society that accommodates personal differences."[19] A new national self-image was emerging, and it looked like gay people, or at least some of us if we behaved well, would be included.

The MVAAA had portrayed itself as the representative of a beleaguered minority, activating Canadian values of tolerance and multiculturalism. Svend Robinson spoke at the opening ceremonies and, to his credit, did mention the importance of drag queens, leather men, and youth. Social Credit politicians from the government that had denied the games funding were onstage at the opening ceremonies. And God intervened, providing a huge free rainbow in the sky over the closing ceremonies. The games were a resounding success for most of those participating. And for Vancouverites and those following the media across the country, they cemented the notion of lesbians and gays as a legitimate Canadian minority facing a backward and hateful opposition.

The size and complexity of the event also had other consequences. Organizing a multi-day festival involving thousands of international athletes and spectators required specialized skills and organization. It needed event management, long-term planning, paid staff, a hierarchical organization that could make fast decisions, government and corporate connections, and legal and financial expertise. But such skills and social locations are concentrated in professional strata of society. That had an important impact on the leadership. For example, when the struggle to gain access to UBC facilities was at its height, nine of twelve MVAAA board members were UBC alumni, many of them holding two degrees from the institution. While that was enormously useful, it was far from representative of the community.

Because of racism and sexism, the pool from which those skills were drawn was predominantly white and male. Even with its rhetoric of inclusivity and goal of gender parity, the MVAAA board was made up of a well-established segment of the community who reflected mainstream attitudes and values. While that was useful in selling the event, it led to systematic exclusions and even a downplaying of gay identity.

Sports analyst Helen Lenskyj noted that the words "lesbian and gay" were not part of the organizing group's name. Another analyst, Judy Davidson, pointed out that "promotional posters were incredibly bland, reinscribing heterosexist imagery with the word Gay in tiny, almost indiscernible print."[20]

Lenskyj went on to question the effects of the attempt to normalize gay people.

The choice whether to "be oneself" or to "pass" as a member of the dominant group is not available to lesbians and gays who are Black, or to those
who have disabilities, for example. . . . Liberal individualistic notions of
self-discovery and self expression are insufficient for authentic universal
empowerment, because they overlook the double or triple oppressions suffered by minority members of lesbian and gay communities.[21]

"Inclusivity" meant that the women's events sanctioned by the MVAAA
could not be advertised as women-only. Men had to be permitted to attend. In
the end, only 25 per cent of the participating athletes were women. An affiliated event, Queers in the Arts, had to change its name because the MVAAA
thought that the word "queer" did not promote a positive image. So great was
the anxiety about mixing "politics" with "culture," that although Vancouver's
Little Sisters bookstore was still having over 75 per cent of its imported books
seized by Canada Customs, there was no mention of the case in any of the ceremonies.

Poet Dionne Brand, speaking at the parallel literary festival, Words Without
Borders, noted, "Sometimes in trying to say what is most fine about us, we borrow from the wrong terrain. We, as lesbians and gays need to turn over these
terms. We need to fight against the culture rather than fight for inclusion."[22]

Measured by their impact on the mainstream, the games were a resounding success. Assessed on inclusion of emerging and minority sectors of the
community, they left a lot to be desired. Financially, they were a disaster. Like
so many other spectacular sporting events in a neo-liberal world, the games
ended up with a whopping deficit – over $140,000. The MVAAA blamed
homophobia and threatened a human rights complaint, arguing that the
province's refusal to fund the event was discrimination. The Canadian Civil
Liberties Association launched an investigation along the same lines. But in
the end, after more largely futile fundraising attempts, the MVAAA packed it
in and offered creditors twenty-one cents on dollars owed.

VIOLENCE AND RESPONSE

For a brief moment in 1988, AAN! had felt like the activist successor to the
RTPC that would pull the community together in the face of crisis. But the
consolidation of an HIV positive identity distinct from a gay identity, and our
focus on treatment, left those interested in activism around other issues without a home.

Kyle Rae's visibility had increased since becoming director of the 519 in
December 1987. He had deep community roots. Rae was one of the members
of GLARE involved in reviving Pride Day after the bath raids in 1981, and had
continued to work on Pride until late 1987. His office at the 519 overlooked
Church Street and, in the summer, his open window allowed him to regularly
banter with passersby. Rae became known as the Mayor of Church Street, a
reference to Harvey Milk's Mayor of Castro Street moniker.

A battle during the preceding summers had been trying to get Mayor Eggleton to proclaim Pride Day. In 1989, Rae joined the Pride Committee in a court case to force the mayor to proclaim the day.

But the judge seemed genuinely puzzled by the suit against Eggleton, and why the support of a public official might have such importance to gay people. The event would be held, with or without the mayor's support. It was purely symbolic. Pride's lawyer Charles Campbell argued that the mayor's refusal cast Pride and gay people generally "into a public role of disrepute." But the judge wasn't buying it. The request for an injunction was dismissed.

It did seem odd to go to the courts to force someone to declare himself an ally. On the other hand, the mayor's refusal seemed to legitimate other expressions of homophobia. In either case, it was an early indication of the importance the movement was attributing to the approval of those in power. Vertical alliances, even if only symbolic, now overshadowed horizontal ones.

As traditional activists focused on city hall, Toronto saw another of its periodic waves of queerbashing. It was not immediately clear what prompted this. Perhaps increasing gay visibility or our association with death and disease through AIDS were factors. Maybe Eggleton's refusal to recognize Pride contributed. In any case, over one May weekend in 1990, eight incidents were reported in the village. Rae himself was attacked twice on the street during one week. When he asked the police for statistics, it turned out they had none. He was told "there was no evidence of violence happening in this community."[23]

Concerns about violence were in the air, especially after the Montreal massacre in December 1989, in which fourteen women were killed at the École Polytechnique by a young man claiming feminists had ruined his life. The 519 opened up a hotline to report attacks. "We had a form that people could fill out, anonymously or with their name, with dates, explanation, and the words that were used, because the language is important to see if it's a hate crime," Rae explains. "We would get them to fill out the incident report and then fax it to 52 Division so they would have to deal with it. It was hard because people didn't want to believe the police would help. . . . We still weren't talking to the police. There was no liaison. Nothing." Previously, the community had organized self-defence patrols, but broader social concerns about violence and a toehold in institutions such as the 519 made asking for better police protection in the gaybourhood a logical step.

As a result of the hotline, David Boothby, then unit commander of 52 Division, approached Rae about doing educationals with his officers. (Boothby's interest in community policing, considered a breath of fresh air for the force, would eventually lead to his appointment as chief.) "They started coming in for an hour or so during work in the early evening," Rae recalls.

> For about four months, Chris [Phibbs] and I would have fifteen to twenty police sergeants who would arrive in their squad cars. . . . They were tough. They didn't want to be there. They weren't interested in the community.

They were most interested in asking why gay men insisted on having sex in parks and washrooms.

Nevertheless, the program was declared a success and was shifted to the Metro police training centre in Scarborough. Rae and his assistant Chris Phibbs were given an afternoon as part of regular trainings for sergeants from across Metro. Rae considered the trainings a breakthrough. "That was an amazing turnaround. We got more and more officers who were very positive about working with the community. . . . I think that was one of the most important transitions I got involved in."[24]

Rae's leadership further cemented the 519's image as the de facto lesbian and gay community centre. And with the Parkside and the St. Charles taverns on Yonge Street both closed, Church Street was now *the* magnet for community.

QUEER NATION

The wave of violence in our neighbourhood was especially unacceptable to a new generation who had come out after the bath raids to a far more developed community. They heard gay issues discussed in the media and took a range of available services for granted. Homophobia seemed so 1980s. While influenced by the emergence of the new Queer Theory, with its questioning of fixed sexual identity categories, they understood sexual identity as an individual matter, not subject to religion, the state, or anyone else's dictates. Whatever their choices, they expected respect.

A small group calling itself Lesbians and Gays Against Violence began meeting at the 519 during the summer of 1990. Participation swelled to more than a hundred by August. Some argued that violence was just a symptom, and there were calls to deal with deeper issues. On September 10, 150 people packed into a basement room and voted to adopt the name Queer Nation. Some had already been involved in shouting down Family Coalition candidate and inveterate homophobe Ken Campbell at an all-candidates meeting during the September provincial election. A tape of that action was played to rile up the crowd. Queer Nation's pedagogy was to be education through confrontation.

The choice of the term "queer" signalled a new phase of activism and a new generation. The term "gay," adopted by the 1970s movement, had been the coming out of a code word traditionally used to signal homosexual to those in the know, but that to others meant "lively" or "fun." Making "gay" a public word for homosexual mirrored the coming out demanded by the Stonewall generation. "Queer," on the other hand, was a traditional derogatory term for homosexuals already well known to straight people. The new generation went beyond coming out. They appropriated a weapon that had been used against us and made it their own.

Toronto's Queer Nation echoed the emergence of Queer Nation in New York, founded by those who wanted to apply ACT UP's in-your-face tactics to broader LGB issues. In both cities, the group was a reaction to the increasingly mainstream approach of the older generation. Queer Nation was impatient with recognition. Their slogans varied from the assertive – "We're queer, we're here, get used to it" – to a riff on gay pride – "We're queer, we're proud, we're fabulous" – to a critique of the emerging "gay market" – "We're queer, we're here, and we're not going shopping."

As member Livia Resendes told *Xtra*, queer identity "was a mark of distinction, pride, energy and youthful politics. We had arrived at a point with ourselves where our validation was from within and we were tired of negotiating and compromising."[25]

"The sense of those early meetings was of individuals finding their cause – their people – for the first time," explained another member, Lori Lyons.

> As for the embattled minority at Oka [the armed standoff that July over a golf course on unceded First Nations land in Quebec], this was the time to take our stand, to join together as a nation and force our attackers and the broader apathetic majority to acknowledge our existence and our anger. . . . We would rally the community around our "new" word, "queer." . . . The 1981 bathhouse raids brought us the Right to Privacy Committee: the early '90s may well bring us the Right to Publicity Committee.[26]

Queer Nation in Toronto also reflected a much more multicultural and multiracial city. While the 1970s generation had been torn by questions of gender, and the '80s blindsided by debates on race, Queer Nation took "intersectionality" as a given.

The group began with a huge burst of energy. Three days after the founding meeting, it was a presence at the annual Take Back the Night march protesting violence against women. The following evening, QN joined with AAN! and the Ontario Coalition for Abortion Clinics to picket Ken Campbell and U.S. televangelist Jerry Falwell, in town for an anti-abortion rally at the People's Church. As the University of Toronto welcomed new students during its regular September orientation week, QN peppered the campus with posters alternately showing two young women and two young men kissing. Both posters carried the same bold message: "How Goes Your Orientation? Queers are Here."

When a local straight bar, The Loose Moose, published a homophobic ad, fifty QN members descended to kiss, dance, and fondle each other. On October 12, International Coming Out Day, they held a kiss-in at the Eaton's Centre, Toronto's iconic downtown mall. There was a march down Yonge Street on Halloween, a protest against New Beginnings Ministry's seminar on "curing" homosexuality at U of T, and participation along with AAN! in the ongoing Gulf War protests. The queer contingent banners read "Money for AIDS Not for War" and "Fight AIDS Not Arabs." After one young man was convicted of a bashing, QN put up flyers with his picture both in the village and around his high school.

While QN briefly established a Pink Patrol, unlike the RTPC effort a decade before, it never really got off the ground. The new sense of entitlement encouraged demands for the same protection from the police as other citizens. When a hundred lesbians and gay men descended on the Mayor's Committee on Racism to demand action on bashing in October, QN reps gave passionate speeches.[27]

ACT UP in New York was organized around affinity groups that took responsibility for particular actions, subject to the approval of a regular general meeting. Queer Nation similarly established internal collectives. The Action collective organized public actions. A Postering collective postered. The Inreach collective planned educationals for the group around race and gender issues. A Facilitators collective worked on building skills to run the large and often fractious general meetings. The Media collective watched for media homophobia and prepared responses. Finance kept the books, and the Newsletter collective dealt with internal communications. There was a Men's Anti-sexist-Anti-racist group, and a Women's Caucus.

But all was not well. This generation would reflect the social fragmentation produced by neo-liberalism. Queer Nation found its race, class, age, gender, and culture differences increasingly unmanageable. The influence of anarchist-style politics with a deep mistrust of organizational hierarchy only amplified the problem. For example, to prevent the domination of privileged groups, a strict speakers policy was implemented, but with unintended consequences.

"In retrospect, it seems that Queer Nation's attempts to be more inclusive actually pushed many people away," Yuki Hayashi recalled.

> Politically correct policy was overriding common sense. We did not utilize a speakers' list because, for some reason I have yet to have explained to me, it is patriarchal for everyone to just put up their hand, get on a list and speak in order. Instead we produced a situation where five or six hands would be left despondently raised, waiting for the next round of "Person of colour? Woman? Man? Someone who's differently-abled?"[28]

Bentley Ball, a young black man, added, "Meanwhile, this one Black dyke at the back of the room would curl up in her wheelchair every time somebody mentioned inclusive imagery, because she knew she'd end up having to find a sitter for her kids just so somebody else could look good."[29]

Lyons continued:

> Queer nation has been criticized for being too politically correct. The reality is that Queer Nation never had the political depth to resolve its own contradictions. We had no strategy . . . to consolidate the myriad of people who brought their anger to our doorstep. . . . Members drawn in by a gut level sense of purpose clashed over individual priorities. When political attacks turned personal, inexperienced facilitators were rarely able to control the destruction. Such confrontations split the group, all too often along race or

gender lines. People began to leave, insulted at the attacks on their personal visions. These ex-Nationals, along with assimilationist gay men and lesbians, created a formidable a backlash to Queer Nation's radical politic.[30]

In a vain attempt at unity, the group became fixated on producing a mission statement, according to Lyons. The use of the term was indicative of the period. "Mission statements" originated with the military in the 1960s, and became more and more common in the corporate and academic world in the '70s. With the downloading of social services to AIDS service organizations, developing such a generalized statement of purpose became a requirement for government funding. But the fact that a radical organization such as QN, one that would never think of asking for government funding, would find it appropriate to develop a mission statement showed the increasing dominance of corporate culture even on grassroots organizations. *The Body Politic* never saw the need for a mission statement until it was in deep trouble in 1986. If the Right to Privacy Committee ever had one, no one knew about it. AIDS ACTION NOW! had a basis of unity, a mandate, and a constitution, all terms drawn from a political rather than corporate lexicon.

After seemingly endless discussion, the mission statement was finally approved.

> We are a QUEER NATION of unapologetic lesbian, gay and bisexual people of diverse races, abilities, ages, creeds, classes and cultures, working together to promote and celebrate the visibility of Queers though non-violent direct action. We work to eliminate homophobia, heterosexism, sexism, racism, ableism, ageism, classism and discrimination on the basis of religious or gender identity, among ourselves and within society. Queer Nation is Pro-choice. We claim the dignity and freedom which a society that breeds fear and ignorance has taken from us unjustly. We're Queer! We're Proud! We're Fabulous![31]

The effort was so time-consuming that no one could stomach talking about process anymore. Plans for reorganizing meetings and an organizational structure were abandoned.

The problem was deeper than any mission statement could solve. As QN member Bruce Eakin observed, "Toronto is full of homosexuals but there ain't no community. We are irrevocably divided by class, age, race, culture, gender and politics."[32] The hemorrhaging did not stop. In June 1992, little more than a year and a half after it burst on the scene, the remaining six members of Toronto's Queer Nation formally decided to disband.

Queer Nation's brief life reflected the success of the movement that came before it. We had carved out a space for more and more people to come out, but that raised a new set of problems. There were frustrations about the mainstreaming of LGB politics, and difficulties in organizing diverse communities as society became more polarized. Queer Nation both popularized the word "queer" among a younger generation, and revealed the limits to the inclusivity that the term hoped to represent.

OUTING = QUEERBASHING

The new radicalism was often associated with "outing" – revealing someone's sexual orientation against their will. Queer Nation in Toronto never endorsed it as a strategy, but a short-lived Queer Nation Ottawa group did propose it. In February 1989, U.S. activist Michael Petrelis outed a Republican senator from Oregon who was supporting anti-gay legislation proposed by Senator Jesse Helms, the iconic American homophobe. His justification was that if someone in the closet was actively working against the community, they needed to be discredited. Petrelis held that an individual's right to privacy was secondary to the interests of the group. On the other hand, Michelangelo Signorile, one of the founders of Queer Nation in New York, called for the "equalization" of reporting on the sexuality of public figures. He began regularly outing the closeted rich and famous in a regular column in *OutWeek* and later in *The Advocate*.

In October 1990 I was asked by *Xtra* to do a commentary on the issue. I tried to challenge both arguments. Taking a liberal stance, I insisted that coming out must be an individual decision. No one had the right to set themselves up as judge and jury to decide when someone deserved to be outed. But I also insisted that practically, outing was bad for the community. I recalled an early example from Germany in 1907, when frustrated homosexual rights reformers outed a number of people in the Kaiser's inner circle. Rather than promote social change, the move linked homosexuality to an unpopular government and strengthened its association with a decadent aristocracy.

I asked how the public would have reacted if someone had outed Svend Robinson rather than letting him make the decision in his own time. Rather than being a hero, Robinson would have appeared to be another duplicitous homosexual, betrayed by other homosexuals. Outing, I said, was another form of queerbashing. Straight homophobes were immune. Only gay people were vulnerable.[33]

Some readers interpreted the article as an attack on Queer Nation. That was never my intention, but I did want to make a proactive strike in case anyone proposed outing as a serious strategy in Toronto.

CITY SPOUSAL BENEFITS

The 1988 municipal elections had returned an especially progressive city council. For the first time, a reformist coalition of NDP members and independents held a majority. De facto leader of the progressive bloc was Councillor Jack Layton, representing Ward 6, the downtown ward including the gay ghetto. In October 1990, at Layton's instigation, the city moved to extend benefits to the same-sex partners of city employees.[34]

The following month, again over the objections of Mayor Eggleton, council voted to proclaim Pride Day. This time the proclamation stuck. Both of these moves raised expectations for the new NDP government in Queen's Park.

POVERTY, CLASS, COLOUR

AAN! continued to work on diversity. At the AGM when Darien Taylor was elected as the first woman co-chair, two other women, Linda Gardner and Julia Barnett, also joined the steering committee. These women strengthened our connections to another stream of organizing, the Women's Health Movement. For years, women had been battling the same kind of medical indifference faced by gay men and PWAs. We faced homophobia, they faced sexism. HIV positive women found these problems compounded. "Women and AIDS," the lead article in the December 1990 issue of *AIDS ACTION NEWS!* was written by Karen Donnan, head of the media committee and a member of our new Women's Caucus. A few months later, Taylor went on to found a new AIDS service organization, Voices of Positive Women, to provide support services to women diagnosed with HIV.

Several AAN! members were involved with the Ontario Coalition for Abortion Clinics. The two groups regularly publicized and supported each other's actions. When the Supreme Court struck down Canada's abortion law in 1988 as a violation of the Charter, and Parliament failed to pass a new law in 1991, Linda Gardner and her husband Bob were able to pour their considerable activist energies and skills into AAN!

We also asked the service organizations working in racialized communities to nominate representatives to the steering committee. Stefan Collins of the Black Coalition for AIDS Prevention and Terry Sands of Two Spirited People of the First Nations were both elected. Steering committee member Bernard Courte continued to head up the Francophone Caucus. But fifteen of the nineteen members were still gay men, and the vast majority white and university educated.

That autumn George Smith, the architect of much of AAN!'s strategy, left the steering committee to concentrate on the new Community Treatment Information Exchange. James Thatcher, on the other hand, began taking a leading role. Thatcher had graduated in business from the University of Western Ontario and, until his diagnosis in 1988, had worked in the corporate world. He brought exceptional organizational and managerial skills. On the opposite end of the political spectrum was Michael Smith, a wiry British anarchist.

A rather strange man also began attending meetings. Brian Farlinger first arrived wearing well-tailored suits rather than the activist T-shirt-and-jeans uniform. Initially he was very quiet, but as he relaxed over several months, we learned he had been director of commercial affairs for the Canadian Bankers' Association before his diagnosis. Farlinger was an unlikely activist, but his skills allowed him to rise rapidly through the organization. Such were the class alliances generated by AIDS.

Despite the growing importance of people with a managerial background, by the end of 1990, a new focus was also emerging in AAN!: poverty and the high cost of drugs. The policy options document discussed at the AGM noted:

> AAN! needs to continue to work with anti-poverty groups ... to ensure that AIDS is represented as a poverty issue.... The costs of treatments must be subsidized or otherwise regulated so that people are not forced by prohibitive costs to go on assistance in order to get treatments.[35]

As new therapies slowly came on line, drug costs were becoming a crucial issue. If someone had a private drug plan with their employer, like I did at the board of education, they were generally okay. But much of the gay male community, not to mention women and people from racialized groups with HIV, did not work for such employers. They tended to be in service industries offering low wages and no benefits. As the transformation of the economy progressed, the number of people relying on such temporary or precarious employment steadily increased.

The only people eligible to get a provincial drug benefits card, which covered the cost of medications, were those over sixty-five or on public assistance. Most of us with HIV could only dream of reaching sixty-five. Going on public assistance meant you couldn't work or have any significant savings. People who were still relatively healthy were faced with the choice of continuing to work while their health deteriorated because they couldn't afford drugs, or quitting work and impoverishing themselves to qualify for public assistance and a drug card. At the same time, public assistance rates were so low that although drugs were free, it was often difficult to afford proper nutrition and housing, essentials for someone with a damaged immune system. As treatments extended life, AIDS became a poverty issue.

But living longer was still a rarity. *Xtra* listed another ninety people that year in its Proud Lives section. Among them was Dan Wardock. Dan had come to Toronto from Hamilton to finish school and moved into our commune on Seaton Street. He had worked at Buddies in Bad Times Theatre doing publicity, and became central to AAN!'s media committee in the late 1980s. His Kaposi's was sudden and fast-moving. He died at twenty-seven.

In the next two months we lost two more steering committee members. Ross Laycock had joined the group to work on the Montreal AIDS conference interventions. Even as KS spread through his body, he was known for his humorous and irreverent contributions to our often-long meetings. He was thirty-two.

Michael Smith, our resident anarchist, involved in more good causes than anyone could count, spearheaded AAN!'s early prison work and produced a one-man play before his death. *PLWA: Person Livid with AIDS* was performed at Buddies' 1990 Queer Culture Festival, and later as a fundraiser for AAN!

and Gays and Lesbians of the First Nations. His memorial service appropriately turned into a demonstration that marched down Carlton Street. Michael was thirty-three.

PROVINCIAL POSSIBILITIES

The MCC Christmas service in December 1990 symbolized the new relationship between the lesbian and gay communities and the NDP government. Two thousand attended the event at upscale Roy Thomson Hall. In his review in *Xtra*, Brian Mossop noted that the program included a message from the premier, bows from Councillor Jack Layton and his partner, Trustee Olivia Chow, and a gospel reading by Community and Social Services Minister, Zanana Akande. The opening procession featured a Canadian flag, a cross, two rainbow flags, and a woman swinging a censer.[36]

CLGRO had begun lobbying for spousal recognition during the 1990 election and was as surprised as anyone at the victory of the NDP. Hopes for a thorough revamping of provincial laws on relationships were further raised when the extension of benefits to same-sex partners of provincial employees was announced in January 1991, as well as a promised a review of "all pertinent laws and policies pertaining to spousal benefits."[37] That sounded like a prelude to changing laws to include gay relationships, even though the Ministry of the Attorney General soon cautioned that the review might not lead to legal reform. The new government also appointed Laura Rowe, an openly lesbian social worker, to a post on the Metropolitan Toronto Police Commission, a move that suggested police reform might be in the wings. The chair of the Ontario Film Review Board confirmed a decision to allow the depiction of lesbian and gay sex.

But behind the scenes, Premier Bob Rae was having trouble with his own caucus. Many in his cabinet did not see gay rights as a major issue. The NDP was happy to pass resolutions on the issue while in opposition, but once in power, it found itself with a serious case of cold feet. "My own hope," Rae mused later, "was that enough cases would work their way through the courts that opinion in the caucus and the province would move."[38]

It was not just the gay community hoping the courts would do the work. Politicians hoped the courts would save them from difficult decisions.

At the end of January 1991, AAN! finally met with the health minister. We went over the points in our brief – high drug costs, inconsistent standards of care, fragmented community-based health and social services, the effects of poverty, racism, and sexism on the health of PWAs, and the lack of a provincial AIDS strategy. Gigantes seemed informed but noncommittal. Mostly she begged for time, pointing out that the NDP had been in power for less than six months. James Thatcher reminded her that six months could be a lifetime for someone with HIV. Her only concrete commitment was a no-cost promise to increase the number of HIV positive people on the provincial AIDS Advisory

Committee, and she asked us to suggest candidates. Thatcher described the meeting as "lots of warm fuzzies."

Gigantes subsequently came to a public meeting at 519 Church to hear community concerns, put on an AAN! T-shirt and promised major announcements "within weeks." A month later she resigned after inadvertently divulging private medical information in the legislature. The new minister, Frances Lankin, begged off meeting until she "caught up with her portfolio." We were back to square one.

PASSAGES

A decade after the bath raids, the Right to Privacy Committee formally dissolved on February 9, 1991. The group had been inactive for several years, but true to the spirit of the early 1980s, a public meeting was called to officially close things down and disburse the remaining assets. The Gay Community Dance Committee was also in difficulty. It closed down less than a year later. Younger people preferred the new high-tech dance spots that were springing up, and the older generation didn't dance as much. The 1981 bath raids had smashed the individualist values of the closet and deepened feelings of community. The result had been an explosion of volunteerism. But ten years later, a new equilibrium was being established, and with it, a new individualism. People were measuring themselves not so much by what they gave as by what they consumed. New forms of organization would be necessary to motivate them.

CLGRO still hung on. It scratched together enough funds to rehire its long-time staff person Christine Donald and maintain its little office, with the help of supporting organizations such as the Ontario Federation of Labour (OFL), the Canadian Federation of Students, and gay and lesbian caucuses in the larger unions.

But it was becoming a coalition in name only. Many of the founding groups outside Toronto had been university-based. Membership in student groups was always transitory and dependent on the interests of one or two people. Several early CLGRO activists became key organizers of local or regional AIDS service organizations, which, as funded charities, were constrained in their political activism. The Association of Gays and Lesbians of Ottawa and the Homophile Association of London Ontario became primarily focused on running community centres. Groups in Windsor, Thunder Bay, and Sudbury simply died out. By the 1990s, CLGRO was reduced to a rump of Toronto activists.

On the other hand, March 1991 saw the first Inside Out lesbian and gay film festival. Inside Out was pulled together by a collective of activists and filmmakers to bring largely community-based work to those hungry for lesbian and gay images. The event was held at the Euclid, a small non-profit theatre that had been a project of the Development Education Centre, a left-wing organization that focused on anti-colonial struggles. Inside Out was a huge hit, with more than four thousand people attending ten days of screenings. It would soon become a community institution.

NON-TRADITIONAL WORK

CUPE, the union representing Toronto Hydro's largely blue-collar workplace, won a new collective agreement providing same-sex benefits in 1991. But a more basic issue remained: harassment in the workplace. After long-standing demands that Hydro hire more women to a workforce that was 99 per cent white male, in the late 1980s, thirty women were employed for non-traditional work, many of them out lesbians. Unfortunately, Hydro did nothing to prepare them or other employees for their arrival, and the workplace was soon awash with sexual and homophobic harassment.

After protracted negotiations, a joint union/employer program established in 1992 defined harassment as a safety issue, giving workers the right to leave the workplace with pay if they experienced it. Harassment on the basis of sexual orientation was included in the policy.[39] It was a huge step forward, but the issue of equity was far from resolved. All of the thirty women were white.

BUTLER

The question of pornography had taken a back seat since 1986 when the Mulroney government's attempts to broaden anti-porn laws had been beaten back. But in February 1992, the *Butler* decision at the Supreme Court put porn back on the front burner. *Butler* reframed pornography as "the exploitation of sex in a degrading and dehumanizing manner that is perceived by public opinion to be harmful to society and especially to women," and ruled that the obscenity sections of the Criminal Code were a "justified limitation on freedom of expression" otherwise protected by the Charter.[40]

Butler was hailed as a victory by anti-porn feminists, but its impact was immediately felt in the gay community. In April, Glad Day was raided and the lesbian S/M magazine *Bad Attitude* seized. In July, an Ontario court justice found that thirteen items of gay male porn seized by Canada Customs en route to Glad Day were obscene because the portrayal of casual sex and anal penetration was harmful to the community.

There was outrage and a demonstration, but what was most significant was who was not involved. EGALE, the now national lesbian and gay organization, made no attempt to intervene in *Butler* or the Glad Day or Little Sisters cases. Political scientist Miriam Smith noted, "This seems to display a reluctance to take on issues related to sexuality, issues that would have been defined as central from a gay liberation perspective."[41]

DASHING HOPES, RISING FRUSTRATIONS

That spring the big news was oral alpha interferon, an AIDS treatment developed in Kenya. It was cheap and simple. The Kenyans reported dramatic results. Everyone desperately wanted it to work, and not just because it would be the end of the nightmare. There would be a delicious irony if a developing country came up with something that had eluded big American and European pharma. But no one in Kenya had the cash to finance the trials necessary to get a drug approved in the developed world. In the meantime, a bootlegged version was beginning to flow through the buyers' clubs and alternative therapy networks.

It was a tailor-made project for the new Community Research Initiative Toronto. With a grant from the American Foundation for AIDS Research (there was still very little money for AIDS research in Canada), CRIT set up an eight-week trial with input from a community board drawn from AAN!, the PWA Foundation, and ACT. *AIDS ACTION NEWS!* noted it was the first trial to follow AAN!'s three basic ethical guidelines: respect for catastrophic rights; no possibility of harm can occur to participants as a result; and clearly spelled out risks and benefits. Participants could continue to take any therapies they were on. No one was forced into the trial to get treatment.[42]

In the end, however, the drug had no effect. At least the short study saved people money and time trying to access what turned out to be a false hope.

Over the summer of 1991 we lost more members. Michael Lynch, the visionary who brought people together to found AAN!, died on July 9. The last time I saw Michael was a few days before at Pride. A friend was pushing his wheelchair. He was so gaunt I hardly recognized him. I held his hand briefly, but I don't think he knew who I was. True to form, he had meticulously planned his own memorial service, down to the presenters, the music, and the flowers. He was forty-six.

Three weeks later David Kendall, a member of the steering committee, died in Casey House. David continued to do AAN! work even after he was too weak to get out of bed. He was thirty-five.

Finally Peter McGehee, Doug Wilson's long-time partner, died at home in September. A novelist and performer, Peter's a cappella jazz groups The Quinlan Sisters and the Fabulous Sirs toured the country and did more than one benefit performance for AAN! He was thirty-six.

KILLING TIME IS KILLING PEOPLE

Despite our efforts, everything seemed to bog down. The long-awaited treatment registry was nowhere to be found. We still hadn't been able to meet with new minister of health Lankin. We needed to remind the government that time was of the essence.

On September 20 we took things into our own hands, occupying Lankin's office at Queen's Park. I was delivering a workshop at a school and, by the time I arrived, our crew were already installed, handcuffed and chained to various pieces of furniture. Ministry staff were in a panic. I walked in and sat down with the others without anyone even questioning me.

James Thatcher took the lead in the negotiations, even as he tried surreptitiously to wiggle his fingers. In his excitement he had clipped his handcuff too tightly and was losing the circulation in his hand. Our bottom line was that we would not leave until we met with the minister. The press was arriving to document the confrontation.

No one in the ministry wanted media images of AIDS activists being dragged away screaming about government inaction. Lankin duly appeared, and we had an impromptu hour-long meeting where we delivered our brief. First of our "Four Steps to Deliver Treatment" was drug funding: "Treatment for people living with life-threatening illnesses like HIV infection is a basic right." The following day, we organized a die-in to emphasize our points. Two hundred people blocked the intersection at Yonge and Wellesley and then marched on the ministry.

The actions did seem to light a fire. October 6 Lankin addressed the AIDS Walk, the massive annual fundraising event organized by ACT, and announced the formation of an AIDS Bureau in the ministry. This would remove AIDS policy from the immediate control of Public Health. Up to that point, the chief medical officer of health, Richard Schabas, the man whose resignation we were demanding, had to sign off on all the community grants. George Smith had argued for almost two years that the stranglehold of Public Health had to be broken before government could act in the interests of the infected. AIDS service organizations had begun to chorus that message. The ministry finally responded.

As well, anonymous HIV testing would be available from January 1, 1992. The government also added ddI to the program that distributed AZT free of charge. It was still a long way from a comprehensive drug program, but in a January 1992 speech, Lankin acknowledged the "growing pressure to develop a catastrophic drug policy" and said it was under consideration.

Finally, the previously secretive AIDS committee that advised the minister would be reconfigured. The composition of the new organization, the Ontario Advisory Committee on HIV/AIDS would be one-third people living with AIDS, one-third community organizations, and one-third health providers and researchers. As the gay movement increasingly turned to the law, AIDS activism demonstrated that political action could still be effective.

"Killing Time Is Killing People" was not just a slogan. Bernard Courte died two weeks after Lankin's AIDS Walk speech. Bernard, who had been on the steering committee since 1988, was the architect of our Équipe francophone, which translated all our major documents into French and gave AAN! a national scope.

CITY POLITICS

When Jack Layton announced that he would run for mayor in the November 1991 election, the Ward 6 councillor's seat was up for grabs. Kyle Rae, now in his third year as director of the 519 community centre, quickly threw his hat into the ring. Rae had refused to play quiet city bureaucrat during his tenure at the 519. In addition to the unsuccessful suit against Mayor Eggleton, he regularly deputed at city hall on everything from gay rights to anonymous testing. Rae was the left candidate, carrying the NDP banner. Everyone wondered if this was going to be a replay of the George Hislop fiasco in the same ward a decade earlier. But then it got even more interesting. Peter Maloney, the long-time Liberal gay activist, also decided to run. There went any hopes of a gay voting bloc. They both faced off against Simon de Groot, a Church Street businessman.

The gay vote was in the news again. Gay activism was pulled into municipal electoral politics, and we were suddenly important enough that the long-promised Committee on Lesbian and Gay Issues in Toronto materialized, with lawyer Harvey Brownstone as chair.[43]

In May, things were further complicated when Eggleton announced he would not run again and three candidates – Liberal June Rowlands, independent Betty Disero, and former Progressive Conservative cabinet minister Susan Fish – all pursued the conservative vote, while Layton united progressives. But Disero and Fish ultimately pulled out and their votes went to Rowlands, who won easily to become Toronto's first woman mayor. Layton's partner, Olivia Chow, successfully transitioned from the board of education to become the downtown Metro councillor. And in another significant win, John Campey, an openly gay man, was elected to Chow's former seat at the school board. Finally, Kyle Rae was elected as Toronto's first openly gay city councillor. Although Rae represented the gay village, he would speak for the broader lesbian and gay community.

METRO POLITICS

At that point, Toronto had two levels of government. The City of Toronto was the downtown core. Surrounding it were several more suburban boroughs – North York, York, East York, Scarborough, and Etobicoke – each with its own council. Metro Council, made up of representatives from the city and each of the boroughs, managed joint services such as police, public transit, firefighting, and libraries.

With so many employees, the stakes were higher when it came to same-sex benefits, but Metro was a different kettle of fish from the downtown. The boroughs were far more conservative, certainly around lesbian and gay issues.

Same-sex benefits were first raised before the 1991 election by Metro's access and equity officer Mary-Woo Sims and other employees. Administrative efforts proved fruitless, and the political route was also blocked. When Councillor Roger Hollander moved that Metro follow the city in extending benefits, his motion lost by a wide margin. Sims and others launched a human rights complaint.

After the election, newly minted Metro councillor Olivia Chow resolved to try again. Her assistant, Bob Gallagher, the long-time activist who had worked with *TBP* and the RTPC, had a personal stake in the issue. His HIV positive partner's health was failing. They needed the benefits package.

Since the extension of benefits had been rejected only months before, careful planning was necessary. Metro chair Alan Tonks was a visceral homophobe who could be counted on to do what he could to block the measure. The Metro solicitor was also strongly opposed. Chow's office brought together the caucus of lesbian and gay employees organized by Sims, progressive city councillors like Kyle Rae, and city staff who had helped win the measure in Toronto. But the real foot soldiers in the battle turned out to be a group of lesbian and gay youth whom Chow had cultivated in her previous post as school board trustee.

The youth interviewed Metro councillors to learn their views on the issue. With that reconnaissance, they began to tailor specific arguments for specific councillors. Councillor Ila Bossons, for example, said that she was personally supportive but her constituents would never agree. According to Gallagher, "the youth pulled together a petition and went up and down Albany Road, the centre of her ward, and got a signature in support from every single house on both sides of the street."[44] Presented with the petition, Bossons agreed to vote in favour.

Councillor Raymond Cho said he couldn't support it for religious reasons. Chow's office contacted his bishop, who wrote to say that giving people health care wasn't supporting homosexuality. Cho, too, changed his vote. Another key player was Councillor Mario Gentile, a staunch Roman Catholic who had been a mainstay of the opposition in the previous vote. It turned out he had a lesbian niece. She agreed to talk to him and convinced him that even sinners deserved health care.

Meanwhile at MCC, Brent Hawkes asked members of his congregation to call their councillors and ask for their support. Gallagher and Chow also had access to the supporters list for the unsuccessful Layton mayoralty campaign. Those names were contacted to do the same, while Kyle Rae lobbied other councillors.

When the vote came in June 1992, the result was still uncertain. But Tonks had been kept in the dark about the organizing and hadn't bothered to rally his own troops, confident that Chow's motion would do no better than Hollander's. "We had Mario Gentile be the first speaker," Gallagher recalls.

> He got up and said, "I don't condone homosexuality. It's a sin. I'm a Catholic. They will have to face God. But I believe that they should have health care in the time being, and I support this." That changed the tenor of the discussion. Tonks lost control of the frame and we ended up getting a couple of extra votes on the spot because of Gentile.[45]

The motion passed. And Chow's youth group, who congealed and learned how to do politics from the experience, went on to establish the Lesbian and Gay Youth Line.

AIDS BUREAU

Jay Browne began as the first manager of the new provincial AIDS Bureau on January 1, 1992. Browne had been a Catholic priest for thirteen years before leaving to marry, start a family, and teach at the Department of Psychiatry at McMaster University.

After chairing the Ontario Ministry of Health's Public Health Education Program on AIDS for more than a decade, Browne was well placed to take over the bureau. At first, we regarded him with some suspicion. He was already in his sixties, always appeared tired, and with his slight Kentucky drawl and conservative suits, didn't seem likely to light much of a fire under the provincial government.

Our first impressions were wrong. Browne was a consummate bureaucrat, but he was also passionate about social justice and saving lives. He immediately identified with AAN! and soon bonded with James Thatcher. Browne saw his job as figuring out how to get our wild ideas through the bureaucracy and make things happen.

Browne joined Frank McGee and Anne Bowlby, who had come on earlier to get the bureau set up. Bowlby, who had a social work background, had been working with the Ontario Public Education Panel on AIDS since 1986. McGee was a gay man who had worked in Public Health for several years administering the grants to AIDS service organizations. His funding and responsibilities were transferred to the bureau along with him.

The funding of service organizations was critical in the face of the crisis. People in the community had a far better understanding of community needs than large government bureaucracies, and community groups had already jumped in to fill the void left by state inaction. On the other hand, this trend also represented the neo-liberal downloading of state responsibilities to small, independent groups with less overhead and lower staff salaries, relying on volunteer community labour and additional private fundraising.

The bureau was small enough to work as a team. Its first challenge was getting anonymous testing sites running across the province. Advisory and working groups had to be set up. Regional locations had to be chosen. The opposition of many local public health units needed to be overcome. The system had to become operational quickly. No one wanted any more embarrassing occupations by AIDS activists.

There was a last-minute wrinkle. AAN! realized that although the initial testing would be anonymous, as soon as people went to their doctors for treatment, their status still had to be reported. Ministry officials went into high-anxiety mode, fearing the whole thing would unravel. Browne got

Robert Trow from the Hassle Free Clinic to convince us that anonymity for PWAs throughout the health care system was an unrealistic demand. Since Hassle Free had taken the lead on the issue, AAN! backed down.

When the anonymous sites opened, the bureau earned well-deserved praise for bringing community, ministry bureaucracy, and public health officials together. "I remember that because it was a relief that people weren't yelling at us," McGee recalled.

Browne turned the next challenge into an opportunity. Burroughs Wellcome, the pharma giant with the patent for AZT, heard that the government was only planning to put generic AZT on the government formulary. The NDP saw generics as cost-effective – generic AZT was considerably cheaper than the name brand – and the party was ideologically committed to dealing with local generic companies as opposed to large multinational corporations. Burroughs Wellcome threatened to sue.

Browne knew that one of the chief complaints of activists was the paucity of research funds in Canada. He initiated delicate negotiations with Burroughs Wellcome, the ministry, drug programs, and the legal branch. In the end, the government agreed to purchase AZT from Burroughs Wellcome for distribution through the Special Project Centre run by Dr. Anita Rachlis at Sunnybrook Hospital. To help compensate for the extra cost, the company agreed to a rebate, which would go into a special research fund.

Half of the Burroughs Wellcome rebate money went to fund the HIV Ontario Observational Database. The idea for a province-wide database to follow people with HIV had been kicking around AAN! for years. With a public health care system such as Ontario's, a wealth of data was available on how people with HIV were faring over time. It could tell us about which therapies were associated with longer survival or with particular side effects, as well as geographical anomalies and a host of other information. But there had to be a system to collect and make sense of the data while meeting patients' fears about confidentiality. It was Thatcher who took the lead in developing the idea and selling it to Browne. Browne sold it to the ministry.

The other half of the money went to the Positive Action Fund. The fund's board was made up of clinicians, researchers, and community reps who met regularly to choose the best innovative research proposals for funding. Until better therapies began coming on line and AZT use dropped, Browne's deal with Burroughs Wellcome generated over ten million dollars for HIV research in the province.

Thatcher and I were appointed reps to the new Ontario Advisory Committee on HIV/AIDS. He sat on the committee evaluating the rollout of anonymous testing, chaired a sub-committee that drafted a strategic plan for the province, and helped launch a comprehensive needs assessment of the HIV-infected population. I sat on the Positive Action Fund research panel. Although we could never be satisfied, a whole new set of AAN!'s demands was being met. We now had anonymous testing across the province, a major research fund with community input, and free provision of the three key antiviral medications. Community members had a place at the table to influence the decisions that affected our lives.

The AIDS Bureau under Browne and later McGee became adept at manoeuvring the Byzantine environment at Queen's Park. Among other things, they drew on a network of gay men throughout the system. Even if they were closeted, they understood the crisis. McGee recalls, "You would always try to find them and they would facilitate things at different levels."[46] Unlike other minorities that faced barriers to access, white gay men were already present within the state apparatus.

COP SHOP TALK

As a new city councillor, Kyle Rae moved quickly to capitalize on his relationship with police brass. A decade after it was proposed in Arnold Bruner's post–bath raids report, a formal community-police liaison body was established. Its composition and mandate, though, reflected a different notion of community than had existed in 1981.

The police had created a foot patrol program for the Church-Wellesley area in 1991. The new committee was officially an advisory committee for this program. Originally the Church Wellesley Community Patrol Advisory Committee, the name was soon changed to the Church Wellesley Neighbourhood Police Advisory Committee. So rather than representing the broader lesbian and gay communities, the committee reflected a particular neighbourhood. Made up of homeowners, tenants, institutions, and business owners within that geographical area, it reflected the demographics and concerns of those who could afford to live or own property in the village. When describing the 150 people who came to the 519 to elect committee members on January 29, 1992, *Xtra* noted, "Noticeably absent were faces of colour and young people."[47]

HAPPY FAMILIES

In April 1992, CLGRO released its *Happy Families* report. Although the report still gestured towards allowing people to choose their own beneficiaries in alternative kinds of relationships by quoting the group's *On Our Own Terms* document, in practice, *Happy Families'* focused completely on recommendations to achieve equality between same- and opposite-sex couples. It identified seventy-nine statutes that needed to be amended to achieve that equality.

Over the summer, CLGRO and the Lesbian, Gay, and Bisexual Committee of the NDP lobbied key cabinet ministers. When Attorney General Howard Hampton refused to meet, a sit-in was held at his office. In response, the government set up a working group of ministers to prepare an option paper for cabinet. But opposition to the proposed changes was already growing inside the party. The working group suggested a compromise that wouldn't involve redefinition of "spouse" or the right to adopt, but the activists refused to endorse anything but full reform. Negotiations broke off. That fall the government was distracted by the Charlottetown Accord, a national referendum on the Constitution. The working group's options paper was never even discussed.

Pressure kept building, though. The province might have been able to ignore activists, but it couldn't ignore the Ontario Human Rights Commission. Michael Leshner worked as a Crown counsel with the Ministry of the Attorney General. In 1988 he complained that his benefits package was discriminatory, since his same-sex partner was denied coverage. Most of the complaint had been dealt with when the NDP extended coverage to same-sex partners of provincial employees in January 1991, but one major item remained – pensions. The province argued that the federal Income Tax Act prevented it from providing survivor benefits under the pension plan, since the definition of "spouse" in the act was restricted to opposite-sex partners.

The Ontario Human Rights Commission begged to differ. In response to Leshner's complaint, a board of inquiry cited the Charter and two recent cases from British Columbia and Manitoba that had extended employee benefits, and ordered the provincial government to make every effort to persuade the federal government to change the Income Tax Act. In the meantime, it was ordered to establish a separate plan that would provide equal survivor benefits to the partners of gay and lesbian employees.[48]

CLGRO made sure the *Leshner* decision got national media coverage, but the ruling also galvanized the opposition. Fundamentalist Protestants took the lead. Their tactics this time were different from in 1986, when their bigotry had helped demonstrate the need for inclusion in the code. Guides were distributed to evangelical churches on how to present arguments without quoting scripture or making extreme statements. Church members were encouraged to write personally to members of the provincial legislature so that letter campaigns appeared to be spontaneous.[49] CLGRO, countering with its own phone and fax campaign, delivered seven thousand postcards to the premier by the end of the year. But supportive voices tended to be concentrated in a few metropolitan areas, while groups like the Evangelical Fellowship of Canada had access to hundreds of churches across the province and could target political representatives from rural ridings and the suburbs.

It was an ironic reversal of positions. In the 1970s the lesbian and gay movement had counted on grassroots organizing to bombard conservative and religiously influenced state institutions. In the '90s, the apparent grassroots campaign came from the religious right and was directed against the gay-friendly NDP government.

As if to put a seal on the changes in the community, *Rites* magazine ceased publishing that April. *Rites* suffered from the same malaise that had killed *TBP* five years before: its material base of volunteer labour slowly evaporated. Shawn Syms joined the collective as an eighteen-year-old student in 1988, and supported himself doing odd jobs for the next four years in order to focus on activism. He was one of the last three people on deck when *Rites* finally went down in 1992. "We had volunteer nights to try and drum up interest but it became a struggle," he says. "There didn't seem to be that many people interested in taking it over. The feeling we were getting was that things had run their course."[50]

There were also deepening financial problems. At its height, *Rites* subscriptions had never exceeded 2,500. It had problems attracting advertisers. Even though the magazine shifted from ten to six issues a year, bills from the printer continued to mount up. Tensions increased as the shrinking collective looked around for some way out. "It was really fatigue that was a big part of it," Syms recalls. "There was a bit of drama at the end. Some of us were thinking of starting a new publication and there were rival groups doing that, but in the end, nobody ended up doing anything."[51]

THERE GOES THE ARMY

The relentless advance through the courts continued at the federal level. In August 1992 the Supreme Court ruled on *Haig and Birch*. Joshua Birch, a captain in the Canadian Armed Forces, was denied eligibility for postings, promotions, or further training after he came out. His complaint to the Canadian Human Rights Commission was rejected because the Canadian Human Rights Act did not include sexual orientation.

When his appeal was heard at the Ontario Court of Appeal, the court cited the Charter and decided in his favour, "reading in" sexual orientation. The federal government did not appeal, and the Canadian Human Rights Commission began accepting complaints on the basis of sexual orientation.[52] The armed forces had to abandon its long-standing policy of discrimination against lesbians and gay men.

A few months later, the government settled a parallel case with Michelle Douglas, an armed forces special investigator who had been dismissed when she was found to be a lesbian. Douglas was offered a hundred-thousand-dollar settlement.

AYA

As politics moved to the courts, among black lesbians and gay men – as in the broader community – grassroots organizing shifted to community building. Zami's disappearance had left a void, and by 1991, with Black CAP firmly established, many of the old Zami hands, like Doug Stewart and Courtnay

McFarlane, began talking about something new. For black gay men, white bars and baths were often unwelcoming, and carding by bouncers was a regular occurrence. A new community space was needed.

The new group began as a salon held in people's homes. McFarlane became the first co-ordinator. He was studying at the Ontario College of Art and had developed a keen interest in African textiles. McFarlane came up with the name Aya, the fern symbol representing defiance from Ashanti Adinkra cloth. "So even though we were a salon, there was still this political edge, the notion that black gay men organizing or even meeting socially, given our context, was a defiant act," he recalls.[53]

Aya was by invitation only, but as friends invited more friends, the salon soon outgrew anyone's home. The group moved to the 519 Church Street Community Centre. There, twenty to thirty black men would meet on Sunday afternoons. Unlike Zami, which had seen itself as black and Caribbean and was organized around both race and culture, Aya was specifically a group for black gay men. While Zami had taken on the work of being both black in the gay community and gay in the black community, McFarlane describes Aya as "very much black in the gay community." Nevertheless, many Aya members had different levels of engagement with the broader black communities or were active volunteers in Black CAP's anti-homophobia and HIV prevention work.[54] And although Aya was a men's group, relationships with black lesbians remained close and women often helped organize events.

Aya was also a less sexual space than the largely white bars and baths, and therefore comfortable for a wide range of backgrounds and ages. That diversity generated an equally wide range of activities: a newsletter, brunches and parties, contingents in Pride, speakers and discussions, meetings with visiting black filmmakers and artists, and even an annual Kwanza event. Aya hosted Toronto performances of *Fierce Love*, a show by an African American troupe, Pomo Afro Homos, focused on the stories of black gay lives. The group was perhaps best known for its fashion/variety shows, which could attract hundreds and garnered national attention after coverage by the fashion correspondent for *The Globe and Mail*.

Meanwhile, radical black lesbian singer-songwriter Faith Nolan was developing a vision for a retreat for Indigenous lesbians and lesbians of colour in the Haliburton Highlands, north of Toronto. Nolan was known for her activist work in prisons. Her performances – a mix of blues, folk, and jazz with a taste of funk and reggae – were a mainstay in labour and progressive gatherings. Through Multicultural Women in Focus, a critical mass of women raised money to buy the land and began clearing and building Camp Sis.

YONGE STREET RIOT

As black lesbians and gay men worked to construct more hospitable community spaces for themselves, the Yonge Street riot in the spring of 1992 signalled growing frustration in the broader community. The Rodney King verdict had just come out in Los Angeles. Despite video evidence showing a group of police brutally beating King, a black man, the cops were all cleared. LA erupted into days of rioting. In Toronto, there had been eight recent police shootings of young black men, not to mention regular harassment. On May 4, 1992, a bright spring day, a demonstration linking police racism in LA and Toronto marched up Yonge Street. Richard and I attended, but we were tired and, just before the conclusion and another round of speeches, we jumped on the subway home. When we turned on the TV later, we learned that moments after we'd left, all hell had broken loose.

It was a very Toronto riot: no deaths, a few arrests, some broken windows, and an overturned hotdog stand. But in a city complacent with its reputation for benign multiculturalism, it was a shock. At the board of education we got a reluctant upper administration to authorize a city-wide student meeting. When administrators arrived to talk about all the wonderful things the board was doing to combat racism, they faced angry students who wanted to vent about their everyday experiences. The meeting demanded thorough implementation of the board's existing anti-racism policies, a provincial inquiry into media racism, an independent authority to deal with accusations of police racism, and a jobs program for young people. A new organization was created, Students of Toronto Against Racism. I was surprised when I realized how many of the group's leadership identified as queer.

Premier Rae had a new hot potato in his hands. He tapped elder statesman Stephen Lewis to conduct an inquiry. Lewis delivered his report in less than a month. He pulled no punches. The problem was anti-black racism.

> It is Blacks who are being shot, it is Black youth that is unemployed in excessive numbers, it is Black kids who are disproportionately dropping out, it is housing communities with large concentrations of Black residents where the sense of vulnerability and disadvantage is most acute, it is Black employees, professional and non-professional whom the doors of upward equity slam shut.[55]

Lewis's recommendations demanded changes in the criminal justice system, policing, education, social services, community development, and employment programs for youth. Unfortunately many of the recommendations did not fare well. Those on policing were largely resisted by the deeply racist Metro police force, encouraged by support from the Progressive Conservative party at Queen's Park. In a joint press release with the Metro Police Association, Conservative spokesperson Bob Runciman accused Lewis of capitulating to "vocal interest groups." He said, "Mr Lewis focused exclusively on equality of opportunity and treatment of visible minorities while ignoring issues of public safety, police morale and individual responsibility. It is shameful."[56]

The education recommendations were most fruitful. In July 1993 the ministry released PPM 119, a directive requiring all boards of education in the province to develop policies on anti-racism and ethnocultural equity. PPM 119 detailed ten areas of focus to be taken into account. The new policies needed ministry approval by March 1995.

Despite that success, the conversation was still a vertical one between black communities and the government. With the NDP in power, everyone was orienting their politics towards the state. Unlike the bath raids crisis a decade earlier, there was no attempt to build cross-community alliances demanding police reform. *Rites,* which might have at least raised the issue, had ceased publishing a few months before. *Xtra* did a short, impressionistic story on the riot, comparing it to the march of five hundred lesbian and gay demonstrators who closed down the intersection of Yonge and College to protest a seizure at Glad Day only two days before. No gay or lesbian organization emerged in solidarity with the black community.

Rising expectations after the election of the NDP government affected different groups in different ways. For the largely white gay mainstream, better integrated into circuits of power, it created a burst of energy focused on demands to the state. For black youth, the contrast between expectations and daily experience produced frustration and anger. The limitations of government promises would soon be visible to the gay mainstream as well.

10

Seduction

BOARD OF EDUCATION

Since his election in November 1991, openly gay trustee John Campey had been carefully laying the groundwork for change at the board of education. It was a propitious moment. The margin of manoeuvre was narrowing for homophobic or cautious administrators and trustees. The inclusion of sexual orientation in the Ontario Human Rights Code, the mounting number of Charter-based legal decisions in support of gay rights, the new provincial government's talk about spousal benefits, and research showing the dire situation for many lesbian and gay kids in the school system all increased the pressure.

I also personally helped raise the stakes. Although I regularly put together student conferences on racism and sexism, in 1991, my proposal to organize one on homophobia was blocked by the superintendent in charge of curriculum. I did an end run around him by helping one of the alternative schools organize an anti-homophobia conference for other alternative schools across the system. Such a school-initiated event didn't require central approval, and our organizing went on under the Curriculum Department radar. A hundred and forty students from six schools attended. There was the predictable right-wing media hysteria after the fact. But senior officials were in a corner. They had to defend the conference or look either homophobic or incompetent. It didn't do my reputation as a team player any good, but it created a precedent.

Campey began by encouraging the formation of a Lesbian and Gay Employees Group while still a trustee's assistant before his election. Shortly after the election, in January 1992, the employees group created an agenda for change. Campey framed their proposals as an equity issue, like racism or sexism, and modelled his motions on policies and programs already in place for other groups. He called for Tony Gambini's position in the Human Sexuality counselling program to become full-time, and for the additional of a lesbian counsellor. The anti-homophobia curriculum document, held up in the bureaucracy for six years, should be approved for use. The proselytization policy should be revoked, and a Consultative Committee on the Education of Lesbian and Gay Students set up.

We rallied lesbian and gay students, teachers, and Parents and Friends of Lesbians and Gays (PFLAG) to speak to the motions. Supportive local residents were identified in every ward and encouraged to call their trustee. The board's Labour Education Committee and Status of Women Committee were brought onside. Because Campey had worked with the Heritage Language Committee as a trustee's assistant, he also could rally support from immigrant communities. Despite the expected fulminations from the *Toronto Sun* about the "lunatics" at the board "brainwashing our children," and the emergence of a new group called Citizens United for Responsible Education (CURE), all of Campey's motions passed.

Practically, the victory consolidated services to lesbian and gay students and began the re-education of teachers. It probably saved a number of vulnerable young lives. Symbolically, as the largest board of education in the country, the Toronto board set an example for others to follow. The consultative committee constituted the first official recognition of the community.

This victory was the result of years of often thankless, even risky, work inside the institution, building alliances, mobilizing community, and researching the lives of lesbian and gay students. The tipping point was the emergence of a champion within the system who was able to draw on pre-existing networks and frame the issue to fit institutional practices and policy frameworks.

TREATMENT, TREATMENT, TREATMENT

That summer I finally started on antivirals. I had already been doing pentamidine for almost a year after it had become clear that my CD4 levels had permanently fallen below 200, the point at which the risk of PCP pneumonia soared. By the summer of 1993 my levels had dropped to 50. Given that a normal immune system has between 700 and 1,000 CD4s, that level was like trying to cross a six-lane highway blindfolded at rush hour. It was just a matter of time before something major hit me.

It may have been another point when activism saved my life. There were only three antiviral drugs at that point: AZT, ddI, and DDC. The standard approach was to take one until it lost efficacy and then move on to the next. But at AAN! there was a buzz among those of us monitoring research about combination therapy. Theoretically, it meant that one could take less of each drug, thus limiting side effects, and also hit the virus from different angles. My doctor tried to dissuade me – combinations were not the approved protocol – but I insisted and left his office with two prescriptions. I began taking half-dose AZT plus DDC. My levels crept up to almost 200, not enough to get me off pentamidine but better than 50. I started making trips monthly to Wellesley Hospital to pick up drugs, and twice a month to the new "Puff

Parlour" on Sherbourne Street to take pentamidine. I was one of the lucky ones. Others had several doctors' appointments a week.

AAN! had two major committees at this point. The Provincial Issues Committee badgered the provincial government, largely about drug funding. It was co-ordinated by Bob Gardner, who, as second in command at the province's Legislative Library, had privileged access to what was happening at Queen's Park. For obvious reasons, he had to keep a low profile in his work with us. Although he was often their principal author, his name never appeared on any of our documents.

I worked with the Treatment, Access and Research Committee (TAAR) chaired by Darien Taylor. We followed research developments and promising treatments, pursued the pharmaceutical industry, and monitored clinical trials and drug access. In December 1991, TAAR published a *Guide to HIV Drug Trials in Canada* to help people make informed choices about participating in research. We organized a research conference with the Canadian HIV Trials Network in May 1992. And when the province still hadn't established standards of care, we consulted with clinicians and published our own *AIDS and HIV Treatment Management Guide* in December 1993.

By 1993, TAAR members could hold our own in conversations with doctors and scientists. But the committee also became less accessible to new people unless they already had a scientific background, privileging those with access to education.

That inexorable shift made us more effective. And once again, our lag behind New York alerted us to a potential danger. In January 1992, ACT UP New York's Treatment and Data Committee split off to become the Treatment Action Group. For those remaining in ACT UP, TAG was a privileged bunch of white boys who wanted to hobnob with pharma and government. From TAG's perspective, "shouting at people in the street" wasn't effective anymore. Activists had to be on the inside, at the table.

In Toronto we could not afford such splits. George Smith's mantra of documents and demos needed to guide the organization. We had to develop expertise and be at the table, *and* remain a presence on the street. In June we organized a die-in at Pride. In the middle of the march up Yonge Street, thousands stopped, lay down on the pavement, and had their outlines chalked like victims at a crime scene. It was a reminder to the government and the community that people were dying because of lack of drug funding.

It was not just a performance. In September, our old friend Lim Pei Hsien died in Vancouver. Lim had continued his activism there as one of the organizers of the annual AIDS vigil. His partner, Joseph, died a year before. A mutual friend had told us Lim was very ill, but Vancouver was on the other side of the continent. I felt guilty that we hadn't been able to see him before he passed. A few nights after his death, I dreamed he walked up to me on the street. He was wearing the kind of plaid shirt he always did in the 1980s when he wanted to butch it up. We embraced. I started to sob. I knew he was dead. He said, "It's all right, man. I have to go now. Take care." Then he squeezed me tight and walked away. I woke up crying.

Two weeks later, Doug Wilson died. It was an end to a remarkable activist career, beginning with his challenge to the University of Saskatchewan in 1975 after it refused him a supervisory position. He had chaired the Saskatchewan Human Rights Association and worked with the Saskatoon Gay Community Centre, Central American solidarity, *Rites* magazine, the Toronto Board of Education, the NDP, the Canadian Network of People with HIV/AIDS, and the steering committee of AAN! Doug died at Sunnybrook Hospital. Darien Taylor phoned me in the evening to say things were getting bad, but I was swamped with work and put off going up. I got the call the next day to say it was too late. Doug was forty-two.

JAMES THATCHER

As the winter of 1992 deepened, James Thatcher's health began to seriously deteriorate. He tried to keep up his work as co-chair of AAN! as best he could, but he soon lost sight in one eye and had increasing trouble speaking.

James was a passionate advocate for a catastrophic drug plan. He convinced Jay Browne at the AIDS Bureau to pull together an advisory panel that included senior Ontario Drug Benefit Program officials, the director of the HIV clinic at Sunnybrook Hospital, the chair of the HIV Primary Care Physicians Group, and patient advocates. In two months they hammered out a proposal for a comprehensive drug funding policy for AIDS that the bureaucracy thought should work. The document was presented to the minister in May 1992. She passed it on to her Drug Reform Secretariat. There it disappeared. For seven months all our inquiries were ignored. When a meeting was set up in December, the secretariat's representative, a senior official with specific responsibility for AIDS, hadn't even bothered to read it.

James had been diagnosed with lesions to his central nervous system, likely caused by cytomegalovirus (CMV). His doctor recommended high-dose acyclovir. But James did not have a private drug plan, and once he was diagnosed with AIDS, no one would insure him. He already had high drug costs and couldn't afford the additional acyclovir. If he exhausted his savings and impoverished himself to become eligible for social assistance and a drug card, he would lose his apartment and potentially find himself homeless. Without a public drug plan for people with AIDS, he had to take his chances and forgo treatment.

On December 30, with the help of Linda and Bob Gardner, James recorded a final video message. He was hoping to speak at a planned press conference in early January, but there was some doubt that he would be well enough.

In the video, his once handsome face is gaunt. He wears a black eye patch over his blind eye and a sombre black suit. He has difficulty pronouncing many words. But over twelve minutes, he struggles onward, explaining AAN!'s repeated calls for a drug program, his work with the AIDS Bureau to prepare a model, the failure of the Drug Reform Secretariat to take it seriously, his diagnosis, his inability to afford therapy, and his resultant impending death.

Two days later James was gone. He was thirty-seven.

Our January 6 press conference featuring his video message generated "unprecedented media attention to the drug funding issue."[1]

IMPATIENCE

St. George–St. David was the downtown riding that encompassed much of the gay village. Ian Scott had won the riding for the Liberals in 1990, beating NDP candidate Carolann Wright, a black anti-poverty activist, by only seventy votes. It had been a bizarre election campaign. Scott was a progressive, a former Liberal cabinet minister, widely known to be gay but in the closet. The third candidate was former Tory cabinet minister Keith Norton, who had come out only after he decided to run in the gay-heavy riding. Two white gay men versus a black activist. By 1992 Scott had become disillusioned with politics and resigned, provoking a by-election set for April 1, 1993.

The local NDP riding association, reflecting growing frustration over the government's failure to introduce same-sex spousal recognition, debated refusing to nominate a candidate until legislation was tabled. But when AAN!'s Mark Freamo moved that a catastrophic drug plan also be part of the demand, his motion was defeated, another example of the space that was opening up between gay and AIDS issues. The decision to refuse to nominate a candidate passed. Bob Rae and his cabinet were furious. They went over the riding association's head to appoint George Lamony, a young gay African man, a former theology student, and local co-ordinator of the White Ribbon Campaign, which addressed violence against women.

Kyle Rae and other high-profile local gay NDPers lobbied Lamony to withdraw. I ran into him on the street and did the same. He didn't have a snowball's hope in hell. The party was cynically exploiting the fact that he was black and gay just to keep its name in the race. His running was widely seen as a betrayal of community solidarity. The riding association had already announced that it would refuse to fund or work on his campaign. But Lamony naively insisted that we would all be surprised by the result. We weren't. The NDP vote collapsed and the election was easily won by Tim Murphy for the Liberals. Perhaps Lamony just wanted to make his mark. I hadn't known he was sick, but he died a year later.

CONFLICTING SIGNALS

Mossop was the first same-sex couple case to reach the Supreme Court. The decision in the spring of 1993 was both disappointing and promising. The court rejected the argument that not allowing Mossop to attend his partner's father's funeral was discrimination on the basis of family status, contrary to the Canadian Human Rights Code. But it suggested that making an argument under the Charter (which Mossop's lawyers hadn't done) might have made a difference. A few months later, in a similar case around bereavement leave that did argue the Charter (*Lorenzen v. Treasury Board*), a Public Service Staff Relations Board found that denial of bereavement leave to a same-sex spouse constituted discrimination on the basis of sexual orientation.

If the courts were getting their heads around same-sex benefits, marriage was still outside the pale. When Todd Layland, an American, tried to marry his partner, Pierre Beaulne, in Ottawa, they were refused a marriage licence. Although they argued that their Charter rights had been breached, in March, an Ontario court dismissed their complaint on the grounds that marriage between two individuals of the same sex had traditionally not been permitted under common law. However, one dissenting judge noted, "surely it is in the interests of the state to foster all family relationships, be they heterosexual or same sex relationships."[2]

KIDDIE PORN

That the legal regularization of lesbian and gay relationships might be "in the interests of the state" was still a novel idea in 1993, and as elections approached, the federal Progressive Conservative government needed to mobilize its social conservative base. In June, it passed a new anti-porn law criminalizing possession of "written materials or visual representations depicting, portraying, describing, advocating, or counseling sex with children."[3] Sex with children was defined as sexual activity with a person under the age of eighteen, even though the actual age of consent was fourteen. The *Butler* decision was widely cited, suggesting that the portrayal of anyone who appeared to be less than eighteen in a sexual situation was violence against children. The counselling provision was especially problematic. Potentially, giving safer sex materials or a condom to someone under eighteen could result in criminal charges.

Both *The Globe and Mail* and the *Toronto Star* condemned the legislation. But CLGRO was one of the few voices in the lesbian and gay communities that dared point out that "hysteria against pedophilia has traditionally been used against lesbians and gay men" and that the portrayal of perfectly legal acts was being criminalized. The decision caused internal dissent. Many members of CLGRO's working group on relationship recognition felt that opposing the legislation might harm their efforts to portray lesbians and gays as "happy families." Tom Warner even got a call from Svend Robinson's office in Ottawa "expressing real concern about CLGRO's position on the child pornography law and how damaging that was going to be for the campaign for equal rights and relationship recognition."[4]

In a way they were right. Working group members were associating lesbians and gay men with the positive affective response that ideas like "happy" and "family" produced to shape public logic in favour of relationship recognition. But child pornography, sex work, and adult-child sex were pretty widely associated with a negative affective response. If that was what came to mind when people thought of us, they would be less likely to support apparently pro-gay legislation.

The divide between the old CLGRO activists and the new upwardly mobile professionals in the relationship working group was expressing itself in attitudes towards sexual politics. The old activists were quite comfortable defending those denigrated because of unconventional sexual behaviour. They had been doing so since the day when all gay people were similarly denigrated. The working group wanted to be associated with relationships, family, and lesbians and gay men as normal parents. Talk of sex outside that framework, especially if children were involved, was counterproductive.

EGALE remained silent until after the bill passed, and only half-heartedly raised it as an issue later. In the end, no political party wanted to be on the wrong side of child pornography during an election year. Parliament passed the bill unanimously.

BRIAN FARLINGER

James Thatcher's dramatic message from the grave was the opening salvo of AAN!'s relentless campaign for drug funding. In May we marched up Yonge Street and closed the intersection at Wellesley with a die-in. In June there was a second Pride Day die-in. By now, the parade involved hundreds of thousands, and we were better organized. On cue, the music from the sound trucks stopped and marchers collapsed on the street, where their outlines were again chalked on the pavement. In December, we brought giant cardboard pills, each addressed to a different member of the provincial legislature, to Queen's Park to protest the province's World AIDS Day ceremony. Inside, Brian Farlinger jumped onto the stage and called for immediate drug funding.

Farlinger had undergone an astounding transformation. Gone were the expensive business suits, now replaced with a more activist-appropriate T-shirt and jean jacket. Once the quiet fly on the wall, in the fall of 1992 he was elected AAN! co-chair along with James Thatcher. With James's death, he shouldered the work alone for the rest of the year. He worked with both the Provincial Issues and the Treatment Access and Research committees, and soon developed an encyclopedic knowledge of provincial policy development and the ethical and scientific issues surrounding research. He spearheaded the organization of a national conference of treatment activists in August 1993. In the federal election that fall, he went nose to nose with Liberal leader Jean Chrétien during a Toronto campaign stop, demanding that the Liberals commit to more AIDS research funding.

If the child porn bill was a Tory election strategy, it failed. Beset by corruption scandals, after almost a decade in power they were reduced to a rump of three seats in the October 1993 elections. Their alliance of neo-liberal elites, small-town social conservatives, and Quebec nationalists flew apart. The Reform Party, a populist social conservative formation, bled off Tory votes in the West; the Parti Québécois replaced them in Quebec. Chrétien led the Liberals to a majority government. Although Chrétien was not trapped in an uneasy alliance with social conservatives the way Mulroney had been, no one expected any bold initiatives. The Liberal party had a time-honoured strategy of sticking to the centre. Still, with Clinton in the United States, Thatcher gone in the United Kingdom, and the NDP in Ontario, things seemed to be getting better.

The fragility of that progress was revealed within months. The Tories had left a legacy with their child porn bill. In November, newspapers in leafy London, Ontario, shocked the province, announcing "Child Porn Bust May Be Largest in Ontario." A sack of discarded videotapes had been discovered, and ambitious London police chief Julian Fantino saw an opportunity. He launched Operation Scoop and then Operation Guardian, and over the next year, local papers would be filled with lurid stories about child porn and child sex rings.

Hundreds of charges were laid, all against gay men and youths. Only two involved pornography. Several men were sentenced to prison time for contacts with underage sex workers; most were acquitted or had charges dropped. There were no rings, just some underaged hustlers and amateur video makers. Most of the seized videos on display at police press conferences turned out to be Hollywood blockbusters. As CLGRO had warned, the child porn legislation was carte blanche for a witchhunt against gay men.[5] In the public imagination we were re-associated with porn and pedophilia, despite attempts to link the community to the more salubrious notion of happy families. It did not bode well for the ongoing same-sex relationship campaign.

As Fantino's moral panic rolled out in London, in December, Toronto Morality Squad officers raided the downtown Mercer Union Gallery and seized forty paintings and drawings by a young artist, Eli Langer. Langer and gallery director Sharon Brooks were charged with offences of making obscene material, possession of child pornography, and exposing obscene material to the public. The drawings and paintings, which had not involved live models, depicted young people in various stages of undress, sometimes engaged in sexual acts, and explored intimacy beyond cultural taboos. Although charges against Langer and Brooks were ultimately dropped, bizarrely, the works themselves went on trial before being finally acquitted on the defence of their artistic merit.[6]

As 1994 dawned, the NDP's time in Ontario was running out. Both AAN! and CLGRO saw the window closing on our respective issues – drug funding and spousal benefits. CLGRO had reason to be more hopeful. There was another ruling from British Columbia that the denial of employment benefits to same-sex spouses was discrimination under the Charter.[7] And during the April 1993 by-election in St. George–St. David, Liberal leader Lynn McLeod had publicly stated that if she were elected the next premier, she would end discrimination against same-sex partners. McLeod followed up in a letter to CLGRO profess-ing her support for the *Happy Families* brief. It was largely an attempt to score points and embarrass the Rae government for its failure to act, but it was a public commitment. With both the NDP and the Liberals supportive, what could go wrong?

Two months later, Tim Murphy, the victorious Liberal candidate in St. George–St. David, introduced a private member's bill in the provincial legisla-ture. But McLeod's support for *Happy Families* had produced a behind-the-scenes revolt in her own party. Murphy's bill was limited to changing the defi-nition of "spouse" in the Human Rights Code, a far cry from CLGRO's demand to amend all the relevant provincial statutes. Most private members' bills die in the House; Murphy had been given permission to introduce his because his colleagues assumed it wouldn't go anywhere. But the NDP turned the tables and supported it, forcing McLeod to vote for it, even as most of her Liberal caucus stayed away. Spousal rights had become a shuttlecock in a par-tisan game of "gotcha."

The terrain was further complicated by a cabinet shuffle. Early in 1993, Marion Boyd became the new attorney general and made clear her support for the full package of reforms. Since Murphy's bill passed first and second readings, it could go to public hearings. Boyd hoped that the hearings could be used as a Trojan horse to promote more comprehensive changes. But the hearings on Bill 45 kept being put off and, by December, it was clear they couldn't happen until 1994.

Meanwhile the Christian right used the delay to flood members of the leg-islature with letters and petitions. Lesbian and gay activists, as they continued to badger the government, were repeatedly told not to worry, everything was in hand. Finally Murphy announced that he was opposed to using his bill as a cover to discuss broader changes. The NDP strategy fell apart, and the govern-ment, caught between its own promises and a panicked caucus with an eye to the next election, abandoned the idea of hearings. The lesbian and gay com-munity turned up the pressure. At a party retreat in February 1994, as gay activists protested outside the premier's office, Boyd got permission to intro-duce legislation, its content yet unspecified. But the party was divided. Her proposal was approved by a majority of only one vote.

Then, in March 1994, there was another by-election. Victoria–Haliburton was the riding where I had grown up. It sprawled from mixed farming areas in the south to the Canadian Shield in the north. The population was predominantly of British stock and Canadian born. It was an area of small towns, small farms, small businesses, and cottage country. There was little industry and few unionized workers, and much social life still revolved around churches. Although things had probably improved since I left home at the end of the 1960s, unsurprisingly, it continued to be a deeply socially conservative area.

The Liberals expected to take the riding. But the Tories, now under the hard-right-wing leadership of Mike Harris, placed attack ads in local papers, excoriating McLeod for her support of lesbian and gay spousal benefits. Progressive Conservative candidate Chris Hodgson won handily on a wave of homophobia.

That further panicked the Liberals and the NDP. Nevertheless, Boyd again narrowly won the go-ahead to introduce the full package of legislation based on *Happy Families*. But there was a trade-off. The legislation would be put to a free vote. Members would not be required to vote with their party but could follow their conscience. Rae hoped that, given McLeod's assurance of support, there would be enough Liberals in favour of the legislation to make up for any NDP members against it. Bill 167, An Act to Amend Ontario Statutes to Provide for the Equal Treatment of Persons in Spousal Relationships, was introduced May 19.

Everything unravelled. The Progressive Conservatives voted against the bill en bloc, as did most Liberals and ten NDP members. It narrowly passed first reading. McLeod, caught like a deer in the headlights, first refused to comment on the legislation and then did her famous flip-flop. She had ducked the first vote, issuing a statement that she would vote against the legislation when it came back to the house for second reading. The right-wing Protestants were already on the rampage. Then the Roman Catholic archbishop of Toronto piled on, calling on parishioners to protest the bill. The Ontario Conference of Catholic Bishops was quick to follow him.

LABOUR TAKES A STAND

As the NDP government found itself backed into a corner, the Canadian Labour Congress, representing more than two million Canadian workers, held its annual meeting in Toronto on May 26, 1994. On the agenda was a motion on gay and lesbian rights, calling for workplace education on harassment and political action on lesbian and gay equality, including public campaigning and legal action. It read, in part: "The CLC clearly understands that sexism, racism, ableism and heterosexism share common roots. We acknowledge that we can change attitudes and behaviours if we stand united. We know we will fail if we allow ourselves to be divided."[8]

The debate was preceded by intense caucusing and, on the floor, LGBT delegates rushed to the microphones in order to put a human face on the issue.

Straight allies talked about overcoming their homophobia. Public Service Alliance of Canada president Daryl Hean confessed that a few years ago he would have opposed lesbian and gay rights, but now his mind had been changed. Harry Hynd of the United Steelworkers explained to delegates, "As a young man I used to mistreat gays and reacted to them with violence. Only lately I've come to realize how foolish and wrong that was. I've found out they're the most loving, caring people in the world."[9]

It was a bit over the top, but the years of activists coming out in their workplaces and supporting their co-workers paid off. The motion was passed with a large majority. It was further ammunition for lesbian and gay activists to take back to their workplaces and to raise at the bargaining table, and put more pressure on the hapless NDP government.

An *Xtra* article on the convention included a box comparing the achievements of the major unions on lesbian and gay rights. Carolyn Egan of the Steelworkers felt that her union had not been given due credit, and wrote a stern letter in the following issue setting the record straight. Support for lesbian and gay rights was becoming a badge of honour that unions aspired to.[10]

CAMPAIGN FOR EQUAL FAMILIES

The sudden introduction of Bill 167 also provoked a crisis on the other side. No one had expected a free vote. CLGRO's strategy had been to push the NDP to introduce the legislation and then use its majority to pass it. Now the legislation was introduced, but every vote counted, regardless of the party. A broad coalition of all political stripes needed to be assembled to lobby undecided members. CLGRO's relationships working group split off and formed the Campaign for Equal Families (CEF).

According to Tom Warner, "CLGRO activists had serious misgivings about the CEF strategy and rhetoric, but remained active in the campaign in order not to abandon [the] issue . . . and to maintain a united front publicly." Warner continued as co-chair of the new organization. "But CLGRO activists were massively out-numbered, and relations between a minority of 'liberationists' and the vast majority of equality-seekers within CEF remained rocky."[11]

Notably absent from the legislation was CLGRO's initial demand that people be able to opt out of relationship categories that they rejected. This was of specific concern to AAN! It would mean that if two people were deemed to be in a relationship and one was on social assistance in order to get a drug card, that person might lose benefits because as a couple, their joint income had to be considered. It was a new twist on the old spouse-in-the-house tactic, where single mothers would be denied benefits if Social Services workers determined that they had a live-in boyfriend.

The class implications of the push for equality had already been pointed out in an article by Patricia Lefebour in the *Journal of Law and Social Policy*:

The inclusion of gay and lesbian couples in the definition of marital status will have a polarizing result. Employment-related benefits will pass to those lesbians and gays whose partners receive these benefits through their employment. However, for those whose source of income is social assistance, the recognition of same sex spouses will represent a reduction in benefits received. This reduction in benefits, it will be argued, will pose serious problems especially where one or both of the partners is HIV positive or where the couple experience other serious disability or health problems.[12]

In the scramble for equality, the poor were being thrown under the bus.

None of this was the concern of the Campaign for Equal Families. The sole focus of the new professional class was to see the legislation passed. CEF was largely made up of downtown Toronto members of the NDP's Lesbian, Gay, and Bisexual Committee with a few lesbian and gay Liberals. Bob Gallagher took leave from Olivia Chow's office to co-ordinate the campaign, which quickly hired three other full-time workers and opened an office in the village. Hundreds volunteered to help.

Gallagher disputes Warner's analysis of a class shift in the CEF. "The differences had to do with politics, not class. . . . You could argue that these activists were speaking in a way that was actually in the interests of the middle class, but the people doing it . . . were not new."[13]

Money was a key issue. Bathhouse owner Peter Bochove chipped in, as did Woody's bar and other businesses and the Steelworkers and the CAW. Gallagher had access to the Chow-Layton fundraising lists, and MCC appealed for funds and volunteers through its congregation. Volunteers collected signatures at Church and Wellesley, and those who signed got a fundraising letter. More than sixty thousand dollars was raised in a few weeks.

Two major press conferences were organized, one featuring well-known entertainers and a second with religious figures. Four hundred clergy from across the province signed a petition in support. There were endorsements from the Ontario Association of Professional Social Workers, Children's Aid Societies, the CLC, the OFL, and other unions. Big business remained largely unconcerned. "Same Sex Plan Just Ho-hum to Bosses," read a *Toronto Star* headline. Within weeks the campaign was able to generate over twenty thousand letters in support of the legislation. When it came to public action, CEF was weaker on the ground. It fell to the International Socialists and Steelworkers to organize the major demonstration on June 3.

In the end, it was all for naught. Between the Liberal betrayal and the NDP free vote strategy, there weren't enough votes in the house. The NDP frantically sought a compromise with McLeod, but she refused any contact. At second reading, June 9, 1994, Bill 167 was defeated by eight votes. CEF supporters who had packed the public galleries erupted in cries of "shame, shame." The galleries were cleared by police wearing latex gloves to protect themselves from AIDS. That evening, Church Street filled with angry lesbians and gay men. The crowd marched to Queen's Park in protest.

In his detailed analysis of the campaign, political scientist David Rayside notes several reasons for its failure: the wide-ranging scope of the legislation and its implicit challenge to heterosexist norms, the mobilizing strength of traditional churches, the opportunism of both the Liberals and some of the NDP, the NDP's ineptitude, and the CEF's Toronto-centred campaign that could not bridge the rural-urban divide.[14]

It took a Progressive Conservative member of the legislature to point out the class implications of that divide. He noted that most workers in his riding did not have benefits at all. "We're talking about people who have full-time, good paying jobs who want ice cream afterwards, and I'm really having trouble getting the meal on the table."[15] While workers in large unionized industrial workplaces and in public service had made impressive gains during the Keynesian period, those working for small rural businesses had been left behind. This divide was accentuated by neo-liberalism. Ironically, the success of urban lesbians and gay men in our alliances with government and unions was now contributing to the stereotype that we were a privileged minority who always wanted more. The resentment of those left behind was being turned against us.

The message the new professional leadership of the movement took from the defeat was clear – community mobilization to influence political actors was a dead end. Even with the most supportive government in the province's history, we could not win basic equality. While the CEF died out very quickly after the defeat, some of its key activists launched the Foundation for Equal Families to use litigation to push the issue. The rights movement turned its efforts towards the courts. From then on, our fate was in the hands of lawyers. Community became a fundraising constituency centred on those with more disposable income.

BUDDIES IN BAD TIMES

As what Tom Warner called assimilationist tendencies dominated gay politics, the same could not be said of the arts. Buddies in Bad Times Theatre had been founded in 1979 with Sky Gilbert as artistic director. The new company reflected his vision – "unapologetically political, fiercely pro-sexual, and fundamentally anti-establishment." In a 1989 interview, Gilbert said, "Buddies is not about assimilation and never has been about glossing over the differences between gays and straights. We are interested in life on the edge, the avant-garde, forbidden territory."[16]

Buddies was itinerant until 1991, when it rented space in an old auto repair shop in the east end of the city. The site hosted not only plays by Gilbert and others, but also Dungeon Parties featuring S/M performances.

By 1990, the old Toronto Workshop Productions theatre in the heart of the village was slated for replacement by condos. After a public mobilization, city council intervened and put out a call for proposals to keep the site a community theatre. Gallagher, who was housemates with Gilbert, helped craft a submission. Buddies came in second, but when the winning proposal didn't follow through, Kyle Rae lobbied city cultural staff to grant the building to Buddies rather than put out a new call. "Rita Davies, Barbara Hall and I went to [Mayor] June Rowlands and said this is what we wanted to do," Rae recounts. "Rowlands said, 'that's a great idea. The gays will look after it.'"[17] Using their NDP connections, Rae and Gallagher secured promises of provincial and city funding. Buddies took over the building in 1994.

"The money that we got was only barely able to get the building into operating condition," Gallagher remembers. "There weren't plans to be able to run it. We went for many years operating illegal booze cans to keep it afloat."[18] After years of robbing Peter to pay Paul, the theatre finally got a liquor licence that generated enough cash to continue presenting provocative theatre true to Gilbert's original vision.

MA BELL

The fight for rights continued on other fronts, even in the halls of corporate Canada. Carl Miller and Jari Dvorak both worked as managers for Bell Canada, the huge telephone monopoly. It was considered a bad career move to be out at work, but one Monday morning in January 1991, the two had recognized each other in the elevator after cruising at a GCDC dance over the weekend. They started having lunch together, and as time went on, they were joined by several other lesbian and gay employees.

The lunches turned into the Gay and Lesbian Organization of Bell Employees. GLOBE decided to support Tom Stewart, another employee who had thrown caution to the winds and was seeking spousal benefits for his partner. Their request was rebuffed by Ma Bell. "At the present time, our policies in this area are formed on the basis of legislative requirements and the general acceptance of this issue by the external environment."

GLOBE availed itself of a new cutting-edge technology called email, which Bell employees had recently been given access to. More employees were recruited, and another request for benefits was made. The answer was much the same: "By deciding not to extend eligibility of benefits to same-sex partners, the company wishes to express its preference to let society make its choices known through legislation and high court decisions prior to proceeding with any changes." It was not only the NDP and the Liberals who wanted to hide behind the courts. And when the province extended benefits in response to the *Leshner* decision, the company reminded its employees it was governed by federal, not provincial, legislation. Nor did Bell feel comfortable creating "guidelines or terminology" to deal with anti-gay harassment in the workplace.

Nevertheless, as insiders in the corporate hierarchy, GLOBE knew how to exploit divisions. Miller, who "personally delighted in putting Bell in moral dilemmas," asked the company's Employment Equity group to sponsor GLOBE's banner in the 1992 Pride parade and got space in the company lobby for a Pride display. He then arranged for Premier Rae to write a congratulatory letter, which was distributed to the company's executives.[19]

Shortly after the 1992 Pride, Carrie Brown, another GLOBE member, upped the ante, coming out as a lesbian in a mass email to all Bell employees and managers. That move produced media interest. As a result, a positive story about the group appeared in the company's employee newsletter in 1993, again rattling upper management and provoking a heated discussion among employees. Ma Bell was slowly being pushed into a corner.[20]

The corporation found itself facing down both GLOBE and its unions. In 1994 Laura Davis was elected national representative of the Canadian Telecommunications Employees Association, the union that represented Bell's forty thousand predominantly female clerical and sales workers. Bell regulations required female employees to wear "female" clothing such as dresses, but Davis, an open dyke, was having none of it. She informed her less-assertive union colleagues that she intended to wear pants and a jacket on the job. When other female employees asked why Davis could wear pants and they couldn't, they were told it was because of her "sexual preference." That did not seem like a very good reason. Other women began to openly flout the dress code as well. A lesbian won the right for women to wear pants at Bell Canada.

The courts finally pushed Ma Bell over the edge. Both Bell unions joined a GLOBE discrimination complaint to the Canadian Human Rights Commission. In 1994, Bell lost the case.

GLOBE's business plan also included personal development (largely encouraging employees to come out), education, and outreach to other corporations. IBM was one of GLOBE's early targets. "Our strategy was to counter the 'we don't want to be the first' argument, by demonstrating that it was a corporate Canada trend," Miller explained. Lesbian and gay employees at IBM and Royal Bank were soon demanding spousal recognition as well.[21]

The writing was on the wall. Bell finally extended benefits to all its employees and managers in 1995. Corporate Canada was on notice. Spousal benefits and out lesbian and gay employees could not be resisted.

STONEWALL 25

June 28, 1994, was the twenty-fifth anniversary of Stonewall. The Fourth Gay Games were held in New York, as was the International Lesbian and Gay Association World Conference. Richard and I drove down and stayed with Jonathan Ned Katz and his partner, David Gibson, in the West Village.

Toronto's ILGA support group disappeared after the 1985 conference, and I was so focused on AIDS, I had lost touch and didn't attend the New York conference. The major conference news was the expulsion of the North American Man/Boy Love Association and two other pedophile groups.

The ILGA official statement noted that these groups had joined "at an earlier stage of ILGA's development, at a time when ILGA did not have in place administrative procedures to scrutinize the constitutions and policies of groups seeking membership." This was not true. The group always knew what NAMBLA was, but it had joined when intergenerational sex was still seen as part of the continuum of sexual liberation. Despite controversy, it always had majority support at ILGA gatherings. But by the 1990s, the aims of pedophile organizations were deemed "incompatible with those of ILGA."[22]

Xtra wasn't buying it. Ken Popert called the move "without apparent foundation in principle, squalid, and cruel in its execution." He added, "I now deeply regret our life-saving $15,000 grant to ILGA, and I have no doubt that our board of directors will shortly reconsider our commitment."[23]

The main motivation for the change was the threat to ILGA's standing at the United Nations. After a long struggle, the group had been granted consultative status to the UN Economic and Social Council in 1993. But a subsequent campaign launched by right-wing senator Jesse Helms led to a unanimous vote in the U.S. Senate to withhold $118 million owed by the United States to the United Nations until the president could certify that no pedophile organizations were accredited by UN bodies. Helms's goal was to disrupt both ILGA and the United Nations by linking them to pedophilia.

ILGA's expulsion of NAMBLA to avoid its own expulsion from the United Nations turned out to be futile. A U.S. motion resulted in ILGA's suspension in September 1995.[24] ILGA would not regain its UN status until 2011.

It was not just American politics that turned the tide. The explosive growth of child-focused international sex tourism had laid bare the exploitative character of much child-adult sex. In that context, NAMBLA's insistence on an ethical ground for such relationships seemed naive and self-serving. As the rights movement became more mainstream, association with pedophilia became a serious liability.

But the ILGA meeting was hardly a footnote to the celebration in New York. Museums had displays of queer history. There were concerts, dances, and performances everywhere. A Dyke March went up Fifth Avenue on the twenty-fifth. The same day ACT UP staged a demo to promote its AIDS Cure Project, a demand that riffed on the Manhattan Project's mobilization of national resources to produce the atomic bomb in the 1940s.

The main Pride parade on June 26 was the most massive I had ever seen. Richard, Tony Souza, and I clambered on top of a bus shelter and watched for hours as hundreds of thousands of lesbians and gay men from every part of the globe marched from the United Nations to Central Park. There was so much joy and celebration that it almost seemed that AIDS didn't exist.

Hours later, as we lay on the grass in Central Park listening to the speeches, a familiar voice echoed out over the loudspeakers. It was Simon Nkoli. Our letters had become more sporadic as our mutual AIDS work had intensified, and although Nkoli had mentioned he was coming to the ILGA conference, we hadn't managed to arrange to meet. The stage was so far away that I could barely see his tiny figure. By the time I got close enough, he was gone.

It was the last time I saw him.

CATASTROPHIC DRUG FUNDING

AAN! disrupted the legislature in April 1994, dumping bags of fake money on the politicians from the visitors' galleries to represent the NDP's false promises. A week later, in the middle of the night, we dressed up the statues in Queen's Park as AIDS activists, with signs and banners calling for the drug program. But the spousal rights battle sucked up the political oxygen during the rest of the spring. Its defeat left our demand for a catastrophic drug plan the only one standing.

The Pride march on July 3 turned into an expression of community anger against the NDP government. AAN! led the parade in a flatbed truck where long-time steering committee member Brent Southin, dressed in a suit and Bob Rae mask, spun a huge Wheel of Fortune as he gambled with the lives of people with AIDS. He was accompanied by two drag versions of Vanna White providing commentary. The march veered off its usual Yonge Street route and passed Queen's Park to condemn the Rae government for its inaction.

On September 23 we were back at the Ministry of Health stringing clotheslines with underwear across the entrance to emphasize our theme: "Bob Rae is hanging PLWAs Out to Dry." Brian Farlinger appeared in drag as a washerwoman.

Finally, in November, a group of AAN! members stormed the stage at the provincial NDP conference in Hamilton. It caused a ruckus and, to defuse the situation, Rae agreed to meet with several activists. In private, he gave assurance that a drug plan was in the works. This time he was as good as his word. On November 30 there was an official announcement that a catastrophic drug plan would be implemented by April 1995. It would be called the Trillium Drug Program. We called off a demonstration and public effigy burning of Rae planned for World AIDS Day the next day.

The beauty of Trillium was that it wasn't AIDS-specific. It covered anyone in the province suffering from an illness requiring drugs that cost more than a certain percentage of their income. During the campaign, we had tried to strike alliances with other "disease groups" that would benefit from such a program. But after a couple of meetings we realized that they were run as professional charities, with no interest in advocacy or activism. People who were actually sick had no control. So the Trillium program was AAN!'s gift to the people of Ontario.

George didn't live to hear the announcement of the Trillium program that he had been so instrumental in achieving. He died on November 6, after pouring the last two years of his life into establishing a solid foundation for the Community AIDS Treatment Information Exchange. George instructed that there was to be no memorial service, so this man who had made such decisive impact on the theoretical and political development of the community over almost twenty years slipped away unheralded.

Later that winter we lost two more steering committee members, Ric Hatt and Robert Van Dusen. Ric was the first straight man with AIDS to join the steering committee. He, like Darien Taylor, was an example of the strength of the emerging poz identity. He concentrated on establishing the national network of people with AIDS, and he represented AAN! on the Ontario AIDS Network, the provincial coalition of AIDS service organizations. Robert represented AAN! on the Wellesley Hospital Community Advisory Committee and helped make that hospital the leading downtown centre for AIDS care.

DUSK

The Trillium Drug Program was the last major piece of legislation from the NDP. As promised, Trillium opened for business in April 1995. A few days later the election was called.

The NDP came to power promising many things to many groups, but found itself unable to make good on those promises. At first, it had tried classic Keynesian policies, increasing social spending to combat the recession. That pleased its base, but the economy got worse and the government deficit ballooned. Under pressure, it switched to a neo-liberal austerity budget that alienated traditional supporters.

The NDP's Social Contract, freezing civil service wages and forcing public workers to take twelve days unpaid leave, undermined its traditional support among unions. Cutbacks to education and health care funding angered school boards, teachers, health care professionals, and patients. A promise to create a public auto insurance plan never materialized. Rae came to power promising to eliminate food banks; their proliferation as the recession deepened disappointed anti-poverty activists. Although the NDP had tried to cater to gay people, appointing Tom Warner as the first openly gay man to the OHRC and adopting progressive policies on AIDS, its failure to implement same-sex spousal benefits led to a mass exodus of lesbians and gays from the party.

On the other hand, what progressive policies the government had implemented enraged traditional conservative voters. Landlords hated new rent controls. Business was opposed to legislation facilitating union organizing. An employment equity program that encouraged the hiring of women, visible minorities, Aboriginals, and disabled people generated resentments among traditional white male voters. Rae's support for a woman's right to choose alienated staunch Catholics, while his opposition to the proposed North American Free Trade Agreement confirmed Bay Street's worst fears. In Toronto, the police were up in arms after the appointment of Susan Eng, a long-time police critic, to the Police Commission, and the recommendation for more hiring of visible minorities after the Yonge Street riot.

Few expected that the NDP would win the upcoming election. But none of us imagined what was in store for the province.

EGAN AND NESBIT

Jim Egan may have been Canada's first gay activist. Born in Toronto in 1921, by 1949 he was writing letters to local papers chastising them for sensationalist anti-gay articles. In 1951, he wrote a parliamentary law reform committee under his own name to argue for the repeal of "gross indecency." In touch with the Mattachine Society and other homophile groups in the United States, Egan became a mentor to early pioneers such as George Hislop and Sarah Ellen Dunlop, introducing them to the new homophile literature from south of the border. In the mid-1960s, he helped organize political discussion groups in The Music Room, one of the city's most popular early gay clubs. But his partner, Jack Nesbit, whom Egan met in 1948, was decidedly not political. Nesbit prevailed on him to move to British Columbia in the late '60s, where the couple lived a quiet life.

In the late '80s, however, both men were eligible for old age security, and they applied for a spousal allowance. They knew it was a political act. As expected, the application was denied. The Old Age Security Act only recognized opposite-sex spouses. That denial began a new round of activism for Egan, but in 1989, the logical course of action was no longer letter writing or pressing politicians for law change. The couple took the Department of National Health and Welfare to court, alleging discrimination. By October 1994, *Egan and Nesbit* had made its way to the Supreme Court. Most of the cost was covered by the federal Court Challenges Program.

EGALE was a major intervenor in the case. A normative aging couple, denied benefits despite being together for more than forty years, was about as good as it could get. MCC also intervened. The list of other supporting groups illustrated a broader coalition around the basis of unity of equal rights: the Canadian Human Rights Commission, the Quebec Human Rights Commission, and the Canadian Labour Congress.

Only one intervenor opposed the recognition of same-sex spouses, the Inter-Faith Coalition on Marriage and the Family. That, too, demonstrated a new constellation – of conservative religious groups. The coalition included Focus on the Family, The Evangelical Christian Fellowship, the Ontario Council of Sikhs, the Canadian Conference of Catholic Bishops, the Islamic Society of North America, a Hindu association and two Jewish groups.[25]

Meanwhile, Tom Warner – the veteran CLGRO activist who had co-chaired the Campaign for Equal Families while arguing for recognition of a broader range of relationships – was approached to speak at the rally the day the Supreme Court decision on *Egan* was to come out. But someone on the organizing committee apparently had second thoughts. "I got a call just before I was going to go over to Church and Wellesley for the demonstration," he recalls. "They were really worried that I was going to get into an anti-marriage rant."[26] Warner assured the organizers that he would not rant but refused to let them vet a copy of his speech.

The May 1995 decision was a mixed bag. The court confirmed that sexual orientation was an analogous ground under the Charter, and that the opposite-sex definition of "spouse" in the Old Age Security Act was in violation. But although several judges wrote dissenting opinions, the majority found that the refusal of a spousal allowance was still "justified." Although Egan and Nesbit did not get their pension, the case was a watershed that cleared the way for others. It also raised EGALE's profile. In a further move to mainstream, the group set up the EGALE Human Rights Trust, a registered education-focused charity that could issue charitable tax receipts for donations. Political advocacy work would continue to be the responsibility of EGALE itself.

HATE AND DISCRIMINATION

The *Egan* case overshadowed another legislative victory that June. Federal hate crimes legislation, including sexual orientation, was passed. It had been a Liberal campaign promise, and although it had never been a major issue for lesbian and gay activists, hate crimes legislation had been a key demand by Jewish groups and was widely supported by other minorities. Although there was little evidence that harsher penalties ever deterred a hate crime, the legislation allowed for longer sentences if hate could be demonstrated as the motive. Nonetheless, the inclusion of sexual orientation stirred up vocal opposition from several homophobic Liberal backbenchers and the Reform Party, spooking the Liberal government.

So it took another year to convince the Liberals to live up to their second promise – to formally add sexual orientation to the Canadian Human Rights Act. (Sexual orientation had already been "read in" to the act by the 1992 Ontario Court of Appeal decision.) Despite support from Minister of Justice Alan Rock and promises by Prime Minister Chrétien himself, a vocal minority of Liberals again opposed any changes.

When the government appeared to be dragging its feet, EGALE took a leading role in reminding them of the disastrous outcome of Lynn McLeod's flip-flop over spousal rights in Ontario. Using a backdrop of a huge pair of flip-flop sandals at press conferences, EGALE executive director John Fisher made Chrétien's "integrity" the issue, backing the notoriously prickly prime minister into a corner.

Luckily, the opposition Reform Party, the social conservative party that had split the right-wing vote with disastrous results for Mulroney's Progressive Conservatives, had become intoxicated by the rhetoric of the U.S. right and quickly isolated itself by indulging in strident homophobic language. Their remarks were framed in the press as extremist. Media coverage again established "tolerance" as a Canadian value.

Nonetheless, Chrétien allowed a free vote on this issue to minimize dissention in his caucus, and Justice Minister Rock repeatedly assured everyone who would listen that the bill would have no bearing on same-sex spousal benefits or marriage. The bill passed easily with the support of the Bloc Québécois and the NDP opposition.[27]

Despite the political timidity, the legislation was an assertion that lesbians and gay men were worthy of protection like other minorities, another step towards being embraced by the nation.

THE PRIDE THAT ALMOST WASN'T

The *Egan* decision was a watershed in the rights trajectory. Egan and Nesbit were grand marshals in the 1995 Pride parade. But their triumphal procession down Yonge Street almost didn't happen. In the spring, the simmering contradictions within Pride burst into the open and the festival almost collapsed.

Pride was still run by a volunteer board, elected by whoever showed up to general meetings. The festival itself continued to grow, and after the 1994 mobilization around spousal benefits, attendance had been estimated at 300,000. But in March 1995, five board members including the president and vice-president resigned, leaving only three active directors, not enough for quorum. Without quorum, preparations ground to a halt.

Committee member Tari Akpodiete warned that unless the remaining board members stepped down, the Pride Committee was finished. "These people are incredibly disorganized … they are very anti-business. … They still think it is a party where 5,000 people come." Akpodiete told *Xtra* that meeting minutes were rarely available, deadlines seldom met, and members not accountable.[28]

Councillor Kyle Rae stepped in and applied for the permits himself. He also commandeered the next Pride meeting and constituted a new board. But it was clear to everyone that Pride's volunteer organizational structure was not up to managing a huge festival that carried increasing symbolic weight. Part of this was the loss of so many activists to AIDS and the involvement of others fighting the epidemic. Part had to do with the reassertion of liberal individualist values as the battles of the 1980s receded into history. Pride needed competent people working full-time year-round to meet the demands of the event. This was no longer going to come free.

The problems in Pride mirrored the malaise that had led to the demise of other organizations that sprang up in the 1980s after the bath raids, such as the GCDC. But Pride had become too big to fail.

Spousal benefits was not the only issue that flowed through the courts. In 1985, the age of consent had been lowered to fourteen, except for anal intercourse, set at eighteen. Straight male legislators' anxieties about anal penetration had expressed themselves once again. But in 1992, an Ontario judge ruled that the special age of consent served no legislative purpose and violated the Charter. When the case (*Carmen M*) was heard in the Court of Appeals in May 1995, The Canadian Foundation for Children, Youth and the Law; the Canadian AIDS Society; and CLGRO argued against the higher age of consent. The court obligingly struck down the offending section of the Criminal Code. The only female judge on that panel stated that the law discriminated against young gay men. By this point a Federal Court had come to the same conclusion.[29]

The original movement had called for abolition of age of consent laws but had settled on equality. It was the courts, not the political process, that finally delivered it.

TRIANGLE

Back at the board of education, Tony Gambini and I were hosting a weekly lesbian and gay students' group, and Gambini's counselling load expanded as more queer students surfaced. He noticed a disturbing trend. Despite his support, many of the kids found their school environment so hostile that they were dropping out.

In 1994 he had approached trustee John Campey with the idea of creating an alternative school for queer kids at risk. The school would have lesbian and gay teachers and develop a queer-focused curriculum.

Campey worried that no one would have the stomach to deal with the controversy of establishing such a new school just before a provincial election. Right-wing trustees, who could be expected to oppose such a move, were already emboldened by the expected demise of the NDP government.

So Campey worked behind the scenes. While a new school would require board approval, a new program in an already existing school would not. He approached Oasis Alternative School with the idea of developing a queer-positive satellite program. The school was enthusiastic, and as Oasis staff and Gambini met to iron out the details, Campey went to the director of education to get him onside.

The project was made easier by the fact that a First Nations School had recently been approved and the black community had been demanding a black-focused school for some time. The director took Campey's idea and ran with it, so both a black-focused program, Nighana, and a gay-focused one, Triangle, quietly made their way through the bureaucracy. By the time the right-wing press and homophobic trustees caught on in the spring of 1995, they were too late. Triangle and Nighana were approved. They opened in

September, three months after the provincial election. We got in just under the wire. A few months later the board would face massive cutbacks and its own dissolution. New programs of any kind would no longer be on the agenda.

BACK TO TREATMENT

In a third victory that spring, CATIE received the federal contract for the National AIDS Treatment Information Service in June. Universities in Toronto and Montreal had both failed to make progress, and the feds finally turned to community. Our Community AIDS Treatment Information Exchange became the Canadian AIDS Treatment Information Exchange to offer bilingual treatment information services to physicians and PWAs across the country. Sean Hosein, who had started our little *Treatment AIDS* bulletins six years before as a column in *Rites*, continued as principal researcher.

It was a remarkable transformation. What had begun as a small volunteer committee searching for glimmers of hope and trying to make sense of research had become a major national institution with dozens of employees.

Brian Farlinger finished two years as co-chair in 1994. After the NDP announced the Trillium Drug Program, he focused on treatment issues. He already represented the Canadian AIDS Society on Health Canada's Expert Advisory Committee on HIV Therapies and was chair of the CAS Therapies Committee. He wrote up the results of our 1993 national treatment activist conference in *Confronting the HIV Research Crisis: Treatment Activists' Perceptions of the Canadian Research Effort,* and doggedly demanded that its recommendations be implemented by government, researchers, and pharma. He also challenged discrimination by insurance companies and, with the AIDS Bureau, developed recommendations adopted by the Canadian Life and Health Insurance Association.

AIDS activists were now also in demand for research ethics committees. All research in Canada had to pass an ethical review. Our demand that people with AIDS be at the table, and our growing expertise, meant that AAN! members were increasingly called on to be the community voice. In 1994, Farlinger found himself on the ethics committee evaluating the phase three trial of a new drug, Saquinavir. Property of a Swiss company, Hoffman La Roche, Saquinavir was the first of a new family of anti-HIV drugs called protease inhibitors (PIs). All the previous drugs had attacked HIV at the same point in its life cycle, but PIs blocked the virus in a novel way.

The trial that Roche submitted had no compassionate arm. Once again, desperate PWAs would be forced into research in the hope of getting treatment, something that George Smith had defined as unethical in 1989. After a discussion with other activists, Farlinger refused to give approval, and without unanimous approval the trial could not go forward.[30]

We were never able to ascertain how much pharma talked among themselves, but his position may have been strengthened by another ethics committee that I had been on the year before. This had been a trial of the effect of alcohol on a new HIV saliva test. Participants would submit to the test, and then would drink until they were totally wasted and do the test again. Their before-and-after tests would be compared to see if drunkenness had any effect on the result.

I argued that the first ethical requirement for an HIV test was that the subject must be able to give informed consent, not to mention pre- and post-test counselling. The only reason to know the effect of alcohol was to be able to test people who were drunk, people who were, by definition, unable to give informed consent. Any trial that would pave the way for such unethical use was not ethical.

The researchers were astonished. I think it was the first time anyone had said no, never mind someone from the community. They convened a special meeting with more senior people to ask me to reconsider. In the meantime, I opened the question to a community consultation. There was consensus on my position. Our generation remembered police raids of bars and baths where people were forced to submit to sexually transmitted infection (STI) tests. Were HIV tests now to be added to that list? The other possibility was that people would pick up someone in a bar and demand that they take the test before going home. No one should find out that they were HIV positive when drunk and rejected by a trick. Despite some strong-arm tactics at the special meeting, I dug in my heels. The trial did not proceed.

So Roche knew that Farlinger was not bluffing. He had the power and will to stop the trial. Despite having argued that it would be technically impossible to provide enough of the drug for compassionate use, the pharma giant blinked first. A compassionate arm was added.[31] It was an important precedent and a message to the pharmaco-industrial complex that compassionate access was an indispensable component of clinical trials.

That was probably the third time that activism saved my life. When the Saquinavir trial eventually opened in late 1995, I was one of the first to get the new drug through the compassionate arm, a much-needed boost to my failing regimen.

Farlinger worked tirelessly, but his health was failing. He had been an avid runner, but peripheral neuropathy in his feet made that too painful. Then his sight started to go. He was soon diagnosed with CMV retinitis. In the summer of 1994 when he and I were unexpectedly invited to the International AIDS Conference in Yokohama, he had to arrange to have special seats in order to set up his IV drip on the flight. When we arrived, I began to suspect just how important his family might be. Whether it was that, or just that the Japanese were freaked out by the arrival of two such obvious people with AIDS, we were met at the plane by men in dark suits who spirited us through immigration and customs and put us into taxis to our respective hotels. It was surreal.

One evening shortly after Kalpesh Oza arrived in Toronto in the early 1990s, Richard, he, and I were walking back from an event and were accosted by a young proselytizer for some Christian religious group. I smiled (the guy was cute) and told him he was barking up the wrong tree. We were two atheists and a Hindu. Oza snapped at me that he was every bit as much an atheist as I was.

A microbiologist by training, Oza was one of the few people in AAN! who actually had a scientific background. He was a fierce critic of those whose approach to HIV he felt lacked scientific rigour.

Wearing his poz identity on his sleeve, he had made a name for himself as an activist in Montreal, both with that city's short-lived ACT UP chapter and on the board of the Comité des Personnes Atteintes du VIH du Québec (CPAVIH). When he arrived in Toronto to do AIDS research at the Hospital for Sick Children, he burst into the activist milieu. He was soon a major force in the Alliance for South Asian AIDS Prevention, working with the Canadian HIV Trials Network, an organizer and performer at the Desh Pardesh community arts festival, and on the steering committee and Treatment Access and Research committee at AAN! plus the board of the Canadian AIDS Society.

In late 1994, Kalpesh suddenly took a turn for the worse. Friends in the South Asian community organized a twenty-four-hour care team. He died June 4, 1995. His memorial service was held that summer in front of the AIDS Memorial in Cawthra Park, complete with political speeches, safe sex information, and a community feast of Indian food. His ashes were scattered in Cawthra Park, in Montreal, and in New Delhi.

THE COMMON SENSE REVOLUTION

Three days after Kalpesh's death, the Progressive Conservative party under the leadership of Mike Harris swept to power in the June 8, 1995, provincial election. Harris's platform, the Common Sense Revolution, was a mix of neo-liberal tax cuts and slashing of government services, gift-wrapped in thinly disguised racist, anti-immigrant, anti-poor, and homophobic populism. The NDP and Liberal vote collapsed. Both Bob Rae and Lynn McLeod resigned their party leaderships shortly afterwards. It would be hard to imagine a more dramatic reversal in provincial politics.

If anyone expected Mike Harris's government to return to old-fashioned patrician Tory rule, they were deeply mistaken. Harris assembled a coalition similar to Reagan's in the 1980s: big-city finance capital allied with small-town social conservatives. But unlike Reagan, he was not tentatively beginning a process of displacing an entrenched Keynesian elite. He had power and a blueprint, and was determined to play catch-up with the neo-liberal reforms that had transformed other jurisdictions. His was to be a revolution.

At Toronto Pride a few weeks later, behind the open convertible carrying Jim Egan and Jack Nesbit, thousands of marchers carried AIDS ACTION NOW! placards. Rather than march as a group, we had decided to distribute our signage to everyone who would take them in all the contingents. The uptake was good. We were still riding high from the Trillium victory. As a result, the march looked like one massive AAN! demo. In the face of the new, more hostile provincial government, we wanted to put the Tories on notice that AIDS could not be forgotten nor our achievements dismantled.

Brian Farlinger was too ill to help out at Pride that year. But Richard drove over to his place in the afternoon and brought him down to see the parade. The rest of us were all consumed with applying temporary AAN! logo tattoos on different parts of people's anatomy, and by the time Brian and Richard got there, we were distributing our thousands of placards to the marchers. I didn't get to see him. It was one of those hot, humid Toronto summer afternoons and he wasn't up to staying long. He was almost blind by that point, but Richard said he seemed to enjoy himself. Brian died the next day.

HALCO

Alan Cornwall and his partner, Charles Roy, hosted a party at their home later that Pride Day afternoon. Alan was so ill that he had to stay in bed with an oxygen mask. We took turns going upstairs to visit him.

Alan was a long-standing member of the AAN! steering committee. A lawyer with a corporate background, he had been instrumental in making sure CATIE was on a sound legal basis before it took on the federal contract. He and Mark Freamo also took the lead in the establishment of what became the HIV and AIDS Legal Clinic of Ontario (HALCO). By the early 1990s we realized that more and more PWAs were not just dealing with difficulties accessing drugs. Income security, housing, discrimination, employment, immigration, insurance, wills, and criminal matters were all compounded by illness. Although many of these were systemic, they demanded immediate individual resolution.

Assistance for such issues was fragmented, and none of the existing legal clinics had expertise in AIDS. Alan and Mark realized the need for a new legal service. The first meetings to set up HALCO were held in Alan's home, and he became co-chair when the clinic first opened its doors in 1991 as a project of the Advocacy Resource Centre for the Handicapped (ARCH), a legal clinic specializing in disability law.

Alan died a few weeks after the party, July 25, 1995. He was thirty-four. HALCO began operating as a standalone legal clinic five months later that December.

The same July 25, just over a month from taking office, Harris announced a minibudget, slashing almost two billion dollars of provincial spending. The poor were first in his sights, with a 21 per cent cut to social assistance benefits. Rae had mulled about making food banks unnecessary. Harris turned them into a growth industry. Youth welfare was restricted, with serious impact on young lesbians and gay men thrown out of their homes. The spouse-in-the-house regulation cutting single mothers off welfare if they lived with a man was reinstated. Ironically, though, because of the defeat of the NDP same-sex partner legislation, the new rules still couldn't be used against lesbian or gay couples.

The Ministry of Health's program to co-ordinate long-term care services was disbanded. In August the Workplace Health and Safety Agency was axed. Along with it went the workplace accident prevention program and mandatory inquests when workers were killed on the job. The wage protection fund was cut back and slated for termination. In October almost four hundred co-op and non-profit housing projects were cancelled, exacerbating Toronto's housing crisis and forcing up rents. Twenty-five halfway houses were closed. NDP labour law reforms were repealed to facilitate strike breaking and discourage union organizing. Ministry of Labour staff was cut in half.

Pinochet's terror in Chile in 1973 had been the first great experiment at installing a neo-liberal economy. The method, as Naomi Klein called it, was the "shock doctrine." Come down hard everywhere at once, and when people are too stunned or too afraid to react, impose your will. Harris was democratically elected, and did not unleash a wave of murder and torture. But the strategy of hitting everywhere at once was the same.

Just how ruthless he could be was revealed less than a month after the election when a group of First Nations protesters occupied part of the Ipperwash Provincial Park. The park lands had been seized from the Stoney Point Band under the War Measures Act in 1942, when the federal government decided it wanted the land, including a burial ground, for a military camp. Despite promises, the land was never returned.

On September 4, thirty-five protesters from the reserve moved into the park. The Ontario Provincial Police responded. A newly elected Progressive Conservative member served as intermediary between the police and the premier. The government pressed the police to remove the occupiers as soon as possible. Harris was quoted by the attorney general as saying, "I want those fucking Indians out of my park." On September 6, after a confrontation, police opened fire on the protesters, hitting Dudley George and wounding two others. George died shortly afterwards.[32]

In November, an additional $3.5 billion in cuts was announced, including an almost 20 per cent cut in hospital budgets over three years. Grants to school boards and universities were slashed by a billion dollars, and child care subsidies were eliminated. Ontario Welcome House, the internationally acclaimed one-stop service centre for new immigrants to Toronto, was closed. The Anti-racism Secretariat was eliminated and the Employment Equity Act repealed. Although those did not involve big money, they were a nod to the racist and anti-immigrant currents of Harris's coalition.

Municipal grants were cut by almost 50 per cent over two years, transportation grants by 21 per cent. Libraries lost twelve million dollars. Recycling program funding was eliminated. Conservation authorities were cut by 70 per cent. Public broadcasters, art galleries, and museums lost 28 per cent of funding. Environmental and Freedom of Information laws were gutted.

In December, the government announced further cuts to 1995 spending levels that would total $8.2 billion. Finally, plans were announced to amalgamate the notoriously left-leaning City of Toronto with the five surrounding more conservative municipalities to create one "megacity." That would also mean the end of the Toronto Board of Education, where I worked, and potentially, all its progressive policies.[33]

All this in order to balance the budget in a time of recession and simultaneously deliver a 30 per cent tax cut to benefit large corporations.

There was immediate resistance: strikes, demonstrations, petitions, public statements, sit-ins in the legislature. A union/community group coalition organized a series of massive Days of Action. But because of the overwhelming nature of the assault, efforts were fragmented. Short of a general strike that would make the province ungovernable, the new government was implacable. It had the votes in the legislature and nothing would stand in its way.

In the midst of this mayhem, two pieces of infrastructure remained unscathed – the AIDS Bureau and the new Trillium program. AAN! organized a demonstration on World AIDS Day, December 1, 1995, to protest the cuts to social services. We figured it was just a matter of time before we would be protesting the axe falling on those two NDP-associated programs. But to everyone's surprise, it didn't. We later figured out why. It was Brian Farlinger's last contribution from the grave.

Until he retired in 1993, William Farlinger was chair and chief executive officer of the Canadian branch of Ernst and Young, the third-largest professional services firm in the world and one of the "big four" international accounting firms. He was a personal friend of Mike Harris and a major link between the Progressive Conservative party and Bay Street capital. When Harris took power, Farlinger was immediately appointed chair of the transition team. Some called him the brains behind the Common Sense Revolution. He was certainly a trusted and influential adviser. When his transition team duties were over, Harris appointed him chair of Ontario Hydro, the provincially owned electrical utility – one of the largest fully integrated electricity corporations on the continent.

William Farlinger was Brian Farlinger's father.

Frank McGee at the AIDS Bureau confirmed the connection years later.

It came to us through different sources that Farlinger, the father, had spoken to Harris and said, "Do not touch HIV." That was because of his son, Brian. It sounds almost mythic and not real, but it really happened. In the first briefing that we had with the new Conservative minister of health, Jim Wilson, he came into the room and literally said, "Well, here's the special people that I'm not supposed to touch."[34]

I tend to think of history as the result of social processes, the cumulative decisions of millions of people responding to their understanding of their interests and values. But occasionally things hinge on singularities. People with AIDS were certainly hugely disadvantaged by the Harris cuts, and the province's public health effort was seriously compromised. But the two key programs that AAN! had won survived, in no small part because William Farlinger's son had died of AIDS.

REMMINGTON'S

In February 1996 police raided Remmington's, a gay men's strip club on Yonge Street. They charged nineteen staff, dancers, and customers with bawdy house and other indecency charges. The pretext was the club's Monday Night Sperm Attack, where dancers ejaculated on stage. It appeared that police saw the Harris government as a green light to renew their attacks on the community.

Other than a short-lived attempt at a new coalition against the bawdy house laws between the gay National Leather Association and the sex workers' group, Maggies, there was little public mobilization. After a series of meetings with police brass, Councillor Kyle Rae and Bob Gallagher, assistant to Councillor Olivia Chow, urged calm. They assured the community that this was not a return of the bad old days of the bath raids.

"I think . . . there have been some very encouraging sounds coming from the police. It's clear a lot of senior people in the department are leery about backing this kind of operation," Gallagher told the *Globe*.[35]

In a sense he was correct. The Remmington's raid did not lead to a return to the bad old days of bath raids. The integration of out gay men at city hall and our newfound political influence in the system sent a message to police brass that at least some of us should no longer be considered part of a quasi-criminal class. Although Rae and Gallagher, as old activists, still spoke the language of community unity, the police would increasingly restrict their repression to what they considered especially unsavoury expressions of our desire. It was all a matter of where the line would be drawn.

But neither were things as good as Rae and Gallagher hoped. Despite assurances, it wasn't until three years later that charges were dropped against the dancers and customers. Remmington's management was ultimately found guilty in 1999 of permitting an indecent performance and keeping a bawdy house.

AAN!'s provincial efforts were soon reduced to largely ineffectual protests against the Harris onslaught, until a new federal issue emerged to take our attention.

The National AIDS Strategy provided a secure package of funding and co-ordination for prevention efforts, education, research, and community services. Despite its shortcomings, it had been considered one of AAN!'s significant victories in 1990. It had been renewed once in 1993, and was now up for renewal again. The scuttlebutt was that Chrétien's Liberal government intended to let it lapse and move to a "population health strategy," focusing on demographic groups rather than specific diseases. Small AIDS organizations would have to compete with large, well-funded lobbies for funds and attention. There was a consensus in the broader AIDS movement that renewing the AIDS strategy had to be a priority.

We also had an important window of opportunity. The International AIDS Conference was scheduled for Vancouver in July. The eyes of the world would be on Canada. It would be our opportunity to hold the Liberals to account.

In January, we organized a press conference with the new Canadian Treatment Network and the Canadian Association for HIV Research to draw attention to the fact that the strategy was running out of time. Research money was already finishing. In mid-March, we distributed fifteen thousand postcards to be sent to the prime minister calling for renewal. At the end of the month, I took on a campaign to raise money to print a full-page ad in *The Globe and Mail*, still the country's major national newspaper.

It was the third time I had co-ordinated such an effort. The first was to call for dropping the appeal against *The Body Politic* in 1980. The second was for the repeal of the bawdy house laws for the RTPC in 1982. This time, however, everything had to be done in four months – and the cost of an ad had doubled since the 1980s.

We used the same template. I assembled a team not involved in AAN!'s day-to-day work. We developed a concise statement for supporters to sign, and had it approved by the AAN! steering committee. Well-known figures representing key interest groups were identified and engaged, and when the material was ready, we used the mailing lists of sympathetic groups to reach out to their members. We had a network of AIDS service organizations across the country whose funding was in jeopardy. They were motivated to gather signatures and money in their respective regions.

In April, David Dingwall, the minister of health, came to Toronto to launch a stamp issued by Canada Post in honour of the upcoming AIDS conference. When he made his announcement at the 519, we staged a noisy demonstration pointing out that no one had asked for a stamp; we wanted a national AIDS strategy. His photo op stolen, Dingwall, who had a notoriously bad temper, was furious. At a hastily arranged meeting at CATIE that afternoon, his language was most unparliamentarily. He threatened that if we ever "blind-sided" him again, we would pay. As politely as possible, we explained that if he had been blindsided, he should fire his aides, since we had been calling for the renewal of the strategy for months. The conference was coming up, and the government had a choice: the prime minister could appear and announce the renewal of the strategy or the government could face embarrassment in front of the world media.

Dingwall didn't like deadlines. He said he was looking at the file but not to expect anything by July. We reiterated our position. After the conference, we had no leverage.

By the beginning of June, we were down to the wire and still short of money for the full-page ad. Then an ethical dilemma presented itself: a pharmaceutical company offered to pitch in several thousand dollars. AAN! had a policy of not accepting pharma money. Desperate, I argued at the steering committee that this wasn't accepting money for, or compromising, the organization. The company was showing support for a position statement we had already arrived at. Their money had no influence on our policy. And besides, the ad was a project. The organization itself would not be accepting pharma money. The argument carried the day, but people were still worried about the optics. In the end, however, the company didn't want to risk a public stand that might upset the government and gave us the money anonymously.

Throughout June we tried to keep up the pressure, lobbying local members of Parliament. At Pride, June 30, our banner called for renewal of the strategy and we distributed thousands of placards to demonstrate community support. But there was still no movement from the feds, and Chrétien confirmed he wasn't going to attend the conference. We knew that political action was a dead end with the provincial Tory government. Perhaps the Liberals in Ottawa had become similarly insensible.

SOUTH AFRICA – A CONSTITUTION

As apartheid crumbled, the ANC set up a group to draft a post-apartheid constitution for a new, democratic South Africa. Because the ANC was still illegal back home, the working group was based in London. Through his anti-apartheid solidarity work, Peter Tatchell, who had helped provoke the ANC's public statement in support of gay rights in 1987, was in touch with Albie Sachs, a member of the working group. Tatchell raised the issue of including a ban on discrimination based on sexual orientation. Sachs was sceptical, but after studying several European anti-discrimination statutes, he warmed to the idea. In December 1989, Tatchell brokered a meeting in London between Sachs and a rep from the Cape Town group, the Organization of Lesbian and Gay Activists.

Back in South Africa, both OLGA and Simon Nkoli's Johannesburg group, GLOW, had already participated in the Conference for a Democratic Future on December 9. With two thousand organizations represented, it was the largest assembly of democratic and community organizations since 1955, before the ANC was banned. Nkoli wrote me to express his excitement.

> Last Saturday, GLOW and OLGA were part of the Conference for a Democratic Future. We really felt that there is a real change and acknowledgment of our existence within our community. It is the first time in our history in South Africa that Gay and Lesbian organizations received a formal invitation to a conference where the future of our country is being discussed.[36]

The ANC was unbanned early in 1990, and meetings with lesbian and gay groups were able to continue inside the country. In September that year, OLGA, with the support of eleven other lesbian and gay organizations, made an official submission to the ANC's Constitutional Committee and began lobbying other anti-apartheid organizations such as the United Democratic Front. As a result, the ANC included sexual orientation in its draft constitutional proposals later that year. That wording was included in the interim constitution of 1994, and finally in the permanent constitution approved by the South African parliament on May 8, 1996. The only party to vote against the constitution was the small African Christian Democratic Party.[37]

Nkoli and his comrades in South Africa and the international solidarity movement around the world had established horizontal alliances with other oppressed groups in the anti-apartheid movement. Those alliances were transformed into a vertical alliance when the ANC took power after the fall of apartheid. In Toronto, in 1989, Nkoli had asked how we would answer the question Where were you? after apartheid fell. The answer he and his comrades were able to give was, We were there with you. The constitution responded, Now we are here with you. South Africa was the first country in the world to specifically prohibit discrimination on the basis of sexual orientation in its constitution.

Ironically, although the constitution protected individual rights, it abandoned the social rights to the country's wealth envisaged in the anti-apartheid movement's foundational document, *The Freedom Charter*.

> The national wealth of our country, the heritage of South Africans, shall be restored to the people; The mineral wealth beneath the soil, the banks and monopoly industry shall be transferred to the ownership of the people as a whole; all other industry and trade shall be controlled to assist the wellbeing of the people. . . . Restrictions of land ownership on a racial basis shall be ended, and all the land re-divided amongst those who work it to banish famine and land hunger.[38]

As the ANC negotiated the dismantling of apartheid, Thabo Mbeki, who led the group's commitment to gay rights in 1987, applied the same liberal principles to the economy. In 1995, Mbeki, as deputy prime minister, committed the country to privatization of state-owned enterprises. In the midst of a run on the country's currency, in 1996, as the constitution was being ratified and under pressure from the International Monetary Fund, the ANC committed the country to more cuts to government expenditures, privatization, and deregulation, in order to attract international investors. Such policies increased poverty among the black majority. With one hand, neo-liberalism offered individual rights; with the other, it took away most people's ability to enjoy them.

ONE WORLD, ONE HOPE

As delegates arrived for the Vancouver International AIDS Conference on June 6, 1996, our ad appeared in the national edition of *The Globe and Mail*. Its headline: "Prime Minister Chrétien: Don't Give Up on AIDS." The message was surrounded by a wall of individual names in fine print calling for the renewal of the National AIDS Strategy. As well as the range of AIDS service organizations across the country, a solid array of mainstream groups signed, including the Canadian Labour Congress, the National Action Committee on the Status of Women, the Wellesley Central Hospital, and the Toronto Department of Public Health.

The opening was held in Vancouver's cavernous GM Place Sunday evening. Chrétien's absence was resounding. A hapless David Dingwall was sent in his stead. Conference organizers had already publicly excoriated Chrétien for his absence, and British Columbia's NDP premier Glen Clark received a huge ovation from fifteen thousand delegates when he twisted the knife, telling us *he* wouldn't miss this conference for the world.

A broader coalition, Wake Up Canada, had formed to demand renewal of the strategy. As well as service organizations, it included key researchers and several conference organizers, so there was lots of help on the inside. Banks of seats directly in front of the stage were reserved for PWAs and AIDS activists. We distributed thousands of flyers to delegates headlined "Canada has turned its back on us, now we'll turn our back on Canada." When, as the last speaker of the evening, a visibly nervous Dingwall took the stage, we all stood up on our seats and turned our backs, chanting "shame." Thousands of delegates did the same. Dingwall was so flummoxed that when, as part of his speech, he tried to say the word "tragedy," it came out "strategy." The crowd howled in laughter. He managed to finish and left the stage humiliated amid waves of boos and chants of "Where's Chrétien?"

He had been warned.

Dingwall left the conference early a few days later, complaining of the flu. At the closing ceremony, an activist in a wheelchair rolled on stage to present organizers with a bouquet of flowers from Canadian PWAs to send on to him, telling the crowd, "We know how it feels to be under the weather, and hope he feels better soon."[39]

The Liberals turned what could have been a moment of leadership in the international limelight into a debacle. The government feebly announced that discussions about the renewal of the strategy would begin in September, and Dingwall scheduled several meetings with Wake Up Canada reps. It took continuing pressure over the rest of the year, including demonstrations at a meeting of provincial and federal health ministers and at Liberal fundraisers, phone lobbying, and finally the interruption of one of Chrétien's first speeches of the 1997 election campaign by AAN! activists Maggie Atkinson and Louise Binder, before the Liberals announced the extension of the National AIDS Strategy. It was a stark reminder that polite lobbying without public pressure was impotent, a validation of George Smith's documents and demos maxim.

The big conference news was the trial results of the new protease inhibitors, including Saquinavir, the drug that I had recently started. Everyone was talking about the "Lazarus effect" of combination therapy. For the first time, there seemed to be hope.

Darien Taylor and I walked away from the stadium after the closing ceremonies, exhausted after almost a week of early morning sessions and late-night activist meetings. After a silence, she turned to me and said, "I know it could just be more hype, but it's really hard not to feel that this whole thing may be over. Do you think I'm crazy?"

If protease inhibitors might have emerged as our "One Hope," the other half of the conference slogan, "One World," was still a cruel joke. Vancouver had also exposed the extent of the growing devastation of the epidemic in the developing world. Millions were infected and dying without access to even the most basic health care, never mind hugely expensive protease inhibitors. I heard the words of my hustler buddy from Montreal in 1989 echoing from the grave: AIDS is a lens that magnifies society's problems.

THE LEGAL ROUTE

The experiences with the National AIDS Strategy and the South African constitution indicated the continuing viability of politics as a route for social change. But in Canada, the fight for gay rights was now essentially being channelled through the courts, and it focused on relationship recognition.

A major influence promoting the legal strategy was a combination of the Charter and the Court Challenges Program. The program had evolved out of federal support for minority-language cases in the late 1970s and had been expanded to facilitate civil society groups' attempts to clarify the impact of the Charter on a range of discrimination issues. It provided resources for groups such as EGALE that engaged in legal challenges to promote lesbian and gay rights. The availability of such resources helped channel social protest through the courts and ensured that it stayed within the parameters of "equal rights."

Secondly, the union movement had become a major ally in the fight for gay rights. Traditionally, unions dealt with complaints of discrimination through grievance procedures; if that was unsuccessful, they had the resources to proceed upward through the legal system. Benefits to workers and their families were also familiar to the union environment, so fighting for same-sex spousal recognition in the courts became a logical part of the agenda.

The lawyers representing these cases – Charles Campbell, David Corbett, Doug Elliott, Cynthia Petersen, and Susan Ursell, to name only a few – had a commitment to social justice and often worked long hours for free. Most were community members. But the parameters of their arguments were bounded by the logic of the courts. They could argue for equal benefits, but they could not argue for a different kind of benefits regime to overcome pervasive social inequality. In terms of immediately improving the lives of particular groups and ensuring they received the same benefits as their peers, it was hard to dispute the logic of litigation and the demand for equality.

Like any course of action, progress had unforeseen consequences. Our politics were now shaped by what was legally possible. Lawyers worked to achieve benefits for clients that would hopefully be generalized to others. But for those not in a similar situation, without benefits to share, or whose relationships were not sufficiently similar to straight ones to benefit from equality, progress remained little more than symbolic. We were winning by the rules of the game, but for many people the game was rigged.

Old liberationists like Chris Bearchell were far from happy with the legal turn.

> It seems to me that there is this belief that a chore can be assigned to a group of appropriate professionals who can go off and navigate the waters of the judicial system and come up with solutions that don't involve either the masses of the population of lesbians and gay men or attempting to influence the social attitude(s) of the world around us. . . . [It] assumes that there is a kind of expertise that you can buy or that might be donated . . . that can be applied to solve your political problems without having to get into the messy business of grassroots and mass democracy and public actions.[40]

The shift to the courts was a vertical address to the judiciary, whose decisions were shaped by the liberal logic of the Charter. But the strategy left some people behind. It could also feed resentment that a powerful gay minority, thanks to its access to a cabal of judges, was imposing its values on society against the will of the people.

PART IV

Model Minority

11

Courtship

ELLEN COMES OUT

On April 30, 1997, like millions of others across North America, I was glued to the TV. Ellen was about to come out.

Ellen was a prime-time sitcom starring Ellen DeGeneres. She played Ellen Morgan, an awkward bookstore owner who would babble uncontrollably when nervous, which was often. It was an open secret that DeGeneres was lesbian, but in mid-1996 she began dropping hints about coming out in real life and on the show. On April 14, 1997, the front cover of *Time* featured her picture and the headline "Yep I'm Gay." At the end of the month, she talked about coming out on *The Oprah Winfrey Show,* and later that evening, in a very funny episode, so did her character on *Ellen.*

It was a watershed moment. Oprah got hate mail. The American Family Association tried to pressure ABC not to run the episode. J.C. Penney and Chrysler refused to buy advertising time, and Wendy's dropped the show altogether. Jerry Falwell called her Ellen Degenerate, and an Alabama ABC affiliate refused to broadcast the episode. But thousands of Ellen Coming Out House Party Kits were distributed across the United States, and after weeks of media frenzy, more than 42 million viewers tuned in. The episode won an Emmy, and was described as "the most hyped, anticipated and influential gay moment on television."[1]

It was a first for a lead character on prime-time TV. As the storyline continued, Ellen came out to parents, friends, and at work, and discovered the quirks of the lesbian and gay community. The program was a primer about the life of the new white gay middle class in the United States and opened the way for similar characters on network television. We lapped it up. If only real life were so rosy.

SYSTEMS FAILURE

Less than a month later, in May 1997, a report issued by CLGRO was ample evidence that real life was not a sitcom. *Systems Failure* was the result of five years' work by CLGRO's Project Affirmation, funded by a $350,000 grant from Health Canada. The report analyzed problems in accessing health care by LGBT individuals across Ontario.

When the project was announced in 1992, AAN! grumbled, fearing it would draw attention away from AIDS. *Systems Failure* did not ignore AIDS, but it identified a range of other pressing health issues. Most remarkable was the attention to issues facing transsexuals. A report specifically on transsexual issues, *Access Denied*, authored by Ki Namaste, had been released in July 1995 as part of the project. The chapter in *Systems Failure*, drawn from that report, identified problems in access to hormones, contemptuous treatment in hospitals and emergency rooms, difficulty in accessing the homeless shelter system, and lack of alcohol and drug abuse support. It discussed restrictive policies at the Clarke Institute Gender Identity Clinic, the only provincial body authorized to approve sex reassignment surgery (SRS). For example, the Clarke – later renamed the Centre for Addiction and Mental Health (CAMH) – refused to approve SRS for sex workers.

Systems Failure was foundational for future programs and a trans rights struggle. It also illustrated a new relationship with the state that had emerged out of the AIDS epidemic. For the first time, authorities were taking the health of LGBT communities seriously. For a group like CLGRO, which had lived hand to mouth since 1975, the grant constituted unprecedented recognition.

INSIDE OUT

In 1995 the Inside Out lesbian and gay film festival had begun the shift to institutionalization, opening an office and hiring an executive director. In 1997, Elle Flanders, the festival's second director, moved the screenings from the Euclid to the Cumberland, a major multiscreen cinema. Flanders also dived into an American-style funding model based on private donors and sponsors. That brought in its wake galas and trendy parties. Inside Out had learned the vulnerability that came from public funding in 1993 when Toronto pulled a four-thousand-dollar grant because the word "fuck" was in the program. As well, as the state reduced its support for the arts, arts councils were explicitly calling on organizations to diversify funding.

There was some grumbling about the festival leaving its community roots behind, but with a more accessible location, increased audiences, and a continuing commitment to young, diverse, and local filmmakers, it was hard to argue with success.

REAL LIFE

In the summer, the board of education regularly laid off clerical staff, custodians, and student support workers like me. We went on unemployment insurance for two months and waited to be recalled in September. It was a way for the board to subsidize its wage bill by shifting it to another part of the state.

We received about 60 per cent of our regular wages after a two-week waiting period. Technically, we were supposed to be looking for work, but there wasn't much point, since our regular jobs started again in two months. It had always been painless – some forms to fill out, reports every two weeks, and cheques would come in the mail.

By the mid-1990s things had changed. To start, we had to go to a site in the far north of the city to learn about our "rights and responsibilities." That year, a middle-aged man came in and yelled at the thirty of us in the room. He told us that not actively looking for work constituted fraud. They would be checking up to make sure than no one was taking a vacation. As well as the regular forms, we would be required to submit lists of twenty employers a week that we had approached and that had turned us down. If anyone's list was short they would be cut off. The abuse continued for twenty minutes or so. An older man with a heavy Italian accent put up his hand and said he didn't understand. Our "counsellor" turned on him. He said he didn't care if he understood or not. It didn't matter. He had to sit there and listen. After another ten minutes of lecturing, without asking for questions, he closed his notebook and walked out. Some applicants were close to tears.

I played the game that year, but it was the last time I bothered. Benefits had been reduced to about half our wages and, for me, pretending I was looking for work when I had a full-time job waiting for me in a few weeks wasn't worth the trouble. I had no dependants and Richard was working. I could manage. But many of my colleagues, especially secretarial staff, didn't have that kind of choice. Even at half wages, they needed the money to support themselves and their families over the summer. I imagined this scenario playing itself out in thousands of places. This was what neo-liberal reforms felt like in real life.

And it worked. Between those who were disqualified, those who were discouraged from applying, and the lower benefit rates, the employment insurance system started turning a profit for the federal government. There was a difference between the Ontario provincial government under Harris's Tories and the federal government under Chrétien's Liberals. While Harris applied the shock doctrine, Chrétien preferred the slow death of a thousand small cuts.

By the mid-1990s more than 46 per cent of people in Metropolitan Toronto were living in below-average income areas, up from 19 per cent in 1970. The new poverty was increasingly racialized. In the 1996 census, the family poverty rate for non-European groups in Toronto was 34.3 per cent, more than twice that for European immigrants and the Canadian born.[2] And as the *Three Cities in Toronto* report showed, immigrant groups increasingly lived in an outer suburban ring around a wealthier central core.[3]

This affected the gay village. As condos proliferated and inner-city rents climbed, village residents became older, wealthier, and whiter. There was more friction between residents and those who played there. The city's politics would be shaped by the resentments and fears generated by disparity.

MEGACITY

No one wanted the "megacity." At the end of 1996 the Conservatives introduced Bill 103, the City of Toronto Act, and Bill 104, the Fewer School Boards Act. The bills would amalgamate the six cities that made up Metropolitan Toronto and their six local school boards would become the Toronto District School Board (TDSB).

The pretext was cost-cutting, despite studies of other amalgamations showing higher costs and less responsive services. The real reason was to wipe out the old city of Toronto, a traditional NDP stronghold, by merging it with more conservative suburbs. Citizens for Local Democracy organized a huge demonstration that closed down Yonge Street in February 1997. A municipally conducted referendum on March 3 found 75 per cent of voters opposed amalgamation. Harris was unmoved. Both bills passed in April, and amalgamation was scheduled for January 1, 1998.

Elections for the new council were held in the fall of 1997. The new Toronto mayor was former North York mayor Mel Lastman, who defeated former Toronto mayor Barbara Hall thanks to his strong support in the suburbs. As mayor of North York in 1978, Lastman had mused publicly about awarding Anita Bryant a medal for her "crusade against homosexual activists." While Kyle Rae was re-elected in the old city of Toronto along with most of the progressive downtown councillors, they were now heavily outnumbered by conservatives on the far larger council. The vertical connections that the gay community had built with the city over a decade no longer held sway. Rae was determined to rebuild them.

SOLIDARITY AND PRIDE

As a result of the 1994 convention resolutions, the first Canadian Labour Congress Solidarity and Pride Conference was organized in Ottawa in October 1997. Three hundred delegates attended. When CLC vice-president Nancy Riche welcomed lesbian and gay delegates, there was a five-minute standing ovation. "People were crying for what that statement meant to them," remembered Sue Genge, one of the conference organizers. "Even I was crying. They were so relieved that they could be gay and lesbian and out in their unions."[4]

Many of the delegates were not actually out. They had taken holiday time and covered their own costs. Nearly a third were not comfortable being in the video of the conference deliberations. Homophobia was still an issue in the workplace.

But there was little time for catch-up. A new issue was raised. Gail Owen from the Public Service Alliance of Canada came out as trans and argued forcefully that the union movement had to take up trans issues as well. Her intervention led to consultations across the country and the 2001 publication of *Trans Issues for the Labour Movement*.

When AAN! celebrated its tenth anniversary in February 1998, the event filled the auditorium of the downtown YMCA. We premiered *Demanding a Cure*, a new documentary by Pam Davenport-Earle, Brian Farlinger's sister. The film, about Farlinger's activism and the last years of his life, included footage of our actions at the International AIDS Conference in Vancouver. One person fainted during the scene where gancylovir is injected directly into Farlinger's eyeball to stave off his growing blindness.

The AIDS Memorial that Michael Lynch had started for Pride in 1988 was transformed into a permanent structure in 1993. Made up of a gentle arc of concrete pillars shaded by trees on a knoll adjacent to 519 Church Street, each pillar displays stainless steel plaques engraved with the names of individuals who died that year. The plaques for 1995 list 288 names. For 1996, when some of us were able to get protease inhibitors as part of the compassionate release arm of the trial, there are 198. For 1997 the number drops to 76, and there are 46 names on the plaques for 1998. The dying was coming to an end.

The effectiveness of the new treatments produced a subtle power shift between people living with HIV and the medical establishment. In the early days we joked that most of us knew more about AIDS than our doctors. But as the science around HIV developed, it became harder to keep on top of it. The old "doctor knows best" relationship gradually reasserted itself.

And as the brutality of the crisis waned, so did activism. One no longer saw emaciated men with Kaposi's hobbling down Church Street. A new generation emerged for whom AIDS was just another fact of life. Authority figures warned about it, but there was no visceral impact. As well, so many of us had died. Of the HIV positive members in the original group that met at Michael Lynch's house in 1987, by 1998, I was the only survivor. And for survivors, after more than a decade of crisis, the desire to forget the horror and reconstruct a normal life was hard to resist. That fall, Maggie Atkinson, who had already served as AAN! co-chair from 1995 to 1997, was re-elected for an unprecedented third term. There were no longer new faces around the table.

The tsunami that had ravaged the community in the 1980s and early '90s had passed, leaving behind professionalized agencies whose job it was to clean up the debris. But AIDS was now swamping other people in other places. In February, I received a letter from Simon Nkoli.

> I have given up my combination therapy for a while for the AZT and ddI brought some terrible side-effects. My liver became swollen and I developed yellow jaundice. I became sick and my doctor had to put me off this therapy. The doctors have managed to get my liver to normal and I will be starting with my treatment soon. . . . Personally I am very lucky because a good Samaritan from England is paying my medication which is about R 4,500 a month. I don't know what would I do without his help.[5]

I wrote back immediately to tell him about the wonders of the new drugs and that we needed to get him access. I didn't hear back. Nine months later, on November 20, 1998, Simon was dead.

For anyone in the developing world, AIDS was just as much a death sentence as it had been for us in 1987. Before he died, Simon had been considering a hunger strike to protest the lack of access to treatment, and his death sparked others to action. The same week that more than a thousand people attended Simon's funeral, Zackie Achmat and ten others organized the Treatment Action Campaign to fight for drug access in South Africa. Achmat, a long-time ANC and gay activist who was also poz, declared a treatment strike. Although he himself was able to access treatment, he vowed to take nothing until all South Africans had access. TAC would soon be one of the most militant AIDS activist organizations in the world, and it would change the face of AIDS in South Africa.

In Toronto, we were fighting to hold on to what we had won. Part of Harris's strategy to shrink the state and the deficit (which had been exacerbated by tax cuts during a recession) was to download traditionally provincial responsibilities such as public housing and public health onto the new megacity. Without the required resources, municipal politicians would take the heat for program and service cuts. AAN! spent much of January lobbying city councillors to preserve important public health programs.

A second fight was to keep the Wellesley Hospital. Wellesley had become the centre for AIDS care downtown, but the Tories slated it for closure. Its services would be transferred to nearby St. Michael's, a Catholic hospital. When AAN! steering committee member David Kendall died at St. Mike's in 1991, his partner, Mark Freamo, was not allowed to visit since he wasn't "family." The hospital also prohibited condom distribution and wouldn't perform abortions. Despite news conferences, protests, petitions, and lobbying, Wellesley closed on schedule that spring.

If that wasn't enough, AIDS denialists started to organize in the city. A new group, Health AIDS Education Liaison (HEAL), brought U.S. writer Christine Maggiore to Toronto in April 1998. (Maggiore's three-year-old daughter, Eliza, died of PCP in 2005. An autopsy found the child was HIV positive. Maggiore had refused to have her daughter tested or treated. Maggiore herself would die of AIDS-related causes in 2008.)

Maggiore and other "AIDS dissidents" discouraged people from taking treatments and cast doubt on HIV as the cause of AIDS. Although HEAL organizer Carl Strygg claimed the group took no position on HIV and only wanted to provoke dialogue, HEAL's website said it wanted "to reassure people that simply testing HIV-positive is far from being a health problem that needs to be treated."[6]

HEAL was a serious concern to AAN! In 1994, ACT UP San Francisco had been taken over by such dissidents and became a centre of HIV denialism.

The group's behaviour was increasingly bizarre. Several ACT UP SF members were put under restraining orders after attacks on AIDS charities; others were found guilty of making threatening phone calls to journalists and public health officials. At the Vancouver AIDS conference, an ACT UP SF member assaulted other activists.

I went to a HEAL meeting held at the University of Toronto and was alarmed to find several hundred people there. At AAN!'s report back after the 1998 International AIDS Conference in Geneva, HEAL members monopolized the question period until Atkinson refused to recognize them. With our diminishing numbers and open meetings to elect the steering committee, we could have been vulnerable to a San Francisco–style takeover. That fall, we changed our membership form to declare that AAN! membership recognized HIV as the cause of AIDS. The decision was sent out to our list of members. Despite some previous sceptical coverage of HEAL, *Xtra* was appalled by our "loyalty oath,"[7] and Colman Jones predictably denounced the move. It was annoying, but by then we were accustomed to HIV negative people telling poz people what was best for us.

HEAL turned out to be a flash in the pan, though. The efficacy of the new drugs was increasingly evident, and those who refused to take them eventually sickened and died.

T FOR TRANS

Although Pride was still known as Lesbian and Gay Pride, a new acronym was developing. First a *B* was added for bisexual, and then a *T* for transsexual. At the end of 1996 a general meeting moved to replace the odd term "transgenderal" on the papers of incorporation (no one seemed to know where it had come from) with the increasingly popular term "transgender" – LGBTT. The hard feminist line against transgender people had faded away, and other than in places like the Michigan Womyn's Music Festival, trans people were increasingly seen as part of the community.

So it was an affront when Harris's common sense revolutionaries delisted sex reassignment surgery from medical insurance coverage in 1998. Suddenly, surgery and hormone therapy were out of reach for most trans people. It was a vindictive rather than a cost-cutting move. Only a handful of people managed to pass the difficult approval process mandated by the Clarke Institute's Gender Identity Clinic. The total cost of surgeries came to less than $200,000 a year.

The move generated a wave of activism in trans communities. There were protests and letter-writing campaigns. Martine Stonehouse, in the process of transitioning when the change took place, joined with others to lay a human rights complaint. Michelle Josef, who was in a similar position, sued the province for damages. But the Harris government was unmoved. Given the whirlwind of protests around a range of issues, and the slowness of the OHRC process and the courts, this was the least of their worries.

The University of Toronto has a reputation for smug conservatism. Nonetheless, the first gay group in the city was the University of Toronto Homophile Association in 1969. By 1998, U of T had come a long way since Michael Lynch first daringly began introducing gay sexuality topics in his English courses in the mid-1970s, and John Allan Lee began co-ordinating the Gay Academic Union at Scarborough College in 1975. The Homophile Association had morphed into Gays and Lesbians at U of T (GLAUT), and student activists and staff unions had pushed the institution on many questions.

David Rayside initiated the university's first undergraduate course in Sexual Diversity Politics in 1985. A political scientist, Rayside taught at prestigious University College, the "founding college" of the U of T system. A long-time community activist, he had cut his teeth with *TBP* and the RTPC. In 1989 he helped set up a new group to encourage faculty, managers, and staff to get involved in what previously were largely student driven efforts. The Committee on Homophobia attracted a large membership and helped co-ordinate activism, focusing on both awareness programs and policy change.

By the late 1990s, thanks to such activism, the university had an anti-discrimination policy, campus police had been "sensitized" to queer issues, and same-sex benefits programs were the norm. Yet, it still lagged in course offerings on sexuality issues.

Students clamoured to have this gap filled. In 1993, two graduate students, Fadi Abou Rihan and Julia Creet, organized an enthusiastically received conference, Queer Sites. In response, Rayside, by then vice-president of University College, brought together faculty, graduate students, and others. A committee was struck to develop an interdisciplinary undergraduate curriculum on a Women's Studies model. "The only condition," Rayside told them, "was that you have no money."[8] The Harris cutbacks had seriously affected even august institutions like U of T.

But the neo-liberal transformation of the university had already begun. As well as tuition increases, U of T had beefed up private fundraising to make up for declining state support. Rayside's group found out that a "double match" program had been set up for faculty donations. So the faculty began contributing their own money, and with the university doubling their donations, by 1998 there was enough cash to establish the first Sexual Diversity Studies (SDS) undergraduate program. It was a watershed. That same year, a student referendum rejected a proposal for a small increase in fees to fund lesbian and gay programming. The homophobia expressed during the referendum was an embarrassment. The university responded by establishing an Office of LGBTQ Resources and Programs, which would later morph into the Sexual and Gender Diversity Office.

Thanks to student interest and community fundraising, SDS grew quickly over the next decade. Local investment manager Mark S. Bonham made an early donation, allowing expansion at a time when other programs were contracting. An undergraduate major program was established in 2004, and the next year, the Centre for Sexual Diversity Studies was established. Thanks to a million-dollar endowment from the philanthropist, it was christened the Mark S. Bonham Sexual Diversity Studies Centre. Michael Lynch also contributed from beyond the grave. A $100,000 endowment he had left to establish a community-based centre for lesbian and gay studies was transferred to the new centre. Invested endowments earned the centre approximately 4 per cent a year for operating expenses, as long as the economy didn't tank.

About 30 per cent of operating costs and all scholarships were the result of private fundraising. Rayside explains that the strategy "aimed for a broad range in size of donations." The annual campaign was sending out around nine hundred letters by 2012. Although many small donations added up, an important key to success was "a few quite substantial donations." Rayside notes, "We've benefited enormously from having major donors who are hugely impressed by our students ... and give us the freedom to grow.... We've never once had supporters press us to move in directions that we on the academic side didn't want. ... We've been very lucky."

Casey House, Inside Out film festival, and the 519 Church Street Community Centre would all benefit from major donors in the new century. The success of these LGBT institutions in a time of declining state support was largely predicated on the disposable wealth of lesbian and gay members of neo-liberal elites, and the new willingness of those elites to associate themselves with the community.

Many lesbian and gay institutions were in a position to adapt to the neo-liberal world. But other minorities without such elite access were left behind. The idea that lesbians and gay men were a privileged rather than an oppressed group would gain traction.

LASTMAN AT PRIDE

As mayor of the old Toronto, Barbara Hall had always walked in the Pride parade. The theme for the 1998 Pride, Megapride, was chosen the previous September in honour of the impending amalgamation. It raised eyebrows among many activists who were still fighting to block the unpopular move. But now that amalgamation was a *fait accompli* the question was, Would new megacity mayor Mel Lastman come? We were back in the world of the symbolic.

Kyle Rae and councillors Layton and Chow began lobbying the mayor early in the year, but Lastman was scared. People walked around naked. That kind of thing didn't happen in the suburbs. According to Rae, he began consulting his trusted business advisers.

"He was a businessman, so to get him to understand that there was a community, a business community, a queer community that works and thrives in the neighbourhood, I thought that that might be an entree," Rae explains. "So we ended up at the Second Cup. We sat on the steps and . . . explained that this was a community that had worked really hard for identity, equality rights and you are now the mayor and you have to represent this very vibrant part of the city. . . . People were thrilled to see him."

A month later Lastman came to Pride. "He brought all these business-people with him . . . to give him the energy to last through this. . . . He was really thrilled to be on this fire truck. And then this other truck came up beside him. It was . . . the Toronto Bears. They all had their shirts off, they had leather, it was hilarious."[9]

But Lastman thoroughly enjoyed himself, and participated in Pride through his two terms as mayor. According to Doug Kerr, later a co-chair of World Pride's Human Rights Conference: "That Lastman, a suburban somewhat conservative-ish old guy who didn't get our votes, would join the downtown queers in their parade sent a positive message across the city and maybe even the country. . . . I remember thinking that we were turning a corner towards a more inclusive city."[10]

Lastman's willingness to participate paralleled changes that Pride itself was undergoing. A *Globe and Mail* article the day before the big parade was head-lined "Corporate cash rains down on gay parade: No longer a fringe festival, Pride Week becomes a marketer's dream." It noted that 700,000 people would spend over $40 million on restaurants, hotel rooms, shopping excursions, and entertainment. Not one but two major beer companies were sponsors. It went on, "Mr. Lastman knows Pride events fit in perfectly with his economic agenda to both bring tourists to the city and keep Torontonians at home on the weekends."[11] The *Globe* cited a 1996 economic impact study to explain the importance of the festival. Other corporate supporters included pharma com-panies SmithKline Beecham and Abbott Laboratories, Häagen-Dazs ice cream, and Pizza Pizza. Pride was not just a gathering of our tribes, it was developing the pink market.

Amid all this money, community organizations began to be priced out of the action. CLGRO complained that it was unable to participate in the com-munity fair after the cost of table space was raised to $250. Other groups like ACT and the Toronto PWA Foundation resorted to private sponsorship for their booths. At the ACT beer tent, Molson's signage overwhelmed ACT mes-saging. The PWA table was sponsored by Swatch. "All you could see was Swatch watches," complained Darien Taylor. "You couldn't even tell it was for the PWA."[12]

Others, however, tried to distance themselves. For the third year, Pride fea-tured a Dyke March on the Saturday before the main parade. The Dyke March had begun in 1996 as a reaction to male dominance, lack of politics, and increasing corporatization of the main parade.

For the first time in years, Pride made a substantial profit. "The money has got to come from somewhere, and it's not going to come from the tooth fairy," said Pride co-chair David Clarke. It was hard to dispute. The logic of big business did not distinguish between a gay dollar and a straight one, and Pride needed resources to put on a festival. Corporations controlled such resources. Pride, too, was growing and entering the mainstream. Its goals were short-term – putting on the next festival. Forging vertical alliances with business was the solution.

Lastman was not the only one to experience Pride for the first time that year. Susan Gapka presented as male when she ran away from home as a teenager. Like many young people at the time, she quickly fell through the ravaged social safety net and found herself homeless. After several years she managed to get off the streets and into stable housing, and enrolled in the Community Worker Program at George Brown College. Struggling with her gender identity, she began hanging around the Church Street drag scene. That led her to Pride. "It was a tremendous experience," she recalls, "like the biggest drag show ever, thousands of people cheering you on. It was very empowering."[13] The "thousands of people" included friends from school who knew her as a man. The experience accelerated her resolve to transition.

BYE BYE HARRIS?

As the recession eased, the Tories were riding high and Bay Street was happy with their reduction of the provincial deficit. But those hurt by the massive transfer of wealth from the poor to the rich hoped for change. When Harris called an election in the spring of 1999, AAN! spearheaded the AIDS Provincial Election Campaign. It was our first serious attempt to intervene in electoral politics.

Paul McPhee co-ordinated the campaign for AAN!

> I took the results for every provincial riding in Ontario from the 1995 election, and presented who I thought should be supported at the OAN [Ontario AIDS Network] annual conference. We then worked with the OAN member agencies and PHAs [people living with HIV/AIDS] at the conference to choose the most progressive/AIDS-friendly candidates to support. It was also strategic voting. We were looking at candidates who would have the best chance of beating the Tories. Every OAN member organization and PHA was supposed to go back to their riding and actively canvass for the chosen candidate.[14]

The process was far from smooth. Many AIDS service organizations were conditioned to vertical alliances. They were used to ingratiating themselves to those in power, not intervening for change. Also, the effort had to be less than public; as charities, service organizations were prohibited from engaging in partisan politics. McPhee remembers his frustrations.

It was shocking how many people liked their Tory members . . . the [AIDS service organizations] in particular were more interested in the status of their organizations than in the well-being of PHAs, even with all the cutbacks and policies that were detrimental to PHAs. "Oh, but [Minister of Community and Social Services] Janet Ecker is so supportive of our organization." . . . ugh.[15]

The results were disappointing. Although the Harris Conservatives lost seats, they retained a majority in the legislature. The Liberals increased only slightly, despite the labour movement, traditional NDP supporters, having opted for strategic voting and thrown in its lot with the lesser of two evils. The NDP continued to bleed.

So we were facing another five years of Progressive Conservative rule. That September AAN! handed out postcards in a vain attempt to reverse cuts to funding for nutritional supplements for those on public assistance. Such supplements could be a lifesaver for people with HIV. For the Tories, they were a frill.

EQUITY FOR ALL

At the board of education, however, a victory had been won, thanks to the alliances lesbian and gay activists had developed with other marginalized groups.

The Toronto board had developed a range of policies on anti-racism, anti-sexism, anti-homophobia, anti-ableism, and class bias. But most of the suburban boards that were now part of the TDSB had only an anti-racism policy, as required by the province. Without a significant gay voting bloc outside the downtown, suburban trustees and bureaucrats had little interest in dealing with homophobia in the schools. In the fall of 1998, the new board began harmonizing its equity policies. Would the new policy focus narrowly on race or on a broader range of equity issues?

Things didn't get off to a good start. In the task group discussing the policy, old City of Toronto people were in a minority. The majority refused to consider anything but the required anti-racism policy. They knew that other issues would open the door to a discussion of homophobia. Given the Harris government, involvement in anti-homophobia work was not a good career move. The new director of education, Margarite Jackson, previously of North York, certainly did not want to deal with such an explosive issue in an already difficult job. Our efforts to broaden the discussion were blocked. But we Toronto folks knew that with a race-only policy, our other work would disappear. So we stopped playing by the rules.

We had good contacts with AMENO, the Anti-racism Multicultural Educators Network of Ontario, a group that had gone through a long process of integrating different kinds of equity work. Under their auspices, we developed an alternative policy, *Anti-racism and Equity for All*. It closely resembled the one drafted by the official task group, except it included all the issues. When trustees ignored it, we sent out hundreds of copies to administrators and schools through the internal mail system. Jackson was apoplectic about this "unauthorized use of the mail," but the cat was out of the bag. Comparison of the two approaches had begun.

Public consultations were scheduled for January 1999. In December we pulled together a coalition of community groups including the Chinese Canadian National Council, Education Wife Assault, Culturelink, several disability activists, and CLGRO, as well as the Labour Council, university faculty, and teachers from across the system. Kyle Rae spoke out. We arranged for a legal opinion from the Law Union of Ontario and for articles in the *Toronto Star*. Deputations were organized.

Few people were willing to publicly argue a homophobic position. Bureaucrats knew that by doing so, they risked running afoul of the Human Rights Code. So that fell to an small ultraconservative Muslim group calling itself the Toronto District Muslim Educational Assembly, which also opposed music, dancing, sex education, and social activities that involved the "intermingling of the sexes." They soon alienated everyone, no matter their position, and unfortunately also contributed to stereotypes about Muslims, despite support for the inclusive policy by more liberal Muslim voices.

In May 1999, the task group capitulated. To save face, it didn't just adopt *Equity for All* but rather called for the development of four parallel documents: on race and ethnocultural equity, gender, sexual orientation, and socio-economic status. We got them to include disability as well. A new, inclusive equity policy for the country's largest school district was adopted by the Toronto District School Board in June 1999.[16]

THE BENEFITS NOOSE TIGHTENS

Meanwhile, the legal juggernaut rolled on. That year, the federal government agreed to settle with Wilson Hodder and Paul Boulais, making them the first gay men in Canada to receive Canada Pension Plan survivor benefits. Ironically, the most significant case of the year involved a lesbian relationship gone sour. In May 1999, a landmark 8–1 decision of the Supreme Court of Canada in *M. v. H.* overturned the opposite-sex definition of "spouse" in the Ontario Family Law Act that prevented same-sex partners from applying for spousal support after a relationship breakdown. The court ordered the province to amend the act to comply with the Charter within six months.

Premier Harris was in a tight spot. If he did nothing, the opposite-sex parts of the act would be permanently invalid. If he put the whole thing off by invoking the notwithstanding clause allowed him by the Constitution, he would lose control of the issue. If he did what the court told him, his conservative base might revolt. CLGRO got a meeting with the attorney general and began a postcard campaign, urging broad amendments like those lost in the

NDP debacle over Bill 167 five years before. But something queer was happening in the Progressive Conservative party.

Jaime Watt was a gay neo-liberal poster boy, socially liberal, economically conservative. He was widely credited as a key architect of Harris's first election victory with its emphasis on bashing imagined "welfare cheats." Although Watt had his own shady past – a 1985 fraud conviction – his smarts and skill at media manipulation allowed him to rise to the top. In 1999, he was still Harris's communications director.

In an interview with Jonathan Kay in *The Globe and Mail*, Watt described his work inside the party after the 1994 defeat of spousal benefits. "At the time, there were a bunch of us here in Toronto – strategists, lawyers and other professionals – who wanted equality, and we were tired of leaving the issue to the activist left. . . . We started to convince people that this was an issue of Canadian values."[17] Watt was in a position to push his boss. It was a situation that few in the movement could have previously imagined.

Harris finally held his nose and jumped. There were no real financial consequences, so Bay Street was unconcerned, and Conservative small-town Ontario had no place else to go. Still, in a petulant attempt to ensure traditionalist supporters that he was doing this against his will, the bill was called "An Act to amend certain statutes because of the Supreme Court of Canada decision in M. v. H." To further assure homophobes that he was on their side, rather than changing the definition of "spouse," he added a new category, "same sex partner."

That move produced community division. CLGRO supported the bill and pushed for its immediate passage. A rose was a rose by any other name. The bill did the job and gave people the benefits they needed. EGALE, however, was as concerned with the symbolism as with the substance. It condemned the bill as establishing a "separate and unequal" category that sent a message that "same-sex relationships are qualitatively different than opposite sex relationships." EGALE wanted a sex-neutral definition of spouse, "simple equality – nothing more, nothing less." Ultimately, the Supreme Court refused to hear EGALE's challenge to the legislation.

On October 27, 1999, the Ontario Legislative Assembly adopted the act, amending sixty-seven provincial laws to provide same-sex couples with the same statutory rights and responsibilities as applied to opposite-sex common-law spouses. Bob Rae's instinct to put the issue off until the courts laid the groundwork had been right. But he had sadly misjudged how long it would take. In the end, it was the Tories rather than the gay-friendly NDP that could take credit for the legislation.

The only thing left on this trajectory was marriage. EGALE's insistence on the symbolic rather than the practical laid the groundwork for that fight.

Church Street was a depressed area when it first became the focus of the gay village in the 1980s. But as the new century approached, Church was becoming prime real estate. Condominiums were replacing rentals. Small businesses were squeezed by higher rents. Because it was still safer than nearby Yonge Street and gay men were supposedly a softer touch, the village was simultaneously becoming a magnet for panhandlers and homeless youth. A 1999 study by Shout Health Clinic, *Making Money*, estimated that a thousand queer homeless kids were sleeping on the street every night.[18] Widening class disparities became ever more visible in the village.

Xtra printed letters from the more well-to-do complaining about the decline in the neighbourhood. There were calls for intensified policing to keep the area "safe." In the summer of 1999, Kyle Rae initiated a Community Action Policing project. Foot patrol officers became a visible presence and began to demand information from "undesirables" – squeegee kids, panhandlers, sex workers, men having sex in the park at 519 Church. A few years later, even the iconic Steps on Church Street would be demolished to discourage the wrong kind of people from loitering.

The stage was being set for a very different kind of community politics. A more upscale neighbourhood needed to be protected from outsiders.

FROM BIJOU TO PUSSY PALACE

The Bijou opened on Church Street early that year, featuring multiple porn screens, dark rooms, and a slurp ramp to facilitate blowjobs. In June, there were incursions by plainclothes police. Nineteen men were charged with indecency and the bar was served with liquor licence violations. At one point, a Bijou employee was handcuffed and detained after helping patrons escape through a back exit. A newly formed group, the June 13th Committee, warned of impending bath raids. Kyle Rae, on the other hand, declared "there is absolutely no interest on the part of the police to go into the bathhouses."[19]

The Bijou revealed a growing political divide. While *Xtra* rallied the troops with editorials and articles condemning the raids, John Kennedy, editor of *Fab*, a less political bar rag, declined even to characterize the events as raids. He told readers that "we're not above the law," and accused *Xtra* of trying to create a flap in order to sell papers.

After a press conference with the participation of CLGRO, Kyle Rae brokered meetings with the police. Charges against the patrons, but not the business, were dropped. In an interview with *Fab*, Rae broke with the June 13th Committee.

> There are some people who are one-tune activists ... they have only one way in which they think issues can be resolved, and that is by confrontation. ... We're victims again. There's other people who want to get angry and have a demonstration. That's what I used to do in '81 but now we've

had changes to the Ontario Human Rights Code . . . we have a Charter of Rights and Freedoms. The world isn't 1981 anymore, but there's a bunch of dinosaurs who can only react in one way. . . . You've elected me and I'm now at the table making decisions and working with the City, with the police, with the community trying to resolve them.[20]

Brent Hawkes, also in *Fab*, chimed in on a similar note. "Times are changing and we have to change our tactics, change our style to what's more effective today. . . . Be careful that the extremes in our community don't cause people to be paranoid."[21]

There were two entwined issues. The first was whether the community should defend unseemly sexual activity at all, or whether, now that we had been accepted, such activity was an embarrassment. Second, what form should our response take, public mobilization or negotiations through our elected representatives?

Established figures with access to the table, like Rae and Hawkes, were willing to defend sex-focused businesses but insisted that negotiations were the best option. Others, like Kennedy, cut loose slurp ramps from what was considered community. Rae and Hawkes tended to downplay the seriousness of police actions. Activists talked in apocalyptic terms about new bath raids.

Below that political divide was the fault line between affluent residents and the broader community that frequented the village. *Xtra* reported that at a rowdy community meeting on the issue at the 519 on July 22, "One side was chastising police sex raids and demanding that coppers back off. The other pole made a case for more law and order – complaining about dope smokers, loud music, public sex and people dancing in the street."[22] One man recounted that he had difficulty getting to the new bathhouse on Carlton because of all the prostitutes and johns, and said he just wanted the cops to stay away from queers.

Although Rae tried to separate sexual activity in bars and baths that didn't affect residents from street activity that did, in practice, police were not making such a distinction. While there were no immediate bath raids, police pressure closed several back rooms in bars, and charges of permitting disorderly conduct were laid against The Barn for hosting "naked night" parties for Totally Naked Toronto Men (TNT Men).

Rae was object of an anonymous poster campaign. "Resident associations vote more often then [*sic*] squeegee kids. . . . Wealthy condo owners vote more often then [*sic*] club fags. Just ask Kyle."[23] He was accused of trying to drive the homeless out the neighbourhood, blocking a new dance club, and supporting police campaigns against backrooms and park sex. Rae called the posters cowardly, cited zoning bylaws, and reminded *Xtra* readers that park sex was illegal. He insisted that "the protection of the residential neighbourhood comes first."[24]

The next flashpoint was the appointment of Julian Fantino as the new megacity police chief. *Fab* was granted an exclusive interview, and Fantino openly criticized CLGRO and others who had opposed his appointment. "We can't allow radical elements of any community to jeopardize our efforts to understand each other."[25] *Xtra* fulminated about Fantino's homophobia in contriving London, Ontario's kiddie porn panic.

Nine months later, on September 14, 2000, five male police officers from 52 Division marched into the Club Baths where hundreds of women were frolicking at the Pussy Palace, a popular women's bathhouse night. On the pretext of a liquor licence infraction, cops spent an hour and a half taking down people's names, demanding private rooms be opened, and intimidating organizers. Two were charged with disorderly conduct and liquor licence violations.

After his assurance that there would be no more bath raids, Rae was humiliated and furious. In a press release, he characterized the police as "cowboys" and denounced the action as a "panty raid" and a waste of public resources. Gay Liberal member of the provincial legislature George Smitherman brought Fantino into the mix. "I believe that Julian Fantino empowers rogue cops by giving them a sense that he will protect them."[26]

The Women's Bathhouse Committee called a public meeting at the 519 a few days later, and I found myself one of the few men in a room full of furious lesbians. It felt very much like the meetings after the 1981 raids. As people spoke up, the anger of the nearly four hundred people crammed into the room began to build. It was agreed to march to police headquarters. I was about to leave, but Loralee Gillis, one of the WBC organizers, called out to me and asked me to organize the marshals. I was shocked. It didn't seem right for one of the few men to take on that kind of leadership. But when I looked around, I realized that most of the people there were too young to remember the bath raids and many may have never been to a demonstration.

As the marchers got ready, I asked for volunteers, determined who had any experience, and assured everyone that four hundred people didn't need a permit to do anything. I threw together ad hoc teams to manage the front, back, and sides of the march. Once out of the 519 we quickly took Church Street and then College as we marched to police headquarters through the cool September night. The demonstration was on relatively safe territory and there were no problems with either bashers or the cops. But after the rally at headquarters, I still reminded marshals to keep people in groups until they got back to Church Street. I left feeling tickled to be appointed honorary lesbian for the evening, but also old, like a blacksmith, someone whose skills were becoming increasingly rare.

A follow-up demonstration, the Pussy Palace Panty Picket Protest, was held in front of 52 Division on October 28. Led by a giant vulva, the theme was panties and underwear. Everyone brought a pair to wave. As well as the chants "Keep your hands off our panties" and "What do we want? Pussy!

When do we want it? Now!" the crowd even revived the old 1981 slogan, "Fuck You 52."

Between the demonstrations and a general outcry from progressive politicians, the police received a clear message. If this was a trial balloon to see how far they could go under the new police chief, the balloon had been popped. In retaliation, two months later, seven officers filed a suit against Rae for his remarks, claiming $500,000 in damages for defamation. Although in her instructions to the jury the judge said that nothing the police had done on the evening of the raid had to do with police work, the jury ultimately ordered Rae to pay $170,000 damages.

In a denouement in January 2002, Justice Peter Hryn stayed the charges against the two Pussy Palace organizers. Twenty years before, Hryn had been one of the lawyers defending found-ins for the RTPC. He called the Pussy Palace raid inappropriate law enforcement, compared it to a strip search, and suggested that the women's Charter-based privacy rights had been violated. The Toronto police were ordered to pay $350,000, issue an apology, and commit to sensitivity training for their 7,260 members.[27]

Police could still harass the street kids, black youth, and the homeless. But members of the lesbian and gay community who could pay to enter a venue were now officially out of bounds.

CLEAN COUPLES VS. DIRTY BOOKS

In February 2000, after repeated court rulings that denying benefits to same-sex couples violated the Charter, the federal government introduced Bill C-23, the Modernization of Benefits and Obligations Act. Passed in April, the legislation gave same-sex and opposite-sex couples the same benefits rights. EGALE and the Foundation for Equal Families considered the legislation a victory, but it was also subject to an emerging queer critique. "By pursuing benefits for same-sex couples only, our movement misses the unique opportunity to demonstrate the power of nominally queer issues to speak out and embrace many people whose relationships and living arrangements do not conform to dominant models," historian Steven Maynard wrote in *Capital Xtra*. "There has been far too little discussion . . . about how this will actually limit the freedom of many queer people by propping up punitive distinctions between those who will be deemed legally and socially acceptable and those who will not."[28]

Although the queer critique was articulate, it could never fully break with the legal equality approach. Remarks were always prefaced with "while the legislation is important," before continuing with the inevitable *but* . . . More importantly, such critique was never capable of organizing any practical alternative course of action.

Though the legal approach won benefits for normative same-sex couples, it was less effective in dealing with other queer issues. In December the same

year, the B.C. Supreme Court issued its decision in the case of Little Sisters. The
Vancouver bookstore's case against Canada Customs had been battling its way
through the courts since 1987, and a Charter challenge had been mounted in
1990.

Canada Customs cited the *Butler* case equating pornography with violence
against women to justify the seizures. Little Sisters argued that, since the power
imbalance between men and women was absent in lesbian and gay pornography, *Butler* should not apply. While the court agreed that customs officials' targeting of Little Sisters was "prejudicial and demeaning to their dignity,"[29] it
refused to find the Customs Act itself in violation of the Charter. And even
after the court ordered the federal government to pay $170,000 in costs and to
remove Little Sisters from its "lookout" list in 1996, Canada Customs continued its regular border seizures of literature bound for the bookstore.

SUSPENDED ANIMATION

At the end of 1999, with no one left willing to take on the responsibility of co-
chairing AAN!, Maggie Atkinson and I reluctantly agreed to step up again. In
the fall of 2000, the situation was unchanged. What was left of the steering
committee decided to put the organization in suspended animation.

We didn't want to kill it. We had a good reputation, or brand, in the emerging parlance, but there was clearly no energy to continue. A three-person
administrative committee was appointed who could call together the network
on an ad hoc basis in case of crisis. AIDS service organizations would continue
with their polite advocacy, but AIDS activism as we had known it seemed to
have run its course in Toronto.

CAAT

As AAN! faded away, issues of access became more bound up with questions
of marginalization, requiring a different kind of organizing. Alan Li was still
working at the Regent Park Health Centre, serving poor immigrant communities in Canada's largest public housing development. Realizing there were
serious barriers to treatment among new arrivals, refugees, and undocu-
mented immigrants, in 1999 he convinced organizations from the legal,
health, settlement, and HIV/AIDS sectors to form the Committee for Accessible AIDS Treatment.

The group received a grant from the Ontario HIV Treatment Network – a
collaborative group of researchers, health service providers, policy makers,
community members, and people with HIV – to conduct community-based
participatory action research in the affected communities. Its 2001 report
documented the challenges faced by vulnerable PWA groups, and engaged
various sectors to develop projects to address these barriers. This would be the
first of many such projects.

CAAT could have been just another service providers' coalition, but Dr. Li was committed to seeing it serve as a vehicle to empower marginalized PWAs. In 2003, the first training for peer educators for people from affected communities was organized. I helped out and found myself in a world that reflected the isolation, desperation, and determination I remembered from AAN!'s early days. Despite all our work, there were still people in Toronto dying from lack of treatment.

Graduates from that program were mentored to facilitate subsequent ones and went on to manage research projects. Many found their first employment in Canada in service organizations. Others ultimately took over the management of the network. One of my fondest memories was sitting around the campfire at a weekend retreat, as the group started taking turns singing their national anthems. I bridled at the nationalist performance of singing *O Canada* under the circumstances. Sitting beside a Chinese refugee, I asked him if we could sing the *Internationale* together, he in Mandarin and I in English. The rest of the group was amazed that both of us knew the same song in different languages. To their further amazement, we explained it was a communist anthem about international solidarity.

CAAT truly was a new form of organization. It touched those that AAN!'s strategies could never reach. It made a concrete difference in their lives and allowed them to become community leaders. It built a powerful, authentic voice for change at a time when Canada's increasingly xenophobic government was undermining the lives of immigrants and refugees. At the same time, it depended on government funding. CAAT embodied all the contradictions of the neo-liberal age, but was an example of perhaps the best that could be produced under the circumstances.

WEDDING BELLS

On January 14, 2001, the pews at MCC's imposing Romanesque revival church on Simpson Avenue were packed with more than eight hundred congregants, reporters from dozens of national and international media, and a strong security team. Fifty police huddled in the basement. The occasion was a double same-sex wedding, conducted by Rev. Brent Hawkes, who wore a bullet-proof vest under his gleaming white cassock.

The previous year, several same-sex couples were turned away when they applied for marriage licences at city hall. They were now suing the city, the province, and the federal government. But MCC lawyer Kathleen Lahey had discovered another way to legally marry people, a little-used part of the Marriage Act that referred to the "reading of the banns." A church only needed to announce its intention to marry a couple in the congregation on three successive Sundays, and barring valid objections, the couple could be legally married. The section on banns in the Marriage Act referred to "persons." Somewhere along the line, someone had left out the boilerplate "of the opposite sex."

The church first announced the impending marriage of two couples – Elaine and Anne Vautour, and Kevin Bourassa and Joe Varnell – in December 2000. When word got out, several fundamentalist Christians came to object. But since the disqualifications in the act referred to parties being brother and sister, already married, underage, or mentally incompetent, Hawkes ruled them out of order. Despite death threats, demonstrations, and an attempted assault against Hawkes at an earlier service, the ceremony went ahead, the first "legal" same-sex marriages in Canada.

It was all too much for Ontario registrar-general Bob Runciman, who sputtered, "A same-sex marriage simply doesn't meet the definition, and as such we're not going to be certifying it."[30] The newly married couples then joined with the other legal cases to challenge Runciman's position in court.

EGALE GETS ON THE TRAIN

In Ottawa, EGALE also increasingly turned to marriage. Hilary Cook had joined EGALE's Legal Issues Committee in 1999. While she herself was not particularly interested in the issue, committee chair Laurie Aaron – a business lawyer, former Canadian National Railway development manager, and investment analyst – was. "There was no question that he was a huge driving force towards marriage in both the legal committee and EGALE as a whole," Cook recalls.

> He felt very strongly that marriage was a big deal and would make a huge difference. . . . I remember him talking about realizing he was gay as a kid, and looking around and feeling like he would never be a normal part of society. He wanted kids to be able to look and see a more mainstream gay community.[31]

EGALE used Court Challenges money to fly in people from across the country for a consultation. Attending was Lambda Legal, the oldest, largest, and arguably most conservative of the American gay rights groups. Equal marriage was one of Lambda's goals, and they were interested in a Canadian precedent. As deliberations went on, it became clear that the ground had changed. According to Cook, "We realized that there were no longer arguments that could be made against marriage when you took into account all the other decisions that had been made on the Charter. We couldn't lose it."

EGALE took the unusual (and expensive) step of actually looking for litigants. Normally the group had intervened only in pre-existing cases. That generated a debate about the criteria for couples. Did they need to be monogamous? "There was a concern that if we had a case and our perfect couple was quirky and individual as most couples are, that might turn out to be an issue." Cook put her foot down. "We are not fucking asking people if they are monogamous. We're just going to have to take pot-luck on that. That's our community."

As the marriage issue gained momentum, it began to swamp EGALE's Legal committee. For members such as Cook, it seemed like other issues were being neglected. Finally, in the spring of 2001, Aaron left the Legal committee to chair a new EGALE Equal Marriage Committee. According to Cook, who took over as chair of the remaining Legal committee, marriage was like a train leaving the station. "You were on the train or not on, and we had to be on. It was going."[32]

WHERE IS THE TRAIN GOING?

I remembered being slightly bemused by these developments. People did all sorts of foolish things, and I supposed that there was no reason why getting married shouldn't be one of them. Certainly Richard and I, by then together for almost thirty years, didn't "need no piece of paper from the city hall," as Joni Mitchell sang,[33] to authorize our relationship.

Others were not so liberal in their response. The relationship between EGALE and *Xtra* had been growing increasingly testy since 1999 when Brenda Cossman, associate professor in the University of Toronto's law faculty, published a column entitled "No Sex Please: National Lobby Group Stands Up for Respectable Rights Only."[34] While crediting EGALE for its interventions in spousal rights cases, she also pointed out that the organization had been conspicuously absent from issues such as age of consent and censorship of sexually explicit material.

> The group sticks to the straight and narrow, the "nice" rights. Its issues are more respectable, more mainstream, more marketable. EGALE represents itself as the unthreatening face of the gay and lesbian community, the face that looks just like mainstream Canadians. It's gay and lesbian politics without the nasty edge – basically, without sex.[35]

With marriage now squarely on the table, things heated up. In April 2001, *Xtra* published a piece on Jane Rule's opposition to marriage. Rule, the groundbreaking lesbian author who had stuck with *TBP* through thick and thin in the 1980s, told *Xtra*, "I think the old lion just felt like roaring, to tell you the truth. . . . I've worked long and hard in the gay movement, and I don't like the energy that's being spent on this." Rule said:

> Over the years when we have been left to live lawless, a great many of us have learned to take responsibility for ourselves and each other, for richer or poorer, in sickness and health, not bound by the marriage service or model but singularities and groupings of our own invention. To be forced back into the heterosexual cage of coupledom is not a step forward but a step back into state-imposed definitions of relationship. With all that we have learned, we should be helping our heterosexual brothers and sisters out of their state-defined prisons, not volunteering to join them there.

Even the recognition of common-law spouses hurt the most vulnerable, she said. "Whether they want it or not, any couple must now declare themselves if they've [been] together for a year. Single moms and those with disabilities will have to choose whether to live alone or surrender government benefits if they have a working partner."

Rule had the integrity to live up to her beliefs. Although Helen Sonthoff, her partner of forty-five years, had died the year before, Rule refused to apply for available survivor benefits.[36]

The next month, *Xtra* publisher David Walberg penned "Mad Vow Disease."

> I'm surprised divorcing couples don't plead temporary insanity at the time of their wedding. Love has often been compared to madness, and who but a complete loony toon would, at 25, vow publicly that they'll still be supporting someone 50 years hence. . . . Yes, it's mad vow disease. Surely those unspeakably garish bridesmaids outfits could be offered as evidence.[37]

In September Gareth Kirby, managing editor of *Xtra West* wrote, "No, No, No to Marriage Rights." He said, "I hope they lose the legal fight for marriage equality rights."[38]

Nevertheless, when the Ontario cases got to the Ontario Superior Court in July 2002, three judges unanimously found that defining marriage in opposite-sex terms violated the Charter. It gave the government two years to rectify the situation. But the couples were not satisfied with a two-year wait. They appealed, asking for immediate relief.

Despite the sometimes barbed back and forth between *Xtra* and EGALE over marriage, once the path was clear, hundreds of lesbians and gay men started lining up to register. For a moment, Toronto became the gay marriage capital of North America. People were voting with their feet. Many, it turned out, just wanted to be included.

The court decision was a sign of the huge cultural shift that had taken place, a testament to all our work. But there had also been a shift in the goals of lesbian and gay activism. If in the 1970s anyone in *The Body Politic* had suggested demanding the right to marry, they would have been run out of town.

MOVING ON

By 2001 I was seriously considering throwing in the towel at the TDSB. The workplace was getting more frustrating and toxic. Most of the programs I had spent years developing were cut. Despite the new cocktail, my CD4s remained low, and I still did regular sessions at the pentamidine clinic. Others were now scoring undetectable on their viral load, but mine was stubbornly high and I continued to lose weight.

One evening in late April 2001, after a particularly frustrating workshop, I took my "walk in the snow." Actually it was a beautiful spring evening among the high-rises at Yonge and Sheppard. I knew that the work we had done around racism, sexism, and homophobia in the school system was being lost and forgotten in the ungainly and ungovernable TDSB. The new policy was good on paper, but with the cuts there were few people or resources left to do the work and no political will to make it a priority. I decided it would be better for my waning health, and a more productive use of my time, to stop working and write a chronicle of our efforts over more than twenty years before it was forgotten. That became my first book, *Race to Equity*.

ACTIVISTS VS. PHARMA

Four years after Nkoli's death and the organization's founding, South Africa's Treatment Action Campaign was a force to be reckoned with. TAC developed a focus on treatment literacy and trained hundreds of HIV positive people to spread the word in their communities. It embedded itself in the poor black townships where AIDS was rampant. TAC was constantly in the streets and in the media, demanding access to treatment for the almost six million HIV positive South Africans. And together with the AIDS Law Project, it took its fight to the courts.

TAC drew on the organizing experience of both the anti-apartheid movement in South Africa and AIDS activism in the United States and Canada. With demands framed by the human right to health care enshrined in the South African constitution, it championed a grassroots approach where poz people were their own advocates.

Its first challenge came in 2000 when Durban hosted the International AIDS Conference, the first held in the developing world. A month before the conference, Thabo Mbeki, now South African president, began flirting with AIDS denialism to justify government inaction on the epidemic. It was one of those occasions where a politician said something true to promote something false. In his opening speech to the conference, he concentrated on poverty and malnutrition as causes of immune deficiency in Africa, rather than a single virus. His minister of health went farther, suggesting that traditional African medicines like beetroot, garlic, olive oil, and lemon could cure the disease. She actively opposed the use of antivirals as prevention against mother-to-child transmission.

Few disagreed that poverty was a serious factor in the spread of HIV, or that malnourishment contributed to illness. But TAC activists knew that the only hope for those infected was antiviral treatment and that even short-term use could dramatically reduce mother-to-child transmission. Demanding treatment access, TAC led a huge march to the conference site. Their position was strengthened when Nelson Mandela himself, in his closing remarks, called the South African government's position "irresponsible."

By 2001, TAC faced a second challenge. Free trade was the overarching goal of the neo-liberal World Trade Organization, formed six years before. But when that conflicted with the interests of big corporations, it was a different matter.

The WTO's 1995 TRIPS (trade-related aspects of property rights) agreement attempted to strengthen patent protection for the international pharmaceutical industry and discourage cheaper generic alternatives. But a loophole allowed countries to purchase generic drugs in a "medical emergency."

South Africa, stung by international criticism at the conference, reluctantly began studying the economics of providing antivirals to its huge HIV positive population. It was obvious that the only cost-effective way to do it was to develop its own generic industry or purchase generics produced in India. The Pharmaceutical Manufacturers' Association (PMA), representing thirty-nine of the world's largest international pharma firms, sued the country, demanding only high-priced, name-brand products be used. The Clinton administration sided with pharma and threatened South Africa with sanctions if it moved to generics. It was a classic people-versus-profits scenario. Without access to generics, South Africa couldn't afford to treat its millions of HIV positive citizens.

TAC intervened in the case and led a march of five thousand people to the Pretoria High Court. The Global Treatment Access Campaign, an international network of AIDS activist organizations, was mobilized. As part of the effort, AAN! revived and, with the Canadian Treatment Action Council, held a rally in Toronto. ACT UP in New York occupied the investor relations office of GlaxoSmithKline in Manhattan, and there were actions in dozens of cities in eight countries around the world.

Under intense pressure and facing disastrous publicity, the PMA capitulated, withdrawing its suit on April 19, 2001.

GLAMOROUS OUTCASTS

In April 2001, the Summit of the Americas took place in Quebec City to negotiate the Free Trade Area of the Americas, a new neo-liberal trade deal to encompass both North and South America. In the light of anti-globalization protests in Seattle in 1999, Quebec was turned into an armed camp with a three-metre concrete and wire perimeter wall around the part of the city centre where the conference would take place. More than twenty thousand people from unions, environmental, student, and religious groups and progressive political parties came to protest. There was an Alternative Summit, marches, costumes, street theatre, radical cheerleaders, and a teddy bear catapult that lobbed furry stuffed animals at the police. The response was more prosaic – teargas, rubber bullets, and police truncheons. Hundreds were injured. A parliamentary investigation later concluded, "RCMP members used excessive and unjustified force in releasing tear gas to move the protesters when a more measured response could have been attempted first."[39]

Among the protesters were queer activists from Toronto. After returning home energized and still smelling of teargas, they held a public debriefing at the 519. It was decided to bring an anti-capitalist message to Pride, to challenge increasing corporate influence on the festival. The Glamorous Outcasts were born. In the 2001 parade, a boisterous crowd marched to cheers behind a banner reading "Fight Oppression – Fight Capitalism – Make Love."

Inclusion was now the name of the game at Pride. The 2001 festival officially became LGBTTIQ (lesbian, gay, bisexual, transgender, transsexual, intersex, queer) Pride, and for the first time, the city's Official Proclamation of Pride Week included "bisexuals, transsexuals, and transgendered persons." Grand marshal trans video maker, animal rights activist, and sex worker Mirha Soleil-Ross organized a contingent promoting the Animal Liberation Front. Marchers in animal masks carried placards highlighting the front's actions to free animals from laboratories and fur farms. The Animal Liberation Front had already been labelled a domestic terrorist threat in the United States. In interviews, Soleil-Ross criticized AIDS activists for colluding in animal experimentation to develop AIDS drugs, and the leather community for fetishizing leather. "The whole queer leather scene with its grotesque clowns trying to have their taste for dead skin recognized as an 'oppression' is nothing short of an elaborate and sick joke to me."[40]

Pride seemed to be shifting back to its cranky, anti-establishment roots. But events were about to unfold that would fundamentally change the political landscape.

9/11

I was preparing to work on my book about the board of education when I got a call from Pat Case, my former boss in the Equal Opportunity Office. "Turn on the TV!" he commanded. Every channel was showing pictures of the burning World Trade Center in New York. A month later the United States would invade Afghanistan and overthrow its former allies, the Taliban, in a futile search for Osama bin Laden. Like Frankenstein's monster, fundamentalist Islam, cultivated and supported by the United States and Saudi Arabia to fight communism, had turned on its creators.

9/11 was an act of brutalist performance art aimed at sending a message. Knocking down two buildings, no matter how tall, was not going to bring that military and economic juggernaut to its knees. But it showed that resistance to empire was prepared to be every bit as cavalier with innocent lives as the United States had been securing its interests in the developing world. The 9/11 attacks scared the wits out of Americans who ran in circles, asking each other, "Why do they hate our freedoms?"

It had two contradictory effects. First was an authoritarian response – the Patriot Act increased security and surveillance powers and set the tone throughout the West. Stunts like storming the stage at the International AIDS Conference or occupying the offices of the minister of health would no longer be tolerated. Connected was a hysterical rise in Islamophobia that spilled over onto anyone brown.

9/11 was a frontal assault on the bastions of liberal power from a traditionalist reaction to liberal imperialism. Suddenly, for many Americans, gays, who called for the realization of liberal values of individualism, equality, and rational discourse, seemed far less dangerous than Muslims. As the frame clash of civilizations and jihad vs. McWorld fell into place, lesbians and gay men, the white ones anyway, belonged to McWorld. A website to honour gay and lesbian victims of 9/11 was dedicated to "The Lovers Who Awaken Each Morning without Their Gay Patriot & Hero beside Them."[41]

The Glamorous Outcasts appeared at Pride once more in 2002, this time allied with Salaam, the queer Muslim group, to challenge growing Islamophobia. The groups leafleted Church Street, but found the atmosphere changed and the response "less than friendly." LGBT communities were just as susceptible to xenophobia and racism as anyone else.

A year later, despite huge anti-war mobilizations around the world, George W. Bush launched a second war against the United States' old friend Saddam Hussein, this time on the fabricated charge of developing weapons of mass destruction. Once one of the most developed, secular Arab states, Iraq's infrastructure was destroyed, its oil wealth looted, and the country engulfed in chaos and sectarian civil war. American brutality and the resulting power vacuum provided another reason for resentment and fed yet more fundamentalist jihadist groups. In the never-ending war against terror, liberals embraced gay into the nation, but gay Iraqis faced only persecution and murder in the new Iraq the Americans had created.[42]

MARC HALL

In the spring or 2002, Marc Hall, a seventeen-year-old student, was told by the principal of his Catholic high school in Oshawa, near Toronto, that he couldn't take his boyfriend to the prom. With the support of his family, Hall and his friends started a website and took the school board to court. Overnight, he became a media sensation, and he and his school were besieged. George Smitherman stepped in to shield Hall from the feeding frenzy and contacted the local Canadian Auto Workers union. Oshawa is the site of one of the largest auto assembly factories in the world, and the CAW is a major institution in the largely working class town.

Mike Shields, president of CAW local 222, agreed to take over managing the media, but the union's support was not without controversy. "Some workers were very negative that I had gotten involved to support Marc," Shields explained. "Union reps told me to lay off and focus on grievances. . . . Afterwards, when some of them heard the Court's verdict, they said, 'I guess Shields was right after all.' "[43]

A support group, the Coalition to Support Marc Hall, included a who's who of LGBT organizations and supporters: Egale Canada (recently renamed); Parents, Families and Friends of Lesbians and Gays (PFLAG, also renamed); the 519 Church Street Community Centre; the CLGRO; and Toronto city councillors Kyle Rae and Olivia Chow. Even Ontario Liberal leader Dalton McGuinty wrote a letter to the Durham Catholic District School Board advocating for Hall's right to attend the prom.[44]

High-profile gay lawyer Doug Elliott took the case on Hall's behalf, arguing Hall's Charter rights. The Catholic board claimed its Charter rights to religious freedom. In the end, Justice Robert MacKinnon granted an injunction preventing the school from excluding Hall or cancelling the prom. Traditionalist institutions like the Catholic Church found themselves ever more isolated, as institutions such as unions and the courts adopted the liberal logic of individual rights.

PUBLIC HEALTH CARE

One of the major achievements of the Keynesian state in Canada had been the public health care system. Medical care was largely free to all citizens under the universal government program. The cornerstone to public health, it worked well as long as there was money to pay for it. But with neo-liberalism's corporate tax cuts and the resulting fall in government revenue, the health care system was increasingly underfunded. As wait times increased, the wealthy demanded access to private care.

In 2002 the federal government launched a Royal Commission on the Future of Health Care in Canada, led by Roy Romanow, former NDP premier of Manitoba. Romanow, like Tony Blair in the United Kingdom, was a proponent of the "third way," basically neo-liberal economic policy without social conservative baggage. Fear spread across the country that the commission was a Trojan horse for health care privatization.

There was a massive mobilization to intervene in the public consultations. AAN! was especially aware that without a public health care system, the devastation of AIDS would have been far greater. If we had lived in the United States, many of us would not still be alive. We regrouped to turn Pride 2002 into a health care rally.

Pride was now a huge undertaking with dozens of floats, thousands of marchers, and hundreds of thousands of onlookers. To make an impact on something so large, we organized teams of volunteers, assigned distribution sites, printed thousands of placards, and rented a van for a headquarters. It helped that Pride was already in a militant mood that year. The theme was "Uncensored" and J.P. Hornick and Rachel Aitcheson, the two women charged from the Toronto Women's Bathhouse Committee, were grand marshals. Glad Day Bookshop was the honoured group for its continuing fight against censorship. We added public health care to the mix, and thousands of marchers carried our signage.

Just in time for Pride 2002 the new Immigration and Refugee Protection Act came into effect. For many of those involved in immigrant and refugee rights, the legislation was a step backwards. It undermined the civil rights of those seeking refugee status and increased government powers to detain those it suspected of terrorism on the basis of secret evidence. But for the first time, the legislation set out rules for sponsoring same-sex partners. That shift was the result of legal challenges and a decade of lobbying by Egale and LEGIT (Lesbian and Gay Immigration Taskforce).

The case of Pierre Beaulne and Todd Layland had already come to public attention after Beaulne unsuccessfully applied for a marriage licence in 1992 in order to sponsor his partner. LEGIT was founded by Christine Morrissey and others after Morrissey's application to sponsor her partner, Bridget Coll, was rejected. The same year Andrea Underwood also launched a Charter case after immigration officials refused her application to sponsor her partner, Anna Carrott. More cases followed in 1993.

Immigration Canada dodged the bullet by agreeing to accept same-sex partners on a case-by-case basis through independent applications or humanitarian grounds. Underwood's lawyer suggested that immigration officials were "afraid to lose." That policy left the issue up to the discretion of individual immigration officers and, although it worked in many cases, such discretionary decisions could be arbitrary and were not open to appeal. LEGIT and Egale pushed for more. The 1997 Immigration Legislative Review Advisory Group agreed,[45] and with all the other cases on same-sex spouses piling up, in 1999 the minister of immigration introduced legislation. After a great deal of back and forth about cohabitation requirements, the final legislation allowed same-sex partners to apply as common-law or conjugal partners, whichever worked best.[46]

Refugee law had undergone a similar transformation – but without legislation. The first gay refugee case accepted by an Immigration and Refugee Board was that of Jorge Inaudi, an Argentinean man who had been arrested, raped, and tortured by Argentine Federal Police because of his sexual orientation. In a 1992 decision on Inaudi's case, the board found that sexual orientation constituted membership in a particular social group, and anyone facing persecution because of that membership would therefore be eligible for refugee status.[47] From that point on, lesbians and gay men facing persecution because of their sexual orientation were able to apply for refugee status, although they were often required to "prove" their gayness to straight refugee board officials.

Despite undermining refugee rights in general, for those focused only on "gay issues," the Chrétien government had given most of what had been asked for.

Frank Chester's background was in information technology. With the support of his partner, he took a sabbatical after twenty-three years to do community development. He landed in Pride, and in 1999 was hired as part-time office manager. In 2002 he was promoted to managing director, becoming the festival's first full-time staff. The title was soon changed to executive director.

During his tenure, Pride experienced a growth spurt as it cultivated both business and government sponsorship. Its operating budget increased from $400,000 to just over a million dollars by 2005, the year Chester left. The same year, Pride won the Best Festival in Canada prize from the Canadian Event Industry Star Awards.

"Frank has really gotten us organized," Pride co-chair Fred Pitt told *Xtra* in 2005. "We're running a bit like a business now."[48]

The first infusion of major government money came in 2003. That spring there were a number of deaths from severe acute respiratory syndrome in the city. SARS killed quickly and did not respond to antibiotics. Originating in China, it quickly spread through global travel circuits. The World Health Organization issued a travel advisory for Toronto in April, the beginning of the tourist season. Hospitals went on lockdown, and the downtown Chinatown restaurant strip turned into a ghost town. The travel advisory was soon lifted, but the damage was done. The local economy tanked, and the government desperately tried to revive tourism. Pride received $112,000 from the province and $100,000 from Ottawa, and had more expenses picked up by the city.[49]

"We were like drunken sailors," remembers Pride board member Mark Smith.

> The SARS money meant we had to get big name acts. Production values went up. But getting grants meant we started changing the structure to fit the grants, and at the same time, staff started making decisions rather than the board. The grants often required that we had to hire more staff.[50]

Two years later, describing Pride as "one of the five signature events" recognized by the City of Toronto, Kyle Rae got the festival reclassified as one of eleven major cultural institutions.[51] Pride had previously applied for funding through the Toronto Arts Council, but as one of the majors – like the symphony, the Art Gallery of Ontario, and the Toronto International Film Festival – it now received direct city funding. This dramatically increased available money, but also meant that every year, funding had to pass council rather than peer assessment at the Toronto Arts Council.

Pride remained a largely volunteer-run festival in the early 2000s but, as it grew, its organization became more complex. It had to balance the needs of paid staff, the elected board, volunteer co-ordinators, general membership (volunteers and anyone attending three public meetings), and the wider community. It was a potentially unstable system. Pride's next executive director,

Fatima Amarshi, former director of Desh Pardesh, had strong community roots and was able to keep all those balls in the air at once. But as the community became more complex and disparities increased, that would become an ever harder act to pull off.

MARRIAGE IN THE COURTS

Giles Marchildon, Egale Canada's new director, signalled in *Xtra* that he understood criticisms that the national organization had focused too much on squeaky clean issues like spousal benefits and marriage to the detriment of sexuality issues. Nevertheless, marriage continued to claim pride of place as an Egale priority.

After the Ontario Superior Court finding that the opposite-sex definition of marriage was unconstitutional, the Liberals in Ottawa saw the writing on the wall. In November, the federal government released a discussion paper, *Marriage and Legal Recognition of Same-Sex Unions*. After three months of hearings, the Justice Committee was preparing to release its findings when on June 10, 2003, the Ontario Court of Appeals not only confirmed the lower court ruling supporting gay marriage, but struck down the two-year delay.[52] The MCC marriages were retroactively recognized. Ironically, one of the deciding judges at the Court of Appeals was Chief Justice Roy McMurtry, who as attorney general had pursued the prosecutions in *The Body Politic* and bathhouse raids in the 1970s and '80s. Times had changed.

Just in case, two applicants – Michael Leshner and Michael Stark – headed to city hall and became the first to be married under the new regime. They needn't have rushed. The Justice Committee passed a motion to support the Appeals Court decision, and a week later, June 17, 2003, Prime Minister Chrétien announced that the federal government would not appeal. Gay marriage had become legal in Canada.

Leader of the opposition Stephen Harper fulminated, "They wanted to introduce this 'same sex marriage' through the back channels. They didn't want to come to Parliament. They didn't want to go to the Canadian people and be honest that this is what they wanted. They had the courts do it for them, put the judges in they wanted, then they failed to appeal, failed to fight the case in court."[53] Harper was dead on in terms of Liberal strategy, although it was a stretch to conclude that the judges in the case were appointed with gay marriage in mind. But he was also sheltered from a shift in public sentiment by the social conservative company he kept in the Canadian Alliance (the successor to the Reform Party and official opposition in Parliament, 2000–2003). When he introduced a motion to reaffirm that marriage was "the union of a man and a woman" that September, it was roundly defeated.

Refusing to appeal a court decision was not the same as writing something into law. In August, Egale initiated a new coalition to push for parliamentary change in the definition of marriage, Canadians for Equal Marriage. CEM included PFLAG Canada, the Canadian Labour Congress, the Canadian Federation of Students, the Canadian Psychological Association, the Canadian Association of University Teachers, and the Canadian Association of Social Workers, among others.

The change in names illustrated the changing politics of the movement. The question of spousal benefits had first been raised by the Coalition for Lesbian and Gay Rights in Ontario. That situated the fight as a group effort involving different organizations within a rights framework. The organization that supplanted it and managed the unsuccessful 1994 push to extend spousal benefits was the Campaign for Equal Families. "Campaign" signalled some sort of militancy, but "Families," although open-ended enough to include alternative notions of family, produced the positive affective response to the traditional notion of family. "Equal" inserted the liberal value of individual equality. Canadians for Equal Marriage, however, began with a reference to the nation. "Marriage" referenced the traditional religious sacrament and its legal recognition by the nation. "Equal" signalled that Canada was a liberal nation.

CEM and Egale had interlocking boards. The focus was on lobbying, petitions, and celebrity endorsements. "Our website is very action-oriented," explained Laurie Aaron, who had moved from the board to staff and was Egale's director of advocacy. "We are focusing on putting together a national network of local chapters. And we're focusing on putting in place a grassroots campaign to lobby members of Parliament in their ridings." The strategy worked for Egale. The focus on marriage rapidly expanded its donor base. The group was soon receiving $22,000 per month in donations, and staff increased to a dozen. Over a million dollars was raised for the campaign.

THE END OF HARRIS

In October 2001, Mike Harris abruptly announced that he was planning to resign. Although he claimed "personal reasons," it was generally felt that the chickens of the Common Sense Revolution were coming home to roost. The impact of his cuts was being felt in public health and public safety. In the little town of Walkerton, several people died from E. coli in the town's poorly supervised water supply. Harris had halved the welfare rolls and dramatically increased homelessness and reliance on food banks. A pregnant disabled woman, Kimberly Rogers, died in her sweltering apartment in Sudbury after being found guilty of welfare fraud and cut off of under the draconian new regulations. She had been banned from public assistance for life. Wait times in hospitals were becoming intolerable. Education was in crisis after years of underfunding and strikes. Evidence was mounting about Harris's involvement in the Ipperwash shooting. His popularity was at an all-time low.

His successor, Ernie Eves, was left to deal with the mess. He was defeated in a general election in October 2003.

But Ontario's 1 per cent still thought of Harris as a hero. When he left the
legislature after a leadership convention in March 2003, Harris was immediately hired by one of Toronto's major corporate law firms, Goodmans LLP, even though he was not a lawyer. He also joined the Fraser Institute, a right-wing think tank.[54] From there he moved on to a life of well-paid corporate directorships.

LIBERAL ONTARIO

Dalton McGuinty led the Liberal party to victory in 2003. Like Chrétien, Clinton, and Blair, McGuinty was not burdened by an alliance with far-right social conservatives. His cabinet included Smitherman, an openly gay man whose riding included Toronto's gay village. Smitherman was given responsibility for health care reforms as minister of health and long-term care. He became McGuinty's attack dog in the legislature and would subsequently rise to the position of deputy premier.

Another rising star in the new government was Kathleen Wynne, an open lesbian. Wynne had been a progressive parent activist at the Toronto Board of Education and was elected as trustee to the amalgamated TDSB in 2000, just as I was leaving. She was instrumental in getting the board to purchase material in 2001 reflecting lesbian and gay families. Although she was a newly elected backbencher, McGuinty appointed her assistant to the minister of training, colleges and universities, and later, minister of education.

After eight years of Tory rule, Toronto's gay communities gave a collective sigh of relief. Some of "our people" were finally in positions of power.

It was a new political phase. We had begun by contemplating horizontal alliances to overthrow power. We had shifted to a mix of horizontal and strategic vertical alliances to press those in power to enshrine our rights. Now we were becoming those in power.

But the neo-liberal transformation of the economy was not easily undone. Even if the Liberals had wanted to, it is always easier to make a small group of people extraordinarily rich and powerful than it is to redistribute that wealth and power. Like the Tories before them, the Liberals represented the interests of elites. McGuinty did smooth some of the rough edges of Harris's revolution, raising social assistance rates by 3 per cent (after Harris's 21 per cent cut) and cancelling a planned corporate tax cut. He made significant reinvestments in health care and championed the public character of the system. But he also cut coverage for eye care and physical therapy, putting those services out of reach for the poor. He hired new teachers, but didn't change Harris's funding formula, which continued to strangle the education system. There were initiatives to slow urban sprawl and to cut greenhouse gases. But the bottom line would remain balancing the budget.

As marriage took the limelight, behind the scenes, another stream of organizing was taking place. In the fall of 1999, Susan Gapka had received a placement for her Community Worker Program at the offices of Councillor Olivia Chow. In her initial interview, Gapka still presented as male, but she had decided she was going to come out as trans at school. At a second meeting with Chow's assistant Bob Gallagher, Gapka confided her plans to transition. "When I left the office he said, 'See you next week, Susan.' The next week I came into the office as Susan."[55] She met Helen Kennedy, also working in Chow's office, and the pair talked for hours. Despite some "fuss" about washroom use, Gapka found being in the public eye "exciting and challenging simultaneously." She was on her way to becoming a trans activist, and a few months later, with Rupert Raj, she helped found the Health Advocacy Group.

In 2001, CLGRO's 1997 *Systems Failure* report spawned the Rainbow Health Network, a group of individuals who continued to work on the report's many recommendations, including trans issues. In the fall of 2003, RHN's Sexual Reassignment Surgery Committee merged with Gapka and Raj's Health Advocacy Group and was renamed the Trans Health Lobby Group. They were joined by Martine Stonehouse, one of those who had laid the human rights complaint about the delisting of sex reassignment surgery.

According to Gapka, organizing under the Rainbow Health umbrella made the group more accountable, with regular minuted meetings, monthly reports to the RHN, and annual general meetings. The lobby group's major goals at the time were better access to health care – specifically the relisting of SRS – and changes to the Vital Statistics Act to make it easier for trans people to change their sex classification on official documents.

The Liberals seemed to open a window of opportunity after almost a decade of hostility from the Harris government. The long-standing human rights complaint about the abrupt delisting of SRS went back to mediation. Things were looking promising.

"By the beginning of 2004 we thought we had a mediated agreement," Gapka recalls.

> As a result of the negotiations, George Smitherman had agreed to fund the relisting of SRS. They were supposed to sign an agreement to fund SRS and to add protections to the Human Rights Code for trans people. George mentioned it a little at an event Thursday night. The contract was supposed to be announced on Friday. A reporter picked up on the story and called the premier's office. The person on the other end said no, we're not doing that, absolutely not. That was just before the May 2004 budget when they delisted chiropractic services, physiotherapy and eye examinations. That was an enormous setback. We were devastated.[56]

Even with a supposedly supportive gay minister of health, the neo-liberal logic about shrinking state services to save money trumped the rights of trans people.

With mediation a failure, the complaint moved on to the tribunal stage. The tribunal's decision in late 2005 was a disappointment. It ruled that the government had to pay for SRS for those such as Stonehouse who had been stranded in mid-process in 1998, but not for others who had not started the procedure at the time. It did not require relisting. Smitherman announced that coverage for SRS would not be reinstated.

"Smitherman always supported us but he worked for a government and a premier's office that didn't," says Gapka. "My view is that George felt his career as a Liberal was at stake. He felt more loyal to his political future and being deputy premier than to our needs."[57]

THE LAST DOMINO

After the Ontario Superior Court ruling allowing gay marriage in Ontario, it was only a matter of time before the other provinces followed suit. The logic of equality was unassailable. Quebec was first in March 2004, when the Quebec Court of Appeal refused to hear religious objections and rejected an appeal against a same-sex marriage case. Over the following months, five other provinces came on board.

In July, the federal government referred draft legislation to the Supreme Court to ask for its opinion. The court said it was in the government's power to change the definition of marriage, that gender-neutral proposals were consistent with the Charter, but that religious groups could not be compelled to perform same-sex marriages.

The Christian right did not give up. For them, Canada was a traditional nation. But it also realized it had to shed its white, small-town image in an increasingly multicultural and multiracial country, and began to mobilize conservative sectors of racialized groups. In the summer of 2003 a major demonstration against same-sex marriage brought hundreds of fundamentalist Christian Chinese Canadians to Ottawa. The strategy was to portray same-sex marriage as anti-multicultural, in conflict with the traditional values of immigrant groups. In response, Asian Canadians for Equal Marriage was formed in early 2004 "to ensure Asian Canadians see a gay-positive, non-discriminatory representation of their true, tolerant community." Organized by the Chinese Canadian National Council, Asian Community AIDS Services, Gay Asians Toronto, and Asian Lesbians of Toronto, the group soon expanded to include twenty-five sponsoring groups.

Avvy Go, director of the Metro Toronto Chinese and Southeast Asian Legal Clinic, published an op-ed piece in the *Toronto Star* asserting that opposition to same-sex marriage was not grounded in cultural belief, but in the religious teachings of Christian groups that had expanded their influence in minority communities. Referring to the CBC reports on the Chinese demonstrators in

Ottawa, she asserted, "The voices of this small, yet visible, fundamentalist group effectively drowned out the silent majority and successfully created a perception that all racial minorities and immigrants are opposed to same-sex marriage." She went on, "This cannot be further from the truth. Apart from the fact that some immigrants and racial minorities are gays and lesbians themselves, there are many of us who recognize the right to form a family of our choice as a fundamental one."[58] Countering Harper's argument that Parliament, not the courts, should decide, she concluded that minority rights were protected by the Constitution and interpreted by the courts precisely to protect them from majority prejudices.

The new Conservative Party of Canada – formed in December 2003 by the merger of the traditional Progressive Conservatives and the far-right Canadian Alliance – rolled out an anti–gay marriage ad campaign aimed at immigrants in 2005. In response, the National Anti-Racism Council of Canada (NARCC), along with the chair of the Canadian Race Relations Foundation (my old boss from the board of education, Pat Case) spoke out. They were joined by more than a hundred prominent labour, religious, and community activists across Canada. The group held a press conference to express its "strong objection to the announced campaign of Stephen Harper's Conservatives to target racial minority communities in its efforts to deny gays and lesbians the equal rights that they are entitled to under the Canadian Charter of Rights and Freedoms."

"The ad campaign introduced by Stephen Harper and the Conservatives is in our view, divisive, panders to prejudice, seeks to pit one minority community against another, and reinforces unfounded and in fact, racist stereotypes that visible minorities are intolerant,"[59] explained spokesperson Mary-Woo Sims, former chief human rights commissioner in British Columbia. Nonetheless, the need for communities to make such arguments was not just a function of Harper's campaign; it underscored that most of those visibly leading the charge for marriage equality in CEM were white.

In January 2005, Egale announced that for the next three months, all the group's resources would be dedicated to the marriage fight. It was too much for board member Susan Gapka, who had helped establish Egale's Trans Issues Committee. She resigned in protest. But by this point, anti-marriage voices within the community had largely fallen silent. It was Us vs. Harper. Although it published one think piece arguing that the state should get out of the marriage business altogether,[60] even *Xtra* provided office space and sponsorship to CEM.

On February 1, 2005, Bill C-38, the Civil Marriage Act, was introduced in the House of Commons. As befits a gay issue, there was high drama to the end. The Liberals led a minority government, and unless the bill passed first, a likely spring election would kill the legislation in its tracks. As the Conservatives tried to stall the bill in committee, the Liberal government narrowly won a confidence vote in May, after a key Tory member of Parliament, Belinda Stronach, abruptly switched sides and joined the Liberals. But it still looked like the bill would not pass before summer recess. The Liberals vowed to extend the sitting, but then reneged when a Liberal member resigned his seat, once again putting the party's control of Parliament in question.

Egale frantically worked the phones and media. The Liberals again changed their position and agreed to extend the session. But the next day, that strategy almost collapsed when the opposition Bloc Québécois announced they would only vote for an extension if the Liberals gave them a written guarantee that the marriage bill would come to a vote. The NDP managed to bridge the traditional animosity between the Liberals and the Bloc, and the extension was again on. Then the Conservatives tried to bring down the government in order to kill the bill, but were outmanoeuvred in a snap vote.

Only then did the legislation legalizing same-sex marriage across Canada pass third reading in the house, on June 28. It was approved in the Senate July 19 and proclaimed as law July 20, 2005. Canada was the fourth country in the world to approve same-sex marriage, after Belgium, the Netherlands, and Spain.

Alex Munter, national co-ordinator for Canadians for Equal Marriage, could barely contain his patriotism in Egale's newsletter. "This is a proud and exciting time to be a Canadian. Today we made history. Today, we affirmed once again our world-wide reputation as a country that is open, inclusive and welcoming."[61]

From then on, there was only some cleanup to do. The *Hislop* case won arrears of survivor benefits under the Canada Pension Plan at the Supreme Court in 2007. Hislop received a cheque of $14,000 shortly before he died at seventy-eight in 2005. The money covered unpaid survivor pension benefits owing since the death of his long-time partner, Ron Shearer, in 1986. The case won over $50 million in benefits for other aging same-sex couples. Lesbians and gay men were now full citizens, officially equal. According to some, the fight in Canada was over. We had been included.

MERGER

But in this new world of equality, inequality was deepening. In 2004, the Ontario HIV Treatment Network conducted a study on HIV and housing, *Positive Spaces, Healthy Places.* It generated a wealth of socio-economic data on more than six hundred people living with HIV/AIDS that were interviewed. Seventy-five per cent of the sample had income less than $18,000 per year. Sixty per cent of the subjects were living in the Greater Toronto Area, and the poverty line in Toronto was approximately $17,500 per year at the time. More than half of those interviewed reported difficulties buying sufficient food and clothing, and 31 per cent felt their housing was insecure.[62]

The sample was probably not representative, since the study focused on people who were already clients of AIDS service organizations. But gay men were almost 60 per cent of those living with HIV, and it was clear that poverty was a serious and growing problem.

The issue came to a head that fall, when both the ACT and Toronto PWA Foundation boards of directors proposed amalgamating the two organizations. Downloading had contributed to the creation of the plethora of AIDS service organizations in Toronto, but the continued shrinkage of state revenues, still a significant part of their budgets, now argued for further efficiencies. Why should there be two general service organizations, each with its own administration, offices, and boards in the same city? ACT and Toronto PWA actually shared the same building, with their offices on different floors.

Although ACT voted for the merger by 80 per cent, there was serious disagreement among the membership of Toronto PWA. The required two-thirds majority could not be mustered at a general meeting.

I was a member of Toronto PWA, but I hadn't attended the first meeting. When a second was called to reconsider, I thought I had better see what was going on. The banked seats of the downtown YMCA auditorium were full and, to my surprise, the arguments against merger were all about class. ACT was seen as serving the white, middle-class gay population, but Toronto PWA members were largely drawn from the new urban poor, including more racialized people. Although there was overlap in counselling and education services, Toronto PWA had a well-used food bank, for example, while ACT ran insurance benefits clinics.

At the second meeting, despite entreaties from the Toronto PWA board, the vote was still short of the necessary two-thirds majority. The merger could not proceed. Toronto PWA subsequently moved out of the building it shared with ACT and struck out on its own. It wasn't long afterwards when one night in the baths I realized that the ACT safe sex poster in my room had been defaced. Someone had scrawled on it, "Fuck ACT. They don't give a damn. The ED makes $70,000 a year." The ship of a common HIV identity had hit the reef of underlying class disparity. Would gay identity follow the same trajectory?

12

We're Not in Kansas Anymore

DEMOGRAPHY

By 2005, Toronto's demography had changed dramatically. Only 29 per cent of the city remained middle income, down from 66 per cent in 1970. Fifty-three per cent of the population was now low or very low income, up from 19 per cent in 1970. The high-income group was now 18 per cent, up from 15 per cent.[1] A majority of working people were now relegated to precarious employment – temporary, part-time, sporadic, usually without benefits, often ineligible for unemployment insurance.

There were clear patterns in this increase in inequality. New immigrants and racialized people were especially hard hit. More than twice as many immigrants experienced a state of chronic low income than did the Canadian born. Ethno-racial minority families made up 37 per cent of Toronto families but 59 per cent of poor families. Since 1980 the poverty rate among racialized families had climbed 361 per cent.[2] Gender and age also played a role. An annual special feature in the *Toronto Star*, "Toronto's Vital Signs," pointed out: "In 1980, recent immigrant women earned 85 cents for each dollar earned by Canadian-born women. By 2005 the ratio was 56 cents, even though the education levels of immigrant women had risen faster." Half of TDSB students were now from lower-income families.[3]

The geography of immigrant settlement and poverty had also changed. When I began working at the Toronto Board of Education, we referred to schools that needed extra resources because of poverty and large immigrant and racialized populations as "inner-city schools." By 2005, the centre of the city was fast gentrifying and becoming whiter. Immigrants, racialized people, and the poor were living in the outer suburbs where rents were cheaper, but public transport and other services were poor. From the vantage point of Scarborough or Etobicoke, a gay community associated with the downtown village looked more like a privileged than a marginalized group.

THE NEW NORMAL

On January 23, 2006, Stephen Harper's Conservative party narrowly won a minority government. The victory had less to do with a shift in public sentiments than with the decline of the Liberals, mired in corruption and scandal after eighteen years of power. The main factor in Harper's victory was the merger of the socially conservative Canadian Alliance based in the West and the Progressive Conservative party in the East. With the left split between Liberals and a centrist NDP, the right squeaked into power.

That left Harper with a debt to social conservatives. During the campaign he'd promised to revisit same-sex marriage if elected. The new prime minister was not just opportunistic. He attended an evangelical church and seemed to believe in old-time family values. Since his party was in a minority, he put off the issue as long as he could, while Canadians for Equal Marriage pushed for a vote.

In December, Harper was finally shamed into reopening the issue. As expected, the motion was defeated, and the prime minister told reporters that he didn't see reopening the question in the future. Harper was playing a long game to deepen the neo-liberal transformation of the economy. He had bigger fish to fry, and his social conservative allies were expendable.

TINA

While marriage was secure, sex among gay men was changing. Once seen as the basis of our social networks and community solidarity, recreational sex was increasingly portrayed as sleazy and dangerous. The perception was amplified by the spread of crystal meth, or Tina. Meth made users confident, horny, uninhibited. A synthetic, it was cheaper than drugs that required raw materials from exotic locations. It was also very addictive, and both physically and psychologically corrosive. Because it affected judgment, "partying" increased risk of HIV transmission.

Rock Bottom,[4] a documentary by former ACT UP activist Jay Corcoran, began doing the rounds. The film detailed the individual and community destruction caused by the crystal meth epidemic, linking it to a new wave of HIV infections. A cautionary tale in a world where promiscuous sex and drug use were intimately entwined, *Rock Bottom* certainly did not portray a positive image of the gay recreational sex scene. ACT developed a harm reduction campaign – *Hi My Name is Tina* – to address crystal in Toronto, but more and more people in the baths seemed to be using. Even the fear of HIV infection was less of a deterrent. The new cocktails worked. HIV was no longer a death sentence.

A TIME TO DELIVER

In mid-August 2006, more than 26,000 delegates descended on Toronto for the sixteenth International AIDS Conference. Things had changed since 1989.

Established PWA organizations were officially at the table. The International Council of AIDS Service Organizations (ICASO), the Global Network of People Living with HIV (GNP+), and the International Community of Women Living with HIV (ICW) were all official partners of the Geneva-based International AIDS Society (IAS) in conference planning.

AIDS had also become a celebrity issue. There were an unprecedented number of high-profile speakers, including Bill and Melinda Gates, actor Richard Gere, and former U.S. president Bill Clinton. Social issues now rivalled medical ones. Getting drugs to people who would die without them was a major theme, as were the barriers to health care and prevention produced by gender inequity, poverty, homophobia, and discrimination against sex workers and drug users.

The IAS was also managing activism differently. It helped arrange a site close to the conference where activists could meet and strategize, and recruited Alain Volney-Anne to work as the conference/activist liaison. He in turn recruited me, Andy Velez, an old ACT UP activist from New York, and Fabienne Hejoaka, a young French woman working in Africa, as his volunteer team. All of us were poz. It was an odd position. Officially we were supposed to be facilitating activism, and we did prevent some of the ACT UP Paris people from getting arrested at one point, but we also made sure they didn't cause too much trouble. Meanwhile, at the same time as reaching out to activists, the IAS was tightening up security and rules around acceptable protest.

The major controversy was the absence of the freshly elected prime minister. Harper probably declined to attend as a sop to his social conservative base. But this time, AIDS activists did not lead the charge. In his opening remarks, conference co-chair Dr. Mark Wainberg openly attacked the absent prime minister.

> We are dismayed that the prime minister of Canada, Mr. Stephen Harper, is not here this evening. . . . The role of prime minister includes the responsibility to show leadership on the world stage. Your absence sends the message that you do not consider HIV/AIDS as a critical priority, and clearly all of us here disagree with you.[5]

RESURRECTION ONE

Unexpectedly, the conference sparked a revival of AAN! Weeks of media hype made AIDS hot again. After an exploratory meeting that fall, a very different organization emerged under the same name. Although a few of us old-timers hung on to provide continuity, a new generation of young people had been energized. They were interested in a range of issues from IV drug use to homelessness, welfare cuts, and international development.

Although most were still white, there was significant participation of racialized people. Sexuality hardly seemed an issue. "Queer" had replaced gay or lesbian as the term of choice, and although it was supposed to be out there and cutting edge, it also seemed to provide a cover for a new closetry. Everyone was ambiguous and few talked about the sex they had anymore.

Poz identity also seemed less relevant. The steering committee was more ad hoc, and in practice, there was little distinction between who was poz and who wasn't. In fact, poz as an identity seemed to be collapsing. Broader social determinants rather than serostatus determined people's health. Poz folks had once all been in the same boat, but now, some of us were tethered securely to the shore by antivirals, while others still drifted inexorably towards the cataracts.

There was also participation of those involved in various AIDS service organizations. Harper made them anxious about funding. They had programs, organizations, and careers to protect. It appeared that activism might be necessary again.

GAY YOUTH

As AAN! was reviving, one of Toronto's original queer organizations passed away. Lesbian and Gay Youth Toronto had provoked a crisis at 519 Church Street Community Centre when it first applied for membership in 1976. Over the years, the group had changed its name, first adding a *B* for bisexual to its acronym, and finally, as the expected list of letters became too cumbersome, becoming Welcoming All Youth to the Village (WAYV). For thirty years, the youth-run, all-volunteer group held weekly drop-ins at the 519. They provided a space for isolated young people to come out, establish queer friendships, and explore issues.

I led several anti-racism and anti-oppression workshops for the group over the years, and when Tony Gambini established the queer youth support group at the board of education, we met Tuesdays after school so that those who wanted could drop in to LGBYT later. LGBYT was an incubator for many young activists, including Kristyn Wong-Tam, who would later become Toronto's first openly lesbian city councillor.

"Walking into The 519 auditorium and seeing other young kids ... was electrifying and nerve-wracking all in the same emotional breath," Wong-Tam recounted to *Xtra*. "Knowing that I was no longer alone and that I belonged to a larger community alleviated many of my social insecurities."[6]

WAYV was a victim of the much-demanded expansion of professional youth services. As agency-driven programs for queer youth – such as Central Toronto Youth Services' Supporting Our Youth – began to host more staff-supported youth groups, attendance at WAYV declined. By the summer of 2006 only a handful of young people were showing up, and no one was in a position to take leadership. The group folded. WAYV was probably the longest surviving of the grassroots organizations that made up the community in the 1970s.

It took a new coalition of youth and youth advocates, the Age of Consent Committee, to issue a media release accusing the Harper government of a "regressive move to repress and criminalize youth sexuality."[7] The Tories had begun the process of raising the age of consent from fourteen to sixteen on the pretext of "protecting youth." Twenty-one-year-old spokesperson Andrew Brett explained that the Criminal Code already criminalized exploitive sex with anyone under eighteen.

The committee warned that youth would be less likely to seek out safe sex, STI, and birth control information. Nor did the changes deal with the long-standing issue of the eighteen-year age of consent for anal sex, still on the books although invalid under the Charter, or recognize that many queer youth sought out older partners.

Community allies spoke out against the changes, including CLGRO, the Canadian Federation for Sexual Health, the Canadian AIDS Society, Planned Parenthood Ottawa, the Sexual Health Division of Toronto Public Health, and late in the day, Egale Canada. But Harper's legislation faced little opposition in Parliament. Under pressure from its youth wing, the NDP did manage to strengthen an exemption for young people less than five years apart in age, but in the end, all parties supported the bill. The legislation was passed and came into law May 1, 2008.[8] The Conservatives were playing to a crowd that would support anything to limit sex outside marriage, especially for young people. The Liberals and the NDP, having put all their eggs in the more salubrious marriage equality basket, were reluctant to get involved in issues outside those parameters, especially if they involved young people and sex.

The ideal of youth liberation had sparked so many battles in the early lesbian and gay movement and inspired the creation of Gay Youth Toronto in the 1970s. It was now a thing of the past, squeezed out by the embrace of a protective state.

EGALE ON THE ROPES

In the spring of 2007, Egale's new director, Helen Kennedy, loaded the contents of the organization's Ottawa office into a rented van and drove to Toronto, where she deposited sixty-two boxes of records at the Canadian Lesbian and Gay Archives. There was no room in Egale's new digs, the small third-floor space donated by Jaime Watt, the former Harris Conservative operative, above his Toronto-based consulting company. Egale, on the brink of collapse, had to issue a press release to deny it was already dead after a report in *Xtra*.

"When I took over, it was really a bit of a shock," Kennedy recalls. "I was the only staff person. I closed the office in Ottawa because we couldn't pay the rent. They could barely pay my salary."[9]

Egale had received two body blows. First, everything had gone into marriage, and it was now rudderless. The board squabbled over future directions.

There were resignations and infighting. The donor base collapsed. At the height of the marriage fight, the group boasted a dozen employees and was receiving upwards of $22,000 a month from hundreds of donors. By early 2007, donations had fallen to less than $6,000. For those focused on marriage, the fight was over and Egale was no longer needed.

Then, the Harper government abruptly cut the Court Challenges Program that had financed Charter challenges. "The Court Challenges Program was our livelihood," says Kennedy. "That was supporting all our legal cases."

Kennedy tried to resuscitate the organization. She visited corporate equity offices to ask for funding but no one was interested. Still the group hung on. Despite the resignation of most of the education committee in May, Egale released a long-awaited survey for secondary students about safety in schools in December 2007. Those results would be the foundation of the group's focus on educational issues. The second focus was trans issues, but there the priority was to rebuild trust. Many trans activists had felt ignored and disrespected when the priority had shifted to marriage.

One thing was clear. Youth and trans people did not have deep pockets like those who funded the marriage fight. If it was to survive, Egale was going to need a new model.

REHABILITATION

On June 11, 2007, in the ballroom atop the Sutton Place Hotel, "Ontario's LGBT Communities" hosted a hundred-dollar-a-plate soiree to honour retiring chief justice of Ontario Roy McMurtry. "There is a definite buzz, up here on the 33rd floor with its wraparound windows, its nonstop vistas, its darling little tables draped in gold or white cloth, each hosting a discreet candle, a tasteful single blossom . . ." wrote Gerald Hannon for *Xtra*.[10]

The event was organized by renowned gay lawyer Douglas Elliot, who had argued the same-sex marriage case before the Supreme Court as well as the Hislop pension benefits case, and Michelle Douglas, the lesbian who launched the challenge against the Canadian Armed Forces that helped overturn the military's anti-gay policies. Legendary Toronto drag queen Michelle DuBarry hosted. According to Hannon, most of the attendees were "smartly dressed gay men and lesbians," along with a few luminaries such as former premier Bob Rae.

McMurtry, as Ontario's attorney general and solicitor general, had overseen the raids, trials, and appeals against *The Body Politic* in the late 1970s, and the bath raids and subsequent trials of hundreds of gay men in the early '80s. At that time, he was perhaps the community's most reviled politician. We had burned him in effigy, denounced him in print, demonstrated outside his campaign headquarters, and occupied his offices.

But in 2007, all was forgiven, or rather, forgotten. In 2003, as senior member of the Ontario Court of Appeal panel, McMurtry had approved same-sex marriage. He was also instrumental in brokering the deal that established the Charter, the game-changer in lesbian and gay equality cases.

Elliott characterized the evening as being about "truth and reconciliation." Hannon snidely commented, "Reconciliation is undoubtedly in the air. I was hoping, though, for a little truth." The rest of Hannon's article tries to answer whether McMurtry was a homophobe who changed, or an opportunist who knew how to bend with the wind. A more interesting question, I thought, was how community leadership had changed, in its politics, its composition, and in whom it chose to honour.

MURDER MUSIC

That same spring, Akim Adé Larcher attended the release of a study by the African and Caribbean Council on HIV/AIDS in Ontario (ACCHO) focusing on HIV stigma and discrimination among African and Caribbean communities. The study pointed out the linkage between HIV infection and homophobia fuelled by lyrics in dancehall music. Larcher, originally from St. Lucia, had recently returned to Canada after studying law in the United Kingdom. There, he had been in contact with Peter Tatchell's Stop Murder Music. Larcher left the ACCHO meeting energized, and when he heard of an impending tour by Elephant Man, an artist well known for homophobic lyrics, he contacted Gareth Henry of the Jamaican gay group J-FLAG (Jamaica Forum for Lesbians, All-Sexuals and Gays) and Tatchell in Britain.

Tatchell's Stop Murder Music campaign, founded in 2004, got a number of concerts and sponsorships cancelled. It had led to the Reggae Compassionate Act, signed by artists who agreed to stop performing lyrics promoting violence against gay people. But it had also resulted in controversy. Both Tatchell and the campaign were accused of racism and colonialism for singling out Jamaica and reggae for criticism.

Similar issues were raised as far back as 1992, when the Gay and Lesbian Alliance Against Defamation (GLAAD) launched a campaign in New York to protest homophobic lyrics in Buju Banton's "Boom Bye Bye." Even Donald Suggs, the African American man spearheading the effort, worried that mainstream media would take up the issue "as yet another illustration of the pathology of Blackness." Colin Robinson, later a key organizer of the Trinidad and Tobago lesbian and gay group CAISO, argued that it would be more useful to have the conversation in the West Indian media.

When the issue surfaced again in New York in 2004, Robinson and others helped craft principles to guide a new No More Murder Music effort. Protests should highlight the impact of the music on Jamaica and Jamaicans. Advocacy should foreground Jamaican and Caribbean voices, and protests should benefit LGBT Jamaicans. The goal should be voluntary action by presenters and promoters rather than censorship. Finally, there should be no racism or stereotyping of Caribbean culture. Despite these efforts, Robinson concluded, "the average [No More Murder Music] protester was in fact using his own body to call for homophobic music to be censored, artists banned and concerts cancelled," and "protests were not so much a campaign about Jamaica or LGBT people over there, but one to keep hateful foreign music and its singers out of the metropole." For Robinson, "the 'murder music' picket line in New York was a place of a profoundly ambivalent alliance with racists and people who despised Caribbean culture."[11]

Nevertheless, Larcher decided to form a Canadian group, Stop Murder Music (Canada). Hoping to navigate such issues, he contacted key activists in the black gay community, Doug Stewart, Courtnay McFarlane, and University of Toronto professor Rinaldo Walcott. They drew up a list of groups to approach, and by the time they hosted their first press conference, almost all the AIDS service organizations had signed on.

There was an immediate homophobic reaction. After several death threats, Larcher was fired from his job at a travel agency. The group approached Egale for support, and Stop Murder Music (Canada) began operating out of Egale's new Toronto offices later that summer.

SMM(C) first wrote the minister of immigration urging that entry visas be denied to offending artists. When they received no reply, they concentrated on a more community-based campaign, panels, educational materials, and contacting music promoters and clubs. After national media coverage, several venues cancelled concerts. Archambault, a major Montreal book and music store, removed some offending music from their shelves. iTunes North America was convinced to drop violent homophobic work from its online selections. Larcher also credited the campaign with allowing "racialized queers to be visible and vocal within the predominantly white gay community in Canada."[12]

In February 2008, SMM(C), Egale, and CUPE held a meeting at the University of Toronto. Although it was a snowy night, the lecture hall was packed with a largely black and Caribbean crowd. They expressed anger and frustration at continuing anti-gay violence in Jamaica. Calls for a boycott were raised. "It came from the floor, not from the panellists. And we took that back and followed up," Larcher recalls. Walcott concurs, "We knew that boycotts in other situations had brought attention to particular issues and pushed forward reform, even when they were not economically successful."[13] The most obvious target was tourism.

Group representatives met with the Jamaican high commissioner. They outlined examples of abuse and demanded a response "or there would be a boycott."[14] The high commissioner was receptive, acknowledged there was a problem, but insisted that people in Canada didn't have any right to tell Jamaica what it should do. The boycott was on.

It was not easy going. Although conversations between SMM(C) and J-FLAG continued, the Jamaican group feared a backlash. *Xtra*, always on edge about censorship, questioned why Egale was spending so much energy on the issue and sent a white reporter to Jamaica for three days to check out the situation. Critics charged that the campaign was promoting racial stereotypes by focusing on black singers from Jamaica. Then Egale's sponsorship began affecting the optics. "By the time we got to the big meeting at the U of T, SMM(C) had shifted . . . and had become basically an in-house program of Egale," Walcott notes.

> A lot of folks in the Caribbean region looked at that and said, Why is this white community organization making these claims without discussing it with us? I think that at that moment, one thing that we missed was that in parts of the global South there was the beginnings of a rejection of what people saw as the white gay international. Egale and SMM got caught up in that.[15]

Harper's immigration minister, Jason Kenney, finally stepped in on the visa issue. That raised the stakes: a government widely considered to be racist was denying visas to Jamaicans. Larcher countered that the issue was incitement to violence and while he was "a staunch advocate of freedom of movement. . . . If we accept travel restrictions for people who incite violence against Jews, or Muslims or Christians, then we should do it for gays. Period. Why is religion given some elevated status and not other categories?"

In March 2008 J-FLAG issued a statement opposing the boycott.

> Because of the possible repercussions of increased homophobic violence against our already besieged community, we feel that a tourist boycott is not the most appropriate response at this time. In our battle to win hearts and minds, we do not wish to be perceived as taking food off the plate of those who are already impoverished. In fact, members of our own community could be disproportionately affected by a worsened economic situation brought about by a tourist ban.[16]

But Gareth Henry, J-FLAG co-chair until he fled to Canada for his own safety, was still in support. He argued that while J-FLAG could not publicly support a boycott, "gays and lesbians and queers on the ground" still did.

In May, the boycott was officially called off after Stop Murder Music (Canada) received a letter from the Jamaican consul general reiterating Jamaica's commitment to protect all citizens. The only specific mention of homosexuality in the letter was to point out that J-FLAG did not support the boycott. "It is to be assumed that, naturally, the views of the persons whose interests are ostensibly being promoted will be respected."[17]

Stop Murder Music faced opposition from an anti-censorship position, a Jamaican nationalist position, a pan-Caribbean opposition who felt they had not been properly consulted, and others concerned with the campaign's effect on racial politics in Canada. All of these were amplified by the boycott strategy. Helen Kennedy of Egale took a lot of the flak. "I don't think she should have," Larcher recollects. "But she was the head of the organization so she took the hard questions. I don't think she should have been identified as the person who made this happen."[18]

The Toronto campaign was more grounded in the Caribbean and black communities than the 2004 efforts in the United Kingdom. But what seemed at first a straightforward fight against homophobia became a minefield of racial, colonial, diaspora, and regional politics. It struggled against the frame that "enlightened" (white) countries like Canada were trying to discipline "backward" (black) ones. That frame both pinkwashed continuing homophobia in Canada, and projected it on the racialized other. Solidarity in the age of neo-liberalism would not be a simple matter.

THE CRIMINALIZATION OF HIV

One evening in the baths I bumped into a man I had played with before. He invited me into his room but as soon as the door closed, he began to cry. After our first encounter, he had recognized me speaking on behalf of people with HIV in the media. Now he was sure he had AIDS. "You should have told me," he sobbed.

Our sex had been safe, with no opportunity for transmission, and it had never occurred to me to talk about my medical history. I almost never disclosed unless someone initiated some sort of risky sex. Then I would come out as poz and give them a lecture about protecting themselves. I spent the next forty-five minutes in counselling mode, reassuring him that he certainly hadn't contracted anything from me. I pointed out that if he was going to have sex in the baths, he needed to be prepared to come across poz guys and ensure that he had safe sex with everyone. He couldn't expect people to volunteer their status, and those most infectious were probably recently infected and didn't know it, anyway.

I found the incident unsettling. In the bathhouse culture that I was familiar with, people were supposed to protect themselves, not rely on someone else's disclosure. A few months later, an article appeared in the media about a young gay man accused of not disclosing his status. The article included his picture and instructed anyone who had contact with him to contact the police sex crimes unit. The penny dropped about what was changing our carefully constructed safe sex culture.

In 1998, the Supreme Court found an HIV positive man, Henry Cuerrier, had committed fraud by not disclosing his HIV status to two women before unprotected sex. Neither of the women was infected, but presuming they would not have consented had they known his status, the court ruled that their apparent consent was invalid. Cuerrier was therefore guilty of aggravated sexual assault, one of the most serious charges under the Criminal Code, originally drafted with violent rapes in mind.

The court ruled that HIV positive people were required to disclose our status before engaging in any behaviour involving "significant risk" of infecting others. While suggesting that condom use might mean we didn't have to disclose, the court didn't clarify what significant risk was or how it was to be determined.

The issue of how to deal with HIV positive people, who through negligence or malice exposed others to the virus, had been around for a long time. The Ontario Advisory Committee on HIV/AIDS set up a sub-committee to deal with it in 1990. In those days, Public Health generally assumed responsibility. The Public Health Act gave officials the power to order individuals to refrain from activities that put others at risk, and if they violated the order, to detain them in a hospital setting.

These "Section 22" orders were laid at the discretion of local medical officers of health, and their application varied widely across the province. The right to appeal was limited, and standards of evidence were not those of a court of law. The act had also been drafted to deal with diseases that could be cured. There was no cure for HIV, so theoretically, people could be detained for life. At the time I argued at the AAN! steering committee that it would be better for such cases to be dealt with in the courts. At least there, a concrete charge had to be laid, the accused had the right to a proper legal defence, and they had to be found guilty beyond a reasonable doubt. I should have been careful what I wished for.

With *Cuerrier*, the criminal justice system began to displace Public Health, producing a whole new set of problems. First, there was the lack of clarity about significant risk. Against a background of AIDS phobia and ignorance, courts across the country came to wildly different interpretations. A number of people were convicted for not disclosing before engaging in what was generally considered very low-risk activity.

Since the issue was a matter of fraud, no one needed to be infected. Non-disclosure itself was the crime. Charges began to escalate in number and seriousness. Police began publishing names and pictures of the accused in a hunt for other victims before any finding of guilt. A disproportionate number of racialized people were charged. Lurid media reports of trials exaggerated the risk of HIV transmission, and represented PWAs as irresponsible, dishonest, and potential murderers. The process amplified itself – more publicity, more accusations.

The results were perverse. As fear of being charged spread, poz people were less likely to disclose. Worse, many who suspected they were poz were less likely to test. At least they could plead ignorance. But if they didn't test, they weren't treated and they were more infectious. The law was fanning the flames of the epidemic.

In 2007 a group of women from PASAN, Africans in Partnership Against AIDS, Asian Community AIDS Services, and the 519 Church Street Community Centre began meeting. A client at ACAS had been charged for failing to disclose her status and was facing deportation. The criminalization of HIV had begun to affect women. This was new. Most of the original cases had been against straight men.

The women's group broadened to include others and became the Ontario Working Group on Criminal Law and HIV Exposure (CLHE). Two key member organizations were the Canadian HIV/AIDS Legal Network and the HIV and AIDS Legal Clinic of Ontario. Although the revitalized AAN! sent a rep, the centre of gravity of CLHE was in AIDS service organizations. In the 1990s, AAN! had represented activism by HIV positive people and valued coming out as poz. Ironically, in the new century, advocacy for HIV positive people involved the right not to disclose one's status.

After long discussions, CLHE developed a position paper that opened, "The criminal law is an ineffective and inappropriate tool with which to address HIV exposure." It developed an analysis of the social impact of criminalization – stigma, invasion of privacy, fear of disclosure, decreased testing, and increased transmission. CLHE focused on education for service organizations. But after more cases hit the press, I argued that it needed to step up its work. Lawyers needed to be organized to ensure that those accused received the best possible legal representation. Every conviction and guilty plea created another precedent. We needed a more public campaign to make people aware of the dangers of the situation. I joined as an AAN! rep in 2008.

The roots of HIV criminalization were complicated and diverse. On the surface, they included public health concerns, a desire to protect the vulnerable, and feminist notions of consent generalized and amplified by legal precedents. But they were also based on irrational fears of HIV. The media regularly referenced a vampire narrative, the seductive kiss that converted its victim into the undead carrier of the dreaded disease. Neo-liberalism's focus on individual responsibility fed the conservative tough on crime response. Seroconversion required blame – of oneself, or preferably, of the other.

Finally, criminalization both reflected and reinforced notions of acceptable sex – between intimates, preferably monogamous and married – as contrasted with unacceptable sex – without intimacy and promiscuous. As the single largest group of positive people, it was only a matter of time before gay men began getting swept up.

AZIGA

Discussion of the social and public health effects of criminalization was beyond most people's interpretive frames. That became especially evident during the trial of Johnson Aziga in 2008–2009. Ugandan-born Aziga was accused of not disclosing to a number of women. Several were infected and two subsequently died. Aziga was charged and found guilty of two counts of first-degree murder and ten of aggravated sexual assault. CLHE organized a public forum to try to talk about the broader issues, but right-wing *Globe and*

Mail columnist Margaret Wente, who has made a career out of using wedge issues to isolate racialized minorities and progressive organizations,[19] launched an attack on the "AIDS establishment" for its evasion of the issue of "personal responsibility."

The mainstream narrative was a simple and powerful – a black African, through gross negligence or malice, had deceived his partners and infected them with a virus that killed them. The story fit racist tropes about black men assaulting white women, immigrants as diseased and dangerous, guilt and innocence, love and betrayal, death and sex. It was a story of good and evil that echoed the plot of every TV crime drama. At the end of the program, the bad guy had to go to jail.

On the other hand, CLHE advanced a complex narrative focusing on the cascading of effects of stigma on marginalized groups and its effects on transmission. It was like a second-year sociology lecture. Our messaging was interpreted as giving guilty PWAs a get-out-of-jail-free card. In a neo-liberal world where there was "no society, only individuals," no one wanted to hear talk about social impact.

RELISTING

In May 2008, a decade after the procedure was cut from provincial health insurance by the Harris government, Health Minister George Smitherman announced that the province would relist sex reassignment surgery. By then, Ontario was one of only two provinces still refusing to pay, and Smitherman had felt increasing pressure from a more militant trans community and a growing list of allies. In 2004, Egale initiated a postcard campaign targeting Premier McGuinty, and after the marriage battles were over, it launched its Trans Equality Campaign. When the Human Rights Tribunal ruling failed to force the government to reinstate funding, Cheri DiNovo introduced a private member's bill to include gender identity and later gender expression in the OHRC. There were more postcard and petition campaigns. The Trans Lobby Group made the government's foot dragging an issue in the 2007 provincial elections, and demonstrators crashed Smitherman's annual constituents' picnic.

Smitherman's announcement, while welcome, only returned to the pre-1998 status quo. The Gender Identity Clinic at Toronto's Centre for Addiction and Mental Health was still the only site authorized to approve surgery, and CAMH, because of its restrictive policies, had a long history of conflict with the trans community. A new series of negotiations needed to be launched.

Nevertheless, Smitherman's announcement was a focus during the 2008 Pride celebrations. Trans people finally seemed to be winning acceptance in the community. New issues about who was welcome at Pride, however, were in the wings.

At first glance, the Middle East would seem a long way from Toronto, even though, in a fast globalizing world, distances were collapsing. Still, few would have predicted that Israel/Palestine would be the next flashpoint in Toronto gay politics.

By 2008, Palestinians made up the largest and most long-standing refugee population in the world. Displaced by Israeli ethnic cleansing in 1948, many had been refugees for sixty years. Millions were stateless and living in surrounding Arab countries or scattered throughout the world. In the Gaza Strip and the West Bank, four million had lived under Israeli occupation since 1967. Palestinians had tried many strategies to regain their homeland: armed struggle, spontaneous uprisings, and UN-brokered talks. All had failed. Israel refused to comply with international refugee law and continued expanding its illegal settlements in the occupied territories.

In 2005 Palestinian civil society organizations agreed on a new strategy, an international call for boycott, divestment, and sanctions until Israel complied with international law. That would mean allowing refugees to return to their homes, giving full rights to Palestinians living in Israel, and ending its occupation of the West Bank and Gaza.[20]

The strategy was modelled on the international campaign to isolate apartheid South Africa thirty years before. "Israeli apartheid" was not a rhetorical slogan. It had been used to describe the situation by well-known figures such as former U.S. president Jimmy Carter and South African archbishop Desmond Tutu. It was based on the uncanny similarities between the two systems, as evidenced in a major 2009 study by the South African Human Sciences Research Council.[21] There were separate laws and education systems, housing segregation, a pass system to regulate movement, daily humiliations, huge disparities in wealth, and brutal military repression to keep the system in place. Visiting South Africans often remarked that what they saw in Palestine was worse than what they had experienced in South Africa.

The BDS strategy rejuvenated an international solidarity movement, including Israeli Apartheid Week events on university campuses. Queers Against Israeli Apartheid formed in 2008 after one such event at the University of Toronto. The small group's original membership was mostly young, many already friends. Most had studied equity issues and were acquainted with Queer Theory. About a third were Jewish, and there were a few Palestinians.

That year at Pride, a gaggle of QuAIA activists marched, sandwiched between the CUPE and Canadian Union of Postal Workers. CUPE Ontario had endorsed the Palestinian call for BDS in 2006, and CUPW had become the first country-wide union to do so in April 2008. It was not the first time that Israeli politics had surfaced at Pride. The largely lesbian and bi Jewish Women's Committee to End the Occupation had marched regularly during the late 1980s and early '90s carrying Palestinian solidarity messages.

By 2008, the stakes were higher. Israeli brutality and its occupation of Palestinian lands had seriously tarnished the county's international reputation. In October 2005 after a review of "specialized research conducted by American marketing executives," the directors of Israel's three most powerful ministries, the Foreign Ministry, the Prime Minister's Office, and the Finance Ministry, launched a new public relations campaign, "Brand Israel."[22]

Brand Israel, aimed at U.S. and European audiences, was based on marketing theory: establishing brand loyalty is more important than the merits of a product. It called for downplaying religion and avoiding mention of the Palestinian conflict. Instead, it focused on Israel's contribution to medicine, technology, and culture. The country would be associated with warm, fuzzy, core liberal values: modernity, democracy, innovation, and progress. The resulting brand loyalty, it was hoped, would render the North American and European public impervious to Palestinian arguments about human rights and international law.

In August 2008, the Israeli consulate announced Toronto would be a test market for Brand Israel. The lessons learned would inform the subsequent worldwide rollout. Consul General Amir Gissin revealed plans for an exhibition of the Dead Sea Scrolls and a major presence in the 2009 Toronto International Film Festival.[23]

According to the U.K. *Guardian*, "One of the most remarkable features of the Brand Israel campaign is the marketing of a modern Israel as a gay-friendly Israel." This was not simply aimed at winning friends and encouraging tourism among queer communities.

> Within global gay and lesbian organizing circuits, to be gay friendly is to be modern, cosmopolitan, developed, first-world, global north, and, most significantly, democratic. Events such as World Pride 2006 hosted in Jerusalem, and "Out in Israel" recently held in San Francisco highlight Israel as a country committed to democratic ideals of freedom for all, including gays and lesbians.[24]

Our community was being played to support an apartheid regime.

THE CRASH

In September there was a massive financial crash in the United States. On October 11, 2008, the head of the International Monetary Fund warned that the world financial system was teetering on the "brink of systemic meltdown."[25]

The immediate cause was that major U.S. banks had been selling "securities" to investors based on the projected income owed them from bundles of mortgage payments. But the banks had also been granting mortgages to people who couldn't possibly pay them off. When they started to default, the whole system collapsed. Fifteen U.S. banks failed; others were rescued by government because they were "too big to fail." Dozens of banks around the world soon followed. A complete economic collapse, worse than the Great Depression, was only avoided by massive government intervention. Trillions of dollars were pumped into the international banking system to keep it afloat.

The neo-liberal chickens had come home to roost. The rich, awash in money to invest, found financial speculation more profitable than producing real goods. Without oversight, financial institutions indulged in risky practices to make a fast buck for their clients. Free trade had undermined the U.S. manufacturing system as companies moved offshore to exploit cheap labour in the developing world. Although more people were earning less as better jobs disappeared, the banks made credit easier to keep them consuming. Selling people homes they couldn't pay for was part of that strategy.

The economic crisis produced a political one. It devalued the political currency of neo-liberalism and the politicians most closely associated with it. President George W. Bush looked pathetic by the end of his term. The Democratic presidential candidate, Barack Obama, won election in November 2008 and became president on January 20, 2009. The first black American president, Obama won on a vague platform of hope, a message that many Americans lapped up. The more socially conservative Republicans were relegated to the opposition. But like Clinton's Democratic presidency before his, Obama was not about to take on the powerful elites behind neo-liberalism.

Canada escaped the worst. Our deregulation process lagged behind that of the United States. Canadian banks were still better supervised and not as exposed to rotten loans. Still, after years of talking about reducing government's role in the economy, the Harper government began spending millions on a very Keynesian stimulus package to avoid the worst effects of recession. In 2009, even Toronto Pride was granted $400,000 as part of the program. That grant put the noses of Harper's social conservative friends severely out of joint.

WATT WERE THEY THINKING?

June 5, 2009, at its gala fundraiser in the King Edward Hotel's elegant ballroom, Egale presented its inaugural leadership award to Jaime Watt, executive chairman of Navigator, "Canada's leading high-stakes public strategy and communications firm."

Watt was the "communications guru" for Mike Harris's 1995 Conservative election victory that had unleashed the Common Sense Revolution, closing hospitals, slashing health care funding, delisting sex reassignment surgery, reducing social security benefits, decimating education funding, dismantling labour and environmental protections, and so on, in order to give handsome tax cuts to the super rich. Watt had only resigned from his position as Harris's director of communications in 2002 when his previous fraud and forgery convictions became an embarrassment.

Egale's announcement generated an incredulous reaction, even from normally more circumspect voices in the community. Peter Bochove, owner of the Spa Excess bathhouse, told *Xtra* that he found the honour "personally offensive." "Let's talk about Walkerton, let's talk about Ipperwash, let's talk about the amalgamation of Toronto, let's talk about the 'common sense revolution.' It's the antithesis of everything in the gay community."[26] Gilles Marchildon, former Egale director, pointed out that the erosion of public infrastructure during the Harris government "disproportionately affected people who were already marginalized."[27] Long-time activist Stephen Seaborn noted the irony of the situation. "This year's dinner was billed as a fundraiser for safe schools, and here we are honoring a Harris operative whose efforts totally gutted these initiatives. . . . Jaime Watt spent his entire political career working for politicians who fought against us."[28]

In an article in *NOW*, Andrew Brett pointed out that Watt's close friend, Tory cabinet minister John Baird, was also a guest at the gala. "Despite Baird's vigorous applause for same-sex marriage, when he was Treasury Board president in 2006 he cancelled the Court Challenges Program that allowed citizens to fight discriminatory treatment in the courts, the very program Egale relied on to mount its legal challenges."[29]

But for Egale, having such a well-connected, wealthy, and influential friend was what mattered. Egale's justification was that Watt had helped ensure the passage of Bill 5, the legislation that gave same-sex couples equal rights, "the most significant piece of equality rights legislation in Ontario's history."[30] Egale seemed to have forgotten that Harris only reluctantly passed the legislation when ordered to do so by a court ruling. Helen Kennedy also credited Watt with stepping in when Egale faced collapse after the same-sex marriage campaign. Navigator was still providing Egale free space in its downtown offices.

It was becoming increasingly evident where vertical alliances were taking the ever more mainstream rights movement.

ADIOS CLGRO

In May 2009, CLGRO held its last annual general meeting. A resolution to disband the group carried unanimously. The last of the 1970s political organizations was gone. Over thirty-four years, CLGRO spearheaded the fight to have sexual orientation included in the OHRC, fought censorship, and challenged police homophobia. It mentored organizing in smaller centres across the province and was an LGBT voice in dozens of municipal, provincial, and federal forums. It intervened in education and immigration issues and launched the community discussion on same-sex relationships that eventually led to the Coalition for Equal Families. At a point when the community was focused on AIDS, CLGRO promoted research on the wider range of health issues affecting LGBT people, eventually leading to provincial funding for Rainbow Health Ontario and an early platform for trans activists. It galvanized the LGBT communities in the struggle for equality. And true to its gay liberation roots, it also questioned whether equality was enough, taking unpopular stands on controversial issues such as sexual rights for youth and age of consent.

Remarkably, CLGRO remained a grassroots, volunteer-driven organization that resisted dominant institutional forms. Like AAN! it gave birth to important services without ever becoming a service organization itself.

Several CLGRO organizers went on to found a new organization, Queer Ontario. But Tom Warner, the group's mainstay since inception and one of the early activists working on *TBP* and GATE, took his retirement.

PRIDE 2009

QuAIA was ready to make a bigger splash at Pride 2009. It kicked off the season with a public meeting in mid-May, and asked me to deliver a keynote about my experience with the Simon Nkdoi Anti-apartheid Committee in the 1980s. El Farouk Khaki served as emcee. Khaki, a well-known immigration lawyer specializing in queer refugee cases, was founder of Salaam, an early lesbian and gay Muslim group in 1991. He had recently helped establish the El Tawhid Juma Circle and Unity Mosque, Toronto's first queer-friendly mosque. He had also just been selected as grand marshal for the 2009 Pride festival, the first Muslim ever awarded the honour. The event, at Buddies in Bad Times Theatre, was packed.

I hadn't previously been much involved in Middle East issues, but I was happy to speak about our experience with SNAAC. We had found ourselves doing both support work for Simon in lesbian and gay communities, and anti-homophobia work in the broader anti-apartheid movement. These efforts ultimately helped enshrine lesbian and gay rights in South Africa's post-apartheid constitution. I stressed that queers needed to unconditionally express our solidarity with other groups fighting for human rights and social justice, and the struggle against Israeli apartheid was one of those causes.

A couple of dissenters had come to say that they didn't understand how gay people could support homophobic Palestinians rather than gay-friendly Israel. But the discussion was good, and the meeting a success.

Then the shit hit the fan.

Anyone who has dared criticize Israel's illegal occupation of Palestine has become used to histrionic attacks, but as grand marshal and a Muslim, the attacks on Khaki were over the top. B'Nai Brith's Frank Dimant described him as "part and parcel of the anti-Israel machinery that continues to churn out hateful and divisive propaganda" and demanded he be removed as grand marshal.[31] Once a respected human rights organization, by 2009 B'Nai Brith had become one of the shrillest voices in what QuAIA termed the Israel lobby, a loose coalition of groups who, despite differences in tone, regularly decried any criticism of Israel's policies as anti-Semitic.[32] Even staunch Israel supporter Jonathan Kay of the *National Post* wrote about B'Nai Brith's "absurd contention that anti-Semitism is a growing epidemic in this tolerant country. . . . Older Jews with dark historical memories become terrified, and the donations to B'nai Brith come rolling in."[33]

Others objected to the choice of a Muslim as a grand marshal in the first place,[34] and demanded QuAIA be banned from Pride as a hate group.

Pride felt the heat. Director Tracey Sandilands issued a statement that Khaki would "never under any circumstances speak on the Israeli issue from a Pride point of view." But ultimately, the campaign to have Khaki removed and QuAIA banned went nowhere. No one had ever heard of a queer group being banned from Pride because of its politics.

Even Councillor Kyle Rae found it necessary to speak out.

> I would be angered and offended if someone were able to use Pride for a vehicle to express their anti-Semitism or hatred. My understanding is the use of the word apartheid could be offensive to some, but it is a description of a political regime that is happening on the West Bank. . . . It's not about hate. . . . There are Jews as well as non-Jews who are members of this organization who are opposed to the Israeli government's actions, including the building of the controversial West-Bank barrier. There are Palestinian queer people who are living under that situation. . . . It's a political issue but it does have a gay dynamic to it.[35]

I had expected my talk would be a one-off, but given the virulence of the attacks, I couldn't just speak and run. Richard and I started attending QuAIA meetings, as the group tried to figure out how to deal with the fallout. I soon became aware how much the tools of organizing had changed. QuAIA had a substantial website with key resources and links to other movements around the world. Events were organized through Facebook groups, and we had a Twitter following. While it didn't replace regular meetings, membership also required a deluge of email communications with different lists for core members and supporters. All of this amplified our voice, but it also meant that there was a considerable social media infrastructure to maintain. Organizing had become a much more intense process than in my youth.

When QuAIA marched in Pride, our contingent was swelled by the controversy. Afterwards, we laughed and privately thanked Israel's apologists for giving us so much free publicity. But we seriously underestimated their strength and tenacity. And we hadn't even noticed a middle-aged man studiously filming our contingent.

CHRISTIAN ZIONISM

B'Nai Brith's main spokesperson, Executive Vice-President Frank Dimant, liked to have friends in high places. When Harper was elected, Dimant and former B'Nai Brith president Rochelle Wilner were among the first to meet with the new prime minister. Dimant soon established himself as "chief inter-locutor" between Harper and the "Jewish community."[36]

Dimant also had friends in very low places. He had received an honorary doctorate and was chair of Israel studies at the Canada Christian College, the fundamentalist training camp run by Charles McVety, arguably Canada's lead-ing homophobe.

The connection with McVety was more than just moonlighting on Dimant's part. Dimant was a main architect of the Israel lobby's new alliance with Christian fundamentalists in Canada. In 2003 he pushed a motion through the B'Nai Brith board "authorizing a formal partnership with the Christian right."[37] He also initiated the first evangelical/Jewish delegation to Israel with John Tweedie, senior pastor at the New Covenant Christian Fel-lowship Church in Brantford, Ontario. Tweedie went on to chair Christians for Israel, regularly leading tours to the country and opposing calls for a Palestinian homeland.

Christian Zionism is a powerful tendency within evangelical Christianity drawing on a particular reading of the book of Revelation called Dispensa-tionalism.[38] It proclaims we are approaching "the end of times" when the bat-tle of Armageddon will be fought on the plains of Israel, and Christ will return and set up his kingdom. True Christians will avoid the tribulations because they will be vacuumed up to heaven in the Rapture. But in order for all this to occur, Jews must first return to Israel, rebuild the Temple, and be attacked by their enemies. Christian Zionists therefore want Israel to consoli-date its occupation and the ethnic cleansing of Palestinians, and are steadfast in their support of the most right-wing and bellicose forces within Israel. Anything that brings the region closer to war brings us all closer to Jesus.

McVety was probably the major Canadian propagandist for this theology. He was also tireless in building a new theo-con movement to bring Canada back under Biblical law so that it could play its ordained role as a Christian nation in hastening Christ's return. Although driven by evangelical zeal, the movement had successfully reached out to conservative Catholics, Jews, and more recent immigrant groups such as Sikhs and Muslims around such issues as gay rights and abortion. In 2005 McVety had led the Defend Marriage Campaign, the major opposition to gay marriage legislation.

The Christian right wielded increasing influence in Harper's Ottawa, as detailed in Marci McDonald's book, *The Armageddon Factor*.[39] According to McDonald:

> With funding from a handful of conservative Christian philanthropists and
> a web of grassroots believers accustomed to tithing in the service of their
> faith, those organizations have built sophisticated databases and online net-
> works capable of mobilizing their forces behind specific legislation with
> instant e-mail alerts and updates. Setting up an array of internship pro-
> grams, they are also training a new generation of activists to be savvier than

their secular peers in navigating the corridors of power. Already, their alumni have landed top jobs in the public service, MPs' offices and the [Prime Minister's Office], prompting one official from the National House of Prayer to boast in an unguarded moment, "If the media knew how many Christians there are in the government, they'd go crazy."[40]

The growing influence of Christian lobby groups was facilitated by Harper himself. He gave them personal recognition and unparalleled access to parliamentarians, and allowed his evangelical Christian members of Parliament to test public sentiment with private members' bills. So in 2009, when McVety spearheaded complaints about the $400,000 federal stimulus package grant to Pride Toronto, Harper sacked the minister responsible, Diane Ablonczy.

Christian Zionists, who want Jews to return to Israel to be destroyed in the battle of Armageddon or converted to Christianity, may seem odd bedfellows for pro-Israel Jews. The logic of this alliance was pointed out clearly by Joseph Ben-Ami. "The Jewish community in Canada is 380,000 strong. The evangelical community is three and a half million. The real support base for Israel is Christians."[41] Ben-Ami is a good example of the growing connections between Zionists, Christian Zionists, and the Harper government. Operations director for Stockwell Day's 2002 leadership campaign, he served as a policy aid to Stephen Harper and for two years as B'Nai Brith's chief lobbyist in Ottawa before emerging as McVety deputy in the Defend Marriage Campaign.

At any rate, the alliance of Jewish and Christian Zionists was a marriage made in heaven for Harper. His unquestioning support for Israel won conservative Jews away from their traditional home in the Liberal party and invigorated his support among the much larger Christian evangelical demographic.

So Dimant's attack on QuAIA and Khaki was not just to silence critics of Israel. It also contributed to his boss McVety's attempts to destabilize Pride, and played into the hands of the Harper Conservatives.

DESIRING SOLIDARITY

One of QuAIA's leading members, Natalie Kouri-Towe, was working on a doctorate on the ethics of international solidarity. Some of her concerns were familiar to me from our experience with SNAAC in the 1980s. Solidarity movements develop their own momentum and imperatives, and it is easy to slip into using the object of the work to serve those purposes.

In SNAAC, we had been well aware of the power differential between those of us in the global North, and the patronizing history of charity that depicted those in the South as victims, dependent on our benevolence and deprived of any agency of their own. We talked about recognizing the leadership of those with whom we were in solidarity. Still, there was a moment of discomfort in SNAAC when Nkoli wrote that what he really needed was a warm coat. Shouldn't our meager resources be used to do anti-apartheid work here? Were we just a charity? Again, when Nkoli finally made it to Canada, our triumphant North American tour of thirty cities in thirty days almost killed him.

Despite our best efforts, we had exploited Nkoli as our poster boy. Kouri-Towe warned against looking for a similar "authentic queer Palestinian subjects" to serve our interests. Why would our solidarity be contingent on the existence of Palestinian queers rather than with Palestinians as an oppressed people, regardless of their sexuality? Further, while Nkoli had unproblematically adopted a gay identity intelligible to us in Toronto, Queer Theory's insistence on the discursive production of sexuality (what the old debates had called the social construction of sexuality) warned that the assumption of the universal gay subject was essentialist, and in this context, colonialist.

Kouri-Towe introduced us to Joseph Massad's new book, *Desiring Arabs*. Massad, a Palestinian living in exile, was widely seen as inheriting the mantle of Edward Said, the leading Palestinian intellectual of his day. Said's *Orientalism* (1978) had probed the development of European ideas of "the orient" and how they were tied to western colonial ambitions in the Middle East. Part of that discourse focused on the notion of "oriental sexuality." Massad's book sought to develop those insights. He pointed out that "while the pre-modern West attacked medieval Islam's alleged sexual licentiousness, the modern West attacks its alleged *repression* of sexual freedoms."[42] Either way, Arab sexuality was always something backward, and Europe and the West needed to intervene, whether to control or to liberate.

Massad was less interested in how the West saw Arab sexuality than in how Arabs saw it themselves, and how nationalism, religion, colonialism, and western ideas such as Social Darwinism had affected that vision. Much of *Desiring Arabs* discussed the reception accorded to the more than a thousand homoerotic couplets of Abu Nuwas. The medieval Arab poet holds something of the same esteem among Arabic speakers as Shakespeare does in the English-speaking world. Massad described how Nuwas's homoerotic couplets and his many references to wine, women, and song had alternately been understood as promoting vice, a call to honesty, representative of the golden age of enlightened Arab tolerance, denounced as foreign (Persian), or attacked as anti-religious.

But the two central chapters of *Desiring Arabs* leave literary criticism to focus on what Massad calls "the Gay International," groups such as the ILGA and the International Gay and Lesbian Human Rights Commission. He accused them of working within the parameters of western colonialism to "incite a discourse" to locate same-sex activity within the western category of homosexuality. "I will argue that it is the very discourse of the Gay International, which both produces homosexuals, as well as gays and lesbians, where they do not exist, and represses same-sex desires and practices that refuse to be assimilated into its sexual epistemology."[43] On a practical level, Massad alleged that it was only upper- and middle-class individuals, those most influenced by and complicit with colonialism, who adopted the western category of homosexual.

The result, he argued, was disastrous for the majority of those involved in same-sex practices in the Arab world, regardless of their identity. The attempt to impose homosexual categories from the outside inflamed nationalist and religious reaction and led to the suppression of behaviours that were previously tolerated. That reaction was then exploited by the Gay International as revelatory of the Arab world's backwardness, justifying more colonial intervention.

Personally, I felt that Massad was a much better literary scholar than he was a sociologist. The organizations he derides as the Gay International were tiny and hardly played such a significant role on the international stage. There was a diffusion of identities to parts of the world that had previously not organized identities around sexual practices. But while that took place within the context of western colonialism, it could not be reduced to a western imposition. People in a neo-colonial world were adopting such identities because, on some level, they worked for them. Such identities were, as Foucault might have said, "technologies of self" that individuals used to make sense of and shape their behaviour. Their diffusion could no more be constrained than could the diffusion of any other technology in a globalized world. To try to do so would be to suppose a pre-existing "authentic" Arab sexuality that needed to be protected, despite Massad's denial of such an implication. Finally it was not surprising that such identities were being adopted first by people with most access to global circuits.

Still, QuAIA needed to take into account Massad's point that sexuality had become part of the battle between the "civilizing mission" of western colonialism and the anti-colonial reaction. On the one hand, we were combatting the Israeli generated stereotypes about the backwardness of Arabs. But at the same time, we faced the temptation of finding authentic Palestinian queers to undermine those stereotypes, and to make our politics palatable to western lesbian and gay communities. We were ethically obliged to show solidarity for people persecuted because they had adopted lesbian or gay identities, but when we did so, we ran the risk of becoming part of the civilizing mission. At times Queer Theory, with its anxieties and insights about the potential contradictory and unintended consequences of any action, seemed a paralyzing influence.

RAINBOWS AND RAILROADS

With visible gay rights successes in North America, Europe, and parts of Latin America, more people in cultures with strong traditional values were adopting similar sexual identities. In places without a tradition of individual rights, those attempting to organize around those identities could experience violence in their families and communities as well as persecution. In a world ever more awash with political, economic, and climate refugees, a new category of sexual refugees was emerging. Countries like Canada were considered a safe haven. Faced with individual emergencies, groups with a liberal human rights approach emerged to fill the gap.

In Toronto, MCC was the first off the mark. The church began hosting support group meetings for LGBT refugee claimants in 2005. The program soon expanded to assist claimants with immigration hearings, housing, social assistance, and legal aid. Later, taking advantage of the private refugee sponsorship program, MCC helped bring in selected LGBT refugees and located donors to support their first transition year in Canada.[44]

Toronto's Rainbow Railroad was founded in 2006. The group's chair, Michel Battista, was an immigration lawyer and adjunct professor at the U of T Faculty of Law. Rainbow Railroad soon developed a focus on the Caribbean, Africa, and the former Soviet bloc countries. It supported LGBT refugees in hiding and provided funds to secure passage to safer countries for those facing imminent threat of violence or death.[45]

The same year, the Iranian Queer Organization (IRQO)[46] began organizing among lesbian, gay, bisexual, and trans Iranians in Toronto. In 2008 one of the original IRQO founders, Arsham Parsi, started another group, the Iranian Railroad for Queer Refugees (IRQR).[47] Both Iranian groups worked to provide legal, housing, and financial assistance for Iranian LGBT refugees, to facilitate their passage to Canada or other safe countries, and to document human rights abuses inside Iran.

The timelines facing refugees are short. These groups had to develop relationships with the Harper government. And Harper was more than willing to portray Israel's enemy Iran as repressive, even as the government was tightening rules for asylum in Canada.

Rainbow Railroad won charitable status in 2013. This status legally restricts a group's ability to engage in political advocacy, so both structurally and politically it was difficult for it to criticize the government. But supporting vulnerable refugees requires resources, and charitable status encourages wealthy donors.

Richard pointed out another problem. Asked by El Farouk Khaki to provide a letter for a refugee board hearing for a Trinidadian case, he struggled with reprising stereotypes of Caribbean backwardness and violence. If his letter was to be effective for the individual application, it would also have to reinforce the idea of a tolerant, civilized (white) Canada versus an intolerant, backward (black and brown) Caribbean. These stereotypes were damaging to people from the Caribbean, regardless of their sexual orientation. And while it was true that individuals could experience violence and persecution and that Trinidad and Tobago still had the old British anti-sodomy laws on the books, Richard also knew that reality was far more complex. The country was simultaneously home to a thriving lesbian and gay subculture.

The refugee process also required that claimants display an identity congruent with western conceptions of homosexuality. That problem was brought into focus by the case of Alvaro Orozco, a young Nicaraguan gay man facing deportation in 2011. Orozco had run away from his homophobic, abusive father when he was twelve, and over eight years made his way through Central America and the United States to Canada. He applied for refugee status. After a video hearing with a judge in Alberta in 2005, his claim was rejected. The judge didn't think he looked gay enough. Orozco went underground and established roots in the Toronto gay community. In the spring of 2011, he was picked up in a random police check and incarcerated while awaiting deportation to Nicaragua.

The support and advocacy group No One Is Illegal took up the case with a number of lesbian and gay youth and arts organizations. After public demonstrations, sit-ins blocking Church Street, media coverage, petitions, phone-in campaigns, and legal manoeuvring, at the last minute, Orozco was granted humanitarian status and released.

Orozco didn't fit a judge's preconception of what gay should look like. There were deeper problems for those whose sexual practices didn't fit established notions of sexual identity. Immigration law expert Sean Rehaag pointed out the difficulties faced by bisexual refugee applicants. Since their sexual history may include marriage and parenthood, they were often unable to fit into the straight-gay dichotomy entrenched in Canada's refugee law. In the legal system, those with fluid, queer, or bisexual orientations faced a more difficult time proving they were part of a persecuted class.[48]

PROSECUTORIAL GUIDELINES

CLHE's arguments about the social impact of criminalization had proved unintelligible to the general public. Arguments about individual responsibility were well accepted; arguments about the social were not. After twenty years of neo-liberalism, Thatcher's famous statement about no society, only individuals, had become common sense. People didn't think much about long-term social effects. They saw a world inhabited by rational individuals who made good or bad decisions. Such individuals should be discouraged from making bad decisions. If they insisted on being bad, they should be punished.

CLHE was isolated politically, and not just among the general public. There was division among those who traditionally rallied around AIDS issues. Dr. Mark Wainberg, co-chair of the 2006 International AIDS Conference in Toronto, was one of the first to unequivocally speak out against criminalization. Drs. Philip Berger and Brian Cornelson, two Toronto physicians well known for their AIDS work, said people should be held accountable for non-disclosure.[49] A libertarian current that found voice in *Xtra* argued there should be no role for criminal law in HIV infection, and that it was the individual responsibility of HIV *negative* people to protect themselves. Others echoed the prevailing view that anyone who was positive had an unequivocal responsibility to disclose at all times. Why the hell were these people having sex, anyway? Upright gay people were accepted. We needed to distinguish ourselves from the sleazy and irresponsible.

The current of feminism that had called on state intervention as far back as the pornography debates saw criminalization as a legitimate way to protect women from dangerous or irresponsible men. If someone withheld information, consent was invalid and sex was legally rape. "Sex-positive" feminists landed on the other side of the issue. In the anti-criminalization camp, many racialized people alleged that the Aziga trial and the disproportionate number of black men charged in such cases showed the criminal justice system's racism.

By 2009, 104 charges had been laid across the country, almost half in Ontario. If it was going to stop the damage, CLHE needed a strategy that would allow for a broader basis of unity.

In February, a young gay man named Justus Zela was picked up by the RCMP at a Buddhist retreat in Halifax and flown back to Hamilton in handcuffs. He was charged with aggravated sexual assault for consensual, low-risk sexual activity with another man, and held in solitary confinement to protect him from other inmates. Details were published in the media. He had done nothing that constituted a "significant risk" for transmitting HIV, and no one had been infected.

The idea of prosecutorial guidelines had been bouncing around for some time. In 2008 the Crown Prosecution Service of England and Wales published a "legal guidance" to Crown prosecutors entitled "Intentional or Reckless Sexual Transmission of Infection." The document, which set out how the courts should deal with such cases, was successful in reducing the number of charges.

Guidelines would not satisfy those who argued that there was no place for criminal law whatsoever. But they might reduce the number and severity of charges and the damage to people such as Zela. Just as important, asking for prosecutorial guidelines might serve as a basis of unity in the traditional AIDS community base. Even if it wasn't successful, it could provide a reasonable demand around which we could reach out.

The demand for guidelines would be addressed to the provincial government, which is responsible for the administration of justice. The Criminal Code is a federal matter, but its administration is the responsibility of the provincial Ministry of the Attorney General. And Ontario's provincial Liberals were more likely to listen than the hostile Harper government in Ottawa.

Throughout the fall of 2009 and into 2010, CLHE drafted a call to Ontario's attorney general to establish prosecutorial guidelines. It opened by affirming that the criminal law should be compatible with attempts to prevent the spread of the epidemic. It conceded that criminal prosecutions might be warranted in some circumstances, but insisted that the "current expansive use of criminal law" was cause for concern. It called on the attorney general to "undertake a process to develop guidelines for criminal prosecutors" and to ensure that process involved "meaningful" consultation with stakeholders.[50] It did not suggest what such guidelines should entail or where the line between significant or insignificant risk should be drawn. Around those issues, there would still be divisions. But what could be agreed on, the basis of unity, was that a line needed be drawn somewhere.

We developed supporting background documents, and in a parallel effort through the Ontario HIV Treatment Network, York University professor Eric Mykhalovskiy spearheaded a research effort to produce *HIV Non-disclosure and the Criminal Law: Establishing Policy Options for Ontario*.[51] This more scholarly document spoke to policy makers and lawyers within the ministry. Finally, colourful postcards focusing on the issue were produced for distribution in the community.

The campaign rolled out on the model of the three earlier *Globe and Mail* ad campaigns, only without an ad. We approached opinion leaders in the target sectors – the traditional AIDS community, legal experts, academics, religious figures, unions, feminist leaders, and social justice groups – the wider bloc that could exert pressure on the government. Before going public, we had a long discussion with the editors of *Xtra* to ensure they understood what we were doing and to solicit support.

The campaign was surprisingly successful. By mid-2010 more than a thousand people had signed on and sent messages to the attorney general. In December 2010, in an interview with *Xtra*, the attorney general publicly committed to developing guidelines. We were over the first hurdle. Now we needed to get guidelines that could actually do some good.

THE CITY

City council was dominated by a progressive bloc headed by Mayor David Miller. Although he soon let his party membership lapse, he was a member of the NDP when first elected in 2003 as the second mayor of the amalgamated Toronto. His key support came from the gentrifying old city of downtown Toronto.

Miller's campaign symbol was a broom, with which he vowed to clean up a city hall plagued by backroom deals and shady lobbyists. Miller pushed for greater transparency, better public transit, waterfront renewal, and environmental policies. But he took control at a time when the city's traditional manufacturing base was in decline due to free trade policies, and Toronto was still struggling with the extra service responsibilities downloaded by the province during amalgamation. Neo-liberalism had shrunk the capacity of the state to act.

Enter Richard Florida, urban guru. In a series of books, Florida argued that a new "creative class" had emerged as part of the economy's shift towards technology, research and development, and the internet. This class is the engine of economic growth, and cities around the world now compete to attract its members. One of the elements attracting this class is diversity, which Florida measured in part by "the Gay Index." He claimed a strong correlation between the ability to attract creative class members, and thus economic growth, and more tolerance towards culturally unconventional people such as lesbians and gays.

Florida's theories were widely criticized. The right saw him as a big-spending liberal, throwing public money at a privileged cultural elite and ignoring bread and butter issues. The left accused him of devaluing the contributions of ordinary working people and ignoring their marginalization in the face of gentrification. But liberals loved him.

In 2007, Florida moved to Toronto and was soon the darling of city council. Mayor Miller gushed:

> It is on behalf of all Torontonians and with great pride that I welcome Richard and his wife Rana to our great city. Richard is one of the leading thinkers on cities and his choice to live in Toronto shows that we can compete with any city in the world. I also look forward to the knowledge and insights Richard brings that we can learn from to make Toronto even better.[52]

Florida's ideas were enshrined in Toronto's *Plan for a Creative City*,[53] and he was commissioned by Queen's Park to write a major report, *Ontario in the Creative Age*. When the economy tanked in 2009, Councillor Kyle Rae invited Florida to a special closed-door brainstorming session of the city's economic development committee.[54]

While many in the gay community were seduced by the importance he attributed to queer communities, others pointed out that his notion of gay people as upwardly mobile, well educated, artistic, and "creative" scarcely rose above the level of common stereotypes. But among those seduced was Rae, who told the *Toronto Star*, "Luring Richard Florida is like luring one of the top research scientists from Harvard or Yale. He has a credibility, an expertise and an understanding of the dimensions of urban life that dissect and describe how cities work, improve and excel."[55]

Florida-thought cemented city support for events such as Pride. While queer communities might have interpreted this as a demonstration of increased tolerance and declining homophobia, the arguments were fundamentally about economic competition. In a certain way, the city's motivations were similar to those of Brand Israel. Gay tolerance was used to brand Toronto as a modern, progressive place with the hope of political and economic gain.

While far-right social conservatives had been banished from the corridors of political power in Toronto and Queen's Park, they had not gone away.

Kathleen Wynne was appointed minister of education in 2006. Her status in cabinet was strengthened by her personal defeat of Progressive Conservative leader John Tory in her riding during the 2007 election. The first open lesbian to hold a cabinet post in Ontario, Wynne was determined to deal with the hostility faced by lesbian, gay, and trans kids and parents in the school system.

She proceeded systematically. In December 2008, the ministry released *Shaping a Culture of Respect in Our Schools: Promoting Safe and Healthy Relationships.* The document, prepared by the ministry's Safe Schools Action Team, focused on gender-based violence, homophobia, sexual harassment, and inappropriate sexual behaviour.

In June 2009, the Keep Our Kids Safe at School Act was passed. It required reporting of incidents including "racist/sexist or homophobic remarks."[56] It was followed up by a new policy memorandum called *Bullying Prevention and Intervention.* In December 2009, the ministry convened a conference of all boards of education to help them develop new anti-bullying policies that had to be in place by February 2010.

The new policies were a godsend for Egale. Identified by the ministry as a resource, it was deluged with requests from boards across the province. Outside Toronto, schools had been almost impenetrable to lesbian and gay issues. Now under the gun, they were begging for help in catching up. There were advantages to having friends in power.

The focus on harassment and safety disarmed the opposition. Talking about marriage "equality" had put anyone opposed in the uncomfortable position of arguing for inequality. Similarly, talking about bullying and the safety of lesbian and gay children put homophobes in the awkward position of suggesting that violence and bullying were acceptable.

Wynne also released a broader policy, *Realizing the Promise of Diversity: Ontario's Equity and Inclusive Education Strategy.* It came with a new memorandum #119. The original PPM #119, passed by the Rae government after the 1992 Yonge Street riots, required all boards to have an anti-racism policy. The new policy added the word "equity" and required boards to address other such issues, including sexual orientation.

It was, in a certain sense, a catch-up with the 1999 TDSB policy won after so much community organizing. I suppose I should have been happy. It was a validation of what we had been fighting for for years. When AMENO, the group that had pushed for the broad policy in Toronto, invited me to introduce Wynne at a congratulatory meeting, I said I could do it. But I would have to say such policy, as good as it sounded, was only window dressing without resources for implementation.

The Liberals had reintroduced the language of equity, but had not substantially changed the Harris era funding formula that continued to strangle public education. If they were serious about equity, they needed to reverse the cuts, and not only to education. Increasing poverty and the racialization of that poverty was driving racism. The impoverishment of public education deprived vulnerable kids of basic support and triggered unequal outcomes, scapegoating, and horizontal hostility. Policy documents were not enough. AMENO decided that maybe I wasn't a good fit.

A STEP TOO FAR – SEX

In January 2010, the Ministry of Education posted a new Health and Physical Education Curriculum. It was the result of more than three years of consultations with teachers, parent groups, and other stakeholders including PFLAG, Egale, and CLGRO. It had passed ministry bureaucrats and cabinet. Ironically, the day the curriculum was released, Wynne was shifted from Education to Transport. Perhaps McGuinty figured her job was done or that the optics were better for a straight minister to defend the gay-inclusive initiative.

All was quiet until Charles McVety burst on stage. He issued a press release calling on McGuinty to withdraw the policy, which he said involved teaching "Explicit Sex Ed for 8 Year Olds."

> It is unconscionable to teach 8-year old children same-sex marriage, sexual orientation and gender identity. . . . It is even more absurd to subject 6th graders to instruction on the pleasures of masturbation, vaginal lubrication, and 12 year olds to lessons on oral sex and anal intercourse.[57]

McVety's claims set the media alight, and new Tory leader Tim Hudak vowed "to stand with moms and dads across the province of Ontario." Then, although the Catholic boards had been consulted on the document, the Catholic archbishop of Ottawa encouraged parents to voice their concerns. Members of the legislature began to receive hostile emails generated through McVety's mailing lists. Supporters of the bill were caught off guard. Although the Elementary Teachers' Federation and ACT quickly spoke out in support, CLGRO had just dissolved and Egale was silent.

The government panicked. The election was only a year away, and the Liberals were already in trouble over the harmonized sales tax. Despite the fury of Wynne and newly elected member Glen Murray, who had replaced George Smitherman, McGuinty announced three days after McVety's press release that the sex education segments of the curriculum would be withdrawn for a "rethink." There was no timeline announced for its reintroduction. The Liberals caved. There was still bite left in the homophobic dog.

UGANDA

The strength of social conservatism and the Christian right was also evidenced on the other side of the world. Like other former British colonies,

Uganda inherited British laws criminalizing homosexual behaviour. As part of its civilizing mission, the British hoped to stamp out "unnatural sex" among their licentious native subjects. The Bible came as well as laws, and Christian teaching merged with traditional African patriarchy to reinforce socially conservative values in regard to sex. Nevertheless, as in many former British colonies, such legislation had been largely ignored.[58]

In the 1980s and '90s, the battle against AIDS had seen countries like Uganda flooded with NGOs on a different kind of civilizing mission. They recognized that as long as same-sex activity was underground and couldn't be spoken about, it was a vector for disease. With NGO support, a number of small lesbian and gay rights organizations formed. Under the leadership of Victor Mukasa, four of these groups joined to form Sexual Minorities Uganda in 2004. The group's director, Dr. Frank Mugisha, soon became an internationally known spokesperson for sexual rights on the continent.

In March 2009, American evangelical Christians under the leadership of Scott Lively, president of Abiding Truth Ministries, organized a series of workshops in Kampala. Over four days, several thousand prominent Ugandans including police, teachers, and politicians were exposed to the message that gay people could be cured, that we were a danger to children, and that "the gay movement is an evil institution whose goal is to defeat the marriage based society and replace it with a culture of sexual promiscuity."[59]

The result was a private member's bill by David Bahati calling for the death penalty for "aggravated homosexuality" and life imprisonment for other homosexual offences. Anyone who was aware of such an offence and did not report it would be liable to three years' imprisonment. For Bahati and his followers, homosexuality was un-African and needed to be stamped out. But while homosexual identity might have been new to traditional Uganda, homosexual behaviour certainly wasn't. Ironically, both the homophobes and the gay rights advocates contributed to the development of homosexual identities in the country.

There was immediate international reaction to the bill, and not just from the expected human rights and lesbian and gay groups. The United States and several European governments spoke out and threatened aid cuts. During the Commonwealth Heads of Government Meeting in Trinidad and Tobago in November 2009, both British prime minister Gordon Brown and Canada's Stephen Harper expressed their opposition to the bill to Ugandan president Yoweri Museveni. Back in Canada, Transport Minister John Baird told *The Globe and Mail*, "The current legislation before Parliament in Uganda is vile, it's abhorrent. It's offensive. It offends Canadian values. It offends decency."[60]

Baird was widely, if not publicly, known to be gay, but his strong statement and the involvement of Harper himself were a departure for the Conservatives. This was only three years after Harper had tried to reverse gay marriage. But neo-liberal politics again trumped social conservatism. Gay rights had no discernable effect on the corporate bottom line, and lesbians and gays, especially the marrying kind, had been admitted to full citizenship in the nation. Gay rights had become a marker of civilization that even conservative politicians could deploy.

The pressure was effective in making the aid-dependent Museveni think twice about the legislation, and the death penalty provision was removed. But it also provoked an anti-colonial backlash. When the archbishop of Canterbury, head of the Anglican church, condemned the bill, the Anglican bishop of the Ugandan Diocese of Karamoja wrote: "Ugandan Parliament, the watch dog of our laws, please go ahead and put the anti-gay laws in place. It is then that we become truly accountable to our young and to this country, not to Canada or England. We are in charge." The subtitle of the article set the frame: "Christianity in Africa is under attack by Gays and Christians in Europe and the Americas. Africans do not need Europeans to teach them what the Gospels say."[61]

In 2010 a Ugandan newspaper published a list of names, pictures, and addresses of the nation's "top" gays and lesbians together with headline "hang them." Several months later in January 2011, David Kato, a prominent activist, was beaten to death in his home. (The bill, with the death penalty replaced by life imprisonment, was passed in 2014 but ultimately struck down by the constitutional court.)

Evangelical Christians, who had largely lost the battle to encroaching liberal values in the settler states and Europe, had successfully opened another front in the post-colonial world. An international rift was widening between social conservative repression and neo-liberal inclusion of homosexuality.

13

Homonationalism

PRIDE AND POLITICS

Martin Gladstone, an estate lawyer with connections at city hall, lived in the fashionable Upper Beaches neighbourhood with his partner and their two dogs. He was also an ardent Zionist. He had spent the 2009 Pride parade shadowing QuAIA's contingent with his camera. Over the winter he made a video.

The thesis of *Reclaiming Our Pride* was that QuAIA's participation was an anti-Semitic attack on Canadian multiculturalism. The propaganda techniques were unsophisticated. Happy parade images accompanied by refrains of "Pride Party," which Gladstone composed and performed himself, are replaced by ominous chords once the QuAIA contingent appears. QuAIA chants are distorted in post-production to sound menacing but barely intelligible. An anti-Nazi T-shirt with a crossed out swastika that a marcher wore is shown repeatedly; it was subsequently characterized in the press as "Nazi memorabilia." Right-wing media turned the image into an army of Nazis marching in Pride.

Central to the video are interviews recounting how QuAIA spoiled Pride and frightened people. But one segment gives the game away. Justine Apple, director of Kulanu, a Jewish LGBT social group, recounts receiving a call from the police Hate Crimes Unit before the parade. "The tension in my heart just increased as soon as I received phone calls from the Toronto police," she says. "These people . . . had been built up in everyone's heads, that it was a serious thing that they might pose a security risk, that there might end up being violence, and that's why it led to a lot of tension and fear."

The video didn't mention that Pride asked the police to approach Kulanu because of demands from lobbyists, including Gladstone. It was a page out of B'Nai Brith's playbook, inciting fear in the Jewish community for their own political purposes.

Over the winter, Gladstone distributed his video to city councillors and staff to convince them that QuAIA was a hate group whose participation contravened city policy. In November, Gladstone, Avi Benlolo of the Friends of Simon Wiesenthal Centre, Carol Pasternak from Kulanu, and Daniel Engel met privately with city staff. A briefing note to downtown councillor Kyle Ray reported:

> Gladstone stated that Pride has no mandate to engage in anti-Israel advocacy and that ... allowing marchers, some of whom wore swastikas and carried signs that read "End Israeli Apartheid" and "We stand with Queers in Palestine" is contrary to the City of Toronto Anti-Racism, Access and Equity Policy.[1]

On February 9, 2010, Rae wrote to Pride Toronto. His message was very different from the year before when he had supported QuAIA's right to march. "Over the weekend, I saw the film produced by Martin Gladstone and found the intervention of Queers Against Israeli Apartheid in last year's parade completely out of keeping with the spirit and values of Pride Toronto."[2] He urged Pride to review parade entrance requirements.

It was a dramatic about-face. No one believed Rae was actually swayed by Gladstone's crude video. Several years later, he is candid. Staff who had been positive about Pride were "getting heat from people." The "lefties" on council didn't know what to do and were "freaking out." There were angry calls from constituents, and an election was coming. He himself "got a lot of calls from Jewish developers who were very angry with what QuAIA was doing. . . . All along I knew that what QuAIA was doing was not in violation of the city's human rights policies. . . . The debate for me was keeping the funding and getting it through another year, or watching Pride lose its funding."[3]

A series of meetings including Rae, Tracey Sandilands, and Israel lobbyists to discuss how to exclude QuAIA from Pride then followed. It would be months before anyone found out about them.

Pride wasn't the only place where Palestine solidarity was targeted for censorship. On February 25, at the end of the day when few members were in the House, Progressive Conservative member Peter Shurman managed to manoeuvre an all-party resolution through the Ontario legislature condemning the use of the term "Israeli Apartheid." The non-binding resolution, part of an attempt to suppress Israeli Apartheid Week activities at Ontario universities, would be repeatedly cited in the polemics around Pride.

The first step in Pride's strategy to exclude QuAIA was to organize focus groups to help shape a strategy for community involvement. QuAIA was not cited as an issue, but the Wiesenthal Centre's Benlolo seemed to know what was going on. He wrote to Pride to "express his shock and concern that Pride Toronto has chosen to follow the route of focus groups to determine if Israel- and Jew-bashing is an acceptable practice." He threatened to further pressure sponsors and funders if QuAIA wasn't banned.[4]

On March 11, Pride announced that as a result of the focus groups, all parade messaging would need advance approval by an ethics committee. That provoked an immediate response. Rick Telfer, a doctoral student at the University of Western Ontario, organized a Facebook group called Don't Sanitize Pride: Free Expression Must Prevail, signing up 1,500 members in two weeks. Telfer was not simply concerned about QuAIA; he saw this as the beginning of a cleanup of anything controversial. Within Pride itself, members of the Human Rights Committee, Jane Walsh and Doug Kerr, met with Sandilands and then the co-chairs to demand the ethics committee idea be scrapped. Pride withdrew the idea two weeks later.

BLACKNESS YES!

Pride had another problem on its hands. Blackness Yes!, organizers of Blockorama, the Pride space for black queer and trans people and allies, had called a public meeting.

Blocko had been an important feature in Pride since 1999. It recreated the spirit of a Trinidadian blocko party after the parade. Blocko built on the stream of black community organizing starting with Zami in 1983, and Blackness Yes! included many original Zami and Aya activists.

For years, the Blocko dance party was held in a prominent site at the Wellesley Street parking lot in the centre of the Pride action. But in 2007, without consultation, Pride decided that spot would be given to a TD Bank–sponsored stage and beer garden. Blocko had always resisted becoming a beer garden. It wanted to be open to all ages and welcoming to those with substance issues. So although the Blocko stage was popular, it didn't make money for Pride. The new space was in a much smaller parking lot. As a result, overcrowding led to a number of medical emergencies.

The following year, Pride moved Blocko again, this time to the George Hislop Parkette, an out-of-the-way area four blocks north of the main festival hub. Grassy parks are not well suited to dancing, and the space was soon a muddy mess. Accommodations were made at the same site in 2009, but in 2010 Pride announced, again without consultation, that Blocko would move to an even smaller site, this one hilly and completely unsuitable.

Enough was enough. The Blackness Yes! community meeting at the 519 on April 13 was angry and raucous, and Sandilands was raked over the coals. Under pressure, Pride agreed to allow Blocko to stay at George Hislop Parkette for the time being. But the damage was done. Pride was perceived to have been at least disrespectful, if not racist, in its treatment of the group.

BACK AT CITY HALL

Gladstone and company continued to press the city and Pride sponsors. On April 19, the *Toronto Star* ran a half-page story entitled "Dispute Threatens Funding for Pride: Queers Against Israeli Apartheid Violated Policy, City Says." The *Star* quoted Toronto's general manager of economic development and culture Mike Williams, saying that the city "believes its anti-discrimination policy was likely violated by QuAIA's conduct and even its very presence at last summer's parade." On May 12, city councillor Giorgio Mammoliti introduced a motion to withdraw all funding from Pride unless it banned QuAIA. Mammoliti was well known for his homophobic opposition to spousal benefits as a provincial representative. Council bounced the motion to executive committee for further study. The referral was the weak-kneed response of progressive councillors fearful of taking on a controversial issue or defending free speech in an election year. They hoped Pride would do the dirty work and get the city off the hook.

On May 13, three QuAIA members met with Williams and diversity and community engagement manager Ceta Ramkhalawansingh. Williams denied that the city had been pressuring Pride to exclude QuAIA, and admitted that there had been no investigation and no finding that QuAIA violated any city policy. We asked him to write to the *Star* to "clarify" its misleading article. He agreed but never did so.

That same afternoon, *Xtra* released documents from a Freedom of Information request revealing the secret meetings between Rae, city officials, Pride staff, and Israel lobbyists to establish a rationale to keep QuAIA out of Pride. It was a very different account from the one that Pride had been spinning or that city officials had suggested that morning.[5]

Both the city and Pride were embarrassed, but word leaked out that the Pride board was buckling, nonetheless. On QuAIA's initiative, a last-minute meeting was organized for May 19. It was clear that board members were in over their heads. Although they seemed to understand our arguments, they saw their role as primarily financial. The festival's success was measured by growth in dollar terms. Anything that might interfere with that was expendable. Talk about community accountability was met with blank stares.

I missed that meeting because I was chairing another initiative. Savannah Garmon, one of QuAIA's trans members, had pointed out that Pride seemed to have contracts with everyone except the community. That was the germ of a coalition, The Pride Community Contract. At that meeting, Rinaldo Walcott put his finger on an important dynamic: Pride was addicted to growth. Success was about being bigger – more sponsors, bigger budgets, larger audiences, and higher salaries. Its contracts were aimed at facilitating such growth. That served Tourism Toronto, Pride staff, and its board, but no one asked about its impact on queer communities. The Contract group developed an eleven-point series of principles for a Pride Toronto contract with the community. They included financial, social, and environmental sustainability and accessibility to all; freedom of expression; priority for grassroots community events, local queer and trans artists, and local small businesses; and meaningful commitment of sponsors to the well-being of local queer and trans communities.

Up until the last minute, the idea that Pride might ban us seemed so outrageous that I didn't believe it could happen. Hunkered down in AIDS, I hadn't been paying attention to how much the world, including Pride, was changing.

On Friday, May 21, in a four-to-three vote, the Pride Toronto board decided to ban the use of the term "Israeli apartheid" from all Pride activities.

The decision was to be secret until a press conference on May 25, but word soon leaked out. The group that had convinced Pride to drop sign vetting swung into action, joined by former Pride co-ordinators purged by Sandilands, organizers of Blocko, and trans activists. The Pride Coalition for Free Speech (PCFS) was born.

The Israel lobby made a strategic error in pushing for censorship. They had generally managed to control the discourse on Israel/Palestine through the memory of the Holocaust, Islamophobia, and the War on Terror. Instead, here it became a question of "free speech." When it was revealed that Pride had written in a blanket prohibition against "political statements" in performers' contracts, people were truly enraged.

Anti-censorship was embedded in this community. My first gay protest had been against the *Toronto Star* for its refusal to accept classified ads using the word "gay." Then there were *The Body Politic* trials, the Glad Day and Little Sisters customs censorship battles, the fight against the board of education policy banning gay speakers, and struggles for the right for explicit safe sex education. This tradition gave momentum to the Pride Coalition for Free Speech and extensive coverage in *Xtra*. Although *Xtra* did not take a position on Israel/Palestine, it was firm in its support of the PCFS free speech demand.

The bright spring morning of May 25, Pride held a press conference on the steps of its office, a renovated Victorian building in the village. A crowd of a hundred PCFS and QuAIA members gathered to heckle the announcement of the ban. Some wore tape across their mouths. Others loudly demanded the resignation of the Pride board and director. When beleaguered spokespeople tried to explain their rationale – not that QuAIA had violated any city policy or law, but that Pride feared it might lose funding – they were met with chants of "Fight the city, not the queers."

QuAIA took advantage of media interest to focus on the substantive issue – that queer Palestine solidarity had a place in Pride. We spoke of the history of politics at Pride and Israel's pinkwashing campaign, and pointed out that, because of the country's apartheid regulations, Palestinian queers did not benefit from Israel's gay rights.[6]

Off to a bad start, Pride's crisis management continued to unravel. Dr. Alan Li, chosen as the 2010 grand marshal, rejected the honour. "Pride's recent decision to ban the term 'Israeli apartheid' and thus prohibit the group Queers Against Israeli Apartheid from participating in the Pride celebrations this year is a slap in the face to our history of diverse voices," he wrote in a letter to the board. Li's example was soon followed by the honoured dyke and the Community Service Award winner. On May 29, organizers of the first Pride march in 1981 released an open letter declaring, "We stand totally opposed to the decision of the current Toronto Pride Committee to ban the use of 'Israeli Apartheid' at Toronto Pride events."

On June 7, the 2010 international grand marshals, ILGA co-chairs Gloria Careaga and Renato Sabbadini, announced that they, too, were rejecting their honours and would not come to Toronto. That same morning, more than twenty additional former Pride honourees returned their awards and marched to the Pride offices to present the organization with an "award of shame." Pride's own Human Rights Committee announced it was cancelling its planned events to protest the ban.

That same evening, PCFS and Queer Ontario organized a protest meeting at the 519 Church Street Community Centre, the likes of which had not been seen since the bath raids. Hundreds packed the hall and the meeting was live-streamed by TV news channel CP24. The rowdy meeting brought together all sectors of the community and heard all kinds of complaints about Pride. Groups like Blackness Yes! clearly understood issues of intersectionality and were therefore unmoved by arguments that Palestine was not a queer issue. Others, even those who were unconvinced about Palestine, understood the classical liberal arguments against censorship. *Xtra* editorialized: "In effect, Pride Toronto secures its 2010 city funding by agreeing to limit the free expression of gay and lesbian people. It's an assault on the very foundational root of the sexual liberation movement."[7]

For weeks, the issue raged in the media. The attempt to silence discussion of Israel's apartheid policies spectacularly backfired. There were few in queer communities or the city who didn't hear some reference to Israeli apartheid.

IT'S NOT JUST US

Pride had already alienated many in the black community and it just got worse. Again, without consultation, Pride had decided that the 2010 Dyke March would no longer end back in the gay village. "Expanded" post–Dyke March activities would instead take place in Queen's Park, blocks away from other festival events. It soon became evident that the dykes had been moved out of the village because Pride was partnering with party promoter Prism Toronto to hold Aqua Pride – an admission-only event for the male circuit party crowd – in the village that afternoon.

At first, the change produced only resigned grumbling, as much about the irony of the situation as about the new site itself. A boys' party displaced the dykes on Dyke Day. *Well, that's Pride for you.* Others were happy to leave the heat and the testosterone-soaked village behind to move to the grass and the shade of the park.

But when Pride announced the ban on QuAIA, everything changed. Sex advice columnist Sasha Von Bon Bon and fellow activist Jess Dobkin called for an event to compete with the official Dyke March, Take Back the Dyke.

Then trans issues blew up. It turned out that including a *T* in the acronym hadn't done the trick. Toronto's first Trans March at Pride was spontaneously pulled together in 2009 by an ad hoc committee of trans folk concerned about the lack of trans visibility in the festival. But in 2010, without consultation with the previous organizers, the Trans March was listed as an official Pride event. When the University of Toronto's Trans Inclusion Group wrote Sandilands to find out what was going on, she offered to meet with them on August 12, two weeks *after* Pride.

Nor was it clear who was running other trans events. Nik Redman, who programmed TransAction in 2008 and 2009, offered on several occasions to help out, but was put off. As things fell apart, Pride finally tried to do outreach. One of those contacted, Ayden Scheim, responded, "It's frustrating and upsetting and offensive to be contacted at this stage in the game. If I have to tell you in June that you should probably talk to The 519 or the Sherbourne Health Centre, somebody's not doing their job."[8]

Further, local queer performers had been relegated to less important stages to make way for "international" talent that would draw a more mainstream audience. With rates set to reflect the budgets of corporate sponsors, local businesses were priced out of entering floats. Volunteers who had co-ordinated aspects of the festival for years had been squeezed out by the increasingly hierarchical model promoted by the new executive director. QuAIA's banning was a lightning rod that brought all these issues to the fore.

INTERNAL TENSIONS

Being at the centre of this whirlwind was not easy. Many QuAIA members had little experience in such community politics. And there was what I felt to be a left opportunist current within the group, hostile towards PCFS because of its "liberal" basis of unity around anti-censorship. They complained that the Voltaire quote adorning the PCFS Facebook group – "I may disagree with what you have to say, but I will defend to the death your right to say it" – was an implicit criticism of QuAIA's politics. They were also concerned that the focus on free speech might eclipse the issues around Israeli apartheid. I argued that the last thing we needed was for PCFS to take a position on Palestine. That was our job. And if the issue was eclipsed, it was our fault, not theirs.

At a meeting on June 14 we agreed that we would march despite the ban. Another member and I had met with the police at 52 Division on behalf of the group. We had been assured that police would not intervene if our intention was to march peacefully. Still, we decided to keep open the option of civil disobedience if there was an attempt to prevent us from participating.

Two members, however, were increasingly unhappy with the strategy. They found it difficult to speak about Pride without contempt. They considered free speech to be a "liberal" issue and opposed marching with the PCFS. They were furious that there had been a successful meeting with the police, whom they regarded as the enemy. They proposed "jumping into" the parade rather than taking our rightful place there, a strategy that would inevitably lead to confrontation with parade marshals. When it was announced that the Canadian Auto Workers had also invited us to march with their float, they were opposed to that as well, since the CAW hadn't taken a stand on BDS. They seemed more interested in distancing themselves from Pride than in participating, or in winning lesbian and gay hearts and minds to the struggle for justice in Israel/Palestine. At the end of the meeting, after losing all the arguments, they stormed out.

We were also working on two events, a discussion between Palestinian queer activist Haneen Maikey and Trinidadian activist Colin Robinson on the question of solidarity, and a concert organized in conjunction with PCFS. After the meeting when we broke into sub-committees to focus on these events, the two disgruntled members returned to harangue everyone before storming off again. I found it annoying, but after forty years I was used to political histrionics. Many of the younger members, though, seemed traumatized.

THE G8/G20

Tensions in the city were also building as the police turned the downtown into an armed camp for the G8/G20 meeting the weekend before Pride. The leaders of the world's most important capitalist economies were coming to town to try to sort out the economic crisis. Unions and civil society groups were planning huge demonstrations against neo-liberalism and its consequences. Confrontation seemed likely.

It was worse than anyone had expected. At first, police stood by and allowed a group of masked demonstrators to inflict considerable property damage in the downtown. (It was suspected that this Black Bloc group was infiltrated by police provocateurs.)[9] Then, the damage was used as a pretext for a police riot the next day, with unprovoked attacks on peaceful demonstrators and the largest mass arrest in Canadian history. More than a thousand people, many of them bystanders, were swept up, held in deplorable conditions, beaten, subjected to racist, sexist, and homophobic insults, and denied their most basic rights.[10] This was the unsmiley face of neo-liberal power.

The fallout spilled into Pride Week. In 2005, Police Chief Bill Blair had been cajoled by Kyle Rae to be the city's first police chief to march in Pride. Now the chief hosted an annual reception at 519 Church every Pride Week. But that year it was like attending a wedding the day after the groom was caught cheating. Protesters gathered outside and tried to push their way past the police guard, demanding Blair resign for his role in the police riot. Both Blair and Rae were heckled and booed. The *Toronto Sun* reported that queer activists said they refused to be pinkwashed by Blair's attempt to rub shoulders with the community.

"He's got some nerve coming in here and acting like everything is back to normal and we're all buddy buddy," said protester Michelle Hill, 54. "You attacked our community this weekend, you attacked gay, lesbians and straight people out there who were exercising our basic democratic rights."[11]

RESOLUTION

In the midst of the turmoil there was a breakthrough. Behind the scenes, three prominent community members had been working to broker a resolution. MCC's Brent Hawkes pulled a troika together: himself, Doug Elliott, the lead lawyer in the Supreme Court gay marriage decision and *Hislop*, and Maura Lawless, executive director of 519 Church. Their goal was to head off a confrontation at Pride and win time to deal with the underlying issues.

On June 24 they announced a deal had been struck. Pride would rescind its ban on QuAIA's participation, all groups in the parade would sign an undertaking to abide by the city's non-discrimination policy, and a community advisory panel would be set up to recommend strategic principles and a framework to help shape future festivals.

The deal worked for QuAIA. We had never violated any laws or bylaws and were happy to sign the undertaking – the group's mandate was opposed to ethnic nationalism and racism, after all. But while it solved our immediate problem, it merely postponed the day of reckoning. The fundamental questions about Pride as celebration or politics, free expression or censorship, remained.

The Israel lobby was outraged. Hawkes and his committee soon experienced some of the abuse previously reserved for QuAIA. The Canadian Jewish Congress and the Canada-Israel Committee held a press conference condemning the capitulation to QuAIA's "hateful message." Right-wing city councillors were apoplectic, feeling they had been duped by Pride, which, by this point, had received its city cheque. Councillor Mammoliti and councillor and mayoral candidate Rob Ford drafted a motion demanding Pride return the money and that the festival be stripped of any future city funding.

For others, QuAIA's unbanning was welcome but not enough. Queer Ontario had concerns about the backroom nature of the process that led to the deal. Who would make up this community advisory panel? Whom would they be accountable to? Take Back the Dyke still organized its alternative to the official Dyke March. According to their Facebook post:

> We applaud the hard work of our community's activists who pressured Pride Toronto to rescind the ban. But let's be clear: Pride's reversal should not make us come running back into the arms of this abusive relationship, forgiving and forgetting. We stand by our position that this has never been a single-issue fight. Pride Toronto's 11th hour gesture does not address the many grievous issues that have been of concern for years. Pride Toronto's

policies and agenda has impacted the Dyke March spirit before and beyond the words "Israeli Apartheid" and the current censorship disgrace. Barricades, marching fees, corporate sponsorship and vetting of groups all contribute to diminishing the true sense of community spirit and visibility the Dyke March was originally intended to embody. Pride Toronto still does not represent our community or our interests.[12]

THE MARCH

The day of the main Pride parade broke hot, humid, and sunny. Since Pride director Sandilands had purged most of the experienced volunteer organizers, parade assembly was chaotic. There were only a handful of official Pride Toronto marshals, and assigned sites were too small to accommodate marchers. The contingents ended up on top of each other. Some groups lucked into some cover, but QuAIA and PCFS waited for hours under a broiling sun.

I had participated in almost every Pride since 1981 and co-ordinated security for many groups, but I cannot remember a more stressful occasion. Not far away, the former Jewish social group Kulanu had converted itself into a pro-Israel contingent bedecked with Israeli flags. They had sent out a call through area synagogues for support, and their ranks were filled with aggressive, mostly straight, Israel supporters including the Jewish Defense League (JDL), a thuggish right-wing group on the U.S. terrorist watch list.[13] A steady stream of provocateurs kept infiltrating the QuAIA staging area, jostling and attempting to start fights. Luckily, our marchers followed instructions not to engage, and police were generally co-operative in escorting troublemakers out of the crowd.

When we finally began to move, the PCFS contingent with its sea of yellow "My Pride Includes Free Speech" signs provided by *Xtra*, and QuAIA, with its large "Israeli Apartheid Is . . ." and "Solidarity with Palestinian Queers Is . . ." placards created by John Greyson, numbered more than five hundred. The QuAIA contingent was led by a group of Palestinian and Arab women. Despite small groups of hecklers, we were upbeat and disciplined, and received resounding cheers from hundreds of onlookers.

WTF WAS THAT ALL ABOUT?

When the dust settled, we tried to make sense of what had just happened. Why would our largest community festival alienate the black, women's, and trans communities, and violate a fundamental community value with censorship?

A first clue was the composition of the Pride board. By 2010, most were from management or consulting backgrounds. Well intentioned, they were upwardly mobile types and, with notable exceptions, didn't have much history with the political struggles that had shaped the community. Certainly they believed in community, but a stint on the board of a million-dollar festival was also not a bad thing to have on your resume.

These were people who felt that with gay marriage, we had arrived. Their role was putting on a festival. Above all, they wanted to associate good feelings with the Pride brand. Conflict was to be avoided. It was a board that didn't attract the already engaged. It was politically weak and out of touch with many community currents.

Because of their backgrounds, members also generally bought into a growth model of the festival: bigger is better. That model requires ever-increasing corporate and government sponsorship to sustain itself. As it spent more and more time attracting dollars, Pride Toronto's role had shifted from putting on a festival for our communities, to delivering LGBT bodies to corporate branding and advertising and helping the city market itself as a queer-friendly tourist destination.

Success was measured in increased cash flows, staff salaries, and sponsorships. Such growth required the attendance of more straight people. In 2009, an *A* for allies was officially added to the jumble of initials that Pride now used to define community – LGBTTIQQ2SA. Pride was to be fun for all. Naughty and titillating was okay. To be sexually risqué within limits was tolerated; that could be marketed. Of course they believed in freedom of speech, but politics? Wasn't that one of those things that polite people didn't talk about at dinner parties? To expose Canada's strategic ally as an apartheid state was upsetting to the power structure in which Pride wanted to be included and on which it depended for financial survival.

A glimpse of who Pride Toronto imagined as its community was revealed in the promo materials for its 6th Annual Gala and Awards Ceremony, described as "an evening of exquisite dining and entertainment."

> The queer community provides a demographic comprised of upper-income, well educated consumers. Highly educated (40% have a university degree), nearly 45% are professionals in their field. In today's economy, the acquisition and retention of skilled talent is vital to success in any industry. Demonstrating public support of the queer community by sponsoring the Pride Toronto Gala & Awards ceremony sends a strong message to the queer community that your business is welcoming of this well educated talent pool.[14]

Sponsored tables were a deal at $10,000 for ten. They came with admittance to a VIP reception, priority table placement in the Platinum zone, and complimentary advertising in Pride publications and on the website. Less prominently placed tables with fewer perks went for $5,000 and $3,500. Individual tickets were $350 each.

The bungling of relations with the black communities, dykes, and trans folk could be understood as a matter of incompetence by the largely white, male, and cis Pride board and staff, or less generously, as examples of racism, sexism, and transphobia. But the logic that bound these groups together was class.

This was rational, liberal logic at work. Demographics that were not targets for corporate advertising were irrelevant. Those that might detract from marketing messages by causing offence – whether political, such as QuAIA, or cultural, such as TNT Men – needed to be excised.

One group that cleverly pointed out class issues was the Lesbian Billionaires. They attended Pride functions and PCFS protests in cocktail dresses, carrying martini glasses (often full) featuring slogans such as "Censorship is Tasteful," and "Whose Pride? TD Pride." They handed out Monopoly money asking, "Can we buy your pride?"

AFTERMATH

When Pride was over for another year, QuAIA was still embroiled in city politics. Mammoliti's motion demanding the return of city money went nowhere, but another motion, seconded by Councillor Ford, directed that next year's Pride funding be withheld until after the parade and be conditional on all participants complying with the city's anti-discrimination policy. It also asked the city manager to determine "whether the participation of QAIA [*sic*] and the signs or banners they carry contravenes the City's Anti-Discrimination Policy." The struggle QuAIA had touched off was far from over.

THE CITY ELECTIONS

That fall left little time to muse over the politics of Pride. The municipal election was unfolding. David Miller, the generally popular and liberal mayor, declined to run for a third term. The progressive favourite, Adam Giambrone, flamed out in a sex scandal and withdrew, leaving only three major candidates: George Smitherman, the openly gay former Liberal cabinet minister; Joe Pantalone, Miller's progressive but uncharismatic deputy mayor; and Councillor Rob Ford, the ultra-right-wing buffoon from Etobicoke who had co-sponsored the resolution to defund Pride.

To almost everyone's astonishment, Ford was soon the front-runner. His platform called for cuts to city hall's "gravy train." It was a simple message that resonated with a hard-pressed electorate in the midst of a recession. His base was the ever-poorer outer suburbs, those who lived far from the glittering arts and cultural events emblematic of Florida's creative city. Why should their taxes support entertainment for the downtown elites? Many worked two precarious jobs to make ends meet, or were small businesspeople who could never share in the stable jobs, benefits, and pensions available to unionized city workers. Why should city workers live better than they did? Without public transit, they had to drive to work. What stake did they have in bicycle lanes? Although he had inherited his daddy's millions, Ford knew how to tap into the cauldron of resentment that was building up in an ever more unequal city. He presented himself as an unvarnished, straight-talking man of the people who would set things right.

All this was soon amplified by a retirement party that Kyle Rae threw for himself at a cost of $12,000 out of his city budget.[15] The *Toronto Sun* jumped on the story and milked it for all it was worth. Gay equalled downtown excess.

Councillor Rae's retirement opened up his downtown ward, an unlikely amalgam of old-money Rosedale north of Bloor Street and the gay village to the south. First off the mark to replace him was Kristyn Wong-Tam, a young lesbian businesswoman with a long history of progressive activism in the community. Rae supported Ken Chan, also gay, a former police officer and one-time adviser to Smitherman.

QuAIA soon became an issue. Although Wong-Tam had not been an active member, she had volunteered to be the "owner" of the QuAIA website when it was first set up. Right-wing lesbian columnist Sue-Ann Levy broke the story in the *Sun* in September.[16] The JDL and other sectors of the Israel lobby were already discussing picketing Wong-Tam's home. Anonymous leaflets denouncing her as an anti-Semite were distributed and cost her support among businesses in the Yorkville area.

The smear campaign was not effective. In the October 25 election, Wong-Tam carried the ward. But Rob Ford swept the city to replace Miller as mayor.

OVER TO THE CITY MANAGER

Since the city manager was charged to determine whether QuAIA's participation contravened city policy, QuAIA requested a meeting with him in September. Given our experience in the spring, when officials had maligned us in the press without going through any process, we had decided on a pre-emptive strike. At first we were refused, since we already had a complaint to the city ombudsman about our treatment by city staff. But we insisted, and a meeting was granted for November 25.

City manager Joe Pennachetti was an affable civil servant. Despite the initial concern about interfering in the ombudsman's deliberations, he invited the key figures in our complaint to attend. He said he intended to listen to all points of view, including the results of the upcoming Community Advisory Panel (CAP).

After a year of skirmishes, our arguments were finely honed. We reminded Pennachetti that we had peacefully participated in Pride for three years, and groups calling for an end to Israeli apartheid had marched in Pride parades in other Canadian cities. The Quebec Jewish Congress had clearly stated that it did not call for a banning of the term. Our right to criticize government policy was protected speech under the Charter.

Elle Flanders, a QuAIA member who grew up in Israel, explained that "Israeli apartheid" was widely used in Israel. She supplied examples of recent articles in the mainstream Israeli press using the term.

Richard had served on the board of the Toronto Arts Council and had helped draft equity guidelines for the Canada Council for the Arts back in the

1990s. He pointedly explained to the city's director of culture that cultural funding policy did not exclude political expression, and that the intention of cultural equity is to allow marginalized voices to be heard. The use of such equity policies to silence criticism of a country's human rights violations was a perversion. It would have deleterious effects not only on the arts but also on the credibility of equity.

COMMUNITY ADVISORY PANEL

A few days later, the first Community Advisory Panel began its consultations to develop recommendations for Pride. In December, CAP held six public meetings, three open forums, and one each focused on trans, racialized, and women's communities. Meetings were live-streamed by *Xtra*. There were over forty targeted sessions with different groups, including one with QuAIA. An online survey received 1,600 responses. CAP also consulted Pride groups in Montreal, Quebec, Vancouver, New York, San Francisco, Sydney (Australia), and Tel Aviv.[17]

But events did not wait for the report. On January 25, Pride released the long-delayed audited financial statement revealing "financial irregularities" and a $430,000 deficit. Although former treasurer Mark Singh gamely continued to blame the loss on "political messaging," the auditors' report showed that sponsorship had actually increased by more than $200,000 from 2009. This was a hefty sum, but not enough to meet dramatically increased costs of salaries, office administration, advertising, and rent. Most damning was the revelation that Sandilands had hired her partner, Janine Marais, to the tune of $40,000, without the knowledge of the board. Marais had continued to be paid while other Pride Toronto employees were laid off.[18] The following day, Sandilands's resignation was announced.[19]

That did little to calm waters at Pride's general meeting January 27. *Xtra* described "a storm of anger" that met the board as the financial mismanagement, lack of oversight, and conflict of interest were revealed. Community member Jane Farrow described the event as a "gong show." The best Pride could do was to plead for time until the CAP report.[20]

THE CAP REPORT

The report was released February 17. At 232 pages with 133 recommendations, it covered everything from finances to entertainment to the rift between Pride and the black and trans communities. It called for a scaling down of Pride events and a focus on local talent. While there was discussion of QuAIA's role, the report made no recommendations about our right to participate. Instead, it called for the creation of a dispute resolution process that would be triggered in the event of complaints.[21]

This was not good enough for the Israel lobby. *Sun* columnist Sue-Ann Levy called the report "milquetoast,"[22] and in consultation with Rob Ford's office, she wrote Jewish leaders calling on them to send mass emails to councillors to defund Pride.[23] The letter backfired, however; because of the perceived conflict of interest, Levy was removed from the Pride beat until after the funding decision.[24]

Gladstone, in an op-ed in the *National Post*, called the CAP report a "complete moral abdication" and argued that bringing a complaint about QuAIA to the dispute resolution process "would literally mean putting the state of Israel on trial."[25]

The Friends of Simon Wiesenthal Centre issued a community alert with a blistering personal attack on Brent Hawkes, accusing him of leading efforts to ensure that QuAIA could march. Hawkes replied, "I am neither a member of Quaia [*sic*] nor have I ever been a supporter." He explained, "In my role as Chair [of the CAP], I have to set aside my personal opinions and try to remain neutral." His letter was termed "a very positive development" by the centre, and released below a picture of a smiling Hawkes shaking hands with Wiesenthal Centre president and CEO Avi Benlolo.

At city hall, Mayor Ford reacted to the news by intoning "taxpayers' dollars should not be used to fund hate speech," and reiterated that unless QuAIA was banned, there would be no city funding for Pride.[26] This was no idle threat. The new mayor was on a roll and seemed positioned to marshal votes in council to get his way.

ANXIOUS OPTIONS

In the spring of 2011, QuAIA needed to re-evaluate its strategy. Although the controversy had brought our issue widespread attention in 2010 and we had provoked a cascade of events that resulted in significant changes at Pride, there was a strong feeling that we couldn't just repeat the same scenario.

Pride was in a fragile state. Fresh in everyone's memory was the history of Caribana, the West Indian festival that was Toronto's other signature summer cultural event. After infighting and financial irregularities put that festival's continuation in jeopardy, the city decided that, given its tourist revenue, Caribana was too important to fail, and the city assumed management in 2005. Caribana was now the Scotiabank Toronto Caribbean Carnival, a complete government/corporate takeover.

If Pride lost its funding or was taken over by the city, QuAIA could potentially take the blame. With so much community energy going into trying to hold Pride together, it was far from clear whether we would be able to marshal the same level of support as in 2010. Not marching, on the other hand, could register as a defeat for Palestine solidarity and for those supporting space for progressive politics in Pride.

After a long and emotional meeting on March 18, there was a consensus that QuAIA would not apply to march in the 2011 parade. Instead, we would use Pride Week as a kickoff for an international queer tourism boycott campaign. We ultimately decided to wait until the release of the city manager's report, which we now understood would be favourable.

The report became public the following day, April 13.[27] It began:

> City staff have determined that the phrase "Israeli Apartheid" in and of itself does not violate the city's Anti-discrimination policy. . . . To date, the phrase "Israeli Apartheid" has not been found to violate either the Criminal Code or the Human Rights Code (Ontario). . . . The City also cannot therefore conclude that the use of term on signs or banners to identify QuAIA constitutes the promotion of hatred or seeks to incite discrimination contrary to the Code.[28]

It was a stunning vindication of our position. In a legal system shaped by the Charter, we could not be silenced. Two days later the press release went out, arguing that the city manager's report settled the issue of censorship. Nonetheless, QuAIA would not march in the parade.

> Rob Ford wants to use us as an excuse to cut Pride funding, even though he has always opposed funding the parade, long before we showed up. . . . By holding our Pride events outside of the parade, we are forcing him to make a choice: fund Pride or have your real homophobic, right-wing agenda exposed.

The release not only produced a minor media sensation and lit up the Twittersphere, but it also changed the focus of the dispute.[29] It was no longer about QuAIA or Israel. It was about the mayor and homophobia. All eyes were now on Ford's response. The mayor and his friends seemed unsure what to do. While Ford stated that Pride funding would still be held back, and Mammoliti demanded a letter from Pride guaranteeing QuAIA would not march, Bernie Farber of the Canadian Jewish Congress declared the matter closed. Councillors such as Josh Matlow followed Farber's lead and deserted the Ford camp.[30]

QuAIA's major Pride event took place on June 22. After a preview of experimental filmmaker Mike Hoolboom's new work, *Lacan Palestine*, New York dyke author and activist Sarah Schulman spoke about her pro-Palestinian activism to a full house. She introduced Jasbir Puar's concept of homonationalism as an analysis of what was happening to our communities. And although QuAIA did not march, Dykes and Trans People for Palestine, including many QuAIA members, participated in the Dyke March, July 2.

Their message was given extra visibility by the presence of Councillor Mammoliti, who stalked the parade with a video camera, taking home footage of lesbians. This attempt to gather evidence of anti-Israel activity was widely ridiculed as "creepy" in the press, and even garnered an editorial cartoon in the *Toronto Star*.[31] During the Pride Parade on July 3, QuAIA dropped an enormous banner – Support Palestinian Queers / Boycott Israeli Tourism –

over the Wellesley subway station in the heart of Pride activity across from the Blockorama stage.[32] The banner drop, reminiscent of the tactics of early AIDS activism, went viral. It was much more effective than a parade contingent.

. QuAIA's strategy paid off handsomely. The mayor's refusal to attend Pride events cemented his reputation as a homophobe. This was not the kind of ally that did much to burnish the image of Brand Israel in the queer community. Then on July 12, Mammoliti, deserted by his allies, lost the vote to defund Pride.[33] By that point even Farber said of Mammoliti, "He just doesn't get it."[34]

It was the beginning of the end of Ford's fiscal conservative / social conservative / Israel apologist coalition. The mayor's boorish and often bizarre behaviour, along with growing evidence of his drug and alcohol problems, soon marginalized him at city hall.

HOMONATIONALISM

"While we enjoy an awesome Pride Week celebration in this wonderful country in which we can be free to be ourselves, let's bear in mind there are many who don't have the same freedom we do." That was Tracey Sandilands's message to the community in the 2010 Pride Guide.

Jasbir Puar's *Terrorist Assemblages: Homonationalism in Queer Times*, like much Queer Theory, revels in obscure language and wordplay. But her concept of homonationalism helped us understand what QuAIA was facing at Pride. Puar built on Lisa Duggan's notion of homonormativity: "a new neoliberal sexual politics" that "hinges upon the possibility of a demobilized gay constituency and a privatized, depoliticized gay culture anchored in domesticity and consumption."[35] Puar called homonormativity plus U.S. nationalism "homonationalism." She argued that while the homonormative part of the equation reiterates heterosexuality as the national norm by mimicking such institutions as heterosexual marriage, "certain domesticated homosexual bodies provide ammunition to reinforce nationalist projects,"[36] such as the War on Terror.

The QuAIA experience also seemed to indicate that the notion of homonationalism needed complicating. Where different national imaginaries competed, there were several competing homonationalisms. The Pride Coalition for Free Speech had a vision of a tolerant nation where the right to free expression was sacrosanct. It opposed a conservative national project that envisioned a more jingoistic nationalism with no place for dissent. The conservative project sought to reinforce the apolitical nature of the quasi-ethnic LGBT community. The PCFS project sought to repoliticize it to defend liberal values. Both, however, were happy to celebrate Canada as model for gay inclusion.

The community was not divided into a reactionary homonationalist versus a progressive anti-homonationalist bloc. On the ground everything was, as always, far more messy.

On August 22, 2011, long-time LGBT community ally Jack Layton died of cancer. He had led the federal NDP to a significant success, with the party for the first time becoming the official opposition in Ottawa. After lying in state in Ottawa and Toronto city hall, Layton's body was accompanied by a police escort to Roy Thomson Hall in downtown Toronto for a state funeral on August 27.

In ceremonies broadcast live nationally, politicians and officials of all stripes jockeyed to eulogize the NDP leader. Layton, who had been instrumental in the struggle for LGBT rights as a city councillor in Toronto, made a statement even in death. MCC minister Brent Hawkes gave the sermon, and the MCC choir sung as the coffin was carried in. Lorraine Segato of the Parachute Club sang "Rise Up." In a day of national mourning, lesbians and gay men were visibly part of the nation.

OCCUPY

That fall the Canadian anti-corporate magazine *Adbusters* initiated a call to protest corporate influence and inequality. Its slogan, "We are the 99 per cent," sparked a huge public discussion about growing income inequality under neo-liberalism, and identified the 1 per cent of the population who were its main beneficiaries. In New York, Occupy Wall Street took over Zuccotti Park near the heart of the American finance capital. A month later protesters took over St. James Park in downtown Toronto.

The Toronto occupation was supported by thousands of individuals and seven major unions led by OPSEU. But taking over a park and attempting to house people there was ultimately unsustainable. Toronto police cleared the tents and the few remaining protesters at the end of November. Although Occupy Toronto lasted only a month, the movement was spectacularly successful in drawing attention to growing inequality.

The argument of the protesters was strengthened by statistics on income inequality released by Statistics Canada that year. Based on 2009 income tax figures, the top 1 per cent of families in Canada earned substantially more from wages and salaries than the entire bottom 30 per cent, and their share of such income had more than doubled since 1990. They also captured 57 per cent of total investment income. The top 10 per cent received more than the bottom 60. The bottom 10 per cent both increased in numbers and saw their income fall.[37]

Occupy in Toronto had an LGBTQ committee, and Stefonknee Wolscht, a trans woman, was a key organizer in the protest. But while there were several small queer interventions, no major lesbian and gay organization made a statement of support or engaged with the protesters.[38]

At the end of 2011 it appeared that Pride had turned a page. But there would be more to the saga. In 2012, QuAIA called together key allies from the remains of the PCFS and, based on feedback, decided to apply to march in the parade. At a subsequent meeting, a new group, Queers for Social Justice, was formed to raise other political issues during Pride Week.

City hall delivered an unexpected twist. On June 7, city council unanimously approved Pride funding. But the trade-off was an amendment to the funding motion:

> City Council reaffirm(s) its recognition of Pride Toronto as a significant cultural event that strongly promotes the ideals of tolerance and diversity, but condemn(s) the use of the term "Israeli Apartheid" which undermines these values and also diminishes the suffering experienced by individuals during the apartheid regime in South Africa.[39]

While annoying, the amendment, largely cribbed from the 2010 motion in the Ontario legislature, was little more than a symbolic sop to the Israel lobby. Still, seven councillors voted against it, more than had been willing to stand up for free expression in 2010.

Meanwhile, the impression that *Xtra* was QuAIA's mouthpiece was reinforced with its publication of a feature article on pinkwashing by Israeli journalist Mya Guarnieri. Probably the best of its kind in the queer press to that point, it explained the concept of Israeli apartheid, extensively quoted Palestinian queer activist Haneen Maikey and Israeli anti-occupation activists, and challenged the myth of Israel as a gay paradise. It generated a furious reaction from Israel supporters in the comments section.[40]

QuAIA's application to participate in the 2012 Pride parade sparked a series of complaints to the new Dispute Resolution Committee. In the end, the only one to go forward came from B'Nai Brith. After a full-day hearing under the Arbitration Act, the three-person panel found "that the activities of QUAIA are not contrary to the core missions, or policies, of Pride Toronto" and dismissed the complaint. We had won again.

That was essentially the end of the QuAIA wars at Pride, although there were a few echoes. Gladstone filed an official complaint accusing Uzma Shakir, the city's equity director, of bias because of her role in producing the city manager's report in 2011. When that failed, he made an equally unsuccessful complaint to the city ombudsman. There were also unsuccessful attempts to change the city's human rights policy to ban criticism of Israel. The proposal was rebuked by other equity-seeking groups for trivializing the difficulties they faced, but it required more organizing and more rounds of deputations at city hall. In 2013, another dispute resolution complaint was dismissed.

QuAIA's participation in Pride had become normalized. Public mobilization had played an important role, but success had ultimately been achieved through recourse to the law. With much of civil society cowed by the Harper government, and corporations interested only in money, we had once again found ourselves appealing to the Charter.

GLAD DAY

The new activism in the community also provoked a surprising development. In a period characterized by privatization of community and public resources, Glad Day Bookshop was taken over by a collective.

Jearld Moldenhauer had sold the business to his old friend John Scythes in 1991. While small bookstores went under across the continent, Scythes kept the business afloat for two decades. But by 2011, he had had enough. Scythes announced that if a buyer couldn't be found, Glad Day would close.

Michael Erickson, a secondary school English teacher, had spearheaded anti-homophobia work in the school system and played a leading role in the PCFS. Erickson brought together twenty investors who pooled their money to buy out the business.

"We firmly believe that Glad Day provides a service and books that are not available anywhere else in the world. We hope that with a large group of people willing to put their energy and passion behind the business, we can keep it not only alive, but also growing," he told *Xtra*. The group was remarkably diverse in terms of age, gender identity, and race.

"As a queer [black, mixed race] woman myself, and coming out in Toronto, it was really hard for me to believe it was possible to be queer because I didn't see anybody that looked like me," explained Kim Crosby (now Kim Katrin Milan), one of the investors. "There's an incredible importance in changing what the face of the queer community looks like."[41]

The new model fell somewhere between collective management of a public resource, like the original *TBP*, and a joint stock company. From an economic perspective, taking over a small bookstore in the twenty-first century was not an astute decision. Glad Day's new ownership was motivated primarily by a desire to preserve a community institution and to build and strengthen community in all its diversity. It was heartening to know it was still possible for political ideals to outweigh economic imperatives.

THE STATE IS NOT THE GOVERNMENT

In January 2011, the Ontario Ministry of the Attorney General finally began a process to draft prosecutorial guidelines, but without public consultation. In response, CLHE itself organized community stakeholder discussions across the province and posted an online survey to reach those unable to participate face-to-face. The process was both a consultation and a capacity-building exercise. The resulting thirty-page report submitted to the ministry in June 2011 urged restraint in prosecutions and warned against conflating non-disclosure with aggravated sexual assault. It suggested no prosecutions in cases involving oral sex, condom use, or undetectable viral load.

Despite requests for follow-up meetings, the attorney general's ministry went silent until mid-October when it released arguments it intended to make at the upcoming *Mabior* Supreme Court hearing. We were astounded to see that the ministry planned to call for the *expansion* of the scope of the law to require disclosure, even when there was no risk of infection. Our report had been disregarded.

CLHE had developed a network of support through the earlier call for guidelines. We alerted supporters and flooded the attorney general with emails demanding the intervention be withdrawn. Finally, thanks to behind-the-scenes work by downtown Toronto representative Glen Murray, we got a meeting with the minister on December 7.

It was tense. The attorney general, John Gerretsen, was himself quite amicable, like a friendly grandfather. But his deputy minister, the civil servant behind the intervention, was combative. He and one of our lawyers went nose to nose. We left the meeting depressed, but the following day, Ontario's intervention was withdrawn. It was a significant victory and a serious humiliation for ministry bureaucrats. We had been strong enough to block a step backwards, but not to force a step forward. At that point, we realized that despite our political support, the lawyers in the ministry were not budging. They were beyond democratic control.

Mabior was heard in February 2012, and the ruling came down in October. Though we had blocked Ontario's hard-line arguments, the court's decision was unhelpful. It ruled that non-disclosure was not criminal only when a condom was used *and* the HIV positive person had a low viral load. Lower court rulings had specified that either condom use *or* a low viral load would be sufficient. This ruling would have disproportionate impact on people with HIV in remote areas who couldn't access regular viral load tests, and on HIV positive women now required to ensure their partners used condoms, even if their own low viral load made them uninfectious.

A month later, a young Ottawa gay man was found guilty of three counts of attempted murder, three counts of aggravated sexual assault, and two of administering a noxious substance – his semen. Dubbed the Poz Vampire by Ottawa media, Steven Boone's behaviour was certainly reckless, but even Carissima Mathen, the feminist cheerleader for HIV criminalization, was concerned. She said:

> It can be a little bit tricky, or possibly a slippery slope to start to think that everyone who deliberately withholds that information – maybe because they're just careless or they're not thinking about the other person – will there be a temptation to say, well, they must have intended to kill the person.[42]

Now, more than ever, we needed guidelines to reduce the harm. But with the Ontario Liberal government in a minority, it was unlikely they would buck their bureaucrats.

THE BATTLE OVER BULLYING

Around 2010, reports of gay teen suicides in the United States brought concerns about "bullying" to the fore. The deaths sparked the *It gets better* campaign. *It gets better* exploded in Canada after the son of an Ottawa area councillor committed suicide in 2011. Jamie Hubley had tried to start a Gay Straight Alliance (GSA) in his high school and found the resulting harassment unbearable. Popular CBC comedian Rick Mercer produced a "rant" that went viral. Ontario premier Dalton McGuinty made his own *It gets better* video.

When I googled "anti-bullying" that year, I got 7,650,000 hits. Many were ads, for example: "Stop Bullying (We know the secrets to stop bullying today. Find out how.)" An industry of anti-bullying programs and gurus had emerged.

It appeared that we were faced with a crisis, a bullying epidemic. Perhaps the increased visibility of LGBT communities meant that younger children were coming out and therefore vulnerable. But despite the increased attention, I could find no longitudinal studies demonstrating that bullying had actually increased since my classmate Louis was terrorized in the 1950s and '60s. And we had known for decades that queer kids were more likely to commit suicide.

We were in the thralls of a full-fledged "moral panic," where a heightened awareness of a social problem becomes the focus of more generalized anxieties and symbolizes everything deemed to be wrong in society. Moral panics are generally a conservative reaction against a perceived threat to social values in a time of change. They tend to build support for an authoritarian response. The Salem witch trials are the iconic example, McCarthyism a more recent case. Eugene McCarthy was a classic "moral entrepreneur" who fanned the flames of panic about reds and homosexuals, and used it for his own political purposes. But here, for the first time, gay people were seen as victims in need of protection rather than the danger that needed to be confronted.

As I saw it, the danger of bullies gone wild began in Ontario with the Harris revolution. As cuts, amalgamation, and withdrawal of student supports made schools unmanageable, the idea that they were unsafe justified a demand for stricter traditional discipline. In 2001, the Tories passed the Safe Schools Act, giving draconian powers to principals and teachers to suspend students and requiring mandatory expulsions for a range of behaviours. The material effects of this policy were a rapid increase in the number of expulsions, with a disproportionate impact on racialized and disabled children.[43]

As could be expected, despite the new law, ever more poorly staffed and resourced schools continued to unravel, and the alienation (and behaviour) of students on the receiving end of neo-liberal class changes did not improve. In 2007, fifteen-year-old Jordan Manners was gunned down in the hallway of his Toronto school. A subsequent report by Julian Falconer, *The Road to Health: A Final Report on School Safety,* explained how cuts to student support and the "Safe Schools Culture" had "deeply hurt this City's most disenfranchised. The devastating effect that this style of discipline had (and continues to have) on marginalized communities is borne out by its lasting and ongoing effects."[44]

But Falconer's recommendations ran against the logic of cuts to "trim the fat" from public education, and the logic of fear, surveillance, and privatization could fit together all too neatly. In its article on bullying, Our Kids (a website billed as "Canada's trusted source to help families find top private schools") explained to its readers: "There is a known correlation between supervision and reduced bullying. Bullying festers where teachers, parents and other authority figures are less present. Some schools with bullying problems have helped reduce the issue by adding [a] Closed Circuit TV camera."[45]

One indication that this was a moral panic was the shift in terminology itself. When I worked with the Toronto Board of Education in the 1990s, we talked about "harassment," a legal term with case law behind it. Institutions had legal responsibilities to protect against harassment, which included the concept of "poisoned environment." That meant the institution itself could be guilty of failing to provide a harassment-free environment.

Harassment allowed us to look at systemic practices, but bullying focused on individual bad behaviour, usually that of students. While harassment usually came with an adjective attached – sexual, racial, homophobic – bullying floated outside of these power relationships. When people imagine bullying, they usually think of size, strength, or age differentials.

A front-page article by Catherine Porter in the *Toronto Star* illustrated the consequences of this shift.[46] The article, "Fighting Bullies without Bullying," focused on a commendable program where instances of "bullying" were dealt with through a "restorative conference." The article opened with a description of two students involved in an incident: "One was a slip of a boy in Grade 9, his plaid shirt buttoned right to the Adam's apple. The other was an 18-year-old giant – literally 6-foot-8 – with ear buds and a hoodie." It was clear who the bully and the victim were going to be.

I wondered if the reference to the "hoodie" was code for black, and indeed, the inside picture of the restorative conference was taken from behind the head of a black male. In the background, the "slip of a boy" in his plaid shirt was visible. The image was out of focus, but it was clear that the "slip" was white and, for those in the know, possibly gay.

In the course of the conference, the giant apologized for his "immature" behaviour. Only at the end of the article is his motivation revealed. "The slip" and his friends were making fun of the giant's accent. The black kid was an immigrant. Under TDSB policy, this was racial harassment. But in the universe bounded by the frame of bullying, it had no name. Small white kids could certainly harass, but they weren't bullies.

Bullying as an emotional term lent itself more easily to a moral panic, and a moral panic required government intervention. McGuinty had earned the moniker Premier Dad. As a Liberal, always attempting to occupy the centre, McGuinty tried to manage the crisis by projecting himself as both the nurturing parent and the disciplining father – the two poles that George Lakoff sees as representing liberal and traditional family values.[47]

The Liberals introduced anti-bullying legislation in November 2011.[48] The Accepting Schools Act stressed that "all students should feel safe at school and deserve a positive school climate," and recognized that bullying had to do with a power imbalance. While putting special emphasis on LGBTTIQ students, it referenced all the prohibited grounds of discrimination in the Ontario Human Rights Code, and created an obligation for schools to prevent bullying through progressive discipline and a positive school climate.

The bill also mandated teacher training, the development of curriculum resources, increased support for students wanting to form Gay Straight Alliances, and the designation of Bullying Prevention Week. But it did not contemplate any major reinvestment in education to accomplish these things.

The Progressive Conservatives, the official opposition, could not be seen as soft on bullies, but they also did not want to alienate their base. They introduced a parallel private member's bill.[49] While similar in many respects, it opened with the statement "Bullying, particularly in schools, has become an increasing problem in Canada," portraying it as a growing threat to the social order. It made no mention of LGBT students and focused on the dangers of the Internet and cyberbullying. For Tories, the Internet was one of these new-fangled inventions that needed much more control. Their bill saw bullying as bad individual behaviour, unmoored from broader social inequalities. Its focus was not on empowering victims but on punishing wrongdoers.

Liberal support for GSAs raised the stakes and brought other actors into the drama. GSAs had been popping up in the public schools for some time, but the provincially funded Catholic school system became ground zero for the debate. The Catholic Church was a traditional institution that had made its peace with liberal capitalism. It was granted powers such as the right to conduct marriages, it received tax exemptions, and its religious school system was publicly funded in Ontario. On the other hand, it had opposed the decriminalization of homosexuality in 1969, the inclusion of sexual orientation under the Ontario Human Rights Code in 1986, same-sex relationship recognition in 1999, and gay marriage in 2005. So the Catholics schools were in a tight spot.

The Catholic Schools Trustees' Association document *Respecting Difference* asserted that those dealing with same-sex attractions or gender identity issues should be treated with "sensitivity, respect and compassion." It recognized its "obligation to ensure a safe environment for all students,"[50] but it could not countenance GSAs. After all, the Catechism (Part 3: Life in Christ) defined homosexuality as a "grave depravity" and "intrinsically disordered."[51] This conundrum meant the Catholic system had difficulty even keeping its own troops in line. At least one Catholic trustee called for the establishment of GSAs in Catholic schools.[52]

The Ontario Gay-Straight Alliances Coalition included the Canadian AIDS Society, the Canadian Federation of Students, the Canadian Secular Alliance, CUPE (Ontario), Catholics for Choice, the Centre for Inquiry Canada, Egale, MCC Toronto, the OFL, OPSEU, Rainbow Alliance, and PFLAG. The coalition needed to intervene in a moral panic (which triggers conservative values) in order to achieve a progressive goal, the protection and affirmation of queer and transgender kids.

The coalition didn't talk about an epidemic of bullying that had to be controlled, or even mention teen suicide. Its website was silent on the issues of reporting and discipline. Its single focus was on the rights of students in all schools to establish GSAs. A significant part of the coalition's website consisted of statements by students.

Finally, there was Charles McVety of the Canada Christian College. His latest invention was the Institute for Canadian Values, "a national think-tank dedicated to advancing knowledge of public policy issues from Judeo-Christian intellectual and moral perspectives, as well as awareness of how such perspectives contribute to a modern, free, and democratic society."[53]

The institute had published "Please Don't Confuse Me" ads in the *National Post* and the *Toronto Sun* during the lead-up to the October provincial election. Under pictures of cute, white five-year-olds, the transphobic ads conflated and misrepresented TDSB and provincial curriculum. The child in the ad begs political leaders not to "teach me to question if I'm a boy/girl, transsexual, transgendered, intersexed or two spirited." The *Post* subsequently apologized for publication of the ads. The *Sun* did not.

McVety sought to broaden his appeal through an alliance with other conservative religious groups. His campaign against the Accepting Schools Act, launched at a shambling press conference in December, included representatives from Campaign Life Catholics, the Evangelical Association, and the Council of Orthodox Rabbis. Although no Muslims, Hindus, or Sikhs attended, panellists repeatedly spoke on their behalf.[54] Speakers ritually began their remarks by stating how much they opposed bullying and how stronger measures were needed to prevent it. They then singled out McGuinty as "totalitarian" and denounced the bill as "offensive" to family values. Four months later, at a Queen's Park rally , McVety called the premier "the bully of the province." He called the bill "a violation of our freedom of religion" and "a violation of our ability to parent our own children."[55] Others claimed it violated the constitutional rights of Catholic schools.

But liberal values chipped away at another stronghold of tradition. McGuinty's bill was passed in June 2012. Catholic schools had to permit GSAs. Lesbian, gay, and transgender youth were officially part of the national family, worthy of protection, even in the heart of traditional institutions.

TRANS PROTECTION

That same month gender identity and gender expression were finally added to the Ontario Human Rights Code, prohibiting discrimination against trans people. It was the third time the NDP's Cheri DiNovo had introduced a private member's bill to amend the code. It was named Toby's Bill, after Toby Dancer, an important music producer before transitioning, who slipped into substance abuse and homelessness in the 1990s. She died of a drug overdose in 2004. Dancer had played at Emmanuel Park United Church when DiNovo was pastor. This time the bill was co-sponsored by Liberal member Yasir Naqvi and received support from several Tories.

Although inclusion of gender identity and expression were still stalled at the federal level, the trans rights movement was remarkably successful in achieving its legislative goals in Ontario. The strategy involved the courts, alliances with politicians, and work with lesbian and gay groups. Despite this success, trans people continued to be some of the most marginalized and vulnerable populations in the province.

A LESBIAN PREMIER

Although the anti-bullying legislation and the inclusion of gender identity in the OHRC increased his stature in the LGBT communities, McGuinty's government was beset by scandals, and he announced his resignation in October 2012. After a leadership convention in February 2013, he was succeeded by Kathleen Wynne, the province's first female leader and the first openly lesbian premier in Canada.

RUSSIA

In the spring of 2013, conservative groups in the Russian parliament introduced an amendment to a child protection law criminalizing information to minors that denied traditional family values or advocated for "non-traditional sexual relations." The wording of the widely popular bill was so vague that it could apply to any kind of public gay rights advocacy or even HIV prevention work. Signed into law by President Vladimir Putin on June 30, the law occasioned a wave of violent assaults on gay men and lesbians across the country, and protests against it were attacked by far-right groups. Although more brutal in its execution, the Russian law was not that different in its thrust from Margaret Thatcher's 1988 Section 28 prohibiting the promotion of homosexuality, or even the Toronto Board of Education's 1981 ban on proselytization.

But in Russia there was a new twist. Homosexuality was portrayed as a western plot to undermine the family and Mother Russia. Families were under stress with the fall in living standards after the collapse of the Soviet Union. A handful of corrupt oligarchs helped themselves to public resources and amassed huge fortunes, and although a significant new urban middle class emerged, many were much worse off than before. Alcoholism increased, life expectancy fell, unemployment soared, corruption was rampant, and families fell apart.

Although the authoritarian Putin regime styled itself as the force to set things right, it was no less corrupt. As elites continued to prosper at the expense of everyone else, Putin increasingly relied on conservative social forces such as the Russian Orthodox Church and appeals to Russian nationalism to maintain control. As mature neo-liberalism exploited sexual choice in the West, its authoritarian Russian version hearkened back to the Reagan strategy, using homosexuality as a scapegoat for broader social problems.

There was immediate reaction from the West, heightened by Russia's hosting of the Winter Olympics in Sochi in February 2014. Putin assured the Olympic Committee that the law would not affect those attending the games, and calls for a boycott fizzled.

The issue provoked a split in Harper's neo-liberal/social conservative coalition. Foreign Affairs Minister John Baird said the law was "mean spirited and hateful . . . an incitement to intolerance, which breeds hate. And intolerance and hate breed violence."[56] This was all too much for REAL Women of Canada, traditional Harper supporters, who accused Baird of "abusing his position as a cabinet minister."

"Just who does John Baird think he is, using taxpayers' money to promote his own personal agenda and endeavoring to set standards of the laws of foreign countries?" said spokesperson Gwendolyn Landolt.[57] "It is not, and I repeat not, a Canadian value that homosexuals should usurp religious rights and traditional values." Grumbling was also reported from Conservative backbenchers in Ottawa. "We've got much more important things to be doing in terms of a foreign affairs agenda," complained one.[58]

PINK TORIES

Russia was a flashpoint, but Jonathan Kay discerned a shift in general conservative attitudes towards homosexuality. In a major opinion piece in the *National Post*, "Rise of the Rainbow Hawks: How Conservatives and Canada's Gay-Rights Activists Made Common Cause," Kay argued Harper had not "just come around to gay rights: He has made the issue a centerpiece of Canada's foreign policy."[59]

In that article, Jaime Watt, former Harris henchman, Egale award winner, and public relations consultant, took credit for the shift in Ontario. "As strategists, we started doing for our [gay] community what we'd been doing for our clients." Kay also quoted Mitchel Raphael, former Parliament Hill social circuit reporter for *Maclean's,* who pointed to the socialization of new federal

Tory MPs after their 2006 victory. "A lot of these people who were elected as rookie MPs, they came from areas of the country where they might have never met a gay person. . . . Then suddenly, you're in Ottawa, and gay people are everywhere – and so your attitude changes." Raphael also noted that there were an inordinate number of gay staffers in the Conservative party. "Often it's the young men, the ones without kids, who tend to work the longest hours that [this Prime Minister's Office] demands."

Finally, the War on Terror after 9/11 played a role. "In Canada, especially, the campaign in Afghanistan was not seen merely as part of the war against terrorism. It was also seen as a war against the anti-western, anti-Semitic, murderously misogynistic and, yes, anti-gay hatred promoted by the Taliban, al-Qaeda and hardcore Islamists more generally." Kay also referenced the program facilitating the arrival of gay Iranian refugees, a move that "allowed the Conservative government to poke a stick in Iran's eye, and help a genuinely in-need refugee constituency, all at one blow."[60]

EGALE

When Helen Kennedy took over as director of Egale Canada in 2007, she inherited an organization on the brink of collapse. If it was to survive, the group needed a fundamental reorientation. So Egale shifted from lobbying and advocacy to research and front-line training, "to change the culture," as Kennedy explains. She was a relentless networker. By 2014, Egale's website sported the logos of TD and Royal Banks, several major unions, IBM, the Ontario Trillium Foundation, Winners, Ryerson University, law firms, and the organization for LGBT professionals Out on Bay Street.

The student survey on school safety and a policy scan of boards of education opened the way for training programs with teachers and administrators across the country. Egale hosted conferences on youth suicide, school safety, and GSAs. It opened a crisis centre for street-involved youth next to its Toronto offices, organized community kitchen and arts programs, began an internship program with Loblaws, and in 2014 was in the process of negotiating for a dedicated housing space for queer youth with Toronto Community Housing.

Its Out at Night program raised awareness about homelessness. Other programs focused on seniors. Training sessions on campuses for residence dons focused on trans and intersex students. Other trainings extended beyond Canada with programs for police and social workers in Montenegro. Two Spirits, One Voice offered workshops on Aboriginal issues, and Egale hosted an event with two spirit residential school survivors and the National Truth and Reconciliation Committee.

Kennedy became ILGA co-chair and Egale participated in UN human rights and women's conferences. In 2013, it submitted a report to the UN Human Rights Council on LGBT rights, focusing on Canada's weakness on trans rights, discrimination in the blood donation system, reproductive technology, and other issues. The following year Egale presented a similar report to the Organization of American States (OAS). That caught the attention of the Canadian government, which sent down lawyers, the ambassador, and three researchers to do damage control.

Two months later, Egale received notice that it was being audited by the Canada Revenue Agency. Although the agency denied any political motive, the Harper government had supplied the agency with extra cash to conduct political audits, and dozens of environmental and progressive organizations across the country were targeted, including the David Suzuki Foundation and the Canadian Centre for Policy Alternatives.[61] Such investigations could result in the loss of charitable status. "It was a horrific time for us. It was very stressful," Kennedy notes. "We had three or four staff dedicated to the auditors for an extensive period."[62]

Although it emerged from the audit unscathed, the experience accelerated Egale's shift. By 2014, most of its service and education work, along with donations, were funnelled through the trust, in order to receive a tax deduction. Egale Canada, the original advocacy organization, was essentially moribund. It was allowed to die in October 2014. Its board, with two representatives from six regions across the country, was replaced by a streamlined, largely Toronto-based trust board of six professionals.

Egale's reinvention as a trust was double edged. On the one hand, it was better positioned to negotiate fee-for-service educational programs with governments and institutions, to receive institutional and individual donations, and to develop services. On the other, like all charities, a maximum of 10 per cent of its resources could be allocated to political advocacy. As Kennedy puts it, "We have to be very careful what we do, careful politically."[63]

GAY TORONTO IN 2014

The Toronto community in 2014 was very different from the one I came out into forty years before. Men's spaces still dominated, but much of the friction between men and women had evaporated. As the glass ceiling for (mostly white) professional women shattered, more women took roles in a more professionalized community leadership.

Political advocacy groups had almost disappeared, but there were at least fifty social groups for those interested in a range of recreational activities from music to every possible kind of sport. A well-established network of funded institutions targeted AIDS and other health issues, addiction, youth, trans, refugee settlement programs, and so on.

Trans had emerged as a standalone identity and, while the trans movement followed a familiar rights trajectory, activists such as Susan Gapka, who had spent time on the street, still worked on poverty issues. Rainbow Health concentrated on the social determinants of trans health in a still deeply marginalized community.

Toronto had become a city where half the population was racialized, and the significance of racialization itself had changed. Sectors of some groups did well; others faced deeper marginalization. While groups such as Zami, Khush, and Gay Asians Toronto were long gone, new organizations – mostly focused on cultural expression or youth, such as the Kiki Ballroom Alliance or the Asian Arts Freedom School – replaced them. We were no longer just a city of gay refugees from small towns across the country, but a magnet for queer refugees from around the world. In 1974, what was called "the community" was largely working class, but by 2014, the city and the community were more starkly divided between rich and poor, white and racialized.

Gay relationships, once criminal, were now sanctified by marriage, transformed into a niche market, and part of the national mosaic. On the other hand, charges for HIV non-disclosure among gay men symbolized the abjection of those who did not conform to (homo)normative sexual relationships. And more poz men were hiding their status fearing stigma and vulnerability to criminal prosecution. Long-promised prosecutorial guidelines to limit the damage continued to be blocked in the Ministry of the Attorney General. AAN! launched a new website urging gay men to "think twice" before resorting to the police.

In an education system where talk of homosexuality had been forbidden, LGBT issues had become provincial policy. The Triangle program, in its second decade, had expanded to provide a haven for LGBT youth at risk, with two teachers and thirty students in renovated classrooms at MCC. On the other hand, Triangle was still necessary.

MCC, struggling to survive in the 1970s, now owned a massive church, holding three services accommodating close to six hundred worshippers every Sunday. Its older, 60 per cent male congregation was still 85 per cent white, although thanks in part to its refugee program, it now included people identifying with a range of racial backgrounds. More than 16 per cent of church members identified as straight. Almost 75 per cent had college, university, or post-graduate education and, according to Brent Hawkes, his was "a pretty wealthy congregation." The church continued to grow despite there being at least fifty other "gay affirming" Christian churches in the city, gay-positive synagogues, and a mosque.

The Body Politic, our only community voice in 1974, was replaced by *Xtra*, which was in the process of abandoning paper for an electronic platform, available instantaneously to people on devices around the world but not on the street. LGBT characters were now a prime-time media staple.

The handful of bars and clubs that made up the commercial scene in the '70s were now the Church Street village, and the village itself supplemented, supplanted even, by a growing "queer" scene scattered in the city's west end. Park cruising, which featured heavily in my 1974 gay Toronto guide, had largely collapsed, except perhaps for the old summer evening stalwart,

Queen's Park. Thanks to hook-up apps such as Grindr, gay men no longer need to gather to find sex. Although several baths still thrived, there were fewer than forty years before.

The walls that once surrounded gay life had become permeable. "I always make it a point to be at the table. I find that if you don't have that voice at the table it goes unheard," explains Art Zoccole of Two Spirited People of the First Nations, showing me with satisfaction a copy of the Final Report of the Toronto Aboriginal Research Project. TSPFN is listed as one of the eight sponsors of the project, and is part of the Toronto Aboriginal Support Services Council. "I found it important to be at those meetings and say, we are Two Spirit people, and we are here, and this is what we can contribute."[64]

Alan Li, who came out into Gay Asians Toronto as a university student in 1981, joined the board of the Chinese Canadian National Council, the Chinese community's largest and most militant advocacy group, in 1988. He was national president from 1994 to 1998, and national chair from 1998 to 2001.

Debbie Douglas, one of the founders of Zami, was now executive director of the Ontario Coalition of Agencies Serving Immigrants, the umbrella group representing the interests of immigrant services organizations across the province. Under her leadership, OCASI actively supported the recognition of same-sex relationships in immigration and refugee legislation, and developed a Positive Space Initiative to engage member agencies in anti-homophobia work in their communities.

Much of the corporate world, once synonymous with racism and homophobia, now calculated that inclusion was more rational and profitable. For example, Silvia Alfonso, chair of the Royal Bank of Canada's Pride Employee Resource Group, explained, "What we're trying to work towards is to encourage people to bring their authentic self to work so that they're more productive and happier and more engaged at work."[65]

The premier was a dyke. Politicians of all stripes were openly gay. The city councillor for the gay village, Kristyn Wong-Tam, was a long-time lesbian activist. Nothing could encapsulate these changes better than World Pride 2014.

WORLD PRIDE

The announcement that Toronto would host the 2014 World Pride was initially met with scepticism. London's World Pride in 2012 had been a financial disaster, with major events cancelled at the last minute. Given that Pride had just gotten back on its feet after Sandilands's disastrous tenure, there were fears that it was again overreaching itself.

QuAIA began planning early, despite our depleted energies. Several key members had moved away, others had moved on to other issues, and new members were not taking up the slack. The website was out of date and our Twitter account was dormant. There was debate about whether we should participate at all. Younger members weren't much interested in investing energy in Pride. If it hadn't been for QuAIA, many wouldn't even have attended the festival. World Pride, like the Olympics, it was argued, would inevitably be soaked in homonationalism and displace the poor and marginalized. In fact, it was later leaked that police were already planning to clean up the downtown to ensure the "security" of revellers.

Certainly, for all of its pretensions of inclusivity, Word Pride's immediate goal was to attract the gay tourist dollar. And that had geographic, gender, racial, and class implications. The lion's share of that market comes from Europe and the white settler states, countries whose passports allow us to travel freely. It is also mostly male because of higher levels of disposable income among men, and middle class and above. World Pride is an inclusive project resting on exclusive material foundations.

The debate came down to whether or not QuAIA was primarily an anti-homonationalist organization or a Palestine solidarity organization. If our prime concern was educating people about Israel's apartheid system and building support for BDS, then World Pride was an opportunity to get our message out. Whether it was homonationalist or liberal was irrelevant. I argued that the call for BDS was a classic liberal demand calling on Israel to comply with existing international law, and there was nothing in that basis of unity that precluded participating.

In the end, we agreed to make a splash. Canadians for Justice and Peace in the Middle East had raised money to place ads in the subway system with a series of maps showing the erosion of Palestinian territory over sixty years, but under political pressure, the Toronto transit system refused to display them. Instead, we raised money to place a full-page ad in *Xtra* featuring the same maps during Pride Week.

A second project was to distribute two thousand condom packages labelled "Fuck apartheid," with an insert explaining the loss of land, Israeli human rights violations, and pinkwashing. Now that we were no longer entangled in the freedom of speech issue, we organized a public event to explore Middle East solidarity in a more nuanced fashion. Finally, we came up with the semi-insane idea of floating a massive twenty-five-foot-long banner displaying the same censored disappearing Palestine maps, held aloft by helium balloons above our parade contingent.

The city's mood was appreciably lightened on June 12, when Wynne's Liberals unexpectedly swept to a majority in the provincial election. There had been real fears that the hard-right Progressive Conservatives under Tim Hudak might take power and return us to the Harris era. But Ontario's first lesbian premier defied the odds and humiliated both the Tories and the NDP, whose vote against her previous minority government had sparked the election.

As the date drew closer, it appeared World Pride would come together. A major LGBT Human Rights Conference organized by Sexual Diversity Studies at the University of Toronto would draw activists from around the world. A steep registration fee put it out of reach of many in Toronto, but there were generous scholarships to activists from developing countries.

Dozens of World Pride–affiliated public art shows, performances, innovative history exhibits, talks, and events were planned. A panel of queer people of colour packed the Gladstone Hotel to address "WTF is queer about Settler Colonialism, Racism and Homonationalism?" A mural project promoted by Councillor Wong-Tam redecorated key buildings on Church Street, and the park housing the AIDS Memorial was refurbished. Wong-Tam also planned a mass gay wedding at city hall.

There would be six major stages in the Church Street area with performances by local and international talent. Mariela Castro, director of Cuba's National Centre for Sexual Education, was coming to town. She would receive the OFL's International Workplace Rights Award for her part in reforming the Cuban labour code. Parachute Club announced the release of a remix of its iconic 1983 anthem "Rise Up"; Rise Up was the 2014 festival slogan. Brent Hawkes was chosen as grand marshal, and the international grand marshal would be the young Georgian human rights activist Anna Rekhviashvili.

The buildup was not without missteps connected with the now ubiquitous corporate sponsorship. In April, as part of a million-dollar sponsorship package, CTV began airing a public service announcement asking the meaning of Pride. For the next thirty seconds, a dozen smiling white normative faces said things like "acceptance, harmony, being an equal," and so on. A cop says "tolerance." Two gay dads with their infant say "happiness." At the end, the only racialized person, a young black woman, says "peace." The Pride board had no say in the content, which by the terms of the contract was CTV intellectual property. The ad produced an angry reaction from a number of the ethno-specific AIDS service organizations.

Then *Xtra* revealed that Pride's agreement with Trojan meant that only Trojan condoms could be distributed at events. The commodification of safe sex also produced blowback.

Nevertheless, the opening ceremonies in front of city hall were packed. They featured performances by lesbian icon Melissa Etheridge, Canadian R&B singer Deborah Cox, gay country music heartthrob Steve Grand, and Tom Robinson, whose 1976 "Glad to Be Gay" was one of our first activist anthems. There was something for everyone.

Many of us had feared the human rights conference would be a homonationalist showcase. While the celebratory currents of Canada as a gay-friendly liberal nation were certainly present, the conference was both thought provoking and nuanced, with strong participation from a range of critical activists from around the world. Despite the cost, it was oversubscribed, but every evening there was a free keynote open to the public.

Critical perspectives broke through even in public sessions with a homonationalist cast. The Pathbreakers plenary featured the former prime minister of Iceland, Jóhanna Sigurðardóttir; her wife, Jónína Leósdóttir; and eighty-five-year-old Edith Windsor, whose legal case in 2013 had won the recognition of same-sex marriages in the United States. Conversation revolved around the importance of gay marriage for the panellists, but in the middle of her talk, Windsor went off script. She pointed out that while marriage might be an important issue for older middle-class lesbians and gay men with property to bequeath, it was largely irrelevant to youth and other groups facing violence, discrimination, poverty, homelessness, and substance abuse problems.

Over the week I was in demand as a living gay dinosaur, with seven different speaking gigs on topics as diverse as World Pride and homonationalism, HIV criminalization, the successes and problems of single-issue queer equity work in the schools, and QuAIA.

Richard was also busy. He was producing a follow-up to his first video *Orientations: Lesbian and Gay Asians*, following the activities of the surviving interviewees thirty years later. Pride was the obvious backdrop, and he had to shepherd a film crew through the massive crowds. We briefly met up at the Trans March on Friday evening and the Dyke March on Saturday afternoon, and I waved as the QuAIA contingent with its giant floating banner passed underneath him as he filmed from the roof of Glad Day Bookshop on Sunday.

The 2014 Pride march could not have been more different from the one forty years before when fifty or so of us walked from Allan Gardens to Queen's Park, largely unnoticed, carrying homemade signs. With more than 12,000 marchers and 280 floats and contingents, the World Pride parade went on for six hours. Led by a white balloon-festooned float of the Two Spirited People of the First Nations, it included leading banks and corporations, NGOs, community groups, more than a dozen unions, and at least six local and regional police forces. Hundreds of marchers carried national flags. Political leaders were out in force and the Canadian Olympic Team participated for the first time. Yonge Street was packed with spectators for almost twenty city blocks well before the parade kicked off. The 1974 march had gone unreported. In 2014, media partners included CP24, CTV, Proud FM, Z103.5, and the *Toronto Star*.

In 1974 Pride was organized by an ad hoc group of volunteers on a budget of a few hundred dollars. World Pride had an office, paid staff, and net revenues of more than $5.3 million, of which $2.7 million were from sponsorships and almost $1.4 million from federal, provincial, and municipal grants.[66]

World Pride embodied all the contradictions of neo-liberal Canada and the state of the LGBT movement. Promotion of the inclusive Canadian state and a critique of that notion. Corporate development of the pink dollar niche market and anti-corporate protest. Israeli pinkwashing and anti-pinkwashing activism. Discussion of both the necessity and pitfalls of international human rights work. Community unity and community infighting, inclusivity and the displacement of the homeless, and a celebration of historical struggles that were at the same time conceptualized as a relic of an ever more distant past.

Conclusion

Looking Back, Looking Forward

WHERE WE BEGAN

Growing up in small-town Ontario, I knew failure to properly perform gender would make me subject to contempt, ridicule, and violence. Such failure was related to "homosexuality," a term mentioned only in hushed tones and out of range of children.

The world I was born into was homophobic in the primary sense. Homosexuals were identified as a category, and we were feared and despised. Sexual behaviour outside the management of the church and the patriarchal family was a sin and a threat to society and nation. This threat was amplified by the Cold War. Traditional institutions feared communism and its call for women's equality, radical egalitarianism, and atheism. They were in alignment with owners of capital, for whom communism represented expropriation. Homosexuals were a weak link in the fight to preserve the "free world."

A half century later, the more normative among us are embraced by the nation and are expected to embrace it in turn. We have become ordinary. We are no longer dangerous nor do we carry the germ of a utopian future; we are the mundane present. This book has charted that "progress" based on the experiences of one city, Toronto. I have examined how fundamental economic and social changes and the structuring forces of class, race, gender, and immigration status have affected the process, our identities, our political strategies, and our goals.

NATIONAL IMAGINARIES

I began by observing, based on Andil Gosine, that integration into the national imaginary is the goal to which successful LGBT efforts have aspired. Those who hope to transform the nation in more fundamental ways have generally remained marginalized.

Canada imagines itself as a peaceful, progressive fair broker on the world stage and regularly forgets its national roots in settler colonialism, racism, and exploitation. Lesbian and gay rights has inserted itself into that vision through a complex historical process. But we have struck a Faustian bargain. The state defends our rights, and the tolerance we experience is deployed as proof that Canada is the liberal country it imagines itself to be. We have become complicit in the nation's forgetting and the ongoing damage that it causes. Yet it is an anxious bargain, and we continue to be haunted by our potential vulnerability.

CONTRADICTIONS: ACCEPTANCE AND DISSENT

Riffing on a quote from writer Richard Goldstein, David Rayside noted: "Gays, lesbians, bisexuals and the transgendered carry within themselves both 'the yearning for acceptance and the determination to dissent.' The conflict within us is carried into the movement that we want to be representative of our aspirations."[1]

The post-Stonewall revolutionaries sought to resolve this contradiction by imagining an impending collectivist utopia. Identity was a product of oppression and the new world would dissolve the distinction between gay and straight. Dissent was a pathway to our inclusion there. Our allies in the fight would be horizontal – the working class, women, oppressed and colonized peoples. But the revolution never came.

When the more down-to-earth types settled into the long haul of a rights-based trajectory, they adopted an identity modelled on other minorities. The debate was about which tactics were more effective in winning acceptance. The imaginary nation in which we sought inclusion was a social democratic or at least Keynesian one, stripped of its traditionalist compromises. It was not liberalism's values that we opposed, only its hypocrisy. We would make the nation live up to liberal values of individualism, equality, and rationality. Our allies would be unions, centre-left political parties, and fair-minded, secular, liberal people.

That vision of the future turned out to be as much a hallucination as the workers' paradise. The society in which we are included today is an enormously unequal one. Our successful struggle against the repressive state was accompanied by the dismantling of protective state institutions. As a result, our legal equality has come hand in hand with substantive inequality that, in turn, cuts across and divides our community. The dominant voices in our communities, revelling in their new acceptance, now echo the dominant voices in our society. Dissent has been relegated to the sidelines.

THE PROCESS: 1970S

While the commonality of "gayness" was first imagined as sufficient to hold together community, contradictions quickly emerged. One was between generally poorer, feminist lesbians, and gay men who benefited from a male wage and male privilege. The second was between liberationist radicals – generally younger, relatively well-educated activists of working class origin – and "assimilationists" – based in a more cautious gay petite bourgeoisie. Both sought to represent those whose lives were still regulated by the social contract of the closet.

Simultaneously, variations within feminism divided lesbians on the advisability of working with gay men, and gay men's sexism fuelled the flames of separatism. It was a fractious period, but one of intense learning. A young movement experimented with strategies, tactics, and organizational forms.

Before Stonewall, although a few famous transitions had occurred, there was little or no public distinction among the exotics that have today differentiated into the alphabet of LGBTTIQQ2SA, and so on. Gay, lesbian, bisexual, and trans people moved in the same circles and negotiated the social contract of the closet.

But when coming out became the standard of virtue, the radical politics of gay liberation saw transitioning as an individual capitulation to the status quo. Such positions were reinforced by the political alliance between gay men and feminism, since early second-wave feminism was generally even more hostile to transitioning than were newly liberated gay men.

At the end of the 1970s, the world began to change. A new social conservative movement, deeply anxious about change, was being orchestrated in the United States. The new right, as the chant went, was "racist, sexist, anti-gay." American cultural and economic influences had their effect in Canada, although here, the attraction of social conservatism was softened by a more successful welfare state.

Nevertheless, the fledgling lesbian and gay movements came under attack. After the first raid on *TBP*, there was a short period of unity between lesbian feminists and gay men on the basis of freedom of expression and a common enemy, papering over profound disagreements on other issues. Social conservatism also had other targets, and the same basis of unity brought together artists and publishers with gay communities.

1980S

The neo-liberal shift arrived full force with Reagan's 1980 election. Although his main goal was in economic policy, his alliance with a radical social conservatism gave these groups unprecedented influence.

In Toronto, George Hislop's campaign to become the city's first openly gay councillor reflected a new community unity based on neighbourhood. Even Hislop's radical critics came on side. But in the face of homophobic resurgence, Hislop went down to defeat, as did John Sewell, the progressive mayor who spoke out in favour of press freedom in the *TBP* case. Those defeats opened the door to the 1981 bath raids.

The response to the raids crystallized a decade of often imperceptible changes – the growth of gay men's sexual networks and a higher profile community. An alliance formed between the gay petite bourgeoisie, the radical movement, and previously apolitical gay men who recognized that police were no longer honouring the social contract of the closet. Lesbians, too, grew aware of the dangers of the right-wing backlash, and straight allies emerged among civil libertarians, artists, politicians, and religious figures.

Although the bath raids legitimized street activism, the period also required a robust legal response. Fighting in the courts was a defensive imperative. Yet the resulting victories strengthened the idea that the courts could be a site of redress, a notion that gained more traction after the Charter of Rights and Freedoms was established in 1982.

The increase in economic disparity was still not widely evident in the mid-1980s. But in terms of race and ethnicity, the demographic shift in Toronto certainly was. Racialized communities, especially black communities, were also targets of brutal police violence. The RTPC established important horizontal alliances with groups formed to combat police racism. But while happy to pay lip service to multiculturalism, the overwhelmingly white LGB movement had no idea how to navigate the complex racial politics coming to the fore. New visible minority communities struggled with marginalization, discrimination, state harassment, and daily microaggressions. Lesbians and gay men from racialized communities found themselves with a foot in both camps and secure in neither. They organized independently. Especially after its sexual turn, the libertarian current around *TBP* revealed itself as insensitive to such issues. That poisoned relations with emerging radical people of colour's lesbian and gay groups.

Tighter economic times and the fraying of the social safety net eroded the volunteer gift culture that had been the basis of most of the early organizations. People were more pressured to think about their futures and careers; what they could accumulate rather than what they could give. The new economy was bringing different values to the fore. As Margaret Thatcher famously said, "Economics are the method; the object is to change the heart and soul." Neo-liberalism promoted behaviour congruent with its "economic man" – logical, calculating, and self-serving. Volunteer-based organizations were unable to adapt and began to disappear.

Social conservatism also had profound effects on the women's movement. In the United States, many opted for an alliance with the state to protect women from violence and pornography. Those promoting sexual freedom and women's sexual agency were reduced to a vocal minority. Although in Canada, the women's movement coalesced around the issue of access to abortion, an anti-porn movement also developed. It was soon on a collision course with a libertarian gay men's movement informed by ongoing battles against censorship. What remained of the imagined alliance between gay men and the women's movement fell into disarray, as did autonomous lesbian organizing. Ironically, a more libertarian gay men's movement began to envisage transgender people as part of the community. *T* was added to LGB.

But in the same period, a singularity occurred. Social conservatism lost ground in Ontario with the collapse of the exhausted Progressive Conservative party's forty-year rule. This provided an opening for CLGRO, one of the few original organizations that managed to survive, to win the inclusion of sexual orientation in the Ontario Human Rights Code. It paved the way for the inclusion of anti-homophobia work in other institutions, for example, the Toronto Board of Education.

By mid-decade, AIDS emerged as the worst crisis the young community had ever confronted. Unlike in many U.S. cities, in Toronto the alliance between gay business and activists cemented by the bath raids presented a united front and there were no battles about closing down overtly sexual gay institutions. In the face of government indifference, a surge of energy went into setting up the AIDS Committee of Toronto, the first of many AIDS service organizations. AIDS was a long-term crisis demanding services and an institutional response. That required state and corporate funding, which in turn required more corporate organizational management – mission statements, boards, executive directors, and so on. A professional class began to assume leadership.

But there was a need for more than services. In Toronto, AIDS ACTION NOW! was the activist political voice of the crisis. It focused on treatment accessibility: first material access, then access to information, then ethical access to clinical trials, and finally financial access. While AAN! employed large-scale street activism, the work also required expertise in a number of fields. Although AAN! resisted becoming a funded organization, it experienced the same pressures for professionalization, ultimately reflected in the class character of the leadership.

1990S

The unexpected election of a provincial NDP government and of Kyle Rae, the first openly gay man on city council, opened a window for political change. Both the AIDS movement and the LGBT movement tried to take advantage. AAN! proved more successful, and won the last major social accomplishment of the 1990s: the Trillium Drug Program, extending financial access to medications to Ontarians.

On the other hand, the lesbian and gay movement experienced one of its most resounding defeats: the fight for same-sex spousal benefits was lost. That poisoned relations with the NDP and increased cynicism about politics. It also revealed a changing class dynamic. More established professional lesbians and gay men, who would never have associated themselves with community politics a decade before, dominated the message of the Campaign for Equal Families.

The victory of the Harris Tories in 1995 heralded a neo-liberal revolution on fast forward, with attacks on labour, immigrants, Indigenous people, and the poor. The social safety net, education, public health, labour rights, and environmental protections were devastated. The City of Toronto was amalgamated with more conservative suburbs. Groups like AAN! were on the defensive. AIDS service organizations desperately attempted to diversify funding in the face of cuts. With any prospect of political progress closed, the lesbian and gay movement turned to the courts.

This again helped cement the influence of the professional class. From then on, the goals of the movement were bounded by the parameters of the Charter. Its logic was inclusion rather than social change, vertical alliances rather than horizontal ones. Respectability facilitated inclusion. Those who could perform a normative same-sex family structure or donate money for court cases became more important. Men and women worked together on this struggle. Lesbians raising children were less threatening and less sexualized than gay men, and played a visible media role. As the new strategy developed, independent lesbian organizing largely faded away. In the process of transforming laws, we transformed ourselves.

Unions were an ever more valuable partner in this struggle. Spousal benefits were a good fit with union politics, and unions became instrumental in legal cases that required a large organization's financial resources. But larger unions represented a relatively privileged sector of the workforce, those with stable employment and benefits. That distanced them from the growing number of workers in non-unionized workplaces. The extension of benefits meant little to those who had no benefits at all. For very poor queers on public assistance, the ultimate recognition of gay or lesbian relationships was actually economically detrimental.

In the context of this increasingly liberal movement, trans people became more assertive, and their stories more aligned with the gay coming-out narrative. Gay rights became about each individual's right to pursue happiness within existing social arrangements; transition, one more individual road to happiness. Finally, as gay Main Street became more comfortable with biological explanations – *I was born this way* – the argument "I was born in the wrong body" became more acceptable. A clearer distinction began to be made between gender identity and sexual orientation. After the delisting of sex reassignment surgery, trans struggles were seen as allied community struggles. Many trans activists followed a similar rights-based strategy as lesbians and gay men had done.

2000S

After the 9/11 attack on the World Trade Center, gays seemed potentially less dangerous to the nation than Muslims. For the gay rights movement, radical Islam was just another incarnation of the religious bigotry that had always opposed homosexuality. The foundation of homonationalism was completed. In Canada, where spousal benefits for same-sex partners were already obtained in the courts, the goal became largely symbolic – access to the respectability of marriage. Despite a few detractors, the marriage fight was widely embraced as a symbol of equality within the community. Eventually, governments acquiesced to court decisions and amended legislation. With it, the liberal civil rights agenda was fulfilled.

The rights-based strategy was remarkably successful in achieving its concrete goals and producing a cultural shift in the historically short period of less than one lifetime. At least some of us had been transformed from a group outside the law to full citizens and an important niche market. But marriage was not only a measure of our acceptance. It was becoming the condition for it. Those who still engaged in less seemly sexual activity, as evidenced by our HIV status, for example, became more vulnerable to state policing.

The cultural shift was beneficial to the vast majority of LGBT people in Canada. But for those for whom homophobia was the *only* major barrier to acceptance, it was especially beneficial. Such people, now embraced by the nation, returned the embrace, and emerged as the homonationalist leadership. Early community leadership was a quasi-criminal class defending itself against the state. The new leadership was a propertied class, seeking state protection. Those without significant property and with little market value became more alienated.

INFLUENCES: THE NOTION OF COMMUNITY

Homonationalism in Canada took shape amid several overarching influences. "Community" always obscured class differences among those identifying as lesbian or gay. Class differences first played out as competing political positions, liberation versus assimilation between gay radicals and small gay business.

With the bath raids, both radicals and the petite bourgeoisie were subsumed into the umbrella of community. But gradually, a professional/managerial class became dominant. Without a language to talk about class, it was almost impossible to talk about this process, and the upward class shift that eventually produced homonationalism went largely unnoticed.

GEOGRAPHY AND GENTRIFICATION

This process also had a spatial aspect. With the opening of the 519 Church Street Community Centre in the late 1970s, and new gay-oriented small businesses taking advantage of cheaper rents along Church in the 1980s, the gay village was born. External economies of scale ensured that once a critical mass was reached, the area became a magnet for more such businesses and lesbian and gay residents. A community that imagined itself along the model of Canadian multiculturalism developed its own ethnic enclave.

This enclave provided a voting bloc that elected gay and gay-positive politicians, who in turn became community spokespeople. Such politicians needed to be sensitive to the voices of homeowners and businesses in their districts, and represented their interests and perspectives as those of the community. As downtown property values dramatically increased in the 1990s, and rental accommodation gave way to more condos, the socio-economic status of those with claims to this community space was further elevated.

THE RESILIENCE OF CAPITALISM

Those who felt that 1970s capitalism could not change without shattering were sadly mistaken. Capitalism is flexible. Markets adapt to prevailing conditions like water seeking its level. All in all, the period between 1974 and 2014 saw no earthshaking political changes. The shift from Keynesianism to neo-liberalism was relatively smooth.

While unstable conditions favour horizontal alliances (since one never knows who is going to be in power), stable conditions select for vertical alliances. Power is not vulnerable and one must find favour with it to win concrete change. Vertical alliances therefore became dominant. That in turn selected for those with more class privilege within the movement.

THE SALES EFFORT

Today's capitalist economy is dominated by large monopolies. They produce a huge choice of different products that are essentially the same, and success or failure has less to do with price or cost of production than with marketing and branding. Sex, a major theme in such marketing, saturates our media. Sexual desire constantly renews itself. If a product can be linked to it, demand is infinite.

This has driven a social transformation. In the '70s, talk and depiction of sex was socially unacceptable and potentially illegal. Sexual liberation was about freeing sex from the constraints of marriage, censorship laws, and social disapproval. Now, however, sexual expression is only discouraged among the very young, where it is still subject to legal constraints, and the very old, where it is subject to ridicule.

Our community became a niche market. Its professional/managerial sectors are especially coveted because of their disposable income. Corporations fall over themselves to demonstrate they are gay friendly, empowering homo-nationalist voices.

THE EXHAUSTION OF SEXUAL LIBERATION POLITICS

As advertising made sexual talk and imagery ubiquitous and recreational sex became more commonplace, what did sexual liberation mean? As sexual liberation lost its edge and purpose, the field was left open to those who wanted to assimilate. Gay people and straight people were no longer so different. Straights became more slutty and gay people wanted to get married.

With such convergence, why should we have different rights? Today's dissenters are more likely to be those who want liberation *from* the intrusions of sex and sexual imagery – assexuals, women raised in the West who choose to wear Muslim head coverings – rather than those who want more.

SUCCESS

Surfing on the liberal notion that sexuality was individual expression rather than social duty, the early activists were remarkably successful in laying the groundwork for more people coming out. By making it easier to come out, we allowed those who previously would not have risked their privilege to do so.

We found that we were indeed everywhere, from the top to the bottom of the social pyramid. When those higher up on the social ladder came out, their resources, skills, and connections allowed their investment in the status quo and the nation to dominate the movement.

AIDS

AIDS ironically helped undermine the social contract of the closet and opened the way for homonationalism. When dying Hollywood stars like Rock Hudson tumbled out of the closet, famous colleagues modelled sympathy rather than fear or disgust. Under surveillance by public health systems, gay men became more visible. AIDS service organizations served public health and were supported by the state and corporations.

The timeline imposed by AIDS, where the horizon – death – was often a matter of months rather than years or decades, reinforced the need for vertical alliances. No one could wait for the revolution. As AIDS service organizations became more professionalized and dependent on the state and corporate donations, their vision of the future seldom went beyond the next funding cycle. Success required the recruitment of those with resources and connections, another vehicle for upward class shift in leadership. The professional class in AIDS and other community institutions became a bridge between the community and power.

AIDS also dramatically changed the cost-fuck ratio for recreational sex. The potential of getting a life-threatening disease now had to be included in the calculation. The drudgery of monogamy seemed relatively more attractive. That helped drive the demand for marriage and respectability.

Finally, AIDS wiped out a generation and much historical memory. We lost many seasoned activists who might have challenged the new homonationalist leadership.

INSTITUTIONALIZATION

Early lesbian and gay organizations tended to be volunteer, non-hierarchical collectives. Such organizations often were dependent on individual personalities and circumstances, and often had short life spans.

Collectives that engaged in businesses, such as *TBP*, were gradually forced to adopt more corporate models by business and tax law or by the need for efficiency produced by competition. Collectives that engaged in offering social services were reshaped by laws governing charitable status and funders' demands. In both cases, equality gave way to divisions of labour and then to institutional hierarchy.

INSTITUTIONAL COMPLETENESS

Completeness refers to the range of institutions in a community. In an institutionally complete community, members are able to fulfill most of their needs without recourse to the outside world. For example, I can now live in a gay neighbourhood, shop in gay stores, find employment in gay organizations or with a gay employer, go to a gay doctor and dentist, use the services of a gay lawyer, and go to a gay place of worship.

From the time when our institutions were restricted to a handful of bars and baths, the community has become much more institutionally complete. Advertisers in gay media demonstrate the scope. But it therefore begins to reflect the class structure of the surrounding world. The ward-heeler, the businessperson who provides jobs to their own kind, the community religious leader all become "natural" spokespeople who have an inordinate impact on community politics. Lawyers became important when progress was restricted to the courts. Those with medical and scientific knowledge became more important in the fight against AIDS. The well-connected and the wealthy became more important as groups institutionalized and needed money. Well-educated policy wonks who could negotiate with governments became more important as vertical alliances developed.

In terms of institutional completeness, homonationalism is not exceptional. It is our community's expression of a mundane phenomenon. Lesbian and gay men are much like any other successful minority in a country that ascribes to multiculturalism as part of its national imaginary. We ethnicized ourselves in order to fit into the paradigm of a minority seeking rights. Like most model minorities, our leadership is now made up of those most successful by the standards of wider society. They speak for us, manage our community affairs, and discipline those whose behaviour is unacceptable. In return, they derive status as our leaders, represent us in elite gatherings, market us to large corporations, and deploy us as a political constituency.

THE RISE OF NEO-LIBERALISM

In a Keynesian system, where class disparity was less severe and experience across class lines more homogenous, the incipient professionalization of the early movement was less of a problem. But neo-liberal class structure, with its huge gap between the top and the rest, means that our leadership is more out of touch with how most of us live. This is exacerbated by the racialization of these differences, with the top 10 per cent still largely white and a growing racialized underclass.

Neo-liberalism has also changed social values. Unmoored from any notion of social good, the liberal values we promoted in our struggle against tradition have been transformed into something resembling a destructive psychosis. Individualism justifies unlimited greed and selfishness. When rationalism is stripped of empathy, success can only be measured by dollars accumulated, despite its destruction of people and the planet. This shift in values affects all of us.

But on a political level, neo-liberalism was the wave that carried forward our push for rights. While at first, neo-liberals needed a populist social conservatism to displace the old Keynesian order, once in power, a more mature neo-liberalism could dispense with such embarrassing bedfellows. After all, "irrational" traditional values impede the free flow of capital – the fundamental goal. Reagan gave way to Clinton, Thatcher to Blair, Mulroney to Chrétien. Neo-liberalism became eager to portray itself as socially liberal. People were to be judged by their capacity to produce or consume, not by extraneous factors such as race, gender, or sexual orientation.

The decline in social conservative influence during the 1990s opened the way for rapid change through the courts via the Charter. The demands of the rights movement were in no way antithetical to the mature neo-liberal state, and were bolstered by its basic values of individualism and legal equality. There was a flowering of anti-discrimination legislation, even as neo-liberal economies structurally marginalized certain populations on the basis of intersections of race, ethnicity, immigration status, gender, and so on. More privileged members of groups such as women and gay people, widely distributed across the class spectrum, were able to take advantage of liberal anti-discrimination discourse. But the benefits of this legal equality were more unequally distributed, as class inequality increased within our communities.

HOMONATIONALIST CANADA

In *Money, Myths and Change: The Economic Lives of Lesbians and Gay Men,* Lee Badgett challenges what she describes as the major myths about lesbians and gay men. The myth of privilege – that we are an affluent, well-educated, professional elite, occupying positions of power and influence. The double-income-no-kids (DINK) myth – that we are without family responsibilities to hamper our accumulation of wealth. The myth of invisibility that protects us from stigma and discrimination. The myth of the conspicuous consumer that sees us as an important niche market. Although hers is no class analysis, she does effectively skewer these stereotypes and pulls apart the "data" on which many gay marketing strategies are based.[2]

But if in terms of averages LGBTQ people may still be disadvantaged, the devil is always in the details. Discrimination is not equally distributed. There is a sector of our community for whom those stereotypes ring true. They have become the social base for the homonationalist leadership.

Puar describes homonationalism as associated with whiteness, privatized, depoliticized, anchored in domesticity and consumption, and serving as ammunition to reinforce nationalist projects. How well does this description fit Canadian homonationalism?

The white-dominated gay movement always had difficulty understanding and even recognizing racialized queers, and while the homonationalist leadership is still largely white, our community is not. When the rights struggle was won, the marginalization of white professional gays and lesbians significantly declined in Canada. For many racialized and poor queers, however, it continues. For white professionals, LGBTQ identity was the ticket to the party. Others still find themselves carded at the door. We are divided along racial lines, even when black and brown faces are liberally foregrounded to prove that we are not.

That said, the association with whiteness is complicated. Our society is officially multicultural, and neo-liberal society is different from a traditionally racist one. Highly selected individuals who prove their worth to the system can rise, despite their inconvenient racial origins. LGBTQ ones can become part of the homonationalist leadership.

Certainly the fight to keep inconvenient politics out of Pride in 2010 illustrated a vision of a community anchored in domesticity and consumption. But Pride is a profoundly public event. Lesbian and gay people are incited to make public our existence in the service of the nation, the city, and commerce. In 1974, orgasm with a same-sex partner was an act of ecstatic resistance against a homophobic nation. In homonationalist Canada, being out is our patriotic duty. As such, homosexuality serves as ammunition to reinforce nationalist projects. Here is the contradiction between Puar's notion of the depoliticized homonationalist subject and the political role that that subject is asked to perform.

But homonationalism in Canada is, like the nation, far from homogenous. The fight around QuAIA was less about Israeli apartheid than it was about two conflicting national imaginaries – an authoritarian conservative nationalism, and a more liberal nationalism defending such Canadian values as freedom of expression.

Perhaps, since there are always competing national imaginaries, it would be better to think about homonationalisms rather than homonationalism. We often associate homonationalism with right-wing politics. But there are more progressive national imaginaries as well. It seriously flattens the concept to assume that gay Conservative cabinet minister John Baird and lesbian NDP member of Parliament Libby Davies had the same ideal of what it meant to be Canadian, even though both were involved in a (homo)nationalist project to include gay people in their version of the nation. We are all complicit with homonationalism. Even the most dissident non-normative queer would not advocate return to an officially homophobic nation that singled us out for persecution.

Problems arise when we don't make that distinction, and assume a simple contradiction between a homonationalist faction that wants to celebrate inclusion, versus anti-homonationalist political queers who want to protest injustice. Such an analysis limits our options. We can submit to homonationalist leadership, prioritizing identity. Or we can make a radical break with that leadership on the grounds that, in the face of centrifugal forces accelerated by neo-liberalism, shared sexual orientation is no longer a strong enough glue to hold us together. Queers would therefore need to organize not on the basis of LGBT politics, but on the basis of class or race.

I think we need to look more carefully at homonationalism as it actually exists. If we understand that there are different nationalisms, under what conditions might it be useful to unite with some against others?

That leads to asking what windows of opportunity are open. Are we entering a period of fundamental social change where each must stand in their place – a situation that would call for horizontal alliances for deeper social change? Or do we face many more years of relative stability, where vertical alliances are more effective in protecting what has been gained and winning incremental improvements?

IS THE FUTURE THE SAME?

Homonationalism generally assumes continuity: that with the attainment of rights, we have reached a plateau that stretches into the foreseeable future. This change is irreversible. It is therefore a time for celebration. The fight – other than a bit of mopping up around education, or sensitivity training for the police, and so on – is essentially over.

The assumption that the future will be like the present (except better) is a common wishful illusion among those satisfied with the present. But neo-liberalism has delivered anything but stability over the last twenty years. Canada has still not recovered from the 2008 crash. Growth continues to be slow, wealth ever more unequally distributed, and the economy more vulnerable to external shocks.

IS THE FUTURE CONTESTED?

If there is one thing we can say definitively, it is that prolonged economic crises lead to political crises, and prolonged political crises foster authoritarianism. In periods of political crises, elites often opt for demagogues and scapegoats to deflect public anger.

The Harper government was notable for its suppression of political dissent, draconian changes to the Criminal Code, greater police and surveillance powers, silencing of inconvenient scientific data, and targeting groups such as Muslims, environmentalists, and even sociologists. Even now, after Harper has been replaced, a huge repressive apparatus is constructed and ready for deployment. The foundations have been laid for a more conservative, authoritarian future.

During the Keynesian period, the theory of convergence was popular. Socialist countries would gradually become more democratic, while capitalist ones would gradually develop more social programs and government economic management, until they met in a social democratic middle point.[3] It didn't turn out that way. Socialism collapsed, and today the differences seem to be between the more authoritarian versions of capitalism found in countries such as China, Russia, Saudi Arabia, or Singapore and less authoritarian ones such as Canada, the European Union, or arguably the United States. The difference lies in how society will be managed, through repressive power or by inciting compliance through access to consumer goods.

If there is a new convergence, it seems to be towards the authoritarian end of the spectrum. As economic power becomes more concentrated, political power follows. Class disparity, deepening environmental crises, inter-imperialist rivalries, and expanding technical capacity for surveillance all feed the authoritarian impulse. What would it mean to identify with such a state? Would we even be allowed to?

IS THE FUTURE APOCALYPTIC?

The apocalyptic position is to imagine that the LGBTQ community will find itself in a similar position to the Jewish community in pre-war Germany – enjoying legal rights, some of us integrated into the systems of elite power while most of us do the best we can in a world dominated by others, trusting our friends in the elite to protect us. Yet, in a flash, when it became politically expedient, the Jewish community, elite or not, suddenly found itself no longer part of the nation.

Could gay people serve as a similar scapegoat, or are we now too entangled in society to return to the status of other? Tom Warner confidently entitled his history *Never Going Back*. But I am old enough to also remember the "irreversible gains of socialism." The association of minority community brokers with the status quo and elites can make a whole minority a target for anti-elite resentment. If the dominant image of our community is that of gay elites, there is no reason why anti-elite sentiment could not be turned against us. That, in fact, already happened in Toronto under the Rob Ford administration. Who could have predicted that after so many years of support from city hall, Pride funding could in 2010 once again be controversial?

Capitalist rationality will always sacrifice a niche market in order to save itself. A traditionally homophobic social conservatism waits in the wings. What are the conditions that could once again propel it into power? Are we, who surfed so long on the wave of liberalism, now in danger of being caught in its dangerous undertow?

IS THE FUTURE QUEER?

In reaction to conservatism and respectability, queer has championed dissent. Queer has an eclectic class basis. It includes marginalized young people, trans people who refuse to stealthily conform to gender norms, young intellectuals with few prospects of achieving their class aspirations in the neo-liberal university, the unrespectable and often racialized poor, old radicals consigned to the margins.

Over the past decade, there has been an explosion of spontaneous, grassroots queer organizing in Toronto, much of it arts-based. This work has a much clearer appreciation of the entwined nature of oppressions, and those involved often have a foot in many camps. But while the 1970s radicals drew on a century of socialist analysis and organizing, and imagined their project in the context of fundamental social change, queer's commitment to resisting oppressions has no unifying theory of a different kind of society. We '70s radicals may have been deluded in our vision of the future, but that shared delusion oriented our work.

Part of this has to do with the fact that Queer Theory is generally obtuse and inaccessible to all but the cognoscenti. Those who could provide leadership and social analysis to a radical queer movement have generally retreated to different ivory towers. There, they content themselves with shouting clever and elegant phrases back and forth, each one more radical than the rest.

Queer is also rife with contradictions. It is an anti-identity that simultaneously rejects and fetishizes identity. It so values the role of the outsider that, rather than seeing less radical, more normative lesbians and gay men as a constituency to be organized or won over, it more often uses them as a foil to highlight its own political righteousness. Everyone wants to be a radical activist, but no one wants to organize.

Queer has been shaped by the neo-liberal ethos. Much of the queer generation has grown up in a dog-eat-dog world with profoundly individualistic values. Individual entrepreneurship often replaces a sense of group agency. This is an ethos grounded in the material relations of day-to-day life. With nearly half of Toronto's working population in precarious employment, and younger people especially vulnerable to slipping into poverty, fewer have time to consistently dedicate themselves to unsalaried activism. Unemployment insurance and occasional work can no longer subsidize volunteer organizations as they did in the past. Unlike '70s radicals, today's queer youth are anxious about their economic future. As a result, they can ricochet between left and right opportunism at lightning speed, at one moment indulging in high anti-capitalist rhetoric and the next fantasizing an entrepreneurial start-up. Queer exemplifies individual radicalism in the neo-liberal age with all the attendant contradictions.

Queer demonstrates the energy, enthusiasm, and optimism of youth, but its deep distrust of institutionalization, its hyper-egalitarian rejection of any organizational hierarchy, and its distain for more normative and mainstream politics often results in volatile short-term efforts without long-term goals or strategies. Queer represents a rejection of the status quo, but has been so far unable to imagine a solution to it, and its politics tends to be one of gestures rather than organizing towards concrete goals.

So while queer undoubtedly represents a radical impulse, it remains to be seen if it can serve as a centre for successful resistance to neo-liberalism or a resurgent social conservatism, never mind charting a path to a better future. From this perspective, the problem is not so much homonationalism as it is the lack of capacity of the queer left.

PINKWASHING

Israel's deployment of gay rights to reinforce its nationalist project is the most obvious example of pinkwashing. But many liberal democracies are also employing it. In the face of more unequal, less democratic societies hurtling towards war and threatened by ecological catastrophe, it is tempting to see any celebration of gay rights as a happy story to paint over the grim reality, reinforcing a mirage of liberal equality in a desert of injustice.

But this analysis of pinkwashing can also lead to a position where no celebration can be tolerated lest it distract from misery. Such dourness cannot possibly be transformative. It forgets that the carnivalesque is simultaneously a celebration of the oppressed, a distraction from that oppression, and a ritualistic letting off of steam.

We need to tighten up our definition of pinkwashing to distinguish between the cynical deployment of our community for elite purposes, the social effects our celebrations generate, and their potential as a site of struggle.

INTERNATIONAL IMPLICATIONS

Since the 1970s, LGBT struggles have been conceptualized as struggles for rights. They have therefore generally been directed towards the state as the arbiter of citizenship. The strategy has been to insinuate ourselves into the national imaginary.

But with the globalization of the world economy, flows of capital, labour, and information across national borders have accelerated. Nation states, once independent entities with their own internal logic, are becoming administrative units of transnational capital. They are now subject to increasing pressure for harmonization in their economic, legal, social, and cultural practices. This process seeks to establish international standards by which all nations are to be judged. A positive judgment puts a nation in the realm of the civilized. A negative judgment is to be excluded from the civilized world, to be barbarous, backward, and in need of correction. Among the traditional western imperial powers, forty years of struggle have integrated gay rights into the national imaginary. For them, gay rights are human rights and the treatment of homosexuals has become a litmus test for civilization.

This leads to three interrelated issues. First, globalization does not take place among equals. It benefits the most powerful and takes place in the context of neo-colonial relationships. Second, there is a globalization of sexual identities that have developed in the cultures of the dominant powers.

Finally, globalization has been unable to contain and often amplifies inter-imperialist rivalries. All affect international solidarity around questions of sexuality.

NEO-COLONIALISM

Globalization is not a neutral process. It consists of the penetration of capital and capitalist social relations into the economies and cultures of societies still dominated by other logics. The nation states that first benefited from and still dominate modern capital accumulation are Europe and the settler states. The targets of penetration are often the post-colonial states that they once ruled imperially and, in many cases, still dominate.

For those on the receiving end, the push for harmonization of legal and social rights is often experienced as old-fashioned colonial meddling. It produces a reflex of anti-colonial resistance, dominated nowadays by those who see themselves as guardians and protectors of the traditional (even when such tradition is largely recently invented).

Further, in return for a cut of the spoils, local elites in many post-colonial countries have been happy to adopt policies that expose their societies to the predations of international capital. Portraying themselves as the defenders of tradition, against homosexuality, masks how they are selling out the nation for their own benefit.

In the Middle East, repeated western interventions for control of oil and strategic advantage and the continued support for Israel's occupation of Palestine have produced a deep backlash. For those in the region seeking development and democracy, co-operation with the West only resulted in betrayal. Discontent there is increasingly channelled by fundamentalist currents of Islam. With the West now vaunting its support of gay people as evidence of its superior civilization, it is not surprising that those assuming lesbian and gay identities have become symbols of foreign penetration.

SEXUAL IDENTITY

We have seen how the debate between essentialists and the social constructionists was resolved with social construction relegated to the academy while essentialism became the common sense of ordinary people. The international struggle against homophobia also tends to assume essentialism – that there are LGBT people everywhere, even if some of them don't know it yet or their culture is so repressive they still can't conceive of coming out. They therefore need our help to be liberated.

So, for example, in 2007, when Iranian president Mahmoud Ahmadinejad said, "We don't have homosexuals in Iran," he was widely ridiculed by the common-sense essentialists. However, when one takes his statement in its entirety – "We don't have homosexuals in Iran, *like you do in the West*" – the statement could be perfectly acceptable in any university course on sexual diversity, dominated as they are by social constructionists. They understand the homosexual/heterosexual binary as a recent western invention.

This is further complicated in a globalized world where the borders between different regimes of sexual identities are regularly breached. The problem with Amadinejad's statement is that there are homosexuals in Iran, just like we have in the West. There are men and women who identify as lesbians, gay men, and so on. But such identities are not as ubiquitous, and access to them is mediated once again by factors including class, gender, and urban-rural differences.

The "newness" of such identities contributes to their appearance as foreign, and feeds the persecution of those who adopt them. This persecution often spills over onto those who don't adopt such identities but still engage in same-sex sexual activity.

INTER-IMPERIALIST RIVALRIES

Globalized capital is not seamless. Different sectors, economic actors, and interests still dominate particular nation states. Nations still strive to dominate the global economy. Dominance comes with competitive advantage in capital accumulation and potential imperial tribute.

It was not, for example, homosexual rights that kicked off the recent conflict between the United States and Russia over Russia's anti-gay legislation. Homosexual rights became a weapon to use in a pre-existing fight between two imperial blocs about who is going to dominate Eastern Europe. Two large, aggressive capitalist nations, both with economic ambitions, are playing to respective national ideologies – the United States as the supposed upholder of secular liberal values, Russia waving the banner of traditional Orthodox Christian values.

THE GAY INTERNATIONAL AND ITS DISCONTENTS

All of these fault lines and conflicts mean attempts at international solidarity can become a minefield. In its original use in the union movement, "solidarity" described a horizontal alliance. Workers everywhere needed to stand up for each other. During the anti-colonial period, the term was expanded to include those in one country who supported oppressed people in other countries – solidarity with the fight against apartheid, for example.

But solidarity between relatively wealthy folks in the global North and those facing oppression elsewhere is hardly a relationship between equals. Expressions of solidarity can become colonial. The stock solution is that leadership should always reside with the more oppressed side of the equation. In practice, people on that side probably have enough difficulty figuring out their own local strategy and tactics, never mind managing those on the other side of the world. Our movement here didn't really have any idea what it was doing when we started, and there were all sorts of disagreements. Why should we assume it would be different elsewhere?

But our solidarity and resources can exert powerful pressures on those struggling against oppression to adapt strategies and even identities to please their more powerful partners. Our aid can upset the home-grown ecology of local organizations as groups compete to define themselves in ways that access foreign resources. And all of us can become pawns in international politics that have little to do with us.

Stir into this mix white entitlement, money, and a little missionary zeal, and things can go very wrong. Even with the best intentions human rights campaigners can find themselves reinforcing racist imagery and notions of the white man's burden, projecting identities on others or feeding into national chauvinism.

It would be unfair to imply that many dedicated human rights organizations are not aware of such issues. They are, and they do their best to ensure that what they do has the support and collaboration of those on the ground. But given the imbalance of power, the question always remains: Who is in control?

WHAT IS TO BE DONE?

So under these conditions, what are progressive LGBTQ people to do today?

In Canada, should we be organizing to challenge the homonationalist leadership? Or, given that all nationalisms are not the same, negotiate alliances in the face of the possibility of authoritarianism and resurgent homophobia? And who are "we?" On what basis can we organize people to have a coherent voice either to break with or negotiate with the homonationalist leadership?

Internationally, we can scarcely abandon people facing torture and violence. But if we use our vertical connections to encourage our governments to intervene, we may end up making things much worse. And we may feed into agendas that lead farther away from, rather than towards, human liberation. How do we establish true horizontal alliances with those who seek our solidarity, whether they share our ideas of sexual orientation or not, without recourse to discredited state structures?

It would be foolish and arrogant for me to speculate about an agenda for the future. Such directions will be selected, as they have been in the past, out of many strategies proposed by many people, doing their best as conditions change, involving too many evening meetings. I hope that this reflection on the struggles of the past will help us recognize the broader social forces that need to be taken into account in thinking through such strategies and avoiding pitfalls. Social and class analysis has become much more sophisticated over this forty-year span. We need to take it into account.

I would like to close by channelling Simon Nkoli about one thing I am sure of. In the end, history will judge our communities not by how many friends we had in high places, but by what we did to support social justice for all.

Acronyms and Abbreviations

AAN!	AIDS ACTION NOW!
ACAS	Asian Community AIDS Services
ACCHO	African and Caribbean Council on HIV/AIDS in Ontario
ACT	AIDS Committee of Toronto
ACT UP	AIDS Coalition to Unleash Power
AIDS	acquired immune deficiency syndrome
AL-721	a lipid mixture used as an anti-HIV drug
AMENO	Anti-racism Multicultural Educators Network of Ontario
ANC	African National Congress
APA	American Psychiatric Association
ARCH	Advocacy Resource Centre for the Handicapped
AZT	an antiviral drug (azidothymidine)
BDS	boycott, divestment, and sanctions
Black CAP	Black Coalition for AIDS Prevention
BM	black male
BOOST	Blind Organization of Ontario with Self-Help Tactics
CAAT	Committee for Accessible AIDS Treatment
CAISO	Coalition Advocating for Inclusion of Sexual Orientation (Trinidad and Tobago)
CALGM	Canadian Association of Lesbians and Gay Men
CAMH	Centre for Addiction and Mental Health
CAP	Community Advisory Panel
CAS	Canadian AIDS Society
CATIE	Community AIDS Treatment Information Exchange (later, Canadian AIDS Treatment Information Exchange)
CAW	Canadian Auto Workers
CD4	a type of white blood cell; a measure of the immune system
CEF	Campaign for Equal Families
CEM	Canadians for Equal Marriage
CGRO	Coalition for Gay Rights in Ontario (later, CLGRO)
CHAR	Comité homosexuel anti-répression / Gay Coalition Against Repression

CHAT	Community Homophile Association of Toronto
CIA	Central Intelligence Agency (U.S.)
CIRPA	Citizen's Independent Review of Police Activities
CLC	Canadian Labour Congress
CLGA	Canadian Lesbian and Gay Archives
CLGRC	Canadian Lesbian and Gay Rights Coalition
CLGRO	Coalition for Lesbian and Gay Rights in Ontario
CLHE	Working Group on Criminal Law and HIV Exposure
CMV	cytomegalovirus
COSAS	Congress of South African Students
CPAVIH	Comité des Personnes Atteintes du VIH du Québec
CRIT	Community Research Initiative Toronto
CSAM	Comité SIDA Aide Montréal
CUPE	Canadian Union of Public Employees
CUPW	Canadian Union of Postal Workers
CURE	Citizens United for Responsible Education
CUT	Coalition for Usable Transportation
DDC	an antiviral drug (dideoxycytidine)
ddI	an antiviral drug (dideoxyinosine)
EDRP	Emergency Drug Release Program
EGALE	Equality for Gays and Lesbians Everywhere (later, EGALE Canada; Egale Canada)
EHGAM	Euskal Herriko Gay Askapen Mugimendua (Basque Gay Liberation Movement)
ERA	Equal Rights Amendment (U.S.)
FAGC	Front d'Alliberament Gai de Catalunya (Catalan Gay Liberation Front)
FGG	Federation of Gay Games
GAAP	Gay Asian AIDS Project
GASA	Gay Association of South Africa
GAT	Gay Asians Toronto
GATE	Gay Alliance Toward Equality
GCDC	Gay Community Dance Committee
GLAAD	Gay and Lesbian Alliance Against Defamation
GLAL	Grup de Lluita per l'Alliberament de la Lesbiana (Group in Struggle for Lesbian Liberation) (Spain)
GLARE	Gays and Lesbians Against the Right Everywhere (later, Gay Liberation Against the Right Everywhere)
GLAUT	Gays and Lesbians at U of T
GLOBE	Gay and Lesbian Organization of Bell Employees
GLOW	Gay and Lesbian Organization of the Witwatersrand (South Africa)
GNP+	Global Network of People Living with HIV

GO	Gays of Ottawa
GRID	gay related immune deficiency
GSA	Gay Straight Alliance
GWM	gay white male
HALCO	HIV and AIDS Legal Clinic of Ontario
HEAL	Health AIDS Education Liaison
HIV	human immunodeficiency virus (previously, HTLV-III)
IAS	International AIDS Society
ICASO	International Council of AIDS Service Organizations
ICW	International Community of Women Living with HIV
IGA	International Gay Association (later, ILGA)
ILGA	International Lesbian and Gay Association
IRQO	Iranian Queer Organization
IRQR	Iranian Railroad for Queer Refugees
IV	intravenous
IWD	International Women's Day
JDL	Jewish Defense League
J-FLAG	Jamaica Forum for Lesbians, All-Sexuals and Gays
KS	Kaposi's sarcoma
LAR	Lesbians Against the Right
LEGIT	Lesbian and Gay Immigration Taskforce
LGB	lesbian, gay, bisexual
LGBT	lesbian, gay, bisexual, trans
LGBTQ	lesbian, gay, bisexual, trans, queer
LGBTTIQ	lesbian, gay, bisexual, transgender, transsexual, intersex, queer
LGBTTIQQ2SA	lesbian, gay, bisexual, transsexual, transgender, intersex, queer, questioning, two-spirited, and allies
LGBYT	Lesbian, Gay and Bisexual Youth Toronto
LGSM	Lesbians and Gays Support the Miners (U.K.)
LOON	Lesbians of Ottawa Now
LOOT	Lesbian Organization of Toronto
LSA	League for Socialist Action
MCC	Metropolitan Community Church
MVAAA	Metropolitan Vancouver Arts and Athletics Association
NAMBLA	North American Man/Boy Love Association
NARCC	National Anti-Racism Council of Canada
NDP	New Democratic Party
NGO	non-governmental organization
NGRC	National Gay Rights Coalition (later, CLGRC)
NMI	New Marxist Institute
NOW	National Organization of Women (U.S.) (also, italicized, a free downtown weekly in Toronto)

OAN	Ontario AIDS Network
OAS	Organization of American States
OBOS	*Our Bodies, Ourselves*
OCASI	Ontario Coalition of Agencies Serving Immigrants
OFL	Ontario Federation of Labour
OHIP	Ontario Health Insurance Plan
OHRC	Ontario Human Rights Commission
OLGA	Organization of Lesbian and Gay Activists (South Africa)
OPSEU	Ontario Public Service Employees Union
PASAN	Prisoners AIDS Support and Advocacy Network
PCFS	Pride Coalition for Free Speech
PCP	a kind of pneumonia (pneumocystis)
PFLAG	Parents and Friends of Lesbians and Gays (later, Parents, Families and Friends of Lesbians and Gays)
PHA	people living with HIV/AIDS
PI	protease inhibitors
PIE	Paedophile Information Exchange (U.K.)
PLURA	inter-church coalition with Presbyterian, Lutheran, United Church, Roman Catholic, and Anglican sponsors
PLWA	people with AIDS (people living with HIV/AIDS)
PMA	Pharmaceutical Manufacturers' Association
PTP	Pink Triangle Press
PWA	people living with AIDS
QN	Queer Nation
QuAIA	Queers Against Israeli Apartheid
RCMP	Royal Canadian Mounted Police
RGO	Rand Gay Organization (South Africa)
RHN	Rainbow Health Network
RICC	Riverdale Intercultural Council
RMG	Revolutionary Marxist Group
RTPC	Right to Privacy Committee
SARS	severe acute respiratory syndrome
SDS	Sexual Diversity Studies
SIDA	*syndrome d'immunodéficience acquise* (AIDS)
S/M	sado-masochism
SMM(C)	Stop Murder Music (Canada)
SNAAC	Simon Nkodi Anti-apartheid Committee: Lesbians and Gays Against Apartheid
SRS	sex reassignment surgery
STI	sexually transmitted infection
TAAR	Treatment, Access and Research Committee (AAN!)
TAC	Treatment Action Campaign (South Africa)
TAG	Treatment Action Group (New York)

TBP	*The Body Politic*
TCLSAC	Toronto Committee for the Liberation of South African Colonies
TDSB	Toronto District School Board
TGA	Toronto Gay Action
TGCC	Toronto Gay Community Council
TIE	Treatment Information Exchange
TNT Men	Totally Naked Toronto Men
TRIPS	trade-related aspects of property rights
TSPFN	Two Spirited People of the First Nations
UBC	University of British Columbia
UN	United Nations
U of T	University of Toronto
WASP	*White Assed Super Pricks* (magazine)
WAVAW	Women Against Violence Against Women
WAYV	Welcoming All Youth to the Village
WBC	Women's Bathhouse Committee
WHO	World Health Organization
WTO	World Trade Organization
YMCA	Young Men's Christian Association

Notes

Introduction

1 The material was eventually published as: Andil Gosine, "CAISO, CAISO: Negotiating Sex Rights and Nationalism in Trinidad and Tobago," *Sexualities*, http://sex.sagepub.com, 2015; and "Rescue and Real Love: Same-Sex Desire in International Development," Institute of Development Studies, March 2015, http://opendocs.ids.ac.uk/opendocs.

2 Karl Marx, "The Eighteenth Brumaire of Louis Bonapart," in Karl Marx and Frederick Engels, *Selected Works* (Moscow: Progress Publishers, 1969), 398.

3 See George Lakoff, *The Political Mind* (2008); *Whose Freedom* (2007); *Don't Think of an Elephant* (2004); *Moral Politics* (2002).

4 Tom Crompton, *Common Cause: The Case for Working with Our Cultural Values* (Climate Outreach and Information Network, Campaign to Protect Rural England, Friends of the Earth, Oxfam, and World Wildlife Foundation, September 2010), http://valuesandframes.org.

5 Raymond Williams, *Keywords: A Vocabulary of Culture and Society* (London: Fontana Paperbacks, 1983), 179.

6 Phil Ochs, "I Ain't Marching Anymore," Universal, 1965.

1 Invisible

1 Quoted in Gary Kinsman and Patrizia Gentile, *The Canadian War on Queers: National Security as Sexual Regulation* (UBC Press, 2010), 17.

2 *The Body Politic* (*TBP*) 13 (May/June 1974), 2.

3 Community Homophile Association of Toronto, *Gay Directions: A Guide to Toronto*, rev. Aug. 1974, 1.

4 Michael Ornstein, *Ethno-Racial Groups in Toronto, 1971–2001: A Demographic and Socio-Economic Profile* (Toronto: Institute for Social Research, York University, 2006).

5 J. David Hulchanski, *The Three Cities within Toronto: Income Polarization among Toronto's Neighbourhoods, 1970–2005* (Toronto: Cities Centre Press, University of Toronto, 2008).

6 Wainwright Churchill, *Homosexual Behavior among Males: A Cross-cultural and Cross Species Investigation* (Englewood Cliffs, NJ: Prentice Hall, 1967).

7 Ibid., 74.

8 Ibid., 175.

9 Ibid., 174.

10 Ibid., 181.

11 Ibid., 173.

12 Karla Jay and Allen Young, eds., *Out of the Closets: Voices of Gay Liberation* (New York: Douglas/Links, 1972).

13 Ibid., 1.

14 Ibid., 20–25.

15 Ibid., 331.

16 Ibid., 339.

17 Ibid., 340.

18 Ibid., 315.

19 Ibid., 364.

20 Ibid., 343–45.

21 Gerald Hannon, "Throat-Ramming," *TBP* 18 (May/June 1975), 15.

22 Radicalesbians, *The Woman Identified Woman* (Pittsburgh PA: KNOW INC, 1970).

23 "In 1969, the Criminal Code was amended so as to make certain sexual acts between consenting adults, in private, legal. This was widely misunderstood as 'legalizing' homosexuality and thus putting homosexuals on an equal basis with other Canadians. In fact, this amendment was merely recognition of the non-enforceable nature of the Criminal Code as it existed. Consequently, its effects have done little to alleviate the oppression of homosexual men and women in Canada. In our daily lives we are still confronted with discrimination, police harassment, exploitation and pressures to conform which deny our sexuality." From *We Demand*, quoted in Peter Knegt, *Queer Rights* (Halifax & Winnipeg: Fernwood, 2011), 36.

24 *TBP* 8 (Spring 1973), 17.

25 *TBP* 9 (Summer 1973), 3.

2 Getting Noticed

1 *TBP* 15 (Sept./Oct. 1974), 2.

2 Peter Zorzi, Queer Catharsis, http://onthebookshelves.com.

3 Brian Waite, "Strategy for Gay Liberation," *TBP* 3 (March/April 1972), 19.

4 Bob Wallace, "Wheat and Women: The Failure of Feminism in the West," *TBP* 8 (Spring 1973), 13.

5 Ken Popert, "Gay Rights Now!" reverse of *TBP* insert poster for the National Gay Rights Conference, Ottawa, June 28–July 1, 1975.

6 *TBP* 8 (Spring 1973), 5.

7 Gerald Hannon, "Of Men and Little Boys," *TBP* 5 (July/Aug. 1972), 3.

8 Ed Jackson, "Notes from the Bagnell Closet," *TBP* 6 (Autumn 1972), 10.

9 Gerald Hannon, "Children and Sex," *TBP* 6 (Autumn 1972), 3.

10 Ken Popert, "Gay Rights in the Unions," *TBP* 23 (April 1976), 12.

11 *TBP* 13 (May/June 1974), 7.

12 *TBP* 15 (Sept./Oct. 1974), 10.

13 *Toronto Star*, editorial, Oct. 19, 1974.

14 *TBP* 16 (Nov./Dec. 1974), 2.

15 *TBP* 7 (Winter 1973), 2.

16 Donald W. McLeod, *Lesbian and Gay Liberation in Canada: A Selected Annotated Chronology, 1964–1975* (Toronto: ECW Press/Homewood Books, 1996), 239.

17 Prabha Khosla, *Labour Pride: What Our Unions Have Done for Us* (Toronto: World Pride Committee of the Toronto and York Region Labour Council, June 2014), 6.

18 Sally Gearhart, "The Lesbian and God-the-Father," *TBP* 16 (Nov./Dec. 1974), 23.

19 *TBP* 17 (Jan./Feb. 1975), 6.

20 Ken Popert, "Comment: All Together Now," *TBP* 17 (Jan./Feb. 1975), 10.

21 *TBP* 1 (Nov./Dec. 1971), 2.

22 *TBP* 3 (March/April 1972), 18.

23 *TBP* 7 (Winter 1973), 24.

24 *TBP* 11 (1974), 7.

25 Sander Gillman, *The Jew's Body* (New York: Routledge, 1991), 60–103.

26 Michael Riordon, "Blessed Are the Deviates," *TBP* 21 (Nov./Dec. 1975), 10–11.

27 Editorial, *TBP* 8 (Spring 1973), 3.

28 Ken Popert, "Third National Conference Launches Gay Rights Coalition," *TBP* 20 (Oct. 1975), 3–5.

29 *TBP* 20 (Oct. 1975), 2.

30 Popert, "Third National Conference," 5.

31 "I'm Determined to Win: John Damien," *TBP* 18 (May/June 1975), 12.

32 Ibid., 13.

33 Tom Warner, *Never Going Back: A History of Queer Activism in Canada* (Toronto: University of Toronto Press, 2002), 144.

34 Valerie J. Korinek, "Activism = Public Education: The History of Public Discourses of Homosexuality in Saskatchewan, 1971–93," in *I Could Not Speak My Heart: Education and Social Justice for Gay and Lesbian Youth*, ed. James McNinch and Mary Cronin (Regina: Canadian Plains Research Centre, University of Regina, 2004), 109–138.

35 Gary Kinsman, unpublished notes from Gay Marxist Perspectives course, 1975.

36 Vladimir Lenin, *What Is to Be Done?* 3.3 Political Exposures and Training in Revolutionary Activity (1902).

37 Kinsman and Gentile, *The Canadian War on Queers*, 286.

38 Walter Blumenthal, "Open Male in the Post Office: Not the Same Old Place," *TBP* 10 (Fall 1973), 20–21.

39 Khosla, *Labour Pride*, 7.

40 "Olympic Crackdown," *TBP* 25 (Aug. 1976), 17.

41 *TBP* 25 (Aug. 1976), 1–17.

42 Merv Walker, "The Advocate: The Soft Sell Hardens," *TBP* 23 (April 1976), 10.

43 "Public Struggle," editorial, *TBP* 23 (April 1976), 2.

44 Gerald Hannon, "The Marketing of John Damien," *TBP* 24 (June 1976), 15.

45 Michael Lynch, "The Rise of Gay Capitalism," *TBP* 27 (Oct. 1976), 3.

46 Ed Jackson, "Nudity and Sexism," *TBP* 21 (Dec. 1975), 12.

47 See Warner, *Never Going Back*, 77–84.

48 Chris Bearchell, "Review of Lesbianism and the Women's Movement," *TBP* 22 (Feb. 1976), 5.

49 Ruth Roach Pierson, "The Politics of the Domestic Sphere," *Canadian Women's Issues* 11: Bold Visions (James Lorimer, January 1995), 23.

50 Wages Due Lesbians, "Lesbian Autonomy and the Gay Movement," *TBP* 25 (Aug. 1976), 8.

51 Gerald Hannon, "Marie Robertson: Upfront Dyke and Loving Woman," *TBP* 29 (Dec. 1976/Jan. 1977), 9.

52 Becki L. Ross, *The House That Jill Built: A Lesbian Nation in Formation* (Toronto: University of Toronto Press, 1995), 63.

53 Ibid., 64.
54 Naomi Brooks, personal interview, March 2, 2015.
55 Warner, *Never Going Back*, 179.
56 Any Gottlieb, personal interview, March 26, 2015.
57 The 519, www.the519.org.
58 Gerald Hannon, "Seven Years to Go: The Plight of Gay Youth," *TBP* 26 (Sept. 1976), 15.
59 "Lesbians Call for Autonomy," *TBP* 27 (Oct. 1976), 1.
60 Ibid., 3.
61 *TBP* 28 (Nov. 1975), 2.
62 *TBP* 29 (Dec. 1975/Jan. 1976), 2.

3 Noticed

1 For an in-depth analysis of struggles between assimilationist and liberationalist politics in the Damien committee, see Catherine Jean Nash, *Toronto's Gay Ghetto: Politics and the Disciplining of Identity and Space (1969–1982)*, PhD thesis, Queen's University, 2003.
2 Rick Bébout, *Promiscuous Affections: A Life in the Bar, 1969–2000: 1977*, www.rbebout.com.
3 Ken Popert, personal interview, Feb. 24, 2015.
4 Gerald Hannon, "Men Loving Boys Loving Men," *TBP* 39 (Dec. 1977/Jan. 1978), 30.
5 Bébout, *Promiscuous Affections*.
6 Chris Bearchell, Naomi Brooks, Bob Brosius, Tim Guest, Pat Leslie, Tim McCaskell, David Mole, Gordon Montador, Heather Ramsay, and Lorna Weir.
7 The Canadian Lesbian and Gay Archives, *Inventory of the Records of the Body Politic and Pink Triangle Press*, 29, www.clga.ca.
8 "*TBP* Raided and Charged," *TBP* 40 (Feb. 1978), 8.
9 Amy Gottlieb, personal interview, March 26, 2015.
10 Becki Ross, "Like Apples and Oranges: Lesbian Feminist Responses to the Politics of *The Body Politic*," *Queerly Canadian: An Introductory Reader in Sexuality Studies*, ed. Maureen FitzGerald and Scott Rayter (Toronto: Canadian Scholars Press, 2012), 142.
11 Ibid., 141.
12 Ross. *The House That Jill Built*, 167.
13 Naomi Brooks, personal interview, March 2, 2015.
14 *TBP* 40 (Feb. 1978), 1.
15 Ibid., 7.

16 Warner, *Never Going Back*, 136.
17 Brent Hawkes, personal interview, April 8, 2015.
18 "Judge Slams Gays in Jaques Verdict," *TBP* 42 (April 1978), 4.
19 Robin Hardy, "Commission Head: Gay Rights 'Non-issue,'" *TBP* 41 (March 1978), 1.
20 Ross, *The House That Jill Built*, 179.
21 Ibid.
22 *TBP* 42 (April 1978), 5.
23 Naomi Brooks, personal interview, March 2, 2015.
24 *TBP* 42 (April 1978), 2.
25 *TBP* 44 (June/July 1978), 9.
26 *TBP* 43 (May 1978), 2.
27 *TBP* 42 (April 1978), 28.
28 Ibid., 2.
29 *TBP* 45 (Aug. 1978), 16.
30 TBP 43 (May 1978), 3.
31 Andrea Dworkin, "Pornography: The New Terrorism," *TBP* 45 (Aug. 1978), 11–12
32 Ibid., 12.
33 *TBP* 45 (Aug. 1978), 12.
34 Ibid., 13.
35 Ibid., 5.
36 *TBP* 42 (April 1978), 14.
37 *TBP* 43 (May 1978), 3.
38 *TBP* 44 (June/July 1978), 2.
39 Ibid.
40 Philinda Masters, "Broadside and Beyond," editorial, *Broadside* 10,5 (Aug./Sept. 1989), 2.
41 Brian Mossop, "How to Advance Gay Rights in the Face of Attack," unpublished manuscript, personal files, March 12, 1978.
42 *TBP* 47 (Oct. 1978), 22.
43 Ibid., 23.
44 *TBP* 50 (Feb. 1979), 33.
45 Ibid., 12.
46 Ibid.
47 Ibid., 13.
48 Ibid., 10.
49 *TBP* 51 (March/April 1979), 8.
50 Ibid., 9.
51 *TBP* 53 (June 1979), 20.
52 Ross, *The House That Jill Built*, 186.
53 Ibid., 192.
54 Val Edwards, "The Invisible Community," *Broadside* (Sept. 1980), 4. Quoted in Ross, *The House That Jill Built*.
55 Judith Quinlan, "Response to Val Edwards," *Broadside* (Oct./Nov. 1980), 3, 8. Quoted in Ross, *The House That Jill Built*.

56 *TBP* 52 (May 1979), 8.

57 *TBP 54* (July 1979), 11.

58 Ibid., 25–26.

59 *TBP* 58 (Nov. 1979), 9.

60 Gerald Emmett Cardinal Carter, "Report to the Civic Authorities of Metropolitan Toronto and Its Citizens" (Toronto: City of Toronto Archives, 1979).

4 Shifting Sands

1 Audre Lorde, "When Will the Ignorance End?," keynote speech at the National Third World Gay and Lesbian Conference, Washington, DC, Oct. 13, 1979. In *I Am Your Sister* (New York: Oxford University Press, 2009), 207.

2 "Gay Marchers Flood Washington," *TBP* 58 (Nov. 1979), 17.

3 Ibid.

4 Myrna Kostash, "The 80s: Decade for Digging In," *Broadside* 1,7 (May 1980), 5.

5 *TBP* 48 (Nov. 1978), 6.

6 *TBP* 49 (Dec. 1978/Jan. 1979), 3.

7 Mariana Valverde, personal correspondence, Feb. 18, 2015.

8 Jane Rule, "So's Your Grandmother," *TBP* 54 (July 1979), 20.

9 *TBP* 64 (June/July 1980), 14.

10 *TBP* 66 (Sept. 1980), 13.

11 *TBP* 61 (March 1980), 20.

12 *TBP* 49 (Dec. 1978/Jan. 1979), 8.

13 Arthur Bell, *The Village Voice,* July 16, 1979.

14 *TBP* 59 (Dec. 1979), 4.

15 Susan G. Cole, "Cruising Windows," *Broadside* 1,5 (May 1980), 6.

16 *TBP* 60 (Feb. 1980), 18.

17 *TBP* 61 (March 1980), 9.

18 *TBP* 63 (May 1980), 24.

19 Wikipedia, "Gay Power Gay Politics," citing Frank Browning, *The Culture of Desire: Paradox and Perversity in Gay Lives Today* (New York, Vintage Books: 1993).

20 *TBP* 64 (June/July 1980), 38.

21 Right Wing Watch, "Heritage Foundation," http://rightwingwatch.org.

22 Mariana Valverde, "Viva Gay," *TBP* 47 (Oct. 1978), 31.

23 Ken Popert, "Dangers of the Minority Game," *TBP* 63 (May 1980), 37.

24 Robert A. Padgug, "Casting Light on the Dark Ages," *TBP* 70 (Feb. 1981), 29.

25 *TBP* 53 (June 1979), 22.

26 *TBP* 65 (Aug. 1980), 11.

27 *TBP* 64 (June/July 1980), 12.

28 *TBP* 67 (Oct. 1980), 32.

29 Jane Rule, "Closet Burning," *TBP* 68 (Nov. 1980), 21.

30 *TBP* 70 (Feb. 1981), 5.

31 Ibid., 15.

32 Kathleen A. Lahey, *Are We "Persons" Yet?: Law and Sexuality in Canada* (Toronto: University of Toronto Press, 1999), 364n11.

33 Government of Canada, Justice Laws Website, http://laws-lois.justice.gc.ca/eng/const/page-15.html.

34 *TBP* 62 (April 1980), 9.

35 Chris Bearchell, "Toronto Elections: George Hislop," *Broadside* 2,1–2 (Oct./Nov. 1980), 7.

36 *TBP* 67 (Oct. 1980), 9.

37 Tim McCaskell, *Race to Equity: Disrupting Educational Inequality* (Toronto: Between the Lines, 2005), 51.

38 *TBP* 69 (Dec. 1980/Jan. 1981), 11.

39 *TBP* 68 (Nov. 1980), 8.

40 *TBP* 69 (Dec. 1980/Jan. 1981), 12.

41 *TBP* 70 (Feb. 1981), 10.

5 Onslaught

1 Peter Zorzi, "The 1981 Bath Raids," *Queer Catharsis.*

2 *TBP* 71 (March 1981), 10.

3 *TBP* 72 (April 1981), 9.

4 Naomi Brooks, personal interview, March 2, 2015.

5 *TBP* 72 (April 1981), 16.

6 *TBP* 68 (Nov. 1980), 20.

7 *TBP* 77 (Oct. 1981), 14.

8 McLeod, *Lesbian and Gay Liberation in Canada*, 97.

9 "Gay Liberation Against the Right Everywhere," Connexions, www.connexions.org.

10 Lorna Weir, "Lesbians Against the Right," *Broadside* 2,8 (June 1981), 9.

11 *TBP* 76 (Sept. 1981), 7.

12 *TBP* 79 (Dec. 1981), 9.

13 *TBP* 78 (Nov. 1981), 10.

14 Ibid.

15 Judy Liefschultz, "Womynly Way," *Broadside* 2,5 (March 1981), 19.

16 Brent Hawkes, personal interview, April 8, 2015.

17 See Sharon D. Stone, "Lesbians Against the Right," *Women and Social Change: Feminist Activism in Canada,* ed. Jeri Dawn Wine and Janice L. Ristock (Toronto: James Lorimer and Company, 1991).

18 *TBP* 76 (Sept. 1981), 7.

19 Brent Hawkes, personal interview, April 8, 2015.

20 *TBP* 81 (March 1982), 8.
21 Tim McCaskell, "Gay in Colombia: Hiding, Hustling and Coming Together," *TBP* 69 (Dec. 1980/Jan. 1981), 25–27.
22 Tim McCaskell, "Sex and Sandinismo: Gay Life in the New Nicaragua," *TBP* 73 (May 1981), 19–21.
23 Tim McCaskell, "Untangling Emotions and Eros," *TBP* 75 (July/Aug. 1981), 22.
24 Gerald Hannon, "The Heart of The Mineshaft," *TBP* 75 (July/Aug. 1981), 43.
25 *TBP* 76 (Sept. 1981), 5.
26 Ibid., 4.
27 Ibid., 5.
28 Jane Rule, "Deliberations: Sexual Infancy," *TBP* 85 (July/Aug. 1982), 28.
29 Ken Popert, "Public Sexuality and Social Space," *TBP* 85 (July/Aug. 1982), 29.
30 Joan Nestle, "Butch/fem and Sexual Courage," *TBP* 76 (Sept. 1981), 29.
31 *TBP* 77 (Oct. 1981), 35.
32 Gayle Rubin, "The Leather Menace," *TBP* 82 (April 1982), 33.
33 *TBP* 90 (Jan./Feb. 1983), 16.

6 Sex and Death
1 *TBP* 76 (Sept. 1981), 19.
2 *TBP* 77 (Oct. 1981), 43.
3 Mike Hoolboom, "A Chronology of Censorship in Ontario by Judith Doyle," *Impulse Magazine* 9,2 (Fall 1981), excerpted at http://mikehoolboom.com.
4 *Globe and Mail*, March 24, 1981.
5 Eve Zaremba, "Sisters of Perpetual Arrogance," *Broadside* 4,2 (Nov. 1982), 3.
6 *TBP* 84 (June 1982), 9.
7 *TBP* 86 (Sept. 1982), 9.
8 Ibid., 29.
9 *TBP* 78 (Nov. 1981), 32.
10 *TBP* 85 (July/Aug. 1982), 16.
11 *TBP* 88 (Nov. 1982), 36.
12 *TBP* 90 (Jan./Feb. 1983), 10.
13 *TBP* 92 (April 1983), 31.
14 Jim Bartley, "Charting a Course between Male and Female," *TBP* 94 (June 1983), 30–31.
15 Ross, *The House That Jill Built*, 134.
16 Janice Raymond, *The Transsexual Empire: The Making of the She-Male* (New York: Teachers College Press, Athene series, 1994), 104.
17 *TBP* 94 (June 1983), 34.
18 *TBP* 96 (Sept. 1983), 6–9.
19 Ibid.
20 *TBP* 97 (Oct. 1983), 5.
21 For a fuller discussion of the camps, see

McCaskell, *Race to Equity*, 28–46.
22 Larry Kramer, "1,112 and Counting," *New York Native* 59 (March 14–27, 1983), 1.
23 *TBP* 94 (June 1983), 14.
24 Rick Bébout and Joan Anderson, "ACT: Some History," www.actoronto.org.
25 *TBP* 93 (May 1983), 9.
26 *TBP* 99 (Dec. 1983), 37.
27 *TBP* 100 (Jan./Feb. 1984), 37–38.
28 *TBP* 94 (June 1983), 8.
29 *TBP* 96 (Sept. 1983), 37.
30 *TBP* 100 (Jan./Feb. 1984), 23.

7 Plague and Panic
1 Gary Kinsman, *Rites* 6 (Nov. 1984), 1. See also "What If They Gave an International March and Nobody Came?," The Cahokian, Sept. 30, 2010, http://thecahokian.blogspot.co.uk.
2 Naomi Brooks, personal interview, March 2, 2015.
3 Bébout and Anderson, "ACT: Some History."
4 *TBP* 81 (March 1982), 38.
5 *TBP* 92 (April 1983), 28.
6 *TBP* 103 (May 1984), 7.
7 *TBP* 117 (Aug. 1985), 35.
8 *TBP* 118 (Sept. 1985), 8, 35.
9 *TBP* 101 (March 1984), 12.
10 *TBP* 103 (May 1984), 14.
11 *TBP* 104 (June 1984), 5.
12 *TBP* 106 (Sept. 1984), 31.
13 *Rites* 1 (May 1984), 1.
14 Mariana Valverde, "Lesbian Sexuality Conference: Coming On Strong," *Broadside* 5,9 (July 1984), 5.
15 *TBP* 106 (Sept. 1984), 36.
16 Naomi Brooks, personal interview, March 12, 2015.
17 *TBP* 106 (Sept. 1984), 10.
18 *TBP* 110 (Jan. 1985), 32.
19 Government and media reports on this issue are cited on Wikipedia, "CIA Involvement in Contra Cocaine Trafficking," http://en.wikipedia.org.
20 Diarmaid Kelliher, "Solidarity and Sexuality: Lesbians and Gays Support the Miners 1984–5," *Oxford History Workshop Journal* 77,1 (Spring 2014), 240–62, http://hwj.oxfordjournals.org.
21 Jamie Doward, "The Real-Life Triumphs of the Gay Communist behind Hit Movie Pride," *Observer*, Sept. 21, 2014, www.theguardian.com.
22 Ibid.
23 See Colin Clews, "1984. Lesbians and Gays

Support the Miners. Part One," *Gay in the 80s*, Sept. 10, 2012, www.gayinthe80s.com.

24 *TBP* 108 (Nov. 1984), 32.

25 The group demanded the release of seven hundred of their members, illegally transported to Israel for imprisonment after Israel withdrew from its invasion of southern Lebanon.

26 *TBP* 118 (Sept. 1985), 27.

27 Andrew Lesk, "Six Days of Distraction," *TBP* 115 (June 1985), 18.

28 Taryn Sirove, "Freedom, Sex and Power: Film/Video Regulation in Ontario," *Wreck: Graduate Journal of Art History, Visual Art and Theory* 2,1 (2008), 33.

29 Douglas Stewart, personal interview, March 20, 2015.

30 Ibid.

31 Courtnay McFarlane, personal interview, March 14, 2015.

32 Rinaldo Walcott, personal interview, March 8, 2015.

33 *TBP* 113 (April 1985), 30.

34 Ibid.

35 Ibid., 31.

36 Ibid., 32.

37 Ibid.

38 Ibid., 32, 45.

39 Ibid., 45.

40 *TBP* 114 (May 1985), 5.

41 Ibid.

42 *TBP* 115 (June 1985), 8.

43 For further discussion, see David Churchill, "Personal Ad Politics: Race, Sexuality and Power at *The Body Politic*," *Left History: An Interdisciplinary Journal of Historical Inquiry* 8,2 (2003), 114–34.

44 *Celebrasian* 7 (Summer 1985).

45 There was confusion about the proper spelling of Simon's name. It first appeared in *TBP* as Nokoli. Then we were told it was actually Nkodi. That confusion arose from the fact that the "l" in Sotho, Simon's mother tongue, is pronounced like "d" in English. The correct orthography is Nkoli, although Nkodi was also used in South Africa and was painted on the SNAAC banner.

46 *TBP* 119 (Oct. 1985), 24.

47 *TBP* 122 (Jan. 1986), 14.

48 McCaskell, *Race to Equity*, 93.

49 Ibid.

50 *TBP* 117 (Aug. 1985), 18.

51 See "Art Alter Eros: The Feminist Festival of Erotica Certainly Wasn't Pornographic – but Was It Sexy?," *TBP* 105 (July/Aug.

1984), 37; "Chris Bearchell Looks at Two of the New Crop of Lusty Lesbian Magazines and Has One Overwhelming Reaction: At Last!," *TBP* 108 (Nov. 1984), 37; "Girls on Video: Fear and Loathing and the Search for Pleasure," *TBP* 128 (July 1986), 25.

52 *TBP* 128 (July 1986), 22.

53 *TBP* 129 (Aug. 1986), 17–18.

54 Khosla, *Labour Pride*, 10.

55 Ibid., 11.

56 *TBP* 127 (June 1986), 8.

57 *TBP* 126 (May 1986), 28.

58 *TBP* 129 (Aug. 1986), 15.

59 *TBP* 135 (Feb. 1987), 4.

60 *TBP* 128 (July 1986), 14.

61 See *TBP* 126, 17; 127, 14; 131, 7; 133, 13.

62 *Xtra* 81 (July 31, 1987), 1.

63 Ken Popert, personal interview, Feb. 24, 2015.

64 *TBP* 135 (Feb. 1987), 7.

65 Ibid.

66 Margaret Thatcher Foundation, "Mrs Thatcher: The First Two Years," interview for *Sunday Times*, May 1, 1981, http://margaretthatcher.org.

67 Ken Popert, personal interview, Feb. 24, 2015.

68 *TBP* 135 (Feb. 1987), 5.

69 Ibid.

70 Ibid.

8 By Any Means Necessary

1 Ann Silversides, *AIDS Activist: Michael Lynch and the Politics of Community* (Toronto: Between the Lines, 2003), 124.

2 Ibid., 167.

3 Peter Tatchell, "How the ANC Was Won to Support LGBT Freedom," www.petertatchell.net.

4 Peter Maloney, "Deciphering the Code," *Xtra* 131 (Aug. 25, 1989).

5 Roger N. Lancaster, *Sex Panic and the Punitive State* (Berkeley and Los Angeles: University of California Press, 2011).

6 Silversides, *AIDS Activist*, 145.

7 Ibid., 146.

8 Ibid., 149.

9 *AIDS ACTION NEWS!* 3 (Oct. 1988), 2.

10 The United Church of Canada, "Membership, Ministry and Human Sexuality," social policy (1988), www.united-church.ca.

11 *Xtra* 109 (Sept. 30, 1988), 3.

12 *AIDS ACTION NEWS!* 3 (Oct. 1988), 4–5.

13 Silversides, *AIDS Activist*, 179–80.

14 Graeme Truelove, *Svend Robinson: A Life in Politics* (Vancouver: New Star Books, 2013), 129.

15 *AIDS ACTION NEWS!* 6 (Summer 1989), 2.

16 Ibid., 1–3.

17 Ron Goldberg, "Conference Call: When PWAs First Sat at the High Table," ACT UP website, www.actupny.org.

18 Colman Jones, "Challenging the AIDS Establishment over HIV," *Rites* 6,3 (July/Aug. 1989), 7.

19 Peter H. Duesberg, "Retroviruses as Carcinogens and Pathogens: Expectations and Reality," *Cancer Research* 47 (March 1987), 1199–220.

20 Sharon Fernandez, "More Than Just an Arts Festival: Communities, Resistance and the Story of Desh Pardesh," *Canadian Journal of Communication* 31,1 (2006), www.cjc-online.ca.

21 Ibid.

22 Warner, *Never Going Back*, 330.

23 Art Zoccole, personal interview, Sept. 8, 2014.

24 "Editorial: Broadside's Future Vision," *Broadside* 10,2 (Nov. 1988), 2.

25 Philinda Masters, "Editorial: Broadside and Beyond," *Broadside* 10,5 (Aug./Sept. 1989), 2.

26 Eve Zaremba, "In for the Long Hall," *Broadside* 10,5 (Aug./Sept. 1989), 23.

27 Ingrid MacDonald, "A Funny Thing Happened on the Way to the Revolution: More Lesbians Are Looking at Marriage as an Option – Is It for You?," *Rites* 6,6 (Nov. 1989), 11.

28 *Xtra* 123 (April 28, 1989), 7.

29 *Rites* 6,4 (Sept. 1989), 4.

30 Warner, *Never Going Back*, 224.

31 Bernard Courte, "An AIDS Activist Reflects," *AIDS ACTION NEWS!* 7 (Fall 1989), 7.

32 *AIDS ACTION NEWS!* 8 & 9 (Second anniversary issue, Feb. 1990), 3.

33 "It's Unconstitutional! Federal Court Rules Bias against Gays Violates Charter of Rights," *Xtra* 133 (Nov. 24, 1989), 1; Mary Louise Adams, "Federal Court Rules on Charter in Vesey [*sic*] Case: Section 15 Includes Sexual Orientation," *Rites* 6,7 (Dec. 1989/Jan. 1990), 1.

34 *AIDS ACTION NEWS!* 7, 5; 8/9, 11; 13, 2.

35 "AIDS Test Now a Must," *Xtra* 140 (Jan. 1990), 3.

36 Pierre Tanguay, "AIDS Quarantine Plan Unleashes Storm of Protest," *AIDS ACTION NEWS!* 8 & 9 (Feb. 1990), 2.

37 "Anonymous Testing Approved," *Xtra* 147 (April 27, 1990).

38 Stephen Manning, "Owning AIDS," *Xtra* Supplement (XS) (July 1990), 17–18.

39 Sonya Norris, "Canada's Blood Supply Ten Years after the Krever Commission," Library of Parliament Research Publications, July 10, 2008, www.lop.parl.gc.ca.

40 "Reorganization at the CAS AGM," *AIDS ACTION NEWS!* 10 (June 1990), 4.

41 "A Treatment Registry: One More Step in Managing the Delivery of AIDS Treatments," *AIDS ACTION NEWS!* 10 (June 1990), 3.

42 George Smith, "AIDS ACTION NOW! Responds to Federal AIDS Strategy," *AIDS ACTION NEWS!* 11 (Oct. 1990), 1.

43 Tim McCaskell, "AIDS in South Africa," *AIDS ACTION NEWS!* 11 (Oct. 1990), 8.

9 Great Expectations

1 Hulchanski, *The Three Cities within Toronto*, 28.

2 Anne Vespry, "Lesbian and Gay Pride Day – Politic or Party?," *Rites* 6,7 (Dec. 1989/Jan. 1990), 5.

3 Ken Popert, personal interview, Feb. 24, 2015.

4 *New England Journal of Medicine* 322,14 (1990), 941–49. Quoted in Sean Hossein, "AIDS TREATMENT UPDATE: AZT Effective Dose Lowered in Anti-HIV Treatments," *Rites* 7,2 (June 1990), 8.

5 Warner, *Never Going Back*, 225.

6 Ibid., 226.

7 Ibid.

8 *Xtra* 161 (Nov. 23, 1990), 15.

9 Ibid.

10 The Fraternity, "Table Talk Discussion Notes," Oct. 5, 1992, Canadian Lesbian and Gay Archives files.

11 "Federation of Gay Game Bylaws 1989," quoted in Judy Davidson, "Homophobia, Fundamentalism, and Canadian Tolerance: Enabling Gay Games III in Vancouver," *International Journal of Canadian Studies/Revue internationale d'études canadiennes* 35 (2007), 151–75, www.erudit.org.

12 Davidson, "Homophobia, Fundamentalism, and Canadian Tolerance," 154.

13 Ibid., 156.

14 Ibid., 157.

15 Ibid., 165.

16 Ibid., 163.

17 Ibid., 158.

18 Ibid., 163.

19 Ibid., 164

20 Ibid., 166.

21 Helen Jefferson Lenskyj, "Gay Games or Gay Olympics? Implications for Lesbian Inclusion," *Canadian Woman Studies/Les Cahiers de la femme* 21,3 (Winter 2002).

22 Davidson, "Homophobia, Fundamentalism, and Canadian Tolerance," 166.

23 Kyle Rae, personal interview, Feb. 23, 2015.

24 Ibid.

25 *Xtra* 200 (June 26, 1992), 15.

26 Ibid.

27 *Xtra* 158 (Oct. 12, 1990), 9.

28 Ibid., 14.

29 Ibid., 15.

30 Ibid.

31 "Queer Nation: An Introduction," pamphlet, Canadian Lesbian and Gay Archives.

32 *Xtra* 200 (June 26, 1992), 14.

33 *Xtra* 157 (Sept. 28, 1990), 17.

34 *Xtra* 161 (Nov. 23, 1990), 13.

35 "Policy Options '91," *AIDS ACTION NEWS!* (Dec. 1990), 5.

36 *Xtra* 164 (Jan. 11, 1991), 7.

37 Ibid., 1.

38 Bob Rae, *From Protest to Power: Personal Reflections on a Life in Politics* (Toronto: Penguin, 1996), 251.

39 Khosla, *Labour Pride*, 13.

40 Warner, *Never Going Back,* 268.

41 Miriam Smith, *Lesbian and Gay Rights in Canada: Social Movements and Equality Seeking, 1971–1995* (Toronto: University of Toronto Press, 1999), 87.

42 *AIDS ACTION NEWS!* 13 (March 1991), 9.

43 *Xtra* 171 (April 26, 1991), 15.

44 Bob Gallagher, personal interview, March 25, 2015.

45 Ibid.

46 Frank McGee, personal interview, September 17, 2014.

47 *Xtra* 190 (Feb. 7, 1992), 1.

48 *Leshner v. Ontario* (1992) is discussed in *Human Rights Issues in Insurance,* discussion paper, Policy and Education Branch, Ontario Human Rights Commission, Oct. 1999, www.ohrc.on.ca.

49 David Rayside, *On the Fringe: Gays and Lesbians in Politics* (Ithaca: Cornell University Press, 1998), 156.

50 Shawn Syms, personal interview, March 7, 2015.

51 Ibid.

52 "Sexual Orientation and the *Canadian Human Rights Act*," Human Rights in Canada: A Historical Perspective, Canadian Human Rights Commission, milestone 131, www.chrc-ccdp.ca.

53 Courtnay McFarlane, personal interview, March 14, 2015.

54 Ibid.

55 Stephen Lewis, Letter to Premier Bob Rae, June 9, 1992.

56 McCaskell, *Race to Equity*, 166.

10 Seduction

1 *AIDS ACTION NEWS!* 18 (Summer 1993), 15.

2 Smith, *Lesbian and Gay Rights in Canada*, 160.

3 Warner, *Never Going Back*, 280.

4 Tom Warner, personal interview, Feb. 25, 2015.

5 See "The Trials of London, Parts One, Two and Three," *Ideas,* Oct. 7, 1994, Canadian Broadcasting Corporation.

6 See Katrina Enros, "A Brief Survey of Censorship in Canadian Cultural Institutions," E-merge: Censorship in Canada, May 18, 2010, http://blogs.saic.edu/ emerge.

7 *Guevremont and the Public Service Alliance of Canada v. Canada Post Corporation*, Arbitration Decision, Vancouver, B.C., March 8, 1994.

8 Khosla, *Labour Pride*, 15.

9 Michael Battista, "Planes, Trains and Automobiles: The Labour Movement Is Taking up the Same-Sex Benefits Battle," *Xtra* 251 (June 10, 1994), 15.

10 *Xtra* 253 (July 22, 1994), 9.

11 Warner, *Never Going Back*, 231.

12 Patricia Lefebour, "Same Sex Spousal Recognition in Ontario: Declarations and Denials: A Class Perspective," *Journal of Law and Social Policy* 9 (1993), 272–89, Digital Commons, www.osgoode.yorku.ca.

13 Bob Gallagher, personal interview, March 25, 2015.

14 Rayside, *On the Fringe*, 153–65.

15 Ibid., 154–55.

16 Buddies in Bad Times Theatre, "Our History." http://buddiesinbadtimes.com.

17 Kyle Rae, personal interview, March 23, 2015.

18 Bob Gallagher, personal interview, March 25, 2015.

19 Carl Miller, personal correspondence, Nov. 26, 2014.

20 Rob Salerno, "Just Pick Up Dammit: Archival Documents Show How Bell Fought Queer Employees," *Xtra* (May 14, 2007), www.dailyxtra.com.

21 Ibid.

22 ILGA, "Against Paedophilia," http://ilga.org.

23 *Xtra* 253 (July 8, 1994), 12.

24 ILGA, "ILGA 1978–2007," http://ilga.org.

25 Doreen Beagan, "Top Court Hears Nesbit and Egan," *The Interim: Canada's Life and Family Newspaper*, Aug. 16, 1994, www.theinterim.com.

26 Tom Warner, personal interview, Feb. 25, 2015.

27 For a fuller analysis, see Rayside, *On the Fringe*, 105–140.

28 *Xtra* 272 (March 31, 1995), 11.

29 Warner, *Never Going Back*, 287–98.

30 Louise Binder, personal correspondence, March 17, 2016.

31 Project Remember, Brian Farlinger, www.projectremember.ca.

32 The Honourable Sidney B. Linden, *Report of the Ipperwash Inquiry* (Government of Ontario, 2007), www.attorneygeneral.jus.gov.on.ca.

33 All stats from: Diana Ralph, André Régimbald, and Nérée St-Amand, *Mike Harris's Ontario: Open for Business, Closed to People* (Halifax: Fernwood Publishing, 1997), 20–26.

34 Frank McGee, personal interview, Sept. 17, 2014.

35 Warner, *Never Going Back*, 296.

36 Simon Nkoli, personal correspondence, Dec. 12, 1989.

37 Peter Tatchell, "How the ANC Was Won to Support LGBT Freedom," www.petertatchell.net; International Gay and Lesbian Human Rights Commission, South Africa, "New Constitution Protects Gays and Lesbians," http://iglhrc.org.

38 The Freedom Charter, 1955, www.anc.org.za.

39 Karin Timour, "11th International Conference on AIDS: Activist Perspective," *The Body: The Complete HIV/AIDS Resource*, Sept. 1996, www.thebody.com.

40 Smith, *Lesbian and Gay Rights in Canada*, 104.

11 Courtship

1 Laura Castañeda and Shannon Campbell, *News and Sexuality: Media Portraits of Diversity* (Thousand Oaks, CA: SAGE, 2005), 267.

2 Michael Ornstein, *Ethno-Racial Inequality in the City of Toronto: An Analysis of the 1996 Census* (City of Toronto, May 2000), 97.

3 Hulchanski, *The Three Cities within Toronto*, 28.

4 Khosla, *Labour Pride*, 19.

5 Simon Nkoli, personal correspondence, Feb. 2, 1998.

6 Colman Jones, "Is This AIDS Group More Harm Than Good? HEAL Says Toxic Drugs and Fear – Not a Virus – Cause AIDS," *Now*, April 9–15, 1998, www.virusmyth.com.

7 "AAN Wants Signed Oath," *Xtra* 368 (Dec. 3, 1998), 13.

8 David Rayside, personal interview, Jan. 30, 2015.

9 "The Steps: Interview with Kyle Rae," Queerstory, www.queerstory.ca.

10 Stephanie Chambers, "World Pride Special: An LGBT History of Toronto: Lastman Takes a Ride on the Wild Side," *Globe and Mail*, www.theglobeandmail.com, June 19, 2014.

11 Jane Armstrong, "Corporate Cash Rains Down on Gay Parade," *Globe and Mail*, June 27, 1998, A1, A11.

12 Carl Warren, "Gay Pride Goes Corporate: Split Widens between Grassroots and Organizers," *Varsity* 119,2 (July 1998), 1, 3.

13 Susan Gapka, personal interview, March 6, 2015.

14 Paul McPhee, personal correspondence, Nov. 10, 2014.

15 Ibid.

16 For a fuller analysis, see McCaskell, *Race to Equity*, 255–72.

17 Jonathan Kay, "Rise of the Rainbow Hawks: How Conservatives and Canada's Gay-Rights Activists Made Common Cause," *Globe and Mail*, Aug. 23, 2013.

18 Denise Balkissoon, "Sleeping on the Street," *Xtra*, www.dailyxtra.com, Nov. 17, 1999.

19 Warner, *Never Going Back*, 298.

20 John Kennedy, "On the Record, Interview with Kyle Rae," *Fab*, Aug. 19, 1999, 18. Quoted in ibid., 297.

21 John Kennedy, "Now Those Were Raids," *Fab*, Oct. 14, 1999, 19. Quoted in ibid., 298.

22 Vern Smith, "Top Cop Laughs at Gay 'Domestic dispute'" *Xtra,* www.dailyxtra.com, July 28, 1999.

23 Julia Garro, "The Posters," *Xtra,* www.dailyxtra.com, June 30, 1999.

24 Julia Garro, "Kyle's All over the Place," *Xtra,* www.dailyxtra.com, June 30, 1999.

25 John Kennedy, "Toronto's New Top Cop Speaks," *Fab,* Dec. 9–22, 1999, 12–13. Quoted in Warner, *Never Going Back,* 301.

26 Eleanor Brown, "Cops Sue Kyle Rae," *Xtra,* www.dailyxtra.com, Nov. 15, 2000.

27 Stephanie Chambers, "World Pride Special: An LGBT History of Toronto: 1981 and 2000: The Bathhouse Raids," *Globe and Mail,* www.theglobeandmail.com, June 19, 2014.

28 Steven Maynard, "Modernization or Liberation?" *Capital Xtra,* March 17, 2000, 19. Quoted in Warner, *Never Going Back,* 245.

29 Mary C. Hurley, Law and Government Division, Parliament of Canada, "Sexual Orientation and Legal Rights," revised May 31, 2007, www.parl.gc.ca.

30 Chambers, "World Pride Special: The Bathhouse Raids," *Globe and Mail,* June 19, 2014.

31 Hilary Cook, personal interview, April 1, 2015.

32 Ibid.

33 Joni Mitchell, "My Old Man," 1970.

34 Brenda Cossman, "No Sex Please: National Lobby Group Stands Up for Respectable Rights Only," *Daily Xtra,* www.dailyxtra.com, Feb. 25, 1999.

35 Ibid.

36 Tom Yeung, "Lawlessness as Lifestyle," *Daily Xtra,* www.dailyxtra.com, April 5, 2001.

37 David Walberg, "Mad Vow Disease," *Daily Xtra,* www.dailyxtra.com, May 31, 2001.

38 Gareth Kirby, *Xtra West,* www.dailyxtra.com, Sept. 6, 2001.

39 "RCMP Used 'Excessive Force' at Quebec Summit: Report," CBC news, www.cbc.ca, Nov. 13, 2003.

40 Claudette Vaughan, "Shaking Things UP: Queer Rights/Animal Rights: The Vegan Voice Interview with Mirha-Soleil Ross," *Satya,* www.satyamag.com, Oct. 2003.

41 www.angelfire.com/fl3/uraniamanuscripts/sept11.html.

42 Taylor Asen and Zach Strassburger, "The Gay Iraqi Crisis," *Foreign Policy: Middle East Channel,* http://foreignpolicy.com, June 18, 2010.

43 Khosla, *Labour Pride,* 24.

44 Matthew Guerin, "Hall Drops Case against Catholic School," *Daily Xtra,* www.dailyxtra.com, July 7, 2005.

45 Immigration Legislative Review, *Not Just Numbers: A Canadian Framework for Future Immigration* (Ottawa: Minister of Public Works and Government Services Canada, 1997).

46 Nicole LaViolett, "Coming Out to Canada: The Immigration of Same-Sex Couples under the Immigration and Refugee Protection Act," *McGill Law Journal* 49 (2004), 969–1003.

47 Clyde Fransworth, "Argentine Homosexual Gets Refugee Status in Canada," *New York Times,* www.nytimes.com, Jan. 14, 1992.

48 Tanya Gulliver, "To Be Frank: Pride's First ED Steps Down," *Daily Xtra,* www.dailyxtra.com, June 23, 2005; Kerwin McLeister, "What's Pride Cost?" *Daily Xtra,* June 13, 2002.

49 Paul Henderson, "A Shot of Cash," *Xtra,* www.dailyxtra.com, June 12, 2003.

50 Mark Smith, personal interview, Jan. 26, 2015.

51 Mark Brodsky, "Please Sir, I Want Some More," *Xtra,* www.dailyxtra.com, Feb. 3, 2005.

52 *Halpern v. Canada* [2003] OJ No 2268.

53 "Harper vs the Globe and Mail," *Globe and Mail,* Sept. 6, 2003. Quoted in Knegt, *Queer Rights,* 45.

54 "Goodmans Welcomes Harris, Strengthens Capacity to Service Clients and Manage Change," press release, Oct. 3, 2002, www.goodmans.ca.

55 Susan Gapka, personal interview, March 6, 2015.

56 Ibid.

57 Ibid.

58 Avvy Go, "Minorities and Same-Sex Marriage," *Toronto Star,* Sept. 22, 2004.

59 "Racialized Communities Denounce Harper's Campaign against Same Sex Marriage," press release, Jan. 21, 2005.

60 Daniel Cere, "Get the State Out of Marriage," *Daily Xtra,* www.dailyxtra.com, April 7, 2005.

61 *Info-Egale* 2,5 (Summer 2005), 1.

62 Rourke, O'Brien-Teengs, Koornstra, Hambly, and Watson, *Positive Spaces, Healthy Places* (Ontario HIV Treatment Network, 2004), www.pshp.ca.

12 We're Not in Kansas Anymore

1 Hulchanski, *The Three Cities within Toronto*, 28.

2 The Colour of Poverty Campaign, "Understanding the Racialization of Poverty in Ontario," fact sheet, 2007.

3 Toronto Community Foundation, "Toronto's Vital Signs," *Toronto Star*, Oct. 6, 2009, R4.

4 *Rock Bottom: Gay Men & Meth*, Jay Corcoran, Outcast Films, USA, 2006.

5 "AIDS Conference Opens Without PM," CBC News, www.cbc.ca, Aug. 14, 2006.

6 James Burrell, "EVENTS: WAYV Reunion," *Xtra*, www.dailyxtra.com, Aug. 16, 2007.

7 Gareth Kirkby, "Queer Youth Oppose Raising Consent Age," *Xtra*, www.dailyxtra.com, June 29, 2006.

8 "Age of Consent Legislation Comes into Force," *Xtra*, www.dailyxtra.com, May 1, 2008.

9 Helen Kennedy, personal interview, March 19, 2015.

10 Gerald Hannon, "Roy's Resurrection," *Daily Xtra*, www.dailyxtra.com, Oct. 11, 2007.

11 Akim Adé Larcher and Colin Robinson, "Fighting 'Murder Music': Activist Reflections," *Caribbean Review of Gender Studies* 3 (2009), 3.

12 Ibid., 6.

13 Rinaldo Walcott, personal interview, March 8, 2015.

14 Akim Larcher, personal interview, Nov. 2014.

15 Rinaldo Walcott, personal interview, March 8, 2015.

16 Krishna Rau, "Jamaica's Queer Group Says Boycott Is a Bad Idea," *Daily Xtra*, www.dailyxtra.com, April 11, 2008.

17 Krishna Rau, "Jamaica Boycott Called Off," *Daily Xtra*, www.dailyxtra.com, May 21, 2008.

18 Akim Larcher, personal interview, Nov. 2014.

19 See Wentewatch, http://wentewatch.blogspot.com.

20 Palestinian Civil Society Call for BDS, July 9, 2005, www.bdsmovement.net/call.

21 *Occupation, Colonialism, Apartheid? A Reassessment of Israel's Practices in the Occupied Palestinian Territories under International Law* (Democracy and Governance Programme, Middle East Project, Human Sciences Research Council, May 2009).

22 Nathaniel Popper, "Israel Aims to Improve Its Public Image," *Forward*, www.forward.com, Oct. 14, 2005.

23 Andy Levy-Ajzenkopf, "Brand Israel Set to Launch in GTA," *Canadian Jewish News*, www.cjnews.com, Aug. 21, 2008.

24 Jasbir Puar, "Israel's Gay Propaganda War," *Guardian*, www.guardian.co.uk, July 1, 2010.

25 "Finance Ministers Face Down Crisis as IMF Head Warns of 'Meltdown,'" Canwest News Service, Canada.com, Oct. 12, 2008.

26 Krishna Rau, "Gay Leaders Denounce Egale Award to Jaimie Watt," *Xtra*, www.dailyxtra.com, June 4, 2009.

27 Andrew Brett, "Egale's Gay Gaffe," *NOW*, https://nowtoronto.com, June 16, 2009.

28 Ibid.

29 Ibid.

30 Gala program.

31 Edwin Janzen, "Israel's Critics Will Not Be Silenced?," *Canadian Dimension* 43,5 (Sept./Oct. 2009), https://canadiandimension.com.

32 For instance, on May 5, 2010, the Israeli newspaper *Ha'aretz* ran a story based on B'Nai Brith information claiming that Montreal's Orthodox community was "living in fear." In response, the Quebec Jewish Congress reacted that B'Nai Brith had "limited credibility" in the province, and Montreal Rabbi Reuben Poupko termed the story "a complete and total fabrication of reality." Or see B'Nai Brith's "Back to School Checklist for Jewish students and friends of Israel" which tells students to "Prepare to Face Hate on Campus" and to expect "Harassment of students wearing the Star of David or a kippah, Intimidation by your professor or teaching assistant because of your support for the Jewish State, Swastikas and other anti-Semitic graffiti all over campus."

33 Jonathan Kay, "B'nai B'rith Report on Anti-Semitism Debunked," *National Post*, May 12, 2010.

34 Babble: The rabble.ca Discussion Forum, "Let Pride Toronto Know That You Support Queers Against Israeli Apartheid Marching in Toronto Pride," June 2009, http://rabble.ca/babble.

35 Rob Lamberti and Sam Pazzano, "Pride 'Not about Hate,'" *Toronto Sun*, www.torontosun.com, June 13, 2009.

36 Marci McDonald, *The Armageddon Factor:*

The Rise of Christian Nationalism in Canada (Toronto: Random House, 2010), 320.

37 Ibid., 322.

38 See, e.g., Hillel Halkin, "Power, Faith, and Fantasy by Michael B. Oren," *Commentary*, www.commentarymagazine.com, Jan. 1, 2007; Paul S. Boyer, *When Time Shall Be No More: Prophecy Belief in Modern American Culture* (Cambridge, MA: Harvard University Press, 1992); Chip Berlet and Nikhil Aziz, "Culture, Religion, Apocalypse, and Middle East Foreign Policy," IRC Right Web (Silver City, NM: Interhemispheric Resource Center, 2003).

39 McDonald, *The Armageddon Factor*, 322.

40 Marci McDonald, "How Canada's Christian Right Was Built," *Toronto Star*, www.thestar.com, May 7, 2010.

41 McDonald, *The Armageddon Factor*, 323.

42 Joseph Massad, *Desiring Arabs* (Chicago: University of Chicago Press, 2008), 175.

43 Ibid., 162–63.

44 Metropolitan Community Church of Toronto, Refugee and Immigration Project, www.mcctoronto.com.

45 www.rainbowrailroad.ca.

46 www.irqo.org.

47 http://irqr.ca/2016.

48 Sean Rehaag, "Patrolling the Borders of Sexual Orientation: Bisexual Refugee Claims in Canada," *McGill Law Journal* 53 (2008), 59.

49 Margaret Wente, "To Tell or Not to Tell," *Globe and Mail*, www.theglobeandmail.com, April 11, 2009.

50 http://clhe.ca.

51 E. Mykhalovskiy, G. Betteridge, and D. McLay, *HIV Non-disclosure and the Criminal Law: Establishing Policy Options for Ontario*, a report funded by a grant from the Ontario HIV Treatment Network (Aug. 2010), www.aidslex.org.

52 City of Toronto, "Mayor David Miller Officially Welcomes Leading Urban Thinker, Richard Florida, to Toronto," news release, Oct. 31, 2007, www.toronto.ca.

53 Murray Whyte, "Why Richard Florida's Honeymoon Is Over," *Toronto Star*, www.thestar.com, June 27, 2009.

54 Allison Hanes, "Richard Florida to Visit City Committee," *National Post*, May 8, 2009.

55 Daniel Girard, "Reverse Brain Drain Brings Urban Expert to U of T," *Toronto Star*, www.thestar.com, July 11, 2007.

56 David Rayside, "Sex Ed in Ontario: Religious Mobilization and Social-cultural Anxiety," paper presented at the annual Meeting of the Canadian Political Science Association, www.cpsa-acsp.ca (Concordia University, Montreal, June 2010), 9.

57 Ibid., 11.

58 For more background on Uganda, see Adrian Jjuuko, "The Incremental Approach: Uganda's Struggle for the Decriminalization of Homosexuality" in Connie Lennox and Matthew Waites, eds., *Human Rights, Sexual Orientation and Gender Identity in the Commonwealth: Struggles of Decriminalisation and Change* (London: Institute of Commonwealth Studies, 2013), 381–408.

59 Jeffrey Gettleman, "Americans' Role Seen in Uganda Anti-Gay Push," *New York Times*, www.nytimes.com, Jan. 3, 2010.

60 Jane Taber, "Harper to Press Uganda on 'Abhorrent' Anti-gay Law," *Globe and Mail*, www.theglobeandmail.com, Nov. 26, 2009.

61 Joseph Abura, "For Some Anglicans, Vices Are Now Virtues: Christianity in Africa Is under Attack by Gays and Christians in Europe and the Americas, Africans Do Not Need Europeans to Teach Them What the Gospels Say," *Spero News*, www.speroforum.com, Nov. 25, 2009.

13 Homonationalism

1 *Xtra*, June 17, 2010, 20.

2 "The Unravelling of Pride Toronto: Pride Timeline/How a Queer Community Organization Became a Censor," *Xtra*, www.xtra.ca, June 17, 2010.

3 Kyle Rae, personal interview, March 23, 2015.

4 "The Unravelling of Pride Toronto," *Xtra*, June 17, 2010.

5 "Pride Toronto Plans to Censor the Term 'Queers Against Israeli Apartheid,'" *Xtra*, www.xtra.ca, May 13, 2010.

6 QuAIA "Israeli Apartheid – A Queer Issue," handout, Spring 2010.

7 Matt Mills, "Pride Toronto Censorship: How It Came to This," *Xtra*, www.xtra.ca, June 17, 2010.

8 Andrea Zanin, "Pride Toronto Promises Consultation with Trans Community . . . in August: Organizers Scramble on Trans File amid Dissent," *Xtra*, www.xtra.ca, June 11, 2010.

9 Judy Rebick, "Toronto Is Burning! Or Is It?," rabble.ca, June 27, 2010.

10 Wendy Gillis, "G20 Commander Apologizes after Being Convicted of Misconduct," *Toronto Star*, www.thestar.com, Aug. 25, 2015.

11 Jenny Yuen, "Gay Activists Challenge Blair," *Toronto Sun*, www.torontosun.com, June 29, 2010.

12 "Will TAKE BACK THE DYKE still happen? In two words: HELL YES," www.facebook.com/note.php?note_id=133034760059130

13 U.S. Department of Justice, Federal Bureau of Investigation, "Terrorism 2000/2001," www.fbi.gov.

14 Pride Toronto 6th Annual Gala & Awards Ceremony, Feb. 9, 2010, letter of invitation.

15 Don Peat and Antonella Artuso, "Rae Should Pay for Party: Ford . . . and Councilor Should Tender His Resignation, Too," *Toronto Sun*, www.torontosun.com, June 9, 2010.

16 Sue-Ann Levy, "The Other Face of the Ward 27 Frontrunner," *Toronto Sun*, www.torontosun.com, Sept. 23, 2010.

17 Community Advisory Panel, "Our Pride, A Community Effort: Final Report."

18 Andrea Houston, "Pride Toronto Financial Statements Show Big Losses," *Xtra*, www.xtra.ca, Jan. 26, 2011.

19 Andrea Houston and Marcus McCann, "Pride Toronto's Tracey Sandilands Resigns," *Xtra* , www.xtra.ca, Jan. 26, 2011.

20 Houston, "Pride Toronto Board Faces Tough Questions on Deficit," *Xtra*, www.dailyxtra.com, Jan. 27, 2011.

21 Andrea Houston and Marcus McCann, "Advisory Panel Offers 133 Recommendations to Pride Toronto," *Xtra*, www.xtra.ca, Feb. 17, 2011.

22 Sue-Ann Levy, "Pride Panel Won't Touch QuAIA: Levy," *Toronto Sun*, www.torontosun.com, Feb. 19, 2011.

23 "Levy Urges Jewish Leaders to Press City to Defund Pride Toronto," *Xtra*, www.xtra.ca, April 6, 2011.

24 Andrea Houston, "Sun Removes Levy from Pride Beat Pending Council Vote," *Xtra*, www.xtra.ca, April 8, 2011.

25 Martin Gladstone, "Toronto Pride Leadership Ignores Anti-Israel Elephant in Room," *National Post*, www.nationalpost.com, March 2, 2011.

26 Levy, "Pride Panel Won't Touch QuAIA: Levy."

27 Andrea Houston, " 'Hate Speech' Rhetoric Threatens Pride Toronto Debate," *Xtra*, www.xtra.ca, April 10, 2011; updated April 13, 2011.

28 Joseph P. Pennachetti, "Compliance with the City of Toronto's Anti-Discrimination Policy – Pride Toronto," report to Executive Committee, www.toronto.ca, April 2, 2011.

29 See: Natalie Alcoba, "QuAIA Pulls out of Pride Parade, Challenges Mayor Ford," *National Post*, www.nationalpost.com, April 15, 2011; Daniel Dale, "Councilor Demands Pride Promise to Ban Queers Against Israeli Apartheid," *Toronto Star,* www.thestar.com, April 15, 2011; "QuAIA Withdraws from Pride Toronto Parade," *Xtra*, www.xtra.ca, April 15, 2011; Susan G. Cole, "Pride Pullout: QuAIA Pulls out of the Pride Parade. It's the City's Move Now," *Now*, www.nowtoronto.com, April 20, 2011; Justin Skinner, "Controversial Group Opts out of Pride Parade," InsideToronto.com, April 15, 2011; Hamutal Dotan, "QuAIA Withdraws from Pride Parade," Torontoist.com, April 15, 2011; Anna Mehler Paperny, "Queers Against Israeli Apartheid Issues Parade 'Challenge' to Mayor Ford," *Globe and Mail*, www.theglobeandmail.com, April 15, 2011; " 'Israeli Apartheid' Group Pulls out of Toronto Pride," CBC News, www.cbc.ca, April 15, 2011; Don Peat, " 'Israeli Apartheid' Group Bows out of Pride Parade," *Toronto Sun*, www.torontosun.com, April 15, 2011.

30 Andrea Houston, "Pride Toronto Must Guarantee a QuAIA-Free Pride Week," *Xtra*, www.xtra.ca, April 21, 2011.

31 Theo Moudakis, editorial cartoon, *Toronto Star,* July 5, 2011.

32 Marcus McCann, "QuAIA Drops Banner from Wellesley Subway Station," *Xtra*, www.xtra.ca, July 3, 2011.

33 Andrea Houston, "Mammoliti Fails in Attempt to Defund Pride Toronto," *Xtra*, www.xtra.ca, July 12, 2011.

34 Andrea Houston, "Jewish Leader Says Mammoliti Went Too Far in Quest to Cut Pride Funding," *Xtra*, www.xtra.ca, July 9, 2001.

35 Jasbir Puar, *Terrorist Assemblages: Homonationalism in Queer Times* (Durham: Duke University Press, 2007), 38.

36 Ibid., 9.

37 Garson Hunter, Miguel Sanches, and Fiona Douglas, *Poverty Papers 5* (University of Regina, March 2012), www.uregina.ca.

38 Katie Toth, "Dispatch: Toronto's Occupy Movement," *Daily Xtra*, www.dailyxtra.com, Oct. 27, 2011.

39 Toronto City Council, 2012 Major Cultural Organizations Allocation, ED14.4, June 6, 2012, www.toronto.ca.

40 Mya Guarnieri, "Pinkwashing and Israel: Apartheid, Gay Rights and Military Occupation in the Middle East," *Xtra*, www.xtra.ca, June 18, 2012.

41 Carolyn Yates, "Update: Glad Day Investors Want More Diverse, Accessible Shop," *Xtra*, www.dailyxtra.com, Feb. 8, 2012.

42 "HIV-Positive Ottawa Man Guilty of Attempted Murder," CBC News, www.cbc.ca, Nov. 1, 2012.

43 The Ontario Human Rights Commission, "The Ontario Safe Schools Act: School Discipline and Discrimination," www.ohrc.on.ca.

44 Julian Falconer, "The Road to Health: A Final Report on School Safety," www.falconerschoolsafetyreport.com, 2008, 4.

45 "Bullying: Facts, Statistics & Effects," Our Kids: The Trusted Source, www.ourkids.net.

46 Catherine Porter, "Fighting Bullies without Bullying," *Toronto Star*, www.thestar.com, April 24, 2012.

47 George Lakoff, *Moral Politics: What Conservatives Know That Liberals Don't* (Chicago: University of Chicago Press, 1996).

48 Bill 13, Accepting Schools Act, 2012, http://ontla.on.ca

49 Bill 14, Anti-Bullying Act, 2012, http://ontla.on.ca.

50 Ontario Catholic School Trustees' Association, *Respecting Difference: A Resource for Catholic Schools in the Province of Ontario* (Jan. 25, 2012), 2, www.tcdsb.org.

51 Catechism of the Catholic Church, Article 2357, www.vatican.va.

52 Louise Brown, "Catholic Board Trustee Launches Bid to Let Gay-Straight Clubs Broach Taboos," *Toronto Star*, April 30, 2012.

53 Institute for Canadian Values, www.canadianvalues.ca.

54 youtu.be/cUvt7QfTzuE.

55 Evan Boudreau, "Queen's Park Protesters Oppose Bill 13," *Catholic Register*, April 2, 2012.

56 Mike Blanchfield, "John Baird Blasts Russia's 'Hateful' Anti-gay Law, after Pushing Privately for Change," *National Post*, www.nationalpost.com, Aug. 1, 2013.

57 REAL Women of Canada, "John Baird's Abuse of Office," media release, Aug. 7, 2013, www.realwomenofcanada.ca.

58 Lee Berthiaume, "Canadian Conservatives Divided over Harper Government's Defence of Gay Rights," *National Post*, www.nationalpost.com, Aug. 10, 2013.

59 Jonathan Kay, "Rise of the Rainbow Hawks: How Conservatives and Canada's Gay-Rights Activists Made Common Cause," *National Post*, Aug. 23, 2013.

60 Ibid.

61 "Stephen Harper's CRA: Selective Audits, 'Political' Activity, and Right-Leaning Charities," Broadbent Institute, Oct. 2014, www.broadbentinstitute.ca.

62 Helen Kennedy, personal interview, March 19, 2015.

63 Ibid.

64 Art Zoccole, personal interview, Sept. 8, 2014.

65 Quoted in *Re:Orientations*, Richard Fung, July 2016.

66 Pride Toronto, Audited Financial Statement, 2014, www.pridetoronto.com.

Conclusion

1 David Rayside, *On the Fringe: Gays and Lesbians in Politics* (Ithaca, NY: Cornell University Press, 1998), 314.

2 M.V. Lee Badgett, *Money, Myths and Change: The Economic Lives of Lesbians and Gay Men* (Chicago: University of Chicago Press, 2001).

3 For example, J. Galbraith and P. Sorokin in the United States, J. Tinbergen in the Netherlands, R. Aron in France, and J. Strachey in Great Britain.

Index